DUNGEONS & DRAGONS®

MONSTER MANUAL™ IV

CREDITS

DESIGN
Gwendolyn F.M. Kestrel, Jennifer Clarke Wilkes, Matthew Sernett, Eric Cagle, Andrew Finch, Christopher Lindsay, Kolja Raven Liquette, Chris Sims, Owen K.C. Stephens, Travis Stout, JD Wiker, Skip Williams

DEVELOPMENT TEAM
Stephen Schubert, Mike Mearls, Matthew Sernett, Jesse Decker, Andrew Finch

EDITORS
Jennifer Clarke Wilkes, Chris Thomasson, M. Alexander Jurkat, Chris Sims

EDITING MANAGER
Kim Mohan

DESIGN MANAGER
Christopher Perkins

DEVELOPMENT MANAGER
Jesse Decker

DIRECTOR OF RPG R&D
Bill Slavicsek

PRODUCTION MANAGERS
Josh Fischer, Randall Crews

SENIOR ART DIRECTOR D&D
Stacy Longstreet

ART DIRECTOR
Karin Jaques

COVER ARTIST
Henry Higginbotham

INTERIOR ARTISTS
Daarken, Wayne England, Carl Frank, David Hudnut, Howard Lyon, Raven Mimura, Jim Nelson, Steve Prescott, Wayne Reynolds, Ron Spencer, Anne Stokes, Arnie Swekel, Francis Tsai, Eva Widermann, Sam Wood, James Zhang

CARTOGRAPHER
Mike Schley

GRAPHIC DESIGNERS
Karin Jaques, Leon Cortez

GRAPHIC PRODUCTION SPECIALIST
Angelika Lokotz

IMAGE TECHNICIAN
Bob Jordan

Based on the original DUNGEONS & DRAGONS® rules created by E. Gary Gygax and Dave Arneson, and the new DUNGEONS & DRAGONS game designed by Jonathan Tweet, Monte Cook, Skip Williams, Richard Baker, and Peter Adkison.

This product uses updated material from the v.3.5 revision.

U.S., CANADA, ASIA, PACIFIC,
& LATIN AMERICA
Wizards of the Coast, Inc.
P.O. Box 707
Renton WA 98057-0707
+1-800-324-6496

EUROPEAN HEADQUARTERS
Hasbro UK Ltd
Caswell Way
Newport, Gwent NP9 0YH
GREAT BRITAIN
Please keep this address for your records

620-95376720-001-EN
9 8 7 6 5 4 3 2 1
First Printing: July 2006

ISBN-10: 0-7869-3920-6

ISBN-13: 978-0-7869-3920-6

Visit our website at **www.wizards.com/dnd**

Contents

Introduction

Welcome to *Monster Manual IV*. This book contains new creatures for use in DUNGEONS & DRAGONS® adventures. The monster entries are generally alphabetical by name, with closely related monsters grouped together. In addition to the table of contents at the front of this book, monsters are also listed by type and subtype on page 221, and by Challenge Rating and ECL on page 204.

This introduction explains how to read each creature's writeup. It often mentions terms in the glossary, which is found on pages 205–221. Refer to those pages for definitions of terms you might not be familiar with.

READING THE ENTRIES

Each monster description is organized in the same general format, as outlined below. For complete information about the characteristics of monsters, consult the glossary of this book, the *Player's Handbook* (PH), or the *Dungeon Master's Guide* (DMG).

We want this book to be as useful to DMs as possible, so we've adopted our new statistics block format for use here. The new format is divided into four main sections separated by horizontal lines. Each section serves a specific purpose; you will need to reference different sections at different times during an encounter.

IDENTIFICATION AND ENCOUNTER

The top section identifies the creature and gives the information you need at the start of an encounter.

Name: This word or phrase identifies the creature. Sometimes a number is given with the name to indicate how many creatures appear in the encounter.

CR: This value is the Challenge Rating of an individual creature of this kind.

Race, Class, and Level: This information is provided only for characters with class levels.

Alignment: The one- or two-letter abbreviation that appears here denotes the creature's alignment.

Size and Type: The creature's size category and its type (and subtype or subtypes, if applicable) are given here.

Init: This value is the creature's modifier on initiative checks.

Senses: The Senses entry indicates whether the creature has darkvision, low-light vision, scent, or some other sensory special quality, along with the creature's modifiers on Listen and Spot checks (even if the creature has no ranks in those skills).

Aura: This indicates special abilities that take effect anytime another creature comes within a certain distance, such as a devil's fear aura.

Languages: This entry gives the languages the creature speaks or understands, as well as any special abilities relating to communication (such as telepathy or *tongues*).

DEFENSIVE INFORMATION

This section provides the information you need when characters are attacking the creature.

AC: This entry gives the creature's Armor Class against most regular attacks, followed by its AC against touch attacks and its AC when flat-footed. If the creature has feats or other abilities that modify its Armor Class under specific circumstances (such as the Mobility feat), they are noted here as well as in the Feats entry.

hp: This entry consists of the creature's full normal hit point total (usually average rolls on each Hit Die), followed by the creature's Hit Dice in parentheses. If the creature has fast healing, regeneration, damage reduction (DR), or some other ability that affects the amount of damage it takes or the rate at which it regains hit points, that information also appears here.

Immune: Any immunities the creature has are indicated here. This includes immunity to specific types of energy as well as specific immunities (such as immunity to poison or to *sleep* effects).

Resist and SR: If the creature has resistance to certain kinds of attacks, that information is given here. Altered saving throw bonuses for specific circumstances appear on this line. The creature's spell resistance, if any, appears after the other resistances on the same line.

Fort, Ref, Will: This entry gives the creature's saving throw modifiers.

Weakness: This entry details any weaknesses or vulnerabilities the creature has, such as light sensitivity or vulnerability to a type of energy.

OFFENSIVE INFORMATION

Refer to this section when it's the creature's turn to act in combat. All a creature's combat options are detailed here, even those that are not strictly offensive.

Speed: This entry begins with the creature's base land speed in feet and in squares on the battle grid, followed by speeds for other modes of movement, if applicable.

ADAPTABLE ADVENTURE SITES

One of the new features in *Monster Manual IV* is a set of full-page maps that aren't associated with a particular kind of creature. Instead, they depict some archetypal adventuring venues: a great tomb (page 23), a typical wilderness lair (page 66), an underground lair (page 89), and a subterranean mining camp (page 113). Each of these maps can be used "out of the box"—all you, as the DM, need to do is populate them with appropriate monsters and treasure. Any of them, of course, can be modified to suit the needs of a particular story that's being played out in the campaign.

The Deephollows, a sample underground lair that appears on pages 200 and 201, differs from the other full-page map presentations—it comes with extensive text descriptions of each keyed location within the site. It serves both as an adventure site in its own right and as an example of how the other archetypal locations can be expanded by adding the same sort of detailed information.

Melee/Ranged: Typically, these entries give all the physical attacks the creature can make when taking a full attack action. The first attack described is the creature's preferred form of attack, usually a melee attack of some sort but possibly (as in the example below) a ranged attack. If the creature can make only a single attack (for instance, when it is taking an attack action), use the first indicated attack bonus. Occasionally, a creature has separate options indicated for single attacks and for full attacks. For example, a halfling ranger with the Manyshot and Rapid Shot feats might have the following entries:

Ranged *+1 longbow* +8 (2d6+2/×3) with Manyshot or
Ranged *+1 longbow* +10/+10/+5 (1d6+1/×3) with Rapid Shot
Melee masterwork longsword +8/+3 (1d6/19–20)

Each set of attack routines is prefaced by a boldface word indicating whether the attacks are melee or ranged. Next comes the weapon used for the attack, the modified attack bonus, the amount of damage the attack deals, and information about critical hits. If the weapon has the "default" critical hit characteristics (threat on a 20 and 2 damage), this portion of the entry is omitted.

Space and Reach: This entry defines how large a square the creature takes up on the battle grid, as well as how far a creature's natural reach extends and any reach weapons it might use.

Base Atk: The Base Atk entry gives the creature's base attack bonus without any modifiers.

Grp: This entry gives the creature's grapple bonus (base attack + size modifier + Str bonus).

Atk Options: Special abilities that the creature can employ to modify its normal attacks appear here. Such abilities might include feats such as Power Attack or Combat Expertise, or special abilities such as smite evil or trip.

Special Actions: This entry gives any special actions that the creature can take on its turn in place of making attacks.

Combat Gear: Possessions that the creature can choose to employ on its turn as an action appear here. Such items might include doses of poison (applied poisons, not natural ones), scrolls, potions, oils, wands, staffs, rods, and other wondrous items.

Spells Known or Spells Prepared: This entry appears for spellcasters. It is listed as "spells known" for sorcerers and members of other classes who do not prepare spells, and "spells prepared" for wizards, clerics and others who do prepare them in advance. It begins with the creature's caster level for spells. If its rolls to overcome spell resistance are based on a number other than its caster level (because the creature has the Spell Penetration feat, for example), its total modifier is given after the expression "spell pen." Spells known are listed from highest level to 0 level, and each includes an attack bonus and a saving throw DC, if appropriate. If the character casts some spells at a different caster level than others, that information is also specified here.

A cleric's statistics block also includes the name of his deity (if applicable) and the domains to which he has access. Each domain spell he has prepared is marked with a superscript D. The granted powers of his domains might appear as combat options or resistances or not at all, if they only modify information presented elsewhere.

Power Points/Day and Powers Known: This entry gives the number of power points per day to which a psionic character has access, as well as any psionic powers known. It begins with the creature's manifester level. Powers known are listed from highest level to lowest, and each power includes an attack bonus and a saving throw DC, if appropriate. If the character uses some powers at a different caster level than others, that information is also specified with the affected powers.

Spell-Like Abilities: Any spell-like abilities the creature possesses appear here. The entry begins with the creature's caster level for these abilities. As with spells, this entry includes attack bonuses and saving throw DCs where appropriate.

OTHER INFORMATION

Most of the information presented in this section is not relevant during a combat encounter with the creature.

Abilities: The creature's ability scores appear here in the customary order (Str, Dex, Con, Int, Wis, Cha).

SQ: Any special qualities not presented earlier in the statistics block appear here.

Feats: This entry lists all the feats the creature possesses, including those that appear elsewhere in the statistics block.

Skills: This entry shows all the skill modifiers for skills in which the creature has ranks. Modifiers are also provided for skills to which racial modifiers, bonuses from synergy, or other modifiers apply, whether or not the creature has ranks in those skills.

Possessions: This entry lists the items the creature is wearing or carrying. The expression "combat gear" appears first when applicable to remind you of other possessions referenced above.

Spellbook: This entry gives the spells in the creature's spellbook, if it has one. The notation "spells prepared plus" indicates that the spells the creature has prepared are part of this list, but are not reiterated here.

The final portion of the statistics block consists of paragraphs explaining special abilities noted in the various entries above as necessary.

STRATEGIES AND TACTICS

This section contains guidance for running the creature. Does the creature favor charging into combat or attacking at range? Does it prefer weapons or spells? Is it a solitary monster or does it tend to gather in hordes?

SAMPLE ENCOUNTERS

The older monster write-ups had a one-line entry titled Organization. This adds more depth and detail. The encounter section lists sample ELs and often includes name and adventure seeds.

ECOLOGY

Where do the monsters live? What do they hunt or eat? What hunts or eats them? What's their life cycle? When appropriate, the ecology section offers insights into the life cycle of the monster in question.

Environment: Here, we continue to use the specific terms we've developed to describe climate (warm, temperate, or cold) and terrain (plains, hills, forests, marshes, mountains, or deserts). Some creatures are subterranean and live underground. Some that have no place in the natural environment (particularly constructs and undead) might be found anywhere. Extraplanar outsiders are assigned a plane of origin. On that plane, they are considered native outsiders. If encountered elsewhere, they have the extraplanar subtype.

Typical Physical Characteristics: This section states the average height of a bipedal creature or whatever's most appropriate for a nonbipedal one and the creature's weight. It discusses any significant physical differences between ages or genders.

Alignment: The creature's statistic block lists a sample alignment. Here is a discussion of its philosophy. Is it is always, usually, or sometimes that alignment?

LORE

Monster Manual IV offers information about each monster that can be gleaned from an appropriate Knowledge check. The description of the Knowledge skill indicates that in general, the baseline DC of checks to identify monsters and remember one bit of useful information about their special power or vulnerabilities is equal to 10 + the monster's HD. Every 5 points by which the check result exceeds the DC yields another useful piece of information (PH 78).

That addresses specific creatures very well, but there's more to be said about creatures of general types. Consider the whisper demon as an example. It's a 15 Hit Dice creature. That means that identifying it is a DC 25 check. This generally check will generally yield one bit of information, but since there are lowly 2 HD demons such as the dretch out there that share many of the demon and tanar'ri traits, it's reasonable to give more information about it with the initial identification of the creature as a tanar'ri.

As a general rule of thumb, a DC 15 check or higher will reveal all of the base creature's type and subtype traits as defined in the glossary. This often includes information about energy resistance or various immunities. For instance, a DC 15 Knowledge (arcana) check reveals that dragons have high hit points (12-sided HD), all good saves, and have darkvision out to 60 feet and low-light vision. They are immune to magic sleep effects and paralysis effects. They eat, sleep, and breathe.

Information specific to the creature, such as its type of damage resistance, spell-like abilities, or immunities come with the high DC check results.

SOCIETY

Intelligent creatures often form their own societies and have particular worldviews and norms. Here, you'll find entries that include details about their thoughts, social interactions, religion, or government. How do creatures view themselves, each other, other races? What do they value? What's "normal" for them?

SAMPLE LAIR

Some creatures have an entry showing a sample lair complete with area descriptions.

TYPICAL TREASURE

This information expresses typical treasure values and treasure preferences.

Some creatures don't have treasure. Others have their treasure merely expressed in their Possessions stat block line. This section of the description is where you can find more information if it applies.

For cultured societies, sample art objects, jewelry, and other creature-specific flavor pieces might be described.

A creature that has been advanced by class levels, has treasure equal to an NPC of its Challenge Rating, not its effective class level. For example, a githyanki soldier (3rd-level fighter) is CR 4, and has an ECL of 5 (class levels +2). He has treasure equivalent to a 4th-level NPC.

FOR PLAYER CHARACTERS

If the creature can be useful to a player character as an animal companion, familiar, planar ally, mount, summoned monster, relevant information is included here.

CREATURES AS CHARACTERS

If a creature offers exciting possibilities for play as a character, this section provides the statistics and level adjustment.

CREATURES WITH CLASS LEVELS

If the creature advances by class, but is not suitable for play as a character, this section discusses its favored class and might offer information about its deity and domains or other class-based information.

ADVANCED CREATURES

If a creature advances by Hit Dice, the Advancement line in its statistics block gives the break points. This section of the description, when present, discusses the whys and wherefores of the creature's increased size and abilities. For example, given a subterranean creature, are the larger specimens found deeper in the earth? Is its growth a result of good feeding, good environment, age, or simple happenstance?

CREATURES IN EBERRON OR CREATURES IN FAERÛN

These sections (not present for every creature) describe the creature's niche in the EBERRON campaign setting or in the FORGOTTEN REALMS campaign setting.

AVATARS OF ELEMENTAL EVIL

The Princes of Elemental Evil—Imix, Ogremoch, Olhydra, and Yan-C-Bin—have long sought to extend their influence to the Material Plane. They believe that the deity known as the Elder Elemental Eye holds the key to their plan. The avatars of Elemental Evil, foremost among the princes' servants, are powerful forces of destruction that aid and serve the high priests of Elemental Evil.

The Elemental Princes believe that the Elder Elemental Eye is their forebear, a mighty being who can elevate them to godhood and herald their domination of the Material Plane. However, this deity is trapped in a strange void between the planes from which the princes seek to free it. Unknown to them, the Elder Elemental Eye is actually a front for the malevolent god Tharizdun.

Long ago, both good and evil deities allied against Tharizdun, who seeks the annihilation of all reality, and sealed the god in a mighty prison. The ever-greedy Princes of Elemental Evil, too young to remember that ancient war, allowed their ambition to blind them to Tharizdun's deception. Should they succeed in freeing the Elder Elemental Eye, the resulting destruction would spell the end of all existence. The secretive cult of Tharizdun failed in its initial attempt to use the Elemental Princes to restore their dread lord, but the princes' ambition and avarice remain.

Symbol of the Elder Elemental Eye

The avatars of Elemental Evil represent the princes' first steps in reestablishing their power. Since the destruction of the Temple of All-Consumption (see the *Return to the Temple of Elemental Evil* adventure), the four princes have been actively spreading their foul progeny across the Material Plane. Luckily for the world, the princes rarely cooperate. Each competes against the others for the Elder Elemental Eye's favor. Their cults also quarrel with each other, and at times they resort to open warfare to achieve dominance in a region.

Followers of the Elder Elemental Eye worship one of its elemental aspects: air, earth, fire, or water. Clerics choose one elemental domain plus either Destruction or Evil. They wear ochre robes marked with the deity's symbol, modified according to the elemental aspect they worship. The cult appeals to people on the fringes of civilization, individuals who feel wronged by society, and those who seek vengeance against powerful enemies. Each of the four sects attracts a different variety of creatures.

Clerics who worship the Eye's air aspect wear white-trimmed robes. They build temples in the highest mountain peaks, where screaming winds continually sweep through the rocks. The mightiest air clerics reside in castles that float among the clouds. Harpies, cloud giants, and renegade djinn inhabit these temples, as well as humanoids riding captive hippogriffs, griffons, and rocs.

Earth clerics wear amulets set with dozens of small gems, silver and gold beads, and other earthly treasures. Their robes are trimmed in yellow, and they delve temples deep within the earth. Greathorn minotaurs (see page 100) have a natural connection to these places, owing to their link with Ogremoch. They serve as guardians and, in some cases, priests of the Elder Elemental Eye. Evil dwarves, duergar, troglodytes, and grimlocks also flock to this temple's banner.

Clerics of the Eye's fire aspect wear robes with red trim and usually have *continual flame* cast upon amulets or bracelets. They have secret bases within volcanic tunnels and caves, but they are the most nomadic of all the Eye's agents. Fire priests journey to cities and drought-stricken areas to set fires that sweep over wide swaths of land. Fire giants, salamanders, azers, efreet, and similar creatures worship this aspect.

The water aspect attracts mariners and pirates to its cause. Water clerics wear robes with dark blue trim. Many of them carry small jugs filled with seawater for special ceremonies and blessings. Aboleths, sahuagin, and krakens worship the water aspect. Many evil sea druids, particularly those who seek to destroy seaside towns, also revere the Eye's water aspect.

WORSHIP OF THE ELDER ELEMENTAL EYE

All beings that worship the Elder Elemental Eye in truth offer prayers and sacrifice to Tharizdun. Few know of, or even suspect, the truth of the god's identity.

The Dark God, Tharizdun
Intermediate Deity
Symbol: A black triangle with an inverted yellow Y inscribed within, each arm ending at the midpoint of one of the triangle's sides
Home Plane: None (sealed in a prison plane)
Alignment: Neutral evil
Portfolio: Ruin, elemental power, vengeance
Worshipers: Fanatic nihilists, evil elemental beings
Cleric Alignments: LE, NE, CE
Domains: Air, Destruction, Earth, Evil, Fire, Water
Favored Weapon: Curved dagger

PLANS AND AIMS

The cult of the Elder Elemental Eye aims to destroy civilization and usher in a new age. The Elemental Princes foresee a world of pure chaos dominated by elemental forces. The earth will shudder and crack, swallowing cities whole. The seas will rise and smash into the land, dragging living creatures to a watery grave. Volcanoes will blast forth torrents of lava, consuming all in their path. The winds will howl with rage, sweeping away civilization and tearing it into dust. The cultists believe they alone will be saved because of their diligence, obedience, and faith.

Cults can operate behind innocent façades. For example, clerics of the Eye's earth aspect might infiltrate a mining operation under the pretext of uniting the miners into a union or guild. The rank-and-file members pay a few coins for dues each month; in return, the guild ensures safe working conditions. Skilled and ambitious guild members work their way up the ranks, with the most trustworthy initiated into the clergy. The clerics build a small temple deep within the mine, a protected base of operations near a city or town. This gives them a pool of unwitting minions who see adventurers who challenge the clerics as thugs sent to break up the guild. The clerics use divine healing to put the miners in their debt: A worker is unlikely to turn against the guildmaster who used *remove disease* to save a relative's life. As the guild grows more powerful, it is a useful shield against investigation and suspicion.

THE ELEMENTAL NODES

The Elder Elemental Eye commands its followers to seek out and claim sacred places throughout the world. The Elemental Princes believe the Eye uses these sites as conduits for its great power. By sanctifying and properly attuning such a location, the cult transforms it into an elemental node. When enough nodes are prepared, the energy flowing through them grows great enough to allow the Elder Elemental Eye to return to the world. Clerics of the Eye erect temples in and around the nodes and recruit beasts, outsiders, and elementals to guard them against intrusion.

Each node requires a specific, complex ritual to activate its powers. Such rituals can require months, if not years, of research to uncover. Once established, an elemental node usually contains strange edifices, artifacts, and landmarks. A fire node might consist of a sphere of crackling energy floating in the middle of a lava lake deep within a volcano. An air node could be a set of powerful winds that blow in a regular pattern high above the clouds, with a silver, latticelike structure floating amid them and a stone altar at the center. Regardless of their exact forms, these places are inimical to good creatures.

THE ELEMENTAL AVATARS

The avatars of Elemental Evil have only recently appeared. Each avatar is the living will of an Prince of Elemental Evil. It contains a tiny fragment of the corresponding prince's essence and exists solely to advance its creator's cause on the Material Plane. The avatars gather at important sites such as recently discovered elemental nodes or other places that might be key to returning the Eye to the world. Sometimes they serve as mighty engines of war for the clerics of the Elder Elemental Eye.

The simmering war between each faction of the Elder Elemental Eye's priests draws in the avatars as well. These creatures are just as likely to turn against each other as they are to ally against a powerful threat.

BLACK ROCK TRISKELION (EARTH AVATAR)

A living pillar of black rock towers over the ground before you. Its angular body is covered with spikes and sharp ridges. It unfurls three long arms, each ending in a long, vicious point: Two extend slightly forward, while the third sprouts from the center of its back to loom over its head. Three short, powerful legs support it like a tripod.

BLACK ROCK TRISKELION   CR 18
Always NE Large elemental (earth, extraplanar)
Init −1; **Senses** darkvision 60 ft., tremorsense 60 ft.; Listen +13, Spot +13
Languages Terran

AC 30, touch 8, flat-footed 30
   (−1 Dex, −1 size, +22 natural)
hp 377 (26 HD); fast healing 5; **DR** 10/adamantine and magic
Immune elemental immunities
Resist endure pain, stability (+8 against bull rush or trip); **SR** 23
Fort +27, **Ref** +9, **Will** +11
Weakness vulnerability to sonic

Speed 20 ft. (4 squares), burrow 20 ft.
Melee 3 piercing arms +30 each (2d6+11/19–20/×4)
Ranged 6 spikes +17 each (1d8+11/×3)
Atk Options Cleave, Great Cleave, Power Attack, magic strike, metal strike
Space 10 ft.; **Reach** 10 ft.
Base Atk +19; **Grp** +34

Abilities Str 33, Dex 8, Con 31, Int 5, Wis 12, Cha 8
SQ elemental traits
Feats Alertness, Cleave, Great Cleave, Great Fortitude, Improved Critical (piercing arm), Iron Will, Lightning Reflexes, Power Attack, Weapon Focus (piercing arm)
Skills Climb +20, Listen +13, Spot +13
Advancement 27–40 HD (Large)

Endure Pain (Ex) Whenever a black rock triskelion fails a Reflex or Will saving throw against an effect that deals damage, it takes half damage if it succeeds on a Fortitude saving throw against the same DC. This additional saving throw affects only damage, not any other conditions that might apply from failing the original save.
Stability (Ex) A black rock triskelion is exceptionally stable on its feet. It gains a +8 bonus on ability checks made to resist being bull rushed or tripped when standing on the ground (but not when climbing, flying, riding or otherwise not standing firmly on the ground).
Metal Strike (Ex) A black rock triskelion's natural attacks are treated as adamantine, cold iron, and silver for the purpose of overcoming damage reduction.

A black rock triskelion is a powerful elemental creature spawned by Ogremoch, the Prince of Evil Earth Elementals. It smashes its enemies with three powerful arms that pierce armor and flesh like heavy picks.

Strategies and Tactics

Black rock triskelions operate under the close supervision of powerful earth clerics of the Elder Elemental Eye, warding off attacks to protect the clerics' spellcasting. A cult might leave a triskelion to guard a newfound earth node until it can be properly fortified. Triskelions form the front line against invaders or heretics.

The dimmest of the four elemental avatars, a black rock triskelion is a simple brute. It wades into its foes and lashes out with its three arms, exulting in the chaos and pain it causes. It can reduce lesser opponents to bleeding carcasses with a few strikes. If it finds an opponent easy to hit, it uses Power Attack to further increase its devastating damage. In some cases, an earth cleric rides a triskelion into battle. The cleric hammers a thick adamantine chain into the creature's upper body to hold onto while perched on one of its spikes. Triskelions accept no other riders.

Sample Encounters

Black rock triskelions defend the earth temples that Ogremoch bids them serve.

Guard (EL 18–21): Any temple led by a 12th-level or higher earth cleric of the Eye receives one triskelion as a guardian. Ogremoch might dispatch more to protect an elemental node or to assist the sect against a powerful air, fire, or water faction of the Elemental Eye.

EL 18: A lone triskelion stands watch over a hidden passage leading into an earth temple of the Eye. It hides beneath the surface, just past a magic trap that causes a *wall of stone* to block the passage 30 feet behind the party. When the trap activates, the triskelion emerges in front of the intruders and attacks.

Ecology

Black rock triskelions are not natural beings but are sent to the defense of Ogremoch's temples and earth nodes. They do not reproduce; the Elemental Prince must create a new avatar at need. Once created, a triskelion serves its elemental masters until destroyed.

Environment: Black rock triskelions are native to the Elemental Plane of Earth but are usually found in subterranean locales, typically in an earth temple of the Elder Elemental Eye or an earth node.

Typical Physical Characteristics: A black rock triskelion stands 16 feet tall and weighs around 6,000 pounds. It resembles a great pillar of dark stone.

Alignment: As the creation of Ogremoch, a black rock triskelion is always neutral evil.

Typical Treasure

Black rock triskelions rarely have any treasure of their own. As guardians of earth temples, they turn valuables looted from enemies over to the priests of the Elder Elemental Eye.

Black rock triskelion

Illus. by J. Nelson

BLACK ROCK TRISKELION LORE

Characters with ranks in Knowledge (the planes) can learn more about black rock triskelions. When a character makes a successful skill check, the following lore is revealed, including the information from lower DCs.

Knowledge (the Planes)

DC	Result
18	This strange, rocky creature is obviously an elemental. This result reveals all elemental traits and the earth subtype.
28	This creature is a black rock triskelion, a servant of Ogremoch, Prince of Evil Earth Elementals. Its rocky body reduces damage from physical attacks.
33	A black rock triskelion's fearsome arms strike like heavy picks and can penetrate even adamantine to deal devastating damage.
38	Triskelions are incredibly durable and can resist spells and magical effects with their innate toughness rather than reflexes.

CYCLONIC RAVAGER (AIR AVATAR)

The air before you seems to explode in fury. Dirt and debris funnels upward, creating a rough outline of a whirlwind with humanoid features. The creature extends its arms from its body and begins to spin in place, blasting you with hurricane-force winds.

CYCLONIC RAVAGER CR 15

Always NE Large elemental (air, extraplanar)
Init +14; **Senses** darkvision 60 ft., scent;
Listen +26, Spot +16
Languages Auran, Common, Infernal

AC 25, touch 25, flat-footed 15; Dodge,
Mobility, deflecting winds
(−1 size, +10 Dex, +6 deflection)
Miss Chance 50 % (invisibility)
hp 169 (26 HD); **DR** 10/magic
Immune elemental immunities
Resist improved evasion; **SR** 23
Fort +10, **Ref** +27, **Will** +11

Speed 30 ft. (6 squares), fly 90 ft.
(perfect); Flyby Attack
Melee smite of seven winds +28 touch
(4d6+7 or 1d6+7; see text)
Space 10 ft.; **Reach** 10 ft.
Base Atk +19; **Grp** +28
Atk Options Combat Reflexes
Special Actions buffeting winds

Abilities Str 21, Dex 31, Con 15, Int 12,
Wis 12, Cha 16
SQ elemental traits
Feats Alertness, Combat Reflexes, Dodge, Flyby
Attack, Improved Initiative, Iron Will, Lightning
Reflexes, Mobility, Weapon Finesse
Skills Escape Artist +32, Hide +29, Knowledge (the
planes) +13, Listen +26, Move Silently +32, Spot +16,
Survival +23 (+25 on other planes), Use Rope +10
(+12 involving bindings)
Advancement 27–40 HD (Large)

Deflecting Winds (Su) A cyclonic ravager controls the air
around it to knock aside sword blows, arrows, and even
magical rays. The ravager gains a +6 deflection bonus
to AC.
Smite of Seven Winds (Su) A cyclonic ravager can make
a melee touch attack that generates a brief, rending
gust of wind within its target. This attack deals 4d6+7
points of damage. Creatures that are not subject to
critical hits instead take 1d6+7 points of damage.
Buffeting Winds (Su) As a standard action, a cyclonic
ravager can cause a tremendous surge of storm-
strength winds in a 100-foot-radius burst centered
on itself. A creature within this area must succeed
on a DC 28 Reflex save or be pushed up to 30 feet
in a direction of the ravager's choice. A creature can
choose to fail this save voluntarily. A ravager can
push a creature to a location outside the area of
this effect, but the pushed creature can't end up in
another creature's or object's space. The save DC is
Strength-based.

    A creature takes a −4 penalty on this save per size
category below Medium. Bigger creatures gain a +4
bonus per size category above Medium.

Cyclonic ravager

    When the ravager activates this ability, it can choose
to affect some creatures within its area while ignoring
others.
Skills A cyclonic ravager has a +10 racial bonus on Escape
Artist, Hide, Listen, Move Silently and Survival checks.

CYCLONIC RAVAGER LORE

Characters with ranks in Knowledge (the planes) can learn
more about cyclonic ravagers. When a character makes a successful skill check, the following lore is revealed, including the
information from lower DCs.

Knowledge (the Planes)

DC	Result
15	This creature composed of howling winds is obviously an elemental. This result reveals all elemental traits and the air subtype.
25	This creature is a cyclonic ravager, an avatar of Yan-C-Bin, Prince of Evil Air Elementals. Its transparent body is made only of violent wind.
30	The cyclonic ravager's command of air allows it to move its opponents and allies around the battlefield.
35	A cyclonic ravager can tear a creature apart with blasts of wind, but creatures immune to critical hits take far less damage.

Illus. by J. Zhang

Yan-C-Bin, the Prince of Evil Air Elementals, sends the cyclonic ravager to toss enemies about like kites in a hurricane.

Strategies and Tactics

Its ability to generate mighty winds allows a cyclonic ravager to take control of the battlefield. It flings its opponents through the air, sending them crashing into each other and disrupting their tactics and spellcasting.

A cyclonic ravager works best when it fights alongside the other denizens of an air temple of the Elder Elemental Eye. It generates air currents within an opponent's body that rip apart its organs. However, this attack form has little effect against creatures such as elementals and constructs, which are immune to extra damage from critical hits. Against such opposition, the ravager hangs back to direct the others in melee, using its buffeting winds to unbalance and interfere with opponents or blast them into disadvantageous positions. It can also move allies into better tactical situations.

Sample Encounter

Cyclonic ravagers fight best side by side with big, strong monsters that can take advantage of the chaos they produce.

Strike Force (EL 16): A cyclonic ravager and three cloud giants form the primary strike force for an air temple. The ravager's buffeting winds prevent melee combatants from closing with the giants, who exploit their great reach while forcing spellcasters into melee range. The ravager also uses its winds to move the giants into flanking positions or rescue them from dangerous situations.

Ecology

A cyclonic ravager assists air priests of the Elder Elemental Eye. It is a cunning tactician and an excellent complement to a temple's spellcasting forces. Yan-C-Bin dispatches a ravager when the temple is hard pressed, especially when servants of the other Elemental Princes attack.

Environment: Cyclonic ravagers are native to the Elemental Plane of Air and are usually found in an air temple of the Elder Elemental Eye or an air node. Ravagers ride the winds wherever their duties take them.

Typical Physical Characteristics: A cyclonic ravager stands 16 feet tall and weighs around 5 pounds. It looks like a tall, thin column of dust-roiled air but has humanoid features.

Alignment: As the creation of Yan-C-Bin, a cyclonic ravager is always neutral evil.

Typical Treasure

Cyclonic ravagers collect treasures for their prince, Yan-C-Bin. They prefer coins and gems, which they catch within their winds and swirl about in complex patterns that serve as paeans to their dread lord. A cyclonic ravager has standard treasure for its Challenge Rating, about 22,000 gp.

HOLOCAUST DISCIPLE (FIRE AVATAR)

A tall, human-shaped creature composed of pure flame stands before you. It wears a plain red robe that seems to float and billow in the tremendous heat, while the air shimmers around it. Its lower body is a stream of flame that coils behind it like a snake's tail.

HOLOCAUST DISCIPLE	**CR 15**

Always NE Large elemental (extraplanar, fire)
Init +9; **Senses** darkvision 60 ft.; Listen +23, Spot +23
Aura heat (15 ft., DC 27)
Languages Common, Draconic, Ignan, Terran

AC 21, touch 14, flat-footed 16
    (–1 size, +5 Dex, +7 natural)
hp 221 (26 HD); fast healing 5; **DR** 10/magic
Immune fire, elemental immunities
SR 23
Fort +20, **Ref** +28, **Will** +21
Weakness vulnerability to cold

Speed 30 ft. (6 squares), fly 40 ft. (perfect)
Melee fire bolt +24 touch (8d6 fire/19–20)
Ranged fire bolt +24 touch (8d6 fire/19–20)
Space 10 ft.; **Reach** 10 ft.
Base Atk +19; **Grp** +28
Atk Options magic strike
Special Actions flame wave
Spell-Like Abilities (CL 18th)
    At will—*fireball* (DC 19), *fire shield* (warm only, DC 20)
    3/day—*wall of fire*
    1/day—*meteor swarm* (DC 25)

Abilities Str 21, Dex 21, Con 19, Int 14, Wis 20, Cha 22
SQ elemental grace, elemental traits
Feats Ability Focus (flame wave), Alertness, Combat Casting, Great Fortitude, Improved Critical (fire bolt), Improved Initiative, Iron Will, Lightning Reflexes, Weapon Focus (fire bolt)
Skills Climb +21, Concentration +24, Knowledge (arcana) +18, Knowledge (the planes) +18, Listen +23, Spellcraft +20, Spot +23, Survival +5 (+7 on other planes)
Advancement 27–40 HD (Large)

Heat Aura (Su) At the end of each of their turns, creatures within 15 feet of a holocaust disciple must succeed on DC 27 Fortitude saves or be fatigued. A successful save negates the effect. A fatigued creature that fails its save becomes exhausted. A creature must attempt this saving throw each round it is within range, whether or not it has succeeded on an earlier save. A creature that has resistance or immunity to fire damage is immune to this effect, as is a creature that is not subject to the effects of extreme heat conditions. The fatigued and exhausted conditions end 1 minute after leaving the aura's area of effect. The save DC is Constitution-based.

Fire Bolt (Su) A holocaust disciple can aim a bolt of fire at a single target as a melee or ranged touch attack. The ranged touch attack has a maximum range of 200 feet with no range increment.

Flame Wave (Su) Once per round as a standard action, a holocaust disciple can generate a wave of flame that rolls out from its body. Any creature within 60 feet of the holocaust disciple must succeed on a DC 29 Reflex save or take 13d6 points of fire damage. A successful save results in half damage. The save DC is Constitution-based.

Holocaust disciple

The flame wave damage increases by 1d6 for every 2 additional HD the flame holocaust disciple possesses.

Elemental Grace (Su) A holocaust disciple gains a bonus equal to its Charisma bonus on saving throws. Included above.

A holocaust disciple is an elemental avatar crafted by Imix, Prince of Evil Fire Elementals. This fearsome creature bakes the area around it with withering heat.

Strategies and Tactics

Holocaust disciples relish spreading destruction and misery with their searing flames. Their impressive intellects are bent solely to this purpose. In battle, a disciple uses sound tactics to burn its foes while minimizing risks to itself; for example, it might fly over opponents and rain flame down on them. It prefers to work with fire giants and red dragons, relying on such powerful creatures to engage enemies in melee while it indiscriminately fills the area with fire.

A disciple's flames affect creatures both near and far. It can project bolts of fire up to 200 feet away or wash the area around it in a wave of flame. As well, the air around it is incredibly hot, sapping the vitality from the stoutest warrior in mere moments.

Sample Encounter

Holocaust disciples often team up with fire giants. While the giants wade into melee, the disciples hang back and provide ranged support.

EL 16: Four fire giants protect a holocaust disciple that leads raids to destroy human towns and villages. When the giants engage a foe, the disciple surrounds the melee with its flame wave. It then flies above the battle and attacks with its fire bolts.

Ecology

Holocaust disciples are unnatural beings of malevolent fire. One's presence in an area is unmistakable—flames and destruction spread everywhere. Imix sends a disciple to provide support to fire priests who are on campaign. The creature is wickedly clever, but its attention rarely strays from laying waste to everything in site.

Environment: Holocaust disciples are native to the Elemental Plane of Fire but often accompany wandering fire priests of the Elder Elemental Eye. Occasionally one occupies a fire node, but its thirst for destruction causes it to chafe if it remains in such a stable location for long.

Typical Physical Characteristics: A holocaust disciple stands 16 feet tall and weighs around 4 pounds.

Alignment: As the creation of Imix, a holocaust disciple is always neutral evil.

Typical Treasure

A holocaust disciple has standard treasure for its Challenge Rating, about 22,000 gp. Holocaust disciples prefer materials that can withstand great heat, such as gems and magic items. They also love to collect coins to melt them down and reshape into strange art objects. Collectors who specialize in alien, planar art forms pay good prices for such finished works.

HOLOCAUST DISCIPLE LORE

Characters with ranks in Knowledge (the planes) can learn more about holocaust disciples. When a character makes a successful skill check, the following lore is revealed, including the information from lower DCs.

Knowledge (the Planes)

DC	Result
15	This creature composed of pure fire is obviously an elemental. This result reveals all elemental traits and the fire subtype.
25	This creature is a holocaust disciple. It serves Imix, Prince of Evil Fire Elementals. It can fill the area around it with deadly flame.
30	The disciple's blazing aura causes fatigue and exhaustion in creatures that draw close to it.
35	A holocaust disciple targets vital spots with its deadly fire bolts. A single such strike can slay even the stoutest warrior.

WATERVEILED ASSASSIN (WATER AVATAR)

The walls around you groan, buckle, and bulge outward as a torrent of water sprays out from a dozen rents. The water flows together, forming a monstrous shape. Bits of rock, dirt, and bones float within it, along with the shredded remnants of weapons, armor, and clothing. The shape rushes toward you like a tidal wave as it attacks.

WATERVEILED ASSASSIN   **CR 15**

Always NE Large elemental (extraplanar, water)
Init +10; **Senses** darkvision 60 ft., blindsight 60 ft.;
    Listen +20, Spot +20
Languages Aquan, Common

AC 25, touch 15, flat-footed 19
    (–1 size, +6 Dex, +10 natural)
hp 169 (26 HD); fast healing 5; **DR** 10/—
Immune elemental immunities
Resist liquid body; **SR** 23
Fort +17, **Ref** +16, **Will** +13

Speed 30 ft. (6 squares), swim 60 ft.; malleable form
Melee slam +26 (4d8+10)
Space 10 ft.; **Reach** 20 ft.
Base Atk +19; **Grp** +30
Atk Options Combat Reflexes
Special Actions churn, engulf

Abilities Str 25, Dex 23, Con 15, Int 10, Wis 16, Cha 12
SQ elemental traits, one with water
Feats Alertness, Combat Reflexes, Lightning Reflexes,
    Improved Initiative, Improved Natural Attack (slam),
    Iron Will, Skill Focus (Hide), Skill Focus (Move Silently),
    Weapon Focus (slam)
Skills Hide +19, Listen +20, Move Silently +23, Spot +20,
    Swim +15
Advancement 27–40 HD (Large)

Liquid Body (Ex) A waterveiled assassin exercises supreme control over its watery form, allowing it to flow around attacks, flatten itself against the ground to avoid a spell's blast, and so forth. Any effect or spell that allows a Reflex save for half damage has a 50% chance to have no effect on a waterveiled assassin.

Malleable Form (Ex) A waterveiled assassin's control over its form allows it to flow through tiny cracks in objects and move through the earth, walls, and other obstacles. The assassin moves at normal speed through terrain that slows movement. It can move through permeable objects at half speed, but it cannot move through completely solid barriers. For example, an assassin could flow through a wooden or brick wall by squeezing into cracks and channels, but it could not move through a wall of solid iron or rock, such as that produced by *wall of stone*.

   If the assassin ends its movement completely within an object, opponents do not have line of sight or line of effect to it. Its reach drops to 0 feet. Any creatures engulfed within the assassin (see Engulf below) fall out, dropping prone at the edge of the object. If only part of the assassin is in an object, but its remaining space cannot hold all the creatures within it, the assassin chooses which ones to release.

Churn (Ex) As a swift action, a waterveiled assassin can create mighty currents within its body that grind engulfed creatures, dealing 5d6 points of bludgeoning damage. An engulfed creature that succeeds on a DC 30 Fortitude save takes half damage. The save DC is Strength-based.

Engulf (Ex) As a standard action, a waterveiled assassin can flow over Medium or smaller creatures, entrapping them within its liquid form. The assassin simply moves into the opponents' space; any creature whose space it completely covers is subject to the engulf attack. The assassin cannot make a slam attack during a round in which it engulfs. It can engulf as many creatures as fit in its space.

   Opponents can make attacks of opportunity against the assassin, but if they do so they are not entitled to a saving throw. Those who do not attempt attacks of opportunity must succeed on DC 30 Reflex saves or be engulfed; on a success, a creature moves aside or back (opponent's choice) to move out of the assassin's path. The save DC is Strength-based.

   Engulfed creatures are considered to be grappled within the assassin's body, and they are subject to its churn attack (see above). Engulfed creatures that breathe air might drown (*DMG* 304).

One With Water (Ex) Since a waterveiled assassin's body is liquid, it can simply disappear into water. An assassin in a volume of water at least 15 feet wide, 15 feet long, and 15 feet deep is invisible. It remains invisible as long as it remains within water, even if it attacks.

Skills A waterveiled assassin has a +8 racial bonus on any Swim check to perform some special action or avoid a hazard. It can always choose to take 10 on a Swim check, even if distracted or endangered. It can use the run action while swimming, provided it swims in a straight line.

A waterveiled assassin is a creature of living water sent by Olhydra, Prince of Evil Water Elementals, to slay her cult's enemies. This deadly killer can flow through the smallest cracks to ambush and engulf foes, and its fluid form lets it strike at opponents from a great distance.

Strategies and Tactics

Waterveiled assassins are cunning hunters that take full advantage of terrain and their special abilities to surprise foes. An assassin prefers to lurk within a wall, a large statue, or another similar object that can contain its bulk. From there, it watches its targets, attacking when they least expect it. The creature is clever enough to focus on spellcasters and other opponents with dangerous abilities. Its liquid form makes it difficult to injure, so it ignores physical attacks. This confidence sometimes leads to rashness: An assassin might leap on a party's wizard, disregarding melee combatants until they have dealt it serious damage.

A waterveiled assassin travels through a river or stream to infiltrate a city or enemy camp. Once there, it relies on information from the temple's spies and scouts, or clerics' divination magic, to find its target. The assassin attempts to engulf and drag off the victim to an isolated spot for the kill. It usually lets weaker creatures drown within its liquid body. Stronger targets require coordinated attacks; for example, the assassin might drag a foe to a nearby river and a waiting team of sahuagin.

Waterveiled assassin

WATERVEILED ASSASSIN LORE

Characters with ranks in Knowledge (the planes) can learn more about waterveiled assassins. When a character makes a successful skill check, the following lore is revealed, including the information from lower DCs.

Knowledge (the Planes)

DC	Result
15	This creature composed of liquid water is obviously an elemental. This result reveals all elemental traits and the water subtype.
25	This creature is a waterveiled assassin, an avatar of Olhydra, Prince of Evil Water Elementals. Its watery body simply ignores many physical attacks and spells.
30	A waterveiled assassin's most fearsome attack is its ability to engulf opponents within its liquid form and grind them in its currents.
35	A waterveiled assassin can flow through tiny cracks in seemingly solid material. It can seep into the earth, move through holes in a wall, and hide within porous objects.

Sample Encounters

Waterveiled assassins specialize in hunting down and slaying the enemies of the Elder Elemental Eye. An assassin is usually encountered alone, but one might work with assistants against challenging foes.

Individual (EL 15): A solitary assassin relies on information from the temple that called it.

EL 15: A waterveiled assassin lurks within the well near a busy inn, lying in wait for a band of adventurers that have caused trouble for the Elder Elemental Eye. When the targets arrive at the inn, a half-orc spy for the water temple gives the signal to attack. That night, the assassin flows through the ground and the inn's floor and walls to fall upon its enemies one at a time.

Assassination Team (EL 16–17): Stronger targets require coordinated attacks, often using sahuagin minions.

EL 16: A waterveiled assassin teams up with a pair of sahuagin assassins (LE rogue 5/assassin 6) who swim within its body. It engulfs one opponent at a time, which the sahuagin attack with their claws and teeth while the avatar wards off the target's allies. It does not use its churn ability in this case, since it does not want to harm the engulfed sahuagin.

Ecology

A waterveiled assassin is the highest gift that Olhydra can bestow upon priests of the Elder Elemental Eye. Within water temples, assassins occupy hallowed positions as embodiments of Olhydra's will. In addition to being a weapon against powerful foes, an assassin offers advice and counsel to the clerics and might even lead the temple. Underlings, usually sahuagin rogues or rangers, help it track down the temple's enemies.

Environment: Waterveiled assassins are native to the Elemental Plane of Water but are usually found in aquatic locales, typically in a water temple of the Elder Elemental Eye or a water node. Any body of water might contain an assassin that is on a mission.

Typical Physical Characteristics: A waterveiled assassin stands 16 feet tall and weighs around 3,000 pounds. It looks like a towering wave of murky water.

Alignment: As the creation of Olhydra, a waterveiled assassin is always neutral evil.

Typical Treasure

Waterveiled assassins are greedy creatures that seek to accumulate as much wealth as possible. A waterveiled assassin has standard treasure for its Challenge Rating, about 22,000 gp. It displays its status among Olhydra's followers by displaying gems, gold, and other durable items suspended within its body. Although it leaves behind such valuables when on a mission, within a water temple, an assassin takes great pains to show off its trophies—at least one from each of its victims.

BALHANNOTH

A hulking creature with an ovoid body drops from the ceiling. It moves on six long tentacles instead of legs, and from between its shoulders protrudes a slavering mouth full of jagged, ripping teeth.

BALHANNOTH   **CR 10**
Usually CN Large aberration
Init +7; **Senses** blind, dweomersight 120 ft.; Listen +6
Languages —
Aura dimensional lock

AC 21, touch 12, flat-footed 18
   (−1 size, +3 Dex, +9 natural)
hp 147 (14 HD); **DR** 15/magic
Immune gaze attacks, illusions, visual effects
SR 18
Fort +10, **Ref** +9, **Will** +12

Speed 50 ft. (10 squares), climb 50 ft.
Melee 2 slams +18 each (2d6+9/19–20) and
   bite +13 (1d8+4)
Space 10 ft.; **Reach** 10 ft. (15 ft. with tentacles)
Base Atk +10; **Grp** +23
Atk Options Power Attack, constrict +1d8, improved grab,
   magic strike
Special Actions antimagic grapple

Abilities Str 28, Dex 17, Con 23, Int 3, Wis 12, Cha 8
SQ camouflage
Feats Improved Critical (slam), Improved Initiative, Iron Will,
   Lightning Reflexes, Power Attack
Skills Climb +17, Hide +16, Jump +17, Listen +6, Move
   Silently +13
Advancement 15–20 HD (Large); 21–30 HD (Huge)

Dweomersight (Su) A balhannoth can sense the presence and position of magic auras within 120 feet of itself, and knows the strength and school of each one. It can pinpoint the location of any creature with ongoing spells cast on it, carrying magic items, or otherwise using magic, and it can notice anything within the area of a magic effect (including its own dimensional lock aura). This otherwise functions like blindsense.

Dimensional Lock (Su) As the *dimensional lock* spell, 20-foot radius centered on the balhannoth, CL 10th. This effect moves with the creature.

Constrict (Ex) A balhannoth deals 1d8 points of damage with a successful grapple check, in addition to damage from its slam attack.

Improved Grab (Ex) To use this ability, a balhannoth must hit an opponent of up to Large size with a slam attack. It can then attempt to start a grapple as a free action without provoking attacks of opportunity. If it wins the grapple check, it establishes a hold and can constrict.

Antimagic Grapple (Su) When a balhannoth grapples an opponent, all the magical properties of that opponent's magic items are suppressed. In addition, a creature grappled by a balhannoth cannot cast spells or use spell-like or supernatural abilities. A balhannoth automatically suppresses magic items by holding or wearing them.

Camouflage (Ex) A balhannoth's skin changes color to match its surroundings. As a result, a balhannoth can use the Hide skill in any sort of natural terrain.

Skills A balhannoth has a +15 racial bonus on Hide checks due to its camouflage ability. It has a +8 racial bonus on Climb checks and can always choose to take 10 on Climb checks, even if rushed or threatened.

Illus. by C. Frank

Even the deadly drow fear the lurking might of a balhannoth

Horrid aberrations of the subterranean realm, balhannoths hunt by tracking magical energy. They can "see" magic but are otherwise blind. Nothing magical functions in their powerful grips, making these predators especially deadly to those who rely on spells or magic items.

STRATEGIES AND TACTICS

Balhannoths hunt by ambush, not stalking. While swift in short sprints, a balhannoth is too bulky to pursue quarry through the narrow, twisting passages of the underground. The most common balhannoth tactic is to wait motionless in a large cavern, blending in with a natural rock wall or clinging to the ceiling with its powerful, prehensile limbs. When it detects potential quarry using its dweomersight, the balhannoth charges in to attack the creature with the most or the strongest magical effects. It readily uses Power Attack to smash down its most threatening opponents.

SAMPLE ENCOUNTER

Balhannoths usually hunt alone, but in areas of plentiful and powerful magic, they might gather in groups of up to six members.

Bodyguards (EL 12–14): Powerful creatures sometimes employ balhannoths as guardians, feeding them meat and occasionally giving them magic items from which they can draw power.

EL 14: A pair of mind flayers have *charmed* three balhannoths, which they now use as bodyguards while they travel through the underground. They set the balhannoths on other creatures encountered on their journey and allow the creatures to feed on the auras of any magic items. The mind flayers confiscate the items after the creatures grow tired of their tastes. Once they find a good location for a lair near a humanoid settlement, the illithids plan to station the balhannoths on its perimeter—the aberrations are too dangerous to keep nearby for long.

ECOLOGY

Balhannoths evolved to fill an unusual niche in the magic-permeated underground realms. They are attuned to magic and use its presence to detect their prey.

Balhannoths feed on both flesh and magical auras. A magic item with a faint aura sustains a balhannoth for a day, one with a moderate aura gives food for a week, and one with a strong aura is sufficient for a month. How long a balhannoth might survive on an overwhelming magical aura is unknown, but some scholars believe an item of such power might sustain it for life. A balhannoth enjoys the taste of magic but does no permanent harm to an item. Eventually it tires of the magic's flavor and must seek out a new source of nourishment.

The strange feeding needs of balhannoths drive them to attack and kill magic-bearing individuals. The creatures can't tell the difference between a magic item and an ongoing spell effect, so they attack anything they can detect with their dweomersight. A creature without magic is in no danger unless it enters the area of a balhannoth's dimensional lock aura, rendering it "visible" to the predator.

Once a balhannoth has killed its prey and dealt with any other threats, it takes the corpse back to its lair. There it devours the flesh and separates out any magic items the creature possessed. It chooses one item to carry and feed on, placing the others in a hidden or hard-to-reach place. Common hiding places for such food stores include cavities beneath large boulders or cracks in cavern ceilings.

Balhannoths have no gender—any one can impregnate any other. They do not mark mating with ritual but simply touch tentacles in greeting, which impregnates each of them. One year later, each balhannoth lays a single egg about the size of an ale keg. The egg must remain in contact with a magic item or within the area of a magic effect until it hatches. Most balhannoths keep their eggs with their food stores, but some establish separate caches. A balhannoth that can't find suitable food near its lair carries the egg to a better location. While so engaged, a balhannoth can use only one slam attack; it usually flees combat rather than risk breaking the egg. Balhannoth eggs hatch after a month, and the young reach maturity in three years.

Although intelligent enough to learn the rudiments of a language, few balhannoths can speak. Only those kept in captivity and trained as guardians gain some understanding of their masters' tongue, speaking in deep, growling voices. They possess small vocabularies and have little grasp of syntax.

Environment: Balhannoths can be found in any underground terrain.

Typical Physical Characteristics: A typical balhannoth stands approximately 9 feet tall at the shoulder and weighs about 4,000 pounds.

Alignment: Balhannoths are ravenous predators, unpredictable in their behavior but not inherently evil. They are usually chaotic neutral.

BALHANNOTH LORE

Characters with ranks in Knowledge (dungeoneering) can learn more about balhannoths. When a character makes a successful skill check, the following lore is revealed, including the information from lower DCs.

Knowledge (Dungeoneering)

DC	Result
20	This bizarre creature is a balhannoth, an aberration native to the underground. This result reveals all aberration traits.
25	Balhannoths are specially adapted to hunt by sensing magic. If you carry no magic items and aren't the subject of an ongoing spell, you are invisible to a balhannoth unless you are very close.
30	Balhannoths eat flesh but also absorb magical energy, feeding off magic items without harming them. They store magic items in their lairs like meat in a larder.
35	Balhannoths suppress any magic items they touch and magical effects of any creatures they grapple. A balhannoth is surrounded by a dimensional lock effect. This prevents magical escape and allows the creature to discern its surroundings.

"I lost another mining crew today. The priests say nothing, but rumors stir among the soldiers. They call it balhannoth, 'death without magic,' and mutter about refusing patrol. I might have to institute lashing soon."
—Vulfur, duergar captain

SAMPLE LAIR: BALHANNOTH CAVERN

This broad, high-ceilinged cavern lies not far from a major subterranean trade route. The balhannoth that dwells here preys on herd animals, beasts of burden, and the occasional sentient being that loses its way in the caverns.

1. Balhannoth Ambush (EL 11)

This large cavern is crowded with thick natural pillars that reach to the 20-foot-high ceiling.

A balhannoth clings to the ceiling in the space labeled "1," waiting for unsuspecting travelers to pass beneath.

2. The Broken Bridge (EL 4)

A narrow ribbon of worn stone stretches into the darkness. The roar of rushing water echoes from below.

This narrow stone bridge is crumbling and unstable. Moving over the surface requires a DC 20 Balance check to avoid falling. The current in the water below is swift and flows toward area 4. Characters in the water must succeed on a DC 20 Swim check or be dragged under, taking 1d6 points of damage before emerging in area 4.

3. Balhannoth Lair

This chamber is where the balhannoth sleeps and consumes its prey. Several partially eaten bodies remain here and still have useful items: A search of the remains uncovers 40 gp, a gem worth 55 gp, a suit of *rhino hide* armor, and a *potion of delay poison*.

4. Underground River

This is a continuation of the river beneath the bridge in area 2. It is deep and swift-flowing. A character in the water who fails a DC 20 Swim check is swept away under the wall, taking 3d6 points of damage from the battering before emerging in a new area. This can be a good way to draw the PCs on to the next leg of an adventure.

5. Subterranean Trade Road (EL 11)

A winding pathway extends for miles into the underground.

If the PCs are having too easy a time with the balhannoth, have a drow patrol of three dark snipers and two arcane guards (see the Drow entry on page 55) happen along the road and engage the party from the rear.

Balhannoth Cavern
One square = 5 feet

TYPICAL TREASURE

Because of the way they feed, balhannoths are more likely than other creatures to have magical treasure. Most of this is kept in the creature's lair and has a value appropriate to a CR 10 creature, about 5,800 gp. Balhannoths have one-half the normal amount in coins but have double items.

BALHANNOTHS IN EBERRON

Balhannoths can be found throughout Khyber, but they are most common in the deep caverns below the continent of Xen'drik. There they frequently come into contact with drow nomads, and among certain tribes the word "balhannoth" means a particularly skilled, cunning hunter.

BALHANNOTHS IN FAERÛN

Balhannoths are mostly found scattered through the North-dark, with particular concentrations along the borders of Anauroch. This unusual distribution has led sages to hypothesize that the creatures were created by Netherese wizards to assassinate their rivals.

BLOODFIRE OOZE

This disgusting pool of blood occasionally manifests a face twisted in torment. It seethes and boils, reeking of brimstone, and extends a gory pseudopod toward you.

BLOODFIRE OOZE   CR 7

Always NE Huge ooze (fire)
Init +1; **Senses** blind, blindsight 60 ft.; **Listen** +0
Languages —

AC 16, touch 9, flat-footed 15
    (−2 size, +1 Dex, +7 natural)
hp 150 (12 HD), fast healing 5
Immune fire; ooze immunities
Resist acid 10, electricity 10; **SR** 19
Fort +11, **Ref** +5, **Will** +4
Weakness vulnerability to cold

Speed 30 ft. (6 squares)
Melee slam +14 (1d8+10 plus 2d6 fire)
Space 15 ft.; **Reach** 10 ft.
Base Atk +9; **Grp** +24
Atk Options burning blood
Special Actions flame burst

Abilities Str 24, Dex 13, Con 24, Int —, Wis 11, Cha 4
SQ empower fire spells, ooze traits
Feats —
Skills Listen +0
Advancement 13–24 HD (Huge); 25–48 HD (Gargantuan)

Burning Blood (Ex) A bloodfire ooze's body produces tremendous heat. Any creature that strikes or touches a bloodfire ooze with its body or a weapon, or that grapples a bloodfire ooze, automatically takes 2d6 points of fire damage. A creature takes damage from this ability only once per turn.
Flame Burst (Su) A bloodfire ooze can activate a flame burst as a standard action once per round. Any creature within 10 feet must succeed on a DC 23 Reflex save or take 6d6 points of fire damage. A successful save results in half damage. The save DC is Constitution-based.
Empower Fire Spells (Su) Any spell or spell-like ability with the fire descriptor that is cast within 60 feet of a bloodfire ooze is empowered as if by the Empower Spell feat. In order to trigger this effect, both the spellcaster and the spell's origin point must be within the affected area.

A bloodfire ooze is the unholy result of mixing an immense quantity of blood from innocent beings with the ichor of a demon. It is dimly aware of its surroundings and burns with intense heat.

BLIGHTED BLOODFIRE   CR 12

NE Huge outsider (augmented ooze, fire)
Init +1; **Senses** blind, blindsight 60 ft.; **Listen** +0
Languages —
Aura negative energy (10 ft.)

AC 17, touch 9, flat-footed 16; DR 10/magic
    (−2 size, +1 Dex, +8 natural)
hp 162 (12 HD), fast healing 5
Immune fire, gaze attacks, illusions, visual effects
Resist acid 15, electricity 15; **SR** 22 (27 against positive energy)
Fort +12, **Ref** +5, **Will** +4
Weakness vulnerability to cold

Speed 30 ft. (6 squares)
Melee slam +15 (2d6+10/19–20 plus 2d6 fire)
Space 15 ft.; **Reach** 10 ft.
Base Atk +9; **Grp** +24
Atk Options burning blood, magic strike, true strike 1/day
Special Actions alternate form, flame burst, negative energy ray

Abilities Str 24, Dex 13, Con 26, Int 3, Wis 11, Cha 6
SQ empower fire spells, negative adaptation
Feats Ability Focus (flame burst), Improved Critical (slam), Improved Natural Armor, Improved Natural Attack (slam), Weapon Focus (slam)
Skills Escape Artist +16, Hide +8, Listen +0, Move Silently +16, Sense Motive +15
Advancement 13–24 HD (Huge); 25–48 HD (Gargantuan)

Negative Energy Aura (Su) Any living creature within 10 feet of a blighted bloodfire loses 1 hit point per round. Characters with immunity to negative energy effects, as well as other entropic creatures, are not affected by this aura. If conscious, the blighted bloodfire can repress this aura as a standard action, but takes 1 point of Strength damage for each full minute that the aura is inactive. *Planar Handbook* 124.
Burning Blood (Ex) As standard bloodfire ooze.
True Strike (Su) As the *true strike* spell.
Alternate Form (Su) As a standard action, a blighted bloodfire makes itself even more hideous, imposing a −1 morale penalty on attack rolls against it. *Complete Arcane* 161.
Flame Burst (Su) As standard bloodfire ooze; Reflex DC 26.
Negative Energy Ray (Su) Once every 1d4 rounds; range 60 feet; ranged touch attack; 1d4−2 negative energy damage. This attack damages living creatures and heals undead. *Planar Handbook* 123.
Empower Fire Spells (Su) As standard bloodfire ooze.
Negative Adaptation (Ex) Blighted bloodfires do not lose hit points or need to attempt Fortitude saves due to being in a negative-dominant environment. *Planar Handbook* 124.

Truly twisted or extraplanar creators shape bloodfire oozes into even more alien and horrific beings. A blighted bloodfire is created by adding the pseudonatural creature template from *Complete Arcane* and the entropic creature template from *Planar Handbook* to a bloodfire ooze.

BLOODFIRE OOZE LORE

Characters with ranks in Knowledge (dungeoneering) can learn more about bloodfire oozes. When a character makes a successful skill check, the following lore is revealed, including the information from lower DCs.

Knowledge (Dungeoneering)

DC	Result
17	This puddle of smoking gore is a bloodfire ooze. This result reveals all ooze traits.
22	A bloodfire ooze's smoldering mass deals fire damage to any it touches. Its affinity with fire increases the power of fire-based magic cast in its vicinity.
27	Bloodfire oozes are created through unspeakable rituals that blend the blood of innocent beings with fiendish essence.
32	Beings of fire and evil evokers often keep bloodfire oozes nearby to enhance their own fiery abilities.

STRATEGIES AND TACTICS

As mindless creatures, bloodfire oozes do not employ any tactics beyond "overwhelm" and "burn." Intelligent creatures often create them to serve as guards and to enhance their own magical abilities. Evil evokers especially favor these oozes because they empower fire spells cast nearby in addition to providing physical defense. Evil outsiders that can use fire spells or abilities seek out or create these creatures as well.

SAMPLE ENCOUNTERS

Bloodfire oozes often accompany spellcasters or more powerful fire creatures.

Guards (EL 10): Kalamaz Al'Anar, an efreeti hiding on the Material Plane, keeps two bloodfire oozes in a small cave system that he has claimed. The efreeti now raids the surrounding area for slaves and supplies. Alternatively, Kalamaz and the two oozes are mercenaries holding their own section of a larger dungeon complex.

Fire Team (EL 12): Melzeer, a noble salamander of fearsome reputation, leads a raiding party of four average salamanders and one bloodfire ooze. These creatures fill the air with flame as they slam into a settlement where the PCs are staying, attempting to plunder quickly and then flee under the cover of raging flames.

Bloodfire ooze

ECOLOGY

Bloodfire oozes come into existence only through twisted rituals and have no place in the natural world.

The more blood a bloodfire ooze consumes, the larger it grows; the blood of good creatures provides superior nutrition. Gargantuan and larger bloodfire oozes require the blood of hundreds of creatures to create. Once an ooze comes into existence, it mindlessly pursues further nourishment.

Environment: Bloodfire oozes are found in evil temples (abandoned or otherwise), the demesnes of evil evokers, and the territories of powerful fire creatures. They roam the underground realm in places, but few survive long that wander aboveground—the fires they create rapidly draw attention. Bloodfire oozes frequently remain inside the massive cauldrons that spawned them or lie in wait in shallow pits.

Typical Physical Characteristics: A bloodfire ooze resembles an enormous, living mass of burning blood. As the creature moves, faces of tormented souls appear on the surface, only to be reabsorbed moments later. Wisps of sulfurous smoke constantly rise from a bloodfire ooze. A Huge ooze is about 15 feet on a side and weighs around 8,000 pounds, but much larger specimens have been observed.

Alignment: Although mindless, bloodfire oozes are created and motivated by evil acts. They are always neutral evil.

TYPICAL TREASURE

A bloodfire ooze has treasure appropriate to its Challenge Rating, about 2,600 gp. This represents discarded gear and money of previous victims.

FOR PLAYER CHARACTERS

The creation of a bloodfire ooze involves a horrific ritual, requiring the blood of at least 100 good- or neutral-aligned humanoids and all the ichor of a single demon having 10 or more HD. These ingredients must be mixed in an enormous cauldron scribed with special runes, worth at least 3,000 gp. The ritual takes 24 hours to complete, during which time the caster can do nothing else, beyond occasional breaks—combat, spellcasting, or other arduous tasks ruin the ritual, which must started over from the beginning. The ritual must be performed within the area of an *unhallow* spell, and the creator spends 500 XP on its completion.

A bloodfire ooze obeys simple commands from its creator, such as "guard this temple" or "attack anyone who enters but me," but it ignores more complicated orders. Commanding a bloodfire ooze requires the creator to be within 30 feet.

BLOODFIRE OOZES IN EBERRON

Bloodfire oozes are commonly found in the Demon Wastes, the result of hideous rituals conducted by the rakshasas and other vile beings. Adventurers also report the presence of bloodfire oozes protecting long-forgotten temples underneath Sharn and the cyclopean ruins of Xen'drik.

BLOODFIRE OOZES IN FAERÛN

Bloodfire oozes are most common in Thay. The Red Wizards create them to guard laboratories, temples, and other important locations.

Illus. by A. Stokes

BLOODHULK

Bloodhulks are corpses reanimated through an infusion of the blood of innocent victims in a dark and horrible ritual. Their bloated bodies are filled with viscous gore and unholy fluids, providing them with the endurance to absorb an amazing amount of punishment before falling.

Although bloodhulk fighters are the most common form of this undead, necromancers and vile priests sometimes create larger, more ferocious versions, such as bloodhulk giants and bloodhulk crushers.

BLOODHULK FIGHTER

This might have been a human, once. Now it is a bloated horror, distended veins sprawling across its livid skin. Scraps of rotting cloth are all that cover its swollen body. Its empty eyes fix on you, and it lurches forward swinging massive fists.

BLOODHULK FIGHTER   **CR 4**

Always NE Medium undead
Init −1; **Senses** darkvision 60 ft., low-light vision; Listen +0, Spot +0
Languages understands creator's orders

AC 11, touch 9, flat-footed 11
    (−1 Dex, +2 natural)
hp 140 (10 HD)
Immune undead immunities
Fort +3, **Ref** +2, **Will** +7
Weakness fragile

Speed 20 ft. (4 squares)
Melee slam +8 (1d8+4)
Space 5 ft.; **Reach** 5 ft.
Base Atk +5; **Grp** +8

Abilities Str 16, Dex 9, Con —, Int —, Wis 10, Cha 1
SQ blood bloated, undead traits
Feats —
Skills Listen +0, Spot +0
Advancement see text

Fragile (Ex) A bloodhulk fighter takes an extra 1d6 points of damage whenever it takes at least 1 point of damage from a piercing or slashing weapon.
Blood Bloated (Ex) A bloodhulk fighter always gains the maximum hit points possible per Hit Die. In addition, it gains 2 bonus hit points per Hit Die.

BLOODHULK GIANT

This towering, swollen giant looks as if its skin is about to burst and rip away. Thick veins run across its body, and here and there it pulses and shifts with a great quantity of fluid.

BLOODHULK GIANT   **CR 6**

Always NE Large undead
Init −2; **Senses** darkvision 60 ft., low-light vision; Listen +0, Spot +0
Languages understands creator's orders

AC 13, touch 7, flat-footed 13
    (−1 size, −2 Dex, +6 natural)
hp 196 (14 HD)
Immune undead immunities
Fort +4, **Ref** +2, **Will** +9
Weakness fragile

Speed 20 ft. (4 squares)
Melee slam +17 (2d6+16)
Space 10 ft.; **Reach** 10 ft.
Base Atk +7; **Grp** +22

Abilities Str 33, Dex 6, Con —, Int —, Wis 10, Cha 1
SQ blood bloated, undead traits
Feats —
Skills Listen +0, Spot +0
Advancement see text

Fragile (Ex) As bloodhulk fighter.
Blood Bloated (Ex) As bloodhulk fighter.

Bloodhulk crusher

Illus. by J. Nelson

Bloodhulk giant   *Bloodhulk fighter*

A bloodhulk giant is a larger, tougher version of a bloodhulk fighter. It can absorb scores of attacks, making it ideal as a guardian or bodyguard. Necromancers, evil clerics, and other evil spellcasters use bloodhulk giants to fend off enemies while they attack with their magic.

BLOODHULK CRUSHER

A twisted, swollen form the size of a castle tower looms over you. Its bloated, swollen body is covered with thick, ropy veins that throb with viscous blood. It looks down upon you with hollow, empty eyes.

BLOODHULK CRUSHER	**CR 8**

Always NE Huge undead
Init –2; **Senses** darkvision 60 ft., low-light vision; Listen +0, Spot +0
Languages understands creator's orders

AC 14, touch 6, flat-footed 14
   (–2 size, –2 Dex, +8 natural)
hp 280 (20 HD)
Immune undead immunities
Fort +6, **Ref** +4, **Will** +12
Weakness fragile

Speed 30 ft. (6 squares)
Melee slam +24 (3d6+24)
Space 15 ft.; **Reach** 15 ft.
Base Atk +10; **Grp** +34

Abilities Str 43, Dex 6, Con —, Int —, Wis 10, Cha 1
SQ blood bloated, undead traits
Feats —
Skills Listen +0, Spot +0
Advancement see text

Fragile (Ex) As bloodhulk fighter.
Blood Bloated (Ex) As bloodhulk fighter.

The most powerful version of this undead, a bloodhulk crusher is a living engine of destruction. Evil clerics use these beasts as walking engines of war. Their tremendous durability and great strength allow them to batter down castle gates, smash apart buildings, and crush smaller creatures.

STRATEGIES AND TACTICS

A bloodhulk can absorb a tremendous amount of punishment, though its vulnerability to piercing and slashing weapons gives adventurers an advantage against it. This mindless, bloated automaton sloshes about, following the orders of its creator without thought. Because of its utter lack of intelligence, the instructions given to a newly created bloodhulk must be very simple, such as "Kill anyone who enters this room."

Bloodhulks can be encountered singly or in groups, depending on the proclivities of their creator and their purpose. Their immense strength and ability to absorb damage makes them useful as guards, tougher than zombies but not as expensive or complex as flesh golems. Bloodhulks are commonly found shuffling alongside other minor undead servants in a necromancer's lair or a temple to an evil god of death.

Most evil spellcasters who employ bloodhulks use them as bodyguards. While a bloodhulk holds back a band of adventurers, its master can rain spells and ranged attacks upon them. A bloodhulk's durability makes it possible to drop area attacks upon both the bloodhulk and those it is fighting. In most cases, the undead can better absorb the punishment than its opponents.

"It took me a moment to realize what this horror was. We'd lost Inthord to an attack by undead weeks earlier, and we never found the body. I only recognized him by the birthmark on his cheek."

—Rous, explorer

SAMPLE ENCOUNTERS

Adventurers are most likely to encounter bloodhulks as second-tier guardians. The creatures can be found individually or in small groups.

Individual (EL 4–8): A single bloodhulk usually serves as a guardian assigned to slow down intruders while a general alarm is raised.

EL 4: A bloodhulk fighter guards the entrance to a temple of Erythnul hidden within a dungeon. If it spots intruders, it walks over to a huge bronze gong and strikes it each round unless it is attacked, at which point it retaliates in kind. The ringing gong alerts the temple inhabitants.

Patrol (EL 6–10): When deployed in groups, bloodhulks form a daunting, almost impenetrable line of defense.

EL 9: A pair of bloodhulk giants blocks a 40-foot-wide corridor within a dungeon. The bloodhulks stand watch over the passage to prevent adventurers or wandering monsters from disturbing a hobgoblin necromancer and his assistants. The necromancer and his followers are in the process of excavating a tomb hidden within the dungeon.

BLOODHULK LORE

Characters with ranks in Knowledge (religion) can learn more about bloodhulks. When a character makes a successful skill check, the following lore is revealed, including the information from lower DCs.

Knowledge (Religion)

DC	Result
10 + CR	This is a bloodhulk, a kind of mindless undead. It can withstand tremendous physical punishment. This result reveals all undead traits.
15 + CR	A bloodhulk is created through a foul ritual that saturates a creature's flesh with the blood of sacrificed victims.
20 + CR	A bloodhulk is full to bursting with blood. Whenever it takes damage from edged weapons, its flesh ruptures.

Bodyguard (EL 10–20): A high-ranking priest or necromancer might be accompanied by one or more bloodhulks that act as "meat shields" against physical attack.

EL 13: A 12th-level cleric of Hextor uses two bloodhulk fighters and a pair of bloodhulk crushers as personal bodyguards. The monsters surround him while he casts his spells. The crushers' great reach allows them to swat at opponents who move close to the cleric, while the fighters protect his flanks and make it impossible for his foes to get next to him.

ECOLOGY

Bloodhulks are completely mindless. Their wretched existence is at the pleasure of their creators, and their destruction is inconsequential (though unpleasantly messy). Creating a bloodhulk requires a ritual of bloody sacrifice culminating in a spell of animation. Most living corporeal beings can be made into these horrors.

Environment: As created beings, bloodhulks can be found in any environment. Typically they patrol grim temples, moldering tombs, and precincts devoted to blasphemous observances.

Some spellcasters display a preference for creating bloodhulks over more standard undead servants. In particular, evil blood magi (*Complete Arcane* 26) who specialize in necromancy can't resist innovative methods of using blood.

Typical Physical Characteristics: Bloodhulks are disgusting to behold, resembling swollen, muscle-bound corpses whose skin writhes with purulent veins. They stink of festering wounds and make an unsettling slurping sound as they move. They wear no armor and at most are covered with ragged fragments of clothing, having outgrown their former garments.

A bloodhulk is the same height as the typical creature for its size but has a much bulkier build. The sheer volume of blood sloshing around within makes a bloodhulk twice as heavy as a base creature of comparable size.

Alignment: Bloodhulks are incapable of independent thought or moral judgment, making them neutral in outlook. However, the horrible ritual of their creation, the cruelty of their makers, and the grim tasks to which they are set lend them a taint of evil. All bloodhulks are therefore of neutral evil alignment.

TYPICAL TREASURE

Bloodhulks are servitors and possess no treasure of their own, although they might be set to guard items of value. Even those that were once champions of battle no longer wear even a vestige of armor, nor do they wield weapons.

FOR PLAYER CHARACTERS

The *animate dead* spell normally allows the creation of only skeletons and zombies. It can also create bloodhulks, though the process is more difficult.

- You can create bloodhulk warriors, giants, or crushers based solely on the size of the corpse you wish to animate: A Medium corpse is required for a bloodhulk fighter, Large for a giant, and Huge for a crusher. Smaller and larger corpses cannot be made into bloodhulks. The creation of a bloodhulk changes the original corpse too much for it to retain most of its original features.
- In addition to the usual material components, you must supply blood from three recently slain creatures the same size as the potential bloodhulk.
- Bloodhulks are considered to have double their Hit Dice for the purpose of creating and controlling them. Thus, the number of bloodhulks you can create is equal to your Hit Dice (instead of twice your Hit Dice) if you are not in a *desecrated* area. You can control no more than 2 HD worth of bloodhulks per caster level; if you are attempting to control different sorts of undead creatures, the bloodhulks are considered to have twice as many Hit Dice as are shown in their entries for the purpose of determining the total number of undead you can control.

BLOODHULKS IN EBERRON

Some worshipers of the Keeper create bloodhulks in rituals offered to the lord of death and decay. The grossly swollen creatures are thought to reflect the form of the dark god.

Karrnathi clerics might know of the rituals that create bloodhulks but would never use them for their armies. Such honorless monstrosities do not deserve to stand with the tireless soldiers who serve their nation in death.

BLOODHULKS IN FAERÛN

The most notorious necromancer in the Realms is Szass Tam, the Zulkir of Necromancy in Thay. In addition to creating dread warriors (*Monsters of Faerûn* 46) for Thay's armies, he has been experimenting in recent years with other forms of undead. Bloodhulks are useful ways to "recycle" the waste products of his necromantic research. Szass Tam constructs bloodhulks with the cold dispassion of a magical researcher. The requisite creatures are quickly slaughtered, bled, and animated.

Velsharoon is the patron and creator of undead, with cults dedicated to his worship hidden throughout Faerûn. Some of these dark servitors produce bloodhulks from captured townsfolk and send the bloated parodies back to torment and terrify their kin.

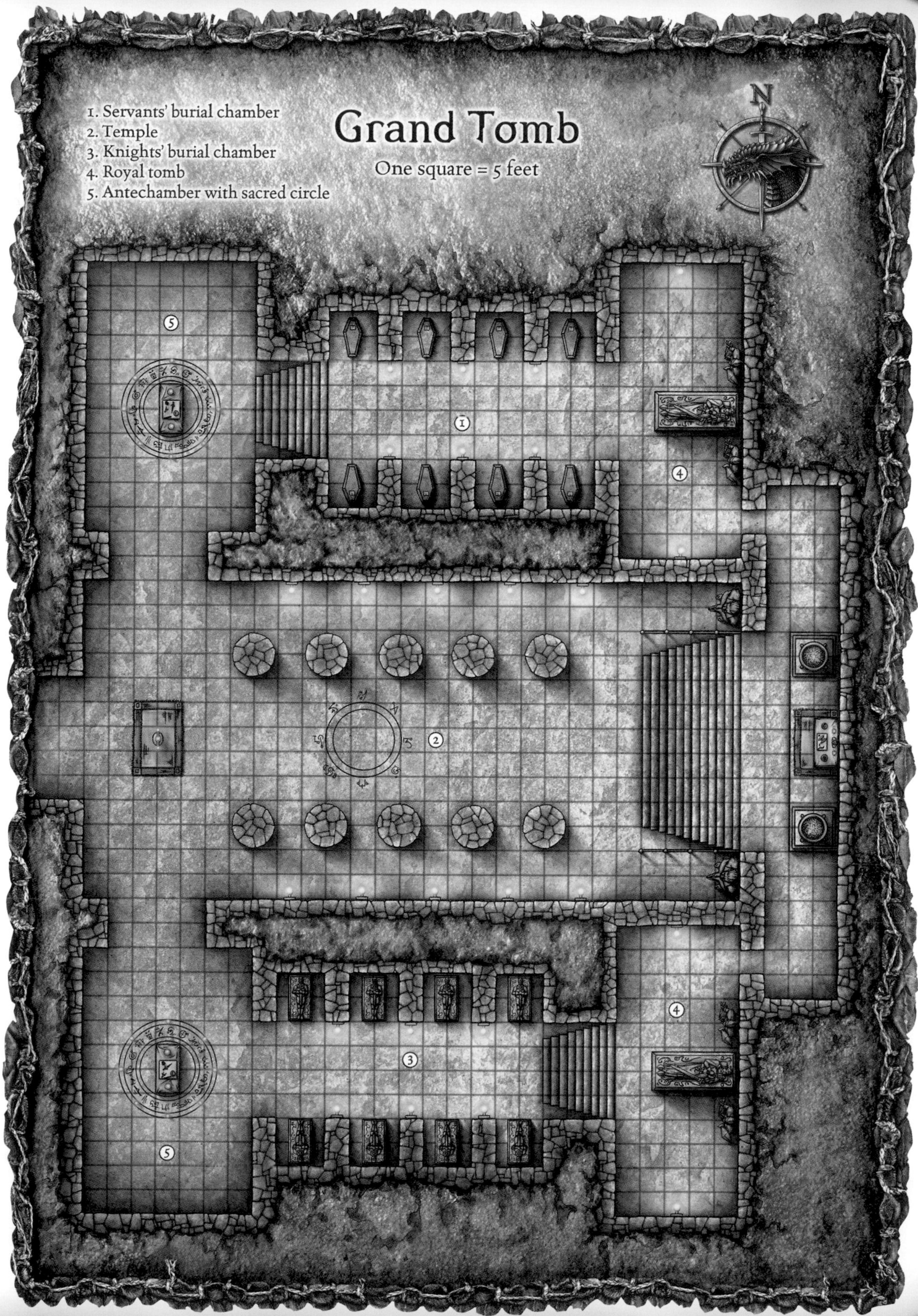

Grand Tomb

One square = 5 feet

1. Servants' burial chamber
2. Temple
3. Knights' burial chamber
4. Royal tomb
5. Antechamber with sacred circle

BLOODHULK

BLOODSILK SPIDER

This bloated spider is as big as a wolf, with thick, powerful legs and a heavy, red blister of flesh on its back.

BLOODSILK SPIDER   CR 2

Usually N Small magical beast
Init +3; **Senses** darkvision 60 ft., tremorsense 60 ft.;
    Listen +0, Spot +4
Languages —

AC 16, touch 14, flat-footed 13
    (+1 size, +3 Dex, +2 natural)
hp 11 (2 HD)
Fort +3, **Ref** +6, **Will** +0

Speed 30 ft. (6 squares), climb 20 ft.
Melee bite +6 (1d6–1)
Ranged blood web +6 ranged touch (entangle)
Space 5 ft.; **Reach** 5 ft.
Base Atk +2; **Grp** –3
Special Actions blood drain

Abilities Str 9, Dex 16, Con 10, Int 2, Wis 10, Cha 2
Feats Weapon Finesse
Skills Climb +11, Hide +12*, Listen +0, Move Silently +3*,
    Spot +4
    *When a bloodsilk spider is in its web, its racial bonus
        on Hide checks increases to +8, and it has a +8 racial
        bonus on Move Silently checks.
Advancement 3–4 HD (Small); 5–8 HD (Medium);
    9–12 HD (Large)

Blood Drain (Su) As a swift action each round, a bloodsilk
    spider can command its webs to drill into ensnared
    creatures, drain their blood, and channel it to the
    spider. The spider must be in contact with its webs
    to use this ability. A bloodsilk spider's webs deal 1d4
    points of damage at the beginning of each round to
    an opponent entangled in them. This ability does
    not affect elementals, plants, or creatures that lack a
    Constitution score.
        A bloodsilk spider gains temporary hit points equal
    to the damage dealt. A bloodsilk spider can gain no
    more than 10 temporary hit points in this fashion. These
    temporary hit points last for up to 24 hours.
Blood Web (Ex) A bloodsilk spider can throw a blood-red
    web eight times per day. This is similar to an attack with
    a net but has a maximum range of 50 feet, with a range
    increment of 10 feet, and is effective against targets up to
    one size category larger than the spider. The web anchors
    the target in place, allowing no movement. Attempts
    to escape or burst the webbing gain a +5 bonus if the
    trapped creature has something to walk on or grab while
    pulling free.
        An entangled creature can escape with a DC 11
    Escape Artist check or burst the web with a DC 15
    Strength check. Both are standard actions. The check
    DCs are Constitution-based, and the Strength check
    DC includes a +4 racial bonus. The web has 12 hit
    points and hardness 0. The blood that soaks it gives
    the web immunity to fire damage, unlike ordinary
    spider webs.
        A bloodsilk spider can create sheets of sticky webbing
    from 5 to 20 feet square. The webs are red with blood
    drained from its victims, and in some places they drip
    blood. The spider usually positions these sheets to
    snare flying creatures but can also try to trap prey on the
    ground. Approaching creatures must succeed on a DC 20
    Spot check to notice a web; otherwise they stumble into
    it and become trapped as though by a successful web
    attack. Each 5-foot section of webbing has 12 hit points
    and damage reduction 5/—.
        A bloodsilk spider can move across its own web at its
    climb speed and can pinpoint the location of any creature
    touching its web.
Skills Bloodsilk spiders have a +4 racial bonus on Hide
    checks (except when in their webs; see above) and a +4
    racial bonus on Spot checks.
        A bloodsilk spider has a +8 racial bonus on Climb
    checks and can always choose to take 10 on Climb
    checks, even if rushed or threatened. It uses either its
    Strength or its Dexterity modifier for Climb checks,
    whichever is higher.

Bloodsilk spiders, like their mundane cousins, are ambush
predators that feed on the vital fluids of their prey. They
lurk in reddened webs, which they use to drain blood from
trapped creatures.

STRATEGIES AND TACTICS

Unlike mundane or even monstrous vermin, bloodsilk spiders possess a cunning intelligence. They attack any living thing for its blood, using their webs to catch and slay even more prey. They are not powerful individually, so they prefer to attack in numbers, usually groups of four to eight. One of the spiders leads off the attack with a blast of webbing, after which the others charge any snared opponents.

A lone bloodsilk spider strings its webs between two trees, rocks, or similar landmarks along a forest path. The spider lurks nearby, using its tremorsense ability to detect a foe's approach. Once a creature is trapped within the webs, the spider leaps to attack. Its web soaks up the prey's blood while the spider bites with its mandibles.

Bloodsilk spiders fighting opponents larger than themselves always wait until they have slain some lesser prey (and thus gained temporary hit points) before attacking more dangerous foes.

"It was on the third day that we encountered a pair of woodsmen with a tale of red webs. Prince Lumien determined to see these webs for himself, and he persuaded the holy man Ilix to accompany him. We did not see them again—not living."
—Guldur of the Royal Guard

SAMPLE ENCOUNTERS

Bloodsilk spiders are patient, cunning killers.
    Individual (EL 2): A single bloodsilk spider uses hide-and-pounce tactics to surprise prey. In about one in ten cases, a lone bloodsilk spider has recently fed and has 5 temporary hit points stored up.
    Cluster (EL 6–8): Clusters of four to eight bloodsilk spiders lurk in foliage or rubble, waiting for prey to pass by.
    Nest (EL 8–10): A bloodsilk spider nest can contain anywhere from eight to sixteen individuals. At least half the spiders in such nests have fed recently, each with 5 to 10 temporary hit points.

ECOLOGY

Bloodsilk spiders live and reproduce much as other spiders do. They prefer areas of heavy foliage for their lairs, particularly if the region contains plenty of animals to feed upon. When it has exhausted the local stock of prey, a spider moves on to another area.

A bloodsilk spider might instead inhabit ruins if the local forest has a significant number of giant wasps or spider eaters—both of which are its deadly foes. Even other varieties of giant spider are troublesome to bloodsilk spiders, if prey in the area is scarce.

Environment: Bloodsilk spiders are found in warm and temperate forests and marshes, particularly amid larger trees or areas of thick undergrowth, where they can blend in more easily.

Typical Physical Characteristics: A typical bloodsilk spider is about 3 feet long and weighs 40 to 50 pounds.

Alignment: Bloodsilk spiders are predators and rarely take moral stances. Those inhabiting an area tainted by malice might tend toward evil.

TYPICAL TREASURE

Like other monstrous spiders, bloodsilk spiders do not collect treasure, but there is a 50% chance that a bloodsilk spider nest contains some coins, goods, or items left over from its victims. Roll separately for each type of treasure.

BLOODSILK SPIDERS IN EBERRON

Bloodsilk spiders are among the many dangers that await adventurers who travel through the Towering Wood of the Eldeen Reaches. An unwary explorer could easily wander into a nest of the beasts if he ignores the tell-tale web signs of a bloodsilk brood. Large populations infest the Gloaming, where their webs fade into the continual dimness of that twisted forest. Bloodsilk spiders occasionally wander closer to the edge of the wood, posing a threat to homesteaders of the Reaches.

BLOODSILK SPIDERS IN FAERÛN

In Faerûn, bloodsilk spiders inhabit the great forests of the south, most notably within the Chondalwood, where exceptionally large spiders live among the dangerous flora. Halfling rangers and druids also occasionally muster to battle infestations within the Lluirwood, and nests of bloodsilk spiders can be found in many other forests near the Shaar, including Qurth Forest and the Thornwood of the Border Kingdoms. Rumors hold that bloodsilk spiders were born of the Calishite sorcerer's curse that poisoned the Qurth forest, a new form of deadly spider that bred true long after the sorcerer's death.

Bloodsilk spider

Illus. by J. Nilson

BLOODSILK SPIDER LORE

Characters with ranks in Knowledge (arcana) can learn more about bloodsilk spiders. When a character makes a successful skill check, the following lore is revealed, including the information from lower DCs.

Knowledge (Arcana)

DC	Result
12	Bloodsilk spiders are magical beasts named for the blood-red webs they spin. This result reveals all magical beast traits.
17	Bloodsilk spider webs drain blood from trapped creatures by boring into the flesh. The spider consumes blood drained by its web, growing tougher in the process.
22	A bloodsilk spider is a patient and cunning hunter. When hunting a creature larger than itself, it first feeds on smaller prey to gain vitality for the fight.
27	A nest of bloodsilk spiders is especially dangerous, because those that have recently fed throw webs over intruders, trapping them to feed the rest.

BRIARVEX

This creature appears to be a large humanoid-shaped plant, roughly the size of an ogre. Glistening with sticky amber sap, wicked spikes protrude from its body, and a pair of writhing, tentacular vines extend from its hips.

BRIARVEX   **CR 6**

Usually NE Large plant
Init +0; **Senses** low-light vision; Listen +7, Spot +7
Languages Common, Sylvan

AC 19, touch 9, flat-footed 19
   (–1 size, +10 natural)
hp 68 (8 HD); **DR** 5/slashing
Immunities plant immunities
Fort +10, **Ref** +2, **Will** +5
Weakness vulnerability to fire

Speed 30 ft. (6 squares); improved woodland stride
Melee 2 spiked fists +12 each (2d6+7 plus thorn burrow)
Space 10 ft.; **Reach** 10 ft.
Base Atk +6; **Grp** +17
Atk Options Power Attack, thorn burrow
Special Actions entangle

Abilities Str 25, Dex 10, Con 19, Int 11, Wis 12, Cha 11
SQ plant traits
Feats Improved Natural Attack (spiked fist), Iron Will, Power Attack
Skills Hide +1*, Listen +7, Spot +7, Survival +6
   *A briarvex has a +16 racial bonus on Hide checks made in forested areas.
Advancement 9–12 HD (Large); 13–25 HD (Huge) or by character class; **Favored Class** druid; see text

Improved Woodland Stride (Ex) A briarvex can move through any sort of undergrowth (such as natural thorns, briars, overgrown areas, and similar terrain) at its normal speed and without taking damage or suffering any other impairment. In addition, thorns, briars, and overgrown areas that have been magically manipulated do not impede its motion or otherwise affect it.

Thorn Burrow (Su) A briarvex's spiked fist attack deals piercing as well as bludgeoning damage.

   Each time a briarvex hits with its spiked fist, thorns break off and bore into the struck opponent. As a swift action, the briarvex can cause embedded thorns to twist and burrow into a single creature's flesh, dealing 3d6 points of piercing damage; damage reduction applies. The target of this ability must be within 100 feet of the briarvex. The briarvex must also have line of effect to the target. A creature can remove the thorns with a standard action.

Entangle (Su) As the *entangle* spell; at will; DC 18; caster level 8th.

   This ability affects a 60-foot-radius area around the briarvex and lasts for 1 round. The save DC is Constitution-based.

A briarvex is a vicious, aggressive plant creature that haunts old-growth forests, dense swamps, and other areas choked with plant life. Briarvexes are able to control plants, thereby entangling their foes, or pierce opponents with spiny thorns that animate to drill into the flesh. These creatures are commonly referred to as "vine ogres."

STRATEGIES AND TACTICS

Existing only in limited numbers, briarvexes are preoccupied with their own survival and prosperity. They seek to populate forested lands with their spawn, migrating to new areas to expand their influence and control.

When they encounter other creatures, briarvexes attempt to appraise any possible threat from hiding. They are particularly wary of intruders who bear sources of fire. They generally assault only creatures that appear weaker than themselves, and they prefer surprise. A briarvex begins combat by entangling opponents, then closes to melee range; it is unaffected by the entangle effect. When facing a powerful opponent, a briarvex tries to buy time for reinforcements to arrive. It first attempts to intimidate the opponent (typically lying about its companions' numbers), and then resorts to wheedling if that is unsuccessful. Combat is the last resort.

Briarvexes hate treants (the feeling is mutual) and attack them on sight. They see treants as their most powerful competition in the war for control of the forest, and they attempt to eradicate their woodland cousins whenever possible. As always, they do this from a position of strength, gathering in greater numbers before launching such an assault.

SAMPLE ENCOUNTERS

Briarvexes prefer their own kind, existing in stands of two to four creatures that migrate from one forested area to the next, spreading their seed wherever they go. Powerful specimens are occasionally encountered alone, particularly those devoted to the druid's arts. Evil briarvex druids aggressively patrol their territory, driving out or slaying all nonplant creatures.

Individual (EL 6): A single briarvex hides within a stand of trees near a campsite commonly used by travelers. It waits

BRIARVEX LORE

Characters with ranks in Knowledge (nature) can learn more about briarvexes. When a character makes a successful skill check, the following lore is revealed, including the information from lower DCs.

A successful DC 26 Knowledge (nature) check identifies a briarvex in its immature stage.

Due to the creature's extraplanar origins, Knowledge (the planes) can also be used, but all check DCs increase by 5.

Knowledge (Nature)

DC	Result
16	This creature is a briarvex, a malevolent plant being. This result reveals all plant traits.
21	A briarvex is capable of controlling the plants around it, causing them to grapple and hold its foes.
26	A briarvex's strikes implant thorns into a creature. These thorns can animate and burrow into the flesh, causing grievous injuries.
31	A briarvex spends the first two years of its life in an inert state, similar to a normal plant. During that time, it can be easily uprooted and burnt.

patiently until the party approaches and beds down for the night. It then creeps up to the campsite and attacks the nearest sleeping traveler, using its entangle ability to prevent any sentries from interfering. If the travelers openly carry any expensive goods or treasure, the briarvex presses the attack to steal as much as possible.

Pair (EL 8): A pair of briarvexes form a daunting combination. One uses its entangle ability each round to lock down enemies. The other wades into melee to rip into the trapped creatures.

ECOLOGY

Briarvexes seek only to propagate, spreading their seeds across any lands with habitable soil. They view all other creatures—especially treants—as potential threats to their continued existence. Against stronger beings, briarvexes might attempt diplomatic maneuvers while they grow their population to unstoppable numbers. However, they seek to remove weaker creatures forcibly from areas they inhabit. A rare few briarvexes have attempted to establish peaceful relations with other creatures that live nearby, particularly gnolls, but most consider such "lesser beings" to be nuisances fit only to fertilize the soil.

A newly sprouted briarvex seedling spends the first two years of its life inert and rooted in the ground, looking like a large, gnarled bush. Once it has fully matured, it awakens, uproots itself, and moves out into the world.

Briarvexes can sow tremendous numbers of their kind, though excessive planting greatly strains the soil and water table. However, in areas blessed with rich soil and plentiful rain, their numbers can explode, leading to disaster. At least twice in recorded history, briarvexes have managed to plant almost a thousand of their kind in the course of a year near a city that poorly patrolled the nearby wilds. Two years later, the unlucky city found itself under attack by a horde of the creatures.

Environment: Briarvexes seek out the darkest parts of large forests, where their distinguishing features are less noticeable. Once there, they clear an area of the canopy to gain access to daylight, but do so as unobtrusively as possible.

Sages and druids who know of the briarvexes believe they originated somewhere in the Nine Hells of Baator but at some point were transported wholly to earthly realms.

Typical Physical Characteristics: Briarvexes stand from 9 to 12 feet tall at maturity and can weigh as much as 1,500 pounds. They do not eat, but they do require a reliable source of water and access to sunlight.

Alignment: Briarvexes are almost always neutral evil. Older, more powerful individuals grow more malign with age, tending toward chaotic evil.

TYPICAL TREASURE

Briarvexes have an innate love of shiny gems and gold coins. These creatures weave such objects into their thorns and vines to display trophies of past victories. A briarvex has standard treasure for its Challenge Rating, about 2,000 gp.

BRIARVEXES WITH CLASS LEVELS

Briarvexes are generally not suitable as player characters, but some learn druid magic. Briarvex druids usually become leaders of their kind, though a few strike out on their own.

Level Adjustment: +4.

BRIARVEXES IN EBERRON

Nobody is quite sure when briarvexes appeared in Khorvaire, though stands of the creatures began wandering out of the Mournland shortly after the end of the Last War. They seem to migrate in patterns, but the meanings of these patterns are unclear. Perhaps the elder races and the giants know, but they are not telling. Meanwhile, the dragons study this new thread in the fabric of the Prophecy.

BRIARVEXES IN FAERÛN

These creatures spontaneously appeared in the High Forest, and almost simultaneously in the jungles of Chult. Scholars and sages interested in the briarvexes' movements are funding expeditions to observe them. So far, none have reported solid information regarding the strange new creatures.

Illus. by R. Mimura

Briarvex

CLOCKROACH

Chewing on the ground is a whirring, scuttling metal bug about the size of a large dog. Glass eyes dotting its body look in all directions as it sinks sharp pincers into the ground and spews a stream of acid onto a bit of debris.

CLOCKROACH CR 1

Always N Small construct
Init +3; **Senses** darkvision 60 ft., low-light vision, tremorsense 60 ft.; Listen +0, Spot +0
Languages —

AC 14, touch 14, flat-footed 11
    (+1 size, +3 Dex)
hp 15 (1 HD)
Immune construct immunities
Fort +0, **Ref** +3, **Will** +0

Speed 30 ft. (6 squares), burrow 15 ft., climb 30 ft.
Melee 2 pincers +1 each (1d4)
Space 5 ft.; **Reach** 5 ft.
Base Atk +0; **Grp** −4
Special Actions breath weapon

Abilities Str 11, Dex 17, Con —, Int —, Wis 11, Cha 10
SQ construct traits
Feats —
Skills Climb +8, Hide +7, Listen +0, Spot +0
Advancement 2–3 HD (Small)

Breath Weapon (Su) 30-foot line, once every 5 rounds, damage 3d4 acid, Reflex DC 14 half. The save DC includes a +4 racial bonus.
Skills A clockroach has a +8 racial bonus on Climb checks and can always choose to take 10 on Climb checks, even if rushed or threatened.

Clockroaches are automatons designed to clean up messes in dungeons, workshops, and the like. A clockroach is controlled by a command amulet, through which the owner can give it simple instructions.

CLOCKROACH LORE

Characters with ranks in Knowledge (arcana) can learn more about clockroaches. When a character makes a successful skill check, the following lore is revealed, including the information from lower DCs.

Knowledge (Arcana)

DC	Result
11	This creature is a clockroach, a mindless construct incapable of independent thought. This result reveals all construct traits.
16	Clockroaches are tough, buglike automatons equipped with magically replenishing reservoirs of powerful acid, which they can spray up to 30 feet.
21	Clockroaches can burrow into stone and earth, and they can climb at the same speed they walk.
26	A clockroach's carapace contains an indention to hold a command amulet. When the amulet is in place, the clockroach can be programmed.

STRATEGIES AND TACTICS

As mindless constructs, clockroaches exercise limited, preprogrammed tactics. A clockroach attacks only when defending itself or if a creature is in an area it's been instructed to clear. In either case, it uses its breath weapon as often as possible, using its pincers while recharging its reserve of acid. A clockroach also uses its acid to bore through obstacles between it and its objective.

"So far, all my efforts to control the silly thing have failed. Clearly there's some secret to this I have yet to unravel. As long as it's doing nothing but clearing the dungeons of refuse, I'm not concerned. But if it should decide my familiar is trash—or I am . . .
    Clearly, further research is called for."
                —Final journal entry of
                   Ingalla Asterian, artificer

SAMPLE ENCOUNTERS

Clockroaches are most often found in subterranean compounds, usually in cleaning crews of up to six individuals. Hordes of clockroaches descend on the battlefields of the planes, posing hazards to the unwary traveler.

Guardian (EL 1): A single clockroach can be programmed to attack anything that it sees or any creature that doesn't give an approved signal or password.

EL 1: Guarding the entrance to a brigand's cave is one clockroach. It never moves more than 30 feet from the entrance, and it doesn't enter the cave or attack anything within it. It ignores any creature that either gives the password "Cinnamon" or waves with just two fingers raised. It otherwise attacks anything that moves.

Clean Sweep (EL 2–6): On extraplanar battlegrounds, clockroaches scour the refuse of old combats clean, leaving the field fresh for new battles.

EL 6: On one of the endless battlefields of Acheron lie the remains of thousands of orcs and goblins, killed over and over in ceaseless warfare. The war has long since moved on, but the stinking piles of bodies linger. Six clockroaches move slowly through the area, spraying acid on everything until they reduce the corpses, broken weapons, and other refuse down to clean earth. They see everything as trash in need of disposal and attack any creature that comes into range. An opponent that survives more than 1 round becomes the focus of all six clockroaches, who all direct their acid against the troublesome "garbage."

ECOLOGY

Clockroaches are mindless constructs. They do not eat, sleep, or breathe. They exist as tools, working only to the purposes they have been set. They follow their programming from the moment they are built to the day they fall apart.

Each clockroach is constructed with a command amulet. This small round disk of metal fits into an indention in

Clockroach

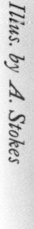

Illus. by A. Stokes

FOR PLAYER CHARACTERS

A clockroach is crafted from metal plates that protect finely wrought gears and other mechanical elements, with a total cost of 75 gp. Constructing the body requires a DC 14 Craft (metalworking) check.

A clockroach with more than 1 Hit Die can be created, but each additional Hit Die adds 2,000 gp to the cost.

The creation cost also includes the materials for the command amulet attuned to that clockroach. The amulet is part of the clockroach, not a mechanical key. It is not possible to recreate a destroyed amulet, nor to somehow bypass the amulet's function and program the clockroach without it.

CL 4th; Craft Construct, *arcane eye, Melf's acid arrow, message*; Price 2,150 gp; Cost 1,075 gp + 80 XP.

CLOCKROACHES IN EBERRON

Clockroaches are believed to have been developed at the same time as warforged, possibly to serve as their assistants. Many still exist in the Mournland, and some warforged keep clockroaches as pets.

Some artificers also create clockroaches as homunculi (*Magic of Eberron* 151). A homunculus clockroach requires as an additional ingredient a pint of the creator's blood. It has an Intelligence score of 10, the Weapon Finesse feat (raising its melee attack bonus to +4), and a +4 bonus on Spot checks. It does not have a command amulet.

CLOCKROACHES IN FAERÛN

Clockroaches first appeared in Lantan, products of Gond's wondermakers. Word of their usefulness spread rapidly, and they can now be found up and down the Sword Coast. Most are purchased by wealthy merchants, but a few inadvertently migrated to the mainland in the holds of passing vessels. Tales tell of explorers who released a massive horde of clockroaches into the jungles of Chult, hoping to blaze a roadway to a newly discovered ruin. The experiment failed, and now the creatures rove the landscape devouring old trash and priceless historical artifacts with equal zeal.

---

the clockroach's carapace. When fitted with its amulet, a clockroach can be given a simple program. Programmed instructions must depend only on sight and hearing and allow no cognitive function; they can be no longer than twenty-five words.

Environment: Though clockroaches can be found anywhere, they were originally built by extraplanar generals to clean up battlegrounds taken from eternal foes.

Typical Physical Characteristics: A clockroach is 4 feet long and 1-1/2 feet wide. Eight spindly metal legs carry it about 1 foot off the ground. Its feet are lined with tiny hooks, allowing it to burrow into the ground or walk up a wall. Glass eyes are randomly located on its body. It constantly produces a slight whirring noise, like a wheel spinning very fast. Most clockroaches are made of brass or bronze, but a few steel or iron specimens have been encountered.

The carapace of a clockroach has a round indention in it, which is ridged and inscribed with many small runes.

Alignment: As mindless automatons, clockroaches are always neutral.

TYPICAL TREASURE

Clockroaches do not carry or store treasure of any kind. However, a clockroach with its command amulet is worth 2,150 gp.

CLOCKWORK MENDER

This minuscule mechanical creature flits about on wings that beat like a hummingbird's. Its tiny face vaguely resembles a human's, and its tail ends in a sharp stinger.

CLOCKWORK MENDER   CR 1/2
Always LN Tiny construct (extraplanar, lawful)
Init +4; **Senses** darkvision 60 ft., low-light vision; Listen +1, Spot +1
Languages Abyssal, Celestial, Infernal (can't speak)

AC 18, touch 16, flat-footed 14
    (+2 size, +4 Dex, +2 natural)
hp 5 (1 HD)
Immune construct immunities
Fort +0, **Ref** +4, **Will** +1

Speed 10 ft. (2 squares), fly 30 ft. (perfect); Spring Attack
Melee sting +6 (1d2–4 plus poison)
Space 2-1/2 ft.; **Reach** 2-1/2 ft.
Base Atk +0; **Grp** –12
Atk Options aligned strike (lawful), poison (DC 12, 1d4 Dex/1d4 Dex)
Special Actions repairing touch

Abilities Str 3, Dex 19, Con —, Int 4, Wis 12, Cha 10
SQ construct traits, repairing touch
Feats Skill Focus (Craft), Spring Attack[B], Weapon Finesse[B]
Skills Craft (any one) +4, Hide +12, Listen +1, Spot +1
Advancement —

Poison (Ex) The save DC includes a +2 racial bonus.
Repairing Touch (Su) Once per day as a standard action, a clockwork mender can touch an object or construct to repair 1d8 points of damage.

Clockwork menders live on the Clockwork Nirvana of Mechanus, where they serve a vital role in that plane's ecology. Wizards and sorcerers of the Material Plane who craft constructs find them to be useful familiars and guardians for their creations.

CLOCKWORK MENDER SWARM   CR 3
Always LN Tiny construct (extraplanar, lawful, swarm)
Init +4; **Senses** darkvision 60 ft., low-light vision; Listen +3, Spot +3
Languages Abyssal, Celestial, Infernal (can't speak)

AC 18, touch 16, flat-footed 14
    (+2 size, +4 Dex, +2 natural)
hp 22 (4 HD)
Immune construct immunities, swarm immunities
Resist half damage from slashing and piercing
Weakness swarm vulnerabilities
Fort +1, **Ref** +5, **Will** +2

Speed 10 ft. (2 squares), fly 30 ft. (perfect)
Melee swarm (1d6 plus poison and distraction)
Space 10 ft.; **Reach** 0 ft.
Base Atk +3; **Grp** —
Atk Options aligned strike (lawful), distraction, poison (DC 14, 2d4 Dex/2d4 Dex)
Special Actions swarm repair, swarm sacrifice

Abilities Str 3, Dex 19, Con —, Int 4, Wis 12, Cha 10
SQ construct traits, swarm traits
Feats Alertness, Skill Focus (Craft)
Skills Craft (any one) +7, Listen +3, Spot +3
Advancement —

Poison (Ex) The save DC includes a +2 racial bonus.
Distraction (Ex) Fortitude DC 12, nauseated 1 round. The save DC is Constitution-based.
Swarm Repair (Su) A clockwork mender swarm can choose not to damage a construct with its swarm attack. When the clockwork mender swarm occupies a construct's space at the end of the swarm's turn, it can repair of 1 point of damage to that construct. The swarm can use its swarm repair on itself if it does not move for 1 round.
Swarm Sacrifice (Ex) A clockwork mender swarm can choose not to damage a construct with its swarm attack. When the swarm occupies a construct's space at the end of the swarm's turn, it can repair damage to that construct, up to the swarm's current hit points. The swarm loses an equal number of hit points as its members sacrifice themselves to become building material to repair the construct. If the swarm sacrifice reduces the clockwork mender swarm's hit points to 0, it breaks up.

STRATEGIES AND TACTICS

Clockwork menders exist to repair damaged objects and constructs, but when agitated they attack any creature fearlessly. Menders attack when disturbed in their repairing efforts or when commanded to do so by their masters.

Clockwork menders spend most of their time on the wing and use their speed and Dexterity to their advantage, swooping in for hit-and-run attacks with their stings. They target nonconstructs first, using their poison to weaken those opponents before moving to construct or undead creatures. If damaged in combat, a clockwork mender uses its repairing touch on itself.

Clockwork mender swarms are more dangerous. They surround a target and batter it with their metallic wings while injecting poison. A swarm's ability to heal itself repeatedly makes it especially deadly.

SAMPLE ENCOUNTER

Clockwork menders exist in great numbers on the Clockwork Nirvana of Mechanus, where they tend to the environment and aid inevitables. They most often appear on the Material Plane in the company of wizards and others intrigued by constructs.

Golem Rampage (EL 8): A flesh golem went berserk almost immediately after its creation and killed its master. It smashed its way free of the dead wizard's home and now stalks the streets, followed by two clockwork mender swarms. The clockwork menders once served the wizard, but they were in another room when the golem attacked and don't know of their master's passing. They now dutifully flit about his creation as it wantonly attacks people in the city, repairing it whenever it sustains damage.

ECOLOGY

On Mechanus, clockwork menders work to repair damaged parts of the mechanized plane and heal its construct inhabitants, striving to maintain perfect order. Since they do not originate on the Material Plane, they do not fit into its ecology in any way. Once brought there, clockwork menders rarely leave the presence of the person who summoned them, usually remaining indoors.

Clockwork menders feed on small bits of metal and rust as they go about their repairs. Their masters often leave scrap metal about as nourishment—over the course of a month, a clockwork mender devours about 4 pounds of metal.

Although clockwork menders do not propagate as living creatures do, they can build more of their kind. On Mechanus, swarms of menders gather according to a strict schedule, carrying materials to a long-established "mating" ground. There they construct a new batch of clockwork menders, numbering roughly half the swarms' population. The mender swarms fiercely guard this process from interruption. As yet, clockwork menders have not reproduced outside Mechanus; sages speculate that some peculiarity of the plane grants them "life" and sentience.

Environment: Clockwork menders are native to the Clockwork Nirvana of Mechanus but can be found in any environment. They prefer dry and cool settings—wet locales irritate them, and extremely hot places such as deserts make them lethargic.

Typical Physical Characteristics: A clockwork mender is close to a small cat in size. It has the same general shape as a wasp, including a sharp stinger, but bears a vaguely humanoid head devoid of distinct features. A clockwork mender has two minute arms that can perform incredibly delicate repairs.

Alignment: As creatures of Mechanus, clockwork menders are always lawful neutral. They pursue their tasks with single-minded efficiency.

TYPICAL TREASURE
Clockwork menders never have treasure.

CLOCKWORK MENDER LORE
Characters with ranks in Knowledge (the planes) can learn more about clockwork menders. When a character makes a successful skill check, the following lore is revealed, including the information from lower DCs.

Knowledge (the Planes)

DC	Result
11	This creature is a clockwork mender, a construct used by some wizards as a familiar. This result reveals all construct traits.
16	Clockwork menders hail from the Clockwork Nirvana of Mechanus. They spend their time repairing broken objects and other constructs. They're usually harmless unless threatened or impeded in some way.
21	Clockwork menders have stings that inject poison. They sometimes travel in swarms of hundreds.

Clockwork mender

FOR PLAYER CHARACTERS
Clockwork menders might appeal to PCs as familiars, homunculi, or summoned monsters.

Clockwork Menders as Familiars
A clockwork mender can be summoned as an improved familiar (DMG 200). An arcane spellcaster must be lawful-aligned, be at least 5th level, and take the Improved Familiar feat to acquire a clockwork mender familiar.

Summoning Clockwork Menders
Spellcasters can summon a clockwork mender with *summon monster II* or a higher-level *summon monster* spell. Treat the clockwork mender as being on the 2nd-level list on the Summon Monster table (PH 287).

A clockwork mender swarm can be summoned with the following spell.

Summon Clockwork Mender Swarm
Conjuration (Summoning) [Lawful]
Level: Cleric 4, sorcerer/wizard 4
Effect: One swarm of clockwork menders

This spell functions like *summon monster I*, except that you summon a single clockwork mender swarm. The swarm can be directed to attack opponents, to use its swarm repair ability, and even to use its swarm sacrifice ability.

Arcane Focus: A broken metal gear.

CLOCKWORK MENDERS IN EBERRON
Clockwork menders in Eberron exist as creations of artificers. They are relatively common sights wherever artificers congregate, and they often accompany warforged artificers. The gnomes of Zilargo make extensive use of clockwork menders, and it's considered a source of status for a workshop to host as many as possible.

Artificers can create a clockwork mender as a homunculus following the rules presented in the *Eberron Campaign Setting*. For expanded rules and advancement of homunculi, see *Magic of Eberron*.

Construction
A clockwork mender is made of bronze, steel, silver, gold, and a pint of the creator's blood. The materials cost 400 gp. Creating the body requires a DC 15 Craft (blacksmithing) check.

A clockwork mender with more than 1 Hit Die can be created, but each additional Hit Die adds 2,000 gp to the cost to create.

CL 5th; Craft Construct, *mending, repair light damage*; Price — (never sold); Cost 1,250 gp + 68 XP.

Illus. by A. Stokes

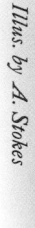

CLOCKWORK STEED

This creature resembles a horse crafted of sturdy metal plates and taut springs. A whistle of steam and the ratcheting click of gears accompany its movements.

CLOCKWORK STALLION   CR 3

Always N Large construct
Init –1; **Senses** darkvision 60 ft., low-light vision; Listen +0, Spot +0
Languages —

AC 15, touch 8, flat-footed 15
  (–1 size, –1 Dex, +7 natural)
hp 63 (6 HD)
Immune construct immunities
Fort +2, **Ref** +1, **Will** +2

Speed 50 ft. (10 squares)
Melee 2 hooves +8 each (1d6+5)
Space 10 ft.; **Reach** 5 ft.
Base Atk +4; **Grp** +13

Abilities Str 20, Dex 8, Con —, Int —, Wis 10, Cha 1
SQ construct traits, rider response, upgrades
Feats —
Skills Jump +13, Listen +0, Spot +0
Advancement —

Rider Response (Ex) A clockwork steed is built to respond to physical commands given to it by a rider holding its reins or guiding it with the knees. A riderless clockwork steed immediately stops and stands motionless, regardless of threats to itself, until mounted by a rider. A clockwork steed also stops and stands still if its rider becomes unconscious, stunned, paralyzed, dead, or otherwise unable to function.

  A clockwork steed cannot be taught tricks like a real horse or pony. A rider can direct it to move and attack foes, just like a war-trained mount, but cannot spur it to greater speed.

Upgrades (Ex) The creator of a clockwork steed can imbue it with more abilities at greater expense. See For Player Characters for more information.

CLOCKWORK PONY   CR 3

Always N Medium construct
Init +0; **Senses** darkvision 60 ft., low-light vision; Listen +0, Spot +0
Languages —

AC 17, touch 10, flat-footed 17
  (+7 natural)
hp 53 (6 HD)
Immune construct immunities
Fort +2, **Ref** +2, **Will** +2

Speed 40 ft. (8 squares)
Melee 2 hooves +8 each (1d4+4)
Space 5 ft.; **Reach** 5 ft.
Base Atk +4; **Grp** +8

Abilities Str 18, Dex 10, Con —, Int —, Wis 10, Cha 1
SQ construct traits, rider response, upgrades
Feats —
Skills Jump +8, Listen +0, Spot +0
Advancement —

Rider Response (Ex) As clockwork stallion.
Upgrades (Ex) As clockwork stallion.

A clockwork steed presents its owner with a perfectly tractable and battle-ready mount that never grows tired or requires food. Clockwork stallions are built for Medium riders, while ponies serve Small riders.

STRATEGIES AND TACTICS

Clockwork steeds are utterly mindless and simply stand inert unless commanded by a rider. Commanding a clockwork steed is a simple matter for anyone trained to ride an ordinary mount. As a free action, a character with at least 1 rank in Ride can direct the steed to perform a move action or an attack action, or as a move action, command it to make a full attack or perform a full-round action relating to movement (such as a charge). A rider without any ranks in Ride must instead use a move action or a standard action, respectively. Commanded actions cannot be complicated tactical choices such as tripping or overrunning or aiding another's attack, but clockwork steeds can be directed to charge and jump like horses. No command words are needed.

  Clockwork steeds serve at least as well as battle-trained mounts in combat, despite their lack of intelligence.

SAMPLE ENCOUNTER

People use clockwork steeds just as they do horses. However, most clockwork steeds belong to wealthy individuals or people powerful enough to steal from the wealthy. Thus, any encounter with a clockwork steed likely involves an owner who presents the real threat.

  Repossession (EL 7): A janni made a bargain with a wizard she saved from death in the desert, and she has come to collect. The wizard refused to acknowledge the debt to the janni, so she stole his clockwork stallion. Now she and two compatriot jann seek to escape the city. Everyone knows the wizard owns the clockwork stallion, and the alarm goes up as soon as someone sees a stranger riding it. The two jann on foot move invisibly and *enlarged* to block anyone attempting to reach their mounted companion. They bull rush opponents, and this action combined with their sudden appearance should frighten off most people; they attack with their scimitars if that doesn't work. The mount has the Improved Overrun and Trample upgrades (see below), which its janni rider uses against opponents that get by her fellows.

CLOCKWORK STEED LORE

Characters with ranks in Knowledge (arcana) can learn more about clockwork steeds. When a character makes a successful skill check, the following lore is revealed, including the information from lower DCs.

Knowledge (Arcana)

DC	Result
13	This creature is a clockwork steed, a construct mount designed to replace ordinary horses. This result reveals all construct traits.
18	Clockwork steeds do nothing without a rider, and anyone can command one by mounting it. No command words are necessary.
23	Although clockwork steeds themselves are not dangerous, beings wealthy enough to afford them might be serious threats.

ECOLOGY

As clockwork constructs, clockwork steeds don't contribute to the environment. Without a rider, a clockwork steed simply stands, gathering dust and slowly rusting away.

A forgotten wizard created the first clockwork steeds for a warlord's forces in a long campaign, but when the warlord learned how expensive the mounts were, he refused to pay. The wizard ended up selling his creations (and the warlord's plans) to the nobility of the city-state the warlord was planning to attack. Since then, others have learned how to create the mounts, and now they can be found in the service of anyone with enough gold.

Environment: Clockwork steeds, being constructs, have no natural environment. Like real horses, they fare best on hard, open ground such as plains, hills, and deserts. Massed cavalry gets bogged down in forests and marshes, but lone outriders or scouts mounted on clockwork steeds might be encountered even in such terrain.

Typical Physical Characteristics: A clockwork stallion is roughly the size of a heavy warhorse, standing nearly 6 feet at the shoulder. A clockwork pony is about the size of a warpony, slightly under 5 feet tall at the shoulder. The steeds' metallic construction makes them significantly heavier than their living equivalents: A clockwork stallion weighs upward of 2,500 pounds, while a pony weighs around 2,000 pounds.

TYPICAL TREASURE

A clockwork steed is itself treasure, usually found as part of an opponent's possessions. Many adventurers would pay well for a mount that never tires, never needs stabling, and needs no time-consuming care. As well, the saddlebags of clockwork steeds often hold items useful to their owners, such as *potions of cure light wounds* and emergency rations.

FOR PLAYER CHARACTERS

Player characters can create or purchase clockwork steeds, provided the necessary resources are available. In addition, they can pay for a steed's upgrades during creation or upgrade it later as though adding new abilities to a magic item (DMG 288).

Carrying Capacity: A light load for a clockwork stallion is up to 400 pounds; a medium load, 401–800 pounds; and a heavy load, 801–1,200 pounds. A clockwork stallion can drag 6,000 pounds.

A light load for a clockwork pony is up to 150 pounds; a medium load, 151–300 pounds; and a heavy load, 301–450 pounds. A clockwork pony can drag 2,250 pounds.

Construction

A clockwork steed's body is constructed from finely balanced gears, springs, and pistons treated with special alchemical agents and made from rare alloys costing 150 gp.

Assembling the body requires a DC 18 Craft (blacksmithing) check.

CL 4th; Craft Construct, *animate objects, mount*; Price 2,150 gp; Cost 1,150 gp + 80 XP. Upgrades increase the base cost as described below.

Upgrades

The following abilities can be added to a clockwork steed. Upgrades cost the same for both stallions and ponies.

Armor Proficiency: The steed gains proficiency with all types of armor (but not with shields). A clockwork steed without this upgrade that wears barding takes the appropriate armor check penalty on attack rolls and Strength- and Dexterity-based checks. Price 100 gp; Cost 50 gp + 4 XP.

Damage Reduction: The steed gains damage reduction 5/magic or adamantine. Price 500 gp; Cost 250 gp + 20 XP.

Improved Battle Readiness: This upgrade allows a skilled rider to use a swift action instead of a move action to command the steed to take full-round actions. Price 500 gp; Cost 250 gp + 20 XP.

Improved Bull Rush: The steed gains the Improved Bull Rush feat and lets a rider command it to make bull rush attempts. Price 150 gp; Cost 75 gp + 6 XP.

Improved Overrun: The steed gains the Improved Overrun feat and lets a rider command it to make overrun attempts. Price 150 gp; Cost 75 gp + 6 XP.

Improved Trip: The steed gains the Improved Trip feat and lets a rider command it to make trip attempts. Price 200 gp; Cost 100 gp + 8 XP.

Trample: To qualify for this upgrade, the steed must have the Improved Overrun upgrade. This upgrade allows a rider to use the Trample feat while making overrun attempts with the steed. Price 150 gp; Cost 75 gp + 6 XP.

Illus. by D. Hudnut

Clockwork steed

CONCORDANT KILLER

This creature resembles a tall, scarlet-skinned fiend with a pair of dusky feathered wings. Its loose-fitting robes are decorated with polished bits of blades taken from fallen enemies, and a gray-indigo vapor rises from the top of its head.

CONCORDANT KILLER · CR 19

Always N Large outsider (extraplanar)
Init +7; **Senses** darkvision 60 ft., low-light vision, true seeing; Listen +28, Spot +28
Languages Abyssal, Celestial, Common; telepathy 100 ft.

AC 39, touch 12, flat-footed 36
(−1 size, +3 Dex, +4 armor, +4 shield, +19 natural)
hp 200 (19 HD); **DR** 10/—
Immune acid, cold, electricity, fire, petrification, poison
SR 30
Fort +17, **Ref** +14, **Will** +17

Speed 40 ft. (8 squares), fly 90 ft. (good)
Melee +2 concordant greatsword +29/+24/+19/+14 (3d6+14/17–20) or
Melee 2 slams +26 each (2d8+8)
Space 10 ft.; **Reach** 10 ft.
Base Atk +19; **Grp** +31
Atk Options Cleave, Power Attack, Quicken Spell-Like Ability (*greater dispel magic*), Quicken Spell-Like Ability (*wall of force*), concordant greatsword
Spell-Like Abilities (CL 19th):
　At will—*analyze dweomer* (DC 23), *greater dispel magic*, *mage armor*†, *magic missile*, *Otiluke's resilient sphere* (DC 21), *shield*†, *greater teleport* (self plus 50 lb. of objects only)
　3/day—*forcecage*, *greater invisibility*, *Mordenkainen's sword*, *Otiluke's telekinetic sphere* (DC 25), *plane shift* (self only), *wall of force*
　1/day—*blasphemy* (DC 24), *dictum* (DC 24), *holy word* (DC 24), *mind blank*, *word of chaos* (DC 24)
　†Already used

Abilities Str 27, Dex 17, Con 23, Int 16, Wis 22, Cha 24
SQ aligned defenses, know alignment
Feats Cleave, Improved Critical (greatsword), Improved Initiative, Power Attack, Quicken Spell-Like Ability (*greater dispel magic*), Quicken Spell-Like Ability (*wall of force*), Weapon Focus (greatsword)
Skills Concentration +28, Diplomacy +9, Hide +21, Intimidate +29, Jump +12, Knowledge (arcana) +25, Knowledge (the planes) +25, Listen +28, Move Silently +25, Sense Motive +28, Spellcraft +27 (+29 with scrolls), Spot +28, Survival +6 (+9 on other planes), Use Magic Device +29 (+31 with scrolls)
Advancement 20–40 HD (Large)
Possessions +2 concordant greatsword

True Seeing (Su) As the *true seeing* spell; continuous; caster level 19th.
Concordant Greatsword (Su) Carried by every concordant killer, these blades are an extension of their carrier's will. Such a blade is treated as though it possessed the anarchic, axiomatic, holy, and unholy special abilities simultaneously. The sword can be sundered (it has hardness 14 and 30 hp), but if the concordant killer relinquishes its grip, the weapon dissipates. A concordant killer can create a new blade as a move action.
　If the concordant killer is destroyed, the sword it bears disappears forever.

Aligned Defenses (Su) A concordant killer can increase its defenses against creatures of a specific alignment component (good, evil, law, or chaos). Against attacks made or effects created by creatures of the chosen alignment, this ability grants the concordant killer a +4 deflection bonus to AC and a +4 resistance bonus on saving throws. At will, as a standard action, the concordant killer can change the alignment to which this effect is attuned.
　This ability also blocks spells of up to 3rd level cast by creatures of the specified alignment, as a *lesser globe of invulnerability* spell (CL 19th).(These defensive benefits are not included in the creature's statistics.)
Know Alignment (Su) As the *detect chaos, detect evil, detect good,* and *detect law* spells; continuous; caster level 19th. A concordant killer can suppress or resume some or all of this ability as a free action.

Possessing both celestial and demonic heritage, these powerful entities are dispassionate killers who frequently deliver the wrath of the gods. Concordant killers seek always to perfect their killing abilities and, when not in the employ of a higher power, hunt down those they deem worthy prey.

STRATEGIES AND TACTICS

A concordant killer prefers to study its opponent before entering combat, to discern the creature's alignment and appropriately prepare its defenses. If possible, it first casts *mage armor, shield, mind blank,* and *greater invisibility* on itself, in that order.

Once combat begins, the concordant killer starts by casting a quickened *greater dispel magic* against its target, or against the greatest threat when facing multiple opponents. It follows up with *blasphemy, dictum, holy word,* or *word of chaos,* as appropriate for the opponent's alignment, which

CONCORDANT KILLER LORE

Characters with ranks in Knowledge (the planes) can learn more about concordant killers. When a character makes a successful skill check, the following lore is revealed, including the information from lower DCs.

Knowledge (the Planes)

DC	Result
20	This creature is neither wholly fiendish nor celestial but possessed of both natures. It has traits that can be found in either kind of outsider. This result reveals all outsider traits.
29	A concordant killer is surrounded by an ever-changing defensive field that shifts to repel creatures of any given alignment. Other abilities, including its sword, are even more lethal to those whose alignment strays from neutrality.
34	Many of a concordant killer's spell-like abilities manipulate force energy. The creature is also resistant to all types of physical damage.
39	Concordant killers believe they were created to maintain the cosmic balance. They have since become assassins that pursue their quarry across the planes with cold-blooded, methodical ease.

also helps it gauge the strength of its foes. It uses Power Attack where appropriate against enemies with relatively poor defenses. If it faces a large group of enemies, it breaks the group into manageable numbers with one or more uses of *wall of force*.

If the fight becomes unmanageable, or if the concordant killer is being overwhelmed, it uses *greater teleport* or *plane shift* to escape combat altogether, then returns later when it is fresh and ready to battle on its own terms.

SAMPLE ENCOUNTER

A concordant killer often works alone. More dangerous assignments might require a group of four to five killers. If the PCs encounter a concordant killer, they are either linked somehow to its current target or are themselves the targets.

Individual (EL 19): A lone concordant killer might serve a deity to destroy one or more deserving transgressors.

EL 19: The PCs have run afoul of the servants of a demigod, who has since contracted with a concordant killer named Drexsalles to "take care of the matter." Drexsalles appears a short distance away, raising its +2 *concordant greatsword* in a grim salute before using *greater invisibility* to disappear. It advances invisibly and utters the appropriate sonic evocation once the party is within range.

ECOLOGY

Some say concordant killers were an experiment by gods of neutrality, who sought to create the perfect stewards for maintaining the cosmic balance. Others hold that they were created by a long-forgotten demigod to serve as bodyguards. They failed in that endeavor, and their master was lost to a shadowy rival. Without direction, they settled into the role of mercenaries.

Whatever the truth, as beings of neutrality, concordant killers are concerned with the balance of all forces in the planes. They understand that defeating a powerful foe might tip the scales one way or another. Therefore they track their kills as a group, endeavoring to distribute their prey evenly among the alignments. They keep the location of such meetings secret, though many sages believe they congregate near the central spire of the Outlands. Even deities' magic is impeded there, making it a perfect spot for clandestine gatherings.

Concordant killers do not reproduce, so every one that falls in battle forever reduces their number. Anyone who destroys a concordant killer becomes the target of its irate kin.

Environment: Infused with both fiendish and celestial essence, concordant killers are beings of the Outer Planes but are not native to any one. A killer might be found anywhere its mission takes it.

Typical Physical Characteristics: A concordant killer is between 10 and 11 feet in height and weighs from 900 to 1,200 pounds.

Alignment: A concordant killer is always neutral, seeking balance in its life even as it serves and hunts those of more extreme alignments.

Illus. by W. Reynolds

Concordant killer

SOCIETY

Concordant killers exist to hunt down and destroy other powerful creatures. Effective yet discreet, they are highly sought after by powerful entities such as demon lords, demigods, and even deities to do their dirty work. A concordant killer is dismissive of any prospective employer, though, unless offered substantial payment.

Concordant killers trade their services for favors, having little need for material possessions. Sometimes they request these favors at the time of hiring, but usually a contract for future payment suffices. Even gods are indebted to the concordant killers and so might look the other way, leave a planar portal open, provide information on a target's whereabouts, or undertake other favors that help the killers achieve their objectives.

TYPICAL TREASURE

Concordant killers have standard treasure for their Challenge Rating, about 61,000 gp, but carry no coins (replace these with gems of equal value). They care little for magic weapons or armor, so they typically carry powerful wands, staffs, or wondrous items.

CORRUPTURE

A hideous avalanche of flesh rolls down upon you, undulating like a wave of skin. Warts full of thick, yellow liquid swell up continually across its mass, bursting with loud pops and spraying corrosive fluids into the air.

CORRUPTURE   CR 9

Always N Huge ooze (aquatic)
Init –5; **Senses** blind, blindsight 60 ft.; Listen –5
Languages —

AC 3, touch 3, flat-footed 3
    (–2 size, –5 Dex)
hp 159 (11 HD); **DR** 5/—
Immune acid, gaze attacks, illusions, visual effects; ooze
    immunities
SR 18
Fort +12, **Ref** –2, **Will** –2

Speed 20 ft. (4 squares), climb 20 ft., swim 20 ft.
Melee slam +16 (2d6+15 plus 2d6 acid)
Space 15 ft.; **Reach** 10 ft.
Base Atk +8; **Grp** +26
Atk Options acid sheath, trample 2d6+15 plus 2d6 acid
Special Actions acid burst

Abilities Str 31, Dex 1, Con 29, Int —, Wis 1, Cha 1
SQ amphibious, ooze traits
Skills Climb +18, Listen –5, Swim +18
Advancement 12–22 HD (Huge); 23–33 HD (Gargantuan)

Acid Sheath (Ex) A corrupture's body produces corrosive slime. Any creature that strikes or touches a corrupture with its body, or that grapples a corrupture, automatically takes 2d6 points of acid damage. A creature takes damage from this ability only once per turn.

Trample (Ex) Reflex DC 25 half. The save DC is Strength-based.

Acid Burst (Ex) A corrupture can activate an acid burst as a standard action. Any creature within 20 feet must succeed on a DC 24 Reflex save or take 6d6 points of acid damage. A successful save results in half damage. The save DC is Constitution-based.

Amphibious (Ex) A corrupture can survive indefinitely on land or underwater.

Skills A corrupture has a +8 racial bonus on Climb checks and can always choose to take 10 on Climb checks, even if rushed or threatened. In addition, it has a +8 racial bonus on any Swim check to perform some special action or avoid a hazard. It can always choose to take 10 on a Swim check, even if distracted or endangered. It can use the run action while swimming, provided it swims in a straight line.

Disgusting bags of acid-filled flesh, corruptures result from the warping of nature. They hunger for meat and mindlessly attack living things even as they dissolve the environment that supports their prey.

STRATEGIES AND TACTICS

A corrupture instinctively moves toward any moving object or creature larger than Tiny size and attacks it, trampling others in its rush to dissolve and taste flesh. Stubborn in its mindless hunger, a corrupture doggedly continues attacking the creature it first tastes. It uses its acid burst whenever its prey and at least one other creature are within range, or if it is blocked by a creature larger than it can trample. If a group of foes flee a corrupture, it follows only its prey, following the nearest creature if it has not yet tasted flesh. Once its initial prey dies, the corrupture attacks the largest fleshly creature of which it is aware; if no others are nearby, the ooze begins consuming its meal at leisure.

A corrupture ignores creatures it cannot taste after its first attack, such as those not susceptible to its acid or those lacking flesh—at least until they move out of the range of its blindsight. (The mindless ooze cannot recognize a new moving object as one that it hit before.) Skeletal undead, many constructs, and creatures immune to acid can escape harm simply by not attacking back after first being struck. The oozes seem to instinctively recognize that other corruptures aren't prey.

"Foul things! Corruptures come to punish us for our sins against nature. What have you done to invoke nature's wrath?"

    —Craggar, half-orc druid, shortly before his death

SAMPLE ENCOUNTER

A corrupture might be encountered with more of its kind or with other creatures that despoil the natural world.

Guards (EL 12): A young adult black dragon uses two corruptures to guard its lair, keeping them in a huge pit that surrounds the submerged entrance. The dragon, being immune to acid, is ignored by the oozes and keeps them from wandering by bringing them meat whenever it enters the cave. The oozes attack anything that comes within range

CORRUPTURE LORE

Characters with ranks in Knowledge (dungeoneering) can learn more about corruptures. When a character makes a successful skill check, the following lore is revealed, including the information from lower DCs.

Knowledge (Dungeoneering)

DC	Result
19	Corruptures are acid-spraying oozes that feed on flesh. This result reveals all ooze traits.
24	Corruptures are equally at home on land or underwater. They move relatively swiftly and can climb and swim as well.
29	Corruptures come into being wherever the wilderness has been horribly befouled or natural laws have been repeatedly broken. They hunger endlessly for flesh, which they dissolve with their acid.

of their blindsight. The dragon flies over the battle and uses its breath weapon on as many invaders as it can. It continues to use this strategy for as long as the corruptures live and its breath weapon seems to be harming foes. While it waits for its breath weapon to recharge, it takes the opportunity to cast *shield* and *mage armor* on itself. The *Monster Manual* presents statistics for a young adult black dragon on page 72: Replace the dragon's Wingover feat with Flyby Attack and its *protection from good* spell with *shield*.

ECOLOGY

Corruptures come into being wherever the wilderness has been horribly befouled or natural laws have been repeatedly broken. In such places, nature reacts with a rent in existence that births a corrupture before closing, an embodiment of the cancerous damage to the world. Corruptures commonly appear in wilderness areas that have been poisoned or diseased, or that are heavily influenced by magic or another plane. Rarely they appear in civilized areas. Mundane defilement, such as razing a forest or draining a swamp, isn't enough to create a corrupture, but an arcane laboratory used for magical experimentation on creatures might well do so.

A corrupture is a mindless hunter, driven by instinct to hunt down the nearest prey of fair size. It draws food and water directly through its skin, first dissolving flesh with its acid and then moving over the gooey remains. Corruptures are able to survive on plant matter for a short time but need meat at least once a week. They can feed on carrion if necessary, but they prefer fresh, fluid-filled prey.

Corruptures have no gender and do not mate: They just get bigger. An undamaged corrupture with plenty to eat molts its outer flesh as it grows. This process takes a month of uninterrupted hibernation. After this time, the corrupture has an even more voracious appetite for several weeks. Larger, ancient corruptures begin to lose the ability to move under their own power. Such massive sacks of flesh can actually become stationary and starve.

Environment: Corruptures can appear in any sullied environment, even the sea.

Typical Physical Characteristics: A corrupture is a large mass of semifluid flesh approximately 15 feet in diameter. It constantly undulates and pulses, making its exact mass difficult to determine, but a typical example weighs about 6,000 pounds. Corruptures' flesh varies in color from tan to pink to angry red, and is covered in a web of veins, bruises, and sores. Boils of thick, yellow acid swell up on its surface every few seconds, bursting to spray the area. The

skin of a corrupture is covered with the residue of these eruptions, coating it in a caustic slime.

Alignment: Mindless feeding machines, corruptures are always neutral.

TYPICAL TREASURE

A corrupture never carries treasure, but the equipment of the ooze's victims might be left behind if it can survive the ooze's acidic touch. A corrupture has only a 50% chance of having goods or magic items, which must be metallic or stone, and 1/10 standard treasure in coins.

CORRUPTURES IN EBERRON

Corruptures roll out of the dead-gray mist bordering the Mournland to attack those foolish enough to approach. Hundreds exist within that foggy fringe surrounding the war-torn landscape, but corruptures can also be found wandering in Thrane, Darguun, and the Talenta Plains. It was long thought that the mists somehow made the creatures, but recently adventurers returned from Xen'drik with tales of corruptures in the cyclopean ruins. What connection the Mournland might have with events on that mysterious continent remains unknown.

CORRUPTURES IN FAERÛN

Corruptures roam many places in Faerûn, but they are most common in sites tied to failing mythals and the Netherese arcanists of old. Undermountain hosts its share of corruptures, as do Myth Drannor and the Dire Wood in the High Forest. Rumor holds that dozens of corruptures inhabit secret places in the city of Shade, and that the shades who live with them keep the oozes for some plot. Of course, no investigation has confirmed the rumor, and the shades laugh off such a preposterous suggestion.

Illus. by J. Nelson

Corrupture

DEFACER

The screaming and wailing you've been hearing for some time seems to be coming from the stone beneath your feet. Suddenly a gray shape looms up from the ground. Its muscular form looks solid and strong, but its featureless head is surrounded by many ghostly faces. As it swings a heavy fist at you, one of the faces rushes up its arm.

DEFACER   CR 6
Always NE Medium undead
Init +2; **Senses** darkvision 60 ft., tremorsense 60 ft.;
    Listen +15, Spot +15
Languages understands creator's orders
Aura frightful keening (60 ft.)

AC 19, touch 12, flat-footed 17; Dodge, Mobility
    (+2 Dex, +7 natural)
hp 71 (11 HD); **DR** 10/silver
Immune undead immunities
Fort +3, **Ref** +5, **Will** +8

Speed 30 ft. (6 squares); Spring Attack, earth glide
Melee 2 slams +10 each (1d8+4 plus stunning possession)
Space 5 ft.; **Reach** 5 ft.
Base Atk +5; **Grp** +9
Atk Options stunning possession
Special Actions steal face

Abilities Str 18, Dex 15, Con —, Int 7, Wis 13, Cha 14
SQ undead traits
Feats Dodge, Mobility, Spring Attack, Weapon Focus (slam)
Skills Listen +15, Spot +15
Advancement —

Frightful Keening (Su) The faces that whirl about the head of a defacer constantly wail and scream. This noise can be heard through earth and stone as easily as it can through air. A defacer cannot stop this keening. Any creature that can hear the sound and that is within 60 feet of a defacer is automatically shaken. This is a sonic, mind-affecting fear effect.

Earth Glide (Ex) A defacer glides through stone, dirt, and any other sort of earth except metal as easily as a fish swims through water. Its burrowing leaves behind no tunnel or hole, nor does it create a ripple or any other signs of its presence (although its frightful keening can still be heard).

Stunning Possession (Su) A creature with an Intelligence of 3 or higher that is struck by a defacer's slam attack must succeed on a DC 17 Will save or be stunned for 1 round. The save DC is Charisma-based.

> While stunned, the creature's face takes on the shape of one of the defacer's victims and screams for help and release using the languages that soul knew in life. When the effect ends, the ghostly face returns to the defacer.

Steal Face (Su) If a defacer's slam attack kills a creature with an Intelligence of 3 or higher, or if the defacer touches the body of such a creature within 1 day of its death, the defacer steals its face as an immediate action. This physically erases the facial features of the body, including bone structure, mouth, and teeth, leaving a smooth and blank surface. Attempts to cast *speak with dead* on victims of this attack always fail.

> This defilement of the corpse also draws the soul of the creature to the defacer, and it becomes one of the keening faces that whirl about the defacer's head. This prevents the soul from reaching the afterlife, becoming undead, or being raised or resurrected. Nothing short of

destroying the defacer restores a corpse's face and frees the soul.

> For 1 day after stealing a face, the defacer's blank visage takes the shape of that creature's face in the same manner as a creature affected by its stunning possession. This effect ends if the defacer uses its earth glide ability, which it is loath to do unless it thinks it can take another creature's face that day.

> If a defacer stole a creature's face by killing it and is destroyed within 24 hours of that act, its victim returns to life (stable at 0 hit points) if its body is largely whole. Its face is restored. This return to life does not result in level loss or ability drain.

A defacer arises when a spellcaster creates an undead being from the corpse of a doppelganger or other creature that assumes others' visages. Tortured by its inability to mimic others, a defacer steals the faces of those it kills and of the recently dead, trapping their souls by defiling their corpses.

STRATEGIES AND TACTICS
A defacer typically attacks from beneath the earth's surface, using Spring Attack to glide up toward a foe, strike it, and then disappear underground. When it stuns a creature, a defacer moves up to make a full attack, hoping to keep the creature stunned and kill it to steal its face. Once it steals a face, a defacer typically flees aboveground so that it can keep the captured soul's visage for a whole day.

Evil spellcasters use defacers as guardians, exploiting their frightful keening to create ambiance—one that also serves as an alarm system of sorts. Movement of the keening indicates that the defacers are attacking, allowing the spellcaster to take appropriate measures. When traveling with their creations, such spellcasters usually cast a *silence* spell on defacers to suppress their keening if they desire stealth or are not immune to fear.

"I created a defacer once. It was a grave error."
    —Black Orthal, human necromancer

SAMPLE ENCOUNTER
A defacer typically accompanies the spellcaster who created it, along with other undead minions.

A defacer without a controller might be encountered alone or in the company of incorporeal undead attracted by its frightful keening. Although the defacer does not communicate with the other undead, it doesn't concern itself if they follow it and aid its attacks against the living.

Bodyguards (EL 14): An 11th-level wizard lich (*MM* 166) uses two defacers and two bodaks as bodyguards. The defacers attack foes to stun them and prevent them from approaching the lich while the bodaks simply stand guard, allowing their death gazes to do their work. The lich casts spells from behind the bodaks.

ECOLOGY
As undead beings that prey only on intelligent life, defacers do not contribute to the ecology of an area. Even so, they have an effect on the region. A defacer seeks to take a face at least once a week, adding the unfortunate victim to its host

Defacer

Illus. by R. Mimura

Environment: Defacers can exist in any environment but typically accompany the spellcasters who created them. Some roam free, whether created by mistake, released on purpose, or abandoned after the death of a controller. These defacers seek out civilized areas and gravitate toward burial grounds. A defacer might leave a community alone, preferring to visit a nearby graveyard to steal the face of someone recently buried and spend a day in that individual's coffin before leaving. The screaming of the trapped souls gives the graveyard a dire reputation.

Typical Physical Characteristics: The body of a creature turned into a defacer loses the characteristics it had in life and gains the typical defacer shape and appearance. Faceless and gray, a defacer's thick-skinned and muscular body stands roughly 6 feet tall and weighs nearly 260 pounds.

Alignment: Defacers are always neutral evil.

TYPICAL TREASURE

Defacers do not carry treasure and cannot carry objects with them as they glide through the earth.

FOR PLAYER CHARACTERS

A spellcaster of 14th or higher level can create a defacer by casting *create undead* on the corpse of a creature that mimics other creatures, such as a doppelganger.

DEFACERS IN EBERRON

Intrigued by defacers' ability to keep souls from returning to life and to prevent bodies from revealing secrets, agents of Karrnath tried to use the creatures as assassins during the Last War. They met with some success, but the program was halted after high-ranking members of the Karrnathi army were found faceless. The head of the program, a human necromancer named Clavius Kreel, disappeared at that time and hasn't been seen since.

Changelings turned into undead sometimes spontaneously rise as defacers instead of what their creators intended. When Dolurrh is coterminous, dead changelings become defacers under circumstances when they might otherwise become ghosts.

DEFACERS IN FAERÛN

Rumors from Skullport insist that a sorcerer lich hailing from Chessenta recently arrived in the underground city with several defacers as bodyguards. The lich apparently went into Undermountain to set up a base of operations. With the spells and magic items at its disposal, and the ability to take other's shapes, the lich presents a serious threat to the Lords of Waterdeep. The recent appearance of a faceless corpse near the City of the Dead confirms the Lords' suspicions, and now they quietly seek powerful adventurers willing to take on the difficult task of locating and destroying the lich and its guards.

of captured souls. Although only half a dozen or so of these spirits appear on a defacer's head at any given time, no limit seems to exist on the number of faces one can steal, and it is always hungry for more.

Defacers have no society and do not communicate. They lack the ability to speak and don't seem to understand any language, although they still obey the instructions of those who can command them.

DEFACER LORE

Characters with ranks in Knowledge (religion) can learn more about defacers. When a character makes a successful skill check, the following lore is revealed, including the information from lower DCs.

Knowledge (Religion)

DC	Result
16	This creature is a defacer, an undead creature that steals faces from corpses. This result reveals all undead traits.
21	A defacer's attacks can stun creatures and cause them to be momentarily possessed by one of the defacer's victims. Defacers are vulnerable to silvered weapons.
26	A defacer that steals a face doesn't like to move through the earth for a day afterward unless it plans on stealing another face very soon.

DEMON

Evil and chaotic to the core, demons like nothing more than to maim and destroy. They are native to the Infinite Layers of the Abyss, and their environment complements their natures. Demons take pleasure in the pain and misfortune of others. Some are sneaky and sly, while others are more direct and brutal.

A number of demons belong to a race (and subtype) known as the tanar'ri. The tanar'ri form the largest and most diverse group of demons, and they are the unchallenged masters of the Abyss (at least in their own eyes). Tanar'ri possess a number of racial traits, summarized in the glossary.

Except where otherwise noted, demons speak Abyssal, Celestial, and Draconic.

DEATHDRINKER

This massive creature is the size of a giant, and it sports chipped, antlerlike horns from which hang desiccated bodies and skulls. The creature wears intricate armor, and dark, pitted plates cover legs that end in hooves. Its many-fingered hand holds a broad longsword.

DEATHDRINKER   CR 18

Always CE Huge outsider (chaotic, evil, extraplanar)
Init +6; **Senses** true seeing; Listen +30, Spot +30
Aura unlife (10 ft.)
Languages Abyssal, Common

AC 35, touch 10, flat-footed 33
  (−2 size, +2 Dex, +7 armor, +18 natural)
hp 337 (27 HD); **DR** 15/good and lawful
Immune negative energy, poison
Resist acid 10, cold 10, electricity 10, fire 10; **SR** 29
Fort +23, **Ref** +17, **Will** +17

Speed 35 ft. (7 squares) in breastplate; base speed 50 ft.
Melee *+3 adamantine longsword* +38/+33/+28/+23
  (3d6+13/17–20)
Space 15 ft.; **Reach** 15 ft.
Base Atk +27; **Grp** +45
Atk Options Cleave, Combat Reflexes, Great Cleave, Power Attack, Quick Draw, Quicken Spell-Like Ability (*greater teleport*), Quicken Spell-Like Ability (*greater dispel magic*), aligned strike (chaotic, evil), glory in slaughter
Combat Gear *oil of align weapon, oil of bless weapon, oil of corrupt weapon*
Spell-Like Abilities (CL 20th):
  At will—*air walk* (self only) *greater dispel magic, greater teleport* (self plus 50 lb. of objects only)

Abilities Str 30, Dex 14, Con 27, Int 10, Wis 11, Cha 11
SQ deathdrink
Feats Cleave, Combat Reflexes, Great Cleave, Improved Critical (longsword), Improved Initiative, Iron Will, Power Attack, Quick Draw, Quicken Spell-Like Ability (*greater teleport*), Quicken Spell-Like Ability (*greater dispel magic*)
Skills Concentration +38, Hide +21, Intimidate +30, Jump +37, Knowledge (the planes) +30, Listen +30, Move Silently +29, Spot +30, Survival +0 (+2 on other planes)
Advancement by character class; **Favored Class** cleric; see text
Possessions combat gear plus *+2 breastplate, +3 adamantine longsword,* gems and jewelry (13,000 gp).

True Seeing (Su) As the *true seeing* spell; continuous; caster level 20th.
Aura of Unlife (Su) Creatures take 2d6 points of damage at the end of each of the deathdrinker's turns if they are within 10 feet of it. This is a negative energy effect. Undead are instead healed of a like amount of damage.
Glory in Slaughter (Ex) A deathdrinker gains a +5 morale bonus on attack rolls, damage rolls, and saving throws for 1 minute after it kills a worthy opponent (a creature with at least 10 HD).
Deathdrink (Su) If a deathdrinker deals enough damage to a creature to kill it, with either its death aura or a melee attack, it instantly heals 1d8 points of damage per HD of the creature it killed.

A deathdrinker collects souls from those hapless enough to cross its path. Creatures of brute force and gory battle, they seek out combat with sadistic glee, spreading fear even among other demons.

Strategies and Tactics

A deathdrinker is very mobile on the battlefield, using quickened *greater teleport* to reach spellcasters or archers who hang back from melee. The demon has *air walk* active at all times, allowing it to teleport next to flying creatures. It enjoys the fear and panic that ensues when it uses quickened *greater teleport* to move next to a flying spellcaster before unleashing a barrage of powerful melee attacks. It does not hesitate to use quickened *greater dispel magic* to soften up foes before engaging in melee. It generally employs Power Attack unless an enemy is difficult to hit.

A deathdrinker uses its allies to great personal advantage, since it is often accompanied by undead that bask in its aura of unlife. A wounded deathdrinker does not hesitate to kill one of its injured or minor minions to heal itself and then use Cleave to attack an enemy within reach.

DEATHDRINKER LORE

Characters with ranks in Knowledge (the planes) can learn more about deathdrinkers. When a character makes a successful skill check, the following lore is revealed, including the information from lower DCs.

Knowledge (the Planes)

DC	Result
15	This horrible creature is clearly a demon of some kind. This result reveals all outsider traits.
28	This demon is known as a deathdrinker. It revels in slaughter.
33	A deathdrinker is resistant to acid, cold, electricity, and fire. Negative energy does not harm it, nor does poison, but its attacks emphasize the powers of death.
38	Killing another creature heals a deathdrinker and improves its battle prowess. A deathdrinker sometimes even kills its allies to gain these benefits.

Sample Encounters

A deathdrinker makes a formidable opponent. It is often accompanied by lower-CR undead or demons. Although these additional creatures rarely add significant threat to the encounter in themselves, a deathdrinker's willingness to sacrifice its minions to bolster itself usually increases the expected Encounter Level.

Dread Company (EL 18+): A deathdrinker is usually accompanied by undead, frequently by other deathdrinkers, and occasionally by other demons of various kinds.

EL 18: Barrow-walker is a deathdrinker with ambition. It keeps a troupe of undead as allies (and fodder if it needs to heal itself reliably in combat). Its minions include two dread wraiths (*MM* 258) and an elite vampire (*MM* 251).

Ecology

Deathdrinkers reproduce by dripping some of their blood into specially prepared pits of vile essence. The blood mingles with the muck, then clots and grows. Lesser demons tend to a breeding pit, regularly stirring its contents and adding fresh corpses and blood. Eventually a fully formed deathdrinker emerges.

As outsiders, deathdrinkers do not need to eat, sleep, or breathe. However, they enjoy creating and personalizing lairs, decorated with skulls and other symbols of death, where they lounge on large piles of corpses or bones.

Environment: Deathdrinkers live in the Infinite Layers of the Abyss. They prefer to make their lairs near recent battles, enjoying the bounty of corpses.

Typical Physical Characteristics: A deathdrinker stands approximately 18 feet tall and weighs about 3,000 pounds, most of it muscle. It has broad shoulders, bulging biceps, and a flat, muscular chest.

Alignment: Deathdrinkers are always chaotic evil. They are self-serving, egocentric creatures that happily kill their allies if doing so suits them—or if they simply feel like seeing some blood.

Society

Deathdrinkers live in the Abyss but are not tanar'ri. They use this distinction to set themselves apart from political intrigue and power struggles, viewing themselves as above such petty concerns. They're tough and powerful combatants, but they are not evil masterminds or clever generals.

Deathdrinkers have only one overriding interest: themselves. They are extraordinarily egocentric. They see their race as superior to all others, and each considers itself the ultimate representative of the race. When they come together in social situations, they prefer to associate with other deathdrinkers, but they also enjoy the company of creatures that praise, admire, and flatter them (although they might not publicly admit as much). Crafty, powerful individuals sometimes acquire the services of a deathdrinker by sending it many gifts and fawning emissaries.

Typical Treasure

A deathdrinker has treasure appropriate to its Challenge Rating, about 36,000 gp. Most of its treasure is in the form of its magic weapon and armor. If given access to other magic, it favors items that make it a more effective killer, such as better armor or items that overcome damage reduction. The remaining treasure it typically carries in the form of jewelry, usually featuring grisly motifs such as skulls, faces distorted in anguish, or torture implements.

Deathdrinker

Illus. by A. Swekel

Deathdrinkers with Class Levels

A deathdrinker usually lacks the ambition to pursue a class. For one that does, its favored class is cleric, usually of a neutral evil or chaotic evil god of death. Many choose not to worship a god (believing that no one is more worthy of worship than themselves) and instead simply choose domains. The most popular are Death, Destruction, and Evil. A deathdrinker cleric most enjoys creating undead that it can use to bolster its talents.

A deathdrinker automatically qualifies for the assassin prestige class (*DMG* 180).

Deathdrinkers in Eberron

Deathdrinkers inhabit Dolurrh, the Realm of the Dead, acting as lords of the place. Deathdrinkers in Eberron are even more ambitious, active, and power-hungry than described above. Undead flock to the sides of deathdrinkers to enjoy the benefit of their aura of unlife.

Deathdrinkers in Faerûn

Deathdrinkers often lead demonic raiding parties that seek to steal souls from the Fugue Plane. Their aura of unlife attracts dead souls, so these excursions typically result in large harvests.

KASTIGHUR

This hideous demon's body ripples with muscle. Its massive head is heavy with long horns while its powerful legs end in cloven hooves. Most of its head is hidden by an enormous steel helm that has been bolted to the creature's neck. A breastplate fastened onto its body provides additional protection for its already tough hide.

KASTIGHUR   CR 11

Always CE Huge outsider (chaotic, extraplanar, evil, tanar'ri)
Init −1; **Senses** darkvision 60 ft., scent; Listen +19, Spot +19
Aura frightful presence (60 ft., DC 18)
Languages Abyssal, Celestial, Draconic; telepathy 100 ft.

AC 23, touch 7, flat-footed 23
    (−2 size, −1 Dex, +7 armor, +9 natural)
hp 172 (15 HD); **DR** 10/cold iron or good
Immune acid, electricity, poison
Resist cold 10, fire 10; **SR** 17
Fort +16, **Ref** +8, **Will** +10

Speed 30 ft. (6 squares) in breastplate; base speed 40 ft.
Melee gore +21 (2d6+8) and
    2 slams +19 each (1d8+4)
Space 15 ft.; **Reach** 15 ft.
Base Atk +15; **Grp** +31
Atk Options Improved Bull Rush, Improved Overrun, Power Attack, Powerful Charge, Quicken Spell-Like Ability (*teleport*), aligned strike (chaotic, evil), fear bolstered, stunning charge 5d6+12
Spell-Like Abilities (CL 18th):
    At will—*feather fall, teleport* (self only)

Abilities Str 27, Dex 8, Con 25, Int 8, Wis 12, Cha 8
SQ tanar'ri traits
Feats Ability Focus (frightful presence), Improved Bull Rush, Improved Overrun, Multiattack, Power Attack, Powerful Charge, Quicken Spell-Like Ability[B] (*teleport*), Track[B]
Skills Concentration +15, Diplomacy +1, Intimidate +17, Knowledge (dungeoneering) + 4, Knowledge (nature) +6, Knowledge (the planes) +5, Listen +19, Search +8, Sense Motive +13, Spellcraft +8, Spot +19, Survival +19 (+21 on other planes, +21 following tracks, +21 in aboveground environments, +21 underground)
Advancement 16–30 HD (Huge); 31–45 HD (Gargantuan)
Possessions +2 breastplate

Frightful Presence (Su) A kastighur can inspire terror by charging or attacking. Affected creatures must succeed on a DC 18 Will save or become shaken, remaining in that condition as long as they remain with 60 feet of the kastighur. The save DC is Charisma-based and includes the bonus from the Ability Focus feat.
Fear Bolstered (Ex) A kastighur delights in attacking terrified opponents and gains a +2 bonus on attack rolls against shaken, frightened, or panicked creatures.
Stunning Charge (Ex) A kastighur typically begins a battle by charging at an opponent. In addition to the normal benefits and hazards of a charge, this allows the kastighur to make a single gore attack with a +23 attack bonus that deals 5d6+12 points of damage. The struck creature must succeed on a DC 25 Fortitude save or be stunned for 1 round. The save DC is Strength-based.

Cruel and sadistic, the brutish kastighurs act as hunters and prison wardens among the tanar'ri. In combat, they teleport about the battlefield and use stunning charges to incapacitate and terrify foes.

Strategies and Tactics

A kastighur loves melee combat and takes to battle with great relish. It charges foes as often as possible, trying to stun them and leave them shaken as it lands lethal blows.

A kastighur typically begins combat by charging a foe, stopping at the limit of its reach (15 feet). If it stuns its target, it charges again on the following round, closing the remaining distance to stand adjacent to its enemy. It then begins to make full attacks with its gore and slams, dealing horrific damage with Power Attack.

A kastighur can teleport at will, and three times per day it can use its Quicken Spell-Like Ability feat to *teleport* as a swift action. In combat, a kastighur often uses a quickened *teleport* to move 10 feet or more away from a particular foe and then charge it. A kastighur might also use this ability to attack a flying creature by teleporting above the enemy in the hopes of grappling it and bearing it to the ground.

Kastighurs use teleportation tactics with some trepidation because they do not possess the *greater teleport* ability enjoyed by many fiends and generally don't have time to become familiar with most battlefields. They are loath to teleport great distances and keep even battlefield teleports as short as possible.

Sample Encounter

Since a kastighur doesn't possess a reliable means of transporting itself from one plane to the next, it typically depends upon more powerful demons or even magic items to provide the means to travel in this manner. A kastighur also enjoys the pain and suffering that it can inflict on the Material Plane when called by a powerful evil spellcaster using *gate* or *greater planar ally.*

An encounter with a kastighur should emphasize its charge tactics and how much it enjoys terrifying other creatures. Kastighurs might pair up with other creatures that cause fear (such as evil dragons) or that can provide ranged support. Flying allies make a particularly potent combination.

KASTIGHUR LORE

Characters with ranks in Knowledge (the planes) can learn more about kastighurs. When a character makes a successful skill check, the following lore is revealed, including the information from lower DCs.

Knowledge (the Planes)

DC	Result
15	This horrible creature is clearly a demon of some kind. This result reveals all outsider traits.
21	A kastighur is a kind of tanar'ri and shares many of that race's traits, but it is also immune to acid. It is difficult to hurt, and it is resistant to most magic.
26	These demons work as jailers and hunters in the Abyss. A kastighur loves to charge enemies and gore them with its horns. A physical blow from a kastighur can terrify those struck by it.
31	Unlike many tanar'ri, a kastighur teleports with some risk and might end up elsewhere than its intended destination. Occasionally it can teleport as quick as a blink, appearing and attacking before anyone can react.

Kastighur

Alignment: A kastighur is always chaotic evil—capricious, depraved, and fiendish. Its greatest delight is in breaking the will of other creatures, either through physical torture or the relentless hunt.

Society

Not terribly bright by nature, kastighurs typically serve more intelligent and powerful demons. They work as hunters and jailers among the tanar'ri, roles in which they take great pleasure. When a tanar'ri needs to find a creature but lacks the power to create a retriever, it calls upon a kastighur or two to hunt the individual down.

A kastighur's appetite for fear and the hunt sometimes gets the better of it—a fact that can frustrate its master. A kastighur sometimes intentionally allows one of its prisoners to escape, just so it can hunt down the fleeing creature. On a battlefield, a unit of kastighurs often breaks ranks to chase enemies who seem frightened.

Left to its own devices, a kastighur roams the Abyss hunting and killing whatever suits its fancy, whether a damned soul or even another kastighur. It sees others of its kind as competition for the attention of the great generals and demon lords who can take it to hunting grounds on other planes. Thus, kastighurs despise one another unless they serve the same master. Even then, they view their service as a competition, and each always attempts to outdo the other in feats of combat. A kastighur that has managed to survive, and thrive, for a long time might grow to Gargantuan size. Such a fiend looks for opportunities to enslave and torture creatures of great power, including dragons, powerful mortals, and other potent outsiders.

Typical Treasure

A kastighur typically possesses half the standard treasure for a creature of its Challenge Rating, usually in the form of the magic breastplate bolted to its body. A kastighur travels light, and any treasure it finds usually goes to its masters.

These creatures might also seek magic items that grant movement beyond their normal capabilities. Items that allow them to fly, burrow, and climb are all good, but kastighurs prize items that confer *plane shift* above all others.

Kastighurs in Eberron

Kastighurs inhabit Mabar, the Endless Night. Here they maintain prisons and torture creatures in the eternal darkness of the plane. They travel to the Material Plane when the opportunity presents itself, where they hunt in the deepest reaches of Khyber.

Kastighurs in Faerûn

Kastighurs make their home on the Barrens of Doom and Despair, where they compete for service under Loviatar and Talona. They are frequently summoned to Toril to serve powerful spellcasters, such as Larloch, Manshoon, and Fzoul Chembryl.

Fox Hunt (EL 16): Two kastighurs riding fiendish rocs and led by a flying pack of six half-fiend digesters tracked an escaped hound archon prisoner through a *gate* to the Material Plane. Now they seek the celestial but gleefully attack any other creatures in their path. The kastighurs use *teleport* or *feather fall* to land when they spot foes so they can set up stunning charges. The half-fiend digesters use spell-like abilities and acid sprays to harry aerial and landbound foes without regard to the kastighurs. The rocs make flyby attacks against flying enemies and snatch up those without the ability to fly.

Ecology

Although kastighurs don't eat or drink in the traditional sense, they do feed off the fear, panic, and hopelessness of those they imprison or track down. They delight in the hunt and physical torture, and prolong both over great lengths of time to savor the rich emotions.

Environment: Kastighurs live in the Infinite Layers of the Abyss.

Typical Physical Characteristics: Kastighurs stand anywhere from 15 feet to 20 feet tall, and can weigh as much as 10,000 pounds. The horns on their massive heads grow slowly but constantly, and the demons enjoy filing them or carving them with symbols or words.

Illus. by A. Swekel

NASHROU

A nightmarish amalgamation of bony spikes and talons leaps at you from an Abyssal plateau. Its lithe form is covered by thick, glistening chitin, and it glares at you balefully from a cluster of eyes in the center of its body.

NASHROU	CR 2

Always CE Large outsider (chaotic, evil, extraplanar)
Init +6; **Senses** darkvision 60 ft., scent; Listen +7, Spot +7
Languages —

AC 15, touch 11, flat-footed 13
   (–1 size, +2 Dex, +4 natural)
hp 42 (4 HD); **DR** 5/cold iron or good
Fort +10, **Ref** +6, **Will** +4
Weakness vulnerability to criticals

Speed 50 ft. (10 squares)
Melee 2 gores +5 each (1d8+2) and
   2 claws +3 each (1d6+1)
Atk Options aligned strike (chaotic, evil)
Space 10 ft.; **Reach** 10 ft.
Base Atk +4; **Grp** +10

Abilities Str 15, Dex 14, Con 22, Int 2, Wis 11, Cha 8
Feats Improved Initiative, Multiattack
Skills Jump +17, Listen +7, Spot +7, Survival +7
Advancement 5–9 HD (Large); 10–15 HD (Huge)

Vulnerability to Criticals (Ex) A nashrou has a unique weakness that can allow a clever or lucky opponent to slay it in a single blow. A successful critical hit instantly reduces the creature to –10 hit points; no saving throw or damage reduction applies. The attack must deal sufficient damage to overcome the nashrou's damage reduction.

Nashrous are vicious, animalistic predators that roam the blasted volcanic plains of the Abyss. Reaving claws extend in four directions from a nashrou's central body, and many legs propel it rapidly across the ground. Nashrous are swift, tireless hunters that have been known to pursue prey for days

NASHROU LORE

Characters with ranks in Knowledge (the planes) can learn more about nashrous. When a character makes a successful skill check, the following lore is revealed, including the information from lower DCs.

Knowledge (the Planes)

DC	Result
12	Nashrous are evil, predatory demons from the Abyss. This result reveals all outsider traits.
17	Nashrous are difficult to injure unless struck with a weapon of cold iron or one blessed by the powers of good.
22	Nashrous form hunting packs. The weakest members seek out prey, while the strongest terrorize and slaughter victims.
27	Nashrous have a weak spot, and if you hit one in the right spot—or just really hard—it might simply die.

or even weeks. Occasionally, their tenacity is such that they will follow prey through a portal to another plane.

Strategies and Tactics

A nashrou is a fierce fighter that presents a significant challenge to even seasoned planar travelers. When fighting in a pack, the demons charge headlong into the thickest groups of enemies, seeking to disrupt formations and deal as much damage as possible with their goring arms and scythelike secondary claws.

A solitary nashrou fights more cautiously, preferring to stalk in the shadows until it can catch its prey at a vulnerable moment. A lone nashrou rarely if ever attacks a group of more than two creatures, and it often flees if outnumbered in a confrontation.

"We were coming across the first layer of the Abyss when they scented us. First there were three or four, then ten, then a hundred. Mali and Skrit went down in the first few seconds; the rest of us ran. I don't know where the others are—hells, I don't know where I am. All I know is that diving through that portal kept me alive."

—Berrin Orlan,
former adventurer and
unwitting planar traveler

Sample Encounter

A nashrou is usually encountered in the Abyss, but it might pursue prey through planar portals and end up far from home.

Individual (EL 2): A lone nashrou is usually the sole survivor of a decimated pack.

EL 2: In the desert village of Ahlmad, the people whisper of the "poisoned taker from the desert." A nashrou pursued a planar traveler through a *gate* and ended up alone on the Material Plane.

Pack (EL 5–8): Roving packs of three to ten nashrou are "natural" hazards of the Abyss.

EL 5: This group of five nashrous stalks the Plain of Infinite Portals, hunting wayward travelers.

Ecology

Like most creatures of the Abyss, nashrous have no true ecology as the sages of the Material Plane understand the concept. They exist only for the pleasure of rending and devouring any other creature that crosses their path. Some scholars hypothesize that they are Abyssal perversions of natural predators such as wolves or lions.

Environment: Nashrous dwell in the Infinite Layers of the Abyss. They are most commonly encountered on the Plain of Infinite Portals, the first layer of the Abyss, which appears to be their native habitat. Through their use as "hunting hounds" by many Abyssal lords and other powerful demons, however, they might be encountered on any layer. They are sometimes found on the Material Plane, having inadvertently passed through a portal or been summoned to serve a powerful spellcaster. Packs of nashrous rove the

Abyss, while solitary demons are more common on the Material Plane.

Typical Physical Characteristics: A nashrou stands approximately 10 feet tall, with four long, thin legs excellently adapted to running or jumping. Its six fighting limbs are designed to counter a wide variety of threats, although the demon can use only four limbs at a time while fighting. The massive goring arms impale dangerous foes while the lighter, faster claws allow the creature to deal with other threats. An average nashrou weighs about 800 pounds. Nashrous do not grow larger by any natural process but seem to grow more powerful with every creature they shred and devour.

Alignment: Nashrous have only a rudimentary intellect at best, but they are sadistic and twisted creatures of the Lower Planes through and through. They are always chaotic evil.

Society

Nashrous are no more intelligent than animals, but within the pack structure a "society" exists after a fashion. A strict hierarchy of importance and privilege exists within a nashrou pack, which determines when and how much an individual is permitted to feed (nashrous do not require food, of course, but they take a savage joy in devouring the flesh and blood of other creatures).

The smallest, weakest members of the pack are driven ahead of the main body to scout for potential prey. These scouts either grow strong and tough enough to claim a place within the main body of a pack, or they die in short order. The larger, swifter nashrous harry the pack's chosen prey, sometimes for hours, sometimes for days. Students of the creatures have dubbed these pack members "stalkers."

Once the stalkers have worked the prey into a frenzy of fear, the highest rank moves in. Called "slayers," these largest, strongest members of the pack are even more bloodthirsty and savage than their packmates.

Nashrou

Typical Treasure

While corpses left in their wake might retain some former possessions, nashrous do not collect treasure. They have a tendency to devour their prey where it falls, so valuables seldom accrue at a communal lair.

For Player Characters

A nashrou can be summoned with *summon monster III* or a higher-level *summon monster* spell. Treat the nashrou as being on the 3rd-level list on the Summon Monster table (PH 287). Although *lesser planar ally* could call one or more nashrous, the vicious creatures are so intractable that they are nearly impossible to bargain with. Short periods of compelled service are preferable.

Nashrous in Eberron

In Eberron, nashrous hail from the plane of Shavarath, the Battleground. Wild nashrou packs roam the blasted lands claimed by demonic armies, while enterprising demons (and sometimes even devils) seek to capture the feral creatures for use as shock troops. Occasionally nashrous end up on the Material Plane when Shavarath is coterminous, showing up in the Mournland more than any other region.

Nashrous in Faerûn

In the cosmology of the Forgotten Realms, nashrous dwell in the Abyss. They are varyingly said to be debased creations of Malar the Beastlord or Garagos the Reaver, god of destruction and war, though they do not share either deity's home plane. Possibly a bloodreaver (a zealous cleric of Garagos) unleashed the horrors within the Abyss, perhaps to test them against the destructive beings that live there or to toughen them further. The beasts took to the chaotic plane and rapidly spread across its upper layers.

WHISPER DEMON

An insubstantial, ghostly, demonic creature smirks and leers. Though humanoid in shape, it has distorted features. Its brow looms over its face, and its long chin thrusts forward. Its flesh is a mottled green.

WHISPER DEMON   CR 9

Always CE Medium outsider (chaotic, evil, extraplanar, incorporeal)
Init +5; **Senses** darkvision 60 ft.; Listen +14, Spot +14
Aura maddening whispers (60 ft., DC 21)
Languages Abyssal, Celestial, Draconic; telepathy 60 ft.

AC 20, touch 20, flat-footed 15; Dodge, Mobility (+5 Dex, +5 deflection)
Miss Chance 50% (incorporeal)
hp 90 (12 HD); **DR** 5/cold iron or good
Immune *confusion*, electricity, hypnotism, *insanity*, poison, Wisdom damage and drain
Resist acid 10, cold 10, and fire 10
Fort +11, **Ref** +13, **Will** +13

Speed fly 40 ft. (8 squares) (perfect); Flyby Attack
Melee 2 incorporeal touches +17 each (2d6/19–20)
Space 5 ft.; **Reach** 5 ft.
Base Atk +12; **Grp** —
Atk Options aligned strike (chaotic, evil)

Abilities Str —, Dex 20, Con 16, Int 10, Wis 5, Cha 20
SQ create spawn, incorporeal traits, madness
Feats Alertness, Dodge, Flyby Attack, Improved Critical (incorporeal touch), Mobility
Skills Bluff +20, Diplomacy +9, Disguise +5 (+7 acting), Hide +20, Intimidate +22, Knowledge (religion) +15, Knowledge (the planes) +15, Listen +14, Sense Motive +12, Spot +14
Advancement 13–24 HD (Medium)

Maddening Whispers (Su) Any living creature within 60 feet of a whisper demon hears its maddening telepathic whispers and must succeed on a DC 21 Will save or become confused for 1 round. When rolling d% to determine the actions of a creature confused by maddening whispers, on a roll of 51 or higher, instead of the normal confusion result, the creature automatically deals damage to itself equal to its normal melee damage with the weapon it currently wields or its primary natural weapon, whichever deals more damage. A creature that succeeds on the Will save cannot be affected by the same whisper demon's maddening whispers for 1 round. This is a mind-affecting compulsion effect. The save DC is Charisma-based.

This ability does not allow a whisper demon to exercise mental control over a creature, and thus the *protection from evil* spell does not provide immunity to this effect. Demons are immune to a whisper demon's maddening whispers.

Create Spawn (Su) A living creature that kills itself within 60 feet of a whisper demon rises as an allip under the whisper demon's control 1 round later. A whisper demon can control up to nine allips it creates. Allips created by a whisper demon in excess of this limit arise free-willed.

Madness (Ex) Whisper demons use their Charisma modifier on Will saves instead of their Wisdom modifier, and they have immunity to *confusion* and *insanity* effects. In addition, anyone targeting a whisper demon with a thought detection, mind control, or telepathic ability makes direct contact with its tortured mind and takes 1d4 points of Wisdom damage.

Thoroughly evil and insane, whisper demons lust to watch other creatures take their own lives and then to enslave their lost souls. The fiends' maddening telepathic whispers can drive the strongest-willed hero to do herself harm, and their merest touch can rend flesh and break bone.

Strategies and Tactics

A whisper demon typically travels with a cadre of allips under its control. The allips precede the whisper demon, babbling constantly and fascinating creatures to prevent escape. Against enemies that aren't affected by the babble ability, the whisper demon orders the allips to drain the creatures' Wisdom scores, reducing their ability to withstand its maddening whispers. The demon then attacks with its incorporeal touches, hoping that a confused foe will finish itself off with a final lethal blow.

"I'd rather face a balor."

—Lord Windfell,
after losing his son to a whisper demon

Sample Encounters

In any encounter, a whisper demon seeks to drive others to madness and self-destruction. Whisper demons are usually accompanied by allips, but other undead might also associate with one of these insane demons. An undead creature's immunity to the demon's maddening whispers makes it a potent ally. Other demons, and tanar'ri in particular, usually avoid whisper demons, but might risk association to achieve some goal.

Slaving Expedition (EL 10): A whisper demon, accompanied by four allips, is looking for more victims to transform into allip slaves.

It's Your Funeral (EL 14): A mad lich (human lich wizard 11; *MM* 166) used a *planar binding* spell to call and bind a whisper demon. Realizing that its new servant will be

---

WHISPER DEMON LORE

Characters with ranks in Knowledge (the planes) can learn more about whisper demons. When a character makes a successful skill check, the following lore is revealed, including the information from lower DCs.

Knowledge (the Planes)

DC	Result
19	A whisper demon is a kind of demon. It can harm with a touch. A whisper demon is incorporeal, but it isn't undead. This result reveals all outsider and incorporeal traits.
24	A whisper demon emits an aura of maddening telepathic whispers. Those who fall prey to the whispers often attack themselves.
29	Cold iron and good weapons deal better damage to a whisper demon, but if they aren't magical, they pass right through the incorporeal creatures.
34	Allips accompany whisper demons. These creatures are the souls of those who killed themselves while under the influence of the demon's whispers.

more powerful with allip slaves, the lich seeks creatures for the whisper demon to turn into allips, as well as new magic items and spells for itself. The "funeral procession" consists of the lich, nine derro who worship it as a god, and the whisper demon. The hooded derro carry the lich lying in state on a bier while the incorporeal demon rides along, hiding within the lich's body. The derro march solemnly toward any sentient creatures they meet. When the strangers are within the range of the demon's maddening whispers, the group attacks. The derro act as the lich's bodyguards and stay close to the undead, using ranged attacks and their *sound burst* ability against foes. The whisper demon charges, using its incorporeal touches and bringing as many foes as possible within range of its maddening whispers. The lich casts offensive spells with abandon, not caring whether the demon or its derro worshipers are caught in their effects.

Ecology

Whisper demons are strange creatures. Although native to the Abyss, they prefer to visit other planes and ply their powers upon susceptible foes. They can be found anywhere in the multiverse.

Environment: Whisper demons inhabit the Infinite Layers of the Abyss but leave whenever they can to find more sane minds on which to prey.

Typical Physical Characteristics: Whisper demons are roughly the size and shape of humans, but as incorporeal creatures they possess no weight. Their skin is a mottled green. If one is wounded, the area of the injury turns a brighter green and appears to ooze a green, bloodlike substance, though this "blood" is also incorporeal. The demons' brows and chins jut forward, making their wild eyes look very deeply set. A whisper demon's sneering, cunning expression displays its delight in evil.

Alignment: Whisper demons are always chaotic evil. Mad and hateful, they live for the opportunity to see others' misfortune.

Whisper demon

Society

Whisper demons exist to drive others to take their own lives. They find nothing so exquisite as a creature losing all hope or its grip on sanity. Gleefully insane, whisper demons possess no sense of community or fair play. They rarely talk, but when they do, a flood of hateful desires issues forth in every language they can speak.

Whisper demons exist outside the power structures and society of the Abyss. They represent a formidable threat to other fiends. Although their maddening whispers do not harm demons, contacting them with telepathy does damage a demon's Wisdom, while their incorporeal touch ignores damage reduction. In addition, the allips that often accompany them can harm other denizens of the Abyss. Thus, only more powerful demons equipped with magic weapons risk dealing with whisper demons. All others ignore them if possible and flee otherwise. If a creature does decide it wants to use a whisper demon, it usually offers transportation to the Material Plane in exchange for the fiend's service.

Typical Treasure

Whisper demons don't normally have treasure, but one might carry about a ghost touch item, such as a shield, simply for the sensation of manipulating a material object.

Whisper Demons in Eberron

Whisper demons come from Xoriat, the Realm of Madness, and embody much of the plane's atmosphere. They act as weird envoys and visitors to Shavarath, the Battleground, and consort with various demons there.

Whisper Demons in Faerûn

Whisper demons are native to the Abyss. Ever hungry to inflict madness upon mortals, they spend much of their time seeking a means to travel to the Material Plane. Whisper demons often lurk near both sides of a *portal* connecting the Material Plane and the Abyss.

Illus. by W. England

DEMONHIVE

First seen on one of the Infinite Layers of the Abyss, demon-hives are now found throughout the Lower Planes. With their aggressive and bloodthirsty members, demonhives threaten all creatures they encounter and lay waste to the areas they inhabit. If they were allowed to continue their rampage unchecked, demonhives might spread across entire planes.

DEMONHIVE ATTENDANT

A chitinous and horned insectoid creature approximately the size of a dog flaps toward you on translucent red wings. It grins to reveal a mouth of wolfish teeth and reaches toward you with disturbingly humanoid, clawed hands.

DEMONHIVE ATTENDANT	CR 2

Always NE Small outsider (evil, extraplanar)
Init +6; **Senses** darkvision 60 ft.; Listen +7, Spot +7
Languages —

AC 15, touch 13, flat-footed 13
   (+1 size, +2 Dex, +2 natural)
hp 19 (3 HD)
Immune sonic
Fort +5, **Ref** +5, **Will** +4

Speed 40 ft. (8 squares), fly 40 ft. (good)
Melee 2 claws +4 each (1d4) and
   bite +2 (1d4)
Space 5 ft.; **Reach** 5 ft.
Base Atk +3; **Grp** −1
Atk Options aligned strike (evil), frenzied haste

Abilities Str 11, Dex 15, Con 14, Int 2, Wis 13, Cha 1
SQ hive mind
Feats Improved Initiative, Multiattack
Skills Climb +6, Hide +9, Jump +4, Listen +7, Move
   Silently +5, Spot +7
Advancement —

Frenzied Haste (Ex) Whenever a demonhive queen takes damage, all the hive's attendants shudder with nervous energy. When the queen is reduced to −1 hit points or below, attendants enter a state of frenzied haste. Each attendant gains a +2 haste bonus on attack rolls and damage rolls, and one additional claw attack at its highest attack bonus (3 claws +6 each [1d4+2] and bite +4 [1d4+2]). This frenzied haste lasts for the remainder of the encounter, after which the attendant is fatigued for 10 minutes.
Hive Mind (Ex) All demonhive members within 2 miles of a demonhive queen are in constant communication. If one is aware of a particular danger, they all are. If one in an encounter is not flat-footed, none of them are. No demonhive member in an encounter is considered flanked unless all of them are.

Demonhive attendants are the workers and hunters of the hive. They attack nearly any creature they encounter, and they kill regardless of hunger or the colony's needs.

Strategies and Tactics

As the hive's providers, demonhive attendants kill creatures and bring their carcasses back for the queen and demonet swarms to feed on. They attack any creature that enters their hive and any creature larger than Fine size that they encounter while foraging. In combat, attendants prefer to overwhelm a single foe before moving to the next, unless enemies threaten the queen. In such cases, they divide their efforts between blocking approach to the queen and attacking those who come near.

DEMONET SWARM

Hundreds of disgusting, black, larvalike creatures flit through the air on tiny red insect wings, creating a dizzying drone.

DEMONET SWARM	CR 2

Always NE Tiny outsider (evil, extraplanar, swarm)
Init +7; **Senses** darkvision 60 ft.; Listen +7, Spot +7
Languages —
Aura demonic drone (60 ft.)

AC 15, touch 15, flat-footed 12
   (+2 size, +3 Dex)
hp 19 (3 HD)
Immune sonic
Resist half damage from slashing and piercing
Immune swarm immunities
Fort +5, **Ref** +6, **Will** +2

Speed 20 ft. (4 squares), fly 40 ft. (good)
Melee swarm (1d6 plus distraction)
Space 10 ft.; **Reach** 0 ft.
Base Atk +3; **Grp** —
Atk Options aligned strike (evil)

Abilities Str 1, Dex 16, Con 14, Int 1, Wis 9, Cha 1
SQ hive mind, swarm traits
Feats Alertness, Improved Initiative
Skills Hide +17, Listen +7, Spot +7
Advancement —

Demonic Drone (Ex) Creatures within 60 feet of a demonet swarm take a −2 penalty on attack rolls, skill checks, ability checks, and saving throws. This is a sonic mind-affecting effect. Demonhive attendants, demonet swarms, and demonhive queens are immune to this effect.
Distraction (Ex) Fortitude DC 13, nauseated 1 round. The save DC is Constitution-based.
Hive Mind (Ex) As demonhive attendant.

Although individually less dangerous than rats, demonets gather in huge flying swarms, whose buzzing creates a mind-numbing drone.

Strategies and Tactics

A demonet swarm follows the lead of demonhive attendants and the demonhive queen. When attendants or queens seem agitated or enter combat, the demonet swarms do likewise. They do not use sophisticated tactics but simply swarm around whatever the queen or attendants are fighting. A demonet swarm does not attack other demonets.

Demonhives swarm across the Lower Planes, spreading wanton destruction in their wake

DEMONHIVE QUEEN

Swollen with fat and a thousand unborn young, this black, worm-like creature has a toothy mouth flanked by snapping pincers. Wings too flimsy to support its prodigious bulk hang limply from its back, while obscenely human-looking arms reach from its body to slowly drag it along the ground.

DEMONHIVE QUEEN   **CR 6**

Always NE Large outsider (evil, extraplanar)
Init –1; **Senses** darkvision 60 ft.; Listen +14, Spot +14
Languages —

AC 15, touch 8, flat-footed 15
    (–1 size, –1 Dex, +7 natural)
hp 114 (8 HD)
Immune sonic
Fort +14, **Ref** +5, **Will** +9

Speed 20 ft. (4 squares)
Melee bite +10 (3d6+4)
Space 10 ft.; **Reach** 5 ft.
Base Atk +8; **Grp** +15
Atk Options aligned strike (evil)
Special Actions maternal scream

Abilities Str 17, Dex 9, Con 27, Int 2, Wis 16, Cha 2
SQ hive mind
Feats Improved Toughness, Toughness (2)
Skills Climb +14, Listen +14, Spot +14, Survival +14
Advancement 9–11 HD (Large), 12–24 (Huge)

Maternal Scream (Ex) The first time each round a demonet swarm is dispersed or destroyed, a demonhive queen lets loose a terrible screech as an immediate action. If all her demonet swarms are dead, a demonhive queen screams once per round as a free action. This effect deals 3d6 points of sonic damage to all creatures within 60 feet. Creatures in the area can attempt a DC 22 Fortitude save to take half damage. The save DC is Constitution-based.

Hive Mind (Ex) As demonhive attendant.

DEMONHIVE LORE

Characters with ranks in Knowledge (the planes) can learn more about demonhives. When a character makes a successful skill check, the following lore is revealed, including the information from lower DCs.

Knowledge (the Planes)

DC	Result
13	Demonhives are colonies of evil insectlike outsiders. This result reveals all outsider traits.
18	Three kinds of creatures form a demonhive: demonets that gather in swarms, male attendants that hunt for the hive, and the hive's queen.
23	Attendants are the "worker bees" of the hive and go into a frenzy if their queen is severely wounded or killed. The demonet swarms make a hideous droning noise that makes fighting them difficult.
28	The queen is very protective of her demonets and emits a devastating scream if they are killed. The hive members are immune to this and other sonic effects.

A demonhive queen is the heart of the hive and exists only to perpetuate its wanton destruction. Demonhive attendants serve and protect the queen, but she cares little for them. Instead, she values the demonets from which a new queen might arise.

Strategies and Tactics

The queen remains at the center of the hive, barely able to move. She relies on her attendants to defend herself and the precious demonet swarms. If the swarms die, the queen begins to scream. If the queen is injured or killed, the attendants enter a frenzied haste.

SAMPLE ENCOUNTERS

A demonhive presents interesting encounters that can form the backbone of a short adventure. All the members of a demonhive should be encountered together as much as possible, since they rarely stray far from the queen. The abilities of the queen, attendants, and swarms also complement each other. As a result, the difficulty of a demonhive encounter is in large part determined by the tactical choices made by the PCs. From the characters' perspective, an optimal approach is to defeat the attendants first, then the queen, and finally the demonet swarms. In this way, the surviving monsters do not benefit from the others' special abilities.

The PCs might encounter demonhive attendants on the hunt, either alone or in small groups, then clash with more attendants and demonet swarms at the entrance to the hive. Demonhive queens always have a few swarms and attendants nearby, and are normally found in the birthing chamber of the hive. In some circumstances, a party might encounter a queen accompanied by attendant bodyguards and demonet swarms as the hive moves from an uninhabitable lair to find a new one.

Hunting Wing (EL 6): Four demonhive attendants fly through the woods harrying a small herd of deer. When the creatures spot the PCs, they veer off to attack. If the PCs remain in the area after the battle, a new hunting wing soon shows up, alerted to the combat through the attendants' hive mind ability.

Entrance Guardians (EL 7): Two demonet swarms flit about the entrance to a demonhive, eager for the return of a hunting wing with prey. Two attendants stand guard at the entrance, and two others have almost reached the hive along with freshly caught prey—a dying halfling.

Queen and Company (EL 9): The queen lies in the hive's birthing chamber, guarded by five attendants and in the company of three demonet swarms. When the queen or attendants notice a threat, the demonet swarms fly about the enemy while the attendants move to attack those who engage the queen.

ECOLOGY

The ecology of a demonhive resembles that of a beehive. A reproductive queen gives birth to thousands of demonets, most of which grow up to be attendants that care for the queen and her demonets. Attendants hunt in the surrounding territory and work to construct the hive. Demonhives prefer to occupy caves or building complexes that they discover, but attendants can slowly dig out a warren of tunnels for the hive to occupy should the need arise.

Demonhive members eat only carrion and fresh meat. The attendants hunt singly or in small groups and attack any living thing they encounter. A combat that doesn't end quickly in victory draws other hunting attendants to the area within 5 minutes. The attendants hunt throughout a 2-mile-radius area around the hive. This is the range of their hive mind, and they never willingly leave it. An area well populated with prey can sustain a demonhive for several months, but when food runs out, the queen begins to starve. In this state, she continues to give birth but kills one of her attendants each day. The queen does not eat the corpse but instead leaves it for her demonets and other attendants to feed on. When the queen dies, her surviving demonet swarms and attendants separate to create new hives in more bountiful areas.

A queen gives birth to a demonet every 10 minutes, creating enough to constitute a swarm after 1 week. Demonets do not hunt, and indeed they don't even attack intruders unless an attendant or the queen attacks first. Demonets are born genderless, but with a regular diet of meat, most mature into male demonhive attendants. Roughly one in three thousand demonets is female. These females remain immature and swarm with their siblings as long as the queen lives.

When the queen dies, female demonets release a scent that draws surviving attendants to them. The attendants then hunt for and guard the swarm until its members mature into more attendants and a queen. Should several demonet swarms produce queens in this way, the swarms and attendants split up, each seeking a new location for a hive.

Environment: Demonhives once existed only on one layer of the Abyss, but they have since spread to other layers, as well as other planes, through *gates* and deliberate transfers by fiends interested in causing havoc. Such transplants tend to be short-lived in the Upper Planes, where inhabitants take pains to eradicate the threat, but the Material Plane offers a pleasant environment for demonhives to thrive.

Demonhives can exist in any temperate and warm lands, but they are most successful in forests and jungles. With no protection from the elements but their hives and hides, demonhive members find cold lands inhospitable.

Typical Physical Characteristics: A demonet is approximately the size and weight of a rat. A demonhive attendant measures about 3 feet long and weighs about 40 pounds. A demonhive queen is enormous, measuring 10 feet long and nearly as much around. Her wings are feeble things, approximately the size of an attendant's. A typical queen weighs as much as 2,000 pounds, but a well-fed and long-lived queen can grow to Huge size.

Alignment: Demonhives infest any region with a food supply; they don't care about laws or borders. However, their demonic origins make them ruthless predators, and the creatures seem to enjoy the screams of their prey being ripped to pieces. Thus, demonhives are always neutral evil.

DEMONHIVES IN EBERRON

The first demonhive appeared in Eberron only five years ago in southern Zilargo. It was attacked and destroyed by gnome adventurers. The gnomes claim that a shipwreck on their southern coast yielded evidence in a logbook that the demonhive was brought from Xen'drik. Many dispute that claim, choosing instead to believe that the gnomes engineered the demonhive as a weapon. Some others find cause to believe this theory because demonhives appeared in several nations across Khorvaire in the months leading up to the signing of the Treaty of Thronehold. Others agree with the gnomes but still have reason to suspect their motives. One rumor holds that the shipwrecked vessel did not come from Xen'drik, or even the sea at all, but instead hailed from Mabar and somehow sailed the void between planes. The mystery endures to this day, because the gnomes cannot or will not produce the ship or its logbook.

DEMONHIVES IN FAERÛN

Demonhives probably originated in the Demonweb Pits, where they preyed upon the plane's many spiders and were in turn preyed upon by them. Demonhives then spread through *portals* to the Abyss, where some tanar'ri took a special interest in them. From there they traveled to Fury's Heart, where their rapacious nature earned the favor of Malar. Now demonhives can be found in all three planes, but Malar and demons also bring the insectlike outsiders to the Material Plane. Demons sometimes herd them through open *portals*, whereas Malar often inflicts them on the weak but annoying enemies of his vicious hunters, which thus can spend their energy hunting more worthy prey.

DWARF ANCESTOR

A great statue come to life blocks the way threateningly. It looks like a dwarf warrior clad in splint mail, all formed of dark granite. It raises an enormous axe and challenges you in a gravelly voice.

DWARF ANCESTOR   CR 6

Always LG Large outsider (native)
Init −1; **Senses** darkvision 60 ft.; Listen +9, Spot +9
Aura ancestral spirit (30 ft.)
Languages Dwarven

AC 26, touch 8, flat-footed 26
    (−1 size, −1 Dex, +18 natural)
hp 67 (5 HD); **DR** 10/adamantine
Fort +13, **Ref** +3, **Will** +5

Speed 20 ft. (4 squares)
Melee *+1 greataxe* +11 (1d12+10/×3)
Space 10 ft.; **Reach** 10 ft.
Base Atk +5; **Grp** +15
Atk Options Cleave, Power Attack

Abilities Str 22, Dex 8, Con 28, Int 8, Wis 13, Cha 14
SQ blink out
Feats Cleave, Power Attack
Skills Climb +14, Intimidate +10, Jump −4, Knowledge
    (history) +7, Knowledge (the planes) +7, Listen +9,
    Spot +9, Survival +1 (+3 on other planes)
Advancement 6–18 HD (Large); see text
Possessions *+1 greataxe*

Ancestral Spirit (Su) Any dwarf within 30 feet of a dwarf
    ancestor gains a +1 morale bonus on attack rolls and
    damage rolls.
Blink Out (Su) Once per day, a dwarf ancestor can become
    incorporeal until the beginning of its next turn. Activating
    this ability is a free action that does not provoke attacks
    of opportunity.

Illus. by E. Widermann

Dwarf ancestor

A dwarf ancestor is the spirit of an ancient dwarf hero brought back from the afterlife to serve by the will and prayers of a dwarf cleric. It comes to those who plead to Moradin the Soul Forger for aid. When first summoned, a dwarf ancestor takes up residence within a statue of a dwarf hero, animating it. As a result, many mistake the stony creatures for constructs on first encountering them.

STRATEGIES AND TACTICS

A dwarf ancestor is called to aid its people in times of crisis. It defends dwarven halls with grim determination, and it does not retreat or give quarter. It fights until destroyed or until those dwarves it is protecting are safe.

Although of lawful good alignment, the ancestor does not distinguish between enemies on the basis of their moral philosophies. If its descendants are in danger, it attacks all who threaten them. It is not unintelligent, though, and the possessing spirit was usually a warrior in a previous life. It focuses on the most dangerous-looking combatant first and exploits its Power Attack to maximize damage (taking its opponent's armor into consideration) to defeat it quickly, turning on the next with a Cleave attack whenever possible. Despite its impressive damage reduction, it has no special protection against spells, so it targets obvious spellcasters as quickly as possible.

It is unusual to encounter more than one or two dwarf ancestors, although in times of war the priests of Moradin might call for additional assistance. Usually an ancestor provides a bulwark in melee for a group of dwarf soldiers.

SAMPLE ENCOUNTERS

Dwarf ancestors are most often guardians that defend their charges with unflagging zeal.

Guardians (EL 6): A single dwarf ancestor is called to protect a sacred site, such as the tomb of a champion or a temple to Moradin.

EL 6: Ulfgar Silverhand was a dwarven defender who was killed protecting his king from a squad of orc raiders. Now he watches over the king's tomb as an ancestral spirit. Two dwarf crossbow archers also guard the site, allowing the ancestor to engage foes in melee while they attack from range.

Corrupted Guardians (EL 8): Dwarf ancestors were corrupted by duergar invaders. The ancestor spirits now guard the evil duergar as if they were the original dwarves.

EL 8: Duergar made an unholy pact with a group of mind flayers, trading slaves in return for the mind flayers' aid in capturing Fellhammer shrine with little bloodshed. Once the dwarves guarding the shrine were captured, the duergar entered the structure and bound the ancestral spirits to their own purposes. Two corrupted dwarf ancestors and four duergar warriors guard the shrine.

ECOLOGY

Dwarf ancestors appear only when they are called to defend. They are the spirits of heroes long dead, returned to the Material Plane in times of need. They have no need of food, drink, sleep, or air. An ancestor might stand for centuries to guard a holy place, but most often it comes for a specific battle and is released afterward. Dwarves are loath to imprison such valiant souls, preferring to send them back to Moradin's halls as soon as possible.

The bond between dwarf ancestor and its statue host cannot be severed by any means except slaying the creature or banishing it back to Moradin's halls (although the statue remains behind, inert, in the latter case).

Corrupted Ancestors: Dwarf ancestors sometimes fall into the hands of duergar. These unfortunate souls are usually corrupted by the duergar (whom the ancestors see only as dwarves) and turned against their true nature. In lands where dwarf strongholds have fallen to duergar attack, some deranged ancestors patrol ancient corridors, looking to assuage their pain in the blood of living creatures.

Environment: Dwarf ancestors are nearly always found in underground complexes, forming the last line of defense for a community. Royal halls, ancestral homes, and temples are some of the places most likely to be guarded by a dwarf ancestor, although some dwarf priests can summon these champions of Moradin into other battles for a short time.

Typical Physical Characteristics: A typical dwarf ancestor enters a statue 12 feet tall. The statue is carved from the native rock, often granite, and (depending on the kind of stone) weighs 3,000 to 4,000 pounds. The summoned spirit can be that of anything from a relatively low-level fighter to a great champion. The outward appearance of the statue gives no hint as to the strength of the outsider within.

Although the example given here is armed with a greataxe, a dwarf ancestor can wield whatever weapon the statue bears (usually a dwarven waraxe, maul, or greatclub).

Alignment: Dwarf ancestors are always lawful good. They are the spirits of those who fought selflessly for their people, and they are the implacable enemies of all that threaten the dwarf clans. Corrupted ancestors, however, are usually lawful evil.

SOCIETY

Dwarf ancestors answer the call of Moradin's beleaguered faithful, because they were heroes who protect those in need. Many were themselves killed in battle and welcome the opportunity to fight once more against their people's enemies. Their stony bodies suffer no pain, and they can fight to utter destruction without fear, since they return to Moradin's hall at the end of the battle.

Dwarf warriors are fierce and fearless, but these reconstituted champions fight with a ruthlessness and lust for battle that is awe-inspiring. They have nothing to lose, and their cause is the most noble. They shout and sing in their grinding, booming voices as their weapons whirl.

SAMPLE LAIR: CORRUPTED TEMPLE OF MORADIN

A once-proud dwarf temple has been occupied by a foul group of duergar. The place is still protected by a pair of dwarf ancestors summoned centuries ago, and they now follow the will of the duergar.

1. Hall of Worship: This area is where ceremonies dedicated to Moradin took place. Four statues of dwarf heroes stand watch over the temple area (none of them contain ancestors). Two more inanimate statues flank the altar.

2. The Great Forge (EL 4): This chamber was for forging and blessing magic weapons. Only the priests, temple smith, and weapon creators entered this sacred place when dwarves dwelt here, but now duergar come and go as they please, using the forge as they see fit. A *hallow* spell is centered on the forge. Four duergar warriors work the forge.

Duergar Warriors (4): hp 9 each; *MM* 91.

3. Corrupted Dwarf Ancestors (EL 8): Two great statues of Moradin stand in these locations, each desecrated with blood and offal, and greatly damaged by the strokes of hammers and picks. The two statues contain dwarf ancestors, set to guard the inner sanctum but now corrupted by the duergar. When any nonduergar attempts to pass through the doors leading west, they move to attack.

Dwarf Ancestors (2): hp 67 each; see above.

4. Clerics' Cells: These austere sleeping quarters contain ruined cots.

5. High Priest's Quarters: This larger chamber housed the temple's high priest. It is more comfortably appointed than the other cells, though its furnishings have decayed over the years. An unlocked chest contains ceremonial robes and a scroll of *heal*.

DWARF ANCESTOR LORE

Characters with ranks in Knowledge (local), Knowledge (religion), or Knowledge (the planes) can learn more about dwarf ancestors. When a character makes a successful skill check, the following lore is revealed, including the information from lower DCs.

Knowledge (Local)

DC	Result
16	Dwarves revere their ancestral heroes and sometimes call them into battle.
21	Legend holds that these heroes dwell with Moradin the Soul Forger until called by their living ancestors.

Knowledge (Religion)

DC	Result
10	Moradin is a lawful good dwarven deity and the creator of his people.
16	Moradin sometimes answers prayers for help by sending an emissary.
21	A dwarf ancestor is the spirit of a dwarf hero called to aid and defend its people.

Knowledge (the Planes)

DC	Result
16	This creature is a dwarf ancestor, the spirit of a dwarf hero. This result reveals all outsider traits.
21	Priests of Moradin call on dwarf ancestors to defend their people in times of crisis.
26	Dwarf ancestors are extremely resistant to damage.
31	The summoned spirit can range greatly in power—some spirits are the souls of simple warriors who served honorably in their day, and some are the souls of epic heroes. Discovering the strength of the spirit requires entering combat with the ancestor.

Corrupted
Temple of
Moradin
One square = 5 feet

6. Library (EL 5): The temple's religious and secular texts are still on the shelves, but time and damp have made them nearly unreadable. Of greater interest is a trove of engraved stone tablets that contain liturgical lore. Six duergar warriors guard this room.

Duergar Warriors (6): hp 9 each; *MM* 91.

TYPICAL TREASURE

A dwarf ancestor, being a spirit called into this world, possesses no treasure. A slain spirit does not leave behind its weapon, which is destroyed along with the statue that houses the ancestor. When ancestors are encountered with a warband or company of dwarves, the group yields treasure (largely in the form of equipment) commensurate with its Encounter Level. If the PCs dare to plunder a temple of Moradin, they can recover the offerings made to summon an ancestor (if the money has not already been used).

ADVANCED DWARF ANCESTORS

Although the size and appearance of the statue does not change, the spirit within might be that of a very powerful warrior. A dwarf ancestor can have up to 18 Hit Dice (the maximum allowed by the *greater planar ally* spell) but is still Large size. More powerful champions are avatars of Moradin and require epic-level magic to call upon. These spirits are housed in Huge statues; such sculptures exist only in the greatest centers of Moradin's worship. Legend holds that Moradin himself once appeared in the form of an ancestor,

but no magic would summon a god. Only the imminent destruction of his people might bring the Soul Forger to fight in person.

FOR PLAYER CHARACTERS

A cleric of Moradin can summon a dwarf ancestor using *summon monster V* or a higher-level *summon monster* spell or can call on a dwarf ancestor for longer periods of service with a *planar ally* spell. The basic version of the creature can be called using *lesser planar ally*, but advanced ancestors require higher-level versions of the spell.

A summoner must still pay the price required for the ancestor's service. However, because it is called in defense of Moradin's children, the gp cost equivalent is one-half normal. Typically this offering is used to craft superior or magical battle gear for the settlement's defenses. The cleric might instead perform a service for the settlement, such as raising dead combatants at no charge or embarking on a perilous quest.

DWARF ANCESTORS IN EBERRON

The dwarf clans of the Mror Holds are the undisputed masters of finance in Eberron, and the massive vaults beneath Korunda Gate are filled with incalculable wealth in both precious metals and magical artifacts. Dwarf ancestors, themselves often the spirits of long-dead leaders of House Kundarak, stand guard over these riches. Defending the wealth of clients (and of the house) is as vital to these mercantile dwarves as protecting their people in war. However, no one spirit is required to spend more than two centuries performing this duty. Lesser vaults in other centers of House Kundarak might also have ancestor spirits watching over them.

Spirits for such duty are sent by Kol Korran, the Lord of World and Wealth, rather than by Moradin, and they demand the normal price for their service. Those who answer the call to defend their people are summoned through prayers to Dol Dorn and require only one-half normal payment.

DWARF ANCESTORS IN FAERÛN

Although any dwarf community might call on ancestors for aid, the most famed statues of dwarf heroes are found in Mithral Hall. This great city of the shield dwarves in the Silver Marches was reclaimed from the dragon Shimmergloom only a few short decades earlier, and many warriors fell at the side of their champion, Bruenor Battlehammer. King Bruenor is now dedicated to restoring the city's ancient glory and to removing the threat from the Underdark for good. Many spirits of fallen champions now inhabit the statues of Mithral Hall, and they accompany war parties into the Underdark or stand guard over the mithral miners who have once again ventured into the haunted tunnels.

In addition to Moradin, the dwarven deities Berronar Truesilver, Clangeddin Silverbeard, and Gorm Gulthyn sometimes send ancestor spirits in response to prayer. These gods share the portfolios of defending the dwarf community and are receptive to requests for aid.

ELF, DROW

Initially presented in the *Monster Manual*, drow are a depraved and evil subterranean offshoot of elves. The examples below represent four archetypes that can fill out drow encounters: a silent assassin, a mobile archer, a spellslinging fighter, and a fearsome cleric of Lolth.

LOLTH'S STING

A black-skinned elf leaps from the shadows, stark white hair and flashing steel blade only momentarily visible before the creature vanishes.

LOLTH'S STING   CR 5

Female drow ninja* 4
  *Class described in *Complete Adventurer*
NE Medium humanoid (elf)
Init +3; **Senses** darkvision 120 ft.; Listen +11, Spot +11
Languages Common, Drow Sign Language, Elven, Undercommon

AC 18, touch 15, flat-footed 15
  (+3 Dex, +3 armor, +2 Wis)
hp 25 (4 HD)
Immune sleep
SR 15
Fort +3, **Ref** +7, **Will** +3 (+5 with *ki* pool) (+5/+7 against spells and spell-like abilities)
Weakness light blindness

Speed 35 ft. (7 squares)
Melee mwk rapier +7 (1d6+1/18–20 plus poison)
Ranged dagger +6 (1d4+1/19–20 plus poison)
Base Atk +3; **Grp** +4
Atk Options poison (drow poison, DC 13, unconscious 1 minute/unconscious 2d4 hours), sudden strike +2d6
Special Actions
Combat Gear 3 doses of drow poison, 2 bags of caltrops, 2 smokesticks, *elixir of hiding*, *elixir of sneaking*, *potion of cure moderate wounds*
Spell-Like Abilities (CL 4th):
  1/day—*dancing lights*, *darkness*, *faerie fire*

Abilities Str 12, Dex 17, Con 14, Int 12, Wis 14, Cha 10
SQ able to notice secret or concealed doors, ghost step, great leap, *ki* power 4/day, poison use, trapfinding
Feats Dash*, Weapon Finesse
  *Feat described in *Complete Warrior*
Skills Bluff +7, Diplomacy +4, Disguise +0 (+2 acting), Hide +10, Intimidate +2, Jump +7, Listen +11, Move Silently +10, Search +3, Sense Motive +9, Spot +11, Tumble +10
Possessions combat gear plus *+1 leather armor*, masterwork rapier, dagger, *amulet of health +2*

Light Blindness (Ex) Abrupt exposure to bright light (such as sunlight or a *daylight* spell) blinds drow for 1 round. In addition, they take a −1 circumstance penalty on attack rolls, saves, and checks while operating in bright light.
Sudden Strike (Ex) As sneak attack (PH 50), but no extra damage when flanking. *Complete Adventurer* 8.
Great Leap (Su) Always makes Jump checks as if running with the Run feat. *Complete Adventurer* 8.
Ki Power (Su) Expend one daily use to activate *ki*-based abilities (ghost step or *ki* dodge); +2 bonus on Will saves as long as at least one daily use remains. *Complete Adventurer* 8.
Ghost Step (Su) Swift action, one daily *ki* power use, invisibility for 1 round. *Complete Adventurer* 8.

Illus. by F. Tsai

Drow: Lolth's Sting, dark sniper, and arcane guard

In drow culture, assassination is a frequent means of advancement or of keeping one's status. The clerics of Lolth, intent on retaining their top position, train an elite group of female drow assassins. The best of these are given the rank of Lolth's Sting.

The Lolth's Sting presented here had the following ability scores before racial adjustments, Hit Dice ability score increases, and equipment bonuses: Str 12, Dex 15, Con 14, Int 10, Wis 13, Cha 8.

Strategies and Tactics

Stealth and surprise are the cornerstones of a Sting's tactics. When stalking her target, she prepares by consuming her *elixir of hiding* and *elixir of sneaking*, increasing her Hide and Move Silently bonuses to +20.

A Lolth's Sting tries to make her first attack from hiding, gaining her sudden strike bonus without requiring a use of ghost step. Once combat begins, she uses ghost step to remain invisible, attacking with her sudden strike from a different direction each round.

If her foe is formidable and resistant to drow poison, a Lolth's Sting retreats under cover of *darkness* or smoke, courtesy of a smokestick. She lingers in the area long enough to determine if her target succumbs to her poison's secondary effect, perhaps rejoining battle if an enemy falls unconscious and evens the odds against her.

In groups, Stings use invisibility, smoke, and *darkness* to conceal their true numbers. Half the group attacks at once, while the others cover their weapons with drow poison. In alternating rounds the groups switch roles.

DARK SNIPER

A drow holds his bow at the ready, a hunter's gleam in his eye. His cloak makes him seem to blend into the surrounding terrain.

DARK SNIPER   CR 7

Male drow scout* 6
   *Class described in *Complete Adventurer*
CE Medium humanoid (elf)
Init +6; **Senses** darkvision 120 ft.; Listen +12, Spot +12
Languages Common, Drow Sign Language, Elven, Undercommon

AC 19, touch 15, flat-footed 19; Dodge, Mobility, uncanny dodge
   (+5 Dex, +4 armor)
hp 36 (6 HD)
Immune sleep
Resist evasion; **SR** 17
Fort +4, **Ref** +10, **Will** +3 (+5 against spells and spell-like abilities)
Weakness light blindness

Speed 40 ft. (8 squares); Shot on the Run, flawless stride
Melee mwk rapier +6 (1d6+1/18–20 plus poison)
Ranged +1 composite longbow +10 (1d8+2/×3)
Base Atk +4; **Grp** +5
Atk Options Point Blank Shot, poison (drow poison, DC 13, unconscious 1 minute/unconscious 2d4 hours), skirmish (+2d6, +1 AC)
Combat Gear 5 doses of drow poison
Spell-Like Abilities (CL 6th):
   1/day—*dancing lights, darkness, faerie fire*

Abilities Str 13, Dex 20, Con 12, Int 12, Wis 12, Cha 10
SQ able to notice secret or concealed doors, battle fortitude +1, fast movement, poison use, trackless step, trapfinding
Feats Dodge, Mobility, Point Blank Shot, Shot on the Run[B]
Skills Balance +16, Climb +10, Diplomacy +2, Hide +19, Jump +12, Listen +12, Move Silently +14, Search +12, Sense Motive +6, Spot +12, Tumble +15
Possessions combat gear plus mithral shirt, *+1 composite longbow* (+1 Str bonus) with 50 arrows, masterwork rapier, *gloves of Dexterity +2, cloak of elvenkind*

Light Blindness (Ex) As Lolth's Sting.
Flawless Stride (Ex) A dark sniper ignores movement penalties in any terrain that slows movement. *Complete Adventurer* 13.
Skirmish (Ex) +1 bonus on damage rolls and to AC in any round in which the dark sniper moves at least 10 feet. *Complete Adventurer* 12.
Battle Fortitude (Ex) Bonus on initiative checks and Fortitude saves while wearing light or no armor and carrying a light load. Included above. *Complete Adventurer* 12.

Dark snipers patrol the caverns and tunnels near drow settlements and outposts. They use their mobility to harass opponents until stronger reinforcements arrive.

The dark sniper presented here had the following ability scores before racial adjustments, Hit Dice ability score increases, and equipment bonuses: Str 13, Dex 15, Con 14, Int 10, Wis 12, Cha 8.

Strategies and Tactics

Dark snipers choose hiding places along the thoroughfares of the subterranean realm. They fully exploit their superior darkvision, typically launching arrows when targets are still nearly 100 feet away.

In close combat, a dark sniper is constantly on the move, using Shot on the Run extensively after moving at least 10 feet so that he gains the benefit of his skirmish ability. His Tumble skill allows him to safely withdraw from foes that close to melee range. His favorite tactic involves waiting until a target has moved within 30 feet, then making an attack while backing away, preventing opponents from making more than a single attack against him.

A dark sniper uses terrain to his advantage and tries to prevent opponents from charging by moving through terrain that slows movement. In groups, dark snipers split up; if one is attacked, the others are still free to maneuver and attack from other directions.

ARCANE GUARD

This humanoid looks somewhat like a young elf with a shock of white hair and coal-black skin. He swings a spiked chain lazily with one arm, while with the other he makes a magical gesture.

ARCANE GUARD   CR 8

Male drow fighter 2/wizard 5
NE Medium humanoid (elf)
Init +7; **Senses** darkvision 120 ft.; Listen +6, Spot +7
Languages Abyssal, Common, Draconic, Drow Sign Language, Elven, Undercommon

AC 18, touch 14, flat-footed 15; Dodge
   (+3 Dex, +4 armor, +1 deflection)

hp 35 (7 HD)
Immune sleep
SR 18
Fort +5, **Ref** +4, **Will** +4 (+6 against spells and spell-like abilities)
Weakness light blindness

Speed 30 ft. (6 squares)
Melee +1 *spiked chain* +9 (2d4+2) or
Ranged mwk hand crossbow +8 (1d4/19–20 plus poison)
Reach 5 ft. (10 ft. with spiked chain)
Base Atk +4; **Grp** +5
Atk Options poison (drow poison, DC 13, unconscious 1 minute/unconscious 2d4 hours)
Combat Gear 3 doses of drow poison, *wand of magic missile* (CL 5th, 25 charges), *potion of bear's endurance, potion of cure serious wounds, potion of haste*
Wizard Spells Prepared (CL 5th; 10% arcane spell failure chance):
　3rd—*fly, empowered burning hands* (DC 14)
　2nd—*scorching ray* (+7 ranged touch), *invisibility, see invisibility*
　1st—*magic missile, ray of enfeeblement* (+7 ranged touch), *shield, true strike*
　0—*detect magic, ghost sound* (DC 13), *touch of fatigue* (+5 melee touch, DC 13), *resistance*
Spell-Like Abilities (CL 7th):
　1/day—*dancing lights, darkness, faerie fire*

Abilities Str 13, Dex 16, Con 12, Int 17, Wis 10, Cha 10
SQ able to notice secret or concealed doors
Feats Dodge, Empower Spell[B], Exotic Weapon Proficiency (spiked chain), Improved Initiative, Scribe Scroll[B], Weapon Finesse[B], Weapon Focus[B] (spiked chain)
Skills Climb +6, Concentration +10, Intimidate +4, Jump +6, Listen +6, Search +5, Spellcraft +11, Spot +7
Possessions combat gear plus mithral shirt, *+1 spiked chain*, masterwork hand crossbow with 20 bolts, *ring of protection +1*, 12 gp
Spellbook spells prepared plus 0—all; 1st—*alarm, animate rope, identify, silent image*; 2nd—*spider climb, web*; 3rd—*vampiric touch*

Light Blindness (Ex) As Lolth's Sting.

Arcane guards are multitalented male drow who wield both steel and spell. They are not quite powerful enough to continue their wizardly pursuits, but they understand the inner workings of arcane institutes well enough that powerful drow wizards and sorcerers want to keep them in the fold. Arcane guards have also been trained to fight, combining magic with their martial abilities.

The arcane guard presented here had the following ability scores before racial adjustments, Hit Dice ability score increases, and equipment bonuses: Str 12, Dex 13, Con 14, Int 15, Wis 10, Cha 8.

Strategies and Tactics

If he has time to prepare, an arcane guard casts *shield* and *fly* before battle. He then tries to fly up out of reach of his foes, to take advantage of his spiked chain's greater reach, and uses his *potion of haste* if he needs to make more melee attacks.

If flying, an arcane guard first reduces the threat of the most capable-looking melee combatant by using *ray of enfeeblement*. He then tries to place himself within 10 feet of an enemy spellcaster or other ranged attacker, alternating between spiked chain attacks and ranged spells.

In groups, arcane guards focus their spells on the most dangerous target or on a healer, if that individual becomes a nuisance.

DROW PRIESTESS

The humanoid has smooth, black skin and pale silver hair. She is slightly shorter and slimmer than a human. She wears a blackened breastplate with a human-headed spider embossed on it, and she carries a light shield with a similar decoration.

DROW PRIESTESS	**CR 9**

Female drow cleric 8
NE Medium humanoid (elf)
Init +3; **Senses** darkvision 120 ft.; Listen +6, Spot +6
Languages Common, Drow Sign Language, Elven, Undercommon

AC 22, touch 14, flat-footed 19
　(+3 Dex, +6 armor, +2 shield, +1 deflection)
hp 48 (8 HD)
Immune sleep
SR 19
Fort +7, **Ref** +5, **Will** +10 (+12 against spells and spell-like abilities)
Weakness light blindness

Speed 20 ft. (4 squares) in breastplate; base speed 30 ft.
Melee mwk dagger +8/+3 (1d4+1/19–20 plus poison) or
Melee light mace +7/+2 (1d6+1)
Base Atk +6; **Grp** +7
Atk Options poison (drow poison, DC 13, unconscious 1 minute/unconscious 2d4 hours), smite 1/day (+4 attack, +8 damage)
Special Actions rebuke undead 3/day (+0, 2d6+8, 8th), spontaneous casting (*inflict* spells)
Combat Gear 2 doses of drow poison, *wand of cure moderate wounds* (34 charges)
Cleric Spells Prepared (CL 8th, 1d20+10 to overcome SR):
　4th—*air walk, freedom of movement, summon monster IV, unholy blight*[D] (DC 18, CL 9th)
　3rd—*bestow curse* (+8 melee touch, DC 17), *dispel magic, invisibility purge, magic circle against good*[D] (CL 9th), *summon monster III*
　2nd—*cure moderate wounds, death knell* (DC 16, CL 9th), *shatter*[D] (DC 16), *sound burst* (DC 16), *summon monster II*
　1st—*bane, cure light wounds, doom* (DC 15), *entropic shield, inflict light wounds*[D] (+8 melee touch), *summon monster I*
　0—*cure minor wounds* (2), *detect magic, detect poison, guidance, resistance*
　D: Domain spell. Deity: Lolth. *Domains:* Destruction, Evil.
Spell-Like Abilities (CL 8th):
　1/day—*dancing lights, darkness, faerie fire*

Abilities Str 13, Dex 16, Con 12, Int 12, Wis 19, Cha 10
SQ able to notice secret or concealed doors
Feats Augment Summoning, Combat Casting, Spell Penetration
Skills Concentration +12, Diplomacy +5, Knowledge (religion) +4, Knowledge (the planes) +4, Listen +6, Search +3, Spellcraft +12, Spot +6
Possessions combat gear plus *+1 breastplate, +1 light steel shield*, masterwork dagger, light mace, *gloves of Dexterity +2, periapt of Wisdom +2, ring of protection +1*

Light Blindness (Ex) As Lolth's Sting.

No group or organization wields more power in drow society than the clerics of Lolth. Drow priestesses are respected, or at least feared, by nearly all other drow. They act on the will of the Spider Queen, and occasionally on their own whim, always vying for more power and the favor of their goddess. They serve as battlefield commanders, constables, detectives, and judges, as the situation requires.

The drow priestess presented here had the following ability scores before racial adjustments, Hit Dice ability score increases, and equipment bonuses: Str 13, Dex 12, Con 14, Int 10, Wis 15, Cha 8.

Strategies and Tactics

A drow priestess relishes sowing confusion among her opponents. Rarely encountered without other minions, a priestess does not immediately endanger herself in melee, instead using *summon monster* spells to call additional allies to her side.

A drow priestess is willing to convert many of her spells to spontaneously cast *inflict wounds*, though she saves *air walk* and *freedom of movement* in case she needs to escape.

DROW LORE

Characters with ranks in Knowledge (dungeoneering), Knowledge (history), or Knowledge (religion) can learn more about drow. When a character makes a successful skill check, the following lore is revealed, including the information from lower DCs.

Knowledge (Dungeoneering)

DC	Result
15	This creature is a drow, a subterranean and generally evil elf. This result reveals all elf traits.
20	Drow have strong resistance to magic but are vulnerable to light. This result reveals all drow traits (*MM* 103).

Knowledge (History)

DC	Result
12	This creature is a drow, a subterranean and generally evil elf.
17	The drow trace their lineage back to an elf splinter group that rejected the elves' love of freedom and nature.
22	Some drow live on the surface, but most live underground and emerge only at night to conduct trade or make raids.
27	Slaves perform most of the physical labor in drow society.

Knowledge (Religion)

DC	Result
15	Most drow worship Lolth, the spider goddess. She once fomented rebellion against the other elven gods and then literally led her followers underground.
20	Lolth is both cruel and capricious; she demands many sacrifices and demonstrations of loyalty. She also foments internal discord to keep her chosen people tough and ruthless.
25	Religious infighting plagues the drow. Those disaffected with Lolth's rule seek other gods.

If one of her allies should be reduced to negative hit points, the priestess rushes to the side of her fallen comrade—not to heal, but to cast *death knell* to gain power from his ebbing life force.

"The spider is a perfect creature: elegant in her symmetry, silent in her step, and deadly in her hunting. In short, she is much like a drow."

—Kaellara, cleric of Lolth

SAMPLE ENCOUNTERS

Drow usually operate in small groups dedicated to accomplishing some mission. Dark snipers could work in concert with Lolth's Stings, or at the behest of a drow priestess. Most encounters with drow include more than one of the dark elves—an encounter involving four to six is common. A single drow is more likely to find reinforcements before engaging foes, at the very least to provide witnesses to her own prowess.

Patrol (EL 9–11): Groups of dark snipers most often patrol a community's boundaries as the first layer of defense.

EL 11: A squad of four male dark snipers (Krizzun, Lurnad, Tethlar, and Zakphar) are charged with keeping a lookout for intruders. They occupy a remote outpost that overlooks a point where a trade route crosses a deep chasm. The group would love to capture one of their opponents to take home for questioning.

Strike Force (EL 9+): If the leaders of a drow community detect a threat, they mobilize a strike force quickly. Many drow jump at the chance to prove their abilities, curry the favor of superiors, or simply engage in random bloodshed. A strike force includes multiple drow, with one—usually a priestess—in obvious command.

EL 10: A drow priestess has been dispatched to deal with an incursion. Moving quietly through the shadows behind her, three Lolth's Stings await her command to kill. When she gives the word, they eagerly move ahead invisibly to deal death to their foes.

ECOLOGY

Unlike surface-dwelling elves, drow thrive in the light-deprived depths. Their darkvision exceeds that of most of the other denizens and provides a significant advantage. Their spell-like abilities also give them a great deal of control over illumination.

Like most humanoids, drow shape their environment to suit them. They create cities and settlements near valuable resources such as potable water or mithral mines. They use slaves to farm mushrooms and other underground plants, as well as domesticate monstrous spiders for use as mounts and guards.

Environment: Most drow loathe the sun and prefer to dwell deep underground. They construct sprawling underground cities of stone and metal. Their grandest buildings have bizarre shapes with weirdly elegant sculptural adornments. Permanent effects that resemble *faerie fire* cover many of their buildings, giving drow cities a ghostly look.

Typical Physical Characteristics: Like other elves, drow are short and willowy in comparison to humans. Females are slightly larger than males; an adult female is from 5 to 5-1/2 feet tall and weighs between 95 and 120 pounds. Males are around 5 feet tall and weigh between 80 and 110 pounds.

Drow have smooth black skin and finely chiseled features. They have pale hair; white is the most common color, but silver, gray, or white-gold hair is not unknown.

Alignment: Most drow are neutral evil, but many are chaotic evil. In spite of their penchant for status and titles, few drow are lawful. They value unpredictability and a talent for improvisation.

SOCIETY

Drow consider themselves superior to all other mortal beings and harbor a virulent disdain for surface elves and other drow who have returned to sunlit lands. Drow love pleasure and despise physical labor—except for fighting and killing. Slaves perform nearly all the heavy work in drow society. The drow's strange architecture and epicurean tastes are only two aspects of their hedonism.

Drow society is matriarchal. Males are valued but considered expendable. Drow clerics wield tremendous influence, and the faction who can boast the senior priestess of Lolth in a community has enough prestige to claim control, at least outwardly. Drow priestesses jealously guard Lolth's status as the patron of all drow and root out any backsliders who dare put another deity before Lolth.

The priesthood is just one layer in a society that has a preponderance of titles. Drow society is fragmented into many noble houses, merchant families, and guilds, all vying for power. The drow believe that the strongest should rule, and the various drow factions constantly strive to prove that they are the strongest, often by undermining their rivals.

Drow priestess

TYPICAL TREASURE

Drow have standard treasure for NPCs of their Challenge Rating, but most encountered outside their lairs carry little besides fighting gear and a few spare coins. At home, drow covet platinum and adamantine trinkets and jewelry. They also have a taste for fantastic sculptures and tapestries, though most surface-dwellers find these items obscene or at least disturbing.

DROW AS CHARACTERS

See page 103 of the *Monster Manual* for information on drow as characters.

DROW AND THE LOLTH-TOUCHED TEMPLATE

Lolth-touched mounts and beasts of burden (usually vermin) abound in drow society and are mainly used by the nobility and the priestly classes. They are far stronger and hardier than ordinary creatures of their kind, and they ease covert travel. Occasionally, a drow might become Lolth-touched, and such individuals (even males) are highly respected in drow society. For more about Lolth-touched creatures, see page 92.

DROW IN EBERRON

The split between drow and elf occurred long before the giants of Xen'drik enslaved the elves. Secure in their underground enclaves, the drow were spared the humiliation of servitude.

Today, the drow have nominal control of the continent of Xen'drik and the ruins of the giants' fallen empire. Their largest settlements still lie underground in Khyber, partly because of the drow's sensitivity to light but also because the surface of Xen'drik is a wild and dangerous place teeming with giants and other fearsome monsters. Still, the drow believe that they, who have never been slaves, are the true keepers of elven valor and dignity.

The drow of Xen'drik worship the scorpion god Vulkoor. Elsewere, most drow revere the Fury. Lolth is unknown on Eberron.

DROW IN FAERÛN

Drow rule large stretches of the Faerûnian Underdark. Internal strife has driven many back to the surface, where the drow are engaged in a concerted effort to reclaim the forest of Cormanthor from the elves.

Drow merchants handle a lively trade with anyone who values wealth over any moral qualms, including the Zhents and certain merchant houses of Sembia.

Internal strife among the drow is reflected in battles between the drow deities (or perhaps it's the other way around). Lolth remains the patron of the race. Rival deities include Ghaunadaur (the Elder Eye), Kiaransalee (a deity of the dead), and Vhaeraun (patron of rogues and male drow). The goddess Eilistraee is the patron of good-aligned drow who wish to live in peace on the surface of the world.

Illus. by D. Hudnut

GIANT, CRAA'GHORAN

Twisted and deformed, this massive giant appears to have jagged stone formations growing from its body at odd angles. Its expression is wild and frenetic as it shambles forward.

CRAA'GHORAN GIANT   CR 10

Usually NE Huge giant (earth)
Init +0; **Senses** darkvision 60 ft., low-light vision,
  tremorsense 60 ft.; Listen +11, Spot +11
Languages Giant, Terran

AC 24, touch 8, flat-footed 24
  (−2 size, +16 natural)
hp 157 (15 HD); **DR** 5/—
Fort +15, **Ref** +5, **Will** +8

Speed 40 ft. (8 squares); earth glide
Melee 2 claws +20 each (3d8+10)
Ranged rock +9 (2d8+10)
Space 15 ft.; **Reach** 15 ft.
Base Atk +11; **Grp** +29
Atk Options Awesome Blow, Cleave, Power Attack, rend
  4d8+15
Spell-Like Abilities (CL 15th):
  3/day—*spike stones* (DC 13), *wall of stone*

Abilities Str 31, Dex 10, Con 23, Int 12, Wis 13, Cha 8
Feats Awesome Blow, Cleave, Improved Natural Attack
  (claw), Iron Will, Power Attack, Weapon Focus (claw)
Skills Craft (stoneworking) +15, Jump +14, Knowledge
  (nature) +13, Listen +11, Spot +11, Survival +11 (+13 in
  aboveground natural environments)
Advancement by character class; **Favored Class** expert;
  see text

Earth Glide (Ex) A craa'ghoran giant can glide through stone,
  dirt, or almost any other sort of earth except metal as
  easily as a fish swims through water. Its burrowing leaves
  behind no tunnel or hole, nor does it create any ripple or
  other signs of its presence.
Rend (Ex) If a craa'ghoran giant hits with both claw attacks,
  it latches onto the opponent's body and tears the flesh.
  This attack automatically deals an additional 4d8+15
  points of damage.

Craa'ghoran giants are rare stone giant offshoots created millennia ago when earth elemental energy warped and twisted their ancestors. They can glide through stone like earth elementals. Combined with their power to cast *wall of stone*, craa'ghorans excel at building deadly, intricate traps and ambush points high in the mountains.

STRATEGIES AND TACTICS

Though bestial in appearance, a craa'ghoran giant is a canny hunter and uses its environment and its *wall of stone* ability to divide a group before it strikes, eliminating its opponents singly when possible. A typical craa'ghoran carefully builds an intricate series of passages, bridges, and tunnels in and near its lair using *wall of stone*. It delights in creating sharp turns that prevent intruders from seeing too far ahead. In such cramped, tight quarters, the giant can use a single *wall of stone* to divide its opponents. The giant's earth glide ability allows it to ignore stone barriers as it moves to attack.

Once a craa'ghoran has a group split up, it moves in fast, attempting to drop single opponents as quickly as possible, using Power Attack and rend to good effect. It might even rise from below the surface or emerge from the ceiling to attack.

SAMPLE ENCOUNTERS

Craa'ghoran giants gather in small groups. They sometimes ally with evil stone giants, and they often gather orcs, ogres, and other smaller creatures as slaves or grudging allies.

Slaver (EL 10): An ambitious craa'ghoran seeks to capture dwarves to enslave as skilled artisans. The creature uses earth glide to discreetly spy on an adventuring party with a dwarf member. When it finally attacks, it uses *wall of stone* to separate the dwarf from the rest of the group. It then attacks to subdue its victim, initially dealing normal damage before switching to nonlethal blows as the battle progresses. If the craa'ghoran has a clear escape path, it grapples the dwarf and attempts to carry him off.

Twins (EL 12): A pair of craa'ghoran giants use their earth glide ability to confuse and frighten their enemies. These two creatures were born identical twins and use their similarity to misdirect opponents. The giants attack as normal, but they leap into the fray one at a time. The first giant attacks, tears into its foes, and then flees into the ground when it has lost one-half or more of its hit points. After a round or two, when the party finally relaxes its guard, the second giant emerges from the earth. The first giant uses *wall of stone* to protect its sibling and frustrate the party's attempts to coordinate attacks. It then rejoins the melee at an opportune moment.

ECOLOGY

Craa'ghorans were originally created by blending stone giants and the essence of earth elementals. The influx of elemental energy warped and twisted the giants, leaving them with the

---

CRAA'GHORAN GIANT LORE

Characters with ranks in Knowledge (nature) can learn more about craa'ghoran giants. When a character makes a successful skill check, the following lore is revealed, including the information from lower DCs.

Knowledge (Nature)

DC	Result
20	This strange, twisted creature is a craa'ghoran, a giant that has been warped and altered with elemental energy. This result reveals all giant traits and the earth subtype.
25	A craa'ghoran giant's thick, rocky hide absorbs some of the force of every blow that strikes it.
30	A craa'ghoran giant's most dangerous talent is its ability to walk through stone as a fish swims through water. These fierce creatures can emerge from the ground below a traveling party.
35	A craa'ghoran giant can generate walls of stone as a magical ability. It uses these barriers to trap and separate its enemies.

ability to control and shape earth but forever altering their physical appearance. They can subsist on rocks and dirt, but they particularly enjoy the taste and texture of worked stone. Craa'ghorans gather gems, precious metals, and other items as trophies and trade goods.

Environment: Craa'ghoran giants prefer mountainous terrain, particularly if a region contains a great deal of stone nearby. When not hunting or defending their territory, craa'ghoran giants enjoy manipulating their environment to suit their living needs and tastes, and they often create elaborate structures of stone using their magical abilities.

Typical Physical Characteristics: A typical craa'ghoran giant stands up to 20 feet tall and can weigh as much as 14,000 pounds. Infused with the power of elemental earth, these creatures can live up to 800 years.

Alignment: Craa'ghoran giants are usually neutral evil. Extremely selfish and inherently cruel, they are also rarely predictable, switching between spontaneous and planned action at a moment's notice. More contemplative members of the race might be neutral, though they are rare.

Craa'ghoran giant

SOCIETY

Craa'ghoran giants prefer to live alone, since each one needs space to build the intricate passages, mazes, bridges, and other structures it prefers. They are fiercely territorial, but sometimes small families of related craa'ghorans live together. These clans claim wide stretches of territory. They demand tolls for those who use the paths they make in the mountains, and they quickly capture and kill travelers who enter their domain. Evil warlords sometimes pay tribute to craa'ghoran giants for the right to travel unmolested through the mountains they inhabit. The ever-greedy, mercenary craa'ghorans happily take such bribes from multiple sources but allow only the highest bidder access to their mountain passes.

Craa'ghoran giants usually keep orcs, dwarves, goblins, and ogres as slaves and servants. An orc tribe might provide scouts and guardians for the giant's territory. Craa'ghorans love to enslave dwarves in particular: The stout folk's skill in working metal and stone makes them excellent aides and helpers. Craa'ghorans take pride in the stone structures they erect. Among their kind, craa'ghorans judge prestige and ability by the beauty and majesty of their

lairs and territories. Travelers who enter a craa'ghoran's territory might see elaborate statues, massive bas-relief carvings wrought into cliff faces, and other architectural wonders. Few suspect that such beautiful works are the products of fundamentally malevolent creatures. Many dungeons and other old, monster-infested structures were originally crafted by craa'ghoran giants as demonstrations of their skill with stone and earth.

TYPICAL TREASURE

Craa'ghoran giants have treasure appropriate to their Challenge Rating, about 5,800 gp. They frequently demand tribute from lesser giants and other creatures that might be in a position to serve them. While they have little use for magic items they do not understand, and likely believe most such items to be inferior to their own inborn powers, craa'ghoran giants are fond of gems, fine jewelry, gold, and platinum. They use such goods to enhance the natural beauty of their works, as well as to trade for useful magic items and other goods.

CRAA'GHORAN GIANTS WITH CLASS LEVELS

Craa'ghorans do not usually enter a class, but a few become renowned master sculptors and take levels of expert.

Level Adjustment: +4.

CRAA'GHORAN GIANTS IN EBERRON

Though unusual, craa'ghoran giants can be found on the continent of Xen'drik living among others of their kind, most typically stone giants. Here the craa'ghorans are still great builders, looking to relive the glorious past by constructing massive stone monuments. Claustrophobic as a group, they shun the halls of Khyber, preferring to live in more open dwellings of their own construction aboveground.

CRAA'GHORAN GIANTS IN FAERÛN

Created by druids devoted to Gond in ancient times in an attempt to more ably fend off Netherese wizards, craa'ghoran giants have since had the opportunity to spread throughout Faerûn. Wherever large mountains or stone mesas are found, a group of adventurers might encounter one of these creatures, though they tend to be less social the farther north they live. However, this insularity doesn't make the creatures any less dangerous.

Illus. by W. England

GITHYANKI

Initially presented in the *Monster Manual,* the relentlessly militaristic, psionics-using githyanki dwell on the Astral Plane. A dour, brutal, and harsh race, they were once slaves of the mind flayers. Now they travel the planes, conquering worlds and hunting mind flayers wherever they can be found, all in the name of their dreaded lich-queen.

Githyanki are consummate artisans and metalsmiths. When not waging war or staging raids, they keep busy forging the implements they need for future conflicts. They believe that only the strong survive and that the only true freedom lies in power. The githyanki have vowed never to be subjugated again.

Below are several examples of typical githyanki adventurers might encounter, separately or as a marauding raider party.

GITHYANKI SOLDIER

This humanoid is about the size of a human but seems thin and gaunt; the creature's sallow skin gives him a skeletal look. He has long hair the color of drying blood, arranged in loose braids studded with beads. He wears an elaborate, but functional, breastplate, and he carries an equally ornate and deadly greatsword.

GITHYANKI SOLDIER	CR 4

Male githyanki fighter 3
LE Medium humanoid (extraplanar)
Init +2; **Senses** darkvision 60 ft.; Listen +2, Spot +2
Languages Githyanki

AC 19, touch 13, flat-footed 17; Dodge
  (+2 Dex, +6 armor, +1 deflection)
hp 30 (3 HD)
SR 8
Fort +6, **Ref** +3, **Will** +1

Speed 20 ft. (4 squares) in breastplate; base speed 30 ft.
Melee mwk greatsword +7 (2d6+3/19–20) or
Melee dagger +5 (1d4+2/19–20)
Ranged mwk composite longbow +6 (1d8+2/×3) or
Ranged dagger +5 (1d4+2/19–20)
Base Atk +3; **Grp** +5
Atk Options Point Blank Shot, Power Attack
Combat Gear tanglefoot bag, thunderstone
Spell-Like Abilities (CL 3rd):
  3/day—*blur, daze* (DC 9), *mage hand*

Abilities: Str 15, Dex 15, Con 16, Int 10, Wis 10, Cha 8
Feats Dodge, Point Blank Shot[B], Power Attack, Weapon Focus (greatsword)[B]
Skills Intimidate +3, Listen +2, Spot +2
Possessions combat gear plus *+1 breastplate,* masterwork greatsword, masterwork composite longbow (+2 Str bonus) with 20 arrows, dagger, *ring of protection +1*

Githyanki soldiers exemplify the grim attitude of their people. They approach their roles with ruthless efficiency.

The githyanki soldier presented here had the following ability scores before racial adjustments: Str 15, Dex 13, Con 14, Int 10, Wis 12, Cha 8.

Strategies and Tactics

Githyanki soldiers are resourceful combatants who disdain simple frontal attacks. They prefer to fight on their own terms and at times of their choosing. Before a fight, soldiers activate their *blur* abilities for an extra defensive edge.

GISH

This wiry humanoid is clad in a chain shirt with silver and gray links that form bands and swirls like a stormy sky. The creature also wears a buff-colored tunic that nearly matches her sallow skin, and she carries a bow and an elaborate greatsword.

GISH	CR 8

Female githyanki fighter 2/evoker 5
LE Medium humanoid (extraplanar)
Init +2; **Senses** darkvision 60 ft.; Listen +3, Spot +3
Languages Common, Draconic, Githyanki, Infernal, Undercommon

AC 18, touch 13, flat-footed 16
  (+2 Dex, +5 armor, +1 deflection)
hp 42 (7 HD)
SR 12
Fort +6, **Ref** +5, **Will** +5

Speed 30 ft. (6 squares)
Melee mwk greatsword +7 (2d6+3/19–20) or
Melee dagger +6 (1d4+2/19–20)
Ranged mwk composite longbow +7 (1d8+2/×3) or
Ranged dagger +6 (1d4+2/19–20)
Base Atk +4; **Grp** +6
Atk Options Point Blank Shot, Precise Shot
Combat Gear *potion of cure serious wounds, wand of bull's strength* (37 charges)
Wizard Spells Prepared (CL 7th):
  3rd—*haste, hold person* (DC 17), *lightning bolt* (DC 17)
  2nd—*glitterdust* (DC 16), *Melf's acid arrow* (+6 ranged touch), *scorching ray* (2) (+6 ranged touch)
  1st—*magic missile* (2), *ray of enfeeblement* (+6 ranged touch), *shield†, true strike*
  0—*detect magic, ray of frost* (2) (+6 ranged touch), *message, resistance*
  †Already cast
Spell-Like Abilities (CL 7th):
  3/day—*blur, daze* (DC 9), *mage hand, dimension door*

Abilities Str 14, Dex 15, Con 14, Int 18, Wis 8, Cha 8
Feats Githyanki Battlecaster*[B], Iron Will, Lightning Reflexes, Point Blank Shot[B], Practiced Spellcaster†, Precise Shot[B], Scribe Scroll[B]
  *Feat described on page 202
  †Feat described in *Complete Arcane*
Skills Concentration +10, Intimidate +4, Knowledge (arcana) +9, Knowledge (the planes) +6, Listen +3, Ride +7, Spellcraft +11, Spot +3
Possessions combat gear plus *+1 chain shirt,* masterwork greatsword, masterwork composite longbow (+2 Str bonus) with 20 arrows, 2 daggers, *headband of intellect +2, ring of protection +1*
Spellbook spells prepared plus 0—all except illusion and necromancy; 1st—*burning hands, grease, sleep;* 2nd—*darkness, see invisibility, spider climb;* 3rd—*dispel magic*

Gish are the war wizards of the githyanki and lead others into battle.

The gish presented here had the following ability scores before racial adjustments, Hit Dice ability score increases, and equipment bonuses: Str 14, Dex 13, Con 12, Int 15, Wis 10, Cha 8.

Strategies and Tactics

Gish typically lead small squads of soldiers or serve as support for githyanki captains (see below). Though capable in both melee and ranged combat, they prefer to direct a battle from the rear, where they can use their spells to support their followers.

A gish uses *haste* at the outset of combat to improve her allies' offense and defense. The following round, she uses *glitterdust*, hoping to blind some of the enemy. She then targets any nonblinded melee combatant with *hold person* or *ray of enfeeblement*.

If able, before combat, a gish uses her *blur* ability and employs her *wand of bull's strength* to boost her soldiers and captain.

GITHYANKI CAPTAIN

This slim humanoid is as strong and lithe as a hunting cat. He wears a jet-black breastplate that resembles a skeletal torso with ribs outlined in burnished gold. He wields a massive silver sword and carries a composite bow.

GITHYANKI CAPTAIN	**CR 10**

Male githyanki fighter 7/blackguard 2
LE Medium humanoid (extraplanar)
Init +0; **Senses** darkvision 60 ft.; Listen +1, Spot +1
Languages Draconic, Githyanki

AC 17, touch 11, flat-footed 17
   (+6 armor, +1 deflection)
hp 81 (9 HD)
SR 14
Fort +11, **Ref** +2, **Will** +5

Speed 20 ft. (4 squares) in breastplate; base speed 30 ft.
Melee *silver sword* +15/+10 (2d6+9/17–20 plus poison) or
Melee dagger +13/+8 (1d4+4/19–20)
Ranged mwk composite longbow +10/+5 (1d8+4/×3) or
Ranged dagger +9 (1d4+4/19–20)
Base Atk +9; **Grp** +13
Atk Options Cleave, Improved Sunder, Power Attack, poison (purple worm poison, DC 24, 1d6 Str/2d6 Str), smite good 1/day (+0 attack, +2 damage)
Combat Gear thunderstone, 1 dose of purple worm poison, *potion of cure moderate wounds*
Blackguard Spells Prepared (CL 2nd):
   1st—*corrupt weapon, doom* (DC 12)
Spell-Like Abilities (CL 9th):
   At will—*detect good*
   3/day—*blur, daze* (DC 10), *mage hand, dimension door, telekinesis* (DC 15), *plane shift* (DC 17)

Abilities Str 18, Dex 10, Con 16, Int 12, Wis 12, Cha 10
SQ aura of evil, poison use
Feats Cleave[B], Githyanki Dragonrider*, Improved Critical (greatsword), Improved Sunder[B], Iron Will, Power Attack[B], Weapon Focus (greatsword), Weapon Specialization (greatsword)[B]
   *Feat described on page 202

Skills Bluff +5, Concentration +7, Diplomacy +2, Disguise +0 (+2 acting), Hide +4, Intimidate +2, Knowledge (religion) +3, Listen +1, Ride +5, Spot +1
Possessions combat gear plus *+1 breastplate, silver sword,* masterwork composite longbow (+4 Str bonus) with 20 arrows, 2 daggers, *gauntlets of ogre power, ring of protection +1*

A githyanki captain leads strike forces and raids, sometimes flying at the vanguard on a red dragon mount.

The githyanki captain presented here had the following ability scores before racial adjustments, Hit Dice ability score increases, and equipment bonuses: Str 15, Dex 8, Con 14, Int 12, Wis 13, Cha 10.

Strategies and Tactics

Like their underlings, githyanki captains make sure to activate *blur* for defense. They make free use of *dimension door* in combat. If they need to escape, they use *plane shift*.

When given time to prepare, a githyanki captain casts *corrupt weapon* just before battle, so that his critical threats are automatically confirmed against good foes. He also seeks

---

GITHYANKI LORE

Characters with ranks in Knowledge (the planes) or Knowledge (religion) can learn more about githyanki. When a character makes a successful skill check, the following lore is revealed, including the information from lower DCs.

Knowledge (the Planes)

DC	Result
12	This creature is a githyanki, an Astral Plane-dwelling humanoid. This result reveals all humanoid traits and the extraplanar subtype.
17	Githyanki are generally hostile to nongithyanki, but they harbor a special hatred for mind flayers because they are descended from slaves who staged a revolt against the illithids. They also have particularly hostile feelings toward githzerai, another race descended from the original slaves.
22	Githyanki have an array of psionic powers and a small resistance to magic. One of a githyanki's innate abilities enables it to become difficult to discern.
27	Another githyanki ability transports it instantly across a battlefield. Githyanki of especially high level can also travel between the planes.
32	A githyanki *silver sword* can sever an astral traveler's silver cord (*MM* 128). The githyanki relentlessly pursue any nongithyanki who manages to steal one of their *silver swords*.

Knowledge (Religion)

DC	Result
17	The githyanki eschew religion and have no clerics.
22	The githyanki revere a lich-queen as their temporal and spiritual leader. She is said to destroy any githyanki who grow too powerful.

out psionics-using enemies, using his *silver sword* (MM 128) to disrupt their psionic abilities.

When fighting from dragonback, a githyanki captain rains down arrows on his enemies, allowing the dragon to breathe fire once or twice before jumping down into combat.

"Rebellion is a serious crime, abhorrent to our queen. The only excuse for rebellion is success."
—Zetch'r'r

SAMPLE ENCOUNTERS

Except for the occasional scout or spy, githyanki seldom travel or work alone. They are most often encountered in companies of two to four soldiers plus a leader.

Githyanki Company (EL 6–9): A typical githyanki company consists of two to four soldiers led by a gish. Its favorite tactic is to ambush targets who have fallen for simple bait, such as an apparently discarded weapon or a solitary githyanki.

EL 8: A company of four soldiers, led by a gish, are out looking for any loot they can find and have set up an ambush. Most of the company hides behind cover, but one soldier sits in plain sight to act as a decoy. The githyanki fight to the death, having no wish to report failure to their superiors. They will, however, allow their foes to withdraw after each one gives up a weapon or magic item worth at least 300 gp or the equivalent in gold.

Raiding Force (EL 11–16): A githyanki raiding force is commanded by a captain, with nearly a dozen soldiers and a pair of gish for support. A captain of status might also ride a young or juvenile red dragon.

EL 13: The githyanki captain Zymurani and her two gish, Catruuk and Satiim, lead a force of ten soldiers in a lightning raid on a town in search of a lost *silver sword*. Zymurani oversees the raid from the back of her mount, the young red dragon Tournoach, initiating the raid with a flyover of the town and a well-placed cone of fiery breath. PCs might save the town by defeating the githyanki, or by convincing them to stop attacking long enough for the party to find the missing sword.

ECOLOGY

Most githyanki live in massive castles on the Astral Plane. There eating and drinking are not necessary, and the githyanki have lost their appetite for food. They require nourishment when venturing onto other planes, however, and most of their Astral settlements include caves where farmers raise some livestock and tend fungus beds. Githyanki food is notoriously bland, in keeping with their general lack of interest in the culinary arts. Field rations usually include salted meat, dried mushrooms, and a smattering of other preserved foods, such as dried fruit and hardtack, which they have stolen or acquired through trade.

Githyanki consider all other sentient creatures to be enemies, and they harbor a special hatred for mind flayers. In a battle, they usually try to eliminate any mind flayers first. Githyanki might intervene when adventurers are fighting mind flayers, only to turn on the party once the illithids are dead.

Environment: Githyanki are most at home on the Astral Plane, where conditions such as gravity, inclement

Illus. by R. Spencer

Githyanki soldier, gish, and captain

weather, or hunger don't bother them. On the Material Plane, githyanki can be found wherever they can prey on other beings. They usually remain near the fringes of civilization, where they have a good chance of staging successful raids without encountering too much opposition.

Typical Physical Characteristics: See page 127 of the *Monster Manual* for information on typical githyanki height and weight.

Alignment: Most githyanki have evil alignments, although they might be lawful, neutral, or chaotic. The githyanki's evil largely stems from their kill-or-be-killed philosophy. Lawful githyanki embrace their militaristic society, and they thrive on the structure it provides. Chaotic githyanki chafe under the yoke of military discipline and generally do all they can to work independently or in small groups far away from a superior's influence. Neutral githyanki acknowledge the benefits of an established social order but privately doubt that it is the only way their people can survive.

SOCIETY

By their own account, the githyanki once served the mind flayers as slaves and chattel. They won their freedom through a brilliantly and patiently organized revolt—quite an accomplishment in the face of the mind flayers' ability to read thoughts. A female named Gith organized the revolt. When the time to act was right, the slaves rose as one. Small groups escaped into the Astral Plane, where they regrouped and fought off scores of mind flayers that pursued them. Eventually, the mind flayers were forced to give up the struggle (or chose to give it up, according to the mind flayers). When the war finally ended, the slaves chose the name *githyanki*, which means "children of Gith" in the secret tongue the slaves developed for their revolt.

The githyanki have never known peace. Just after helping them win their freedom, Gith ordered the githyanki to begin a full-scale extermination of the mind flayers. But one group among the freed slaves believed that Gith was simply replacing one tyrannical regime with another. A male named Zerthimon led this group of rebels, and the crusade against the mind flayers ended prematurely as civil war erupted among the newly freed slaves. In the end, the race splintered into two factions: those who fled to the Astral Plane and followed Gith (the githyanki) and those who fled to Limbo and followed Zerthimon (the githzerai). To this day, the races cannot stand each other, and githyanki and githzerai attack each other on sight. Only the sight of a mind flayer can cause a githyanki and githzerai to temporarily put aside their differences and unite against the common, most hated foe.

Githyanki live in fortified settlements organized along military lines. Each community has a ruler, whose orders all subordinates are bound to obey. Each community leader in turn has a superior based in a larger settlement. A githyanki leader's position is far from secure. Individuals tend to be loyal to their people as a whole, not to particular leaders. Mutinies that remove incompetent leaders occur from time to time, and these small internal revolts are generally tolerated as long as the mutineers succeed and can demonstrate that they did not act capriciously. Githyanki who rebel and fail face swift execution.

The current leader of all githyanki is Queen Vlaakith, who has reigned for more than a thousand years. Vlaakith is a 24th-level wizard and a lich. She slays all githyanki who become powerful enough to challenge her rule (*MM* 128). Scholars well versed in interplanar affairs suspect that these sacrifices are part of Vlaakith's continuing effort to achieve godhood. Those githyanki who draw the lich-queen's ire or fail in an assignment might be destroyed even before they reach sufficient power to be viewed as a threat. Most githyanki are blissfully unaware of Vlaakith's intentions toward them when they reach higher levels, which is why she has ruled uncontested for so long—and because her actions leave no witnesses.

Whatever Vlaakith's true motivations for slaying her brightest subjects, the githyanki have a culture without a god and largely without religion, which suits their desire for self-sufficiency. They do not have any clerics, but a few pursue alternative divine spellcasting classes, mostly rangers and blackguards. Most githyanki revere Gith, but she is honored as a legendary ancestor and heroine, not as a deity.

TYPICAL TREASURE

Most githyanki have standard treasure for NPCs of their Challenge Rating. They favor masterwork weapons and armor, and usually carry a few other offensive items as well.

GITHYANKI AS CHARACTERS

See page 128 of the *Monster Manual* for information on githyanki as characters.

GITHYANKI IN EBERRON

When the Gatekeepers severed the connection to Xoriat, the githyanki and githzerai took the opportunity to turn on their mind flayer masters, escaping their slavery en masse. The githyanki retreated to the Astral Plane, lured by its timeless qualities. A few githyanki and githzerai stayed on the Material Plane and formed small communities dedicated to maintaining the magic seals imprisoning powerful remnants of the Xoriat interlopers. *Explorer's Handbook* details one such community: Katal Hazath, on the Breland–Droaam border.

Githyanki raiding parties in Eberron are usually encountered as they hunt mind flayers in the depths of Khyber. Unlike those in other D&D worlds, Eberron's githyanki have no special connection to red dragons.

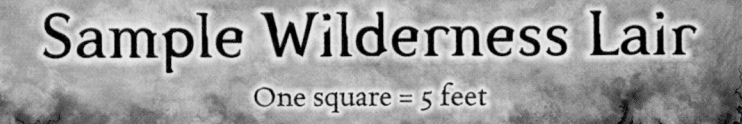

Sample Wilderness Lair

One square = 5 feet

1. Cave
2. Hidden altar chamber
   (search DC 20)
3. Cellar
4. Tents
5. Tree-mounted
   guard platform

GNOLL

Initially presented in the *Monster Manual*, gnolls are savage humanoids that delight in cruelty and are always hungry for the meat of thinking creatures. When gnolls look upon the works of civilization, they see only the towering flames and slaughter they wish to wreak upon them. Yeenoghu, the Demon Prince of Gnolls, watches his children and bares a feral grin with each atrocity they commit.

SLAVE-TAKER

This humanoid is slightly taller than a human. It has a furry body and a head like a hyena's with a brown-gray mane. Its eyes reflect a malevolent glint in the dusk as it hefts a net.

SLAVE-TAKER   CR 3
Male gnoll ranger 2
CE Medium humanoid
Init +1; **Senses** darkvision 60 ft.; Listen +2, Spot +3
Languages Gnoll

AC 17, touch 11, flat-footed 16; Two-Weapon Defense
   (+1 Dex, +4 armor, +1 shield, +1 natural)
hp 37 (4 HD)
Fort +10, **Ref** +4, **Will** +3

Speed 30 ft. (6 squares)
Melee mwk short sword +9 (1d6+4/19–20) or
Melee mwk short sword +7 (1d6+4/19–20) and
   mwk short sword +7 (1d6+2/19–20)
Ranged mwk composite longbow +5 (1d8+4/× 3) or
Ranged net +0 touch (entangle, *PH* 119)
Base Atk +3; **Grp** +7
Atk Options favored enemy humans +2
Combat Gear *potion of cat's grace, potion of bull's strength*

Abilities Str 18, Dex 13, Con 18, Int 8, Wis 12, Cha 6
SQ wild empathy +0 (–4 magical beasts)
Feats Iron Will, Track[B], Two-Weapon Fighting[B], Weapon
   Focus (short sword)
Skills Hide +5, Listen +2, Spot +3, Survival +6
Possessions combat gear plus masterwork chain shirt, 2
   masterwork short swords, 3 nets, masterwork composite
   longbow (+4 Str bonus) with 20 arrows

Gnolls regularly capture slaves in their assaults on other races. They treat slaves harshly and tend to think of the slave population as a living larder, so they replenish their supply at every opportunity. This duty often falls to a gnoll slave-taker. In the hierarchy of the pack, a slave-taker usually occupies the lowest rank above the general population.

   The gnoll slave-taker presented here had the following ability scores before racial adjustments and Hit Dice ability score increases: Str 14, Dex 13, Con 15, Int 10, Wis 12, Cha 8.

Strategies and Tactics

A gnoll slave-taker rarely acts alone. Most often, a mix of gnolls and hyenas accompanies one. Large tribes might foster groups of slave-takers, while smaller tribes might send out a slave-taker with just a few hyenas as support.

   In battle, a slave-taker uses nonlethal tactics so that some foes survive the fight to become slaves. He allows his companions to charge while he hides and sneaks close enough for an accurate net attack. If he has the advantage of surprise, a slave-taker attempts to hold his allies in check while he drinks potions in preparation. Once he enters the fray,

he nets a foe or two. He then administers a few nonlethal blows to entangled creatures, switching to lethal attacks only if pressed or if a foe is resilient. The gnolls and hyenas that follow a slave-taker don't take orders well from their nominal leader, but they know not to feast upon net-covered foes or those a slave-taker stands over. Creatures rendered unconscious by the attack are dragged to the gnolls' camp and imprisoned.

FIENDISH CLERIC OF YEENOGHU

This hyena-headed being has darker fur than others of her kind, and her eyes smolder like red coals. She barks an order and begins to cast a spell.

FIENDISH CLERIC OF YEENOGHU   CR 4
Female fiendish gnoll cleric 3
CE Medium humanoid
Init +4; **Senses** darkvision 60 ft.; Listen +8, Spot +8
Languages Gnoll

AC 21, touch 10, flat-footed 21
   (+8 armor, +2 shield, +1 natural)
hp 41 (5 HD); **DR** 5/magic
Resist cold 5, fire 5; **SR** 10
Fort +10, **Ref** +2, **Will** +7

Speed 20 ft. (4 squares)
Melee mwk flail +8 (1d8+3)
Base Atk +3; **Grp** +6
Atk Options smite good 1/day (+5 damage)
Special Actions rebuke undead 1/day (–2, 2d6+1, 3rd)
   spontaneous casting (*inflict* spells)
Combat Gear *potion of barkskin (+2)*, 2 scrolls of *cure light*
   wounds, scroll of *shield of faith*
Cleric Spells Prepared (CL 3rd):
   2nd—*cure moderate wounds, bear's endurance, spiritual*
      weapon[D] (+6 melee, 1d8+1)
   1st—*bane* (DC 14), *cause fear* (DC 14), *cure light wounds,*
      magic weapon[D]
   0—*cure minor wounds* (2), *detect magic, touch of fatigue*
      (+6 melee touch, DC 13)
   D: Domain spell. Deity: Yeenoghu. *Domains:* Evil, War

Abilities Str 17, Dex 10, Con 16, Int 10, Wis 16, Cha 6
Feats Combat Casting, Improved Initiative, Martial Weapon
   Proficiency (flail)[B], Weapon Focus (flail)[B]
Skills Concentration +7, Knowledge (religion) +2, Listen +8,
   Spot +8
Possessions combat gear plus full plate, heavy steel shield,
   masterwork flail, *cloak of resistance +1*

Although some gnolls worship Erythnul, most tribes pay homage to Yeenoghu, the Demon Prince of Gnolls. As a demon lord, Yeenoghu lacks the power of a true deity, but he "blesses" his worshipers with visitations by demons that communicate his desires. These demons often breed with the gnolls, producing half-fiends that then foster bloodlines of fiendish gnolls. Half-fiend gnolls usually become leaders of their tribes, and their fiendish gnoll offspring serve beneath them as lieutenants. Many half-fiends demand that their children become clerics of Yeenoghu to repay the Demon Prince and give them access to healing magic.

   Fiendish gnoll clerics of Yeenoghu serve as advisors and bodyguards to a tribe's leader rather than as spiritual leaders. The awe gnolls feel for Yeenoghu extends to only those servants who show themselves to be strong enough to lead.

Most fiendish clerics of Yeenoghu choose Evil, Destruction, or War as domains. Typically subservient to a tribe's half-fiend, these clerics save their spells to preserve themselves and their leader.

The fiendish gnoll cleric presented here had the following ability scores before racial adjustments and Hit Dice ability score increases: Str 13, Dex 10, Con 14, Int 12, Wis 15, Cha 8.

Strategies and Tactics

Fiendish gnoll clerics have as much authority as the leader of the tribe grants them at any given moment. When in command of other gnolls, they can be ruthless masters, but if lacking such authority, they tend to keep to themselves. Fiendish gnoll clerics never leave their leader's side unless commanded, relishing the privileges they are granted as advisors and fearing the leader's wrath should they not be present when desired.

In combat, a fiendish gnoll cleric relies on others to occupy foes while she casts spells. Once she has girded herself with magic, the cleric enters melee to attack with her flail and *inflict* spells. She saves her healing magic for herself and her leader, and she uses *touch of fatigue* on a foe already affected by *bane* or *cause fear*.

HALF-FIEND GNOLL WARLOCK

A creature of nightmares, this horned hyenalike humanoid flaps huge membranous wings as she takes to the air, her cloven hooves lifting off the cracked earth beneath her foul form.

HALF-FIEND GNOLL WARLOCK   CR 6

Female half-fiend gnoll warlock* 4
   *Class described in *Complete Arcane*
CE Medium outsider (augmented humanoid, native)
Init +2; **Senses** darkvision 60 ft.; Listen +6, Spot +6
Languages Abyssal, Common, Gnoll

AC 20, touch 13, flat-footed 18
   (+2 Dex, +5 armor, +2 natural, +1 deflection)
hp 50 (6 HD); **DR** 5/magic, 1/cold iron
Miss Chance 20% ranged attacks only (*entropic warding*)
Immune poison
Resist acid 10, cold 10, electricity 10, fire 10; **SR** 16
Fort +9, **Ref** +4, **Will** +6

Speed 30 ft. (6 squares), fly 30 ft. (average)
Melee 2 claws +7 each (1d6+3) and
   bite +2 (1d4 +1)
Base Atk +4; **Grp** +8
Atk Options Point Blank Shot, Precise Shot, magic strike, smite good 1/day (+6 damage)
Special Actions Point Blank Shot, Precise Shot, *eldritch blast* 2d6 (CL 4th, +7 ranged touch)
Combat Gear scroll of *blur*, scroll of *cat's grace*, 4 scrolls of *cure light wounds*, scroll of *glitterdust*, scroll of *greater invisibility*
Invocations Known (CL 4th):
   Least (at will)—*eldritch spear** (*eldritch blast* range 250 ft.), *entropic warding* (as *entropic shield* plus *pass without trace*; cannot be tracked by scent but can be detected), *frightful blast*** (creatures struck by *eldritch blast* must succeed on a DC 15 Will save or be frightened for 1 minute)
   *Blast shape invocation
   **Eldritch essence invocation

Spell-Like Abilities (CL 4th):
   At will—*detect magic*
   3/day—*darkness*
   1/day—*desecrate*, *unholy blight* (DC 17)
Abilities Str 16, Dex 14, Con 18, Int 14, Wis 13, Cha 16
SQ deceive item
Feats Hover, Point Blank Shot, Precise Shot
Skills Bluff +8, Diplomacy +7, Disguise +3 (+5 acting), Hide +4, Intimidate +7, Knowledge (arcana) +4, Knowledge (religion) +4, Knowledge (the planes) +4, Listen +6, Move Silently +4, Sense Motive +6, Spellcraft +7 (+9 deciphering scrolls), Spot +6, Survival +3, Use Magic Device +10 (+12 scrolls)
Possessions combat gear plus +1 chain shirt, *cloak of resistance* +1, *ring of protection* +1

Eldritch Blast (Sp) Standard action; range 60 feet; +7 ranged touch; 2d6 damage. *Complete Arcane* 7.
Deceive Item When making a Use Magic Device check, a half-fiend gnoll warlock can take 10 even if distracted or threatened. *Complete Arcane* 8.

Yeenoghu often grants half-fiend gnolls the dark powers of a warlock. With such obvious blessings, a half-fiend warlock rarely faces challenges to her rule, and her occult abilities often cut such challenges short. Half-fiend gnolls produce fiendish offspring to buttress their positions of power, and they use their uncommon wit and charisma to intimidate and manipulate would-be challengers into allies.

The half-fiend gnoll warlock presented here had the following ability scores before racial adjustments and Hit Dice ability score increases: Str 8, Dex 10, Con 14, Int 12, Wis 13, Cha 15.

Strategies and Tactics

A half-fiend gnoll warlock takes to the air when combat begins, hovering high above while using protective and bolstering scrolls on herself. When ready, she remains aloft to shoot foes with her *eldritch blast*, relying on her resistances, damage reduction, and *entropic warding* to protect her from enemy spells and ranged attacks. She uses *unholy blight* against a group of wounded foes, and if necessary, uses *darkness* to cover her escape.

"Beware the gnolls, for they are a demon's pawns. Let them not breed in numbers, for they will make a wasteland of their lands and yours. Shun them, for they are harbingers of death."
    —Cornelius, satyr cleric of Ehlonna

SAMPLE ENCOUNTERS

Gnolls can make challenging encounters for characters of varying levels.

   Slavers (EL 6): A gnoll slave-taker, two ordinary gnolls (*MM* 130), and four hyenas wander the edge of the woods in search of humanoids to eat and take as slaves. The hyenas charge any likely targets at first sight while the gnolls remain behind to fire arrows. The slave-taker follows the hyenas into melee. Once any spellcasters and archers are netted, he calls the two gnolls to join the melee.

   Raiding Party (EL 9): A fiendish gnoll cleric commands three gnoll slave-takers, eight ordinary gnolls, and four hyenas. Their mission is to burn a nearby settlement to the ground and kill or enslave its people. The slave-takers move in advance of the raiders, hoping to hide in the settlement and identify the most potent defenders before attacking. The gnolls carry torches to set fire to buildings while the hyenas attack whatever gets in their way. The fiendish cleric hangs back and casts spells.

Tribal Leadership (EL 12): A half-fiend gnoll warlock has pleased Yeenoghu enough that the Demon Prince of Gnolls has sent the half-fiend's demonic father to help defend her in her hour of need. When adventurers fight their way to the heart of the gnolls' lair, they find the half-fiend gnoll warlock, four fiendish gnoll clerics, and a hezrou (*MM* 44) waiting for them. The hezrou immediately summons more tanar'ri and then uses its spell-like abilities. The gnolls give the demon a wide berth to avoid its stench. All four clerics charge into melee, but when the hezrou finally enters combat, they retreat to cast their own spells. The warlock flies high above and attacks with her *eldritch blast*, descending only to receive healing.

ECOLOGY

Gnolls eat only meat, preferably uncooked. They hunt and raid under cover of darkness and sleep through much of the day. They take special delight in tormenting and devouring intelligent beings.

A gnoll's life span is around forty years, though an individual that reaches such an advanced age is a remarkable specimen. Most gnolls die in their twenties while in battle or from the rigors of a primitive life.

A female gnoll gives birth to two to four pups about six months after conception. The pups are nearly helpless for eight weeks, doing little besides suckling and sleeping. A warrior gnoll hands off the pups immediately after birth and returns to her normal activities without an-

other thought. The young grow up in crèches, left in the care of wet nurses and slaves until they can fend for themselves. After the first two months, a young gnoll begins to grow rapidly and develop impressive muscle mass. It begins to eat meat at this time. Weaned pups move to a different cave where they practice hunting skills and observe the behavior of adults. It is not safe for them to enter the main body of the tribe until they reach adult size—a pup that gets underfoot makes as good a meal as anything else. Gnolls reach adolescence in two years, when they enter the rest of the tribe and begin to hunt and make war on their own.

A gnoll tribe rarely creates its own dwelling but moves into a cave, ruined building, or dungeon that has been abandoned by previous denizens. Sometimes another occupant inhabits the place, and if it is weak or they outnumber it, the gnolls kill it or drive it out. Occasionally the tribe makes an arrangement to coexist with a powerful inhabitant, but more often the gnolls simply look for another suitable home.

Once a tribe has claimed an area, the dominant female chooses the roomiest, most desirable quarters for herself. The leader then marks her territory, not with musk as an animal does, but with a clan sigil drawn in blood. The "donor" is the nearest lesser tribe member, whose neck the leader bites in a demonstration of authority. She then designates areas for child-rearing and marks them in the same way. After this, the other gnolls compete among themselves for living space. Scraps of fur or leather sometimes mark the den of a moderately high-ranking member.

Environment: Gnolls live on warm plains, preferring lightly wooded hills that border grasslands. They often encroach on forests, mainly for hunting, which brings them into conflict with elves.

Illus. by W. England

Gnoll slave-taker, fiendish cleric of Yeenoghu, and half-fiend gnoll warlock

Typical Physical Characteristics: An adult male gnoll is about 7 feet tall and weighs 250 pounds. Females tend to be larger, about 7-1/2 feet tall and weighing 300 pounds.

Gnolls strongly resemble hyenas, with very powerful jaws and upper bodies. Their brown fur bears spots and streaks, and a bristly mane runs down the back of the head and shoulders.

Alignment: The brutal and competitive nature of their society, as well as their demonic patron, tends to make gnolls chaotic evil in outlook. Some are neutral evil, but a gnoll with a good or lawful outlook is unheard-of.

SOCIETY

Other beings generally view gnolls as vicious, brutish, and filthy—which they are. But they are not stupid, nor are they as simple as many assume. To underestimate them as enemies is to fall to their cunning strategies. The smartest gnoll leaders actually play up this reputation so as to lull opponents into false confidence. Only then do the gnolls strike—with devastating effect.

Like hyenas, gnolls have a matriarchal society. The females grow larger and stronger than males, and the alpha female is the absolute ruler of a tribe for as long as she can defend her rank. She takes for a mate the fittest specimen of the tribe, but they form no lasting relationship. Below the alpha, the other gnolls sort themselves according to the simple rule of might, but the leader of the tribe can elevate or demote any tribe member, regardless of status. The most aggressive males can sometimes hold high rank within the tribe, although they must endure challenges much more frequently than females. Gnolls with the least status, and the old, are relegated

to menial positions within the tribe—especially child-rearing. Yet even these humble individuals far outrank slaves, who must endure constant malnourishment and regular beatings. Gnolls use slaves for cleaning and mending, and for hard labor such as digging or felling trees.

The gnolls' worship of Yeenoghu is closely tied with the phases of the moon and their matriarchal society. Yeenoghu represents the ultimate mate for female gnolls. The new moon is a time for great sacrifices to the Demon Prince, and gnolls increase their attacks during these times to take as many captives as possible. The gnolls bring captured humanoids to a special cave that represents Yeenoghu's den. There, brown-robed and blood-soaked acolytes slaughter the captives while the tribe's leader and her attendant clerics howl for Yeenoghu's favor. A gnoll leader fervently desires Yeenoghu's personal appearance, but the best she can realistically hope for is for him to send a demon. If the tribe lacks a half-fiend leader, or has a weak leader, this demon likely takes command of the tribe and mates with several gnolls to produce half-fiends that will one day rule in its place.

TYPICAL TREASURE

Gnolls have standard treasure for NPCs of their Challenge Rating. They favor armor and weapons, but clerics and warlocks also use scrolls and potions.

GNOLLS AS CHARACTERS

See page 130 of the *Monster Manual* for information on gnolls as characters.

GNOLLS IN EBERRON

The largest populations of gnolls in Khorvaire roam the monstrous realm of Droaam. They form sizable communities throughout that land and refer to themselves overall as a "brotherhood." However, they form the backbone of all the other armies in competition for resources and power in Droaam. The clever gnolls have figured out that this keeps them on the winning side regardless of the final outcome, but they have also created a kind of stability. They don't care whom they work for, and they don't attack other gnolls. As a result, a rough balance of power exists between the various factions in Droaam.

Many gnolls of Eberron are followers of the Devourer, the Shadow, or the Traveler. A few follow dark druidic traditions. Some do revere Yeenoghu as one of the Lords of Dust, especially the fiendish clerics, but most of these gnolls inhabit the Labyrinth in the Demon Wastes.

GNOLLS IN FAERÛN

North of the Moonsea, the Great Gray Land of Thar gives way to the open steppe known as the Ride and the Tortured Land. The Tortured Land holds the ruins of a forgotten city surrounded by countless tribes of flind-led gnolls. Frozen Flindyke, as it is known to bards, might have once been the center of a flind-ruled civilization, or it might have been a bastion of humanity amid a sea of canine humanoids. The gnolls and flinds of the Tortured Land are led by shamans of Yeenoghu, whose predecessors supposedly summoned the Trio Nefarious that laid Myth Drannor low, and they skirmish constantly with each other and the human barbarian tribes of the Ride.

GNOLL LORE

Characters with ranks in Knowledge (local), Knowledge (nature), or Knowledge (religion) can learn more about gnolls. When a character makes a successful skill check, the following lore is revealed, including the information from lower DCs.

Knowledge (Local) or Knowledge (Nature)

DC	Result
11	This creature is a gnoll, a savage humanoid with features of a hyena. This result reveals all humanoid traits, including darkvision.
16	Gnoll society is based on strength and intimidation. The biggest and strongest lead the others, and a female typically leads a tribe.
21	Chaotic as well as evil, gnolls practice some strategy in combat, but they sometimes succumb to their hunger and attack with the savage fury of beasts.

Knowledge (Religion)

DC	Result
11	Gnolls revere the phases of the moon but have few clerics.
16	Yeenoghu, the patron god of gnolls, is actually a demon lord. The phases of the moon have a strange relationship with the worship of Yeenoghu. Gnolls are most prone to violence and raiding during the nights of a new moon.
21	Most clerics among gnolls are fiendish descendants of a half-fiend leader.

Bands of nomadic gnoll hunters also wander the Shaar, hunting the large herds of herbivores that wander the grasslands. Most of the southern gnoll tribes have traditional homes throughout the hills and lower mountain slopes of every range across the Shaar, including the Dun Hills, the Uthangol Mountains, and the Wyrmbones. They are most common in the western half of the Shaar, especially along the various ridges north of the Channath Vale. Gnolls have historically preyed upon settlements along the shores of Lake Lhespen and the caravans that move through that region. Because of this, the Lapaliiyans to the southwest have mounted major drives to eradicate them several times in the past.

SAMPLE LAIR: THE GREAT GEODE

An enormous bubble formed long ago within a range of ancient hills, possibly the result of an intrusion from the Elemental Plane of Earth. The hollow is completely encrusted with amethysts, of little value but breathtakingly beautiful. A recent earthquake cracked the rock over this formation, diverting a surface stream into the hollow so that it now flows out through a fissure in the hillside. A gnoll tribe has taken over this area.

1. Entrance (EL 6): Four gnoll guards (three fighter 2, one fighter 4) are always on duty, two just inside the entrance and one in the brush on each side of the stream. They are armed with battleaxes and light crossbows.

2. The Pool: This immense chamber forms the living area for low-ranking tribe members. Kobold slaves have been digging up gems, starting with those on the floor. Heaps of waste stone form low walls that partially divide the cavern into smaller areas.

3. Sleeping Area: Eighty-seven unclassed gnolls inhabit this large, unfurnished section of the cavern; during the day, two-thirds of them sleep here while a few patrol the region or prepare food.

4. Crèche: Currently sixty-two infants and young pups stay here under the care of low-ranking and old females (see area 5).

5. Nurses: Sixteen noncombatant female gnolls care for the tribe's young.

6. Slave Pen: High heaps of mined-out rock extend natural ridges in the walls to build up a prison area for the tribe's slaves. Thirty kobolds are penned here when they are not working, and two gnolls watch them. Twelve gnolls guard the kobolds when they are at work.

7. Common Area: Food preparation, skinning, and eating take place here. Waste is dumped into the stream where it exits the pool.

8. Chieftain's Quarters (EL 6): The tribe's leader, Gnashtooth (female gnoll ranger 5/adept 1), has appropriated this chamber for herself. Behind a private store of food and drink is a secret exit hatch (Spot DC 22).

9. Elite Quarters (EL 6): The tribe's highest-ranking warriors (six fighter 2, two fighter 4) bunk in this smaller cavern. At any given time, four are on guard in area 1 while the others relax here.

10. Escape Tunnels: A purple worm once tunneled through the area, leaving wide passages suitable for emergency escape. The tunnel entrance in the main chamber is covered by a heap of rubble, which a group of gnolls can clear away in 10 rounds. The secret hatch in Gnashtooth's quarters covers another passage for her own use. These tunnels meander for hundreds of feet and eventually exit through camouflaged openings farther along the hillside.

The Great Geode

One square = 10 feet

GOLEM, FANG

A hulking, bestial form looms from the shadows. It looks like a wild animal, but its shape is jagged and unnatural. The creature rears up, and suddenly the air is filled with spikes!

FANG GOLEM   CR 6
Always N Large construct
Init +3; **Senses** darkvision 60 ft., low-light vision; Listen +0, Spot +0
Languages understands creator's orders

AC 20, touch 12, flat-footed 17
  (−1 size, +3 Dex, +8 natural)
hp 74 (8 HD); **DR** 5/adamantine or bludgeoning
Immune construct immunities, magic
Fort +2, **Ref** +5, **Will** +2
Weakness sonic (see immunity to magic)

Speed 30 ft. (6 squares)
Melee 2 claws +9 each (2d6+4)
Ranged spikes +8 (2d6+4)
Space 10 ft.; **Reach** 5 ft.
Base Atk +6; **Grp** +14
Atk Options verdant surge
Special Actions spikes

Abilities Str 19, Dex 17, Con —, Int —, Wis 11, Cha 1
SQ construct traits
Feats —
Skills Listen +0, Spot +0
Advancement 9–15 HD (Large); 16–30 HD (Huge)

Immunity to Magic (Ex) A fang golem is immune to any spell or spell-like ability that allows spell resistance, except *shout* or *greater shout* and any *orb of sound* spell (*Complete Arcane* 116).

    Any magical attack against a fang golem that deals cold damage heals 1 point of damage for every 3 points of damage it would otherwise deal. If the amount of healing would cause the golem to exceed its full normal hit points, it gains any excess as temporary hit points, up to a maximum of twice its full normal hit point total. These temporary hit points last for up to 1 hour. A fang golem gets no saving throw against magical attacks that deal cold damage.

Verdant Surge (Su) Any creature hit by a fang golem's melee attack or spikes ability takes a −2 penalty on saving throws made to resist the effects of a druid spell or a spell or ability from a fey creature. This effect lasts for 1 minute.

Spikes (Ex) A fang golem can launch a volley of spikes to a range of 80 feet with no range increment. All targets must be within 30 feet of each other. A fang golem can use this ability up to five times in any 24-hour period.

Death Throes (Ex) When killed, a fang golem explodes in a 20-foot-radius burst that deals 8d6 points of piercing damage to everything in the area (Reflex DC 14 half). The save DC is Constitution-based.

A fang golem is the hideous creation of a twisted druid who built it to resemble a wild beast, composed entirely of claws, fangs, and tusks. Such druids often set these constructs to guard unholy groves, but other creators loose fang golems upon nearby populations to terrorize them and thus drive them from untrammeled nature. A number of fang golems still wander long after their creators' deaths, their original purpose forgotten. Powerful fey occasionally construct these creatures to provide a physical threat that complements their own magical abilities.

STRATEGIES AND TACTICS

Fang golems are tenacious in combat and very strong. Being mindless, they do nothing without orders from their creator. They follow instructions explicitly and are incapable of independent strategy or tactics. Emotionless in combat, they cannot be provoked or intimidated.

    A fang golem's creator can command it if the golem is within 60 feet and can see and hear its creator. If uncommanded, a golem usually follows its last instruction to the best of its ability, though if attacked, it responds in kind. The creator can give the golem a simple command to govern its actions in his or her absence, even ordering it to obey the commands of another person (who might in turn place the golem under someone else's command). Reassuming control over the golem is as simple as commanding it to obey its creator alone.

    A fang golem usually accompanies its druid or fey controllers. Without a controller, it executes its last orders relentlessly. Sometimes an evil druid protects her grove with several of these horrors, and a party of adventurers might encounter such a druid accompanied by one or two fang golem bodyguards. The druid launches the constructs against her enemies and hurls *call lightning* and *flame strike* spells into the midst of the melee, knowing this magic cannot harm the golems.

SAMPLE ENCOUNTERS

Fang golems must be created and positioned in a location. Once placed, they do not leave the area unless directed to do so by their creator.

    Fey Guardian (EL 8): Two malicious pixies and a fang golem shaped something like a bear patrol the woods. The pixies scout ahead of the golem, endeavoring to surprise any creatures they encounter. They attack from hiding with their sleep arrows, then order the golem to charge in and slay the sleeping creatures first. After the battle begins, the pixies use their sleep arrows on creatures wounded by the golem (and thus affected by its verdant surge ability).

FANG GOLEM LORE

Characters with ranks in Knowledge (arcana) can learn more about fang golems. When a character makes a successful skill check, the following lore is revealed, including the information from lower DCs. Knowledge (nature) can also be used, but all check DCs increase by 5.

Knowledge (Arcana)

DC	Result
16	This is a fang golem, a kind of construct created by twisted druids to serve as a guardian. This result reveals all construct traits.
21	A fang golem can hurl a volley of sharp spikes to hit multiple targets.
26	Fang golems are immune to most types of energy damage and might be found in dangerous environments. They are somewhat vulnerable to sonic effects.

Bodyguards (EL 10): Arlethin do'Irdrin (NE female drow druid 9), a denizen of the subterranean realms, maintains a sacred "grove" of oversized mushrooms, where she and her circle conduct disturbing rituals. She is accompanied by two fang golems, crafted to combine the features of subterranean lizards and enormous spiders. The druid uses several simple animals as scouts and spies, but these creatures do not join in the fight. In any battle, the druid treats the golems and her animal companion as expendable, seeking only to preserve her own life.

ECOLOGY

Being constructs, fang golems have no need to eat, sleep, or breathe. They can exist wherever their creator places them, be it underwater, in subterranean chambers, or even hostile environments such as volcanic caverns. They have no natural prey but attack whatever and whenever their instructions direct.

Creating such a golem requires killing many creatures (or at least collecting parts from those already dead) and then binding a spirit into the assembled form. Non-evil druids see the very idea as an abomination, and they try to destroy such creations as well as those responsible for their existence.

Environment: As constructs, fang golems can be found anywhere. But as the creations of druids, they usually share the same environment as those who created them. Such places include standing stones in haunted wastelands, underground tunnels, corrupted forests, and similar forbidding locales.

Typical Physical Characteristics: A fang golem is the size of a dire animal, ranging from 8 to 15 feet in length and weighing up to 2,000 pounds. The example presented here is about 10 feet long and weighs around 1,000 pounds.

Fang golems can come in many shapes and sizes. Elephant-sized specimens have been found in remote places, and massive fang golems resembling crabs (often incorporating pincers and sharks' teeth) scuttle on the ocean floor.

Alignment: A fang golem is as mindless as any other golem, existing only to carry out orders. It is always neutral.

TYPICAL TREASURE

Fang golems never have treasure, but their magical bodies might be treasure in their own right. Destroying a fang golem shatters the assemblage of fangs, claws, and tusks that formed, thus releasing the spirit. However, carefully collecting the materials can allow another creator to animate a similar golem for one-half the normal material cost. Alternatively, ivory from these components can be sold for 1/20 the golem's construction cost.

FOR PLAYER CHARACTERS

A player character with a dark edge might consider a fang golem guardian. Its price is not beyond the reach of a mid- to high-level PC. However, most people consider fang golems to be abominations, which makes social interactions more difficult for a party accompanied by such a creation.

Depending on the golem's shape, it might serve as a mount. Since the creature is mindless, the Ride skill is of no use in controlling it. It can carry loads or a rider only in noncombat situations. During combat, the controller is better off dismounting to let the creature fight on its own.

Fang Golem Construction

The cost to create a fang golem includes the cost of the physical body and all the materials and spell components that are consumed or become a permanent part of the golem. Creating a golem is essentially similar to creating any sort of magic item (DMG 282). However, a golem's body includes costly material components that require some extra preparation. The golem's creator can assemble the body or hire someone else to do the job, but the builder must have the appropriate skill, as described below.

Completing the golem's creation drains the indicated XP from the creator and requires casting any spells on the final day. The creator must cast the spells personally, but they can come from outside sources such as scrolls.

A fang golem's body must be assembled from fangs, claws, tusks, and the like, with a total weight of at least 1,000 pounds (more for larger specimens). These are bound with cords or strips of hide to wood laths, all treated with preservative oils costing 500 gp. Creating the body requires a DC 15 Craft (sculpting) or Craft (weaving) check.

The market price of an advanced golem increases by 5,000 gp for each additional Hit Die. Add an additional 50,000 gp if the golem's size increases. The XP cost for creating an advanced golem is equal to 1/25 the increased market price minus the cost of the special materials required.

CL 7th; Craft Construct, *greater magic fang, reincarnate, spike stones*, caster must be at least 7th level; Price 15,000 gp; Cost 8,000 gp + 580 XP.

FANG GOLEMS IN FAERÛN

In the Rawlinswood of Faerûn's Great Dale, the warped followers of the Rotting Man spread corruption through the vast forests from their stronghold of Dun-Tharos. Black-hearted treants rove side by side with fang golems, which are often crafted from the remains of creatures destroyed by the corrupted ones' advance.

Fang golem

Illus. by E. Widermann

HOWLER WASP

Howler wasps are bizarre creatures created by the mighty wizard Otiluke. Otiluke sought to produce a fusion of insect and mammal that would guard his tower against a cabal of slaadi that sought to slay him. The first experiments produced the howler wasps. Otiluke intended to destroy the creatures, since they attacked friendly visitors as well as his enemies. Unfortunately, the slaadi attacked soon after he completed his first experiments. In the confusion of the battle, some of the howler wasps escaped. They and their offspring have since spread their nests throughout the world.

Hovering in the air, its wings buzzing with a constant low drone, appears to be a hornet with a baboonlike head. It screeches at you in fury.

HOWLER WASP   CR 1
Usually CE Small aberration
Init +1; **Senses** darkvision 60 ft.; Listen +3, Spot +4
Languages —

AC 14, touch 12, flat-footed 13
   (+1 size, +1 Dex, +2 natural)
hp 13 (2 HD)
Fort +2, **Ref** +1, **Will** +4

Speed 10 ft. (2 squares), fly 60 ft. (good)
Melee bite +3 (1d4+1) and
   2 claws +1 each (1d3) or
Melee sting +3 (1d3+1 plus poison)
Space 5 ft.; **Reach** 5 ft.
Base Atk +1; **Grp** −2
Atk Options poison (DC 13, 1d6 Dex/1d6 Dex)

Abilities Str 12, Dex 13, Con 15, Int 3, Wis 13, Cha 6
SQ inciting pheromone
Feats Multiattack
Skills Listen +3, Spot +4
Advancement 3–7 HD (Medium); 8 HD (Large)

HOWLER WASP LORE
Characters with ranks in Knowledge (dungeoneering) or Knowledge (arcana) can learn more about howler wasps. When a character makes a successful skill check, the following lore is revealed, including the information from lower DCs.

Knowledge (Dungeoneering)
DC	Result
11	This creature is a howler wasp, a vicious aberration that attacks anything approaching within 10 miles of its nest. This result reveals all aberration traits.
15	A howler wasp flies back to its nest to fetch reinforcements when attacked. A howler wasp queen is much larger than the others, and she rarely if ever leaves the nest.
16	The sting of a howler wasp can paralyze its victim.
21	When wounded, howler wasps spray their attacker with a substance that incites other howler wasps to attack it. Water can wash the substance off.

Knowledge (Arcana)
DC	Result
15	The wizard Otiluke created the howler wasps. He never intended to release them into the wild.

Inciting Pheromone (Ex) If a melee attack reduces a howler wasp to 0 or fewer hit points, or if the wasp takes a critical hit from a melee attack, it can attempt to douse its foe with a pheromone (+3 melee touch). The wasp uses this ability as an immediate action before resolving the effect of the damage.

The pheromone draws other howler wasps to the target, inciting them into a fearsome rage. All howler wasps within 60 feet of a creature doused with the pheromone gain a +1 bonus on attack rolls and a +2 bonus on damage rolls against the doused creature. Howler wasps detect the doused creature as if they had blindsense. The pheromone's effects last for 10 minutes, though a doused creature can wash the substance off by submerging in water.

The example presented above is a typical worker. It builds the nest, forages for food, and defends the colony and its queen.

HOWLER WASP QUEEN
A bear-sized, wingless creature lies in the center of the hive. Its swollen shape combines features of baboons and hornets.

HOWLER WASP QUEEN   CR 5
Usually CE Large aberration
Init +0; **Senses** darkvision 60 ft.; Listen +9, Spot +10
Languages —

AC 18, touch 9, flat-footed 18
   (−1 size, +9 natural)
hp 71 (8 HD)
Fort +6, **Ref** +2, **Will** +8

Speed 20 ft. (4 squares)
Melee bite +9 (1d8+4) and
   2 claws +7 each (1d6+2) or
Melee sting +9 (1d8+4 plus poison)
Space 10 ft.; **Reach** 5 ft.
Base Atk +6; **Grp** +14
Atk Options poison (DC 18, 1d8 Dex/1d8 Dex)

Abilities Str 18, Dex 11, Con 18, Int 6, Wis 15, Cha 8
SQ inciting pheromone
Feats Alertness, Multiattack, Toughness
Skills Listen +9, Spot +10
Advancement —

Inciting Pheromone (Ex) As howler wasp; +9 melee touch.

The colony's queen, like that of a mundane wasp nest, is responsible for laying eggs. Male howler wasps crowd about her at all times.

STRATEGIES AND TACTICS
Individually, a howler wasp attacks whatever is closest to it. In groups, though, howler wasps change their tactics as soon as one of them delivers a spray of inciting pheromone. They all attack any creature doused with the pheromone.

Wounded howler wasps always fly back to the nest, where they gather more howler wasps to eliminate the threat. Thus, it is imperative to defeat every howler wasp encountered or to be far away by the time reinforcements arrive.

SAMPLE ENCOUNTERS

Because howler wasps hunt for food near their homes, they are frequently encountered within a few miles of their nest. Howler wasps are fearless and aggressive. They see all other creatures as either food or threats, and they try to kill anything they find edible or menacing.

Individual (EL 1): A single howler wasp is usually on the prowl for food. It attacks without hesitation, flying back to the nest for reinforcements if injured.

Hunting Group (EL 2–4): Small groups of two to four howler wasps drift, seemingly aimlessly, at distances of up to 10 miles from the nest, attacking any living creature.

Raiding Wing (EL 5–8): A raiding wing comprising five to sixteen howler wasps prowls the countryside, gathering food and resources, as well as defending the nest from possible attackers.

Nest (EL 9–13): A nest can contain anywhere from seventeen to sixty-four howler wasps, in addition to the queen.

ECOLOGY

Howler wasps build nests of paper, dried leaves, and skins of dead animals. Such nests range in complexity from single chambers to multiple consecutive cells, each of which might hold as many as six howler wasps. The wasps incorporate items and gear taken from slain opponents into their nests: Shields, suits of armor, and similar equipment serve as useful framing material. The paper walls of a howler wasp nest have hardness 0 and 3 hit points per inch of thickness.

A queen sits at the center of a howler wasp nest, producing the colony's eggs with the aid of male howler wasps who swarm around her, never leaving the nest. She and her consorts protect the eggs until they hatch. The queen lays anywhere from thirty to sixty eggs each month, each egg hatching in about a week. Because the nest might not be able to support so many new howler wasps, the queen and the healthiest larvae devour the weakest young ones. The survivors reach maturity in about three weeks. The average howler wasp lives for about six months, though the queen's life span might be years.

Female howler wasps that grow to more than 2 Hit Dice are a threat to the queen, who mercilessly dispatches such potential rivals. If the queen dies, the other females in the nest begin to grow freely. They gain 1 extra Hit Die each week until they reach 8 Hit Dice, at which point they vie to

become the new queen. Usually one female slays all her competitors, but occasionally several females leave to start their own nests. The single female builds and enters a cocoonlike structure, there undergoing a biological transformation into a queen, which takes a week.

Giant wasps and giant spiders present the most common threats to howler wasp nests. Apes and dire apes also come into conflict with howler wasps.

Environment: Howler wasps prefer forested environments, but they can make their homes in nearly any warm location. Whenever possible, they occupy derelict buildings. They are especially fond of old libraries and temples, which contain paper for building their nests. They are rarely found underground.

Typical Physical Characteristics: The average howler wasp measures less than 4 feet long and weighs around 30 pounds. The queen is around 8 feet long, and she weighs about 250 pounds.

Physically, male and female howler wasps are nearly identical. The only difference is that a male howler wasp dies 1d4+1 rounds after delivering a sting attack. Howler wasps encountered outside the nest are always female; about 20% of those encountered inside the nest are males.

Alignment: Howler wasps hate all other living creatures and kill them with no provocation, whether the wasps need food or not. They care for nothing other than killing and their own survival, and only a howler wasp queen has any hope of ruling a howler wasp hive without supernatural aid. Thus, howler wasps are usually chaotic evil.

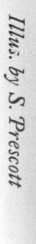

Howler wasp

TYPICAL TREASURE

Howler wasps have no individual treasure, but they use any items they find to build their nests. They particularly love shields and other flat objects that serve as sturdy framing material, or scrolls as a source of paper. Tearing apart a nest's structure reveals a small bounty of magic items, coins, and other treasure with a standard value for the Challenge Rating of the nest.

FOR PLAYER CHARACTERS

A typical howler wasp can be summoned by a cleric with access to the Chaos domain, using *summon monster II* or a higher-level *summon monster* spell. Treat the howler wasp as if it were on the 2nd-level list on the Summon Monster table (*PH* 287).

Illus. by S. Prescott

INFERNO SPIDER

This monstrous arachnid appears to be composed entirely of magma. Liquid flame drips from its fangs, and its eight blazing eyes are devoid of all expression.

INFERNO SPIDER   CR 8

Always N Large elemental (extraplanar, fire)
Init +7; **Senses** darkvision 60 ft., tremorsense 60 ft.; Listen +6, Spot +6
Languages Ignan

AC 22, touch 12, flat-footed 19; Dodge, Mobility
   (−1 size, +3 Dex, +10 natural)
hp 119 (14 HD); **DR** 5/—
Immune fire; elemental immunities
Fort +8, **Ref** +12, **Will** +6
Weakness vulnerability to cold

Speed 40 ft. (8 squares), climb 40 ft.; Spring Attack
Melee bite +14 (2d6+7 plus caustic poison)
Ranged flame web +12 ranged touch (2d6 fire plus entangle)
Space 10 ft.; **Reach** 5 ft.
Base Atk +10; **Grp** +19
Atk Options Combat Reflexes, caustic poison (DC 21, 3d6 fire/3d6 fire), fire shield

Abilities Str 20, Dex 16, Con 18, Int 6, Wis 11, Cha 11
SQ elemental traits
Feats Alertness^B, Combat Reflexes, Dodge, Improved Initiative^B, Iron Will, Mobility, Spring Attack
Skills Climb +13, Hide +8, Jump +9, Listen +6, Spot +6
Advancement 15–20 HD (Large); 21–28 HD (Huge); 29–40 HD (Gargantuan)

Flame Web (Ex) Inferno spiders can throw a burning web eight times per day. This is similar to an attack with a net but has a maximum range of 100 feet, with a range increment of 20 feet, and is effective against targets up to one size category larger than the inferno spider. The web anchors the target in place, allowing no movement. Each round, at the end of the inferno spider's turn, an entangled creature takes 2d6 points of fire damage.

    An entangled creature can escape the web with a successful DC 21 Escape Artist check or burst it with a DC 25 Strength check. The check DCs are Constitution-based, and the Strength check DC includes a +4 racial bonus. The web has 12 hit points and hardness 5. If any part of the flame web takes 5 or more points of cold damage, the flame is extinguished and the web becomes cold and brittle, reducing the difficulty of the Escape Artist check to DC 16 and the Strength check to DC 20.
Fire Shield (Su) An inferno spider's body produces tremendous heat. Any creature that strikes or touches an inferno spider with its body or a weapon, or that grapples an inferno spider, automatically takes 1d6 points of fire damage. A creature takes damage from this ability only once per turn.
Skills Inferno spiders have a +8 racial bonus on Climb checks. An inferno spider can always choose to take 10 on Climb checks, even if rushed or threatened.

Their fangs burning with elemental fury, inferno spiders are deadly predators. These hunters are often aligned with priests of flame deities or groups of cunning salamanders, using their abilities to complement those of other fire creatures.

STRATEGIES AND TACTICS

Inferno spiders hunt and feed on creatures weaker than themselves. They use their flame webs to capture prey that might otherwise be too quick and nimble. In combat, inferno spiders first attempt to entangle prey with their webs and then close to bite with their poisonous fangs. Possessing only limited intelligence, inferno spiders remain cunning and tenacious hunters, using Spring Attack to dart in and out of combat.

SAMPLE ENCOUNTER

Inferno spiders can be found in the company of fire elementals, salamanders, and clerics of fire deities. The spiders are intelligent enough to follow simple orders and to realize the benefits of allying with stronger creatures.

    Temple Guardians (EL 13): Inside a remote volcano, Kaerlak, a pyromaniacal 10th-level cleric of Obad-Hai, has cowed two inferno spiders into guarding his temple. Kaerlak found the spiders in the volcanic chambers beneath the temple, along with a group of four average salamanders. The inferno spiders freely stalk the passages of the fire temple, and Kaerlak and the salamanders have resolved to draw more fire creatures to the site. While Kaerlak and his minions aren't wantonly destructive, their fiery travels through nearby woodlands and their stoking of the volcano's fires have drawn the attention of a small group of druids who are devoted to Ehlonna. These druids now seek help to protect their forest from the threat of Kaerlak's temple.

ECOLOGY

Voracious predators, even among others of their kind, inferno spiders lead solitary lives on the Elemental Plane of Fire. The weaker denizens of that plane universally loathe them, and inferno spiders avoid contact with others of their kind as well.

INFERNO SPIDER LORE

Characters with ranks in Knowledge (the planes) can learn more about inferno spiders. When a character makes a successful skill check, the following lore is revealed, including the information from lower DCs.

Knowledge (the Planes)

DC	Result
18	This is an inferno spider, a kind of fire elemental. This result reveals all elemental traits and the fire subtype.
23	Inferno spiders fling strands of flaming web to immobilize their prey. Composed of a fiery substance, these webs are particularly vulnerable to cold.
28	The bite of an inferno spider delivers a fiery poison that burns a victim from within.
33	Inferno spiders can be summoned by those who learn the proper procedure to do so.

swirling mass of molten rock that forms the creature's internal structure, and flames dance in random patterns across the bulk of its abdomen and legs.

Alignment: Inferno spiders are always neutral. They care only for their own survival as a race, and hunt, live, and mate for this purpose only.

TYPICAL TREASURE

Inferno spiders rarely have any treasure. Their fiery bodies and lairs destroy valuable items quickly.

FOR PLAYER CHARACTERS

An inferno spider can be summoned by a wizard, by a sorcerer, or by a cleric with access to the Fire domain, using *summon monster VI* or a higher-level *summon monster* spell. Treat the inferno spider as if it were on the 6th-level list on the Summon Monster table (PH 287). Clerics with access to the Fire domain can also use a *greater planar ally* spell to call an inferno spider, which usually demands ample food as payment.

To accomplish any of these tasks, a spellcaster must have at least 5 ranks in Knowledge (the planes). Additionally, the spellcaster must complete a magical ritual that requires the powder of fire opals worth 100 gp. Researching the ritual requires two days of intense study.

Once in the life of an inferno spider, typically when it has become advanced in size as well as years, the creature seeks a mate. Two courting inferno spiders fall into a strange, ritualistic dance, during which they circle each other for hours or, in some cases, days. At the end of the ritual, the two inferno spiders charge one another, whereupon they collide and explode, giving birth to hundreds of young. Enemies and predators of inferno spiders often hide near the dancing mates, waiting to slay as many of the offspring as possible. The young also attack one another. Very few inferno spiders survive to become large enough to hunt prey other than their siblings.

Inferno spiders are attracted to individuals who possess great arcane or divine power, finding service with those knowledgeable enough to summon and command them.

Environment: Inferno spiders inhabit any warm region of the Material Plane, as well as the Elemental Plane of Fire. They are occasionally called to service by powerful spellcasters on other planes of existence, particularly by those who serve or revere fire deities.

Typical Physical Characteristics: Inferno spiders stand approximately 4 feet tall and have a diameter of 8 feet. Composed mostly of magma and flame, an inferno spider can weigh as much as 600 pounds. Transparent plates reveal a

Inferno spider

Illus. by Daarken

INFERNO SPIDERS IN EBERRON

Inferno spiders come from Fernia, the Sea of Fire. There, they skip across the surface of the molten landscape like gigantic water striders, hunting, eating, and mating as they continue the endless cycle of life. Sometimes the creatures shift to Eberron when Fernia is coterminous, and there they set up lairs in volcanic caverns. A gigantic specimen is rumored to nest in the crater of Haka'torvhak's peak, miles below the fiendish city.

INFERNO SPIDERS IN FAERÛN

Inferno spiders live on the Elemental Plane of Fire. The vast majority of these creatures are servants of Kossuth, the Lord of Flames, whom they revere. The deity appears to them as an enormous inferno spider of great age and strength. The zealots of the Burning Braziers faction seek to introduce inferno spiders to Toril in their quest to cleanse the world. So far, the Firelord has allowed only limited summoning. Whether the distant and unknowable deity has some other plan in mind for the creatures, or simply does not care, none can say.

JOYSTEALER

You face a cruelly beautiful, insubstantial being. It looks a little like an elf, but the feral smile and glittering, gemlike eyes betray it as something else.

JOYSTEALER	**CR 5**

Usually NE Medium fey (incorporeal)
Init +7; **Senses** low-light vision, sense emotions 60 ft.;
Listen +12, Spot +12
Languages Common, Sylvan, Khen-Zai (*Fiend Folio* 65)

AC 17, touch 17, flat-footed 14
(+3 Dex, +4 deflection)
Miss Chance 50% (incorporeal)
hp 27 (6 HD); **DR** 5/cold iron
Fort +3, **Ref** +8, **Will** +6

Speed fly 30 ft. (perfect) (6 squares)
Melee incorporeal touch +6 (1d4 Cha)
Space 5 ft.; **Reach** 5 ft.
Base Atk +3; **Grp** —
Special Actions drain emotions

Abilities Str —, Dex 17, Con 12, Int 13, Wis 12, Cha 19
SQ incorporeal traits
Feats Alertness, Improved Initiative, Track
Skills Bluff +13, Diplomacy +8, Disguise +4 (+6 acting),
Hide +16, Intimidate +6, Knowledge (nature) +8,
Knowledge (the planes) +5, Listen +12, Sense Motive
+10, Spot +12, Survival +10 (+12 in aboveground natural
environments)
Advancement by character class; **Favored Class** rogue;
see text

Sense Emotions (Su) This ability functions like blindsense,
except that a joystealer can detect only the presence and
positions of living creatures.
Drain Emotions (Su) Once a joystealer has reduced a living
creature to 0 Charisma, it can drain emotion completely
from that opponent as a standard action. A creature so
drained can't be affected by morale bonuses or penalties,
can't rage, and can't receive the benefits of any other
ability derived through inspiration or emotion. The
affected creature is also immune to fear effects.
   The drain emotions effect can be countered only by
finding and destroying the joystealer who caused it or
by casting a *remove curse* spell on the afflicted creature
within the area of a *hallow* spell.
Skills Joystealers have a +4 racial bonus on Hide checks.

Beautiful, haunting, and cruel beyond mortal ken, joystealers hunt passion, feed on fear, and revel in the emotions that they steal from others. Once they labored in servitude for ethereal masters, but now they haunt the streets of cities or stride through forests at the side of other fey creatures.

STRATEGIES AND TACTICS

Individual joystealers seduce mortals with words and deeds, often trying to incite love or happiness, which they find tasty with a touch of surprise and fear. If forced to fight for its sustenance, a joystealer remains in a combat only long enough to reduce one living creature to 0 Charisma. Then it uses its drain emotions ability, fleeing thereafter to digest the passions it has stolen.

A group of joystealers begins an attack from ambush, hiding partially within solid objects. Though they are not invisible, these incorporeal creatures enjoy an excellent racial bonus on Hide checks, and they take advantage of shadows, clutter, undergrowth, and the like. If they achieve surprise, they attack a single target and drain it to helplessness. Their superior reflexes give them an excellent chance of catching opponents flat-footed after the surprise round, allowing them to potentially incapacitate a second target.

SAMPLE ENCOUNTERS

Joystealers often work in teams to feed efficiently. Such gangs consume whatever strong emotions are available—fear being a common one, especially as the joystealers continue to feed. Joystealers sometimes join with other cruel fey, who use their abilities to incapacitate victims that the joystealers then drain of Charisma and emotion. They leave behind hopeless husks that often just give up on living.

Individual (EL 5): Lone joystealers are threats in urban environments or in other places where strong emotions are plentiful, such as battlefields. Occasionally, a single joystealer might be exploring new feeding grounds or be the sole survivor of a larger group.

Dark Pranksters (EL 8): A spiteful pixie enjoys punishing mortals who encroach on its territory, using its sleep arrows or *Otto's irresistible dance* and then allowing its two companion joystealers to drain the victims' emotions.

ECOLOGY

Joystealers lead a strange dual existence. They are bound to the Ethereal Plane but always hunger for the emotions of creatures from the material world.

The ancestors of joystealers were unseelie fey that fed on the emotions of ordinary mortals. When the ethergaunts, or khen-zai as they call themselves (*Fiend Folio* 64), decided to reclaim the Material Plane, they sought slaves that would be

---

JOYSTEALER LORE

Characters with ranks in Knowledge (the planes) or Knowledge (nature) can learn more about joystealers. When a character makes a successful skill check, the following lore is revealed, including the information from lower DCs.

Knowledge (the Planes)

DC	Result
15	This is a joystealer, a fey tied to the Ethereal Plane. This result reveals all incorporeal traits.
20	A joystealer's incorporeal touch saps hope. These creatures feed on the emotions of intelligent beings.
25	Joystealers are the escaped slaves of ethergaunts, who now hunt them down.

Knowledge (Nature)

DC	Result
15	This is a joystealer, an urban fey creature. This result reveals all fey traits.
20	Joystealers became bonded to the Ethereal Plane and cannot take solid form. This result reveals all incorporeal traits.
25	A joystealer's incorporeal touch saps hope. These creatures feed on the emotions of intelligent beings.
30	Joystealers were transformed into ethereal creatures by an ancient race.

useful to their cause of emotional purification and physical eradication. The joystealers were a perfect tool, being material beings that destroyed the emotions of other material beings. The black ethergaunts began to amass large armies of joystealers, whose abilities had no effect on their own "perfected" minds. The fey had never been especially numerous, so it wasn't long before all of them had been taken by the khen-zai. Through magical manipulation and long-term habituation to ethereal existence, the joystealers became insubstantial, partly fastened to the Ethereal Plane.

Joystealers have been bound to the Ethereal Plane for millennia, almost beyond the realm of mortal memory or record. However, they hunger still for the feelings and passions of the mortal world. Under the subjugation of the ethergaunts, joystealers have become cruel and evil to the extreme. Even after escaping ethergaunt rule, they retain their viciousness, willing to drain a mortal of emotion eternally for a moment's revel in the joys of the stolen passion.

Like all fey, joystealers are long-lived and mature slowly.

Environment: Joystealers are inextricably bound to the Ethereal Plane now, but they were urban fey before their enslavement. They are most likely to be encountered within large cities, where plenty of emotion is expressed in the daily lives of residents. Most joystealers restrict themselves to consuming the emotional energy of society's forgotten, unless in desperate straits, to avoid drawing attention to themselves. Slums and waterfronts are their preferred haunts. The presence of other creatures also helps the joystealers conceal themselves from pursuers once they have fed.

Typical Physical Characteristics: A joystealer is a delicate being that resembles an extremely pale elf with long hair and androgynous features. It is coldly attractive by humanoid standards, but its eyes immediately give away its true nature. They resemble gems, luminous and without pupils. A joystealer's eyes are deep ruby red when the creature is hungry but glow golden once it has fed. A typical joystealer stands about 5 feet tall and has a slight form.

Alignment: Joystealers are concerned only with their own well-being, without regard for how their behavior affects others. By that standard, they would have been considered evil even before their transformation. Now their resentment and despair has further darkened their souls. Joystealers are usually neutral evil.

SOCIETY

"Joystealers" is a name conferred on the creatures by frightened survivors of their attacks. They call themselves *insoril*. Insoril are extremely unusual fey in that they adapted to urban environments. When humans spread into the untamed

Joystealer

lands, many fey retreated before them. The insoril lingered, for humans were a rich and plentiful source of intense emotions—far tastier and easier to harvest than those of other fey, elves, and the like. If several insoril previously dwelt by a riverside, they remained in the wharves and alleyways of a river city. If they once inhabited a wood, they haunted the parks and back streets of a growing town.

The insoril saw themselves as a necessary part of the world, draining excess emotions that would only lead to conflict or pain. Indeed, they were proud of their role. They saw their feeding as being on a higher level than the bloodstained hunt or the hard labor of farming. After being enslaved by the ethergaunts, the insoril were put to work as mere hunters, and they resented such debasement. But escape has not freed them, and their feeding is now a desperate scramble instead of the refined culling they once took pride in. They hate the ethergaunts for poisoning their purity so. As far as other intelligent creatures are concerned, though, joystealers are as selfish and terrible as ever.

TYPICAL TREASURE

During their enslavement, joystealers possessed nothing of their own, and being incorporeal, they have no material treasure.

JOYSTEALERS WITH CLASS LEVELS

NPC joystealers advance by character class, most as rogues. A few become spellcasters, though material components are a problem for incorporeal creatures. The rare joystealer cleric usually follows Nerull or Wee Jas.

Level Adjustment: +4.

JOYSTEALERS IN EBERRON

The ethergaunts served the daelkyr, their creators, nearly ten thousand years ago, while the inhabitants of Xoriat ran free on Khorvaire. When the gates to Xoriat were closed, the ethergaunts took refuge on the Ethereal Plane. After the fall of the Dhakaani civilization, humans began to move into the goblinoid lands. The joystealers stayed to feed. Ethergaunts observed them and began to collect them as slaves.

During the Last War, the battlegrounds of Cyre provided an excellent base for the ethergaunts. Amid the wartime horrors, tales of creatures that drained the very heart did not stand out much. Only the passion of an army of Thrane zealots allowed the joystealers to make their escape. Now many of the fugitives linger in the Mournland, hiding in the dead-gray mist. Travelers never suspect that insubstantial creatures within the mist might be responsible for their spiritual deadening.

Illus. by J. Zhang

JUSTICE ARCHON

Archons are celestials from the plane of Celestia. They guard that plane and all who are good or innocent, fighting fiends wherever they find such creatures. Although glorious to behold and created from the essence of good, archons are terrifying enemies of any they see as evil.

A glorious but menacing angel dives toward you. She is a radiant warrior clad in bright full plate, wielding a greatsword that crackles with divine power.

Justice archons consider themselves the purest champions of justice in Celestia. Decisive and self-righteous, their desire to act swiftly on behalf of justice sometimes leads them astray.

Strategies and Tactics

A justice archon does not attack without provocation, but its highly tuned sense of justice and retribution often causes it to become incensed at the mere sight of an evil being or even the suspicion of an evil act. If it is unsure of who was

JUSTICE ARCHON   CR 6

Always LG Medium outsider (archon, extraplanar, good, lawful)

Init +1; **Senses** darkvision 60 ft., low-light vision; Listen +10, Spot +10

Aura magic circle against evil (10 ft.), menace (20 ft., DC 17)

Languages Celestial, Draconic, Infernal, tongues

AC 19, touch 11, flat-footed 18
(+1 Dex, +8 armor)

hp 63 (6 HD); **DR** 10/evil

Immune electricity and petrification

SR 16

Fort +10 (+14 against poison), **Ref** +8, **Will** +8

Speed 20 ft. (4 squares) in full plate, base speed 30 ft.; fly 40 ft. (good) in full plate, base fly speed 60 ft.

Melee *+1 greatsword* +10/+5 (2d6+5/19–20)

Space 5 ft.; **Reach** 5 ft.

Base Atk +6; **Grp** +9

Atk Options aligned strike (good, lawful), justice strike

Special Actions teleport (self plus 50 lb. of objects only)

Spell-Like Abilities (CL 6th):
At will—*aid, continual flame, detect evil*

Abilities Str 16, Dex 12, Con 21, Int 10, Wis 13, Cha 14

SQ archon traits

Feats Iron Will, Improved Toughness (*Complete Warrior* 101), Lightning Reflexes

Skills Concentration +14, Diplomacy +13, Intimidate +11, Knowledge (the planes) +9, Listen +10, Move Silently +4, Sense Motive +10, Spot +10, Survival +1 (+3 on other planes)

Advancement by character class; **Favored Class** paladin; see text

Possessions full plate armor, *+1 greatsword*

Tongues (Su) As the *tongues* spell; continuous; caster level 14th.

Magic Circle against Evil (Su) As the *magic circle against evil* spell; continuous; caster level 14th.

Aura of Menace (Su) –2 penalty on attack rolls, AC, and saves for 24 hours; Will save negates.

Justice Strike (Su) A justice archon that hits with a melee attack can choose to use this special ability instead of dealing normal weapon damage. Justice strike deals the damage of the struck opponent's primary melee attack. This damage includes effects that apply automatically on a hit, such as energy damage or poison, but not those from optional effects or feats, such as Power Attack.

Teleport (Su) As the *teleport* spell; at will; caster level 14th.

Justice archon

responsible for the wrongdoing, a justice archon uses its *detect evil* ability to locate evil creatures and charges headlong into battle with dreadful cries of vengeance, laying into the nearest opponent with its greatsword. It uses the weapon's normal damage until it can discover the nature of its opponent's melee attack (generally as a result of being hit), then uses its justice strike if that is more effective. If the opponent provides a serious challenge, the justice archon teleports away to bring reinforcements or to strike again when it has some other advantage.

JUSTICE ARCHON CHAMPION

This imposing figure appears as an armored knight, swooping on golden wings. His air of authority and menace is almost palpable.

JUSTICE ARCHON CHAMPION	CR 10

Justice archon paladin 4
LG Medium outsider (archon, extraplanar, good, lawful)
Init +1; **Senses** darkvision 60 ft., low-light vision; Listen +9, Spot +9
Aura courage (10 ft., allies +4 against fear), magic circle against evil (10 ft.), menace (20 ft., Will DC 18 negates)
Languages Celestial, Draconic, Infernal, tongues

AC 23, touch 11, flat-footed 22
  (+1 Dex, +10 armor, +2 natural)
hp 129 (10 HD); **DR** 10/evil
Immune disease, electricity, fear, petrification
SR 20
Fort +19 (+23 against poison), **Ref** +12, **Will** +11

Speed 20 ft. (4 squares) in full plate, base speed 30 ft.; fly 40 ft. (good) in full plate, base fly speed 60 ft.
Melee *+1 greatsword* +17/+12 (2d6+8/19–20)
Base Atk +10; **Grp** +15
Atk Options aligned strike (good, lawful), justice strike, smite evil 1/day (+3 attack, +4 damage)
Special Actions lay on hands 12 points/day, teleport (self plus 50 lb. of objects only), turn undead 6/day (+5, 2d6+4, 1st)
Paladin Spells Prepared (CL 2nd):
  1st—*divine favor*
Spell-Like Abilities (CL 6th):
  At will—*aid, continual flame, detect evil*

Abilities Str 21, Dex 12, Con 24, Int 10, Wis 11, Cha 17
SQ archon traits
Feats Iron Will, Improved Toughness, Lightning Reflexes, Weapon Focus (greatsword)
Skills Concentration +16, Diplomacy +14, Intimidate +12, Knowledge (the planes) +9, Knowledge (religion) +5, Listen +9, Move Silently +5, Sense Motive +9, Spot +9, Survival +0 (+2 on other planes)
Possessions *+2 full plate armor, +1 greatsword, amulet of natural armor +2*

Tongues (Su) As standard justice archon.
Magic Circle against Evil (Su) As standard justice archon.
Aura of Menace (Su) As standard justice archon.
Justice Strike (Su) As standard justice archon.
Teleport (Su) As standard justice archon.

Some justice archons take levels in paladin to become more focused champions of their cause. The justice archon champion presented here had the following ability scores before racial adjustments and Hit Dice ability score increases: Str 15, Dex 12, Con 14, Int 10, Wis 8, Cha 13.

Strategies and Tactics

When a justice archon champion decides violence is justified, it makes sure of its overwhelming superiority. In addition to casting *aid* on itself, it casts *divine favor* before joining battle.

A justice archon champion usually leads a large group of other archons, generally six to eight justice archons, several squads of hound archons, or a squad of sword archons (*Book of Exalted Deeds* 160).

Turning evil against itself is the highest form of justice.
—Credo of the archons

SAMPLE ENCOUNTER

Justice archons often fight alone, but they frequently accompany other champions of good. They provide aerial support to squads of hound archons or answer magical summons to aid clerics of lawful good deities. Celestial giant eagles or celestial giant owls regularly accompany justice archons.

Fallen Angel (EL 8): The justice archon Hanzuriel always deals swift judgment and harsh justice to wrongdoers. Over the years, his impetuous decisions have slowly but steadily drawn him off the path of righteousness. Admonished by superiors and accused of falling from grace, Hanzuriel fled the heavens, convinced of his moral superiority over "hand-wringing layabouts that hide in Celestia while evil does its foul works." Now unwittingly lawful neutral, Hanzuriel travels the Material Plane with two like-minded hound archons, judging crimes and punishing "criminals" at will. Hanzuriel's hound archon allies impersonate mortals to root out the malefactors in a community. When they find someone they think has broken a law (by their sense of what is lawful), they report to Hanzuriel, and he and they return to destroy the individual.

ECOLOGY

As an outsider, a justice archon does not need to eat, drink, or sleep. A justice archon does not contribute to the ecology of an area, and an archon avoids taking any action that might alter an area's natural balance, unless pursuit of justice requires doing so.

Environment: Justice archons are native to the Seven Mounting Heavens of Celestia. They inhabit Empyrea, the City of Tempered Souls, on Celestia's fifth layer Mertion, where reflections of their golden wings flash in its crystal-clear waters.

A few justice archons choose voluntary exile from the shining realm of Celestia. These champions remain on the Material Plane to maintain eternal watch on infernal portals that border the Lower Planes, guarding against incursions by fiends.

Typical Physical Characteristics: A typical justice archon stands about 6 feet tall and weighs 190 pounds. It looks like a beautiful humanoid, usually an elf or human, with gleaming golden eyes, skin, and hair. Justice archons favor full plate armor and two-handed weapons, usually greatswords but occasionally greataxes or glaives.

Justice archons have no gender, though one might resemble a male or female humanoid.

Alignment: Natives of Celestia, justice archons always begin existence lawful good. When in the throes of righteous fury, though, they might lash out at all who oppose them, and doing this too often can lead a justice archon to change alignment.

SOCIETY

Justice archons outshine other archons in zealous devotion to what is good and right. They willingly bring succor to the injured and the abused, but their passion lies more in exacting retribution against those responsible for such mistreatment. Justice archons are at the forefront of war parties that hunt down fiends, and they frequently come to the aid of clerics who pray for assistance against evil. They harbor a special enmity toward yugoloths. They despise beings that do not cleave to a philosophy but exist only to cause as much misery as possible.

If justice archons have a weakness, it is that their lust for vengeance can cloud their sense of right and wrong. High priests with ambitions toward great temporal power have exploited this tendency by directing the archons' fury against "evil" rulers. Should a justice archon learn it has been so manipulated, though, its revenge against the true villain is swift, violent, and horrifying. In its fury, it might destroy all who surround the object of vengeance, whether they share guilt or not.

Justice archons consider themselves the purest champions of justice in Celestia. Throne archons (*Book of Exalted Deeds* 162) are the judges of the heavens, but their cold deliberation and resentment of being called to the Material Plane make them too distant in the eyes of the justice archons. The summons to defeat evil and injustice, wherever it might be found, is too loud to ignore, and justice archons eagerly answer.

Cooler-headed celestials recognize the usefulness of such zealotry, but many believe the justice archons are too easily aroused—and thus too prone to act rashly and harm the blameless who get between them and their prey. These other celestials encourage justice archons to engage in raids against the Lower Planes, in which no innocents are at risk.

JUSTICE ARCHON LORE

Characters with ranks in Knowledge (the planes) can learn more about justice archons. When a character makes a successful skill check, the following lore is revealed, including the information from lower DCs.

Knowledge (the Planes)

DC	Result
16	This is a justice archon, a zealous native of Celestia. Such archons frequently lead squads of other archons or earthly champions of good against evil enemies of great power. This result reveals all outsider and archon traits.
21	Justice archons can strike an enemy for the damage it deals, including additional damage from energy or poison. They are resistant to magic and ignore some of the damage dealt by non-evil weapons.
26	Justice archons hate yugoloths. A justice archon that answers a *planar ally* spell usually agrees to fight yugoloths for no payment. However, justice archons can be impetuous in their pursuit of justice, and they are quick to judge.

TYPICAL TREASURE

A justice archon has standard treasure for its Challenge Rating, mostly in the form of magic weapons and armor. It also might wear protective items and use potions to improve its combat abilities. Remaining possessions usually serve to enhance the archon's glorious and imposing appearance. Justice archons favor golden necklaces, torcs, circlets, and other such jewelry, as well as gold enhancements to armor and clothing.

JUSTICE ARCHONS WITH CLASS LEVELS

The abilities of the paladin class mesh well with justice archons' natural desire to combat evil. Their innate spell-like abilities do not increase in caster level with the addition of paladin levels, but their spell resistance does increase.

Level Adjustment: +5.

FOR PLAYER CHARACTERS

A justice archon can be summoned using *summon monster VII* or a higher-level *summon monster* spell. Treat the justice archon as if it were on the 7th-level list on the Summon Monster table (*PH* 287).

When a justice archon is called by one of the *planar ally* spells, it demands only half the usual payment if asked to fight fiends, and no payment if yugoloths are the enemy. A justice archon might continue to fight remaining yugoloths, even if it has accomplished the letter of a bargain struck with its caller.

JUSTICE ARCHONS IN EBERRON

Justice archons are vanguard commanders in the eternal battles that rage across the plane of Shavarath. Yugoloths do not dwell there, though, being denizens of Mabar. The fiendish armies sometimes summon yugoloths, which brings justice archons in swarms. Justice archons might enter Eberron when Mabar is coterminous and yugoloths emerge to plague mortals.

JUSTICE ARCHONS IN FAERÛN

Justice archons are native to the House of the Triad, home to deities of justice and righteous warfare, including Helm, Torm, and Tyr. They are especially hostile to denizens of the Barrens of Doom and Despair, servants of deities who delight in inflicting random pain and misery.

LIZARDFOLK, DARK TALON TRIBE

As detailed in the *Monster Manual*, lizardfolk are primitive reptilian humanoids that lurk in swampy places. Most lizardfolk tend toward neutrality, but the example tribe described here is an exception. Encounters with the Dark Talon lizardfolk can form the basis of an adventure path.

The Dark Talons are murderous lizardfolk, toughened by alchemical infusion with black dragon blood, that seek to conquer lands controlled by other humanoid races. Spurred on by their mad king, Yarshag, and fanatical druids, the Dark Talons march from their swamp on a sinister crusade.

DARK TALON SOLDIER

This hulking, reptilian humanoid has scales tinged with black. He swings an enormous club.

DARK TALON SOLDIER   CR 2
NE Medium humanoid (reptilian)
Init +1; **Senses** Listen +1, Spot +1
Languages Common, Draconic

AC 19, touch 11, flat-footed 18
   (+1 Dex, +3 armor, +5 natural)
hp 19 (2 HD)
Fort +3, **Ref** +4, **Will** +1

Speed 30 ft. (6 squares)
Melee mwk maquahuitl +5 (1d10+4/×3) and
   bite –1 (1d4+1) or
Melee 2 claws +4 each (1d4+3) and
   bite –1 (1d4+1)
Ranged javelin +2 (1d6+3)
Base Atk +1; **Grp** +4
Atk Options Blind-Fight
Combat Gear *potion of bull's strength*, 2 *potions of cure moderate wounds*

Abilities Str 17, Dex 13, Con 16, Int 8, Wis 12, Cha 8
SQ hold breath (64 rounds)
Feats Blind-Fight
Skills Balance +6, Jump +7, Listen +1, Spot +1, Swim +7
Possessions combat gear plus masterwork studded leather, masterwork maquahuitl, 5 javelins

Yarshag's alchemical process makes one out of three Dark Talon lizardfolk stronger, tougher, and meaner. These troops are given special training with the greatclub.

The Dark Talon soldier presented here had the following ability scores before racial adjustments: Str 15, Dex 13, Con 14, Int 10, Wis 12, Cha 8.

Strategies and Tactics

Dark Talon soldiers practice fighting in foggy conditions and excel at making accurate attacks when sight is limited. They use hushed calls in Draconic to keep in contact with each other.

DARK TALON CHAMPION

This hulking, reptilian humanoid has scales tinged with black. He snarls and hefts a jagged spear.

DARK TALON CHAMPION (RAGING)   CR 4
Male lizardfolk barbarian 3
NE Medium humanoid (reptilian)
Init +1; **Senses** Listen +7, Spot +1
Languages Common, Draconic

AC 18, touch 9, flat-footed 18; uncanny dodge
   (+1 Dex, +4 armor, +5 natural, –2 raging)
hp 59 (5 HD)
Fort +8, **Ref** +5, **Will** +4

Speed 40 ft. (8 squares)
Melee mwk falchion +11 (2d4+9/18–20) and
   bite +8 (1d4+3) or
Melee 2 claws +10 each (1d4+6) and
   bite +8 (1d4+3)
Ranged javelin +5 (1d6+6)
Base Atk +4; **Grp** +10
Atk Options Blind-Fight, rage 1/day (8 rounds)
Combat Gear *javelin of lightning, potion of bull's strength*

Abilities Str 22, Dex 13, Con 20, Int 8, Wis 12, Cha 8
SQ fast movement, hold breath (80 rounds), trap sense +1
Feats Blind-Fight, Multiattack
Skills Balance +6, Jump +19, Listen +7, Spot +1, Swim +12
Possessions combat gear plus *+1 studded leather armor*, masterwork falchion, 2 javelins

When not raging, a Dark Talon champion has the following changed statistics:
AC 20, touch 11, flat-footed 20
hp 49 (5 HD)
Fort +6, **Will** +2
Melee mwk falchion +9 (2d4+9/18–20) and
   bite +6 (1d4+2) or
Melee 2 claws +8 each (1d4+4) and
   bite +6 (1d4+2)
Ranged javelin +5 (1d6+4)
Grp +8
Abilities Str 18, Con 16
SQ hold breath (64 rounds)
Skills Jump +17, Swim +10

Most of the Dark Talon tribe's field commanders and champions are barbarians. These berserkers were among the first lizardfolk spawned with Yarshag's alchemical process.

The Dark Talon champion presented here had the following ability scores before racial adjustments and Hit Dice ability score increases: Str 15, Dex 13, Con 14, Int 10, Wis 12, Cha 8.

Strategies and Tactics

Dark Talon champions are straightforward melee combatants who lead Dark Talon charges, raging all the way. Like Dark Talon soldiers, these champions are adept at fighting without the convenience of sight.

Champions lead warbands of six to ten soldiers. They also serve as bodyguards and sergeants for the tribe's druids.

DARK TALON WASP RIDER

An enormous wasp the size of a horse buzzes toward you. On its back is a reptilian humanoid, who levels a lance at your heart.

DARK TALON WASP RIDER   CR 2

NE Medium humanoid (reptilian)
Init +2; **Senses** Listen +0, Spot +0
Languages Common, Draconic

AC 20, touch 12, flat-footed 18
  (+2 Dex +3 armor, +5 natural)
hp 19 (2 HD)
Fort +3, **Ref** +5, **Will** +0

Speed 30 ft. (6 squares)
Melee mwk lance +4 (1d8+3/×3) and
  bite –2 (1d4+1) or
Melee 2 claws +3 each (1d4+2) and
  bite –2 (1d4+1)
Ranged javelin +3 (1d6+2) or
Ranged sling +3 (1d4+2)
Base Atk +1; **Grp** +3
Combat Gear *potion of cat's grace*, 2 *potions of cure moderate wounds*, 5 flasks of alchemist's fire

Abilities Str 15, Dex 15, Con 16, Int 10, Wis 10, Cha 8
SQ hold breath (64 rounds)
Feats Martial Weapon Proficiency (lance)
Skills Balance +7, Jump +7, Listen +0, Ride +7, Spot +0, Swim +9
Possessions combat gear plus masterwork studded leather, masterwork lance, 3 javelins, sling with 20 bullets, giant wasp mount

Wasp riders are chosen for their excellent reflexes, and they receive special training with the lance. The Dark Talon wasp rider presented here had the following ability scores before racial adjustments: Str 13, Dex 15, Con 14, Int 12, Wis 10, Cha 8.

Strategies and Tactics

Wasp riders are the first wave of a Dark Talon attack. These warriors soften up the enemy with a few volleys before the main army engages. Once the warband meets the enemy, the wasp riders patrol the air to guard against the enemy's reinforcements, hunt down foes that flee, and pick off any targets of opportunity.

GIANT WASP MOUNT   CR 3

N Large vermin
Init +1; **Senses** darkvision 60 ft.; Listen +1, Spot +9

AC 14, touch 10, flat-footed 13
  (–1 size, +1 Dex, +4 natural)
hp 32 (5 HD)
Immune vermin immunities
Fort +6, **Ref** +2, **Will** +2

Speed 20 ft. (4 squares), fly 60 ft. (good)
Melee sting +6 (1d3+6 plus poison)
Atk Options poison (DC 14, 1d6 Dex/1d6 Dex)
Space 10 ft.; **Reach** 5 ft.
Base Atk +3; **Grp** +11

Abilities Str 18, Dex 12, Con 14, Int —, Wis 13, Cha 11
Immune vermin traits
Feats —
Skills Listen +1, Spot +9, Survival +1 (+5 to orient itself)

DARK TALON SHAMAN

An imposing reptilian humanoid, festooned with talismans, raises her hands to call lightning from the skies as she shouts a command.

DARK TALON SHAMAN   CR 6

Female lizardfolk druid 5
NE Medium humanoid (reptilian)
Init +0; **Senses** Listen +3, Spot +3
Languages Auran, Common, Draconic, Druidic

AC 18, touch 10, flat-footed 18
  (+3 armor, +5 natural)
hp 49 (7 HD)
Fort +7, **Ref** +5, **Will** +8; +4 against spell-like abilities of fey

Speed 30 ft. (6 squares); woodland stride
Melee 2 claws +4 each (1d4) and
  bite +2 (1d4)
Base Atk +4; **Grp** +4
Atk Options Blind-Fight
Special Actions spontaneous casting (*summon nature's ally* spells), wild shape 1/day (5 hours)
Combat Gear *potion of cure moderate wounds*
Druid Spells Prepared (CL 5th):
  3rd—*call lightning* (DC 16), *poison* (+4 melee touch, DC 16)
  2nd—*barkskin, bear's endurance, fog cloud*
  1st—*entangle* (DC 14), *jump, longstrider, obscuring mist*
  0—*create water, cure minor wounds, detect magic, light, resistance*

Abilities Str 10, Dex 10, Con 15, Int 12, Wis 16, Cha 12
SQ animal companion, hold breath (60 rounds), link with companion, share spells, trackless step, wild empathy +8 (+4 magical beasts)
Feats Blind-Fight, Combat Casting, Multiattack
Skills Balance +9, Concentration +10, Handle Animal +6, Jump +9, Knowledge (nature) +7, Listen +3, Ride +2, Spellcraft +5, Spot +3, Survival +9, Swim +9
Possessions combat gear plus +1 *leather armor*, *cloak of resistance* +1

Animal Companion monitor lizard (*MM* 275)

The typical Dark Talon shaman is ambitious, intelligent, and charismatic. These lizardfolk see Yarshag as a near-divine being whose dictates must be obeyed. They view nature as a destructive force that exists to serve the lizardfolk, and they are responsible for capturing and training monsters, leading warbands, and policing the tribe for heresy. They fight alongside the tribe's soldiers, though they prefer to use their spells to support assaults, wading into melee only if forced to.

The Dark Talon shaman presented here had the following ability scores before racial adjustments and Hit Dice ability score increases: Str 8, Dex 10, Con 13, Int 14, Wis 15, Cha 12.

Strategies and Tactics

A typical Dark Talon warband includes a shaman, who uses spells such as *fog cloud* to cover the troops. *Call lightning* is useful against flying enemies and targets that are too tough for the soldiers to take down quickly. The shaman keeps *obscuring mist* and *entangle* in reserve to cover a retreat or befuddle a potent foe. Other spells augment the shaman's combat potency.

YARSHAG, DARK TALON KING

The king of the Dark Talons stands before you in shining plate made of onyx-colored dragon scales. His form seems large in the bulky armor and horned helm he wears. The shield on his arm is like glistening ebony, and even his curved sword is a lustrous black. Beside him stands a massive horned beetle with a dusky carapace.

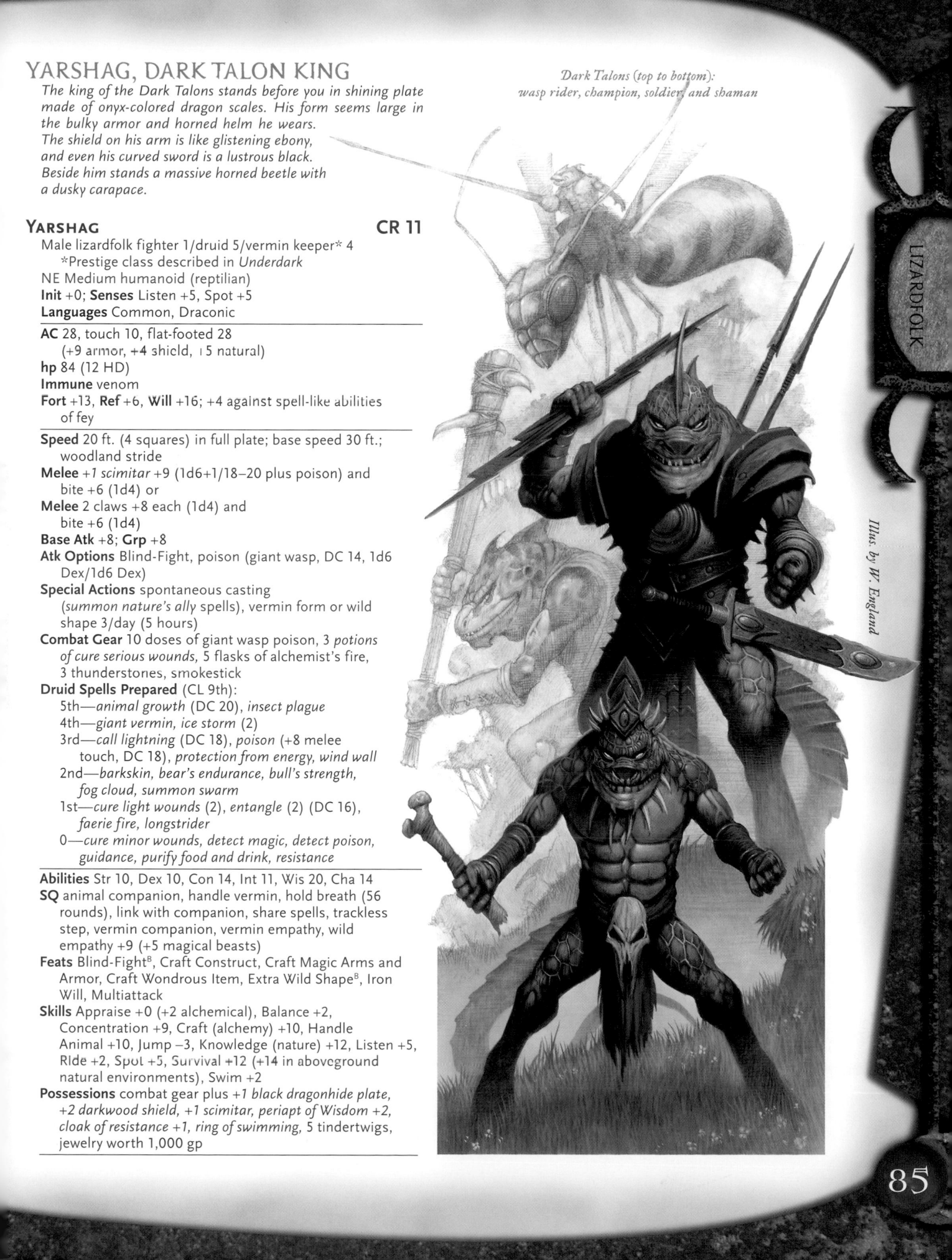

Dark Talons (top to bottom): wasp rider, champion, soldier, and shaman

YARSHAG   CR 11

Male lizardfolk fighter 1/druid 5/vermin keeper* 4
  *Prestige class described in *Underdark*
NE Medium humanoid (reptilian)
Init +0; **Senses** Listen +5, Spot +5
Languages Common, Draconic

AC 28, touch 10, flat-footed 28
  (+9 armor, +4 shield, +5 natural)
hp 84 (12 HD)
Immune venom
Fort +13, **Ref** +6, **Will** +16; +4 against spell-like abilities
  of fey

Speed 20 ft. (4 squares) in full plate; base speed 30 ft.;
  woodland stride
Melee *+1 scimitar* +9 (1d6+1/18–20 plus poison) and
  bite +6 (1d4) or
Melee 2 claws +8 each (1d4) and
  bite +6 (1d4)
Base Atk +8; **Grp** +8
Atk Options Blind-Fight, poison (giant wasp, DC 14, 1d6
  Dex/1d6 Dex)
Special Actions spontaneous casting
  (*summon nature's ally* spells), vermin form or wild
  shape 3/day (5 hours)
Combat Gear 10 doses of giant wasp poison, 3 *potions*
  of cure serious wounds, 5 flasks of alchemist's fire,
  3 thunderstones, smokestick
Druid Spells Prepared (CL 9th):
  5th—*animal growth* (DC 20), *insect plague*
  4th—*giant vermin, ice storm* (2)
  3rd—*call lightning* (DC 18), *poison* (+8 melee
    touch, DC 18), *protection from energy, wind wall*
  2nd—*barkskin, bear's endurance, bull's strength,*
    fog cloud, summon swarm
  1st—*cure light wounds* (2), *entangle* (2) (DC 16),
    faerie fire, longstrider
  0—*cure minor wounds, detect magic, detect poison,*
    guidance, purify food and drink, resistance

Abilities Str 10, Dex 10, Con 14, Int 11, Wis 20, Cha 14
SQ animal companion, handle vermin, hold breath (56
  rounds), link with companion, share spells, trackless
  step, vermin companion, vermin empathy, wild
  empathy +9 (+5 magical beasts)
Feats Blind-Fight[B], Craft Construct, Craft Magic Arms and
  Armor, Craft Wondrous Item, Extra Wild Shape[B], Iron
  Will, Multiattack
Skills Appraise +0 (+2 alchemical), Balance +2,
  Concentration +9, Craft (alchemy) +10, Handle
  Animal +10, Jump –3, Knowledge (nature) +12, Listen +5,
  Ride +2, Spot +5, Survival +12 (+14 in aboveground
  natural environments), Swim +2
Possessions combat gear plus *+1 black dragonhide plate,*
  +2 darkwood shield, +1 scimitar, periapt of Wisdom +2,
  cloak of resistance +1, ring of swimming, 5 tindertwigs,
  jewelry worth 1,000 gp

LIZARDFOLK

Illus. by W. England

Vermin Form (Su) Spend one use of wild shape to transform into a Tiny, Small, or Medium vermin. *Underdark* 45.

Handle Vermin (Ex) Apply Handle Animal to vermin. *Underdark* 45.

Vermin Empathy (Ex) Apply wild empathy to vermin. *Underdark* 45.

GIANT STAG BEETLE VERMIN COMPANION   CR —

N Large vermin

Init +0; **Senses** darkvision 60 ft.; Listen +9, Spot +9

AC 21, touch 9, flat-footed 21
   (–1 size, +12 natural)
hp 68 (9 HD)
Fort +9, **Ref** +3, **Will** +4

Speed 20 ft. (4 squares)
Melee bite +12 (4d6+10)
Atk Options trample 2d8+3
Space 10 ft.; **Reach** 5 ft.
Base Atk +6; **Grp** +17

Abilities Str 24, Dex 11, Con 17, Int 2, Wis 12, Cha 10
Feats Alertness, Cleave, Improved Bull Rush, Power Attack
Skills Listen +9, Spot +9

Trample (Ex) Reflex DC 21 half. The save DC is Strength-based.

A would-be fighter who found his place as a tribal druid, Yarshag looks the part of the lizardfolk warlord he has always wanted to be. He wears the skin of the black dragon that once oppressed his tribe, and he always surrounds himself with able-bodied defenders. Not one to lead an attack from the front rank, Yarshag supports his troops from a safe position where he can observe and cast spells. When a battle is won, he ceremoniously rides his vermin companion in to claim the credit and the best spoils.

Yarshag had the following ability scores before racial adjustments, Hit Dice ability score increases, and equipment bonuses: Str 8, Dex 10, Con 12, Int 13, Wis 15, Cha 14.

Strategies and Tactics

Yarshag is never alone. His personal retinue includes two fang golems (see page 72), a shambling mound (under a *command plants* spell), half a dozen Dark Talon champions, two Dark Talon shamans, and his beetle companion.

When Yarshag fights, he relies on his spells. Selfish to the core, he uses every augmenting spell he has on himself and his companion if he has time. In the first round of combat, he has his fang golems engage the enemy and casts *ice storm* on the ensuing melee. He then casts *call lightning,* so he always has the option of lashing out with a lightning bolt during his turn. If he needs to, he uses *wind wall* to fend off accurate ranged attacks.

To insure his attackers have little chance to get to him quickly without magical aid, Yarshag casts *animal growth* as soon as he can on the monitor lizards that serve the two Dark Talon shamans. The Dark Talon king follows that up with a *giant vermin* spell cast on three spiders he carries in a ceramic flask. Later in the battle, he might spontaneously cast *summon nature's ally* to conjure reptiles or elementals, further stymieing direct assaults.

Should the clash take a turn for the worst, Yarshag casts *entangle* followed by *fog cloud*. He uses *fog cloud* immediately if a melee combatant directly attacks him. He then takes the form of a giant wasp for added mobility and an easy method of escape, using Blind-Fight (or *faerie fire*) to get the better of his assailant. If forced into direct melee, Yarshag uses his scimitar (with poison) or his claws. He casts *poison* on one of his attackers if he can afford the risk. He still uses *fog cloud* and his giant wasp vermin form when the going gets rough.

If defeat seems imminent, Yarshag expects his followers to fight to the death—he gladly sacrifices them for his survival. The king of the Dark Talons would rather die than actually surrender, but he might feign capitulation to buy himself time. In any case, the form of a Tiny vermin provides an easy opportunity for a timely getaway.

Other Creatures and Allies

In addition to the tactics discussed earlier, a Dark Talon army marches into battle with a number of monstrous allies. Shambling mounds use their mighty tendrils to rip apart a town's fortifications. Stirges swarm over the battlefield, descending upon enemy soldiers moments before the Dark Talon's army attacks. Ankhegs burrow tunnels under walls, creating breaches for Dark Talon soldiers, and attack enemy troops from underneath or behind. The appearance of lizardfolk riding giant wasps and a bank of fog is often the beginning of the end for the Dark Talon's foes, most of whom expect a simple, direct attack.

Ankhegs (*MM* 14): The Dark Talons managed to capture several clutches of ankheg eggs. Now these beasts serve as tunnelers (for sieges and home building) and guardians.

Assassin Vines (*MM* 20): The tribe's druids plant these creatures along unused paths and in out-of-the-way places near Dark Talon settlements.

Blackscale Lizardfolk (*MM III* 95): These towering brutes are among the most fanatical members of the Dark Talon tribe.

Fang Golems (page 72): Yarshag has imparted the techniques for making these creatures to his subordinates. A few of the most potent Dark Talon shamanss have made fang golems for themselves.

Giant and Monstrous Vermin (*MM* 285): Dark Talon druids include a number of vermin keepers, who train giant wasps to accept riders and other monstrous vermin to serve as war beasts.

Lizardfolk (*MM* 169): Many of the tribe's combatants are normal lizardfolk.

Poison Dusk Lizardfolk (*MM III* 96): The Dark Talons include several clans of these lizardfolk. They serve as scouts and weaponsmiths.

Shambling Mounds (*MM* 222): Shambling mounds serve as living siege weapons in the Dark Talon war machine. Powerful shamans sometimes ride these monstrous plants into battle.

Stirges (*MM* 236): Dark Talon druids tend several storms of stirges, which in turn serve the tribe in war.

SAMPLE ENCOUNTERS

The Dark Talons' tactics have thus far been effective in overwhelming villages and small towns on the swamp's edge. Tales have spread through the land of a sinister mist that rolls in from the swamp and brings terrible monsters. The fear and uncertainty bred by such rumors sometimes causes the tribe's enemies to flee in panic rather than stand and fight.

Scouting Party (EL 6): Two Dark Talon soldiers, along with a wasp rider and his mount, patrol Dark Talon territory for intruders. The wasp rider locates the enemy and then reports to the soldiers. Once the soldiers strike, the wasp rider attacks from above to pick off spellcasters or outflank the enemy. Sometimes a wasp rider scouts ahead of a single blackscale lizardfolk.

Raiders (EL 8): A Dark Talon shaman and four soldiers form a raiding party to test and estimate defenses before a Dark Talon assault. A raiding band might instead include a shaman, four poison dusk lizardfolk, and a poison dusk lieutenant (ranger 3) on a quick and stealthy survey mission.

HISTORY

The Dark Talon tribe arose from a peaceful lizardfolk clan called the Emerald Eyes. For years, a black dragon ruled over the Emerald Eyes' swamp, and the lizardfolk were forced to give the dragon tribute—usually a few young lizardfolk for its larder—in return for their continued existence. A greedy and ambitious druid named Yarshag, who was the tribe's elder shaman, helped broker the deal. Yarshag thereby won a bit of the dragon's favor, and he undermined or quietly murdered those lizardfolk who spoke out against this ghastly arrangement.

One day, a band of dragonslayers entered the swamp to find and kill the black dragon. They sought the Emerald Eyes' help in finding the dragon's lair. When Yarshag saw that the interlopers were actually strong enough to eliminate the dragon, he gladly betrayed his mistress and offered to lead the hunters to her. However, he secretly bid his beetle companion to bear a message of warning to the dragon. If the slayers won their battle, Yarshag would be hailed as a wise leader who seized the chance to free his people. If the dragon was victorious, surely she would reward Yarshag for leading the intruders to their doom.

The battle between the slayers and the black dragon turned out far better than Yarshag could have dreamt. They slew the dragon, but only one of them, a dwarf berserker, survived. Yarshag hid during the clash and watched from a distance, and when the dragon fell, the treacherous druid leapt upon the dwarf and finished him off. Thus, Yarshag was left with the dragon's hoard and, more important, a small clutch of dragon eggs.

Yarshag believed that he could hatch the dragons and harvest their blood, then employ the liquid to impart draconic strength and cunning to the tribe's young. He perfected this process on his own children, making them stronger, tougher, and faster. With the great wealth looted from the dragon's trove, he instilled greed and ambition in the tribe. Lizardfolk who received his gifts swore personal allegiance to him, cul-

minating in a coup that placed Yarshag on the throne. The few who spoke against Yarshag's plans, particularly his desire to expand his experiments to all the tribe's young, were then cowed or killed.

Since Yarshag's rise to power, he has inflamed the tribe's covetousness and hatred for the outside world. These two passions combine to make the newly renamed Dark Talon tribe into a powerful force. Tribal druids have tamed and raised a number of swamp monsters. Evangelists from the tribe have formed alliances with other lizardfolk. The clans that ally with Yarshag's tribe become part of the Dark Talon's army. Those that resist become targets for conquest.

Unless Yarshag is defeated and his horrific experiments ended, he could leave behind an enduring legacy of destruction, misery, and warfare.

Environment: Lizardfolk usually inhabit temperate marshes, but the Dark Talons prefer underwater, air-filled caves and burrows accessible only by swimming. Such locations are highly defensible and difficult to detect.

Typical Physical Characteristics: The elite of the Dark Talon tribe have been infused with black dragon blood through Yarshag's alchemical process. They are larger, faster, and tougher than ordinary lizardfolk, close to 7 feet tall and weighing nearly 250 pounds. Their scales are dusky, reflecting their draconic heritage.

Yarshag's process warps the young lizardfolk's minds as it enhances and strengthens their bodies. These tendencies breed true in the next generation of lizardfolk, without Yarshag's influence.

Alignment: The Dark Talons' ferocity and cruelty set these lizardfolk apart from others. These stronger, tougher specimens have a natural disposition toward violence. They're not arbitrary in their attacks, however, nor are they wantonly destructive. Dark Talon lizardfolk are often neutral evil, but a great number of them are neutral.

DARK TALON LIZARDFOLK LORE

Characters with ranks in Knowledge (local) can learn more about Dark Talon lizardfolk. When a character makes a successful skill check, the following lore is revealed, including the information from lower DCs.

Knowledge (Local)

DC	Result
11	This is a lizardfolk, a reptilian humanoid, who belongs to the Dark Talon tribe. This result reveals all humanoid and reptilian traits.
16	Many Dark Talon lizardfolk are stronger, faster, and tougher than their ordinary kin. The tribe also includes clans of blackscale and poison dusk lizardfolk.
21	The Dark Talons were once a peaceful clan but have become aggressive conquerors who are spreading rapidly and overwhelming small settlements.
26	Yarshag, the Dark Talon king, developed an alchemical process to infuse lizardfolk with black dragon blood and continues to experiment on the tribe's young.

SOCIETY

Yarshag is the king of the Dark Talon tribe, and his most trusted lieutenants serve as field commanders and lords of smaller settlements and Dark Talon domains. By forcing his most powerful underlings to scatter across a number of villages and regions, Yarshag makes it almost impossible for potential rivals to organize and overthrow him. These feudal leaders have tremendous autonomy in their territory, but they all know that any failure invariably leads to execution. Yarshag rules by fear, yet he richly rewards those lizardfolk who best serve his needs.

Clergy among the Dark Talons are all druids. These lizardfolk have abandoned the worship of Semuanya because Yarshag teaches that the god is dead, slain by the deities of other races. Yarshag claims that the deity's spirit appeared to him in a dream and exhorted him to wreak vengeance upon the civilized races. This philosophy helps stoke the fury of the lizardfolk, particularly those that feel wronged by peoples from beyond the swamps. The emerging Dark Talon cult holds that Yarshag is a deific figure who will one day lead the lizardfolk to control the world. Religious impetus also helps overcome the fears and concerns some lizardfolk feel about mingling black dragon blood with their precious eggs. The strong, vicious lizardfolk born of such tampering seem to confirm Yarshag's teachings that their people must engage in a campaign against all other humanoids.

The Dark Talon tribe measures stature and prestige solely in terms of success in battle. Trophies taken from fallen opponents, treasure looted from cities, and other tangible items serve as an easy barometer for a soldier's success. Females are just as likely to become soldiers as males, particularly those strengthened by Yarshag's process. Dark Talons also win honor and prestige for the deeds of their children. This social impetus ensures the tribe's numbers remain high. It also demands expansion into new territory.

A typical Dark Talon village is a heavily armed and defended fortress. It features a wooden palisade or thick brambles tended by the village's druids—a barrier that serves as cover and a rallying point should the community come under attack. Within these outer defenses, the Dark Talons build their homes with the assumption that they will eventually be assaulted. They prefer underwater, air-filled caves and burrows, but if such dwellings aren't possible, the lizardfolk live in burrowed mounds or huts. Pathways between the burrows are filled with pit traps, snares, and other hazards. If the village is attacked, the noncombatants rush to set these traps before taking cover in the burrows.

The central structure of a Dark Talon village is a labyrinthine collection of narrow tunnels, flooded passages, and tight quarters. This place serves as the living space for the druid who leads the village. A larger settlement, or one recently converted to Dark Talon control, usually holds one of the black dragon hatchlings that provides the blood needed to enhance unborn lizardfolk. The dragon is kept deep within a room in the central complex and fed heavy doses of a poison that reduces its intellect and keeps it docile.

This horrific chamber also holds dozens of lizardfolk eggs, a crude alchemist's lab that processes the blood, and tools used to seed each egg with the vile concoction.

Dark Talon soldiers keep watch at a community's palisade. Contingents of four or more guards protect key points in the settlement, the importance of the post determining the number and strength of its sentinels. If an attack breaches the wall, the soldiers leap from the top of one burrow to another during the ensuing melee, avoiding the traps.

Yarshag and the Dark Talon tribe have one weakness that could potentially spell their doom. Several lizardfolk clerics of Semuanya, along with their followers, have secretly formed an underground resistance. These lizardfolk know Semuanya isn't dead. They are horrified by Yarshag's tampering with their people's eggs. They watch friends and allies being conquered or forced to submit to Yarshag, and they endure while icons to their god are cast down and destroyed. With the right allies, these lizardfolk could lead an uprising that ends Yarshag's evil forever.

TYPICAL TREASURE

Dark Talon lizardfolk have standard treasure for their Challenge Rating. The soldiers adorn themselves with trinkets from fallen foes. A Dark Talon village features dozens of banners, crude statues, and other landmarks festooned with trophies that proclaim each soldier's accomplishments. Each marker stands outside a soldier's dwelling.

FOR PLAYER CHARACTERS

Dark Talon lizardfolk champions wield weapons they call maquahuitl. These martial weapons are greatclubs embellished with teeth or claws so that they deal piercing damage as well as bludgeoning damage.

Dmg (S)	Dmg (M)	Critical	Weight[1]	Type
1d8	1d10	×2	10 lb.	Bludgeoning and piercing

1 Weight is for a Medium weapon. Small weapons weigh half as much, and Large weapons weigh twice as much.

DARK TALON LIZARDFOLK AS CHARACTERS

See page 169 of the *Monster Manual* for information on lizardfolk as characters. Other than their physical enhancements, reflected in game terms by elite statistics, Dark Talon lizardfolk have the same racial abilities as their ordinary kin.

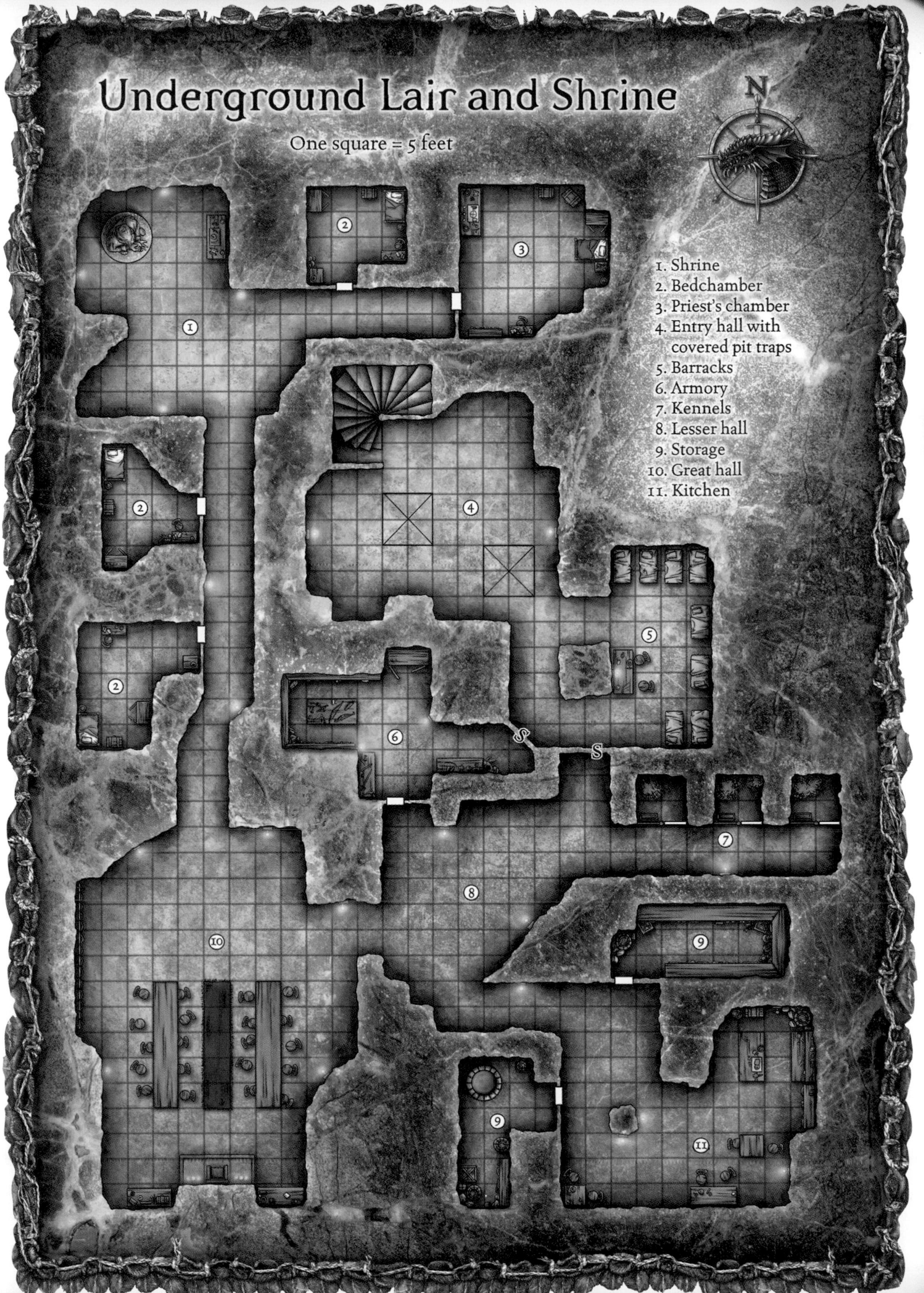

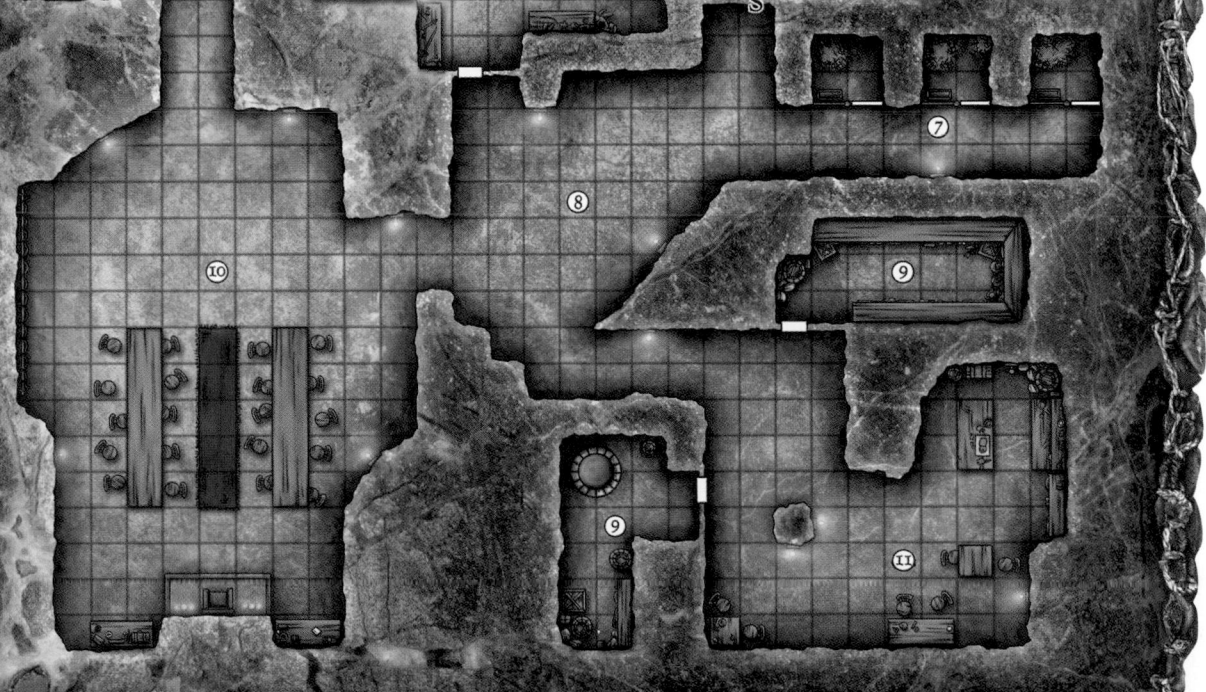

Underground Lair and Shrine

One square = 5 feet

N

1. Shrine
2. Bedchamber
3. Priest's chamber
4. Entry hall with covered pit traps
5. Barracks
6. Armory
7. Kennels
8. Lesser hall
9. Storage
10. Great hall
11. Kitchen

LODESTONE MARAUDER

This frightful creature stalks about on four enormous legs. Its skin resembles dull metal and is covered in rusty spikes.

LODESTONE MARAUDER   CR 9

Usually N Large aberration
Init +5; **Senses** darkvision 60 ft.; Listen +8, Spot +8
Languages —

AC 24, touch 10, flat-footed 23; magnetic defense
   (–1 size, +1 Dex, +14 natural)
hp 115 (11 HD)
Resist stability (+4 against bull rush and trip)
Fort +9, **Ref** +4, **Will** +8

Speed 30 ft. (6 squares), burrow 20 ft., climb 20 ft.
Melee bite +15 (1d8+7) and
   2 claws +12 each (1d6+3)
Space 10 ft.; **Reach** 10 ft.
Base Atk +8; **Grp** +19
Atk Options Power Attack
Special Actions magnetic attraction, magnetic repulsion

Abilities Str 24, Dex 13, Con 22, Int 2, Wis 12, Cha 8
SQ magnetic defense, stability
Feats Improved Initiative, Multiattack, Power Attack,
   Weapon Focus (bite)
Skills Climb +15, Listen +8, Spot +8
Advancement 12–20 HD (Large)

Magnetic Defense (Su) A lodestone marauder gains a +4 deflection bonus to AC against all attacks from sources made wholly or substantially of metal.

Stability (Ex) A lodestone marauder has a +4 bonus on ability checks made to resist being bull rushed or tripped when standing on the ground (but not when climbing, flying, or otherwise not standing firmly on the ground).

Magnetic Attraction (Su) A lodestone marauder can create a pulse of magnetic energy within a 30-foot-radius emanation that sends metal objects hurtling toward it. An affected creature carrying such an object must succeed on a DC 21 Reflex save or drop the object in its space. Objects fastened down in some way, such as properly donned armor, automatically succeed on the save. At the marauder's option, held or unattended objects that fail this save are drawn in a straight line toward it. Such objects stick to its body, and they can be removed only on the marauder's death or with a DC 21 Strength check. The save and check DCs are Constitution-based.

Magnetic Repulsion (Su) This ability works like magnetic attraction, except repulsion pushes objects away from the marauder within a 30-foot-radius burst. An affected creature carrying such an object must succeed on a DC 21 Reflex save or drop the object in its space. All creatures wearing metal armor or carrying metal shields within the area of the marauder must suceed on DC 21 Reflex saves or be knocked prone. The save DC is Constitution-based.

Skills Lodestone marauders have a +8 racial bonus on Climb checks. A lodestone marauder can always choose to take 10 on Climb checks, even if rushed or threatened.

Lodestone marauders are dangerous aberrations with an insatiable appetite for flesh and metal. They are sometimes trained as guardians for vaults, armories, and other strongholds.

STRATEGIES AND TACTICS

A lodestone marauder is not a subtle creature. It knows its most formidable weapons are its magnetic abilities, and it uses them to keep its foes off balance and disarmed. A hungry lodestone marauder first produces a burst of magnetic repulsion and follows this up with attraction. When creatures draw near, it rips into them with its fearsome claws and fangs.

"The marauder tunneled into the armory almost a week ago. Our warriors were tossed around like rag dolls and none could get close enough to harm the beast. One of our tunnel runners reported that the monster was last seen feasting on the racks of hammers and axes."
—Magda Armbrichter, quartermaster

SAMPLE ENCOUNTERS

A lodestone marauder is often encountered individually. It terrorizes a location and moves on once it has gorged itself.

Individual (EL 9): Most lodestone marauders are solitary threats that are attracted to places with large amounts of metal or creatures that carry metallic objects.

EL 9: A mature lodestone marauder recently moved into a small barony. It is drawn to the large amounts of steel to be found there, the result of the baron's recent preparations for a military campaign.

Mated Pair (EL 11): Lodestone marauders seek mates, and breeding pairs lair together.

EL 11: Sahn Ilmat, a powerful necromancer, raised two lodestone marauders, now a mated pair, to act as sentries for his laboratory. They escaped captivity and now roam the wilds looking for food and a place to live.

ECOLOGY

Lodestone marauders are the result of magical experimentation and have no place in the natural world. They were

---

LODESTONE MARAUDER LORE

Characters with ranks in Knowledge (dungeoneering) can learn more about lodestone marauders. When a character makes a successful skill check, the following lore is revealed, including the information from lower DCs.

Knowledge (Dungeoneering)

DC	Result
19	This is a lodestone marauder, a strange aberration. This result reveals all aberration traits.
24	Lodestone marauders eat metal objects and possess the ability to attract or repel metal.
29	Metallic weapons are less effective against lodestone marauders. The creatures have some sort of deflective field.
34	Lodestone marauders are smart enough to be trained as guardians.

originally bred as guardians, but most were too wild for this task and escaped. Some remain in captivity, where they serve in their original roles.

These creatures spend their time hunting for prey and large caches of metal. They can subsist on both meat and metallic objects. Their bodies assimilate metal and use the "nutrients" in the substance to enhance their hides. As a lodestone marauder grows, so too do the number and size of the spikes on its body. A marauder that subsists on raw ore grows more slowly than one that feasts on worked metal objects.

Simple-minded and focused on eating and protecting their hunting grounds, lodestone marauders act much like territorial animals. Larger, older individuals fend off younger interlopers that attempt to take over.

If a lodestone marauder locates an area with plentiful food, it gorges itself and establishes a den. There, it gathers a pile of metallic objects to attract a mate. Courtship is brief, but mates are usually lifelong companions.

After breeding, females lay two to six iron-encased eggs, which are tended by both parents and hatch in two months. Lodestone marauder infants stay with their parents for about six months and then leave to establish their own territories. No familial bond remains.

Environment: Lodestone marauders are commonly found in mountainous areas and underground wherever iron deposits are plentiful. However, some find their way into populated areas, posing a serious danger to the inhabitants.

Typical Physical Characteristics: A bulky quadruped, a lodestone marauder is 10 feet tall and long, weighing 3,500 pounds. Jagged, rusty spikes cover its metal-infused body, and the creature moves about on spindly but powerful legs that end in terrible hooks. Its mouth is filled with numerous mandibles that are capable of shattering iron and steel. Visually, it's impossible to tell the difference between male and female lodestone marauders.

Alignment: Lodestone marauders are typically neutral. As animalistic creatures driven by basic needs, they are unconcerned with ethical matters. Their voracious nature pushes some toward chaos or evil, however, while guardian lodestone marauders are sometimes lawful.

TYPICAL TREASURE

Lodestone marauders often carry a number of metallic objects on their carapaces, which they con-

sider food rather than treasure. A lodestone marauder has standard treasure for its Challenge Rating, about 4,500 gp, which is made up exclusively of metal items.

FOR PLAYER CHARACTERS

Training a lodestone marauder to take orders requires six weeks of work and a DC 20 Handle Animal check. Marauder eggs are worth 4,000 gp apiece on the open market, while young are worth 6,000 gp. Professional trainers charge 2,500 gp to rear or train a lodestone marauder.

LODESTONE MARAUDERS IN EBERRON

Lodestone marauders are common in the Mror Holds, where they are drawn to both the iron deposits in the mountains and the vast armories in the vaults of the dwarves. A few enterprising dwarves capture newborn lodestone marauders and train them as guardians.

LODESTONE MARAUDERS IN FAERÛN

Lodestone marauders can be found all over Faerûn. They are most common in the Underdark, where they prey on the hordes of drow, duergar, and other underground dwellers. The boldest races capture them for training.

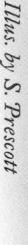

Illus. by S. Prescott

Lodestone marauder

LOLTH-TOUCHED CREATURE

Lolth-touched creatures are blessed specially by the Spider Goddess of the drow. They are stronger, tougher, and sneakier than normal.

LOLTH-TOUCHED BEBILITH

An immense, twisted, spiderlike fiend looms above you. The emblem of a spider is limned faintly on its monstrous head.

LOLTH-TOUCHED BEBILITH	**CR 11**

Always CE Huge outsider (chaotic, evil, extraplanar)
Init +5; **Senses** darkvision 60 ft., scent; Listen +16, Spot +16
Languages understands Abyssal, telepathy 100 ft.

AC 22, touch 9, flat-footed 21
   (–2 size, +1 Dex, +13 natural)
hp 186 (12 HD); **DR** 10/good
Immune fear
Fort +19, **Ref** +9, **Will** +9

Speed 40 ft. (8 squares), climb 20 ft.
Melee bite +22 (2d6+12 plus poison) and
   2 claws +17 each (2d4+6)
Ranged web +11 touch (entangle)
Space 15 ft.; **Reach** 10 ft.
Base Atk +12; **Grp** +36
Atk Options Cleave, Power Attack, aligned strike (chaotic, evil), poison (DC 27, 1d6 Con/2d6 Con), rend armor
Special Actions plane shift (self only)

Abilities Str 34, Dex 12, Con 32, Int 11, Wis 13, Cha 13
Feats Cleave, Improved Initiative, Improved Grapple, Power Attack, Track
Skills Climb +35, Diplomacy +3, Hide +20, Jump +31, Listen +16, Move Silently +20, Search +15, Sense Motive +16, Spot +16, Survival +1 (+3 following tracks)
Advancement 13–18 HD (Huge); 19–36 HD (Gargantuan)

Web (Ex) A Lolth-touched bebilith can throw a web up to four times per day. This is similar to an attack with a net but has a maximum range of 30 feet, with a range increment of 10 feet, and is effective against targets of up to Gargantuan size. The web anchors the target in place, allowing no movement.
   An entangled creature can escape the web with a DC 27 Escape Artist check or burst it with a DC 27 Strength check. The check DCs are Constitution-based. The web has 14 hit points and hardness 0. It has a 75% chance of not burning when any sort of fire is applied to it (check each round).
Rend Armor (Ex) A Lolth-touched bebilith that hits with both claw attacks pulls apart any armor worn by its foe. This attack automatically deals 4d6+24 points of damage to the opponent's armor. Armor reduced to 0 hit points is destroyed.
Plane Shift (Su) As the *plane shift* spell; at will; caster level 12th.
Skills A Lolth-touched bebilith's dark, mottled coloration gives it a +12 racial bonus on Hide checks. It has a +4 racial bonus on Move Silently checks. A Lolth-touched bebilith has a +8 racial bonus on Climb checks and can always choose to take 10 on Climb checks, even if rushed or threatened.

When Lolth so favors a bebilith, she usually has a special purpose in mind. Such spider demons often hunt down and destroy driders. Whether this is an inexplicable further test of those supposedly failed drow or just an expression of hatred, none can say.

Strategies and Tactics

A Lolth-touched bebilith is a cunning predator like its kin, but its improved physical characteristics make its webs harder to escape and its poison more deadly. Its toughness and fearlessness make it bolder, and it's less likely to retreat from battle. It starts out using a generous amount of its base attack bonus with Power Attack, backing off on this aggressiveness only when it finds its targets too hard to hit.

LOLTH-TOUCHED DROW RANGER

This lithe humanoid has ink-black skin and a shock of white hair. She appears stronger than others of her kind, and her shadowy armor is adorned with a spider emblem.

LOLTH-TOUCHED DROW RANGER	**CR 7**

Female drow ranger 5
CE Medium humanoid (elf)
Init +2; **Senses** darkvision 120 ft.; Listen +10, Spot +10
Languages Common, Elven, Undercommon

AC 16, touch 12, flat-footed 14; Dodge
   (+2 Dex, +4 armor)
hp 46 (5 HD)
Immune fear, sleep
SR 16
Fort +8, **Ref** +6, **Will** +2 (+4 against enchantments);
   +4 against spells and spell-like abilities of fey
Weakness light blindness

Speed 30 ft. (6 squares)
Melee +1 *scimitar* +11 (1d6+7/18–20) and
   mwk short sword +10 (1d6+3/19–20) or
Melee +1 *scimitar* +13 (1d6+7/18–20)
Ranged mwk hand crossbow +8 (1d4/19–20 plus poison)
Base Atk +5; **Grp** +11
Atk Options favored enemy aberrations +4, favored enemy humans +2, poison (drow poison, DC 13, unconsciousness 1 minute/unconsciousness 2d4 hours)
Combat Gear 3 doses of drow poison, 2 *potions of cure moderate wounds*, *potion of barkskin* (+3)
Ranger Spells Prepared (CL 2nd):
   1st—*longstrider*
Spell-Like Abilities (CL 5th):
   1/day—*dancing lights, darkness, faerie fire*

Abilities Str 22, Dex 15, Con 18, Int 10, Wis 12, Cha 12
SQ able to notice secret or concealed doors, animal companion, link with companion, share spells, wild empathy +6 (+2 magical beasts)
Feats Dodge, Endurance[B], Track[B], Two-Weapon Fighting[B], Weapon Focus (scimitar)
Skills Hide +14, Knowledge (dungeoneering) +6, Knowledge (nature) +4, Knowledge (religion) +1, Listen +10, Move Silently +19, Search +2, Spot +10, Survival +9 (+11 underground)
Possessions combat gear plus +1 *silent moves studded leather*, +1 *scimitar*, masterwork short sword, masterwork hand crossbow with 20 bolts

Animal Companion Medium viper (*MM* 280).
Skills A Lolth-touched drow ranger has a +4 racial bonus on Hide and Move Silently checks.

A Lolth-touched drow ranger is a fierce hunter who scouts the caverns and corridors of the underground, taking out enemies she can handle alone, and leading her strike team against others. The Lolth-touched drow ranger presented here had the following ability scores before racial adjustments and Hit Dice ability score increases: Str 15, Dex 13, Con 14, Int 8, Wis 12, Cha 10.

Strategies and Tactics

A Lolth-touched drow ranger specializes in surprise attacks. She prefers to track her prey unnoticed until the tactical situation is right, then attack with surprise if possible. Before entering combat, she drinks her potion of *barkskin* and casts *longstrider* on herself. Her viper animal companion weakens opponents with its poisonous bite and helps to set up flanking situations.

LOLTH-TOUCHED MONSTROUS SPIDER

An enormous, dusky spider looms ahead. Its swollen body, marked by a faint emblem, arches up on powerful legs as it lunges.

LOLTH-TOUCHED MONSTROUS
HUNTING SPIDER   CR 3
Always CE Large vermin
Init +3; **Senses** darkvision 60 ft., tremorsense 60 ft.; Listen +0, Spot +8
Languages —

AC 14, touch 12, flat-footed 11
   (−1 size, +3 Dex, +2 natural)
hp 34 (4 HD)
Immune vermin immunities
Fort +8, **Ref** +4, **Will** +1

Speed 30 ft. (6 squares), climb 20 ft.
Melee bite +7 (1d8+7 plus poison)
Ranged web +5 touch (entangle)

Space 10 ft.; **Reach** 5 ft.
Base Atk +3; **Grp** +12
Atk Options poison (DC 16, 1d6 Str/1d6 Str)

Abilities Str 21, Dex 17, Con 18, Int —, Wis 10, Cha 2
Feats —
Skills Climb +13, Hide +7, Jump +15, Listen +0, Move Silently +7, Spot +8
Advancement 5–7 HD (Large)

Web (Ex) A Lolth-touched monstrous spider can throw a web eight times per day. This is similar to an attack with a net but has a maximum range of 100 feet, with a range increment of 20 feet, and is effective against targets up to one size category larger than the spider. The web anchors the target in place, allowing no movement.
   An entangled creature can escape the web with a successful DC 21 Escape Artist check or burst it with a DC 21 Strength check. The check DCs are Strength-based and include a +4 racial bonus. The web has 12 hit points and hardness 0, and takes double damage from fire.
Skills Lolth-touched monstrous hunting spiders have a +10 racial bonus on Jump checks; a +8 racial bonus on Climb, Hide, and Spot checks; and a +4 racial bonus on Move Silently checks. A Lolth-touched monstrous spider can always choose to take 10 on Climb checks, even if rushed or threatened.

This is a monstrous hunting spider exalted to sentinel status in a temple to Lolth.

Strategies and Tactics

A Lolth-touched monstrous spider behaves much like a spider of its size, but it is unafraid of larger or tougher prey.

CREATING A LOLTH-TOUCHED CREATURE

"Lolth-touched" is an acquired template that can be added to any nongood, nonlawful, corporeal living creature (referred to hereafter as the base creature).

    Challenge Rating: Same as the base creature +1.
    Alignment: The creature's alignment changes to chaotic evil.

Illus. by J. Nelson

Lolth-touched bebilith, drow, and monstrous spider

Abilities: Increase from the base creature as follows: Str +6, Con +6.

Skills: A Lolth-touched creature gains a +4 racial bonus on Hide and Move Silently checks.

Special Qualities: A Lolth-touched creature has all the special qualities of the base creature, plus the following special quality.

Fearless (Ex): Lolth-touched creatures have immunity to all fear effects.

Level Adjustment: Same as the base creature +1.

SAMPLE ENCOUNTERS

Lolth-touched creatures are a select few who usually lead or support groups of their lesser kin. They accompany priestesses of Lolth, guard the god's temples, and serve as enhanced mounts or war beasts in drow armies. Occasionally, a favored drow servant of Lolth might be so blessed.

Individual (EL 1–12): A single Lolth-touched creature is usually an elite guardian or agent.

EL 3: A Lolth-touched Large monstrous spider lurks among the spider carvings in a minor temple to Lolth. Its superior Hide skill makes it difficult to distinguish from its surroundings, and it waits until potential prey has wandered close before it strikes. A drow vermin keeper (*Underdark* 44) has trained the spider after a fashion, so that it does not attack anyone displaying the holy symbol of Lolth.

EL 11: A Lolth-touched bebilith prowls the walls of a subterranean chasm, hunting the driders that inhabit cliff dwellings and caves within. Sometimes it takes a web-swathed victim with it to the Abyss, either to eat at its leisure or at the behest of the Queen of the Demonweb Pits.

Patrol (EL 3–15): The Lolth-touched often rise to positions of leadership among the drow, commanding elite squads that patrol the subterranean territory near drow cities.

EL 9: In'zadila, a Lolth-touched ranger as described above, is charged with hunting the choldriths (*Monsters of Faerûn* 27), who lead their chitine followers in raids against her home city. Although she often works alone when spying on chitine activities, when she acts decisively, she leads a squad of four 4th-level drow rangers as a strike team.

LOLTH-TOUCHED CREATURE LORE

Characters with ranks in Knowledge (religion) can learn more about Lolth-touched creatures. When a character makes a successful skill check, the following lore is revealed, including the information from lower DCs.

The base creature and its characteristics must be identified using the appropriate skill according to the base creature's type.

Knowledge (Religion)

DC	Result
15	This is a Lolth-touched creature, a superior specimen. Lolth is the spider goddess of the drow and Queen of the Demonweb Pits.
15 + CR	Lolth-touched creatures can be of almost any kind, and they have greatly increased Strength and Constitution. They are utterly fearless.

ECOLOGY

Lolth-touched creatures exist alongside drow and their allies. Sometimes they serve Lolth directly in the Demonweb or are sent on specific missions by the Queen of Spiders.

Environment: Lolth-touched creatures are usually found underground, regardless of the base creature's normal habitat. Most such creatures were natives of the underground.

Lolth-touched creatures that serve the Queen of Spiders directly dwell in the Demonweb, the 66th layer of the Abyss.

Typical Physical Characteristics: A Lolth-touched creature is more muscular and bulkier than ordinary creatures of its kind. It stands taller if it is bipedal, and its coloration is darker than would be natural for the base creature. This coloration allows a Lolth-touched creature to fade into the shadows more easily. Sometimes it sports a faint emblem of a spider to mark its favored status.

Alignment: A Lolth-touched creature shifts its alignment to chaotic evil, matching that of the Spider Goddess.

TYPICAL TREASURE

If the base creature ordinarily possesses treasure, the Lolth-touched creature does too, according to its Challenge Rating. Lolth-touched creatures favor the same sorts of items as do normal specimens of their kind.

LOLTH-TOUCHED CREATURES IN EBERRON

Lolth is not present in the mainstream pantheons of Eberron, nor is she worshiped among the lesser sects. Most of Eberron's drow revere the Fury, and this sinister goddess of passion fills the role of Lolth in many respects. The Lolth-touched template can be used in an Eberron campaign with no changes, creating "Fury-touched" creatures instead. Drow of Xen'drik worship Vulkoor, a scorpion deity who might favor his followers in the same way.

The Cults of the Dragon Below are numerous and varied. Objects of their worship might be ancient fiends or spirits no longer remembered in the civilized lands, so introducing Lolth into an Eberron campaign is as simple as creating a cult that worships a spider demon. Lolth could even be a rakshasa rajah, a potent fiendish overlord trapped deep within Khyber.

LOLTH-TOUCHED CREATURES IN FAERÛN

Drow judicators (*Underdark* 33) are feared knights who serve Selvetarm, the Champion of Lolth. Their service grants them many fearsome powers, and they can call spiderlike monsters as servants. These dread champions are often blessed as Lolth-touched, which makes them much more dangerous in combat and strengthens their venom while in spider form. A particularly blessed judicator might have a Lolth-touched servant as well.

In the drow metropolis of Menzoberranzan, Lolth-touched guardians protect the training academies on Tier Breche. Lolth-touched bodyguards also attend the high nobles when they venture out of the questionable safety of their estates.

LUNAR RAVAGER

For a moment, the tall, humanoid figure seems to flicker like moonlight reflected on a pond. It hefts a massive, crescent-bladed battleaxe in one hand and a shield emblazoned with crescent moons in the other. Its eyes have a pale, malevolent glint.

LUNAR RAVAGER   CR 7
Usually CE Large fey
Init +7; **Senses** superior low-light vision; Listen +19, Spot +19
Languages Common, Giant

AC 24, touch 12, flat-footed 21
   (−1 size, +3 Dex, +4 armor, +3 shield, +5 natural)
hp 105 (14 HD); **DR** 5/magic and cold iron
Fort +8, **Ref** +12, **Will** +11

Speed 40 ft. (8 squares)
Melee mwk battleaxe +14/+9 (2d6+6/×3)
Ranged javelin +9 (1d8+6)
Space 10 ft.; **Reach** 10 ft.
Base Atk +7; **Grp** +17
Atk Options Cleave, Power Attack
Spell-Like Abilities (CL 14th):
   At will—*air walk, faerie fire*
   3/day—*invisibility* (self only), *pass without trace*
   1/day—*clairaudience/clairvoyance* (see text)

Abilities Str 23, Dex 16, Con 18, Int 11, Wis 14, Cha 8
SQ moon rider
Feats Cleave, Improved Initiative, Power Attack, Track, Weapon Focus (battleaxe)
Skills Hide +15*, Jump +9, Knowledge (nature) +19, Listen +19, Move Silently +19, Spot +19, Survival +19 (+21 in aboveground natural environments)
   *A lunar ravager gains a +10 racial bonus on Hide checks made outdoors at night.
Advancement by character class; **Favored Class** barbarian; see text
Possessions +1 *studded leather armor*, +1 *heavy wooden shield*, masterwork battleaxe, 8 javelins, bronze signaling horn

Superior Low-Light Vision (Ex) A lunar ravager can see five times as far as a human can in shadowy illumination, and ten times as far if moonlight is present.
Clairaudience/Clairvoyance (Sp) Visual only; a lunar ravager can view only areas it is familiar with, which must be illuminated with moonlight at the time of the viewing.
Moon Rider (Su) As the *greater teleport* spell; at will; caster level 18th. Using this ability requires 1 minute of concentration. When outside a lunar ravager lodge, a lunar ravager must stand in moonlight to use this ability, and it can transport only itself and items it carries to the nearest lodge. When inside a lodge, a lunar ravager can use this ability to travel to any point within 10 miles of the lodge. A lunar ravager becomes misty and insubstantial the moment before it teleports.

Lunar ravagers are ferocious fey that live to hunt. These fearsome creatures dwell in hunting lodges nestled among the clouds. On the nights when the moon is visible in the sky, they ride beams of moonlight to the surface world in order to hunt and slay. Lunar ravagers collect grim trophies and treasure from their victims before returning to their lodge to celebrate, rest, and prepare for the next hunt.

STRATEGIES AND TACTICS

When a lunar ravager fights alone, it relies on its spell-like abilities to surprise its foes, using *pass without trace* to leave no sign of its presence and *invisibility* to close with an enemy. A ravager observes its prey for a time to determine its victim's abilities and possibly gain a terrain advantage. If the adversary seems worthy, the lunar ravager uses *air walk* to strike from above. Once engaged in battle, it tests its opponent's defenses before using Power Attack. A lone lunar ravager facing a group usually seeks to slay a single foe, grab that victim's body, and flee with the trophy to a safe place to use its moon rider ability.

Ravagers try to cover a large area during a hunt. They spread out in a ragged line, putting between 100 feet and half a mile between each hunter. Each ravager casts *pass without trace* on itself to evade trackers. Then they sweep across the region, driving all creatures before them. They scream war cries, sound their bronze horns, and call out to each other to remain in contact and track prey.

When one ravager spots a potential mark—anything from a dragon roused from its lair to a hapless farmer caught out at night—it sounds its horn. The entire party then uses *invisibility*. Further horn calls tell the hunters where to go to prepare an ambush, while a single ravager drives the quarry toward its allies. Lunar ravagers fight with vicious abandon after they've encircled their intended kill. Several use *air walk* to attack from above, and the rest close in and use their great size to cut off escape. A few use Power Attack right from the start, with the rest following suit if the bold ones are successful. The hunters continue this process throughout the night, taking trophies and looting the dead. A lunar ravager hunting party usually flees after half its members are slain.

"I've heard the horns that come with the full moon. I've helped bury the headless bodies of those who've ventured into the forest on such nights. Unless you wish to end up as a ravager's trophy, I suggest you spend the night here."
   —Ostler the barkeep, advising Regdar

SAMPLE ENCOUNTERS

Lunar ravagers hunt alone or in groups. The greater a ravager's ability and status, the more likely that it seeks glory alone. Sometimes, younger lunar ravagers embark on solo hunts to prove their mettle and earn the respect of their clan.

Individual (EL 7): A lone lunar ravager is on a quest for blood and fame.

EL 7: Ravnha, a young lunar ravager out to prove herself, has set a trap near a wooden bridge while under the effect of her *pass without trace* ability. She has broken several of the bridge's supports and watches the nearby road for travelers. When she spies a suitable group, she uses *invisibility* and *air walk*. She then pushes out a remaining critical support and leaps to attack from above as the bridge collapses.

Hunting Party (EL 11+): Four or more lunar ravagers form a hunting party.

Lunar ravager

Typical Physical Characteristics: Lunar ravagers stand just over 9 feet tall, on average, and weigh in the neighborhood of 550 pounds. Their skin is fair, though females tend toward pale, and their hair is always blond.

Alignment: Lunar ravagers are bloodthirsty, savage, remorseless killers who pay little heed to the welfare of others even among their kind. Thus, they are usually chaotic evil. Some lunar ravager bands are chaotic neutral, hunting to test their skill and rarely killing weak foes for sport. These neutral fey might even trade with other creatures.

SOCIETY

Lunar ravager society is clannish and based on the principles of strength, battle prowess, bluster, and wealth. Each clan is a family of individuals related by blood or mating. A lunar ravager wins status in its clan by returning from raids with ample loot, fine trophies, and rich food and drink. Female and male lunar ravagers equally earn standing in their society, based on merit.

A clan of lunar ravagers lives in a hunting lodge built on a cloud. The residents of a lodge have basic control over their direction of travel, but the chaotic ravagers usually allow the wind to carry them where it will. They prefer to keep moving rather than linger in one place for too long. This strategy prevents overhunting of an area. It also makes lunar ravagers difficult to handle, since they attack randomly and move on before the local authorities can organize.

Relations between lunar ravager clans are similarly haphazard. In a chance meeting, two clans might clash, trade goods, swap news, engage in a debauched revel, exchange a few members, or rob each other. Often, some or all of these events occur, and in no particular order.

These wicked fey see crafts that lack a direct connection to fighting, status, or easy living as a waste of time. Although they forge their own weapons and armor, build lodges, and make macabre jewelry, they care little for constructing other items. They prefer to take tools and implements from others, along with basic needs such as provisions.

Living as raiders and hunters, lunar ravagers usually seek sustenance in remote locales, spending a few nights each month pillaging and slaying on the surface. They avoid large settlements, where resistance might be a real threat. If the ravagers come across a farm or a poorly defended village, though, they load their sacks with food, casks of ale, livestock, and even a peasant or two. As dawn nears, they sound their horns one final time before returning to their lodge to feast, drink, and celebrate the hunt.

EL 11: Arbha, Clonach, Ebhla, and Nuil prowl a moonlit forest on a midnight hunt. They use characteristic tactics for a hunting party, as described above.

ECOLOGY

Lunar ravagers are supernatural hunters that some say embody nature's viciousness. However, they're largely displaced from the natural world. Little more than overgrown scavengers, they see the land below their lodges as fertile ground for riches and prey. They hunt for meat, and they raid settlements for strong drink and supplies.

Mating among lunar ravagers is thought to be much as it is among humanoids.

Environment: Lunar ravagers hunt in any terrain, though they only rarely venture underground. They prefer areas with a clear view of the sky, close enough to civilization for easy raiding but far enough to avoid large armies and other threats. Lunar ravagers live within lodges that float on the clouds. In this environment, they hunt birds and other flying creatures between raids to the surface world.

Lunar ravagers exult in toying with their victims, and they underestimate smaller creatures. This tendency works against them when they face skilled opposition. Lunar ravagers hate cowardice, but they are not fools, and they retreat before an opponent that seems to have the upper hand. A lunar ravager's belt is much more likely to carry the skulls of dire animals, magical beasts, and common folk than those of dragons, fiends, and heroes.

Some lunar ravagers embark on long journeys to demonstrate their fighting talents and improve their prestige. Such ambitious ravagers are the smartest, bravest, and most cunning of their kind. They ally with other vicious creatures, most notably werewolves and evil fey, to wreak havoc wherever they go. Their aim is to return home laden with enough wealth and fame to attain leadership of their clan.

Stranded ravagers are similarly dangerous. Such an unfortunate usually wanders too far from its lodge or stays on the surface too long, becoming trapped without the moonlight it needs to ride home. Whether this situation arises because of a plot by a jealous rival or mere happenstance, when the next night comes around, the marooned reaver discovers that its cloud lodge has drifted away. Such ravagers seek out weaker but like-minded creatures, particularly orcs and ogres, to torment and command. An orc tribe led by a lunar ravager poses a great threat, for the ravager's intellect, strong personality, and insight make it a keen commander.

A few lunar ravagers intentionally leave their lodges behind, preferring to rule smaller folk on earth rather than serve among their kind amid the clouds.

TYPICAL TREASURE

A lunar ravager lodge is filled with a vast array of treasures and trophies, accumulated through untold centuries of murder and theft. Since these fey are greedy folk who measure their prestige by the possessions they have stolen, they scavenge every coin and valuable object they can find. They take particular delight in robbing mortals of heirlooms and sentimental valuables. Ravager lodges have double the standard treasure for the creatures' Challenge Rating, largely in the form of coins and art objects. However, a lunar ravager encountered alone carries little treasure besides its weapon and armor, along with any trophies it might have taken earlier in the hunt.

Lunar ravagers cherish their hunting horns, handed down through the ages within clans. These ancient bronze horns produce a bone-chilling tone that unmistakably declare the approach of the hunt.

LUNAR RAVAGERS WITH CLASS LEVELS

Lunar ravagers' favored class is barbarian, in keeping with their brutish tendency and love of battle, although rangers and rogues are also common. Among their kind, a swift knife in the back is the preferred method of settling a dispute.

Lunar ravager clerics worship Erythnul. That dread deity's bloodthirsty teachings appeal to their taste for murder and destruction.

Level Adjustment: +6.

LUNAR RAVAGERS IN EBERRON

The lunar ravagers of Eberron dwell primarily in Xen'drik. Legends tell of six floating castles, each positioned high over the continent, that once served as important centers of magical research for the empire of the giants. Lunar ravagers have long since descended into savagery, but their homes are still filled with untold wonders.

LUNAR RAVAGERS IN FAERÛN

Lunar ravagers are spread across Toril. They avoid civilized lands, having learned well the power of a vengeful Harper or a skilled mage. Rumors abound that the Red Wizards of Thay have entered into a pact with several lunar ravager clans. The Thayans pay the ravagers gems, gold, and other riches in return for transport and service as mercenaries. Perhaps the hunter fey are part of the Red Wizards' latest scheme against Rashemen.

LUNAR RAVAGER LORE

Characters with ranks in Knowledge (nature) can learn more about lunar ravagers. When a character makes a successful skill check, the following lore is revealed, including the information from lower DCs.

Knowledge (Nature)

DC	Result
17	This is a lunar ravager, a murderous, aggressive fey. This result reveals all fey traits.
22	Lunar ravagers are expert trackers and hunters. They can follow their prey for miles across rough terrain.
27	Lunar ravagers can turn invisible and walk on the air. They use these abilities to stalk their enemies.
32	A lunar ravager can transport itself back to a hunting lodge in the clouds, but this ability takes a while to use and requires a clear, moonlit night.

MAGERIPPER SWARM

A writhing mass of bizarre little creatures swarms across the floor, myriad tentacles waving like antennae. They are eyeless, their bodies little more than gaping jaws filled with teeth, yet they move unerringly toward you.

MAGERIPPER SWARM   **CR 6**
Always CN Tiny aberration (swarm)
Init +4; **Senses** blind, blindsense 30 ft., sense magic 30 ft.;
    Listen +12
Languages —
Aura dispelling

AC 18, touch 16, flat-footed 14
    (+2 size, +4 Dex, +2 natural)
hp 55 (10 HD)
Resist half damage from piercing and slashing weapons
Immune gaze attacks, illusions, visual effects; swarm
    immunities
SR 21
Fort +4, **Ref** +7, **Will** +8
Weakness swarm vulnerabilities

Speed 20 ft. (4 squares), climb 10 ft.
Melee swarm (2d6 plus magic leech)
Space 10 ft.; **Reach** 0 ft.
Base Atk +7; **Grp** —
Atk Options distraction, magic leech

Abilities Str 4, Dex 19, Con 12, Int 6, Wis 12, Cha 15
SQ swarm traits
Feats Ability Focus (magic leech), Skill Focus (Listen),
    Stealthy, Track
Skills Climb +5, Listen +12, Move Silently +6, Survival +6
Advancement 11–19 HD; see text

Sense Magic (Su) A mageripper swarm automatically detects
    magic auras within 30 feet, and it knows the strength and
    location of each. It can also detect creatures that possess
    the ability to cast spells or use spell-like abilities.
Dispelling Aura (Su) At the end of each of a mageripper
    swarm's turns, it can attempt a dispel check against
    one randomly selected ongoing spell or spell-like effect
    on each creature in its space. This works like the area
    dispel effect of the *dispel magic* spell, with the following
    differences. The dispelled spell is selected randomly from
    those currently active on an affected creature, rather than
    being the one with the highest caster level. This ability
    has no effect on permanent magic items.
        For each spell dispelled by its aura, a mageripper
    swarm gains temporary hit points equal to 2 × that
    spell's level. These temporary hit points last for up to
    24 hours, and a swarm can gain a maximum number of
    temporary hit points equal to its full normal hit point
    total. A mageripper swarm that gains the maximum
    number of temporary hit points and retains them for the
    full 24 hours advances 1 Hit Die at the end of this period,
    increasing its capabilities as normal for advancement.
Magic Leech (Su) In addition to dealing damage to creatures
    whose space it occupies, a mageripper swarm drains
    away the ability to cast spells and use spell-like abilities,
    feeding on the magical energy.
        At the end of a mageripper swarm's turn, each
    creature in its space must succeed on a DC 19 Will save
    or lose one prepared spell or spell slot of the highest level
    available. The save DC is Charisma-based. A creature
    with a spell-like ability that fails its saving throw loses one
    daily use of its highest-level ability. If this spell-like ability
    is usable at will, the creature is unable to use it for 1

minute. If the target has no spells prepared, no remaining
spell slots, and no uses of spell-like abilities remaining,
this ability has no effect. A mageripper swarm cannot
choose which spell to drain; determine this randomly.
        For each spell drained in this way, a swarm gains
    temporary hit points equal to 5 × the spell's level.
    These temporary hit points function as described in the
    dispelling aura ability.
Distraction (Ex) Fortitude DC 16, nauseated 1 round. The
    save DC is Constitution-based.
Skills Mageripper swarms have a +8 racial bonus on Climb
    checks and can always choose to take 10 on Climb
    checks, even if rushed or threatened.

A mageripper swarm consists of around three hundred Tiny
horrors that seek out and feed on magical energy. The creatures are hazards to spellcasters of all kinds.

STRATEGIES AND TACTICS
When it detects nearby magical auras, a mageripper swarm
moves immediately toward the strongest aura or the strongest
spellcaster. It attacks relentlessly, filling the target's space and
draining as much magical energy as it can. It stops only when
destroyed or the source is completely drained.

SAMPLE ENCOUNTER
A mageripper swarm is always encountered alone, although
it might be found near intelligent creatures that use it to
protect against spellcasting enemies. Multiple swarms can
infest the same general area if they get out of control and
the supply of magical energy is plentiful enough, but such
swarms don't work together.
    Individual (EL 6): The lone wizard Edgar (N male human
wizard 4) has become a prisoner in his tower since a mageripper swarm discovered his retreat. After escaping the swarm's
initial assaults, he sealed himself in an inner laboratory. The
windowless room keeps out the swarm, but the supply of food
and air is limited. Occasionally he throws open the door and
blasts the swarm with *scorching ray* spells, but he can't deal
enough damage to overcome it completely. The swarm has
infested his arcane workshop, which is filled with completed

MAGERIPPER SWARM LORE
Characters with ranks in Knowledge (dungeoneering) can learn
more about mageripper swarms. When a character makes a
successful skill check, the following lore is revealed, including
the information from lower DCs. Knowledge (arcana) can also
be used, but all check DCs increase by 5.

Knowledge (Dungeoneering)

DC	Result
10	This is a mageripper swarm, a mass of Tiny aberrations. This result reveals all aberration and swarm traits.
16	Mageripper swarms consume magical energy.
21	These creatures are a serious threat to areas of spellcasting activity. Once they begin feeding, they don't stop until they have consumed everything in the area.
26	Magerippers might have been created to defend against magic. Some creatures keep swarms for this purpose.

and half-finished potions, wands, and the like. During one of his sorties, Edgar activated a *Quaal's feather token (bird)* to take a distress message to the nearby wizards' academy.

ECOLOGY

Mageripper swarms are so bizarre that they are unlikely to have arisen naturally. Most scholars believe that they were created deliberately for some purpose.

A mageripper swarm relies on nonvisual senses to discern its environment. The creatures that make up the swarm can subsist on meat, but they thrive on magical energy and prefer to live where that food source is easy to find. Such swarms are real threats in larger cities, where they infest the magic districts, and in areas inhabited by beings such as elves or fey that use magic routinely.

Although they cannot consume the magical energy stored in magic items, the auras of such items still attract mageripper swarms, much as a candle flame attracts moths. The confused and hungry creatures mill about the item until they are destroyed or find something else to eat.

Consuming magical energy allows the creatures to reproduce, increasing the swarm's size. Individual swarm members live only for a year or so, but when the swarm devours magic, its constituent creatures can double their numbers within days. They reproduce asexually, with young budding from the backs of the adults. If a mageripper swarm grows to double its original size (that is, to 20 Hit Dice), it splits into two swarms with 10 Hit Dice each.

Beings that are inimical to magic sometimes encourage swarms to inhabit their environs. Magerippers make effective guardians, although they move to more fertile feeding grounds if too few spellcasters inhabit the area. Other creatures use them to defend against magical assaults. These keepers sometimes cast spells on a helpless captive or capture and bind a spellcaster, leaving the prisoner as food within the swarm's territory.

Magerippers are sentient, although their intelligence is more the cunning of a predator. They are capable of adapting their tactics to fit new circumstances. Though driven largely by the instinct to feed and reproduce, mageripper swarms can modify their behavior in response to stimuli.

Individuals become sluggish and unresponsive if separated from the swarm, and they soon die.

Environment: Mageripper swarms can be found in any temperate environment and are attracted to urban areas. They can't tolerate extremes of heat and cold. Often a swarm infests the cellar of a wizards' enclave or an ancient dungeon.

Typical Physical Characteristics: A typical mageripper is about 1 foot long and weighs 3 to 5 pounds. It seems to be fashioned from a jumble of unrelated pieces, with big chewing jaws, insectlike legs, and tentacles like those of a displacer beast. Its coloration is unnatural, with overtones of sickly purple, blue, or pink. Circular blotches along the body

mark the location of specialized organs that sense magical energy.

Alignment: Mageripper swarms are solely concerned with acquiring sustenance and multiplying. They are not intentionally destructive or malicious, but they do act erratically. They are always chaotic neutral.

TYPICAL TREASURE

Mageripper swarms do not accumulate money or most sorts of treasure, and most folk have no use for the horrible little things. However, they are often found in the vicinity of hoards of magic items, and the swarm is more likely to gather around stronger magical auras. A mageripper swarm has double standard treasure for its Challenge Rating, about 4,000 gp, all of which is magic items.

MAGERIPPER SWARMS IN EBERRON

The fanatical Ashbound druids regard all arcane magic as unnatural, but they do not believe in wanton killing. They find mageripper swarms to be effective deterrents. The creatures are not common within the Eldeen Reaches, though, and seeking them out can lead into the dangerous territories of the Demon Wastes or the Shadow Marches. Aundair's cities suffer from recurring infestations of mageripper swarms, and they make good sources for Ashbound druids who are willing to enter cities.

With its lingering arcane energy and living spells, the Mournland is a fertile feeding ground for magerippers. The creatures might even have arisen there, perhaps mutated from mundane pests in the aftermath of the Day of Mourning.

MAGERIPPER SWARMS IN FAERÛN

The sewers of Waterdeep lead to innumerable and mysterious places—havens for crime gangs, weird cults, and strange creatures. Mageripper swarms are also found in large numbers in Skullport.

The Red Wizards of Thay have set up trading enclaves throughout Faerûn, where they offer rare and useful magic for sale. Such large concentrations of magic items are magnets for mageripper swarms. Keeping the dangerous creatures under control is a constant worry for the Thayans.

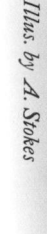

Illus. by A. Stokes

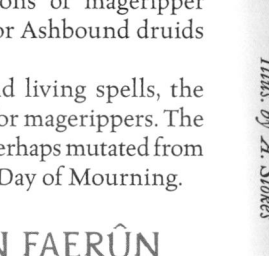

Mageripper swarm

MINOTAUR, GREATHORN

Before you is a tall and thickset minotaur with short, slate-colored fur. Its horns extend nearly 5 feet from its head, and it wields a massive hammer.

GREATHORN MINOTAUR	**CR 7**

Usually CE Large monstrous humanoid (earth)
Init −1; **Senses** darkvision 60 ft., scent, tremorsense 120 ft.;
    Listen +8, Spot +8
Languages Giant, Undercommon

AC 15, touch 8, flat-footed 15
    (−1 size, −1 Dex, +7 natural)
hp 104 (11 HD); **DR** 5/—
Fort +10, **Ref** +6, **Will** +7

Speed 30 ft. (6 squares); earth glide
Melee gore +17 (2d6+10) or
Melee greathammer +17/+12/+7 (3d6+10/×4) and
    gore +12 (2d6+3)
Space 10 ft.; **Reach** 10 ft.
Base Atk +11; **Grp** +22
Atk Options Awesome Blow, Power Attack
Special Actions earth warp

Abilities Str 24, Dex 8, Con 20, Int 9, Wis 10, Cha 10
SQ natural cunning
Feats Awesome Blow[B], Great Fortitude, Improved Natural
    Attack (gore), Power Attack, Track
Skills Intimidate +3, Listen +8, Search +3, Spot +8,
    Survival +3
Advancement by character class; **Favored Class** barbarian;
    see text
Possessions greathammer

Earth Glide (Ex) A greathorn minotaur can glide through
    stone, dirt, or almost any other sort of earth except metal
    as easily as a fish swims through water. Its burrowing
    leaves behind no tunnel or hole, nor does it create any
    ripple or other signs of its presence.
Earth Warp (Su) As a swift action, a greathorn minotaur can
    cause the earth and rock around it to twist and warp in a
    60-foot-radius emanation around it, doubling movement
    costs through that area. Natural stone, finished stone,
    and dirt surfaces are subject to this effect. The effect
    does not move with the minotaur; when the minotaur
    leaves the area, the ground returns to normal. The
    minotaur ignores the movement penalties generated by
    its own or another greathorn's earth warp ability.
Natural Cunning (Ex) Greathorn minotaurs have immunity to
    maze spells, never become lost, and can track enemies.
    They are never caught flat-footed.
Skills Greathorn minotaurs have a +4 racial bonus on Listen,
    Search, and Spot checks.

A greathorn is a powerful subterranean relative of normal minotaurs. It is infused with the power of elemental earth, making it stronger and granting it the ability to manipulate earth and stone around it.

STRATEGIES AND TACTICS

A greathorn minotaur lurks beneath the ground, emerging to attack prey from behind. It prefers to pick off weaker members of a group first, slowing escape and would-be rescuers with its earth warp ability. The beast uses Awesome Blow to knock potent fighters away from it, then renews its assault against the original target. Relying on its greathammer to finish off its intended victim, a greathorn minotaur attacks ferociously and uses Power Attack as much as it can.

SAMPLE ENCOUNTERS

Greathorn minotaurs are likely to be encountered within their lairs or leading other minotaurs underground.

Individual (EL 7): A lone greathorn minotaur has carved a maze close to duergar territory, hoping to capture and devour as many gray dwarves as possible. It ambushes any humanoids that cross its path.

Pair (EL 9): Recently bonded, a mated pair fights as a team. The female launches the initial attack. Once battle is joined, the male emerges from the rock to catch an opponent from a flank.

Templars (EL 11): Four greathorn minotaurs have banded together in service to a temple to the earth aspect of the Elder Elemental Eye (see page 8). They patrol the area near the temple, driving off interlopers. The minotaurs use hit-and-run tactics to slowly sap an enemy group's strength. If hard pressed, they flee or hide within the stone, and the wounded retreat to the temple to rouse its occupants and avenge their fallen comrades.

ECOLOGY

Greathorn minotaurs arose in the untold reaches of the underground realm as an offshoot of the minotaur race. Great wells of elemental earth energy warped and twisted several minotaur tribes, yielding the fearsome beings that now prowl labyrinths and passages deep within the earth.

Greathorn minotaurs hunt for food, eating just about anything they kill. However, they love the taste of the flesh of sentient creatures above all other foods. Humanoid prey is their favorite.

Once every few years, greathorn minotaurs embark on a great migration. Sages believe that the minotaurs follow the ebb and flow of elemental earth energy.

Environment: Greathorn minotaurs live underground and rarely venture to the surface. They steal developed territory from other denizens when possible, altering it to their

GREATHORN MINOTAUR LORE

Characters with ranks in Knowledge (nature) can learn more about greathorn minotaurs. When a character makes a successful skill check, the following lore is revealed, including the information from lower DCs.

Knowledge (Nature)

DC	Result
17	This is a greathorn minotaur, a monstrous humanoid that lives underground and is infused with elemental earth. This result reveals all monstrous humanoid traits and the earth subtype.
22	Greathorn minotaurs have tough, rocklike skin. They use their enormous horns to gore their opponents.
27	These creatures can hide within stone, emerging to slay all who stumble onto their hunting grounds.
32	Greathorn minotaurs can warp the earth, making movement difficult around them. They excel at isolating an opponent from allies.

liking. Otherwise, they carve out long, winding mazes as their lairs, complete with numerous dead ends, pits, and other traps. When on the surface, greathorn minotaurs hide during the day and move about at night.

Typical Physical Characteristics: Greathorn minotaurs are larger and bulkier than their ordinary kin, standing over 9 feet tall and weighing nearly a ton. They get their name from their enormous horns, which can extend 5 or more feet from their massive skulls. Greathorn minotaurs lack the thick, shaggy coats of their mundane cousins, instead sporting short, coarse fur the color of slate.

Males are larger than females, and their horns are longer. The fur of females tends toward lighter colors, and individuals with pure white fur have been documented.

Alignment: Greathorn minotaurs thrive on mayhem and violence, killing and destroying with no regard and seeing only might as worthy of respect. Most greathorn minotaurs are chaotic evil.

Greathorn minotaur

SOCIETY

Greathorn minotaurs are as greedy and vain as they are gluttonous and domineering. They often settle disputes by killing and devouring those that displease them. On the other hand, they gladly work as mercenaries for drow, duergar, derro, and other evil creatures that provide them with wealth and the meat of humanoids. Mind flayers particularly favor greathorn minotaur sellswords, which make excellent guards.

Greathorns go out of their way to murder or browbeat others of their kind, seeing them as rivals—except when the creatures are involved in courtship or mating. Males put on great displays of both prosperity and prowess to attract a mate. Once bonded, a pair stays together for life and has as many children as possible.

In areas with "lesser" minotaurs, greathorn minotaurs are the undisputed leaders. Blessed with higher intelligence than their kin, greathorns unify tribes of ordinary minotaurs into armies that terrorize the surrounding area. An army of this sort is short-lived—the fractious nature of the minotaurs soon tears it apart. When they are not around others of their kind, greathorn minotaurs have been known to dominate evil humanoids such as orcs, bugbears, and gnolls.

Temples dedicated to the earth aspect of the Elder Elemental Eye are strangely attractive to greathorn minotaurs, which are among such temples' most ardent supporters. Given their egotism, piety of any other sort is rare among greathorn minotaurs. They do have clerics, though, all of whom are female. Those females with white fur are groomed from birth to become priestesses of the Elder Elemental Eye and its

servant Ogremoch, the Prince of Evil Elemental Earth. Even the most belligerent male defers to an albino priestess's wisdom and strength.

TYPICAL TREASURE

Greathorn minotaurs relish treasure, which they use to attract mates and show off their power. They have standard treasure for their Challenge Rating, about 2,600 gp, and prefer shiny, gaudy items, including coins, metallic art, and weapons of all kinds. Only the priestesses read or write, so most greathorns discard scrolls, spellbooks, and other paper items they acquire. For a randomly determined hoard, replace any such items with coins.

FOR PLAYER CHARACTERS

Greathorn minotaurs wield these big, heavy hammers, which are considered exotic weapons for other creatures. The incredibly heavy head of the hammer allows it to make devastating strikes against weapons and shields, granting the wielder a +2 bonus on opposed attack rolls to sunder an enemy's weapon or shield.

Dmg (S)	Dmg (M)	Critical	Weight[1]	Type
1d10	1d12	19–20/×4	30 lb.	Bludgeoning

1 Weight is for a Medium weapon. Small weapons weigh half as much, and Large weapons weigh twice as much.

GREATHORNS WITH CLASS LEVELS

Greathorn minotaurs' favored class is barbarian. Naturally aggressive and prone to fits of rage, they take to this class readily. Greathorn minotaur clerics worship the Elder Elemental Eye (see page 7), usually choosing Destruction and Earth as their domains. They have no knowledge of this deity's true nature.

Level Adjustment: +6.

GREATHORNS IN EBERRON

Greathorn minotaurs are most common in Droaam, where they rule entire communities of minotaurs. The tribes view the ascension of a greathorn as an auspicious event, often using the occasion as an excuse to start a grab for more territory. Smarter monsters of Droaam, especially medusas and ogre mages, commonly employ greathorns as officers of minotaur units in their personal armies.

A healthy population of greathorn minotaurs lives in the twisting chasms of the Demon Wastes.

Illus. by C. Frank

NAGATHA

This creature has the lower body of a worm, the head of a snake with milky white eyes, and two long arms that terminate in enormous bone claws. It holds its body at about the height of a human as it rises to attack.

NAGATHA   **CR 4**
Always CE Medium monstrous humanoid
Init –1; **Senses** blind, blindsight 60 ft.; Listen +15
Languages Abyssal, Common

AC 17, touch 9, flat-footed 17
    (–1 Dex, +8 natural)
hp 60 (8 HD)
Immune gaze attacks, illusions, visual effects
Fort +7, **Ref** +5, **Will** +7

Speed 10 ft. (2 squares), burrow 10 ft.
Melee 2 claws +10 each (1d8+2) and
    bite +5 (1d4+1 plus poison)
Space 5 ft.; **Reach** 5 ft.
Base Atk +8; **Grp** +10
Atk Options poison (DC 17, 2d4 Wis/2d4 Wis)

Abilities Str 14, Dex 8, Con 16, Int 6, Wis 13, Cha 9
SQ viper's speed
Feats Great Fortitude, Improved Natural Attack (claws), Skill
    Focus (Listen)
Skills Listen +15
Advancement 9–15 HD (Medium); see text

Viper's Speed (Ex) Whenever a nagatha takes two move
    actions to move twice its land speed or a full-round
    action to run, it gains a 40-foot bonus to its land speed,
    allowing it to move up to 100 feet with two move actions
    or run up to 200 feet.

Nagathas are wormlike creatures created by evil spirit nagas from the bodies of normal humanoids. They enjoy eviscerating their victims and take sadistic glee in the pain and suffering of living creatures. Their cruelty remains the most obvious and twisted expression of the pain they endured during the hideous transformation into their current form.

STRATEGIES AND TACTICS

Nagathas are blind, so they rely on their keen hearing to detect creatures beyond the 60-foot range of their blindsight. They are intelligent enough to fear ranged attacks from outside that distance. If nagathas hear enemies approaching from far away, they burrow just beneath the surface and strike from an ambush position. Similarly, nagathas burrow to protect themselves from attacks by opponents they can't hear or sense with blindsight.

Nagathas guarding an entry often hide beneath the earth in the doorway, waiting to waylay interlopers. Patrolling nagathas space themselves out, using their blindsight for increased effectiveness and mutual protection. When encountered with their naga master, guardian nagathas engage intruders in melee, keeping them stuck in combat as the naga casts spells from afar.

SAMPLE ENCOUNTERS

A given group of nagathas is loyal to the spirit naga that created them, and they are usually encountered in the company of their master or while performing some mission. They patrol their master's domain for intruders. Spirit nagas also throw nagathas against superior forces as fodder.

Guardians (EL 6): A pair of nagathas patrols the marshy outer reaches of a spirit naga's lair, seeking victims.

Sweepers (EL 8): Four nagathas slither through the remains of an ancient churchyard, protecting the nearby sanctum of their master.

Naga Writhe (EL 11): In the heart of a ruined temple, a spirit naga schemes while six nagathas stand watch.

ECOLOGY

Nagathas are the product of a process practiced by spirit nagas that magically corrupts the bodies of captured Medium humanoids into sickening, wormlike creatures with sharp claws. Humanoids that unsuccessfully raid spirit naga lairs provide the most abundant raw material for nagathas. Those left unconscious in battle often end up being harvested for this purpose.

Survivors of such transformation bear no resemblance to their previous forms. Their legs are fused into a wormlike lower body, using up much of the muscle mass from the subject's abdomen and legs. Arm bones re-form and solidify into enormous bone claws. Their heads stretch into the likeness of vipers, and they lose their eyesight. Raw material from snakes provides the basis for a nagatha's poison.

The final and perhaps most invasive alteration is made to the subject's mind. The spirit nagas dull its mental faculties to destroy any potential for arcane spellcasting, and erase memories and knowledge of its previous existence, but they deliberately leave a painful emotional echo, allowing a nagatha to realize that something important has been taken from it.

NAGATHA LORE

Characters with ranks in Knowledge (dungeoneering) or Knowledge (nature) can learn more about nagathas. When a character makes a successful skill check, the following lore is revealed, including the information from lower DCs.

Knowledge (Dungeoneering) or Knowledge (Nature)

DC	Result
14	This is a nagatha, a horrific monstrous humanoid twisted into a wormlike form. This result reveals all monstrous humanoid traits.
19	A nagatha has a poisonous bite that saps a victim's mental alertness.
24	A nagatha is blind beyond 60 feet and ambushes opponents by burrowing underground.
29	All nagathas used to be humanoid, but they were transformed by evil spirit nagas and can no longer remember their former lives.

Environment: Nagathas inhabit temperate marshes, making their homes in an ancient ruin or crumbling fortress with the spirit naga that dominates them. Nagathas leave such areas only if their naga master has been defeated in a battle they survived.

Typical Physical Characteristics: Nagathas have worm-like lower bodies, which elongate and contract when they move. A nagatha's head resembles a large viper's, complete with fangs, and sinewy arms swing its oversized bone claws. These claws make wielding manufactured weapons all but impossible.

The average nagatha is about 7 feet long and weighs 150 to 250 pounds.

Alignment: Nagathas are always chaotic evil, being pain-driven and utterly sadistic. Their spirit naga creators encourage and foster hatred of other creatures, especially humanoids.

SOCIETY

The only solace nagathas can find after being transformed is in the misery of similar company. Nagathas retain no memory of their humanoid existence, but they are filled with a lingering feeling of emptiness: Something important to them has been forever lost. Since this feeling is common to all nagathas, they openly commiserate with each other. Nobody understands the pain a nagatha feels better than another nagatha.

Spirit nagas capitalize on this sense of loss, having cultivated it in their creations, and take care to express understanding. Nagathas consequently look to their sympathetic-seeming "parents" for a sense of purpose. They are happiest when attacking invaders that enter their masters' realm, since battle allows them to focus their painful confusion into a fury that is both cathartic and cruel.

The procedure for creating a nagatha incorporates a *charm person* spell cast on the original humanoid, making the nagatha loyal to the spirit naga even after transformation into a monstrous humanoid. The spell is permanently woven into nagathas so that they always regard their spirit naga creator as a trusted friend or close relative. Nagathas react with rage to any suggestion that their master could in any way be responsible for their pain.

Nagatha

TYPICAL TREASURE

Individual nagathas have no treasure but happily collect riches for their naga masters. A spirit naga with five to eight nagathas has standard coins, double goods, and standard items for the group's Encounter Level. A spirit naga accompanied by nine to twelve nagathas has standard coins, double goods, and double items.

ADVANCED NAGATHAS

Nagathas usually advance by Hit Dice, growing more potent as guardians over the span of their miserable lives. Those that take class levels usually advance as fighters or barbarians, and they never enter a spellcasting class.

Level Adjustment: +2.

NAGATHAS IN EBERRON

Nagathas live where spirit nagas dwell, and the swamps of the Shadow Marches hold the largest number of these abominations. In the ruins left by the Daelkyr War, nagathas guard their masters, while the spirit nagas hoard Eberron dragonshards and seek ways to open the dimensional seals. The Basura Swamp of Q'barra is also home to spirit nagas and their vile creations.

NAGATHAS IN FAERÛN

The sarrukh created nagas to be naturally inquisitive, especially about the Art, but they also made nagas fiercely self-centered. Each seeks a domain where its will is supreme. Independent spirit nagas are common in the caves along the Nagaflow in the Nagalands of Chondath and Sespech, where lie ancient naga spawning grounds. The powerful among these nagas create many nagathas from local folk.

Spirit nagas congregate in Najara, the Kingdom of Snakes, in the Western Heartlands, where a dozen of them serve King Ebarnaje directly. The evil nagas of this realm have crafted nagatha servants from humanoid slaves.

Illus. by A. Swekel

NECROSIS CARNEX

The creature before you is a horrid amalgam of rotting flesh bound to twisted limbs. It walks on all four of its awkward appendages, and great bands of black iron seem to hold the various pieces of putrid tissue together.

NECROSIS CARNEX	**CR 3**

Always NE Medium undead
Init +3; **Senses** darkvision 60 ft.; Listen +5, Spot +4
Languages understands creator's orders
Aura malign (30 ft.)

AC 21, touch 17, flat-footed 18; Mobility
   (+3 Dex, +4 deflection, +4 natural)
hp 26 (4 HD)
Immune undead immunities
Fort +3, **Ref** +4, **Will** +5
Weakness vulnerability to good

Speed 40 ft. (8 squares)
Melee touch +5 (1d6+2)
Space 5 ft.; **Reach** 5 ft.
Atk Options necrotic touch
Special Actions unholy burst
Base Atk +2; **Grp** +3

Abilities Str 12, Dex 17, Con —, Int 3, Wis 12, Cha 7
SQ undead traits
Feats Great Fortitude, Mobility[B], Weapon Finesse
Skills Jump +5, Listen +5, Spot +4
Advancement 5–7 HD (Medium); 8–14 HD (Large)

Malign Aura (Su) Living creatures take a –2 penalty on attack rolls and saving throws when they are within 30 feet of a necrosis carnex.

Vulnerability to Good (Ex) Necrosis carnexes take half again as much (+50%) damage as normal from good-aligned weapons and spells.

Necrotic Touch (Su) If a necrosis carnex hits a living creature with its touch attack, it deals damage equal to 1d6 + 1 per 2 HD of the necrosis carnex. Undead are instead healed by the same amount, gaining any hit points over their full normal total as temporary hit points that last for up to 10 minutes.

Unholy Burst (Ex) When destroyed, a necrosis carnex explodes in a 30-foot-radius spread that deals damage equal to 1d6 + 1 per 2 HD of the necrosis carnex to all living creatures in the area. Undead are instead healed by the same amount, gaining any hit points over their normal total as temporary hit points, as described above.

A necrosis carnex is a ghastly collection of corpse-flesh bound together into an engine of destruction. It is something like an undead flesh golem, but it retains a glimmer of intelligence and can follow simple orders. Necrosis carnexes serve undead armies as both shock troops and combat medics.

STRATEGIES AND TACTICS

Necrosis carnexes employ simple but effective tactics in combat. Usually teamed with other undead, the carnexes know that they are at their most effective when using their foul touch to heal their companions. To facilitate this, they remain just behind the front rank of their undead allies, keeping their foes within their malign aura. These creatures love to slay the living and use their necrotic touch on an unconscious but living foe if an opportunity presents itself.

SAMPLE ENCOUNTERS

Necrosis carnexes are often found in the company of other undead. Powerful intelligent undead keep these creatures as pets and personal companions, knowing that the necrotic energy of a carnex's touch can mend their lifeless flesh.

Gate Guards (EL 5): A pair of bugbear zombies guard the entrance to a secret underground temple, fortified by a necrosis carnex. When combat begins, the zombies lumber forward while the necrosis carnex hangs back to heal them, attempting to keep foes within its malign aura.

Undead Raiders (EL 6): A vampire spawn leads two troglodyte zombies and a necrosis carnex on a raid. The creatures hide within a temple dedicated to Nerull during the day, emerging at night to stalk their prey among the back alleys of a major city. The temple priests deny any involvement with the undead.

Graveyard Lord (EL 7): In a secret warren beneath an ancient graveyard, a wight leads four ghouls and a necrosis carnex. The wight is a strict tactician, ordering the ghouls to move into flanking positions or to aid it in its attacks (with the aid another action). It uses the carnex as a healer for itself and its ghoul minions.

ECOLOGY

Necrosis carnexes are beings outside nature. They have a simple and stark existence, stemming entirely from their origin as purposefully created undead. Their limited intelligence means that they respond to situations on an instinctive level, although they have some capacity to retain instructions and learn the most effective ways to help their allies.

NECROSIS CARNEX LORE

Characters with ranks in Knowledge (religion) can learn more about necrosis carnexes. When a character makes a successful skill check, the following lore is revealed, including the information from lower DCs.

Knowledge (Religion)

DC	Result
13	This is a necrosis carnex, an undead creation that unleashes a burst of life-stealing energy when it is destroyed. This result reveals all undead traits.
18	These creatures exude a debilitating aura out to a range of 30 feet, and their mere touch can cause wounds.
23	Necrosis carnexes are particularly vulnerable to damage from good-aligned weapons and spells.
28	A necrosis carnex is created from several corpses bound together with cold iron bands. It serves to support armies of other undead, though its behavior is largely instinctive.

They make few attempts to communicate and understand only the simplest commands.

Carnexes automatically attack and kill living creatures unless instructed not to by their masters. In the absence of a master, they view the most powerful intelligent undead creature in their presence as a figure of authority and willingly obey that creature's commands. In the rare event that carnexes find themselves on their own, they seek out other undead, preferring potent and sentient undead to which they can ally themselves.

Environment: Necrosis carnexes can be found wherever their abilities are needed. They have no native environment, though they often share the habitats of intelligent undead.

Typical Physical Characteristics: Every necrosis carnex is different, because each one is cobbled together from several corpses. It might walk on four hands, or have no arms at all. Each unholy creation is held together by cold iron bands.

Alignment: Although it is barely intelligent, a necrosis carnex understands its duty—to kill and to protect its undead allies. Their unthinking ferocity, and the horrific process used to create them, make necrosis carnexes always neutral evil.

Necrosis carnex

TYPICAL TREASURE

A necrosis carnex carries no treasure of its own, unless a patron has granted it a protective magic item of some kind. The cold iron bands that hold together its undead flesh weigh 10 pounds and are worth 200 gp. Separating the iron from the moldering meat of a necrosis carnex's corpse requires 1 minute of effort.

FOR PLAYER CHARACTERS

A spellcaster of 11th level or higher can create a necrosis carnex with an *animate dead* spell. To do so requires three corpses from Medium creatures and cold-hammered iron bands worth 200 gp. None of this material is consumed in the casting and but instead becomes the undead amalgam of the carnex. When used to create a necrosis carnex, the *animate dead* spell has a casting time of 10 minutes.

NECROSIS CARNEXES IN EBERRON

Ranks of Karrnathi undead soldiers are seeded with necrosis carnexes whenever possible. A unit's carnex functions as a battlefield healer. Unlike a typical humanoid healer, a necrosis carnex can move to the front of a massed group of undead and, by being destroyed, lay waste ranks of enemy soldiers while rejuvenating its allied troops. Introduced late in the Last War, necrosis carnexes had a decisive influence on several battles involving Karrnath's legions.

Undead servants of the Blood of Vol favor necrosis carnexes as companions and healers. Carnexes occasionally participate in missions with Emerald Claw soldiers who are led by an undead creature. The necromancers of the Emerald Claw also value necrosis carnexes as support for their mindless undead slaves.

NECROSIS CARNEXES IN FAERÛN

Necrosis carnexes are relatively rare in Faerûn, as is the lore of their construction.

Only a couple of groups use these creatures with any regularity. Kiaransalee's worshipers sometimes create necrosis carnexes to protect and bolster their other undead creations. Thayan necromancers produce and keep carnexes in their enclaves scattered throughout Faerûn. These creatures are never allowed to muddy the façade so important to the Thayan representatives, but some enclaves harbor secret reserves of undead troops. A single necrosis carnex can make such a force much more effective.

OAKEN DEFENDER

The thicket seems to come alive around you as a massive form bursts from the earth. It is covered with cruel spikes, and many branchlike tentacles flail about it.

OAKEN DEFENDER	CR 12

Usually NG Huge plant
Init +0; **Senses** darkvision 60 ft., low-light vision, tremorsense 60 ft.; Listen +1, Spot +1
Languages understands Sylvan, empathic link 900 ft.

AC 23, touch 8, flat-footed 23
(−2 size, +15 natural)
hp 207 (18 HD); **DR** 10/magic
Immune plant immunities
SR 24
Fort +18, **Ref** +6, **Will** +7

Speed 20 ft. (4 squares), burrow 10 ft. (loose soil)
Melee gore +23 (2d6+12) and
2 slams +21 each (1d8+6)
Space 15 ft.; **Reach** 10 ft.
Base Atk +13; **Grp** +33
Atk Options Cleave, Great Cleave, Power Attack, Whirlwind Attack, magic strike

Abilities Str 35, Dex 10, Con 24, Int 8, Wis 13, Cha 13
SQ find oaken defender, plant traits
Feats Cleave, Diehard, Endurance, Great Cleave, Multiattack, Power Attack, Track, Whirlwind Attack[B]
Skills Hide −8*, Listen +1, Intimidate +22, Spot +1
*An oaken defender gains a +15 bonus on Hide checks when settled in its grove.
Advancement 19–30 HD (Huge); 31–54 HD (Gargantuan)

Empathic Link (Su) An oaken defender has an empathic link with the dryads of its grove, through which it can sense their needs and feelings. This link extends up to 900 feet.

Find Oaken Defender (Su) As the *discern location* spell; always active; caster level 18th. An oaken defender can use this ability only to find another oaken defender on the same plane as itself. All oaken defenders are considered to have seen one another for the purpose of this ability.

Oaken defenders are ferocious protectors of the sacred groves that dryads inhabit. They are rare creatures, usually appearing only when a dryad's oak is attacked. When roused, an oaken defender remains only as long as is necessary to destroy the dryad's enemies.

STRATEGIES AND TACTICS

As guardians of their groves, oaken defenders immediately attack hostile intruders, unless a dryad or other fey is present to calm them. An oaken defender lurks partially under the ground of its chosen home, hiding in the undergrowth, rising up in the midst of interlopers when most or all of them have moved within its reach.

An oaken defender takes advantage of its great size and overpowering strength, using Power Attack to deal maximum damage. Its multiple limbs can serve as both arms and legs as needed. Against one or two foes, it moves about on four limbs and thrashes with the other two. When it faces a large number of enemies, it prefers to stay in place and smash all its foes using Whirlwind Attack. It commonly uses Power Attack in conjunction with Whirlwind Attack, especially when more than four foes are within reach; in such a case, its gore has a +12 bonus on the attack roll and deals 2d6+23 points of damage.

SAMPLE ENCOUNTERS

To face an oaken defender is to be the enemy of a dryad and its tree. The dryads of a grove lend their support to the defender, as do any treants and other forest protectors in the area. Sometimes dryads adopt a militant stance and draw travelers into hostilities, even those who have no evil intent. Even in such cases, an oaken defender rises to assist.

Guardian (EL 12): The roots of a dryad's tree have grown over and completely enclosed a sacred artifact that is the only hope of repelling a fiendish invasion. The dryad is unwilling to risk death even for such a vital need, and the grove's defender hears her silent cry.

Pair (EL 14): An army on its way to war has camped at the edge of an ancient forest, and a squad of soldiers is cutting down trees for fuel without regard for the dryads that live there. Too many soldiers are encamped for the dryads to influence with their spell-like abilities, and even the grove's defender can't defeat them all. A second defender comes to the aid of the assaulted grove.

ECOLOGY

Oaken defenders are massive, long-lived creatures that embody the fury of nature. They resemble enormous masses of vegetation.

An oaken defender is quiescent for almost all its extensive life, resting just beneath the surface of a faerie grove. It might sleep for centuries, while grass, undergrowth, and small shrubs grow on its hide and obscure its vicious spikes. It is in constant empathic contact with the dryads of the grove, though, and at their alarm, it rises like a mountain to their defense. Once the threat has passed, it sinks again into slumber.

While sleeping, an oaken defender does not eat. The ends of its tentacular limbs sprout absorbent tissues that protrude from the soil around the grove to collect rainwater. The dryads support it with nourishment from their trees, which grow delicate roots into its outer skin. Once

OAKEN DEFENDER LORE

Characters with ranks in Knowledge (nature) can learn more about oaken defenders. When a character makes a successful skill check, the following lore is revealed, including the information from lower DCs.

Knowledge (Nature)

DC	Result
15	This is an oaken defender, a savage and intelligent plant creature. This result reveals all plant traits.
22	Oaken defenders are rare beings that protect dryads' groves, spending most of their time asleep. They can live for more than a thousand years.
27	Oaken defenders are resistant to damage from nonmagic weapons.
32	Oaken defenders can sense each other at any distance, allowing them to come to each other's aid when needed.

an oaken defender has come awake, though, the fury of its attack makes it ravenous. It consumes its fallen enemies and might even pursue those who flee to satiate its rapacious hunger.

When an oaken defender ages to a thousand years, it begins the process of reproduction. The new defender starts out as an acorn from a dryad's tree that incubates within a follicle inside the "parent" oaken defender. There, it absorbs nutrients from the parent's body, causing the parent to draw more nourishment in turn from the grove, and it transforms into an embryonic defender. The seed becomes something like an egg, and the developing creature spends nearly a century slowly growing within. At the end of this period, it is about one-quarter the size of the parent, whose body is visibly distended by the enlarged cyst. The new defender is "born" by bursting from the body of the old, which is killed in the process. The parent's corpse provides nourishment for a new growth spurt, after which the young defender takes up the duties of the old one. Sometimes two acorns are incubated in this way, so that a newborn defender can leave to protect a different grove. None of this takes place in isolation. The dryads of the grove tend to the old defender, comforting it and making their farewells. They then assist the young one with acclimating to its new existence.

Oaken defenders can grow truly massive, depending on their age, the size of the grove they inhabit, and how many attackers they have consumed. Conversely, a defender might decrease in size if the grove is under stress, valuing the health of the trees (and the dryads who depend on them) over its own. In extreme circumstances such as drought, a defender might even allow itself to starve for the sake of the oaks' survival.

Environment: Oaken defenders inhabit the same temperate forests as the dryads they protect. The presence of the defender is signaled by a "faerie ring" that encircles the grove with mushroomlike growths (actually the ends of the creature's limbs).

Variants of oaken defenders might instead take up residence in other sorts of environments. For example, an oread (*Fiend Folio* 134) might have a "rocky defender," which grows from a magical gem, as a guardian. The waterfall of a fossergrim (*Fiend Folio* 79) could host a "cascade defender" that slumbers beneath the falls' ledge.

Typical Physical Characteristics: An oaken defender is a gigantic, disk-shaped being up to 15 feet across and weighing 5 tons. Six flexible limbs resembling tentacles sprout at roughly equal intervals from its body, serving as arms or legs as the situation requires. Its body has a woody appearance, something like an exposed root, and large spikes protrude from the top, as long as shortspears. In most situations, oaken defenders' bodies are covered with soil and vegetation, so that they look like the earth has come to life.

The upper surface of a defender's central body resembles an enormous, angry face, making it even more intimidating in combat. It has an immense mouth, like a jagged split in wood, with which it eats defeated adversaries. Its "eyes" are actually light- and heat-sensitive bulges that let it pinpoint enemies as well as a sighted being can.

Oaken defenders have no gender, reproducing in the manner described above.

Alignment: Oaken defenders are peaceful by nature, as their alliance with dryads suggests. They are merciless when defending their groves, however, making the decision to attack intruders based on the situational needs of the dryads. As such, most oaken defenders are neutral good. The few defenders that fall outside this ethos are usually neutral. If a grove's dryads are corrupt, their defender might also be wicked.

Oaken defender

Illus. by J. Nelson

SOCIETY

Oaken defenders are solitary beings, but they are intimately entwined with the dryads and the trees of their groves. This link is both physical, in that they are sustained by their charges, and spiritual, through the psychic and emotional bond they share. Oaken defenders see themselves as bulwarks of nature's defense, and they are very confident in their ability to protect the sacred groves.

Because they are so widely separated and spend so much of their lives asleep, oaken defenders don't form communities with others of their kind. They do maintain a sort of dream link, through which they are subconsciously aware of one another's moods and concerns.

An individual defender doesn't have a name but rather identifies itself by those it guards. For example, one that dwells in a lakeside grove inhabited by two dryads might be known as Twin Sisters Shore.

TYPICAL TREASURE

Oaken defenders do not collect treasure. The dryads they protect do, however, and these fey certainly keep useful items left after the defender has dispatched a threat. Such dryads might have double the standard treasure for their Challenge Rating.

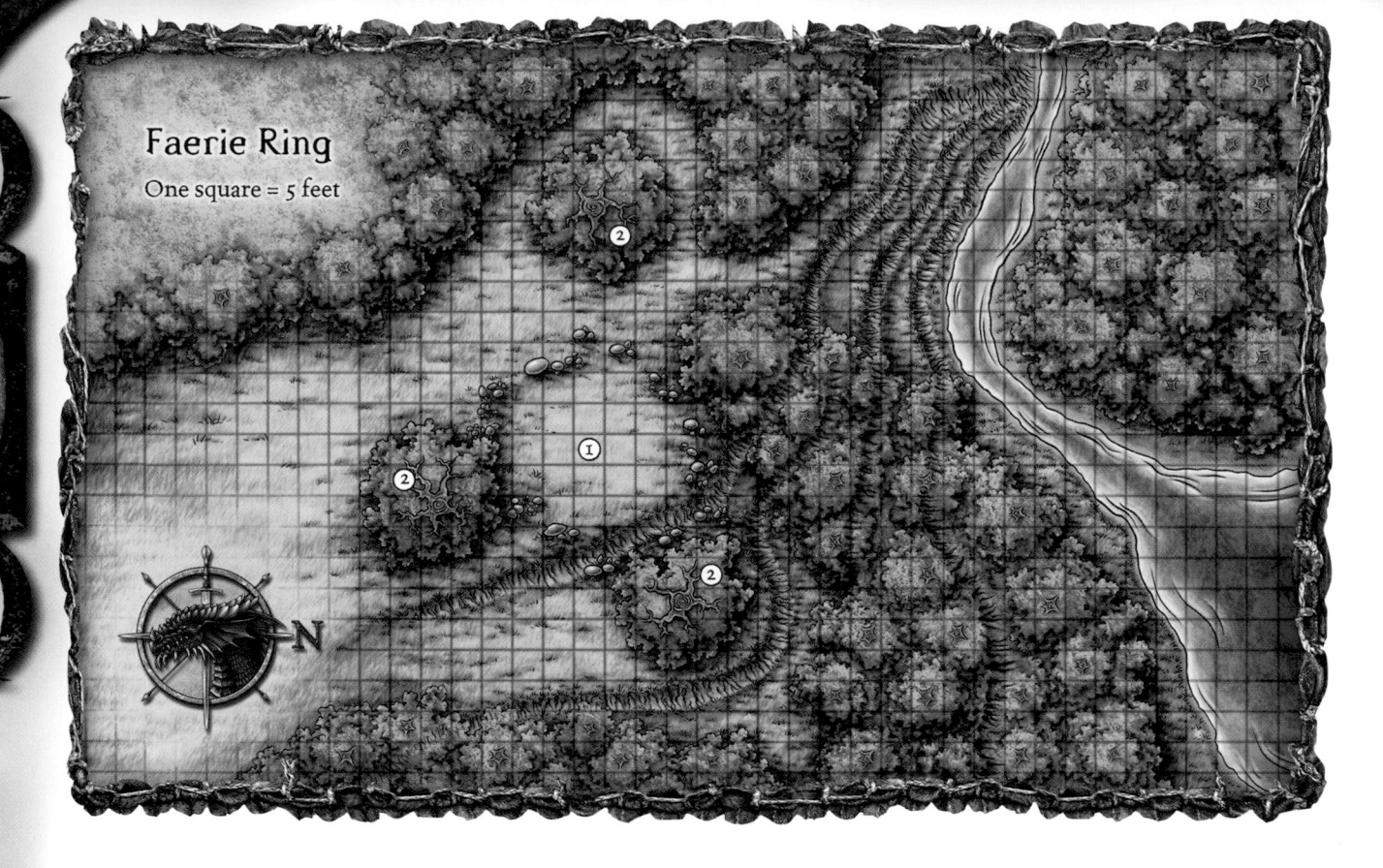

Faerie Ring

One square = 5 feet

OAKEN DEFENDERS IN EBERRON

Ancient trees, some of which are aware, call the Eldeen Reaches home, and in the depths of the forests dwell many fey of all sorts. The western part of the Towering Wood is a manifest zone linked to Thelanis. Here fey powers are augmented, and oaken defenders are unusually large and numerous. The nearness of the Faerie Court might have produced the first defenders, born in the faerie rings and mounds that spring from the earth in this region. The elder Wardens of the Wood also maintain psychic contact with the oaken defenders to supplement the forest's defenses. Oalian is said to speak to them in their dreams, and legend holds that the same Gatekeeper druid who *awakened* the greatpine was responsible for creating the defenders.

OAKEN DEFENDERS IN FAERÛN

The followers of Mielikki revere dryads and other woodland fey, and they consider it a sacred duty to nurture oaken defenders. During the Four Feasts, worshipers bring offerings of nectar to dryad groves and pour these carefully about the faerie rings. The birth of a new defender is a rare and joyous occasion, though tinged with sadness at the death of the old one. When a young defender takes up residence in a heretofore unprotected grove, the local clerics and druids of Mielikki hold a special festival of celebration called Greenhome. For three days, they pray and make offerings of food, and they undertake services for both the grove and its defender.

SAMPLE LAIR: THE FAERIE RING

Three dryads inhabit a rugged hillside deep in the heart of an ancient grove. An oaken defender protects them.

1. Faerie Ring

A clearing lies among the ancient trees. Low berry bushes cluster here and there, and colorful mushrooms sprout in a ring 30 feet across.

The area enclosed by the "mushrooms" is the resting place of the grove's guardian. The clumps of bushes grow around the creature' spines.

Part of the ring extends over a steep hillside. When the guardian awakens, it can move horizontally out of the hill if that is more advantageous.

2. Dryad Oaks

Three magnificent oak trees stand out from the rest of the forest.

Three trees are keyed to this entry. Each is the home of a dryad that has taken the shape of a more ordinary-looking tree in the surrounding woods. Unless intruders actively damage a tree or engage in other destructive activity, the dryads remain camouflaged and wait for them to leave. They use *deep slumber* and *charm person* against threats, calling on the oaken defender only if the opposition is more than they can deal with.

OGRE

Great size and strength make ogres formidable foes in melee, as detailed in the *Monster Manual*—but, handicapped by a brutish culture and poor grasp of strategy, they cannot win wars or command territory. The savage and stupid giants rarely amount to much without the influence of a more intelligent leader. Many other creatures coerce or entice ogres into aiding them and accepting their training.

This entry presents several examples of unusual ogres that present interesting challenges to player characters: a spear-wielding scout, a furious tempest, and a strange servant of mind flayers.

OGRE SCOUT

A female ogre in spiked leather rushes forward with surprising alacrity and lightness of step. As she closes, she points a spear the length of a ship's mast at you.

OGRE SCOUT   **CR 5**

Female ogre scout* 4
   *Class described in *Complete Adventurer*
NE Large giant
Init +3; **Senses** darkvision 60 ft., low-light vision; Listen +4, Spot +8
Languages Common, Giant

AC 20, touch 11, flat-footed 20; Dodge, Mobility, uncanny dodge
   (−1 size, +2 Dex, +4 armor, +5 natural)
hp 71 (8 HD)
Fort +10, **Ref** +7, **Will** +3

Speed 50 ft. (10 squares); Spring Attack
Melee *+1 longspear* +13/+8 (2d6+11/×3) or
Melee mwk armor spikes +13/+8 (1d8+7)
Ranged spear +7 (2d6+7/×3)
Space 10 ft.; **Reach** 10 ft. (20 ft. with *+1 longspear*)
Base Atk +6; **Grp** +17
Atk Options Combat Reflexes, skirmish (+1d6 damage, +1 AC)
Combat Gear *potion of cat's grace*, *potion of bull's strength*

Abilities Str 24, Dex 14, Con 18, Int 6, Wis 12, Cha 4
SQ battle fortitude +1, fast movement, trackless step, trapfinding
Feats Combat Reflexes, Dodge, Mobility, Spring Attack[B]
Skills Hide +9, Jump +16, Listen +4, Move Silently +11, Spot +8
Possessions combat gear plus *+1 studded leather* with masterwork armor spikes, *+1 longspear*, 3 spears

---

Skirmish (Ex) +1 bonus on damage rolls and to AC in any round during which the scout moves at least 10 feet. *Complete Adventurer* 12.
Battle Fortitude (Ex) Bonus on Initiative checks and Fortitude saves while wearing light or no armor and carrying a light load. Included above. *Complete Adventurer* 12.

Most ogres can't fathom the tactics of a scout, but sometimes a member of another race takes the time necessary to train an ogre for the role. Ogre scouts focus on melee attacks to take advantage of their great reach and enormous strength. With the extra speed granted by her class, an ogre scout can charge as far as someone can throw a spear. Even so, ogre scouts usually carry a ranged weapon to attack flying enemies or those who are otherwise beyond their reach.

The ogre scout presented here had the following ability scores before racial adjustments and Hit Dice ability score increases: Str 14, Dex 15, Con 14, Int 10, Wis 12, Cha 8.

Strategies and Tactics

An ogre scout prefers to attack from ambush, so that she can land the first blow. If possible, she drinks her potions before initiating a fight. In combat, she stays on the move, maneuvering toward and away from foes using Spring Attack and thus taking advantage of her skirmish ability. With her longspear in her hands, an ogre scout threatens squares 15 and 20 feet away. She threatens squares up to 10 feet away with her spiked armor. When an enemy stands adjacent to an ogre scout, she moves away, counting on her extreme mobility to protect her from attacks of opportunity.

OGRE TEMPEST

An enormous male ogre in breastplate armor bearing a crude emblem of Gruumsh lumbers toward you. With his thick hands, he spins an oversized axe around himself as he moves.

OGRE TEMPEST   **CR 9**

Male ogre fighter 4/tempest* 2
   *Prestige class described in *Complete Adventurer*
CE Large giant
Init +3; **Senses** darkvision 60 ft., low-light vision; Listen +2, Spot +3
Languages Common, Giant

AC 24, touch 12, flat-footed 21; Dodge, Mobility, tempest defense +1
   (−1 size, +3 Dex, +6 armor, +5 natural, +1 tempest defense)
hp 106 (10 HD)
Fort +16, **Ref** +6, **Will** +2

Speed 40 ft. (8 squares); Spring Attack
Melee *+1 orc double axe* +15/+10 (2d6+8/×3) and
   mwk orc double axe +15/+10 (2d6+3/×3) or
Melee *+1 orc double axe* +16/+11 (2d6+11/×3)
Ranged spear +11 (2d6+7/×3)
Space 10 ft.; **Reach** 10 ft.
Base Atk +9; **Grp** +20
Combat Gear *oil of magic weapon*, *potion of bull's strength*, *potion of cure light wounds*, *potion of protection from good*, *potion of shield of faith (+2)*

Abilities Str 25, Dex 17, Con 18, Int 5, Wis 8, Cha 3
SQ ambidexterity
Feats Dodge, Exotic Weapon Proficiency (orc double axe)[B], Improved Toughness (*Complete Warrior* 101), Improved Two-Weapon Fighting[B], Mobility, Spring Attack[B], Two-Weapon Fighting
Skills Jump +16, Listen +2, Spot +3
Possessions combat gear plus *+1 mithral breastplate*, *+1/masterwork orc double axe*, *cloak of resistance +1*, 3 spears

---

Ambidexterity (Ex) When wielding two weapons or a double weapon, an ogre tempest's penalties for fighting with two weapons are reduced by 1. Included above. *Complete Adventurer* 81.
Tempest Defense (Ex) When wielding two weapons or a double weapon, an ogre tempest gains a +1 bonus to Armor Class. Included above. *Complete Adventurer* 81.

Meetings between orcs and ogres are violent. At times, ogres who win such battles take orcs as slaves instead of killing them; at other times, the orcs triumph and take ogres captive. Orcs recognize the value of ogres in battle, and they treat the captive giants with surprising fairness. If an ogre seems tractable, orcs adopt it into their tribe, converting it to their worship of Gruumsh. Most such ogres become barbarians, but orc tribes that foster fighters sometimes train ogres as tempests.

The ogre tempest presented here had the following ability scores before racial adjustments and Hit Dice ability score increases: Str 15, Dex 18, Con 14, Int 9, Wis 8, Cha 7.

Strategies and Tactics

An ogre tempest acts as an orc tribe's champion and mascot. Wielding an orc double axe and covered with markings in homage to Gruumsh, an ogre tempest making an appearance on a battlefield can strike terror into the enemy and rally shaken orcs.

An ogre tempest uses little strategy. His first attack is usually a charge while swinging his axe with two hands at a foe. Then he moves slowly through the battlefield, making full attacks whenever possible. Brutish and stubborn, an ogre tempest fells one foe before moving on to cut down another. He uses Spring Attack primarily while fleeing from combat, getting in a few blows as he retreats.

OGRE GUARD THRALL

An ogre wielding a greataxe lumbers toward you, its gaze unfocused and its face slack. As it nears, you see four circular depressions in its forehead, each like a scarred-over hole.

OGRE GUARD THRALL	**CR 6**

Always N Large giant
Init –1; **Senses** darkvision 60 ft., low-light vision; Listen –2, Spot –2
Languages —

AC 20, touch 8, flat-footed 20
    (–1 size, –1 Dex, +7 armor, +5 natural)
hp 37 (4 HD); fast healing 5
Immune mind-affecting spells and abilities, stunning
Fort +8, **Ref** +0, **Will** –1

Speed 30 ft. (6 squares) in half-plate; base speed 40 ft.
Melee mwk greataxe +10 (3d6+10/×3)
Special Actions echo mind blast
Space 10 ft.; **Reach** 10 ft.
Base Atk +3; **Grp** +14

Abilities Str 25, Dex 8, Con 19, Int —, Wis 6, Cha 1
SQ guard mind flayer
Feats Toughness[B]
Skills Listen –2, Spot –2
Advancement —
Possessions half-plate, masterwork greataxe

Echo Mind Blast (Su) Being mindless, ogre guard thralls are unaffected by *mind blast*. When a mind flayer catches an ogre guard thrall in the area of a *mind blast*, as a free action, it can choose to emit a second, weaker *mind blast* through the guard thrall. This secondary *mind blast* is a 60-foot cone that stuns those caught in its area for 1d4 rounds; a successful DC 16 Will save negates the stunning effect. An ogre guard thrall can echo only one *mind blast* per round. If a mind flayer catches multiple

ogre guard thralls in its *mind blast,* it must choose one to use this ability. The save DC is Constitution-based.

Guard Mind Flayer (Ex) As long as an ogre guard thrall is not flat-footed or immobilized, it automatically protects any mind flayers within reach, granting each a +2 bonus to AC. If a mind flayer commands it to do so (a free action), a guard thrall can use the aid another action to grant that mind flayer an additional +2 bonus to AC on the next melee attack against it.

Mind flayers regularly attack ogre tribes in subterranean battles, consuming the creatures' ample if underused brain matter. The weak-willed ogres succumb readily to the depredations of the illithids. The mind flayers stumbled upon a strange phenomenon during their feeding—an ogre uses so little of its primitive brain that it can survive having much of it consumed. Of course, treating normal ogres in such a fashion leaves them comatose, but the insidiously clever illithids were intrigued by the idea. They began a process of captive breeding and experimentation that resulted in the creation of ogre guard thralls, powerful but mindless ogres with extraordinary healing ability.

When a mind flayer is within 100 feet, what little remains of an ogre guard thrall's mind picks up the illithid's unspoken desires, and the living automaton does as the mind flayer wishes. This connection alone is not enough to make the transformed ogres into adequate bodyguards, so the mind flayers implant psionically receptive crystals within their skulls. The result is a powerful combatant capable of echoing a mind flayer's *mind blasts.*

Strategies and Tactics

An ogre guard thrall uses whatever tactics a mind flayer commands it to follow. Much like a golem, it is incapable of following complicated commands or thinking on its own. Ogre guard thralls do not innovate, and they cannot interpret commands differently for a new situation. Thus, most illithids keep them close by, so they can direct the thralls in everything. Commanding an ogre guard thrall is a free action that any mind flayer within 100 feet can take. A guard thrall always follows the last command it was given. No illithid has established exclusive control of an ogre guard thrall, and no nonillithid has discovered a means of commanding the creatures.

Mind flayers that are expecting trouble keep ogre guard thralls nearby. If combat begins, an illithid backs away from its thralls in hopes of covering a wider area with its own and the thralls' echoed *mind blast.*

"Dim-witted? Yes. Unpredictable? Yes. But useful, General Aklarl, useful. Why waste the lives of our soldiers killing these ogres when we can convert them?"
—Azthaket, Red Hand war sorcerer and
advisor to a hobgoblin general

SAMPLE ENCOUNTERS

Ogres rarely operate alone, preferring to team up with members of their tribe or another race. Training the chaotic and brutish ogres as specialists takes a great investment in time, materials, and effort. Such an outlay likely means that such ogres are put to use as a core part of a military force. A "minder" that is fluent in Common or Giant accompanies a specialist ogre almost constantly, except when the ogre is given a very simple task or a suicide mission, or the minder is an illithid.

Scouting Party (EL 6): An ogre scout, a bugbear, and two hobgoblins are scouting for a warband of hobgoblins traveling to raid a village. They move at half speed, hiding and moving silently as they go, intending to avoid notice and set up ambushes. The bugbear and hobgoblins hang 50 feet back from the scout so their movement doesn't give them all away. When the ogre sees an intelligent creature, she attacks if she is spotted, but otherwise she waits and attacks from behind when the enemy has engaged the others in her party. When combat occurs, the bugbear charges in, flanking with the ogre when possible. The hobgoblins try to stay out of melee and ready actions to throw javelins at spellcasters.

Rear Guard (EL 9): Four ogre scouts travel about a mile behind a warband of hobgoblins on horseback. The ogres simply follow the obvious tracks of their masters through the woods and attack any intelligent creatures they encounter, including anyone else who follows the warband. When fighting, the ogre scouts attempt to surround enemies, coming from several directions and covering a wide area with their reach.

Tempest Unit (EL 10): An ogre tempest, two orc battle priests (see page 115), and four orcs seek glory in battle. The battle priests stay behind the ogre tempest and use all their spells to heal the giant, while the other orcs charge in to flank foes.

Fighting Core (EL 12): An ogre tempest and two 4th-level barbarian ogres (*MM* 199) form the fighting core of an orc raiding party. Accompanying these ogres are five orc berserkers and a war howler (see page 114). The war howler leads the group, chanting to bolster the ogres and other orcs. He then tumbles into melee to attack vulnerable opponents and enters a rage. Other members of the fighting core simply charge foes, employing flanking attacks if they can.

Hunting Illithids (EL 12): Two mind flayers travel back to their lair along with four ogre guard thralls that are dragging nets filled with stunned and wounded captives. The prisoners are human miners the mind flayers intend to experiment with and use as food. Periodically, a mind flayer takes a moment to use *mind blast* on the guard thralls and captives (affecting the latter twice). When they encounter other creatures, the mind flayers command three guard thralls to attack. The illithids stand adjacent to and behind the fourth thrall, using their *mind blasts* and other psionic abilities.

ECOLOGY

Ogres sleep through the day and hunt at night, although calling such forays "hunting" is misleading. The tribe members arise at sunset and wander in small groups about their territory for hours, attacking and eating any creatures they happen upon. They supplement this diet with fruit and carrion they find along the way. This random lifestyle often leads to some ogres being left hungry and agitated, which causes infighting and makes any encounter with them likely to begin with bloodshed. Winter hits ogres hard, and a tribe resorts to raiding to make it through that season.

Ogres mate and give birth much as humans do. A tribe's members are usually related, so when tribes of ogres meet, mating is foremost on their minds. Ogres lack a sense of emotional attachment. Despite their greedy nature, they aren't possessive about mates or particularly

Illus. by R. Spencer

Ogre guard thrall, scout, and tempest

concerned with a young ogre's parentage. The feast-or-famine nature of the ogre lifestyle harshly affects ogre children, so that just one in three reaches maturity.

Environment: Most ogres live in temperate hills, but nearly any land can host an ogre population, especially if it contains a cave or cavern network in which to take shelter from inclement weather. Ogres also inhabit the grottoes of the underground.

Typical Physical Characteristics: An adult male ogre is about 10 feet tall and weighs roughly 650 pounds. Females are smaller, standing about 9 feet tall and weighing 600 pounds.

An ogre guard thrall is sometimes gray-skinned and has a vapid expression. When not commanded by a mind flayer, it does little but stand and drool. Indeed, guard thralls would starve to death if they were not commanded to feed upon the victims of their illithid masters.

Alignment: Small-minded, selfish, and wrathful, ogres are usually chaotic evil. Ogres taken as slaves by another race might shift alignment if trained and exposed to consistent treatment. Paladins hoping to convert ogres to the side of light should think twice, though. An ogre might become neutral evil or chaotic neutral, but only the most unusual ogre becomes wholly neutral, let alone lawful or good.

SOCIETY

Ogres live in small, primitive tribes. An ogre chieftain leads a given tribe by right of might, relinquishing command of the group when he loses a battle to another ogre. A chieftain that gives up any measure of authority loses it all.

Few ogres are capable of constructing items, so most use crude weapons such as greatclubs and stone mauls, and they wear hide armor. Ogres scavenge what they can from slain foes, but since they possess little ability to think in the long term, few take good care of such items, which often end up broken or lost.

Similarly, ogres rarely construct dwellings, preferring to live in caves, in ruins, or simply under the open sky. Some tribes copy the dwellings they see other creatures using, making crude tents of animal skins or ramshackle buildings of piled logs, but such structures rarely stand for more than a year.

Ogres seldom practice religion unless they are introduced to the worship of a deity by another race. Those that have a great deal of contact with orcs, even as enemies, might revere Gruumsh. Ogres bossed about by other giants worship those giants' deities. Such "worship" consist of little more than howling the deity's name in battle, but ogres can be taught to pray in more conventional ways.

Territorial by nature, ogres come into conflict with any other intelligent creatures they encounter. Unfortunately for ogres, they lack the wits to carry on protracted conflicts. They often flee the area if their first couple of assaults can't crush resistance.

Most ogres have a simple mentality. Other creatures can force ogres to do as they desire by demonstrations of strength. Thus, ogres often end up living and working with such creatures. Even much weaker beings can intimidate a tribe of ogres by consistently defeating them.

TYPICAL TREASURE

Ogres have standard treasure for NPCs of their Challenge Rating. They favor armor and weapons, but ogres subjugated by another race carry whatever equipment is given them.

OGRES AS CHARACTERS

See page 199 of the *Monster Manual* for information on ogres as characters. Ogre guard thralls, being mindless, are not suitable choices for player characters.

OGRES IN EBERRON

Most of Eberron's ogres live in Droaam, where they serve in the monstrous armies of that nation. Long exposure to other races has caused the ogres of Eberron to be more cultured if not more intelligent. Ogres of higher intelligence and charisma appear regularly in Droaam's armies and among the wild ogre tribes.

OGRES IN FAERÛN

Although ogres live all across Faerun, their largest concentration is found in the Great Gray Land of Thar, which was once ruled by a line of ogre "tharkuls" (kings). The Small Teeth of Amn were also once ogre-held territory, until Crown Prince Imnel of Amn prevailed during the Ogre Wars. In recent years, the surviving ogres of Amn have flocked to the banner of the Sothillisian Empire, centered on the newly conquered port city of Murann.

OGRE LORE

Characters with ranks in Knowledge (nature) can learn more about ogres. Characters with ranks in Knowledge (dungeoneering) can learn more about ogre guard thralls. When a character makes a successful skill check, the following lore is revealed, including the information from lower DCs.

Knowledge (Nature)

DC	Result
13	This is an ogre, an evil and savage giant. This result reveals all giant traits.
18	In ogre society, the strongest leads the others. These giants have a primitive lifestyle and make no items of note.
23	Other races, orcs and hobgoblins in particular, sometimes capture and train ogres. Such ogres are usually formidable.

Knowledge (Dungeoneering)

DC	Result
16	This creature is an ogre guard thrall, a mindless giant created by mind flayers. It is immune to mind-affecting magic. This result reveals all giant traits.
21	An ogre guard thrall protects its mind flayer charges with surprising ability. The process of creating a guard thrall renders it immune to stunning attacks and able to heal at an alarming rate.
26	An ogre guard thrall is physically potent, but it also has the dangerous ability to echo a mind flayer's *mind blast*.

Mithral Mines

One square = 10 feet

+0 ft.

+40 ft.

+20 ft.

(1)

+70 ft.

(2)

(3)

+5 ft.
+10 ft.
+15 ft.
+20 ft.
+25 ft.

(4)

(4)

(4)

+10 ft.

(5)

(5)

(5)

+40 ft.

(5)

+10 ft.

(5)

(5)

+20 ft.

+15 ft.

(5)

(6)

(5)

+20 ft.

+60 ft.

+40 ft.

+10 ft.

(7)

+80 ft.

N

(8)

Altar

(9)

1. Royal chambers
2. Slave pens
3. Talus pile
4. Stores
5. Homes

6. Rope bridge
7. Temple
8. Priest's quarters
9. Burial chamber

Curtain

Barred gate

Ladder

ORC

Orcs are among the most dangerous of evil humanoids because of their great strength and relentless, warlike nature. An orc at peace is an orc looking for a fight. As detailed in the *Monster Manual*, orc society is like an army waging continual war against all other creatures. It pauses only to rest between battles. Its allies are temporary.

Orcs are organized into tribes and clans with a hierarchy based solely on personal power. As long as an orc chieftain can continue to lead his tribe to success in battle, they support him. Loot is a measure of triumph. An orc horde might fail to defeat an enemy army, but the orcs see the attack as a victory as long as the warriors sack a few villages, carry off plenty of food, drink, and treasure, and escape to fight another day.

This entry provides several archetypical orc adversaries: a raging berserker, a feral bard, and a battle priest of Gruumsh. In addition, two more unusual orc characters might threaten the PCs: a cleric of pestilence touched by a grim deity, and a spy who can pass for human.

ORC BERSERKER

A brutish, battle-scarred orc charges toward you, his jagged greataxe held high.

ORC BERSERKER (RAGING)   CR 4

Male orc barbarian 4
CE Medium humanoid
Init +1; **Senses** darkvision 60 ft.; Listen +7, Spot +0
Languages Common, Orc

AC 14, touch 9, flat-footed 14; uncanny dodge
(+1 Dex, +5 armor, −2 raging)
hp 48 (4 HD)
Fort +9, **Ref** +3, **Will** +4
Weakness light sensitivity

Speed 40 ft. (8 squares)
Melee mwk greataxe +13 (1d12+10/×3)
Ranged javelin +5 (1d6+7)
Base Atk +4; **Grp** +11
Atk Options Power Attack, rage 2/day (7 rounds)
Combat Gear *potion of jump, potion of shield of faith (+4)*

Abilities Str 24, Dex 13, Con 18, Int 6, Wis 10, Cha 8
SQ fast movement, trap sense +1
Feats Power Attack, Weapon Focus (greataxe)
Skills Jump +17, Listen +7, Spot +0
Possessions combat gear plus *+1 chain shirt*, masterwork greataxe, 3 javelins, *cloak of resistance +1*

When not raging, an orc berserker has the following changed statistics:
AC 16, touch 11, flat-footed 16
hp 40 (4 HD)
Fort +7, **Will** +2
Melee mwk greataxe +11 (1d12+7/×3)
Ranged javelin +5 (1d6+5)
Grp +9
Abilities Str 20, Con 14
Skills Jump +15

An orc berserker is a skilled warrior who has proven himself in combat, both in war and in duels against his rivals in the tribe. He is vicious and selfish. The typical berserker cares only about acquiring personal prestige, treasure, and power. If the tribe also happens to defeat a foe, so much the better.

Berserkers don't so much lead as have retinues of warriors who want to share in their fame. The easiest way for an orc warrior to ascend in the tribe's ranks is to impress a berserker and earn his favor. Orc chieftains look upon their berserkers almost as prized pets. As tribal champions, berserkers are the backbone of the group's fighting ability. Their victories enhance the chief's reputation. To keep them in line and douse any thoughts they might have of taking power for themselves, a chieftain lavishes his berserkers with loot second only to what he takes for himself.

The orc berserker presented here had the following ability scores before racial adjustments and Hit Dice ability score increases: Str 15, Dex 13, Con 14, Int 8, Wis 12, Cha 10.

Strategy and Tactics

In battle, a berserker allows his warrior hangers-on to engage the enemy before joining the melee. He drinks his potions while the warriors move in. A berserker expects his entourage to create flanking opportunities for him, even if they have to submit to attacks of opportunity to do so. When fighting, a berserker aims to deal as much damage as possible, using Power Attack even before learning whether he can hit his opponent.

An orc berserker's bluster hides a core of cowardice. He prefers to terrorize easy targets. Unless a berserker has a number of warriors to back him up, he escapes from a capable foe to fetch reinforcements. The tribe is simply a resource that he uses for sustenance and protection. A wily orc berserker knows that if he flees a losing battle, he can always join a new tribe.

WAR HOWLER

At the forefront of the orc army is a tattooed figure who howls terrible imprecations as his followers roar with fury.

WAR HOWLER (RAGING)   CR 4

Male orc barbarian 2/bard 2
CE Medium humanoid
Init +2; **Senses** darkvision 60 ft.; Listen +6, Spot −1
Languages Common, Orc

AC 14, touch 10, flat-footed 14; Dodge, Mobility, uncanny dodge
(+2 Dex, +4 armor, −2 raging)
hp 34 (4 HD)
Fort +6, **Ref** +5, **Will** +4
Weakness light sensitivity

Speed 40 ft. (8 squares)
Melee mwk greataxe +7 (1d12+4/×3)
Ranged javelin +5 (1d6+3)
Base Atk +3; **Grp** +6
Atk Options rage 1/day (6 rounds)
Combat Gear *necklace of fireballs (type I)*

Abilities Str 16, Dex 14, Con 16, Int 11, Wis 8, Cha 14
SQ fast movement
Feats Dodge, Mobility
Skills Balance +4, Intimidate +8, Jump +16, Listen +6,
Spot −1
Possessions combat gear plus +1 *studded leather armor*,
masterwork greataxe, 4 javelins

When not raging, an orc war howler has the following
changed statistics:
AC 16, touch 12, flat-footed 16
hp 26 (4 HD)
Fort +4, **Will** +2
Melee mwk greataxe +5 (1d12+1/×3)
Ranged javelin +5 (1d6+1)
Grp +4
Special Actions bardic music 2/day (inspire courage +1,
fascinate 1 target, countersong)
Bard Spells Known (CL 2nd):
1st (1/day)—*cause fear* (DC 13), *cure light wounds*
0 (3/day)—*daze* (DC 12), *detect magic, know direction,
prestidigitation, resistance*
Abilities Str 12, Con 12
SQ bardic knowledge +4
Skills Bluff +7, Diplomacy +4, Disguise +2 (+4 acting), Jump
+14, Knowledge (history) +5, Perform +7, Tumble +9

War howlers are rare among orcs, but their talent for inspiring blood thirst in the tribe's warriors makes them highly
valuable. Few of them survive to become practiced warriors—their obvious leadership skills make them prime
rivals for the chieftain's supremacy. Only the greatest orc
warlords, those whose rule and talent are beyond reproach,
have the confidence to field many war howlers.

War howlers are the bards of the orcs. They memorize
ancient chants of hatred against all other races. The clerics
of Gruumsh teach that the other humanoids stole the lands
that were the orcs' birthright. The litanies list their enemies'
many crimes, and the war howlers' stirring delivery drives
the other warriors forward in battle.

The orc war howler presented here had the following ability scores before racial adjustments and Hit Dice ability score
increases: Str 8, Dex 14, Con 12, Int 13, Wis 10, Cha 15.

Strategy and Tactics

True fanatics, war howlers lead from the front. An orc berserker might have a coterie of admiring warriors, but a war
howler is a functional field commander. The courage a howler
stokes, along with his devotion to the orc cause, makes him
an inspiring figure on the battlefield.

Orc war howlers seek out enemy spellcasters, correctly rea-
soning that such enemies can scythe through the orc ranks
with their spells. A howler starts a battle with his inspire
courage ability. He then casts *cause fear* on a spellcaster's nearest defender, and finally he rages. Relying on superior speed
and his Mobility feat, he lunges past the remaining enemy
warriors to attack his chosen foe. Inspired orcs follow him
in, some of them tying up the enemy's front-line fighters and
others protecting the war howler's back.

ORC BATTLE PRIEST

*This shamanistic figure is tattooed with blood-red symbols, domi-
nated by the eye of Gruumsh. Bone fetishes and feathers dangle
from his hair and clothing. He shouts a guttural, savage prayer.*

ORC BATTLE PRIEST   CR 1
Male orc cleric 1
CE Medium humanoid
Init +1; **Senses** darkvision 60 ft.; Listen +1, Spot +1
Languages Common, Orc

AC 17, touch 11, flat-footed 16
(+1 Dex, +6 armor)
hp 10 (1 HD)
Fort +4, **Ref** +1, **Will** +3
Weakness light sensitivity

Speed 20 ft. (4 squares) in banded mail; base speed 30 ft.
Melee mwk spear +4 (1d8+3/×3)
Ranged spear +2 (1d8+2/×3)
Base Atk +0; **Grp** +2
Special Actions feat of strength (+1 Str, 1 round), rebuke
undead 3/day (+0, 2d6+1, 1st), spontaneous casting
(*inflict* spells)
Combat Gear *potion of aid*
Cleric Spells Prepared (CL 1st):
1st—*bless, enlarge person*ᴰ (DC 12), *shield of faith*
0—*cure minor wounds, detect magic, resistance*
D: Domain spell. Deity: Gruumsh. Domains: Strength, War

Abilities Str 14, Dex 12, Con 14, Int 6, Wis 13, Cha 11
Feats Combat Casting, Weapon Focus (spear)ᴮ
Skills Concentration +4, Knowledge (religion) +0, Listen +1,
Spot +1
Possessions combat gear plus banded mail, masterwork
spear, 3 spears

An orc battle priest travels with orc raiding parties and war
bands to provide counsel and religious instruction. The priest
reads the omens, invokes prayers to Gruumsh, and makes the
proper sacrifices before and after battle. A battle priest uses
his spells to enhance other orc warriors. He grants them the
blessing of Gruumsh so that they might slay their enemies
and win glory in the deity's name.

Orcs compete for a battle priest's favor by offering him
bribes and other gifts. They know that warriors who receive
spells from a priest have a much better chance of surviving
a battle.

The orc battle priest presented here had the following ability scores before racial adjustments: Str 10, Dex 12, Con 14,
Int 8, Wis 15, Cha 13.

Strategy and Tactics

A battle priest casts *bless* at the start of an encounter, then
casts *shield of faith* on himself. He saves *enlarge person* for
another warrior who has shown skill and talent in combat.
These priorities change if an enemy cleric, particularly a
cleric of Corellon Larethian, is involved in the fight. In this
case, the priest casts *enlarge person* on himself and charges
forward to slay his rival.

Battle priests illustrate the fundamental contradiction in
orc culture. They love war, exult in slaughter, and lust after
gold, jewels, and other loot, but they value their own skin

over the good of the tribe as a whole. A priest expects the warriors to fight and die for his benefit, as befits a chosen disciple of Gruumsh. Yet Gruumsh's eye watches his priests. The deity can forgive self-interested behavior, but he cannot abide a cleric who cowers in the face of a true adversary. A battle priest might hem and haw at the edge of a battle, but he charges into the conflict when an enemy cleric is revealed.

ORC PLAGUE SPEAKER

A pallid, scrawny orc wearing full plate points a bony claw toward you, muttering terrible words of death and disease.

ORC PLAGUE SPEAKER   CR 7
Male unholy scion* orc cleric 5
  *Template described in *Heroes of Horror*
NE Medium outsider (augmented humanoid, evil, native)
Init +5; **Senses** darkvision 60 ft.; Listen +4, Spot +4
Languages Abyssal, Common, Giant, Infernal, Orc

AC 22, touch 13, flat-footed 21
  (+1 Dex, +9 armor, +2 deflection)
Immune mind-affecting spells and abilities, poison
Resist acid 5, cold 5, fire 5; **SR** 15
hp 36 (5 HD); fast healing 4; **DR** 5/good or magic
Fort +6, **Ref** +2, **Will** +8
Weakness light sensitivity

Speed 20 ft. (4 squares) in full plate; base speed 30 ft.
Melee heavy mace +4 (1d8+1 plus unholy strike) and
  claw −1 (1d4 plus unholy strike) or
Melee 2 claws +4 each (1d4+1 plus unholy strike)
Base Atk +3; **Grp** +4
Atk Options unholy strike
Special Actions death touch 1/day (5d6), rebuke undead 5/
  day (+4, 2d6+7, 5th), smite 1/day (+4 attack, +5 damage),
  spontaneous casting (*inflict* spells)
Combat Gear potion of cure light wounds, Quaal's feather
  token (whip)
Cleric Spells Prepared (CL 5th):
  3rd—contagion^D (+4 melee touch, DC 17), *dispel magic,*
    meld into stone
  2nd—aid, bull's strength, death knell^D (DC 16), *hold*
    person (DC 16)
  1st—bane (DC 15), cause fear^D (DC 15), *deathwatch, cure*
    light wounds, shield of faith
  0—create water, cure minor wounds, detect magic, read
    magic, resistance
  D: Domain spell. Deity: Yurtrus (*Faiths and Pantheons*
    151). Domains: Death, Destruction
Spell-Like Abilities (CL 5th):
  3/day—charm person (DC 13), *protection from good*
  1/day—desecrate, enervation (+4 ranged touch)

Abilities Str 12, Dex 12, Con 14, Int 16, Wis 18, Cha 15
SQ familial charm
Feats Combat Casting, Improved Initiative
Skills Concentration +10, Heal +12, Knowledge (arcana) +8,
  Knowledge (religion) +11, Knowledge (the planes) +6,
  Listen +4, Spellcraft +13, Spot +4
Possessions combat gear plus *+1 full plate,* heavy mace,
  periapt of Wisdom +2

Unholy Strike (Su) A plague speaker's natural and armed
  melee attacks are considered evil-aligned for the purpose
  of overcoming damage reduction, and they deal an extra

2d6 points of damage against good creatures. *Heroes of Horror* 157.
Familial Charm (Su) A plague speaker's mother acts as if under a constant *charm person* spell generated by the plague speaker. *Heroes of Horror* 157.

Orc plague speakers are the accursed representatives of Yurtrus, the orc god of pestilence. Plague speakers do not choose their path but are born to it. Legend holds that once each year, on the winter solstice, Yurtrus reaches out and touches an infant orc in the womb. This orc is born with whitish skin, pink eyes, and a slender, weak frame. Other orcs dare not slay this abomination, for these traits mark the child as Yurtrus's chosen speaker.

A plague speaker is a hallowed figure who strikes terror into the rest of the tribe. Yurtrus is said to visit plagues upon orcs who stray from Gruumsh's directives. Orc tribes that go too long without raiding their neighbors, slaying dwarves and elves, and despoiling the land court destruction at Yurtrus's hands.

A plague speaker is an emissary of Yurtrus, but he is an outcast. Although the rest of the orcs respect his position, they also fear him, his blasphemous origins, and his vile god. He is given a secure place to sleep (well away from the rest of the tribe), ample food and drink, and a share of the treasure from any raids. The speaker spends his days tending a small shrine to Yurtrus, caring for the sick and the dead, and ensuring that the chieftain does nothing to rouse the orc deities' ire. A plague speaker's only company is usually his mother, who idolizes him and might herself be a potent spellcaster.

The orc plague speaker presented here had the following ability scores before racial and template adjustments, Hit Dice ability score increases, and equipment bonuses: Str 8, Dex 10, Con 14, Int 12, Wis 15, Cha 13.

Strategy and Tactics

Since a plague speaker dwells near an orc lair, but usually not within it, he often becomes aware of disturbances in the tribal domain before he is personally threatened. When this happens, he readies himself to come to the tribe's aid and take intruders by surprise. Though the tribe's warriors gladly take advantage of any confusion he causes, they don't fight by his side. A plague speaker stands alone.

Whenever possible, before entering battle, a plague speaker casts *deathwatch*. He then follows with *aid, protection from good, resistance,* and *shield of faith* to protect himself, and *bull's strength* to increase his damage potential. He usually announces his presence with *bane,* followed by *cause fear* or *hold person* against a foe that looks like a tough fighter. If he is able, he casts an area *dispel magic* and then *contagion,* which he delivers on the first chance he gets after entering combat. A plague speaker prefers to confer Yurtrus's special gift of *contagion* by using a claw attack on an opponent that appears frail.

If the situation takes a bad turn, or if the orcs appear to be on the verge of defeat, a plague speaker uses *meld into stone* to escape his enemies. If the attackers destroy his tribe, a plague speaker travels in search of a new home. Any orc tribe he meets must grudgingly accept him, lest they call down Yurtrus's wrath.

HALF-ORC INFILTRATOR

Only close examination reveals the nonhuman ancestry of this traveler. She seems harmless, but in a flash she drives a dagger toward your belly.

HALF-ORC INFILTRATOR	**CR 3**

Female half-orc rogue 3
NE Medium humanoid (orc)
Init +6; **Senses** darkvision 60 ft.; Listen +0, Spot +0
Languages Common, Orc

AC 16, touch 12, flat-footed 14
   (+2 Dex, +4 armor)
hp 16 (3 HD)
Resist evasion
Fort +2, **Ref** +5, **Will** +1

Speed 30 ft. (6 squares)
Melee mwk dagger +5 (1d4/19–20)
Ranged mwk dagger +5 (1d4/19–20)
Base Atk +2; **Grp** +2
Atk Options sneak attack +2d6
Combat Gear *potion of invisibility, potion of reduce person*

Abilities Str 10, Dex 15, Con 13, Int 10, Wis 10, Cha 12
SQ trapfinding
Feats Improved Initiative, Weapon Finesse
Skills Balance +4, Bluff +6, Diplomacy +5, Disguise +9 (+11 acting), Gather Information +6, Hide +8, Intimidate +3, Jump +2, Knowledge (local) +5, Listen +0, Move Silently +8, Open Lock +7, Search +4, Sense Motive +5, Spot +0, Tumble +7
Possessions combat gear plus *+1 studded leather armor,* 2 masterwork daggers, disguise kit, masterwork thieves' tools

A half-orc born to an orc tribe usually fills the same role any other orc might. Sometimes, a half-orc who favors her human parent serves a forward-thinking orc chieftain as a spy.

In most cases, a half-orc infiltrator is encountered in a large settlement. She enters the area, usually posing as a mercenary or vendor, and assesses its defenses from inside. While she gathers information quietly, she also makes maps of the place. An infiltrator might enter the town's sewers in search of a secret entrance that avoids the walls and their guards. If an evil cult or similar group operates in the community, the infiltrator makes contact with them to offer an alliance.

The half-orc infiltrator presented here had the following ability scores before racial adjustments: Str 8, Dex 15, Con 13, Int 12, Wis 10, Cha 14.

Strategy and Tactics

A half-orc infiltrator's goal is to gather intelligence for the tribe and to organize an attack from within. She is not a combatant. An infiltrator either reports her findings to the tribal chief or conducts a guerrilla campaign in the hours before the tribe attacks. She might open a town gate and disable the mechanism used to close it, assassinate or impersonate an officer in the militia, free jailed convicts to help spread confusion, start fires, and so forth. If an infiltrator is exposed, she flees as quickly as possible. She marks those who have harmed her and returns to hound such persons as soon as she can, perhaps using a disguise to get close to her enemies.

A half-orc infiltrator's combat proficiency is weak compared to a typical orc champion's, but her excellent skills make her a subtle opponent. She uses Bluff to feint or to create a diversion to escape when she must fight a tough opponent alone, and she employs Tumble to get an advantageous position on the battlefield.

If an infiltrator is with a tribe under attack, she uses one of two basic strategies. She might hide at the edge of the camp or in a rarely used side passage, trailing her

Orc berserker, war howler, battle priest, and half-orc infiltrator

ORC

enemies and taking them from behind when they engage other orcs. Alternatively, she might pose as a slave to insinuate herself into a group of soft-hearted opponents, choosing a strategic target to eliminate when the time is right.

An infiltrator is no fool. If she is unnoticed but can't use her sneak attack, she doesn't reveal herself. Discretion is the better part of valor, and she flees if the situation looks dire or if attackers target her for elimination.

"You got nothing I can't take, weakling."
—Tareg, orc berserker

SAMPLE ENCOUNTERS

Orcs are raiders and warmongers. They travel in bands and are rarely found alone.

Individual (EL 1/2–3): A lone orc is a rare sight, and such a wanderer is usually a scout for a larger group and a capable individual. Even orc scouts usually travel in pairs.

EL 3: Bruuna is a half-orc infiltrator traveling to the nearest settlement to scope it out for her tribe. She appears to be a somewhat civilized half-orc.

Gang (EL 1–7): Young orcs group into gangs of two to four to undertake small-scale forays into the territory of other humanoids, looking to pick off travelers and raid outlying farms and homes for glory and loot. Sometimes the members of these gangs are redoubtable.

EL 5: Dagu, Gar, and Tareg form a gang that aims to waylay trekkers on a nearby caravan trail. Tareg, an orc berserker, is the group's leader, but even he listens to the counsel of Gar the battle priest. Dagu is a typical orc warrior (*MM* 203) along for the fun.

Raiders (EL 6–9): A squad of orc raiders includes up to twenty warriors and a few elite individuals who lead.

EL 9: On Bruuna's heels comes a crusade led by Shamoz, a war howler. A berserker named Heg has taken up Shamoz's banner, along with four battle priests and a dozen warriors.

ECOLOGY

Orcs are ferocious creatures with no respect for life or their surroundings. Whenever possible, they inhabit natural shelters or settlements built by other creatures, rather than building fortifications from scratch. Wasteful and oblivious to their consumption, orcs strip their territory bare if they can't expand into new lands. Their inefficiency fuels their desire to conquer.

Harsh living and constant warfare, both of which contribute to their high mortality rate, define the existence of orcs. These factors are offset by a strong reproductive urge, and consequently a high birth rate. Orc females carry their children to term in only six months, and multiple births are common. Some orc children die due to the tribe's unforgiving way of life, but many grow up toughened by their upbringing.

Orcs reach physical maturity in about thirteen years, and most are ready to take up the axe for their tribe a year or two later. Orcs age quickly, reaching old age after only thirty-seven years.

Omnivorous and not the least bit picky, orcs can subsist on provisions that other humanoids find unacceptable, including carrion and the flesh of sentient creatures. Still, most orcs prefer fresh meat and blood.

Environment: Orcs usually inhabit temperate hills, but they move into any region where they can exploit the resources. Orcs still prefer areas with natural shelter from direct sunlight.

Typical Physical Characteristics: An adult male orc is a little over 6 feet tall and weighs about 210 pounds. Females are slightly smaller but often just as strong. All orcs have gray skin and sport wild, coarse hair, but individuals vary widely in appearance.

Alignment: Orcs are brutish and bloodthirsty, selfish and devious. They kill and destroy without a thought to the consequences, and they dominate and persecute even other orcs. Every orc craves personal authority and comfort and is willing to eradicate rivals to secure these wants. As such, orcs are often chaotic evil, with chaotic neutral being the

ORC LORE

Characters with ranks in Knowledge (local) can learn more about orcs or half-orcs. A character with Knowledge (religion) can learn more about orc religious practices. When a character makes a successful skill check, the following lore is revealed, including the information from lower DCs.

Knowledge (Local)

DC	Result
10	This is an orc (or half-orc), a strong and usually bloodthirsty humanoid. This result reveals all humanoid and orc traits.
15	Orcs are bellicose and warlike. Their culture is based on the right of might and the warrior ideal, so they often take what they want and need from others by raiding. They hate all other humanoid races but reserve a special loathing for elves.
20	Orc crafts are based on war, religion, or survival. Male orcs dominate, while females form the stable base of an orc tribe.

Knowledge (Religion)

DC	Result
10	Orcs practice a dark religion centered on their war deity, Gruumsh. The orc deities hate the elven and dwarven deities.
15	The orc pantheon includes Gruumsh's war lieutenants; the mother goddess Luthic, Gruumsh's wife; Shargaas, the orc god of darkness and trickery; and Yurtrus, the orc deity of death and disease.
20	Oral orc litanies teach that the gods of other humanoid races, particularly elves and dwarves, cheated Gruumsh out of good places for his people to dwell. This belief is the basis of orc hatred and rage.
25	The orc deities sometimes bless orcs with unholy offspring. These powerful young always rise to positions of power within an orc tribe.

most common exception. An orc individual or group might adopt a differing outlook, but another creature often controls or governs such orcs—one they fear or revere.

SOCIETY

Orc society is tribal, and it is based around the ideals of survival, strength, fear, and war. These principles are, in turn, founded in the orcs' veneration of Gruumsh.

Orcs consider it a gift from Gruumsh that they can survive in places where other sentient creatures can't or won't, but they have nothing resembling racial solidarity. Each values his or her life and comfort above the lives of others. An orc doesn't trust fellow tribe members enough to become attached to them or be willing to sacrifice for them, but seeks as much pleasure, power, and wealth as can be acquired.

These views are an obstacle to racial unity. Orcs focus much of their energy on gaining and maintaining status within the tribe. The strong rule the weak, the clever control the foolish, and the feeble are left with nothing. This world-view spills over into orcs' treatment of everything. Continued existence is a right only of the fit.

Survival requires resources, however, and orcs see the world as theirs for the taking. Orc religion holds that the dwarven and elven deities unfairly cheated Gruumsh out of territory for his creations. So Gruumsh smote the lands to make caves and badlands for the orcs. He also made his children strong, so they could take whatever they needed from others. He made them bloodthirsty and selfish, so the frail couldn't drag down the mighty.

Orcs learn these credos at an early age, mostly from cruel experience. Infants are weaned quickly, lest they weaken the mother. As they grow, orc toddlers are more and more expected to fulfill their needs and wants for themselves. Some long-sighted orc mothers help their children in ways that won't make the child dependent or incompetent, securing the young one's loyalty later in life. Children who succeed at taking what they need become resilient and capable by orc standards, and they earn a place among the adults.

Modeled after Gruumsh's absolute authority over his lessers in the orc pantheon, orc tribes are usually led by a chieftain who is the strongest male in the tribe. Male orcs have complete power over the fate of their mates and children. Clerics of Gruumsh, who are also always male, are very influential. They cull the weak and undermine ineffectual chiefs.

Females among the orcs are commonly subservient, and nothing about orc mating is romantic or monogamous, with the mightiest warriors taking as many mates as they can support. But every orc subconsciously knows that those who provide for the tribal home and give birth to the next generation are the tribe's backbone. Further, while many female orcs do little more than bear children and gather food, strong females are barred only from becoming clerics of Gruumsh. Many powerful male orcs are fiercely loyal to their mothers, giving such females sway in the tribe despite the appearance of male authority. Magical power also grants influence, and a sufficiently strong female orc can carve out a place for herself if she can defeat the males who would subjugate her.

Few professions have specific gender associations in orc culture. Male orcs happen to favor warrior roles, and gifted females favor spellcasting. This latter instance foments a belief among orcs that noncombat magic is a feminine craft; males who practice magic had better be useful in battle to avoid the appearance of weakness.

Orcs of both genders are averse to jobs that are labor-intensive with little quick reward. Thus, orcs take sentient creatures as slaves. Slaves do the work no orc wants to do, such as farming or mining. An orc who owns a slave gains status, wealth, and personal comfort based on the amount of work that slave provides.

TYPICAL TREASURE

Though a tribe's wealth is disproportionately distributed toward the top of the chain of command, orcs have standard treasure for their Challenge Rating. Most orcs favor weapons, armor, and portable treasures that display both affluence and ability. An orc berserker might string the eye teeth of dwarves he has slain into a silver necklace, while another orc might wield a bejeweled elven longsword to show his enemies he has beaten a rich adversary.

ORCS AS CHARACTERS

See page 204 of the *Monster Manual* for information on orcs as characters.

ORCS IN EBERRON

The orcs of Eberron number fewer than most other humanoid races, and they live in inhospitable and remote places. They are unusual in that they are neither as destructive nor as evil, in general, as orcs in other settings. Most orcs live in the Shadow Marches, and the Ironroot and Endworld Mountains hold decent populations. Khorvaire's orcs cling to traditional ways, and those of the Shadow Marches live and interbreed with humans. Many orcs still serve the Gatekeeper druid sect that helped cut Eberron's ties with Xoriat during the ancient war with the daelkyr. Too many orcs, however, have turned against the ancient ways and now worship the Dragon Below, fighting their kin to release the horrors the Gatekeepers trapped in Khyber.

ORCS IN FAERÛN

Orcs in Faerûn are varied. Those from the North and the Spine of the World are known as mountain orcs, and they are the oldest of their kind on Toril. The East is home to gray orcs, which are more civilized and devout than mountain orcs but no less evil. Rare in the lands lit by the sun, deep orcs, or orogs, are descended from mountain orcs that became trapped underground.

PLAGUE WALKER

Staggering forward with an uneven gait, this moving corpse is a large sphere of bloated, rotting flesh. Its bloodshot eyes dart back and forth, and a gurgling sound issues from deep in its throat.

PLAGUE WALKER   **CR 3**

Always CE Medium undead
Init –2; **Senses** darkvision 60 ft.; Listen +10, Spot +1
Languages understands creator's orders

AC 12, touch 8, flat-footed 12
(–2 Dex, +4 natural)
hp 42 (6 HD)
Immune undead immunities
Fort +2, **Ref** +0, **Will** +6

Speed 20 ft. (4 squares)
Melee 2 claws +8 each (1d6+4 plus diseased touch)
Space 5 ft.; **Reach** 5 ft.
Base Atk +3; **Grp** +7
Atk Options diseased touch
Special Actions putrid burst

Abilities Str 18, Dex 6, Con —, Int 4, Wis 13, Cha 3
SQ bloated target, undead traits
Feats Skill Focus (Listen), Toughness, Weapon Focus (claws)
Skills Climb +7, Listen +10, Spot +1

Diseased Touch (Su) Any living creature struck by a plague walker's claws must succeed on a DC 13 Fortitude save or be overcome with racking pain and nausea, causing that creature to become sickened for 1 minute. The save DC is Constitution-based. Creatures that have immunity to disease are not affected by this ability.

Putrid Burst (Ex) When reduced to one-quarter of its starting hit points or fewer, a plague walker can use a swift action to explode. This burst has a 30-foot radius and deals 3d6 points of damage to everything in the area. All living creatures in the area are nauseated for 1 round; a DC 15 Reflex save halves the damage and negates the nauseated effect. The save DC is Constitution-based and includes a +2 racial bonus.

If reduced to 0 hit points before it can activate its putrid burst, a plague walker simply dissolves into a pile of rotting flesh.

Bloated Target (Ex) The –4 penalty for firing into melee does not apply to ranged attacks made against a plague walker. This penalty does, however, apply to other creatures in melee with it.

A plague walker is an undead weapon created by evil mages and clerics. Its tortured body is filled with rotting flesh, diseased matter, and other putrid filth. In battle, it can explode when sufficiently injured, showering the area around it with sickening debris.

STRATEGIES AND TACTICS

Plague walkers are too dim to operate independently; they are usually commanded in battle by their creators or another leader. Due to their putrid burst ability, plague walkers usually roam in advance of their allies. Hobgoblins in particular love to employ these creatures, because their armies and fighting units have the discipline to hold back until after a plague walker detonates. Orcs and other chaotic creatures rush into the fray and get caught in the creatures' blasts,

though that possibility rarely prevents clerics of Gruumsh from making and using plague walkers.

Clever hobgoblin warlords order their archers to target a plague walker when it comes into contact with the enemy, and evil spellcasters typically use *lightning bolt, fireball,* and similar spells against it. In addition to injuring those near the plague walker, such spells often trigger the walker's putrid burst.

Intelligent undead, particularly those spellcasters that can create these monsters, pair plague walkers with incorporeal undead servants. If a walker explodes, its companions ignore the effect and continue to fight. This combination is particularly lethal against enemies incapacitated by nausea.

SAMPLE ENCOUNTERS

In many ways, plague walkers are undead war machines set loose on the battlefield. An improperly deployed plague walker can cause as much trouble for its allies as for the enemy, so these monsters are most popular with evil humanoids and spellcasters, who have the skill and intelligence to form battle plans and use group tactics.

Living Trap (EL 3): Temples of Hextor often use plague walkers as living traps. The high priests order a pit trap constructed just inside the main doors to the temple area. When intruders attack, one of the clerics arms the trap while the rest fortify the temple. A plague walker stands within the pit. When an intruder falls in, the spring-loaded cover snaps back and locks in place, leaving the intruder trapped inside the pit with the undead horror.

Treat this trap like a CR 2 pit trap (DMG 71), except that the cover snaps back in place after it is activated. The cover can support up to 400 pounds. It has hardness 5, 10 hit points, and a break DC of 18. Destroying the mechanism that holds the pit's cover in place requires a DC 15 Disable Device check.

Team (EL 5): A barghest employed as a scout by a hobgoblin warlord accompanies a plague walker. It shadows the walker from afar and waits for an enemy to attack. The barghest uses its spell-like abilities, such as *crushing despair,* to hamper opponents while they deal with the plague walker. Immediately after the plague walker detonates, the barghest uses *dimension door* to appear in their midst and attack.

PLAGUE WALKER LORE

Characters with ranks in Knowledge (religion) can learn more about plague walkers. When a character makes a successful skill check, the following lore is revealed, including the information from lower DCs.

Knowledge (Religion)

DC	Result
13	This creature is a plague walker, a disgusting kind of undead. This result reveals all undead traits.
18	A plague walker's filth-encrusted claws can sicken a creature.
23	When a plague walker takes enough damage, it detonates in a sickening blast. If it is killed outright, before it triggers its body to explode, it collapses into a pile of putrid flesh.

ECOLOGY

As undead creatures crafted for use in war, plague walkers have no place in the natural environment. Tales claim that they arise as the result of a rare contagion, but in truth any diseased corpse serves to produce these monstrosities.

A plague walker that becomes separated from its master remains in place and attempts to fulfill its last orders to the best of its abilities. Thus, a walker ordered to stand guard deep within a dungeon might do so for centuries until intruders disturb it. Although a plague walker is barely intelligent, it can understand simple phrases in Common and can be ordered to ignore creatures bearing a certain holy symbol or speaking a password. Since a walker lacks the intelligence to deal with complex situations or conditions, its must rely on simple signs to distinguish friend from foe. For example, a plague walker might be ordered never to attack a hobgoblin, or to attack only elves.

Clever adventurers who don an opponent's uniform, display an appropriate holy symbol, or pull off some other form of deception can confuse a plague walker or slip by it unmolested. Thus, a plague walker's master must command it carefully, since unclear or easily subverted orders render the creature ineffective.

Environment: Plague walkers are found wherever the dark secret of their manufacture spreads.

Typical Physical Characteristics: A plague walker stands roughly 6 feet tall and weighs 300 pounds.

Alignment: Created only to sicken and destroy, plague walkers are always chaotic evil.

Plague walker

Illus. by A. Swekel

FOR PLAYER CHARACTERS

Creating a plague walker is a relatively simple process, though its cost prevents most spellcasters from producing the creatures in great numbers outside of wartime. Any arcane or divine caster of 6th level or higher who can cast necromancy spells can craft a plague walker. Doing so involves performing a horrific ritual that requires 800 gp worth of unholy water, the corpses of four Medium creatures that died of disease, and two days of prayer. (Two Small corpses are equivalent to one Medium corpse, and one Large body counts as two Medium corpses.) At the end of the ritual, the remains meld into a single plague walker, which obeys its creator's commands to the best of its ability.

A plague walker's creator can order the creature to obey an underling's commands, effectively ceding control of the creature. This arrangement makes it possible for armies to field plague walkers under the control of nonspellcasting officers.

PLAGUE WALKERS IN EBERRON

The necromancers of Karrnath know how to create plague walkers, and that nation employed them during sieges and other special operations during the Last War. However, the walkers were unreliable during large battles unless they were massed in large formations that could not be easily avoided.

Blood of Vol priests, particularly those with the time and resources to create them in numbers, use plague walkers as guardians and enforcers. One faction of the cult in Sharn stations plague walkers in its main temple. If intruders penetrate the inner shrine, the clerics run to a secure room, lock themselves in, and throw a switch. That act drops a portcullis, trapping the intruders in the temple, and opens the secret doors to four cubicles, each of which contains a walker. Even if the intruders defeat the walkers, the subsequent explosions leave them in poor shape to handle the clerics' counterattack.

PLAGUE WALKERS IN FAERÛN

Plague Walkers first appeared centuries ago during the Rotting War of Chondath. The process of creating plague walkers has since spread across Faerûn thanks to the machinations of the Church of Talona. The Red Wizards of Thay produce plague walkers and sell them across the world. Since transferring command of a plague walker is so easy, the creatures make excellent guards and soldiers for a warlord who needs reliable troops. Crime lords and others who face treachery from within their own ranks see plague walkers as intimidating, perfectly faithful bodyguards.

QUANLOS

The size of a large dog, this insectoid creature drones through the air on buzzing wings. A long, vicious-looking stinger protrudes from its abdomen.

QUANLOS   CR 6

Always N Small magical beast
Init +4; **Senses** darkvision 60 ft., low-light vision; Listen +4, Spot +4
Languages —

AC 21, touch 15, flat-footed 17; Dodge
  (+1 size, +4 Dex, +6 natural)
hp 45 (6 HD)
Fort +7, **Ref** +9, **Will** +3

Speed 30 ft. (6 squares), fly 60 ft. (good)
Melee sting +11 (1d8 plus controlling sting or devouring larvae) and
  bite +6 (1d4)
Space 5 ft.; **Reach** 5 ft.
Base Atk +6; **Grp** +2
Atk Options controlling sting, devouring larvae

Abilities Str 10, Dex 19, Con 15, Int 1, Wis 12, Cha 6
Feats Ability Focus (controlling sting), Dodge, Improved Natural Attack (sting)[B], Weapon Finesse
Skills Hide +11, Listen +4, Spot +4
Advancement 7–9 HD (Small); 10–15 HD (Medium)

Controlling Sting (Su) As the *dominate monster* spell; 3/day; Fort DC 19 negates; caster level 10th. The save DC is Constitution-based and includes a +2 racial bonus.

A quanlos can choose to inject a victim of its sting attack with a potent magic toxin, instead of placing its devouring larvae (see below). This poison saps the victim's will and makes it susceptible to mental compulsion by the quanlos.

A quanlos's puny intellect prevents it from exercising a fine level of control over its thralls. The creature lacks the sophistication to order a group of dwarf artisans to build a castle for it, or to command an elf wizard to use a specific spell to protect it. Instead, it relies on a limited set of general commands: attack, defend, gather food, and so forth.

A quanlos can control a number of creatures equal to its total Hit Dice at one time. If it takes control of a creature beyond this limit, it must choose one of its thralls to release from service. Thralls are freed immediately upon the death of the controlling quanlos.

Devouring Larvae (Ex) When a quanlos hits a Small or larger creature with its sting, it injects the foe with a small number of larvae. The target must succeed on a DC 17 Fortitude save or become infested with the larvae, which slowly devour the host from the inside out. This ability's save DC is Constitution-based and includes a +2 racial bonus.

Treat this infestation as a poison that deals 1d6 points of damage as its initial and secondary effects. The poison deals its initial damage as normal and its secondary damage once per round. A successful save does not end the effect. The infected creature must continue to attempt saves until it dies, receives

a *neutralize poison* or *remove disease* spell, or is the beneficiary of a successful DC 20 Heal check to remove the larvae.

If a quanlos takes more than 15 points of cold damage from a single attack, it cannot use its devouring larvae ability for 24 hours.

A quanlos is an insectoid monstrosity that haunts tropical swamps and marshlands. It is a fiercely territorial, solitary creature that uses an insidious poison to control other creatures. A quanlos's thralls defend its territory, hunt for prey, and serve as vessels for its young—literally working themselves to death. Young quanloses burrow through a host's flesh, eating it from the inside out as they grow to adulthood.

Because of their ghoulish means of reproduction and mind-controlling venom, quanloses are often called abyssal wasps and incorrectly identified as a kind of fiend.

STRATEGIES AND TACTICS

Quanloses avoid mingling with their own kind. Instead, a quanlos relies on its thralls to aid in defense, patrol its territory, and slay intruders. A typical quanlos controls several weak-willed animals appropriate to its native environment, such as wolves, bears, and the like. When faced with intruders, it commands such guardians to attack and watches the battle from hiding. If possible, it darts in to seize control of an attacker and turn it against the others.

A quanlos typically avoids direct conflict. It uses its larvae to sap opponents' strength or to encourage them to leave its territory for safer grounds. However, a quanlos without thralls is exceptionally aggressive. It actively seeks out potential victims, targeting lone creatures that it can lure away without interference.

QUANLOS LORE

Characters with ranks in Knowledge (arcana) can learn more about quanloses. When a character makes a successful skill check, the following lore is revealed, including the information from lower DCs.

A successful DC 15 Knowledge (the planes) check debunks the rumor that quanloses are infernal creatures.

Knowledge (Arcana)

DC	Result
16	Quanloses are magical beasts that resemble insects. This result reveals all magical beast traits.
21	Quanloses are tough for their size. It takes several stout blows to defeat one.
26	Quanlos venom has magical mind-controlling properties that the creature uses to secure hosts for its young.
31	Quanlos larvae infestation is potentially deadly, but magic that cures diseases can treat it. Cold damage also inhibits this attack.

SAMPLE ENCOUNTERS

Unlike the insects they resemble, quanloses are solitary from the day they burst forth from their larval hosts as full-grown creatures. Each is its own "queen" and, as with mundane insects, does not tolerate another queen in its territory. Characters are most likely to face a quanlos along with its thralls.

Individual (EL 7): The farmers of a local village tell tales of the "haunted" swamp where cattle, pigs, and people occasionally go missing. The townsfolk are convinced the marsh is haunted, but in fact a quanlos dwells there. This creature has enslaved a pair of hunters (3rd-level human rangers). If the PCs enter the swamp, the quanlos directs the hunters to attack them. To avoid killing these innocent beings, the PCs must overcome them with nonlethal force or find and defeat the quanlos.

ECOLOGY

Quanloses are something of an oddity. They appear to be insects, but each is essentially a self-contained hive. They reproduce asexually, generating anywhere from fifty to five hundred eggs in late autumn to early winter. A quanlos carries its eggs in a thick, rubbery sac beneath its chitinous abdominal plates. The eggs begin to hatch in late winter, and the wormlike larvae immediately fall to devouring each other and any eggs that have not yet hatched. By late spring, only ten to fifty larvae remain, and the parent quanlos enters its final reproductive phase. The creature becomes more aggressive and begins to seek hosts, attacking anything that wanders into its territory. The quanlos uses its controlling sting to keep its victim still while it injects five to ten larvae into the host's belly. The larvae gestate for a week to a month, devouring the creature's vitals, then burst free as adults (these new quanloses are Tiny and have 2 HD). The erstwhile nestmates, sated by their host's flesh, do not attack each other but scatter to find their own territories. The hatchling quanloses reach adulthood in a year, and the cycle begins anew.

Despite their short reproductive cycle, quanloses remain relatively rare. Roughly three-quarters are slain by other quanloses within the first months of their lives as they search for territory, and a significant number fall to other predators.

Quanloses subsist primarily on a diet of small birds, snakes, and mammals. They seldom attack anything even as large as a Small animal unless seeking to inject a host with their devouring larvae. They make no lairs or nests, and sages have never observed any sort of sleep cycle or dormant period.

Environment: Quanloses favor warm marshes but can sometimes be found in jungles or forests in similar climates. They do not thrive in cold regions; the low temperature renders their larvae dormant and temporarily halts their reproductive cycle.

Typical Physical Characteristics: Quanloses are approximately 4 feet long from mandible to stinger, with a wing span of 9 feet. When heavy with larvae, they can weigh up to 120 pounds.

Quanlos

TYPICAL TREASURE

Quanloses accumulate bright, shiny objects such as coins, metals, and so forth for their simple nests. A quanlos might order a humanoid under its control to divest itself of all such objects other than weapons and armor. "Uninteresting" objects, such as scrolls or boots, would not be part of a quanlos's hoard.

Extracted quanlos venom is a prized commodity among those who use such substances. The venom sells for 50 gp per dose, and an adult quanlos yields 1d4 doses.

Quanlos stingers are prized in some regions, where they are made into ornamental daggers (and sometimes crafted into *daggers of venom*). A complete stinger sells for 1,000 gp in regions where this practice is fashionable, or 500 gp elsewhere.

QUANLOSES IN EBERRON

Quanloses are native to the lush jungles and swamps of Aerenal. Some have migrated to the southern reaches of Khorvaire, including the swamps of the Shadow Marches and Droaam.

QUANLOSES IN FAERÛN

Quanloses have spread from the vast jungles of Chult, slowly creeping northward and eastward into more civilized regions of Faerûn. They are most common in the marshes of the south, including the Great Swamp east of Halruaa, but they have been reported as far north as the Marsh of Tun.

Illus. by A. Swekel

SAILSNAKE

Gliding on the warm air currents that rise around the stone pillars is a glittering serpent, its finlike membranes spread to catch the wind. It would be beautiful, except for its long fangs and the cloud of venomous spray it spits toward you.

SAILSNAKE	**CR 2**

Always N Medium animal
Init +7; **Senses** low-light vision, scent; Listen +8, Spot +8
Languages —

AC 15, touch 13, flat-footed 12
  (+3 Dex, +2 natural)
hp 19 (3 HD)
Fort +5, **Ref** +6, **Will** +2

Speed 20 ft. (4 squares), climb 20 ft., fly 30 ft. (poor);
  Flyby Attack
Melee bite +5 (1d8+3)
Space 5 ft.; **Reach** 5 ft.
Base Atk +2; **Grp** +4
Special Actions venom spray

Abilities Str 14, Dex 17, Con 15, Int 1, Wis 12, Cha 10
Feats Flyby Attack, Improved Initiative, Improved Natural
  Weapon[B], Weapon Finesse[B]
Skills Balance +11, Climb +11, Listen +8, Spot +8
Advancement 4–5 HD (Medium); 6–12 HD (Large)

Venom Spray (Ex) 20-ft. cone, once every 6 rounds, blind
  for 1d4 rounds, Fortitude DC 13 half. The save DC is
  Constitution-based.
Skills Sailsnakes have a +8 racial bonus on Balance and Climb
  checks and a +4 racial bonus on Listen and Spot checks. A
  sailsnake uses its Dexterity modifier instead of its Strength
  modifier for Climb checks, and can always choose to take
  10 on Climb checks, even if rushed or threatened.

A sailsnake is an unusual breed of viper that uses its fins to glide from tree to tree, or to coast from the top of a cliff down into a gorge. It is often beautifully colored and always aggressive. Sailsnakes are kept as pets or guardian beasts by yuan-ti.

STRATEGIES AND TACTICS

Sailsnakes are territorial creatures that attack without hesitation, even against threats larger than they are.

A mature sailsnake has bright coloration, which is both a proud display and a dire threat. At the approach of intruders, the animal rears up, flares its forward sail fins (much as a cobra spreads its neck hood), and hisses loudly. It grants just one warning. If the opponent continues to draw closer, the sailsnake lets loose a blast of venom in an attempt to drive it away.

Sailsnakes spend most of their time off the ground, either draped about tree branches or coiled on pillars, natural rock formations, ruined walls, and the like. This puts them in position to ambush potential prey or threats. When on the hunt, a sailsnake lies quietly. When prey comes within range, the snake hurls itself from its perch. It spreads its fins as it nears the target, expelling its venom spray at the same time.

Sailsnakes are hostile to others of their own kind, so the creatures do not work together in combat. One serpent might attack another in preference over other enemies. Sailsnakes have only the most primitive intelligence and do not adapt their standard tactics to new situations.

Sometimes yuan-ti use sailsnakes for recreational hunting in the same way human nobles hunt with trained falcons. The snakes can be trained after a fashion, learning to attack a given target, but cannot learn complex tricks. A large part of a snake's training involves suppressing its instinct to attack other sailsnakes.

SAMPLE ENCOUNTERS

Characters are most likely to run into a sailsnake as a solitary threat within a jungle or a desert ruin.

Individual (EL 2–3): Encountering a sailsnake on the ground is fairly straightforward, and the encounter level is the same as its Challenge Rating. A sailsnake that has the advantage of height and concealment is likely to surprise the party, making the encounter more dangerous.

EL 3: A steamy jungle, filled with flowers and bright tropical birds, has overgrown the ruins of an ancient yuan-ti city. On a vine-covered pillar, a sailsnake lurks.

Hunting Party (EL 5–9): Yuan-ti halfbloods enjoy hunting humanoids with their trained sailsnakes. Hunters might be encountered singly or in gangs of up to four.

EL 8: Ssivileth and Haassorass are a mated pair of halfbloods who delight in hunting down the wild elves that inhabit their forest. Ssivileth has a Large sailsnake she trained from childhood (advanced to 6 HD), while Haassorass has only recently taken up the sport and is in the process of training his pet (Medium size). Because its training is not complete, there is a 50% chance that the pet will not obey his commands and attack a random enemy or the other sailsnake instead.

ECOLOGY

Sailsnakes inhabit warm climates, usually in colorful milieus, and are not found close to civilization except when domesticated by yuan-ti. They hunt small animals and magical beasts, and have a taste for shocker lizards. (They hunt this

---

SAILSNAKE LORE

Characters with ranks in Knowledge (nature) can learn more about sailsnakes. When a character makes a successful skill check, the following lore is revealed, including the information from lower DCs.

Knowledge (Nature)

DC	Result
12	Sailsnakes are mutated vipers that can glide. This result reveals all animal traits and basic information on viper snakes.
17	A sailsnake is an aggressive creature that sprays a blast of venom to blind opponents.
22	Sailsnakes might have been bred by yuan-ti, and the snake people sometimes use these animals as pets, guardians, hunting beasts, or even familiars and animal companions.

dangerous prey only when they find an isolated individual, and do not pursue if the lizard resists the venom spray.) Sailsnakes attack larger creatures that threaten them, and if trained to hunt, will strike without provocation. They are preyed upon in turn by giant eagles, griffons, and larger snakes such as king cobras. A sailsnake also makes a meal for a shocker lizard clutch that survives its attack.

Sailsnakes can live up to twelve years, but in the wild a life span of five to seven years is more typical. The mating season is very short, just a couple of weeks in the early autumn. During this time, the males become vibrantly colored and quest about restlessly in search of females. Females are very picky and might not mate at all in a season if they find no one to their liking. A compatible pair stays together during this time. The sailsnake mating ritual is a rare but wondrous sight—the pair entwine in free fall, then separate and spread their sails just before impact. The snakes go their separate ways after the season ends, and the female locates a suitable nesting area in the hollow of a tree. As birthing time approaches, she becomes pudgy and sluggish, not moving from her nest except in dire emergency.

Sailsnakes are ovoviviparous: Their eggs hatch internally, and the young emerge from the mother's body. A typical clutch contains eight to twelve hatchlings. The mother watches over the young for a few days but then leaves them to fend for themselves. A newborn sailsnake is ravenous, quintupling its size within the first month of life. Its diet during this time consists of tree frogs, tiny mammals such as shrews or baby mice, and even insects. It reaches adult size within a year.

Large specimens are rarely found in the wild. Yuan-ti sometimes breed larger versions of sailsnakes for hunting more challenging prey, or for service as guardians. A yuan-ti druid might choose a sailsnake as an animal companion, so that it gains additional Hit Dice but does not grow in size.

Environment: Sailsnakes are usually found in warm forests, which they share with yuan-ti. Any warm climate will suit, however, and some varieties of sailsnake prefer warm deserts, especially among multicolored, wind-carved rock formations.

Typical Physical Characteristics: A typical sailsnake is 4 to 6 feet long and can weigh up to 50 pounds.

Young sailsnakes have fairly drab coloration that camouflages them until they are large enough to defend themselves effectively. As the serpent ages, its scales become more brilliant, acquiring a metallic sheen. Streaks and splotches of green, scarlet, orange, or blue are common. The sailsnake's environment contributes to its color; minerals in the soil or pigments from prey animals tint its scales. The sail fins are usually golden, bronze, or salmon-pink, with a fine tracery of blood vessels. Females are slightly larger than males, but there is otherwise little difference between the sexes.

Alignment: Sailsnakes have a very basic animal intelligence and are incapable of moral judgments. Hence, they are always neutral.

Sailsnake

Illus. by A. Stokes

TYPICAL TREASURE

Being animals, sailsnakes do not keep treasure. If found in the company of yuan-ti, use the normal treasure for a yuan-ti encounter of the appropriate level (sailsnakes might increase the encounter level depending on their numbers and the Challenge Ratings of the yuan-ti involved).

FOR PLAYER CHARACTERS

Treat a sailsnake as an alternative animal companion available to druids of 4th level or higher. Yuan-ti rangers sometimes use them to help hunt down victims for sacrifices.

A spellcaster who wishes to take a sailsnake familiar must have the Improved Familiar feat (*DMG* 200) and must have an arcane caster level of 5th or higher.

SAILSNAKES IN EBERRON

In Khorvaire, the sort of terrain that sailsnakes favor is found only in the jungles of southeastern Q'barra. Still, the creatures are not common there. Most sailsnakes live on Xen'drik, where they inhabit the ancient ruins along with drow and yuan-ti.

SAILSNAKES IN FAERÛN

In Faerûn, sailsnakes are denizens of the Serpent Hills. They are bred by the yuan-ti as more manageable variants of the larger winged viper (*FORGOTTEN REALMS Campaign Setting* 309). Winged vipers inhabit the same areas and sometimes prey on their smaller relatives, although as often as not, a sailsnake ends up feeding on its would-be predator.

SKIURID

A hissing, chittering sound fills the air in the darkened wood. Out of the corner of your eye, you see a small, black form dash between the tree branches.

SKIURID   **CR 1/2**

Always NE Tiny magical beast (extraplanar)
Init +3; **Senses** darkvision 60 ft., low-light vision; **Listen** +3, Spot +7
Languages —

AC 15, touch 15, flat-footed 12
   (+2 size, +3 Dex)
hp 2 (1/2 HD)
Fort +2, **Ref** +5, **Will** +1

Speed 30 ft. (6 squares), climb 20 ft.
Melee bite +6 (1d3–4)
Space 2-1/2 ft.; **Reach** 0 ft.
Base Atk +1; **Grp** –11
Special Actions chill darkness 3/day

Abilities Str 3, Dex 17, Con 10, Int 2, Wis 12, Cha 12
SQ shadow jump
Feats Alertness, Weapon Finesse[B]
Skills Balance +11, Climb +11, Hide +19, Listen +3, Move Silently +11, Spot +7
Advancement —

Shadow Jump (Su) As the *dimension door* spell; up to 3/day; caster level 1st.

The magical transport must begin and end in an area with at least some shadow. A skiurid can jump up to 30 feet each day in this manner; this can be a single jump or a combination of jumps whose distance totals 30 feet. This amount can be split among several jumps, but each one, no matter how small, counts as a 10-foot increment.

Chill Darkness (Su) As the *darkness* spell; 3/day; caster level 3rd.

A creature within the radius of this effect takes 1d6 points of damage and also takes 1 point of Strength damage unless it succeeds on a DC 13 Fortitude save. The creature takes no further damage as long as it remains within the area, but if it leaves and reenters, it is subject to both types of damage again. The save DC is Charisma-based and includes a +2 racial bonus.

At the end of the effect's duration, if any creature has taken damage within its area, the shadows coalesce into a small nodule, about the size of a peach pit, that provides nourishment for the skiurid.

This ability has no effect on undead or creatures native to the Plane of Shadow. The shadowy illumination created by this ability is sufficient for the skiurid to use its shadow jump ability.

Skills Skiurids have a +8 racial bonus on Balance, Climb, Hide, and Move Silently checks. A skiurid can always choose to take 10 on Climb checks, even if rushed or threatened. A skiurid uses its Dexterity modifier instead of its Strength modifier for Climb checks.

A skiurid is a shadow-born version of a squirrel, disturbingly familiar in appearance but undeniably malicious.

STRATEGIES AND TACTICS

Skiurids operate in colonies, taking advantage of their natural agility and stealth. A nest of them uses chill darkness to cloak as large an area as possible, thus providing food for the entire group. Among creatures of animal intelligence, however, this cooperation is a matter of instinct, not reasoned tactics.

Skiurids prefer not to attack with their feeble bite, using it only as a last resort when they are caught in melee. If things go poorly with a chill darkness attack, they quickly disappear into the shadows.

Skiurids are often encountered with other creatures of shadow. Their chill darkness ability reinforces the hunting methods of the other creatures, which are not harmed by it.

"Go ahead. Laugh. I did, once. Once."
—Gruthark, embittered half-orc

SAMPLE ENCOUNTER

Skiurids might be accompanied by beings from the Plane of Shadow or could be found in the groves of dark fey.

Colony (EL 5–10): Skiurids form colonies consisting of up to several dozen individuals. They are alone only under extraordinary circumstances (such as being caught in a trap).

EL 9: A colony of twenty skiurids inhabits a dark grove in a forest inhabited by shadar-kai (*Fiend Folio* 150). The shadow fey prize the coalesced shadows on which skiurids feed, and they often drive other beings toward the grove to maintain a high level of production.

Umbral Banyan Nest (EL 10–12): Skiurids often live in or near umbral banyans (*Manual of the Planes* 171), which offer protection and a ready supply of captives from which to drain life.

EL 12: This umbral banyan supports a colony of thirty-four skiurids. They wait until the dark tree snares a living creature, then blanket the area with their chill darkness.

SKIURID KNOWLEDGE

Characters with ranks in Knowledge (arcana) and Knowledge (the planes) can learn more about skiurids. When a character makes a successful skill check, the following lore is revealed, including the information from lower DCs.

Knowledge (Arcana)

DC	Result
10	Skiurids are magical beasts native to the Plane of Shadow. This result reveals all magical beast traits and the extraplanar subtype.
15	Sometimes skiurids enter the Material Plane.
20	Skiurids feed on concentrated life energy, which they drain from living creatures and store up.
25	The concentrated life energy is valuable as a spell component for necromancy magic.

Knowledge (the Planes)

DC	Result
10	Skiurids are magical beasts native to the Plane of Shadow. This result reveals all magical beast traits and the extraplanar subtype.
15	They feed on concentrated life energy, which they drain from living creatures and store up.
20	Skiurids often inhabit groves where an umbral banyan grows, and they work with the tree to drain the life from living things.

ECOLOGY

Skiurids are native to the Plane of Shadow and feed solely on life energy. Unlike shadows, which attack victims directly, skiurids blanket an area with chill darkness and let it drain life force from creatures that enter it. They then gather up the "nuggets" of coalesced shadow and store them within their dens for later consumption. This propensity makes skiurids tempting prey for other shadow creatures, which covet the concentrated life energy. Shadow mastiffs and dusk beasts (*Manual of the Planes* 169) are their usual predators, but spellcasters also seek out the coalesced shadow for use in necromantic magic.

Skiurids form large colonies, allowing them to pool their abilities and harvest large quantities of life energy. They often live in or near umbral banyans. Coordinating their efforts helps the tree dispatch its prey more quickly and allows the skiurids to harvest the dying creature's life force before it succumbs. The relationship is mutually beneficial.

A typical skiurid lives two to three years, with five years being the maximum. It is mature at six months of age, and a female can produce several litters in a year, depending on the availability of food. Adults feed their young life energy; they gnaw on a nugget of coalesced shadow to extract the nourishment and then allow the pups to sip from their mouths. A single nugget can sustain a litter of six to eight young for one day.

Environment: Skiurids are native to the Plane of Shadow but often end up in other planes of existence along with the creatures with which they associate.

Sometimes skiurids get left behind accidentally when an umbral banyan shifts to a haunted forest on the Material Plane. Despite the disruption, such migrants usually thrive as long as they remain in the dark heart of the forest. They are occasionally found with the bitter shadar-kai.

Typical Physical Characteristics: A skiurid is around 14 inches in length, excluding the tail. It looks something like a gaunt, outsized squirrel, but a malevolent reddish gleam shines in its eyes. Its body is a deep gray or black, and the creature blends readily into shadows.

Alignment: Skiurids are interested only in feeding and are inimical to most life forms other than those of the Plane of Shadow. Their total disregard for other beings makes them neutral evil.

TYPICAL TREASURE

Skiurids do not collect treasure, but their stores of life energy are prized by many beings. Necromancers in particular seek out skiurid hoards and pay well for them; a nugget of

Skiurids

coalesced shadow is worth 1,000 gp. Skiurids share their dens, so obtaining a hoard usually requires defeating large numbers of them (as well as any other creatures found in the den).

A skiurid nest typically contains one shadow nugget per four adults, representing the excess stored by the colony for lean times and for rearing young.

FOR PLAYER CHARACTERS

A nugget of stored life energy can serve as an optional material component for necromancy spells. It has a 50% chance of increasing such a spell's effective caster level by 2.

SKIURIDS IN EBERRON

Skiurids are usually found in Mabar manifest zones. These are most common in the Shadow Marches, but the jungles of Xen'drik might hide such deadly groves.

When Mabar is coterminous with Eberron, the dark places of the world become blacker and more dangerous. At these times, shadow beings can more easily slip between the worlds, and colonies of skiurids end up in earthly forests, especially the fey woods of the Eldeen Reaches.

SKIURIDS IN FAERÛN

Devotees of the Shadow Weave, dark fey, and creatures of shadow share a mystical connection with Shar, the deity of dark magic. Such creatures not only inhabit her home, the Plane of Shadow, but also favor areas of Faerûn where Shar's influence is strong. The Darkhouse of Saeldoon (*Faiths and Pantheons* 163) is an example of a cult devoted to the Lady of Loss. Adding a colony of skiurids to its groves is a simple matter. Perhaps the cult uses skiurids to extract life energy from prisoners.

Illus. by A. Stokes

SPAWN OF TIAMAT

The deity Tiamat, Creator of Evil Dragonkind, has long sought domination of the world for herself and her progeny. For eons she has struggled against Bahamut, the King of Good Dragons, in a conflict called the Dragonfall War, and most people believed that this battle would last for millennia to come.

Recently, however, Tiamat unveiled her latest and most terrifying tactic. She created diverse and numerous creatures with the blood of chromatic dragons and sent forth these spawn to spread destruction and evil. This incursion of evil dragonblood creatures threatens the balance of the war and, by extension, the world.

To thwart her ambitions, Bahamut created the noble dragonborn (*Races of the Dragon 5*), but the challenge of fighting evil dragonkind demands even more heroes than the Platinum Dragon can produce. Today, Tiamat has the upper hand. It might well fall to the player characters to prevent her spawn from permanently tipping the Dragonfall War in favor of evil.

Every spawn of Tiamat has some vestige of the power of the Queen of Evil Dragons in its blood. Many, though, are born not directly to her but to individual evil dragons throughout the world. Whether chosen by Tiamat herself or only by fickle chance, some chromatic dragon eggs hatch into the spawn described in this section. Usually a single egg is so touched, but occasionally an entire clutch produces spawn of Tiamat (which might not even be all the same kind). A given spawn is born only to a dragon that matches its color, which combined with the word "spawn," forms part of its name. Blackspawn raiders and blackspawn stalkers, for example, are born only to black dragons. Although spawn first began to appear within clutches of dragon eggs, most of them breed true and now are rapidly multiplying.

Evil dragons recognize the birth of a spawn of Tiamat as a fortunate omen, a sign of their creator's favor. That said, spawn rarely remain with their parents for long. They mature much more quickly than true dragons, reaching adulthood in only a few years.

Spawn of Tiamat usually congregate with other creatures, whether in packs of their kind or with like-minded individuals of other races, particularly evil dragons. Reports have surfaced recently of hobgoblin clerics and warlords gathering spawn of Tiamat and other evil dragons for a great battle. Whether this is part of Tiamat's plan for the Dragonfall War or stems from the goblinoids' general antipathy toward other races is unknown.

Regardless of their place in the world, all spawn share an unswerving loyalty to Tiamat, which their would-be allies would do well to remember. The spawn of Tiamat also share her undying hatred of good dragonkind, and they look down upon nondragons of all sorts.

Spawn of Tiamat in Eberron

Tiamat is not pleased with the attitude many of her children have adopted. She is proud of the role chromatic dragons played in defeating the fiends and the quori, but she feels that they now waste time worrying about the Prophecy instead of subjugating the world.

Some chromatic dragons agree with her and have rededicated themselves to her cause. In addition, she has whispered promises of a return of the great Dhakaani Empire to certain hobgoblin warlords in Darguun. Using these contacts, Tiamat has been able to seed the world with her spawn, and they are ready for when the call to battle goes forth.

Chromatic dragons not allied with Tiamat see the spawn's arrival as a dire portent that must somehow be related to the Prophecy, but they are oblivious to the true danger. They continue to do that for which Tiamat condemns them: They wait and watch, hoping to learn the true nature of these new dragonblood through observation and reflection on the Prophecy.

All manner of spawn now inhabit Argonnessen. The different varieties have begun to circulate throughout the world and can be found in Xen'drik, Khorvaire, and Aerenal. Few have gained a foothold in Sarlona.

See specific spawn entries for more details on their place in Eberron.

Holy symbol of Tiamat

Illus. by w. England

TIAMAT

The Chromatic Dragon, Creator of Evil Dragonkind

Lesser Deity

Symbol: Five-headed dragon
Home Plane: Baator
Alignment: Lawful evil
Portfolio: Evil dragons, conquest, greed
Worshipers: Evil dragons, spawn of Tiamat, conquerors
Cleric Alignments: NE, LE
Domains: Destruction, Dragon*, Evil, Greed*, Law, Trickery, [Hatred, Scalykind, Tyranny]
Favored Weapon: Heavy pick (bite)
　　*Domains described in *Draconomicon*.
　　Domains presented inside brackets are found in the *Forgotten Realms*® Campaign Setting. If your campaign is set in Faerûn, you can add these domains to the deity's list (possibly replacing other domains if desired).

Tiamat is the Creator of Evil Dragonkind and the mother of her spawn

Illus. by W. Reynolds

SPAWN OF TIAMAT LORE

Characters with ranks in Knowledge (arcana) can learn more about spawn of Tiamat in general. When a character makes a successful skill check, the following lore is revealed, including the information from lower DCs. Those who recognize the creatures' ancestry can also use Knowledge (religion) to learn more.

Individual spawn of Tiamat entries provide Knowledge check DCs to learn about their specific details.

Knowledge (Arcana)

DC	Result
10	Descendants of a dragon aren't always of the dragon type.
15	This creature doesn't seem to be a half-dragon but clearly has strong chromatic dragon heritage. This result reveals all dragonblood traits.
20	Many strange dragon-descended creatures with chromatic heritage have been appearing recently, perhaps suggesting some new activity on the part of chromatic dragonkind.

Knowledge (Religion)

DC	Result
10	Tiamat is an evil dragon god.
15	Tiamat wages war against Bahamut, the King of Good Dragons, through various mortal pawns, some of which she creates.
20	The spawn are Tiamat's latest escalation of hostilities in the Dragonfall War, and they serve her cause faithfully. Some even work under the direction of her clerics.

Spawn of Tiamat in Faerûn

The first spawn, gifts from the Dragon Queen, were summoned by Tiamat's followers in Unther. Her temples have been secretly breeding more and more spawn and smuggling them out of the country to prevent their discovery by the Mulhorandi occupation force.

The church of Tiamat has since managed to spread spawn throughout the Old Empires and beyond. Many lurk in dark corners of the world, roaming swamps, jungles, and caverns as they hunt their prey and wait for the call to join Tiamat's army. Some have allied themselves with the Cult of the Dragon, though that group's goals never take precedence over serving the will of Tiamat.

Rumors have surfaced of hobgoblins and spawn massing around the Rathgaunt Hills in the southern Shaar. Their appearance could indicate that the Dragonfall War is about to spill over into Faerûn.

See specific spawn entries for more details on their place in Faerûn.

BLACKSPAWN RAIDER

This humanlike creature has black-scaled skin with glints of green. Two horns jut from the sides of its head, curving forward around its skull. It wields a falchion.

BLACKSPAWN RAIDER   CR 4

Always CE Medium monstrous humanoid (dragonblood)
Init +6; **Senses** darkvision 60 ft., low-light vision; Listen +6, Spot +6
Languages Common, Draconic

AC 15, touch 12, flat-footed 13
  (+2 Dex, +3 natural)
hp 60 (8 HD); **DR** 5/magic or good
Immune acid, paralysis, *sleep*
Fort +5, **Ref** +8, **Will** +6

Speed 40 ft. (8 squares)
Melee falchion +10/+5 (2d4+3/18–20)
Ranged javelin +10 (1d6+2)
Space 5 ft.; **Reach** 5 ft.
Base Atk +8; **Grp** +10
Atk Options Power Attack
Special Actions breath weapon
Combat Gear oil of magic weapon, potion of cure moderate wounds, 2 potions of invisibility, potion of jump, potion of pass without trace, potion of protection from good

Abilities Str 14, Dex 15, Con 16, Int 10, Wis 11, Cha 8
Feats Improved Initiative, Power Attack, Track
Skills Jump +6, Listen +6, Spot +6, Survival +10
Advancement by character class; **Favored Class** ninja (*Complete Adventurer* 5); see text
Possessions combat gear plus falchion, 2 javelins, silk rope (50 ft.), 5 tiger eyes worth 10 gp each

Breath Weapon (Su) 40-ft. line, once every 1d4 rounds, 4d4 acid, Reflex DC 17 half. The breath weapon damage increases by 1d4 for every 2 additional HD.

Blackspawn raiders are vicious hunters. They are proud to be descended from Tiamat, and they revel in making her will manifest.

Strategies and Tactics

Blackspawn raiders favor attacking from ambush. They prefer to operate in hunting packs, usually groups of two to four. Together, they set up a good location to lie in wait. If the prey is intelligent, they use feinting tactics: One raider attacks with a ranged weapon and then pretends to flee, luring the quarry into the ambush.

At the start of an ambush, blackspawn raiders are cunning and even cooperate on attacks. They usually start by concentrating on an enemy that can be easily surrounded on the edge of a group. Once they are in the thick of the fight, though, their competitive nature interferes with the plan. Aggressive and bloodthirsty, the creatures value personal glory and bragging rights above all. Thus, each seeks to kill the biggest and best foe.

Good dragons are raiders' preferred prey, and against a mixed group of foes, their first target. The blackspawn raiders' lust to kill good dragons overrides their innate competitiveness, and they work well as a group against such enemies. In these situations, they concentrate on a single foe until it's dead or dying, then shift their focus to the next one.

Blackspawn Exterminator

This humanlike creature has black-scaled skin and two curving horns jutting from its head. A dark strip of cloth covers its face. It sports both a short sword and a shortbow.

BLACKSPAWN EXTERMINATOR   CR 10

Female blackspawn raider ninja* 6
*Class described in *Complete Adventurer*
CE Medium monstrous humanoid
   (dragonblood)
Init +10; **Senses** darkvision 60 ft., low-light
   vision; Listen +14, Spot +14
Languages Common, Draconic

AC 22, touch 19, flat-footed 16; *ki dodge*
   (+6 Dex, +3 natural, +2 Wis, +1 class)
hp 88 (14 HD); **DR** 5/magic or good
Immune acid, paralysis, *sleep*
Fort +6, **Ref** +17, **Will** +10 (+12 with *ki pool*)

Speed 40 ft. (8 squares)
Melee *+1 short sword* +19/+14/+9 (1d6+4/19–20 plus poison)
Ranged *+1 composite shortbow* +19/+14/+9 (1d6+4/×3 plus
   poison)
Base Atk +12; **Grp** +15
Atk Options Cleave, Power Attack, poison (sassone leaf
   residue, DC 16, 2d12 hp/1d6 Con), sudden strike +3d6
Special Actions breath weapon
Combat Gear 2 bags of caltrops, 3 doses of sassone leaf
   residue, *oil of magic weapon*, *potion of cure moderate wounds*,
   2 *potions of invisibility*, *potion of protection from good*, 2 doses
   of purple worm poison (DC 24, 1d6 Str/2d6 Str)

Abilities Str 16, Dex 22, Con 14, Int 10, Wis 14, Cha 11
SQ great leap, *ki* power 5/day, ghost step, poison use,
   trapfinding
Feats Cleave, Improved Initiative, Power Attack, Track,
   Weapon Finesse
Skills Balance +8, Climb +8, Hide +15, Jump +15, Listen +14,
   Move Silently +14, Spot +14, Survival +12, Tumble +14
Possessions combat gear plus *+1 short sword*, *+1 composite
   shortbow* (+3 Str bonus), *quiver of Ehlonna* with 20 arrows,
   10 adamantine arrows, 10 cold iron arrows, and 10 silver
   arrows, *gloves of Dexterity +2*, *Heward's handy haversack*,
   grappling hook, silk rope (50 ft.)

Ki Dodge (Su) Swift action, one daily *ki* power use,
   concealment (20% miss chance) for 1 round. *Complete
   Adventurer* 8.
Sudden Strike (Ex) As sneak attack (*PH* 50), but no extra
   damage when flanking. *Complete Adventurer* 8.
Breath Weapon (Su) 40-ft. line, once every 1d4 rounds, 7d4
   acid, Reflex DC 16 half.
Great Leap (Su) Always makes Jump checks as if running
   with the Run feat. *Complete Adventurer* 8.
Ki Power (Su) Expend one daily use to activate *ki*-based abilities
   (ghost step or *ki* dodge). +2 bonus on Will saves as long as
   at least one daily use remains. *Complete Adventurer* 8.
Ghost Step (Su) Swift action, one daily *ki* power use,
   invisibility for 1 round. *Complete Adventurer* 8.

Ninjas lead smaller groups of blackspawn raiders. A ninja
who attains 6th level earns the title "exterminator."

The blackspawn exterminator presented here had the
following ability scores before racial adjustments, Hit Dice
ability score increases, and equipment bonuses: Str 12, Dex
15, Con 8, Int 10, Wis 14, Cha 13.

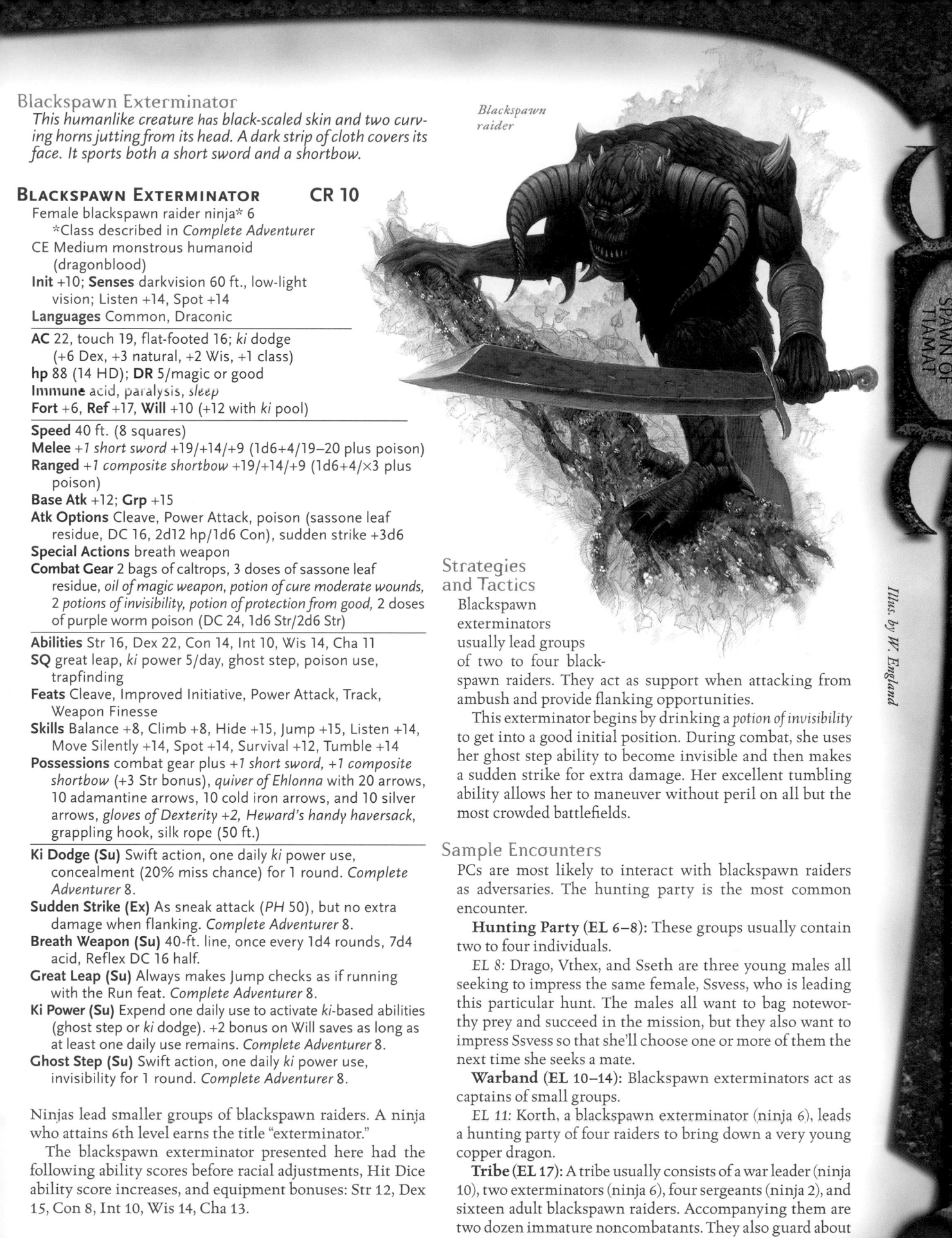

Blackspawn raider

Illus. by W. England

Strategies and Tactics

Blackspawn
exterminators
usually lead groups
of two to four black-
spawn raiders. They act as support when attacking from
ambush and provide flanking opportunities.

This exterminator begins by drinking a *potion of invisibility*
to get into a good initial position. During combat, she uses
her ghost step ability to become invisible and then makes
a sudden strike for extra damage. Her excellent tumbling
ability allows her to maneuver without peril on all but the
most crowded battlefields.

Sample Encounters

PCs are most likely to interact with blackspawn raiders
as adversaries. The hunting party is the most common
encounter.

Hunting Party (EL 6–8): These groups usually contain
two to four individuals.

EL 8: Drago, Vthex, and Sseth are three young males all
seeking to impress the same female, Ssvess, who is leading
this particular hunt. The males all want to bag noteworthy prey and succeed in the mission, but they also want to
impress Ssvess so that she'll choose one or more of them the
next time she seeks a mate.

Warband (EL 10–14): Blackspawn exterminators act as
captains of small groups.

EL 11: Korth, a blackspawn exterminator (ninja 6), leads
a hunting party of four raiders to bring down a very young
copper dragon.

Tribe (EL 17): A tribe usually consists of a war leader (ninja
10), two exterminators (ninja 6), four sergeants (ninja 2), and
sixteen adult blackspawn raiders. Accompanying them are
two dozen immature noncombatants. They also guard about
forty eggs.

Ecology

Blackspawn raiders are nomadic carnivores. They hunt to eat and aren't picky about their prey. Rats, boar, elves—it doesn't matter. Some creatures taste better than others, but they're all edible.

Beyond hunting for mere food, though, blackspawn raiders frequently kill for pleasure. Tracking, finding, and bringing down a challenging foe fulfills a primal desire. After a fight, they ritually sample the flesh of a fresh kill and drink a sip of its blood. One kind of prey thrills a blackspawn raider with the prospect of both the hunt and the great feast after: a good-aligned dragon.

Besides hunting, blackspawn raiders are driven to reproduce. They do this through laying eggs. Females become fertile about four times a year and fight among themselves to choose mates. Gestation takes approximately four weeks. A female lays two to eight eggs at a time, each of which might have been fertilized by a different male.

The eggs are durable, with thick, leathery shells. Each is about 6 inches in diameter. In order to hatch, the eggs must be kept warm and protected from violent motion, such as shaking. After about 4 weeks, Tiny hatchlings emerge. A hatchling develops into an adult in approximately one year.

Environment: Favoring their black dragon heritage, blackspawn raiders are most at home in warm marshes. However, they can live almost anywhere, and they move their camps to find better hunting grounds. They might travel for many miles to follow up a rumor about favorite prey.

Typical Physical Characteristics: A blackspawn raider stands 6 feet tall and weighs 200 pounds.

Females are larger and meaner than males. Males have deeper coloration and more striking green-and-black patterns on their scales. Except for these minor facets, little differentiates the two genders.

BLACKSPAWN RAIDER LORE

Characters with ranks in Knowledge (nature) can learn more about blackspawn raiders. When a character makes a successful skill check, the following lore is revealed, including the information from lower DCs. Those who recognize the creatures' ancestry can also use Knowledge (religion) to learn more.

Knowledge (Nature)

DC	Result
14	This creature is a blackspawn raider, a monstrous humanoid descended from black dragons. This result reveals all monstrous humanoid traits.
19	Blackspawn raiders are immune to acid, paralysis, and *sleep* effects. They have an acid breath weapon.
24	These vicious carnivores favor stealth and ambush. They typically employ potions in combat.
29	The ultimate achievement for blackspawn raiders is killing a good dragon. They are known to bargain for information leading to a good dragon or its lair.

Knowledge (Religion)

DC	Result
14	Blackspawn raiders are some of Tiamat's spawn.
19	Blackspawn raiders worship Tiamat as their creator and their god.

Alignment: Blackspawn raiders are always chaotic evil. Tiamat bestowed much of the look and all the philosophy of black dragons upon these spawn. Social codes forbid killing other blackspawn raiders or directly hindering their ability to reproduce, but everything else is fair game in the drive to advance personal status.

Society

Blackspawn raiders call themselves the Children of Tiamat. Their lives focus on Tiamat and manifesting her will in the world. They revere her as both the literal mother of their race and their spiritual mother.

If a raider sights a good dragon or the tribe gains information leading to a good dragon's lair, everyone in the community bands together. Petty rivalries and social machinations are temporarily laid aside. Everyone works toward the common goal of hunting down and killing this favored prey. (The normal selfishness, greed, and one-upmanship resume once the hunt is over.)

If a group is skillful and lucky enough to bring down the dragon, an extended holiday ensues. The community moves the corpse to its encampment or camps beside a corpse that is too large to move. A tremendous feast celebrates those who actively participated in the hunt. The whole community shares the dragon meat, eating it fresh, raw, and bloody. Consuming the flesh is an act of worship—a paean to Tiamat—and the blackspawn raiders use every scrap. Any meat left from the feast is dried and smoked; the tribe won't hunt again until they have eaten the entire corpse.

Creating more spawn is the second holy duty of blackspawn raiders. The leaders of a tribe are a council of females, each of whom has at least five living adult children, earning her the honorific "spawnmother." The spawnmothers handle all the daily duties of leadership: allocating resources and deciding whether the tribe should move, and if so, where it should go. They also make all the grand strategic decisions.

This form of matriarchy among a chaotic evil people leads to constant machinations and politics. The status of a spawnmother is often in flux: If her living adult progeny ever become fewer than five, she loses her position. Thus, spawnmothers favor enterprises that protect their children (and thus their positions) while putting their rivals' offspring at risk. One common example is stealing eggs from a rival and replacing them with infertile ones or even artificial replicas.

A chosen few blackspawn raiders are indoctrinated into a secret society within the tribe and trained in combat techniques to become even more dangerous killers. This ninja training creates the blackspawn exterminators, the most experienced of whom become war leaders. These tactical leaders handle military matters and run individual hunts, and they might be sent to dispatch any significant threat to the tribe or the spawnmothers.

Being a spawnmother does not preclude tactical leadership. A fertile female with sufficient training could be both a spawnmother (social leader) and an exterminator (hunt leader). It's advantageous for even a very fertile female to hone her ninja skills, since the position of spawnmother is so transitory.

Most races and groups acquainted with blackspawn raiders do not seek diplomatic relations with these brutal hunters. Occasionally a daring, evil organization endeavors to enlist a tribe for a specific mission. An emissary who survives initial contact with a scout or hunting group is brought before the council of spawnmothers. A sufficiently large or important incentive, such as the gift of a good dragon's hide or the location of a good dragon's lair, might buy the tribe's aid.

SAMPLE LAIR: BLACKSPAWN RAIDER ENCAMPMENT

This map shows a typical blackspawn raider camp, set up near a dragon corpse.

1. War Leader's Tent: In addition to housing the war leader, this tent is where planning takes place. Hunting parties gather here before setting out, consulting maps, interviewing scouts, and discussing where to travel and seek prey.

Hand-drawn maps on a rough folding table depict the local area, showing major geographic features and trails. A DC 10 Knowledge (geography) check reveals that several ideal ambush locations are marked. A locked chest contains the personal property of the war leader, who carries the key. A little piece of gold dragon hide adorns the tent's cot.

2. Community Tent: The ruling spawnmothers meet in this larger tent, which is also where the community as a whole meets and where guests stay. Community supplies are stored here.

A few large, misshapen sacks contain dried meat and other surplus supplies, and they are also used as improvised seating. The tent contains nothing of significant value.

3. Family Tents: Each tent shelters two to six individuals (one to three adults and one to three children). A tent almost always contains a blackspawn raider (50% chance of adult,

50% child); females try to keep a close watch on their eggs.

4. Dragon Corpse: This tribe has had a successful hunt, having recently slain an adult copper dragon.

5. Campfire: The blackspawn raiders are smoking and drying excess meat from the copper dragon's corpse.

Typical Treasure

Blackspawn raiders have standard treasure for their Challenge Rating, about 1,200 gp. They store much of their wealth in the form of potions.

A blackspawn exterminator has standard treasure for an NPC of Challenge Rating 10, about 16,000 gp. Exterminators use a variety of poisons, which is included in their treasure.

Blackspawn Raiders with Class Levels

Blackspawn raiders' favored class is the ninja from *Complete Adventurer*. They are sneaky killers. (If you are not using *Complete Adventurer* in your campaign, substitute rogue as the favored class.)

Level Adjustment: +3.

Blackspawn Raiders in Eberron

Eberron blackspawn raiders feel less certainty about their origin, but they suspect the fulfilling of the draconic Prophecy would be very bad for their race. They take pleasure in killing dragonmarked characters and dragons of any alignment, believing that doing so will stave off a great catastrophe.

Blackspawn raiders live in unsettled areas of the world, although hunting parties venture closer to civilization to find noteworthy prey.

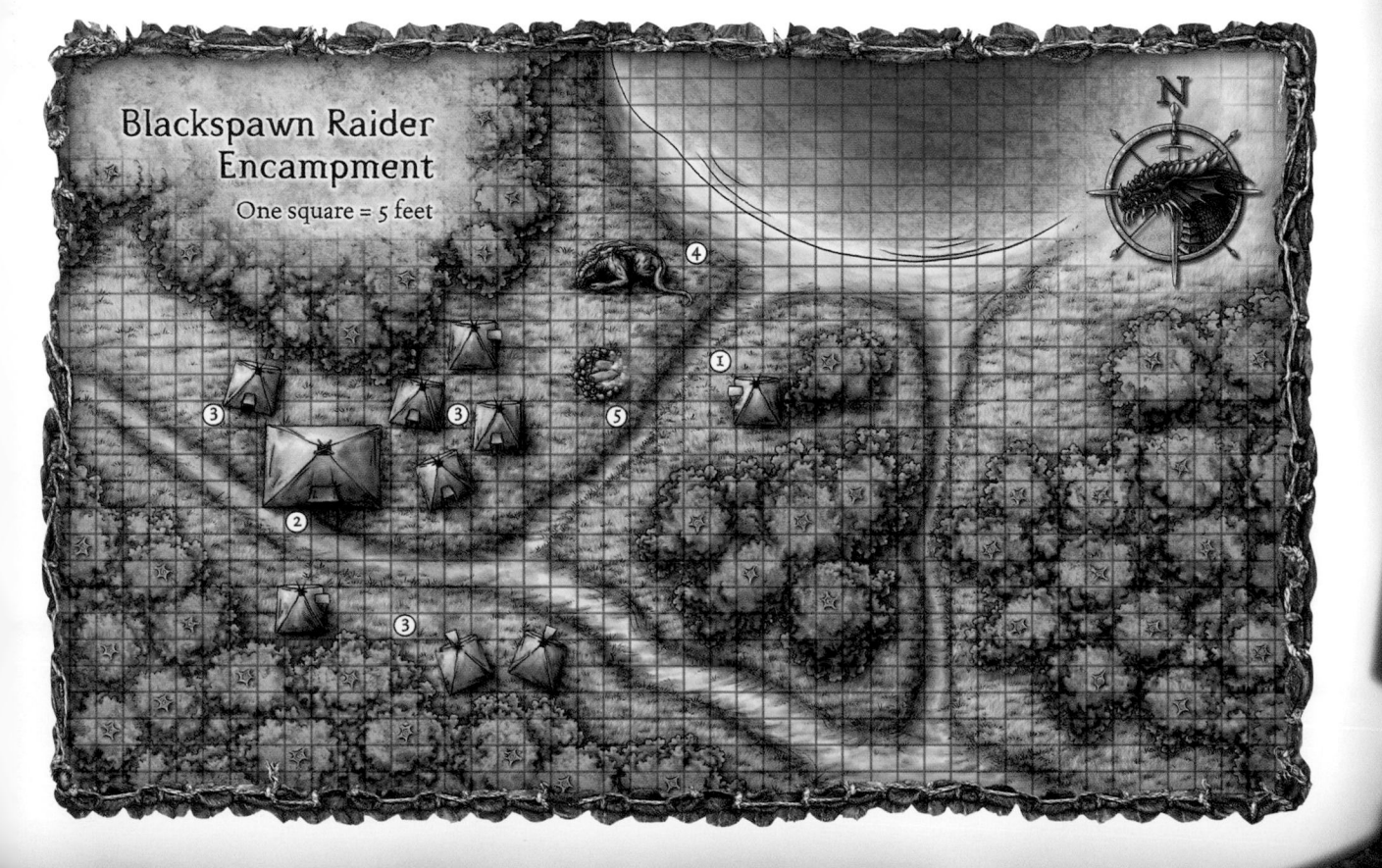

Blackspawn Raider Encampment

One square = 5 feet

BLACKSPAWN STALKER

Looking like a cross between a black dragon and a spider of nightmarish proportions, this creature glares out at the world with six baleful eyes. It drools a putrid green acid that steams and hisses. Two spined tails eject globules of sticky webbing.

BLACKSPAWN STALKER	**CR 9**

Always CE Large magical beast (dragonblood)
Init +2; **Senses** darkvision 60 ft., low-light vision, scent, tremorsense 60 ft.; Listen +3, Spot +3
Languages Draconic

AC 25, touch 11, flat-footed 23
    (–1 size, +2 Dex, +14 natural)
hp 105 (10 HD)
Immune acid
Fort +12, **Ref** +9, **Will** +4

Speed 40 ft. (8 squares), climb 40 ft.
Melee bite +15 (2d6+6/19–20 plus 1d6 acid) and
    2 tail slaps +13 each (1d8+3)
Ranged 2 webs +11 ranged touch each (entangle)
Space 10 ft.; **Reach** 5 ft. (10 ft. with tail slap)
Base Atk +10; **Grp** +20
Atk Options Power Attack, deadly charge 4d6+9
Special Actions spit acid

Abilities Str 23, Dex 15, Con 21, Int 5, Wis 13, Cha 11
SQ Tiamat's blessing (acid)
Feats Improved Critical (bite), Multiattack, Power Attack, Track
Skills Climb +16, Jump +12, Listen +3, Spot +3, Survival +6
Advancement 11–18 HD (Large); 19–30 HD (Huge)

Deadly Charge (Ex) A blackspawn stalker typically begins a battle by charging at an opponent. In addition to the normal benefits and hazards of a charge, this allows the blackspawn stalker to make a single gore attack with a +15 attack bonus that deals 4d6+9 points of damage.

Web (Ex) A blackspawn stalker can throw two webs per round, up to eight times per day. Each of these attacks is similar to an attack with a net but has a maximum range of 50 feet, with a range increment of 10 feet, and is effective against targets up to Huge size. The web anchors the target in place, allowing no movement. Attempts to escape or burst the webbing gain a +5 bonus if the trapped creature has something to walk on or grab while pulling free.

    An entangled creature can escape with a DC 20 Escape Artist check or burst it with a DC 20 Strength check. The check DCs are Constitution-based. The web has 12 hit points, hardness 0, and takes double damage from fire.

    A blackspawn stalker can create sheets of sticky webbing up to 20 feet square. It usually positions these sheets to snare flying creatures but can also try to trap prey on the ground. Approaching creatures must succeed on a DC 20 Spot check to notice a web; otherwise they stumble into it and become trapped as though by a successful web attack. Each 5-foot section of webbing has 12 hit points and damage reduction 5/—.

    A blackspawn stalker can move across its own sheet web at its climb speed and can determine the exact location of any creature touching the web.

Spit Acid (Su) A blackspawn stalker can spit its acidic saliva up to 60 feet as a standard action. This is a ranged touch attack with no range increment that deals 5d6 points of acid damage.

    This acid damage increases by 1d6 for every 2 additional HD.

Tiamat's Blessing (Acid) (Su) All spawn of Tiamat within 5 feet of a blackspawn stalker gain immunity to acid.

Skills Blackspawn stalkers have a +8 racial bonus on Climb checks and can always choose to take 10 on Climb checks, even if rushed or threatened.

Blackspawn stalkers are consummate hunters but lack the intelligence of their draconic progenitors. They were created by Tiamat to instill fear and panic in their prey, from which the Queen of Evil Dragons draws strength. Blackspawn stalkers are voracious, always on the lookout for their next meal.

Strategies and Tactics

Blackspawn stalkers are patient. They set traps, typically laying webs across the ground or up in trees, as the situation demands. If the prey manages to evade its web, a stalker readily takes a more active role, usually slinging webs at the quarry. It first attempts to weaken stronger prey by spitting acid, then charges in for a devastating gore attack.

BLACKSPAWN STALKER LORE

Characters with ranks in Knowledge (arcana) can learn more about blackspawn stalkers. When a character makes a successful skill check, the following lore is revealed, including the information from lower DCs. Those who recognize the creatures' ancestry can also use Knowledge (religion) to learn more.

Knowledge (Arcana)

DC	Result
14	This creature is a blackspawn stalker, a predatory magical beast related to black dragons. This result reveals all magical beast traits.
19	Blackspawn stalkers are immune to acid. Their saliva is extremely acidic, and the stalkers can spit it quite a distance. They can spin webs and sling webbing at their prey when hunting.
24	A blackspawn stalker frequently begins combat by charging and goring an opponent with its massive horns. Male blackspawn stalkers also use their horns in contests of strength to win a mate.
29	Blackspawn stalkers prefer to hunt from the safety of trees, using their climbing abilities to gain an advantage over their prey.
34	Blackspawn stalkers mate annually, creating as many as six nests of eggs. Many large birds or birdlike creatures prey upon the eggs.

Knowledge (Religion)

DC	Result
14	Blackspawn stalkers are some of Tiamat's spawn.
19	Blackspawn stalkers are sometimes found in the company of worshipers of Tiamat, typically black dragons.
24	Blackspawn stalkers seek to breed the ultimate servant of Tiamat.

Sample Encounters

Blackspawn stalkers are solitary creatures, though mated pairs can be encountered. True dragons (particularly black, but sometimes green or red) employ these creatures as guards or assistant hunters.

Pair (EL 11): Two blackspawn stalkers have taken up residence in the swamp just to the north of the Celadon forest. They have created six nests lined with eggs, and they are now hunting for prey to place in these nests for their hungry offspring to feed upon once hatched.

Hunters (EL 10–12): Aconnax, a greenspawn sneak raid leader (see page 148), rides a blackspawn stalker on the fringes of the Dragon Queen's territory. The two patrol in search of interlopers, especially adventurers, then attempt to ambush them. If they run into trouble, they retreat to a preset fallback point where two other blackspawn stalkers lair.

Ecology

Blackspawn stalkers are nearly mindless creatures that view each other as competition for food and mates. They look favorably upon strength, however, and take pride in serving a powerful master. Blackspawn stalkers willingly serve true dragons and other spawn. They prefer black dragons, but red and green dragons also admire the hunting capabilities of these horrid creatures and sometimes team up with them. If a dragon or spawn mistreats a blackspawn stalker, or demonstrates weakness, the servant leaves, often turning on the master first.

Blackspawn stalkers see Tiamat as their ultimate master, and they believe that through breeding, they can create the ultimate servant—one that the Dragon Queen might find worthy enough to take as her own. When left to their own devices, or if their master is slain, blackspawn stalkers reproduce as much as possible.

When blackspawn stalkers mate, they do so for life, unlike the arachnids they resemble. A mated pair lays eggs annually, distributing them in up to half a dozen nests to improve the chances of survival. The eggs are an important food source for many other creatures, so very few manage to hatch. On rare occasions, when an entire clutch remains undisturbed, the hatchlings go on a massed rampage, killing everything they encounter.

Blackspawn stalkers are carnivores. With their unique combination of features, they can switch readily between biting and tearing at prey or dissolving it with acidic saliva and sucking up the remains.

Like dragons, blackspawn stalkers grow larger and more powerful with age. This is especially true of the most capable hunters, particularly those used to hunt good dragons (and allowed to consume the remains afterward).

Environment: Blackspawn stalkers prefer warm or temperate swamps, but they can adapt to dense forests as well. Wherever they live, they seek out the upper branches of trees where they build their nests and lay eggs.

Typical Physical Characteristics: A typical blackspawn stalker stands from 6 to 8 feet tall, with a leg span of 7 to 10 feet in diameter. It can weigh as much as 5,000 pounds. Females tend to be larger, dominating their male counterparts.

Alignment: Blackspawn stalkers are always chaotic evil. They value strength to subjugate others, but they also seek an acceptable master to serve.

Blackspawn stalker

Typical Treasure

Blackspawn stalkers have treasure typical for their Challenge Rating, about 4,500 gp. Unlike their draconic progenitors, these creatures disperse their treasure among many hidden locations, rather than keeping it all in one great hoard.

Blackspawn Stalkers in Eberron

Servants of the dragons of Argonnessen, blackspawn stalkers are rarely found far from their masters. However, those aware of these creatures' existence conjecture that some might be found in the forested land of Q'barra.

Blackspawn Stalkers in Faerûn

These foul creatures can be found roaming the southern jungles of Chult, spreading their progeny at will. They vie for territory against that land's predatory flying dinosaurs.

Illus. by A. Swekel

BLUESPAWN AMBUSHER

The ground trembles, and a blue form bursts from the ground in a shower of dirt and stones. The creature has the shape of a giant badger, but it bears the thick scales, sharp horn, and gnashing teeth of a blue dragon. Suddenly, its body crackles with electricity as sparks leap and arc across its scales.

BLUESPAWN AMBUSHER	CR 4

Always LE Medium magical beast (dragonblood)
Init +0; **Senses** darkvision 60 ft., low-light vision, tremorsense 60 ft.; Listen +4, Spot +4
Languages Draconic

AC 18, touch 10, flat-footed 18
   (+8 natural)
hp 30 (4 HD)
Immune electricity
Fort +6, **Ref** +4, **Will** +3

Speed 20 ft. (4 squares), burrow 20 ft. (earth and stone)
Melee 2 claws +8 each (1d8+4) and
   gore +6 (1d6+2)
Space 5 ft.; **Reach** 5 ft.
Base Atk +4; **Grp** +8
Special Actions electricity burst

Abilities Str 19, Dex 10, Con 14, Int 3, Wis 14, Cha 13
Feats Ability Focus (electricity burst), Multiattack
Skills Climb +7, Hide +0, Listen +4, Spot +4
Advancement 5–10 HD (Medium)

Electricity Burst (Su) A bluespawn ambusher can activate an electricity burst as a standard action once every 1d4 rounds. Any creature within 10 feet must succeed on a DC 16 Reflex save or take 4d6 points of electricity damage. A successful save results in half damage. The save DC is Constitution-based.
   The burst damage increases by 1d6 for each additional HD.

Bluespawn ambushers worship Tiamat as their progenitor, and they willingly serve evil dragons and other followers of Tiamat as guards and hunters. Although dim-witted, they're more than simple beasts and are capable of cunning tactics.

Strategies and Tactics

Bluespawn ambushers live up to their name. They hunt in tight-knit packs containing as many as a dozen members. A pack roams on the surface or lies in wait near a source of water until prey approaches, then swiftly disappears below the ground. Tunneling, the bluespawn ambushers surround their prey, and then claw their way to the surface. Upon resurfacing, they blast the prey with their electricity burst.

The ambushers don't expect anything to survive this assault, so they remain on the surface for a moment afterward to verify the kill. Should prey live to fight back or flee, they burrow underground again the next round. Thereafter, each bluespawn ambusher pursues the quarry from underground, rising to the surface to use its electricity burst, then returning below the surface to wait until the ability recharges.

If this strategy doesn't work, bluespawn ambushers rely on their claw and gore attacks. Ultimately, they prefer to live and fight another day, so they typically flee if overwhelmed.

They fight to the death only when commanded to do so by an evil dragon or a follower of Tiamat.

Bluespawn ambushers that serve as guardians lure intruders into tight, dangerous quarters such as narrow corridors or trails. The ambushers remain out of sight, beneath the surface, then burst from the ground behind their foes to attack. This maneuver cuts off the intruders' escape route, while the ambushers' electricity bursts serve as beacons to draw more guards or alert their masters.

Sample Encounter

Bluespawn ambushers hunt in packs, usually containing an equal number of males and females. An odd number likely represents a group of males protecting a nest or a group of females out hunting after giving birth (see Ecology below). Either makes for a more dangerous encounter, since bluespawn ambushers become much more aggressive in such cases.

Pack (EL 9 or 11): Six males let loose lightning bursts into the night to call back females from the hunt as their young hatch. The young have not yet emerged from the eggs, and the females are some distance off. PCs who investigate the lights on the horizon might encounter the six females dragging

BLUESPAWN AMBUSHER LORE

Characters with ranks in Knowledge (arcana) can learn more about bluespawn ambushers. When a character makes a successful skill check, the following lore is revealed, including the information from lower DCs. Those who recognize the creatures' ancestry can also use Knowledge (religion) to learn more.

Knowledge (Arcana)

DC	Result
14	This creature is a bluespawn ambusher, a predatory magical beast related to blue dragons. This result reveals all magical beast traits.
19	Bluespawn ambushers are immune to electricity. They can release bursts of electricity from their bodies and swiftly burrow beneath the earth.
24	Bluespawn ambushers prefer to attack prey near sources of water in the deserts in which they dwell. They possess a degree of intelligence and can speak pidgin Draconic.
29	Bluespawn ambushers follow regular migration patterns when hunting. Some desert dwellers know these patterns and travel to avoid the creatures.
34	Bluespawn ambushers produce offspring only once every ten years. Females lay eggs underground, then leave to hunt. Males watch the eggs and signal hatching with electricity bursts at night.

Knowledge (Religion)

DC	Result
14	Bluespawn ambushers are some of Tiamat's spawn.
19	Bluespawn ambushers revere Tiamat as their progenitor and often follow the orders of her more intelligent worshipers.

food back to their nests or the whole pack of twelve as they await the emergence of the hatchlings.

Ecology

Bluespawn ambushers eat anything that falls to their electricity burst but rarely trouble themselves with Tiny or smaller prey. Instead, they wait for a suitable number of Small or larger creatures before springing their ambush. A single ambusher can subsist for more than a month on a Small creature.

After a large meal, bluespawn ambushers retreat underground to rest. They lie just beneath the surface, with only the tips of their noses exposed (allowing them to breathe). Most intelligent creatures recognize this and understand the danger (by succeeding on a Spot check opposed by the bluespawn ambusher's Hide check to notice it). Scavengers, attracted to the carcasses, sometimes fall prey to a second surprise attack by the bluespawn ambushers.

Bluespawn ambushers mate for life and produce offspring only once every ten years. After laying eggs underground, the females leave to hunt while the males watch over the clutches. A male signals the hatching with electricity bursts, summoning the female so that both parents can attend the emerging young.

Other spawn of Tiamat value bluespawn ambushers as guardians and sentinels. The ambushers' ability to lurk below ground and their tremorsense form a potent combination. Blue dragons, powerful half-dragons, and blackspawn raiders all make use of these creatures. Though ambushers are desert natives, their masters bring them across the world on campaigns in Tiamat's name.

Environment: Bluespawn ambushers prefer warm deserts, especially those with dunes of loose sand that make burrowing easier. In such environments, packs of four to twelve ambushers migrate from watering hole to oasis to creek, preying on creatures that go to such places to drink. Their travel path depends on the season and what prey is likely to be available in given areas, and it rarely changes. Some desert dwellers have learned these migration patterns and avoid watering holes when bluespawn ambushers are likely to be nearby. They might travel far across the desert to avoid the voracious hunters.

Typical Physical Characteristics: Bluespawn ambushers are thick-bodied, burly creatures. A typical specimen stands about 3 feet tall at the shoulder, and its body is about 4 feet long and nearly as wide. With its dense muscles and thick scales, it weighs about 350 pounds.

Female bluespawn ambushers can be distinguished from males by their slightly narrower heads and longer horns. Young bluespawn ambushers have scales of light blue, which

Bluespawn ambusher

darken as they age. The scales of the oldest are darkly fringed or lined with black.

Alignment: With their simple agenda and loyalty to blue dragon masters, bluespawn ambushers are always lawful evil.

Typical Treasure

Bluespawn ambushers rarely have any treasure, but they do share a hoarding instinct with dragons. Should their prey be carrying treasure, ambushers bury the spoils near a water source on their migration route so they can admire it as they pass through. Only a 20% chance exists that they have coins, goods, or items.

Bluespawn Ambushers in Eberron

Most bluespawn ambushers live mainly in the Blade Desert of Valenar. Scholars trace their ancestry to a blue dragon named Blaphinex, who was killed by other dragons as punishment for what they saw as unnatural interest in the beasts of the deserts.

Bluespawn Ambushers in Faerûn

Bluespawn ambushers can be found wherever blue dragons live, but most dwell in Unther, the seat of Tiamat's power. Several packs serve Hurthoogul, a male hobgoblin worshiper of the Chromatic Dragon, who claimed the title "Talon of Tiamat." He has marshaled a few tribes of goblins and hobgoblins into a small army on the Black Ash Plain, and he hopes to gather more forces to expel Mulhorand's influence and gain dominance over the nation. The Mulhorandi have not discovered this fact.

BLUESPAWN BURROWER

Possessing a head that closely resembles that of a blue dragon and armed with a pair of massive claws, this creature moves through the sand as if it were swimming in water. Its tail is spiked like the head of a great mace, with electricity visibly coursing up and down its length.

BLUESPAWN BURROWER	CR 9

Always LE Large magical beast (dragonblood)
Init +2; **Senses** darkvision 60 ft., low-light vision, tremorsense 60 ft.; Listen +4, Spot +4
Languages Draconic

AC 25, touch 11, flat-footed 23
   (−1 size, +2 Dex, +14 natural)
hp 114 (12 HD)
Immune electricity
Fort +12, **Ref** +10, **Will** +5

Speed 30 ft. (6 squares), burrow 20 ft.
Melee tail slap +18 (1d8+10/19–20 plus shock) and
   2 claws +17 each (2d8+3)
Space 10 ft.; **Reach** 5 ft. (10 ft. with tail slap)
Base Atk +12; **Grp** +23
Atk Options Combat Reflexes, improved grab, shock
Special Actions lightning sweep

Abilities Str 25, Dex 15, Con 19, Int 3, Wis 8, Cha 11
SQ electricity shield, Tiamat's blessing (electricity)
Feats Combat Reflexes, Improved Critical (tail slap), Iron Will, Multiattack, Weapon Focus (claw)
Skills Listen +4, Sense Motive +4, Spot +4
Advancement 13–17 HD (Large); 18–30 HD (Huge)

Improved Grab (Ex) To use this ability, a bluespawn burrower must hit an opponent up to one size larger than itself with a claw attack. It can then attempt to start a grapple as a free action without provoking attacks of opportunity.

Shock (Su) A bluespawn burrower deals an extra 2d6 points of electricity damage with its tail slap attack. In addition to this extra electricity damage, the tail slap attack deals an extra 1d10 points of electricity damage on a successful critical hit.

Lightning Sweep (Su) 60-ft. cone, 3/day, standard action, damage 6d6 electricity, Reflex DC 20 half. The save DC is Constitution-based.
   The lightning sweep damage increases by 1d6 for every 2 additional HD.

Electricity Shield (Su) A bluespawn burrower's body generates a prodigious electrical charge that arcs to nearby creatures. Any creature that strikes or touches a bluespawn burrower with its body or a weapon, or that grapples a bluespawn burrower, automatically takes 2d6 points of electricity damage (Reflex DC 20 half). A creature wielding a metal weapon takes a −2 circumstance penalty on this saving throw. The save DC is Constitution-based. A creature takes damage from this ability only once per round.

Tiamat's Blessing (Electricity) (Su) All spawn of Tiamat within 5 feet of or riding on a bluespawn burrower gain immunity to electricity.

Roaming the desert wastes in organized packs, bluespawn burrowers are used by blue dragons to scout their domains. Other spawn of Tiamat employ bluespawn burrowers to dig out defensive fortifications and erect glass monuments to their dread queen.

Strategies and Tactics

In the wild, a solitary bluespawn burrower bursts from beneath the sand, attempting to grab the closest enemy while using its tail slap and lightning sweep to clear away other foes. If it is seriously injured (in game terms, below 40 hit points), it retreats under the sand, possibly dragging an opponent with it.

Bluespawn burrowers usually hunt in groups. They hide underground with enough distance between them so that they can simultaneously attack from multiple sides.

These creatures are particularly dangerous when led by dragons or more intelligent spawn of Tiamat, who can guide their tactics. In these situations, the burrowers focus on a single target in melee and methodically eliminate it while overlapping their lightning sweeps.

BLUESPAWN BURROWER LORE

Characters with ranks in Knowledge (arcana) can learn more about bluespawn burrowers. When a character makes a successful skill check, the following lore is revealed, including the information from lower DCs. Those who recognize the creatures' ancestry can also use Knowledge (religion) to learn more.

Knowledge (Arcana)

DC	Result
14	This creature is a bluespawn burrower, a predatory magical beast related to blue dragons. This result reveals all magical beast traits.
19	Bluespawn burrowers are immune to electricity. They can generate massive electrical damage when they strike with their tails. Additionally, they can create a cone of electricity by sweeping their tails.
24	Bluespawn burrowers produce so much electricity that when one is struck in melee, electricity arcs from its body to strike the attacker.
29	Bluespawn burrowers attempt to drag single opponents beneath the sands.

Knowledge (Religion)

DC	Result
14	Bluespawn burrowers are some of Tiamat's spawn.
19	Bluespawn burrowers are sometimes found in the company of worshipers of Tiamat, typically blue dragons.
24	In the deepest parts of the desert stand monolithic structures composed entirely of glass, which are somehow related to the burrowers' worship of Tiamat.

Sample Encounters

Whether attacking enemies singly or as a group, bluespawn burrowers always try to use the surrounding terrain to best advantage. They are most likely to be found in small packs of two to four.

Bluespawn burrowers also serve the armies of Tiamat as shock troops that can burrow into an enemy fortress and destroy it from within.

Individual (EL 9): A single bluespawn burrower might lurk near the entrance to a blue dragon's lair, seek a new hunting ground for its pack, or launch an initial foray into a fortification or settlement to gauge its defenses.

Guard Pack (EL 11–13): Occasionally blue dragons or other spawn organize bluespawn burrowers into units that patrol their territory.

EL 13: A quartet of bluespawn burrowers patrol the area around the lair of their mistress, the blue wyrm Thunder Rose. They have instructions to waylay any possible threat, and they report daily on the progress of any creatures too powerful for them to deal with.

Bluespawn burrower

Ecology

Bluespawn burrowers usually form small packs, serving blue dragons or spawn that are more powerful. The creatures organize themselves according to age, size, and ability: Larger members make good soldiers and hunters, while smaller, weaker combatants create and maintain the group's home.

Bluespawn burrowers are ferocious carnivores but can go many days, sometimes weeks, without food; they expend little energy when resting in their burrows. Despite their size, they do not require much water. However, they lurk near oases and watering holes, which draw the desert creatures on which they prey. Once they have depleted the food resources of one area, they move on to the next promising spot.

Other spawn of Tiamat launch expeditions into the desert territories of bluespawn burrowers to enlist the beasts into their armies. The spawn direct the burrowers to fuse sand into glass with their lightning, creating great monoliths that declare the spawn's service to Tiamat.

Environment: Bluespawn burrowers live in the deepest regions of the desert, typically near an oasis or wherever other creatures might congregate.

Typical Physical Characteristics: An average bluespawn burrower is about 5 feet high and 8 to 10 feet in length, weighing as much as 4,000 pounds. The creatures start life with dusky gray coloration, and as they grow, their scales change to a deep, dark blue. In the light of the sun, an adult burrower is somewhat pearlescent.

Like dragons, bluespawn burrowers grow larger and more powerful with age. As they increase in size, they shed their skins like great serpents.

Alignment: Bluespawn burrowers are always lawful evil. These creatures highly value loyalty and obedience. Typically, their association with blue dragons aligns the goals of the group with that of their draconic masters. When left to their own devices, they are less concerned with controlling an area than with simply eating.

Typical Treasure

Bluespawn burrowers have treasure typical for their Challenge Rating, about 4,500 gp. Most of this treasure lies among the remains of past victims, half buried in the sands around the oases where the burrowers lurk.

Bluespawn Burrowers in Eberron

Bluespawn burrowers roam a hidden desert deep in the interior of Xen'drik, awaiting the day their blue dragon masters will return from Argonnessen to lead them against the giants who remain in the continent's jungles.

Bluespawn Burrowers in Faerûn

Roaming the sands of the deep Calim desert, bluespawn burrowers are thought to serve blue dragon masters in that inhospitable land. Scholars speculate that one band of the creatures has come under the control of a powerful mummy lord that has turned the creatures into undead.

Illus. by A. Swekel

BLUESPAWN GODSLAYER

An enormous blue-scaled creature lumbers into view bearing a huge sword and bearing a dragon skull as a shield. Its head looks something like that of a blue dragon, and as it gnashes its teeth and bangs its sword against its shield, electricity sparks from its mouth and weapon.

BLUESPAWN GODSLAYER	**CR 10**

Usually LE Huge monstrous humanoid (dragonblood)
Init –2; **Senses** darkvision 60 ft.; Listen +2, Spot +3
Languages Draconic

AC 23, touch 6, flat-footed 23
    (–2 size, –2 Dex, +2 shield, +15 natural)
hp 138 (12 HD); **DR** 10/chaotic
Immune electricity, paralysis, *sleep*
SR 20
Fort +11, **Ref** +6, **Will** +8

Speed 30 ft. (6 squares)
Melee +2 *bastard sword* +23/+18/+13 (3d8+12/17–20 plus
    2d6 electricity) and
    bite +15 (2d6+5 plus 2d6 electricity)
Space 15 ft.; **Reach** 15 ft.
Base Atk +12; **Grp** +30
Atk Options Awesome Blow, Improved Bull Rush, Power
    Attack, dragon slayer, outsider slayer

Abilities Str 30, Dex 6, Con 25, Int 8, Wis 11, Cha 10
Feats Awesome Blow, Improved Bull Rush, Improved
    Critical (bastard sword), Power Attack, Weapon Focus
    (bastard sword)
Skills Climb +15, Jump +15, Listen +2, Spot +3
Advancement by character class; **Favored Class** fighter;
    see text
Possessions +2 *bastard sword*, heavy dragonskull shield

Dragon Slayer (Su) A bluespawn godslayer deals an
    extra 2d6 points of damage when it hits a dragon or
    dragonblood creature.
Outsider Slayer (Su) A bluespawn godslayer deals an extra
    2d6 points of damage when it hits an outsider.

Bluespawn godslayers live for one purpose: to slay Tiamat's enemies. They delight in combat and take pride in their expertise with weapons. Godslayers guard the lairs of blue dragons and seek out and slaughter good dragons.

Strategies and Tactics

Bluespawn godslayers possess little skill with ranged weapons, and their melee attacks explode with electricity, so they rush to get foes within their reach. A bluespawn godslayer prefers to attack those it can readily identify as enemies of Tiamat. This category includes any dragons or outsiders that oppose them and anyone carrying symbols representing good dragons.

    Against smaller foes, a godslayer moves adjacent and uses Awesome Blow to knock the foe away. When the fallen creature tries to rise from prone, still within reach, the godslayer makes an attack of opportunity against it and then makes a full attack on its next turn (providing that opponent did not flee).

    In groups, bluespawn godslayers surround foes but keep them just within reach. Then, each uses Awesome Blow to knock foes through and into the reach of the others, allowing them to make attacks of opportunity.

Sample Encounters

Bluespawn godslayers are often encountered in small groups or with blue dragons, who protect the spawn from flying enemies. They guard blue dragon lairs or work with other spawn of Tiamat, serving as heavy hitters and anchor points in an army.

    Patrol (EL 11–13): Blue dragons often deploy guard patrols containing bluespawn godslayers and bluespawn burrowers (see page 138).

    EL 11: Brakanax, a bluespawn godslayer, and its "guard dogs," two bluespawn burrowers, patrol the caverns that lead to a blue dragon's lair. They attack any intruders. Brakanax blocks the passage while the burrowers tunnel behind interlopers to flank them and use their electricity sweeps.

    Clutchmates (EL 12–16): Several bluespawn godslayers born to a single dragon might remain with their parent as guards and companions.

    EL 14: Tusenmaug, a young adult blue dragon, soars high above the desert seeking a caravan to raid. Not far behind jog three bluespawn godslayers that attack the dragon's prey while the dragon strafes with lightning.

BLUESPAWN GODSLAYER LORE

Characters with ranks in Knowledge (nature) can learn more about bluespawn godslayers. When a character makes a successful skill check, the following lore is revealed, including the information from lower DCs. Those who recognize the creatures' ancestry can also use Knowledge (religion) to learn more.

Knowledge (Nature)

DC	Result
20	This creature is a bluespawn godslayer, a rarely encountered monstrous humanoid related to blue dragons. This result reveals all monstrous humanoid traits.
25	Bluespawn godslayers are immune to electricity, paralysis, and *sleep*, and their blows deliver a dangerous electrical charge.
30	Bluespawn godslayers hate good dragons and good outsiders. Their attacks against such creatures are particularly potent.
35	Bluespawn godslayers are born only to blue dragons by some twist of fate.

Knowledge (Religion)

DC	Result
20	Bluespawn godslayers are some of Tiamat's spawn.
25	Bluespawn godslayers worship Tiamat and serve her armies as heavy troops.
30	Bluespawn godslayers are born to blue dragons blessed by Tiamat.

Ecology

Bluespawn godslayers are genderless and possess no means of procreation. Instead, they are born to blue dragons blessed by Tiamat. Blue dragons not devoted to the Chromatic Dragon often despise godslayers, but they recognize these creatures' value as guardians. They also fear invoking Tiamat's wrath, which might bring godslayers born of other blue dragons against them.

Godslayers are carnivorous creatures that devour anything that falls to their blades, including other spawn or even chromatic dragons that oppose them. They have the metabolism of dragons, gorging themselves in a spree of slaughter and then not eating for months at a time.

Environment: Bluespawn godslayers live in temperate and warm deserts, along with the blue dragons that gave birth to them.

Typical Physical Characteristics: A bluespawn godslayer stands about 18 feet tall and weighs nearly 18,000 pounds.

Alignment: Bluespawn godslayers are usually lawful evil. Sometimes neutral evil godslayers arise that are willful and often more intelligent. Thus, they are more likely to resist the influences of their mothers and other spawn. Chaotic and good godslayers are unheard-of.

Society

Tiamat designed bluespawn godslayers to kill enemy outsiders and metallic dragons, and to face the aspects of rival dragon gods. They are born to blue dragons who earn Tiamat's favor or who are near to foes of interest to the Chromatic Dragon.

Bluespawn godslayers know they are the favored spawn of Tiamat because they are born only to dragons,

Bluespawn godslayer

and because they hear her distant roars in their dreams. They instinctively recognize all spawn as children of Tiamat, but they believe godslayers to be superior to all the rest. Fortunately for smarter spawn and the blue dragons who foster godslayers as children, the creatures are dull-witted and rarely possess leadership ability.

Nevertheless, all spawn of Tiamat and chromatic dragons are wary around godslayers; their reputation as dragon killers is well known among the worshipers of Tiamat.

Typical Treasure

Bluespawn godslayers carry little treasure. What valuables they find they give to their mothers or to whoever leads them against Tiamat's foes. Most are encountered just with their signature weapons and shields. Godslayers despise being slowed down on the battlefield, but a few leaders convince them to wear light armor, such as a chain shirt fashioned for a giant.

"Yes. I am blessed. I have borne Tiamat's child in Her stead. Holy be Her plans, and may those that use this godslayer come to fruition . . . swiftly."
—*Kazeranthamus, ancient blue dragon*

Bluespawn Godslayers in Eberron

The birth of a bluespawn godslayer is considered a dire omen. Dragon custom dictates that the mother abandon the hatchling godslayer in some distant land and then go into seclusion to contemplate what the birth might mean for the Prophecy. This leaves bluespawn godslayers to live out their lives in solitude or in small groups of siblings throughout Eberron. Since the rise of the humanoid races on Khorvaire, blue dragons have taken to leaving godslayers in the Demon Wastes, the Blade Desert, and in wilderness areas on the continents of Sarlona and Xen'drik.

Bluespawn Godslayers in Faerûn

Bluespawn godslayers live where blue dragons make their homes. In particular, they roam Anauroch, the Calim Desert, and Raurin, the Dust Desert. Blue dragons consider the birth of a bluespawn godslayer to be a great boon. These spawn of Tiamat become able guardians of the dragons' lairs instead of future rivals. The godslayers happily serve in this role until Tiamat calls them to service. Each night, they hope to hear her call to them in their dreams, commanding them to take their place in her great armies.

Illus. by A. Swekel

BLUESPAWN STORMLIZARD

A hulking creature, as big as a horse and twice as wide, circles around you with surprising speed. It looks similar to a wingless blue dragon, but its body shape is more burly. It lowers its horn at you but seems to be waiting for something. Suddenly you notice another of the beasts circling you, taking a similar stance. Electricity crackles along their horns.

BLUESPAWN STORMLIZARD	CR 6

Always LE Large magical beast (dragonblood)
Init –1; **Senses** darkvision 60 ft., low-light vision; Listen +5, Spot +8
Languages —

AC 23, touch 8, flat-footed 23
    (–1 size, –1 Dex, +15 natural)
hp 69 (6 HD); **DR** 5/magic
Immune electricity
Fort +11, **Ref** +4, **Will** +4

Speed 40 ft. (8 squares)
Melee gore +13 (2d6+12)
Space 10 ft.; **Reach** 5 ft.
Base Atk +6; **Grp** +18
Atk Options Improved Bull Rush, Improved Overrun, Power Attack, deadly charge 4d6+12, magic strike
Special Actions electricity arc, electricity link

Abilities Str 27, Dex 9, Con 22, Int 2, Wis 14, Cha 8
SQ Tiamat's blessing (electricity)
Feats Improved Bull Rush, Improved Overrun, Power Attack
Skills Jump +12, Listen +5, Spot +8
Advancement 7–11 HD (Large); 12–17 HD (Huge); 18 HD (Gargantuan)

Deadly Charge (Ex) A bluespawn stormlizard typically begins a battle by charging at an opponent. In addition to the normal benefits and hazards of a charge, this allows the bluespawn stormlizard to deal 4d6+12 points of damage with its gore attack.

Electricity Arc (Su) 100-ft. line, once every 1d4 rounds, standard action, damage 6d6 electricity, Reflex DC 19 half. The save DC is Constitution-based.

Electricity Link (Su) When bluespawn stormlizards gather, electricity surges between them. As a swift action, a bluespawn stormlizard can cause a line of electricity to fire from its horn to that of another bluespawn stormlizard within 100 feet. Creatures in the line must succeed on a DC 19 Reflex save or take 3d6 points of electricity damage. The save DC is Constitution-based.

Tiamat's Blessing (Electricity) (Su) All spawn of Tiamat within 5 feet of or riding on a bluespawn stormlizard gain immunity to electricity.

Tiamat created bluespawn stormlizards to serve her other spawn as mounts, a role they take to readily. Often on the forefront of her forces, stormlizards enjoy charging over foes, or pushing into an enemy line and then blasting creatures between them with their electricity link.

Strategies and Tactics

Bluespawn stormlizards work best in a pack of two to eight. Roughly half of the pack's members charge into melee, while the rest circle around to set up a killing zone with their electricity link, preferably catching several foes at once. The stormlizards continually shift positions to make it harder for the enemy to avoid the lines of lightning. Against creatures with immunity or significant resistance to electricity, stormlizards change their tactics, relying on their gore attacks and setting up flanks.

Sample Encounters

Bluespawn stormlizards are almost never encountered alone. Usually they travel in groups of four or eight, with equal numbers of males and females.

Blackspawn Knights (El 9): Two blackspawn raiders (see page 130) ride on twin bluespawn stormlizards. Eager for glory, both raiders charge their mounts into melee and let the stormlizards decide whether or not to use their electricity link.

Pack (EL 10–12): Packs of stormlizards might be groups of mates or simply siblings.

EL 10: Four bluespawn stormlizards, two male twins and two female twins, hunt together for a meal large enough to sate all of them. The individuals range far apart from one another, keeping their eyes open for Medium or larger creatures. When one spots likely prey, it roars loudly to alert the others and charges in to occupy the quarry until the rest of the pack arrives.

Ecology

Bluespawn stormlizards are always same-sex twins. Each egg holds two stormlizards, and the twins hatch and develop together, inseparable for life. Although an adult can use its

BLUESPAWN STORMLIZARD LORE

Characters with ranks in Knowledge (arcana) can learn more about bluespawn stormlizards. When a character makes a successful skill check, the following lore is revealed, including the information from lower DCs. Those who recognize the creatures' ancestry can also use Knowledge (religion) to learn more.

Knowledge (Arcana)

DC	Result
16	This creature is a bluespawn stormlizard, a predatory magical beast related to blue dragons. This result reveals all magical beast traits.
21	Bluespawn stormlizards are immune to electricity. They attack with their horns and cause terrible damage when they charge. One can release a line of electricity from its horn to strike the horn of another. The boom and crackle of lightning gives them their names.
26	Bluespawn stormlizards are born in same-sex pairs, and twins spend their whole lives together.
31	Bluespawn stormlizard twins hatch from the same egg. If one twin is killed, the other flies into a murderous rage.

Knowledge (Religion)

DC	Result
16	Bluespawn stormlizards are some of Tiamat's spawn.
21	Bluespawn stormlizards often serve followers of Tiamat as mounts or guardians.

electricity link with any other stormlizard, it first learns to use the ability with its twin.

If one of a pair is killed, the other flies into a rage of grief and loss, killing indiscriminately until it is killed itself. If separated for long, both become listless and refuse to eat, slowly starving to death unless reunited. Thus, a pair must seek another pair of twins as mates, and all four use the same lair for egg laying. However, stormlizards don't mate for life, and even within a mated pack, partners might change. All members of a mated group provide for and guard the hatchlings, but once their young are old enough to hunt, the parents split up: Twin fathers take twin sons and twin mothers take twin daughters.

Any creature capable of training wild animals can ride bluespawn stormlizards as mounts. They are surprisingly tractable so long as twins remain within sight or hearing of each another. Fortunately for those who ride them, their electricity link never affects a rider unless one somehow gets between other stormlizards. However, bluespawn stormlizards are driven to kill; if a rider repeatedly spares enemies, the mount grows irritable and eventually rebels. Some riders try to keep their stormlizard mounts in check by "fleeing" from foes they don't wish to kill, but they play a dangerous game by doing so.

Environment: Bluespawn stormlizards live in warm lands. They're more populous in arid regions but can adapt to any temperate or warm environment that provides a dry place to sleep. Mated pairs look for dry caverns in which to lay eggs and tend young; lacking this, they make do with an area of large boulders or even a closely packed stand of trees.

Typical Physical Characteristics: A bluespawn stormlizard stands roughly 6 feet tall at the shoulder and weighs about 4,000 pounds. Males carry slightly more bulk than females, but otherwise they look very similar. With plentiful feeding, though, stormlizards can attain tremendous size. Such behemoths often serve bluespawn godslayers as mounts.

Older stormlizards have darker scales and scarred faces, the result of sparring matches over mates.

Alignment: With their blue dragon heritage and animal intelligence, bluespawn stormlizards are always lawful evil.

Typical Treasure

Bluespawn stormlizards don't carry treasure or eat metal when feeding.

For Player Characters

Bluespawn stormlizards make useful mounts, especially if raised from the egg in captivity and properly handled. Stormlizard twins must remain near each other, and often a pair of twins is trained together. Riding a stormlizard requires an exotic saddle.

Even a domesticated stormlizard retains its evil alignment and takes pleasure in slaughter, so controlling it can be difficult if a rider does not wish to kill an opponent (Handle Animal DC 20). The DCs of Handle Animal and Ride checks increase by 5 for nonspawn riders. All DCs further increase by 10 if a stormlizard is separated from its twin.

Carrying Capacity: A light load for a bluespawn stormlizard is up to 1,040 pounds; a medium load, 1,041–2,080 pounds; and a heavy load, 2,081–3,120 pounds.

Bluespawn Stormlizards in Eberron

Bluespawn stormlizards live in large numbers on Argonnessen and Xen'drik. Far smaller populations eke out an existence in less hospitable regions of Khorvaire, mainly at the edges of Q'barra and within Droaam. The monstrous armies of Droaam have yet to discover the beasts' usefulness as mounts, seeing them only as dangerous predators, but it's only a matter of time until stormlizard cavalry forms the vanguard of their forces.

Bluespawn Stormlizards in Faerûn

Many evil creatures ride stormlizard mounts, including members of the Cult of the Dragon. What their riders don't know is that the beasts have a higher loyalty. Bluespawn stormlizards recognize other spawn of Tiamat as kindred creatures and refuse to attack them. When the time is right for Tiamat's assault on the world, her stormlizards will serve no other master.

Illus. by c. Frank

Bluespawn stormlizard

GREENSPAWN LEAPER

The sound of shaking branches and scrabbling claws grows near. Suddenly you spy a green-scaled, dragonlike creature climbing along the underside of a thick tree limb. About the size of a dwarf, it is clearly a predator built for life in the trees.

GREENSPAWN LEAPER	CR 2

Always NE Medium magical beast (dragonblood)
Init +4; **Senses** darkvision 60 ft., low-light vision; Listen +2, Spot +2
Languages —

AC 18, touch 14, flat-footed 14
   (+4 Dex, +4 natural)
hp 19 (3 HD)
Immune acid
Fort +4, **Ref** +7, **Will** +3

Speed 40 ft. (8 squares), climb 40 ft.
Melee bite +8 (1d6+4)
Space 5 ft.; **Reach** 5 ft.
Base Atk +3; **Grp** +6
Special Actions poison burst

Abilities Str 17, Dex 19, Con 12, Int 2, Wis 15, Cha 8
Feats Weapon Finesse, Weapon Focus (bite)
Skills Balance +14, Climb +17, Hide +14, Jump +17, Listen +2, Spot +2
Advancement 4–9 HD (Medium)

Poison Burst (Ex) A greenspawn leaper can release a burst of poison gas as a standard action once per day. Any creature within 5 feet is affected. This insidious poison is absorbed through the skin and converts to acid. Whenever the greenspawn leaper takes damage from an attack, it can activate this ability as an immediate action. It can still use it only once per day.
   Contact; Fortitude DC 12; initial and secondary damage 2d6 acid. The save DC is Constitution-based.
Skills Greenspawn leapers have a +10 racial bonus on Balance, Hide, and Jump checks. In addition, they have a +8 racial bonus on Climb checks and can always choose to take 10 on Climb checks, even if rushed or threatened.

Predatory and territorial, greenspawn leapers hunt the unwary in the wild and serve the smaller spawn of Tiamat. Greenspawn sneaks (see page 148) use leapers as mounts, beasts of burden, and guardians.

Strategies and Tactics

A greenspawn leaper uses its treetop mobility to approach prey unseen. Although it has little chance of quieting its final approach, the leaper stays hidden behind branches and foliage and uses routes that are impassable on the ground. Once close enough, the leaper jumps onto prey from above or strikes from a nearby branch. It tries to avoid injury, but it stays close to prey so that it can use its poison burst as a last-ditch tactic if it does get hurt. A leaper might even risk an attack of opportunity to make a bull rush attempt against an opponent in the trees, hoping to finish it with poison and the fall.

Sample Encounters

Greenspawn leapers are most often encountered alone or in the company of greenspawn sneaks.

Pair (EL 4): Leapers occasionally pair off, whether for mating or dominance displays, and an interruption usually draws an attack.

EL 4: A pair of courting greenspawn leapers engage in ritual dances and raucous calls, driving most forest animals into hiding. Characters investigating the noise soon find themselves facing two enraged spawn.

Ambush Party (EL 4–7): Patrolling greenspawn sneaks ride leapers through the forest to extend their range and quickly move into ambush positions.

EL 6: Two sneaks and their greenspawn leaper mounts prepare an ambush along a forest path that runs past a small pond. The sneaks lurk in the pond while the leapers crouch nearby in trees. When travelers approach, the leapers roar as they jump down to attack. After a moment, the sneaks rise from the water to surprise and flank their targets.

Ecology

Greenspawn leapers are territorial carnivores that prowl forests and jungles as solitary hunters. They spend most of their lives in the treetops, touching the ground only when they drop on prey from above. They feed mostly on small prey they can surprise or chase down, such as birds and canopy-dwelling mammals. They also hunt bigger creatures that live on the forest floor but rarely attack anything larger than themselves. A greenspawn leaper is careful to avoid damage when attacking prey, despite its poison burst ability. Greenspawn leapers learn early that the acidic spray costs them meals, so they use it only as a last resort.

GREENSPAWN LEAPER LORE

Characters with ranks in Knowledge (arcana) can learn more about greenspawn leapers. When a character makes a successful skill check, the following lore is revealed, including the information from lower DCs. Those who recognize the creatures' ancestry can also use Knowledge (religion) to learn more.

Knowledge (Arcana)

DC	Result
12	This creature is a greenspawn leaper, a predatory magical beast related to green dragons that lives in the forest canopy. This result reveals all magical beast traits.
17	Greenspawn leapers are immune to acid and release a burst of acidic poison from their bodies when wounded. They are vicious and selfish creatures.
22	Greenspawn leapers are very territorial and engage in races against others of their kind through the canopy to determine dominance.
27	Greenspawn leapers dislike being out of their trees and rarely cross open ground or enter water.
32	Greenspawn leapers mate once every three years. A leaper raised in captivity can serve a Small humanoid as a mount among the trees, but it retains its vicious disposition.

Knowledge (Religion)

DC	Result
12	Greenspawn leapers are some of Tiamat's spawn.
17	Greenspawn leapers can sometimes be found among worshipers of Tiamat.

A single leaper claims vast areas of a forest as its hunting grounds, marking trees with scratches and spoor. Most meetings between leapers result in loud fights for dominance that take the form of races about the treetops. The contestants climb swiftly through the trees, each close by the other, trying to be the first to take a risky jump or balance on a narrow branch. The first leaper to fall from the tree or refuse to follow its competitor loses the contest and retreats.

The race pits confidence against bravado as each leaper attempts to outdo and outsmart the other. An experienced leaper often allows its opponent to lead and attempt a foolhardy move. (Of course, this can backfire by giving the other leaper an opportunity to get lucky.) Although of animal intelligence, greenspawn leapers are cunning competitors that engage in malicious "cheating" during such matches. An enterprising leaper might lead a rival toward a branch it knows is weak and then fall behind, or one in the lead might make a jump and then move the branch when its opponent attempts the same maneuver.

One year out of three is a mating year, when males leave their territory to invade the territory of females. Within a given female's territory, males race against each other for the right to mate with her. The winner remains with the female for several days until she grows tired of his presence and chases him away. A retreating male faces a rough homecoming, crossing the territory of other males and undergoing challenges, often returning to find his territory lost to interlopers while he was away.

A pregnant female constructs an egg bed out of interwoven leafy branches. She incubates the eggs for about two weeks, leaving only once a day to hunt for a few hours. Once the young leapers hatch, the female leaves them to fend for themselves within her territory. The hatchlings hone their instinctive abilities to climb, jump, and hide, hunting insects at first but gradually taking on larger prey. When they grow to adolescence, their mother drives them out of her territory, and they must carve out an area of the canopy for themselves.

Greenspawn leapers live for an average of five years in the wild. Living in a forest canopy is difficult for such a relatively large creature, and dangerous races take their toll. In captivity (such as when a greenspawn sneak ranger takes a leaper as an animal companion), a greenspawn leaper can live up to ten years. Only domesticated leapers are likely to live long enough to advance in Hit Dice.

Environment: Greenspawn leapers inhabit warm and temperate forests. They live almost entirely in the canopy, leaving the trees only to attack prey. Large bodies of water, treeless hills or cliffs, and grassy plains form natural barriers against leapers, since they are loath to leave the trees for long.

In regions where trees shed their leaves in winter, greenspawn leapers spend the fall gorging and hibernate in hollowed-out tree trunks. In warmer climes, leapers are active all year round.

Typical Physical Characteristics: A greenspawn leaper is about the size of a leopard or large dog. An adult is about 4 feet long and weighs roughly 100 pounds.

Greenspawn leaper

The scales of leapers bear shades of green appropriate to the forests in which they dwell. Young and domesticated greenspawn leapers often have more uniform coloration as a result of their limited territory. Eggs share this green color for camouflage to protect them from predators.

Alignment: Immensely selfish and territorial, greenspawn leapers are always neutral evil.

Typical Treasure
Greenspawn leapers don't carry or hoard treasure.

For Player Characters
Greenspawn leapers make good treetop mounts for Small riders, if the creatures are raised from the egg in captivity and properly handled. Riding one requires an exotic saddle, and both the leaper and its rider must undergo lengthy and dangerous training to accustom the creature to its role. A greenspawn leaper retains territorial attitudes toward other leapers, and its vicious disposition makes it extraordinarily difficult to handle (+5 on Handle Animal and Ride DCs). The DCs of Handle Animal and Ride checks increase by an additional 5 for nonspawn riders.

Carrying Capacity: A light load for a greenspawn leaper is up to 130 pounds; a medium load, 131–255 pounds; and a heavy load, 256–390 pounds.

Greenspawn Leapers in Eberron
Greenspawn leapers were first discovered in the jungles of Xen'drik. Explorers brought back several captured specimens and eggs to Khorvaire for an exhibition during the Last War, but the creatures escaped. (Some say they were stolen by Seren barbarians.) Where the creatures are now is a mystery yet to be solved.

Greenspawn Leapers in Faerûn
Greenspawn leapers live primarily in the warmer climes of the south, especially the Chultan jungles, but greenspawn sneaks (see page 148) have transplanted them to wherever they live. Typically, sneaks establish a population of leapers around an outpost to serve as mounts and guards. The sneaks sometimes cultivate and shape natural breaks in the forest canopy to serve as barriers, training the leapers to patrol smaller territories.

Illus. by A. Swekel

GREENSPAWN RAZORFIEND

A draconic shape leaps from the water, slashing with razor-tipped, clawed wings. A frill on its forehead and extending down its back suggests a green dragon was somehow involved in the creation of this beast.

GREENSPAWN RAZORFIEND   CR 7

Always LE Large magical beast (dragonblood)
Init +7; **Senses** darkvision 60 ft., low-light vision; Listen +8, Spot +9
Languages Draconic

AC 19, touch 12, flat-footed 16; Dodge, Mobility
   (−1 size, +3 Dex, +7 natural)
hp 85 (10 HD); **DR** 5/magic
Immune acid, paralysis, *sleep*
Fort +10, **Ref** +10, **Will** +5

Speed 50 ft. (10 squares), swim 50 ft.; Spring Attack
Melee 2 wingblades +15 each (2d6+6/18–20/×3) and
   bite +10 (1d8+3)
Space 10 ft.; **Reach** 5 ft. (10 ft. with bite)
Base Atk +10; **Grp** +20
Atk Options augmented critical, magic strike
Special Actions breath weapon

Abilities Str 22, Dex 17, Con 16, Int 5, Wis 15, Cha 12
SQ Tiamat's blessing (acid), water breathing
Feats Dodge, Improved Initiative, Mobility, Spring Attack
Skills Jump +22, Listen +8, Spot +9, Swim +14
Advancement 11–19 HD (Large); 20–30 HD (Huge)

Augmented Critical (Ex) A greenspawn razorfiend's wingblade threatens a critical hit on a natural attack roll of 18–20, dealing triple damage on a successful critical hit.

Breath Weapon (Su) 20-ft. cone, once every 1d4 rounds, 5d6 acid damage, Reflex DC 18 half.
   The breath weapon's damage increases by 1d6 for every 2 additional HD.

Tiamat's Blessing (Acid) (Su) All spawn of Tiamat within 5 feet of a greenspawn razorfiend gain immunity to acid.

Water Breathing (Ex) A greenspawn razorfiend can breathe underwater indefinitely and can freely use its breath weapon while submerged.

Skills A greenspawn razorfiend has a +8 racial bonus on Jump checks. It also has a +8 racial bonus on any Swim check to perform some special action or avoid a hazard. It can always choose to take 10 on a Swim check, even if distracted or endangered. It can use the run action while swimming, provided it swims in a straight line.

Sometimes called "harrowblades" by wood elves and other forest denizens, greenspawn razorfiends are voracious predators of woodland and swamps. Due to their modified wings, they lack the ability to fly, but they can jump a surprising distance.

Strategy and Tactics

Razorfiends are cunning hunters that are fond of hit-and-run tactics. They typically lie in wait under the surface of water or amid undergrowth, then use Spring Attack to great advantage. They know that one blow will eventually strike a vulnerable spot and deal massive damage.

Against multiple foes, a single razorfiend maneuvers to catch as many creatures as possible in its acid breath, even if this provokes attacks of opportunity. A surrounded razorfiend tries to fight its way out, focusing on one enemy until it can clear a path for escape.

Razorfiends are most dangerous in groups. They are intelligent enough to focus all their attacks on one individual, typically the one that most threatens the group. They use their breath weapons liberally, since they are immune to acid, and spray one another with impunity.

Sample Encounters

Razorfiends might be encountered alone or in mated pairs, or used to guard Tiamat's armies.

Mated Pair (EL 7 or 9): The party stumbles upon the nest of a pair of razorfiends. Only one is in the lair, guarding the eggs, and it viciously attacks the intruders. Once combat begins, the razorfiend calls for its mate with a sharp roar. The mate arrives 1d4 rounds later and tries to pick off a PC near the periphery of the battle.

Group (EL 10+): Three or more razorfiends work together to take down large prey or slaughter many weaker creatures.

GREENSPAWN RAZORFIEND LORE

Characters with ranks in Knowledge (arcana) can learn more about greenspawn razorfiends. When a character makes a successful skill check, the following lore is revealed, including the information from lower DCs. Those who recognize the creatures' ancestry can also use Knowledge (religion) to learn more.

Knowledge (Arcana)

DC	Result
17	This creature is a greenspawn razorfiend, a vicious magical beast related to green dragons. This result reveals all magical beast traits.
22	Greenspawn razorfiends are immune to acid, paralysis, and *sleep*. They have an acidic breath weapon and extremely sharp, bladed wings with which they slash at foes.
27	Greenspawn razorfiends live to kill and prefer to ambush opponents, leaping in and out of combat to rip prey to shreds.
32	Greenspawn razorfiends form mated pairs that defend their nests ferociously. One guards the eggs while the other hunts, staying nearby to respond to an alarm.

Knowledge (Religion)

DC	Result
17	Greenspawn razorfiends are some of Tiamat's spawn.
22	Greenspawn razorfiends can often be found among worshipers of Tiamat.
27	Tiamat's armies use greenspawn razorfiends as shock troops to take advantage of their ferocity and love of slaughter.

Greenspawn razorfiend

Those employed by other spawn roam about encampments but are barely under control. In battle, they are released first as shock troops.

In the wild, razorfiends mate for life. Each year, the female produces a clutch of three to six eggs, which she buries under loose dirt or hides in a shallow bog. Mates take turns guarding their nest. One stays with the eggs while the other hunts and protects their territory.

Environment: Greenspawn razorfiends live primarily in temperate or warm forests and marshes. They prefer to build nests near bodies of fresh water, which they also use to ambush prey.

Typical Physical Characteristics: A greenspawn razorfiend stands about 6 feet tall at the shoulder and can reach 20 or more feet in length. An adult weighs roughly 6,000 pounds. Its wings are modified for slashing attacks, and as a razorfiend grows older, the claws become longer and the membranes shrink. When folded, a razorfiend's wings resemble knife blades.

Razorfiends' scales have a dirty green color that helps them lurk in forest pools.

Alignment: Greenspawn razorfiends live for slaughter, but their green dragon heritage and modest intelligence predispose them to a lawful evil alignment.

Treasure

Greenspawn razorfiends have inherited the draconic trait of hoarding wealth, and they collect from their prey anything that glitters or shines. As a result, a razorfiend hoard includes double coins and double goods, with standard items. They never have objects made from cloth, leather, or similar materials, generally preferring metal.

Greenspawn Razorfiends in Eberron

Many greenspawn razorfiends are found within and near the strongholds of hobgoblin warlords in Darguun who have pledged themselves to Tiamat's army. The razorfiends guard hatcheries that incubate eggs of all other kinds of spawn. Other razorfiend populations have been established in Q'barra and the swamplands of the Shadow Marches, as well as the interior of Xen'drik.

Greenspawn Razorfiends in Faerûn

Greenspawn razorfiends are thriving in forests throughout Faerûn. They have been spotted within the Chondalwood, as well as within Thesk and Aglarond. Reports of creatures resembling razorfiends have surfaced around the High Moor and the Serpent Hills, despite their inhospitable climes, and rumors exist of similar beings in the Vast Swamp of eastern Cormyr.

EL 11: Four razorfiends have been let loose by their hobgoblin handler near a busy trade route to perfect their violence in the "wild." They initiate the attack with their acid breath, then use Spring Attack to move in, slash once, and back away. In subsequent rounds, they harry foes from multiple directions, concentrating first on whoever deals the most damage.

Ecology

Greenspawn razorfiends were among the first spawn created by Tiamat, and the first originated in her realm in the Nine Hells. Scores of eggs were distributed to her draconic and hobgoblin servants throughout the world, interbred as troops for Tiamat's grand army.

Now, razorfiends are present in nearly every force of Tiamat's followers, guarding key installations such as dragonspawn hatcheries. Her servants have placed other razorfiends in carefully selected regions to harass settlements and frontier areas in preparation for the great invasion.

Greenspawn razorfiends attack anything that enters their territory. It isn't the hunt they enjoy so much as the killing, and they slay larger and smaller creatures with equal glee.

Illus. by A. Lyon

GREENSPAWN SNEAK

You hear a rustle in the bushes and turn in time to see a green-skinned humanoid burst from hiding. Its obvious speed and agility contrast with its squat body and thick scales. It looks something like a short lizardfolk, but with a distinctly draconic appearance. Wielding two blades and wearing leather armor, it charges toward you.

GREENSPAWN SNEAK   CR 2

Always LE Small monstrous humanoid (dragonblood)
Init +3; **Senses** darkvision 60 ft.; Listen +2, Spot +2
Languages Draconic

AC 19, touch 14, flat-footed 16
  (+1 size, +3 Dex, +2 armor, +3 natural)
hp 11 (2 HD)
Immune acid
Fort +1, **Ref** +6, **Will** +3

Speed 30 ft. (6 squares)
Melee dragonsplit +4/+4 (1d4/19–20 or ×4) or
Melee dragonsplit +6 (1d4/19–20 or ×4)
Ranged dagger +6 (1d3)
Space 5 ft.; **Reach** 5 ft.
Base Atk +2; **Grp** −2
Atk Options sneak attack +2d6
Combat Gear 4 flasks of acid

Abilities Str 11, Dex 16, Con 13, Int 10, Wis 11, Cha 15
SQ water breathing
Feats Two-Weapon Fighting[B], Weapon Finesse
Skills Bluff +9, Hide +14, Listen +2, Move Silently +10, Spot +2
Advancement by character class; **Favored Class** ranger; see text
Possessions combat gear plus leather armor, 2 dragonsplits, 2 daggers

Sneak Attack (Ex) Extra damage to flanked or flat-footed target; *PH* 50. This sneak attack damage stacks with that granted by class levels.
Water Breathing (Ex) A greenspawn sneak can breathe underwater indefinitely.
Skills Greenspawn sneaks have a +5 racial bonus on Bluff, Hide, and Move Silently checks.

Greenspawn sneaks are the eyes and ears of Tiamat's army. Spellcasters might scry on foes, and dragons might spy on enemy troop movement from high in the sky, but greenspawn sneaks are scouts on the ground and in the thick of the action.

Strategies and Tactics

Greenspawn sneaks travel alone or in small groups on scouting missions. They move carefully, staying hidden from potential ambushers. When time is of the essence, they attempt to run silently (−20 penalty on Move Silently checks, with additional penalties for terrain; *PH* 79). On the prowl, sneaks communicate mostly with gesture and body language, but if members of a strike team can't see one another, they call out in short words or phrases of Draconic made to sound like animal noises.

Greenspawn sneaks prefer to attack from hiding. After gaining surprise or at least catching opponents flat-footed, they employ Bluff to feint in combat or create a diversion to hide (*PH* 68). A sneak that successfully feints uses the opportunity to deliver a sneak attack. If able to hide, it continues to make sneak attacks or melts away to attack again later from a different position. In a larger melee, greenspawn sneaks flank foes, usually attempting to surround and eliminate one enemy at a time.

Although not innate swimmers, greenspawn sneaks inherited the green dragon ability to breathe underwater. They prefer to spy from or wait in ambush in bodies of water, usually near bridges or fords that their foes are likely to use. With their poor swimming ability and small size, however, they leave the water to engage foes.

Greenspawn Sneak Raid Leader

An arrow streaks toward you, and a blur of black leather and green scales tumbles in after it. You whirl to face the creature as it pops up behind you, already stabbing with a gleaming blade.

GREENSPAWN SNEAK RAID LEADER   CR 7

Male greenspawn sneak ranger 2/scout* 3
    *Class described in *Complete Adventurer*
LE Small monstrous humanoid (dragonblood)
Init +6; **Senses** darkvision 60 ft.; Listen +7, Spot +7
Languages Draconic

AC 23, touch 16, flat-footed 23; Two-Weapon Defense, uncanny dodge
  (+1 size, +5 Dex, +3 armor, +1 shield, +3 natural)
hp 56 (7 HD)
Immune acid
Fort +8, **Ref** +14, **Will** +7

Speed 40 ft. (8 squares)
Melee +1 *dragonsplit* +12/+7 (1d4+3/19–20 or ×4) and
    dragonsplit +11 (1d4+1/19–20 or ×4) or
Melee +1 *dragonsplit* +14/+9 (1d4+3/19–20 or ×4)
Ranged longbow +12/+7 (1d6/×3)
Base Atk +6; **Grp** +4
Atk Options favored enemy humans +2, skirmish (+1d6, +1 AC), sneak attack +2d6
Combat Gear 4 flasks of acid

Abilities Str 15, Dex 20, Con 16, Int 10, Wis 12, Cha 12
SQ battle fortitude +1, fast movement, trackless step, trapfinding, water breathing, wild empathy +3 (−1 magical beasts)
Feats Iron Will, Track[B], Two-Weapon Defense[B], Two-Weapon Fighting[B], Weapon Finesse, Weapon Focus (dragonsplit)
Skills Balance +7, Bluff +10, Hide +22, Jump +4, Listen +7, Move Silently +16, Spot +7, Survival +5, Swim +7, Tumble +15
Possessions combat gear plus +1 *leather*, +1 *dragonsplit*, dragonsplit, longbow with 20 arrows, *ring of swimming*

Skirmish (Ex) +1 bonus on damage rolls and to AC in any round in which the greenspawn sneak raid leader moves at least 10 feet. *Complete Adventurer* 12.
Sneak Attack (Ex) As greenspawn sneak.
Battle Fortitude (Ex) Bonus on initiative checks and Fortitude saves while wearing light or no armor and carrying a light load. Included above. *Complete Adventurer* 12.
Water Breathing (Ex) As greenspawn sneak.

Raid leaders are rangers, scouts, or rogues who command strike teams of other greenspawn sneaks.

The greenspawn sneak raid leader presented here had the following ability scores before racial adjustments and Hit Dice ability score increases: Str 15, Dex 14, Con 13, Int 10, Wis 12, Cha 8.

Strategies and Tactics

A greenspawn sneak raid leader commands two to four strike teams on a mission to attack an enemy position. Such raids have specific goals beyond mere slaughter and looting: For example, three strike teams might assault a village to divert attention from another strike team that is infiltrating to gather supplies or assassinate an enemy leader.

A raid leader always puts himself where he can most effectively support the mission. This usually means working with the team most likely to encounter difficulty; in the example of the village raid given above, he might accompany the infiltration team if the assassination target seems a tough combatant or the supplies are well defended. Against clever foes, a raid leader might take personal action, using the other strike teams to cover his effort.

Greenspawn sneak raid leaders employ many of the same tactics that sneaks use, but those with levels in rogue or scout also tumble past opponents to flank and use sneak attacks or skirmish. Although they can attack at range, even sniping from hiding, raid leaders prefer melee combat.

Sample Encounters

Adventurers are most likely to encounter greenspawn sneaks singly or in small strike teams. Larger groups assault enemy positions and guard spawn outposts. The strike team is the most common encounter.

Strike Team (EL 5): A strike team usually consists of three sneaks and a single leader with one level in a class.

EL 5: Grayka, Grukex, and Klaykex follow the orders of Kleknax, a 1st-level ranger. The three sneaks are on their first scouting mission, so they are eager to prove themselves, but they're also wary of displeasing Kleknax.

Scout (EL 5–9): A greenspawn sneak found alone is likely to be a low- to mid-level ranger on patrol or sent to scout an enemy strong point.

EL 7: Graxliss is a 4th-level ranger who rides a greenspawn leaper (see page 144), as she roams the sneaks' territory keeping an eye out for intruders. She is eager to charge her mount into battle, where it can use its poison burst, and isn't concerned about its possible injury.

Raid (EL 9–10): In a raid, several strike teams work under a single raid leader.

EL 10: A greenspawn sneak raid leader directs four strike teams against a caravan transporting offerings to a good dragon. The strike teams harry and distract the guardians while the raid leader kills the driver and takes command of the treasure wagon. When he's in place, his whistle signals the strike teams to attack the caravan's other horses so that none can follow as he flees with the treasure.

Outpost (EL 14): An outpost of greenspawn sneaks is hidden in a hill or an underground cave accessible only by water. There, invaders often encounter a prelate (cleric 10), an acolyte (cleric 1), two raid leaders (ranger 2/scout 3), a scout (ranger 4) with a greenspawn leaper mount, twenty adults, and about two dozen immature noncombatants, as well as eggs. Some favored outposts are led by a Talon of Tiamat (cleric 6, talon of Tiamat 4 [*Draconomicon* 134]) instead of a prelate.

Ecology

An outpost of greenspawn sneaks has a surprisingly small impact on the local environment. This isn't due to any love of nature, but rather to a desire to disguise the sneaks' presence in an area.

Omnivorous eaters, greenspawn sneaks have inherited some of dragons' slow metabolism. Each can subsist on less than half the food that a halfling needs, limiting the tribe's impact on the area's flora and fauna. Sneaks are primarily hunter-gatherers, but they tend wild plants they particularly enjoy eating and husband the local animal resources.

Reproduction follows a schedule determined by the tribe's prelate, who sets a limit on egg hatching based on what is best for the tribe and for accomplishing Tiamat's aims. Usually a number of eggs survive each year equal to the number of sneaks in the tribe, but when building up for war, the prelate might allow five to ten times as many eggs to hatch. The tribe sets aside the remaining eggs for use as flasks of acid in battle (these eggs are filled with a caustic fluid that embryonic sneaks breathe and subsist on).

Young greenspawn sneaks are raised communally by tribe members assigned to the task. Parents claim no ownership of offspring—all are children of Tiamat. The prelate judges young sneaks' capabilities and assigns them their adult roles in the tribe. Few greenspawn sneaks ever deviate from these unless retiring from active duty to be caretakers of the young and infirm.

When assigning a tribal role, the prelate also names the hatchling. Greenspawn sneak names have one or two syllables. A hard consonant ("g" or "k") begins the name: "g" indicates a female, and "k," a male.

Greenspawn sneak

Illus. by A. Swekel

Environment: Greenspawn sneaks primarily inhabit temperate or warm forests and marshes. They live in small, hidden settlements in wilderness areas abutting the lands of creatures they consider foes of Tiamat. Sneaks always set up their outposts near a source or fresh water, be it a pond, stream, or underground font. This provides drinking water and a means of escape or concealment for noncombatants should an outpost be attacked.

Typical Physical Characteristics: Greenspawn sneaks average 3-1/2 feet in height and 50 pounds in weight. Females tend to be slightly broader and weigh up to 10 pounds more than males, depending on whether they are carrying eggs.

Alignment: Greenspawn sneaks are nearly always lawful evil. Those that cannot follow the brutal rules of their society rarely live long.

Society

Greenspawn sneaks have a theocratic and orderly society. They are wholly devoted to Tiamat and think of themselves as belonging to a great army with her as their god and general.

Chromatic dragons and other spawn serve Tiamat's army in a multitude of ways, but greenspawn sneaks know their duty with perfect clarity: Strike with surprise, confound and kill, then melt away before the enemy even understands what happened. Every aspect of their lives revolves around this role.

GREENSPAWN SNEAK LORE

Characters with ranks in Knowledge (nature) can learn more about greenspawn sneaks. When a character makes a successful skill check, the following lore is revealed, including the information from lower DCs. Those who recognize the creatures' ancestry can also use Knowledge (religion) to learn more.

Knowledge (Nature)

DC	Result
12	This creature is a greenspawn sneak, a monstrous humanoid related to green dragons. This result reveals all monstrous humanoid traits.
17	Greenspawn sneaks are immune to acid, and they can breathe underwater.
22	Greenspawn sneaks are true to their name. They often use tricks and distractions to overcome foes.
27	Greenspawn sneaks always lair near a source of fresh water, but that source is sometimes underground.

Knowledge (Religion)

DC	Result
12	Greenspawn sneaks are some of Tiamat's spawn.
17	Greenspawn sneaks worship Tiamat and serve her armies as scouts.
22	Greenspawn sneaks have a theocratic society and refuse to follow anyone who doesn't speak for Tiamat. If their clerics are killed, they might leave the region to find and serve another priest of Tiamat.

Three central tenets guide greenspawn sneaks' existence: duty, stealth, and trickery. Duty to Tiamat and tribe comes first. The second most important ideal, stealth, allows them to do their duty. As scouts for the Chromatic Dragon's divine army, greenspawn sneaks live in small settlements, which they call outposts, on the fringes of enemy territory. They know they are the reconnaissance force preparing the way for the great assault. Thus, they must be circumspect, striking when the opportunity presents itself but never revealing their position or intent to others.

Trickery is the tool that gives greenspawn sneaks an edge over foes. Deceit comes naturally to them, and in their social interactions they conceal emotions and disguise their true aims. When the young hatch, the cleverest get attention and training, not the strongest or loudest. These individuals attain the highly honored roles of scouts and strike team members, and one among them might even become prelate. Those with less talent for deceit and strategy become guards, egg incubators, and caretakers for children and the elderly. Of course, trickery must serve the higher goal of helping the tribe and honoring Tiamat; infighting is punished by summary execution.

A high-ranking cleric of Tiamat called a prelate leads a tribe of greenspawn sneaks. As the mouth of Tiamat, the prelate commands complete loyalty. He or she chooses a single successor, called an acolyte, from among the young of the tribe. Although this acolyte has no official authority, in practice, the two clerics act as a unit and are rarely separated. This close relationship prevents power grabs or battles for succession—greenspawn sneaks refuse to follow anyone who cannot speak for Tiamat. Indeed, a tribe that loses both its prelate and acolyte submits to the rule of another tribe's prelate rather than electing a new leader from among their number.

As servants of Tiamat, greenspawn sneaks obey her highest authority. In most cases, this is the prelate, but sometimes a tribe serves a powerful evil dragon or even another group of spawn. Greenspawn sneaks prefer to work with green dragons and other lawful followers of Tiamat. Friction and confusion nearly always result when a leader doesn't appreciate their regimented outlook or the tenets of their society.

Typical Treasure

Greenspawn sneaks have standard items for their Challenge Rating but rarely carry goods or coins. Such wealth is brought back to the outpost and hoarded there as a bed for egg-laying and to offer to evil dragons the sneaks encounter. In addition, an outpost often holds a large cache of nonincubated eggs that serve as acid flasks. Greenspawn sneaks craft their own tools, weapons, and armor, but other items were likely taken from a foe or stolen in a raid.

Greenspawn Sneaks with Class Levels

Although their favored class is ranger, many greenspawn sneaks become rogues, ninjas, or scouts. (The ninja and scout classes are described in *Complete Adventurer*.)

The armies of Tiamat march to war

Illus. by F. Tsai

Rangers often use greenspawn leapers as mounts, and they ride them through the treetops and into battle. A greenspawn sneak ranger who takes the two-weapon combat style gains the Two-Weapon Defense feat in place of the Two-Weapon Fighting feat. Most greenspawn sneak rangers pick humanoid races as favored enemies.

Despite their close relationship with the natural environment, greenspawn sneaks never become druids.

Greenspawn sneaks speak Draconic. Those with a talent for languages learn those of their foes, often Common and Elven.

Level Adjustment: +4.

For Player Characters

A greenspawn sneak wields a pair of dragonsplits, one-handed exotic melee weapons with which all sneaks are proficient. A dragonsplit can be used as a piercing weapon like a short sword. Alternative grips use its long edge for slashing attacks or its short edge for chopping and hacking. It counts as a light weapon for the purpose of Two-Weapon Fighting and Weapon Finesse.

Dmg (S)	Dmg (M)	Critical	Weight[1]	Type
1d4	1d6	19–20/×2 (P) or ×4 (S)	2 lb.	Piercing or slashing

1 Weight is for a Medium weapon. Small weapons weigh half as much, and Large weapons weigh twice as much.

Dragonsplits are not double weapons. Instead, a wielder chooses to use either the piercing edge for a greater critical threat range or the slashing edge for a devastating (but rarer) quadruple-damage critical.

Greenspawn Sneaks in Eberron

Greenspawn sneaks believe themselves to be the favored descendants of green dragons, an idea that most green dragons dispute. Nevertheless, the sneaks revere green dragons and wish to serve them exclusively. Good dragons usually refuse this service; sneaks take such rejection in stride and look for another to worship.

Greenspawn Sneaks in Faerûn

Greenspawn sneaks live undiscovered in many forests and swamps throughout Faerûn. They avoid areas with a large population of elves or other good creatures that might inform the world of their presence. Major communities exist in the Lurkwood, Mere of Dead Men, High Moor, Marsh of Tun, Winterwood, Umber Marshes, and Mhair Jungles, but small tribes live in hundreds of other secret locations. Recent attacks by rogue dragons have the greenspawn hopeful for a new Rage Of Dragons, and they watch the skies for the return of a star the elves call the Kingslayer, which they believe will be a sign from Tiamat that her divine war has at last begun. They trust no humans and thus never work with the Cult of the Dragon.

REDSPAWN ARCANISS

A humanoid, covered in red scales with yellow and orange flame-like markings, leaps at you. It wears studded leather armor and carries a buckler, and it spits harsh sounds as its empty hand reaches into a spell component pouch.

REDSPAWN ARCANISS   CR 6

Always CE Medium monstrous humanoid (dragonblood, fire)

Init +1; **Senses** darkvision 60 ft., low-light vision; Listen +0, Spot +0

Languages Common, Draconic

AC 18, touch 11, flat-footed 17; armored mage
    (+1 Dex, +3 armor, +2 shield, +2 natural)

hp 52 (8 HD); fire spell affinity

Immune fire, paralysis, *sleep*

Fort +4, **Ref** +7, **Will** +6

Weakness vulnerability to cold

Speed 40 ft. (8 squares)

Melee mwk heavy mace +9/+4 (1d8)

Space 5 ft.; **Reach** 5 ft.

Base Atk +8; **Grp** +8

Atk Options Point Blank Shot, Precise Shot

Combat Gear *potion of shield of faith (+3), potion of cure moderate wounds*

Sorcerer Spells Known (CL 6th):
    3rd (4/day)—*fireball* (DC 16; CL 8th)
    2nd (6/day)—*Melf's acid arrow* (+10 ranged touch),
      scorching ray (+10 ranged touch; CL 8th)
    1st (7/day)—*burning hands* (DC 14; CL 8th), *chill touch*
      (+8 melee touch; DC 14), *magic missile, true strike*
    0 (6/day)—*acid splash* (+10 ranged touch), *detect magic,*
      disrupt undead (+10 ranged touch), *ghost sound*
      (DC 13), *message, ray of frost* (+10 ranged touch),
      touch of fatigue (+8 melee touch; DC 13)

Abilities Str 10, Dex 13, Con 15, Int 10, Wis 10, Cha 17

Feats Point Blank Shot, Precise Shot, Weapon Focus
    (ranged touch)

Skills Concentration +13, Jump +4, Knowledge (arcana) +11,
    Listen +0, Spot +0

Possessions combat gear plus masterwork studded
    leather armor, *+1 buckler*, masterwork heavy mace,
    spell component pouch, gold pendant shaped like a red
    dragon's head worth 100 gp

Advancement by character class; **Favored Class** sorcerer;
    see text

Fire Spell Affinity (Ex) A redspawn arcaniss casts fire spells at +2 caster level. In addition, the redspawn arcaniss heals 2 points of damage per spell level each time it casts a fire spell.

Armored Mage (Ex) A redspawn arcaniss can wear light armor and use light shields without an arcane spell failure chance. *Complete Arcane* 12.

Tiamat created the redspawn arcanisses to be her spellcasters in battle, imbuing them with a red dragon's love of carnage and the magic all true dragons inherit with age. The arcanisses serve her as engines of destruction, wildly hurling deadly spells amid the Chromatic Dragon's more melee-oriented forces.

Strategies and Tactics

Redspawn arcanisses enjoy combat and charge into frays. They take a direct approach in combat, rarely using guile or tactics beyond relying on their fire spell affinity and immunity to fire. Even in melee, they prefer to use magic.

An arcaniss casts fire spells recklessly, centering *fireballs* on itself to harm flanking foes and using *burning hands* and *scorching ray* spells, all the while healing itself. Should fire spells be ineffectual, a redspawn arcaniss prefers to retreat, using other magic as it does so. It casts fire spells to heal, then usually returns with other spawn of Tiamat to take revenge.

If in battle it spots a dragonblood character (such as a spellscale or dragonborn from the *Races of the Dragon* supplement) or any creature with a connection to good dragons, a redspawn arcaniss focuses on that enemy. Even dire opposition does not discourage an arcaniss from pleasing Tiamat by killing one of her hated foes.

A redspawn arcaniss typically wears light armor and a light shield, keeping one hand free for spellcasting. It also carries a simple weapon, such as a heavy mace, for the rare occasions when it must resort to physical combat.

Sample Encounter

Redspawn arcanisses know how to handle foes: Burn them to cinders and feast on their charred bones. They usually form raiding parties to maximize the destruction.

Raiders (EL 10): Three redspawn arcanisses and a redspawn firebelcher (see page 154) attack a town at night, setting everything alight as they roam the streets. One arcaniss rides the firebelcher and directs its attacks in the most useful manner. The other two stay close, reserving their *fireball* spells for when the people of the town mount a

REDSPAWN ARCANISS LORE

Characters with ranks in Knowledge (nature) can learn more about redspawn arcanisses. When a character makes a successful skill check, the following lore is revealed, including the information from lower DCs. Those who recognize the creatures' ancestry can also use Knowledge (religion) to learn more.

Knowledge (Nature)

DC	Result
16	This creature is a redspawn arcaniss, a monstrous humanoid descended from red dragons. This result reveals all monstrous humanoid traits.
21	Redspawn arcanisses are vulnerable to cold and immune to fire, paralysis, and *sleep*. They cast spells like sorcerers but can wear armor and use shields.
26	Redspawn arcanisses can heal themselves by casting fire spells, and their fire spells are abnormally potent.
31	Redspawn arcanisses hate good dragons and focus all their attacks on them or creatures that show allegiance to them.

Knowledge (Religion)

DC	Result
16	Redspawn arcanisses are some of Tiamat's spawn.
21	Redspawn arcanisses worship Tiamat and use their potent spellcasting in her service.
26	Redspawn arcanisses believe themselves to be the most highly favored of Tiamat's children, destined to destroy her enemies and rule in her name.

resistance and begin to surround them. The arcanisses have come in search of weapons and armor for their unhatched children. Having overcome resistance at the village gate, they burn their way toward an armorer's shop.

Ecology

Redspawn arcanisses are carnivores that prefer freshly killed, well-roasted meat and blackened bones. They lack skill at hunting and trapping, but can usually bring down game by a well-placed *scorching ray* or even a *fireball*.

Arcanisses live for the destruction of Tiamat's foes. They roam the wilderness in pursuit of her enemies, slaughtering and feeding on the hapless creatures they encounter. Their nomadic natures mean redspawn arcanisses rarely have a great effect on the local environment, although a forest fire can be a sign of their passing.

Bands of arcanisses stay on the move, except when laying and hatching eggs. Females become fertile for one week, once a year. A month after mating, a female lays a single egg. She keeps it in a heated place, such as a hot spring, a volcanic vent, or even a well-tended fire pit. The egg grows quickly in the heat and hatches in approximately two weeks.

Redspawn arcaniss

Hatchling redspawn arcanisses emerge fully formed and adult-sized. They can speak, and they completely understand how to use the spells Tiamat granted them. The band spends another week with the newborns, teaching them about the lay of the land and offering both religious and practical information. Usually, a mother provides her child with a book or a scroll with excerpts from the Scrolls of Fire (see Society) and speaks of the great destiny awaiting their race as children of Tiamat. The parents and children mix and split into two or three new bands, then go their separate ways.

A hundred small flames start a hundred fires that might become a hundred bonfires and a hundred mighty blazes lighting the end of the world. Go forth and burn hot and bright. Fire spreads.

—Excerpt from the Scrolls of Fire

Environment: Redspawn arcanisses haunt the fringes of civilization and move frequently. They don't mind living in the rough for long periods, and they're most at home in large caves in warm hills. Where it is safe for them to do so, they sometimes venture into towns to buy and sell goods and seek information.

Typical Physical Characteristics: A redspawn arcaniss stands about 6 feet tall and weighs approximately 200 pounds. When young, an arcaniss has much more yellow and orange in its coloring. As it ages, these colors grow redder, eventually deepening in color to almost black.

Alignment: Redspawn arcanisses are always chaotic evil. They revel in ruin and pain. They believe that every act of destruction should honor Tiamat, their mother and god.

Society

Redspawn arcanisses call themselves the Burning Ones of Tiamat. They believe themselves to be the most favored of her spawn: Through fire and destruction, they will cleanse the world of nondragons and rule over all dragonkind. Their holy books, the Scrolls of Fire, instruct the arcanisses in these matters. Purportedly written by Tiamat herself, the Scrolls tell arcanisses to go forth and torch the land.

Redspawn arcanisses spend little time in large groups, usually roving the wilderness in small bands of two to six. They wander as whim or rumor takes them, ever careful not to settle in one place too long or grow too dependent on one another. Most meetings between bands are chance encounters, such as when two or more groups seek the lair of a good dragon or other enemy of Tiamat. These meetings provide a brief opportunity to share news, and individuals mingle freely before forming new groups and heading their separate ways. Several bands might work together to defeat a common foe, but more often, the most numerous group wins that honor while the others seek new conquests.

Typical Treasure

Redspawn arcanisses have standard treasure for NPCs of their Challenge Rating. They have a strong hoarding instinct, but they rarely take more treasure than they can carry. Nearly all their combat equipment is stolen from other creatures or crafted for them by a more settled race of Tiamat's spawn. They like to acquire items of fine quality, especially those with draconic themes. Much of an arcaniss's treasure is in the form of art objects and jewelry.

Redspawn Arcanisses with Class Levels

Sorcerer is the favored class of redspawn arcanisses. As an associated class, levels of sorcerer stack with an arcaniss's innate spellcasting ability. Levels of other classes (even spellcasting classes) are nonassociated.

Level Adjustment: +4.

Illus. by R. Spencer

REDSPAWN FIREBELCHER

A red-scaled, dragonlike creature lumbers toward you with surprising speed. As it opens its fearsome jaws to roar, you can see fire flare within.

REDSPAWN FIREBELCHER	**CR 6**

Always CE Large magical beast (dragonblood, fire)
Init –1; **Senses** darkvision 60 ft., low-light vision; Listen +5, Spot +6
Languages —

AC 18, touch 8, flat-footed 18
    (–1 size, –1 Dex, +10 natural)
hp 84 (8 HD)
Immune fire, paralysis, *sleep*
Fort +11, **Ref** +5, **Will** +2
Weakness vulnerability to cold

Speed 40 ft. (8 squares), swim 30 ft.
Melee bite +12 (2d6+6 plus 1d6 fire)
Space 10 ft.; **Reach** 5 ft.
Base Atk +8; **Grp** +16
Atk Options Power Attack
Special Actions belch fire

Abilities Str 19, Dex 8, Con 21, Int 1, Wis 11, Cha 6
SQ Tiamat's blessing (fire)
Feats Power Attack, Weapon Focus (bite), Weapon Focus (ranged touch)
Skills Jump +8, Listen +5, Spot +6, Swim +12
Advancement 9–16 HD (Large); 17–24 HD (Huge)

Belch Fire (Su) A redspawn firebelcher can belch fire up to 60 feet as a standard action. This is a ranged touch attack (attack bonus +7) with no range increment. An opponent hit by this attack takes 6d6 points of fire damage. Creatures adjacent to the target take 3d6 points of fire damage; a DC 19 Reflex save reduces this damage to half. The save DC is Constitution-based.

Tiamat's Blessing (Fire) (Su) All spawn of Tiamat within 5 feet of or riding on a redspawn firebelcher gain immunity to fire.

Skills A redspawn firebelcher has a +8 racial bonus on any Swim check to perform some special action or avoid a hazard. It can always choose to take 10 on a Swim check, even if distracted or endangered. It can use the run action while swimming, provided it swims in a straight line.

Ferocious but stupid, redspawn firebelchers serve Tiamat's more intelligent spawn as mounts. When left to their own devices, they live like crocodiles, lounging around pools of lava instead of water.

Strategies and Tactics

Redspawn firebelchers immediately attack any creature that comes within charging distance, except other spawn of Tiamat and chromatic dragons. A redspawn firebelcher begins combat with its best form of attack: belching fire. It then charges the nearest foe and bites at it savagely, all the while looking for another opportunity to belch fire. It can use this special ability against enemies up to 60 feet away but is content to burn those within reach, especially if they are clustered together.

When used as mounts, firebelchers follow the commands of their riders. Although they are powerful swimmers, they prefer lava and avoid entering water unless ordered to do so.

Sample Encounter

Firebelchers can be encountered individually, but most of the time they form hunting groups of three to twelve. They also serve other spawn of Tiamat as mounts or guard beasts.

Hunting Party (EL 12): A party of twelve blackspawn raiders (see page 130) have commandeered a colony of redspawn firebelchers to serve them. The raiders are looking for a sect of dragon shamans (detailed in *Player's Handbook II*) dedicated to emulating silver dragons, but they readily attack other creatures.

The spawn divide into four smaller groups, each containing three raiders and a firebelcher: One blackspawn is mounted while the other two stay within 5 feet of the firebelcher at all times to gain immunity to fire. The spawn attack from four directions, with the riders first ordering their mounts to belch fire. The group then closes. In melee, the blackspawn raiders on foot try to flank enemies while staying adjacent to the redspawn to avoid damage from splashing flames.

Ecology

Redspawn firebelchers prefer extremely hot locales, particularly volcanic areas. They spend most of their days basking in the sun or sliding slowly through lava flows. This languid life belies the creatures' predatory nature and surprising speed.

When hungry, firebelchers explode into the countryside, setting fires as they incinerate anything larger than a rabbit that crosses their paths. Sometimes they ride the lava flows

REDSPAWN FIREBELCHER LORE

Characters with ranks in Knowledge (arcana) can learn more about redspawn firebelchers. When a character makes a successful skill check, the following lore is revealed, including the information from lower DCs. Those who recognize the creatures' ancestry can also use Knowledge (religion) to learn more.

Knowledge (Arcana)

DC	Result
16	This creature is a redspawn firebelcher, a ferocious magical beast related to red dragons. This result reveals all magical beast traits.
21	Redspawn firebelchers are vulnerable to cold and immune to fire, paralysis, and *sleep*. They live in volcanic areas but periodically leave them to hunt.
26	Redspawn firebelchers spit gobs of fire and have devastating, fiery bites. They possess the chaotic evil nature of red dragons and kill more than they can eat.

Knowledge (Religion)

DC	Result
16	Redspawn firebelchers are some of Tiamat's spawn.
21	Redspawn firebelchers are used as mounts and guard beasts by other spawn of Tiamat.

Redspawn firebelcher

Usually only one hatchling out of a clutch survives. The mothers and surviving young then go hunting. Young firebelchers gorge themselves on fresh meat and grow at a stupendous rate. They reach adult size after ten days, although they do not become fertile for another two years.

Environment: Redspawn firebelchers most commonly inhabit warm hills and mountains, but they can be found in any area with volcanic activity.

Typical Physical Characteristics: A redspawn firebelcher measures about 12 feet from the tip of its nose to the end of its tail. It is solidly built and weighs about 3,000 pounds.

Alignment: Redspawn firebelchers are stupid and destructive, embodying the worst traits of red dragons. They are always chaotic evil.

Typical Treasure

Redspawn firebelchers don't hoard treasure, and their fiery digestive systems destroy any small items of value they might consume.

For Player Characters

Redspawn firebelchers make interesting if challenging mounts. They are exceptionally ornery creatures and difficult to train. Only a very skilled trainer's rearing one from infancy has resulted in successful domestication. For all but the spawn of Tiamat, Handle Animal DCs with redspawn firebelchers increase by 10 and Ride check DCs increase by 5.

Because of the time and effort involved, a domesticated firebelcher mount costs 35,000 gp.

Carrying Capacity: A light load for a redspawn firebelcher is up to 350 pounds; a medium load, 351–700 pounds; and a heavy load, 701–1,050 pounds.

Redspawn Firebelchers in Eberron

Redspawn firebelchers live in the Menechtarun desert and the Skyraker Claws mountains of Xen'drik. Scholars speculate that they might once have been beasts of burden or guardian beasts for fire giants long ago, when giants were cultured builders.

Redspawn Firebelchers in Faerûn

Redspawn firebelchers inhabit many of Faerûn's mountainous areas, often in volcanic caverns hidden beneath snow-covered peaks. Many large colonies of firebelchers exist in the Crags near the Neverwinter Wood and in the Smoking Mountains of Unther. The creatures can also be found in a few areas near civilization. For example, Thraxata, a young adult red dragon, resides at the top of the Blood Horn in Deepingdale and encourages redspawn firebelchers to live near her lair.

of volcanic eruptions, using these upheavals as an excuse to hunt and add to the destruction. Although firebelcher attacks are devastating, the nearby environment adapts to them, as it might to a volcano that periodically erupts.

A firebelcher consumes roughly its body weight in meat at one sitting, then returns to its lair. With a metabolism like that of dragons, it can survive up to two years on such a substantial meal. Redspawn firebelchers inherit red dragons' penchant for cruelty, though, and kill far more than they can eat.

Other, more intelligent spawn of Tiamat capture and train redspawn firebelchers as mounts. Although difficult to tame, firebelchers are receptive to the commands of other spawn—often after eating a few. Such mounts are not allowed to eat their fill; hunger keeps them ferocious and prevents lethargy. Redspawn arcanisses (see page 152) most commonly use redspawn firebelchers, but blackspawn raiders and even greenspawn sneaks have been known to ride them into battle. No one has reported whitespawn riding firebelchers, but this is more likely due to their conflicting environments than to innate hostility.

Adult female firebelchers come into season once every three years, near the height of summer. Several males vie for the privilege of mating with a single female in conflicts that are bloody but rarely fatal. Once the female has conceived, she drives away the victorious male. She then lays a clutch of six to eight eggs, each about a foot long and weighing around 25 pounds. She conceals them with small rocks and debris and guards them against all intruders, including other firebelchers.

After a couple of weeks, the baby redspawn firebelchers break out of their shells, ravenously hungry. They eat anything they can see and overwhelm, including their siblings.

Illus. by F. Tsai

WHITESPAWN HORDELING

A creature the size of a gnome comes howling at you, slashing the air with two short swords made of bone. It has a fang-filled mouth in a head like that of a white dragon, and thick ivory scales cover its body.

WHITESPAWN HORDELING	CR 1

Usually CE Small monstrous humanoid (cold, dragonblood)
Init +0; **Senses** darkvision 60 ft.; Listen –1, Spot –1
Languages Draconic

AC 13, touch 11, flat-footed 13
    (+1 size, +2 natural)
hp 13 (2 HD)
Immune cold
Fort +2, **Ref** +3, **Will** +2
Weakness vulnerability to fire

Speed 40 ft. (8 squares), fly 20 ft. (clumsy)
Melee short sword +3 (1d4/19–20) and
    bite +1 (1d4) or
Melee short sword +1/+1 (1d4/19–20) and
    bite +1 (1d4)
Ranged dart +3 (1d3)
Space 5 ft.; **Reach** 5 ft.
Base Atk +2; **Grp** –2
Special Actions breath weapon

Abilities Str 11, Dex 10, Con 14, Int 4, Wis 9, Cha 9
Feats Multiattack, Two-Weapon Fighting[B]
Skills Balance +10, Climb +5, Hide +4, Jump +4, Listen –1, Spot –1
Advancement by character class; **Favored Class** barbarian; see text
Possessions 2 short swords, 4 darts

Breath Weapon (Su) 30-ft. cone, once every 1d4 rounds, damage 1d6 cold, Reflex DC 13 half.
Skills Whitespawn hordelings have a +5 racial bonus on Balance and Climb checks.

Whitespawn hordelings live for violence. They rove in huge hordes, fighting anything they encounter.

Strategies and Tactics

Whitespawn hordelings employ little strategy. All the members of a group charge and mob foes. Some attack with swords and bites, while others who can't yet get into melee hurl darts and use their breath weapons against enemies. If their melee attacks cannot pierce a target's armor, they turn to their cold breath; if neither tactic works, they flee.

Sample Encounters

Whitespawn hordelings are almost never encountered alone. Most groups include at least six members.

Pair (EL 2): A pair of whitespawn hordelings are probably the only survivors of a recent battle.

EL 2: Two blood-spattered hordelings seek more of their kind after a deadly fight with orcs. They carry two severed orc limbs as food.

Pack (EL 5): Whitespawn hordelings group into packs of about six that form war parties. A single pack has most likely split from the larger group to attack a separate target.

EL 5: Six whitespawn hordelings scout ahead of the rest of a war party. They attack anything except chromatic dragons or other spawn.

War Party (EL 7–9): A war party comprises two to four packs. War parties range apart from the main horde, either at the behest of a powerful and intelligent leader or when most of the hordelings are involved in some other activity, such as egg-laying.

EL 8: Twelve whitespawn hordelings attack a town, charging into the outlying houses in the dead of a winter night. They were sent to test the town's defenses by a blackspawn raider (see page 131), who watches from nearby.

Horde (EL 10–18): Larger than war parties, hordes contain up to 150 members, all of whom are combatants. One hordeling barbarian exerts some control over the group, but it is not much of a leader.

EL 11: Thirty-two whitespawn hordelings descend from the mountains, led by a 5th-level hordeling barbarian. Fleeing frost giants that attacked their tribe, they destroy everything in their path.

Ecology

Whitespawn hordelings subsist as nomadic hunters, the whole horde moving as one group. When prey is sighted, the horde splits into packs and war parties. They approach the quarry from several sides, then charge in to kill as many creatures as they can. Because hordelings aren't adept at stealth, such attacks rarely catch all of a herd. Thus, they fill the role of natural predators: The healthiest and most alert prey survive to propagate.

A horde never remains long in one place. The hordelings leave lands they've hunted out or those whose inhabitants drive them away. Only mating season slows them down.

After the eggs are laid, the hordelings hunt down large or numerous prey. They place the eggs within the carcasses and

WHITESPAWN HORDELING LORE

Characters with ranks in Knowledge (nature) can learn more about whitespawn hordelings. When a character makes a successful skill check, the following lore is revealed, including the information from lower DCs. Those who recognize the creatures' ancestry can also use Knowledge (religion) to learn more.

Knowledge (Nature)

DC	Result
11	This creature is a whitespawn hordeling, a monstrous humanoid related to white dragons. This result reveals all monstrous humanoid traits.
16	Whitespawn hordelings are immune to cold and vulnerable to fire. They can breathe cones of cold.
21	Whitespawn hordelings are most commonly found in cold lands. They travel in great hordes and attack en masse.
26	Whitespawn hordelings are nomadic but wander with little direction. They abandon lands they've overhunted or that other creatures drive them from.

Knowledge (Religion)

DC	Result
11	Whitespawn hordelings are some of Tiamat's spawn.
16	Whitespawn hordelings worship Tiamat and serve her armies as expendable troops.

await hatching. The reason for doing so is unclear, since the bodies provide little warmth to the eggs, and hordelings are unaffected by cold. Whitespawn hordelings say they want the young to "hear the call of blood," and this practice ensures an immediate source of nourishment for the hatchlings. The eggs hatch in about a week, and the young mature swiftly. Hordelings rarely live long past their prime.

Environment: Whitespawn hordelings roam cold lands, rampaging from one area to the next. Any sort of cold terrain, from mountains to deserts, might contain them.

Typical Physical Characteristics: Whitespawn horde-lings average 3-1/2 feet in height and 40 pounds in weight. Females have slightly narrower shoulders than males and weigh a bit less.

Alignment: Whitespawn hordelings are usually chaotic evil. Their society is savage and dedicated to the maleficent Tiamat. Rarely, a neutral evil hordeling appears; such individuals are usually clerics. Lawful or good hordelings are unheard-of.

Whitespawn hordeling

Illus. by A. Swekel

Society

Whitespawn hordelings are barely more intelligent than animals, ruled by emotion and instinct more than by rational thought. Some nevertheless can craft crude tools and weapons of bone or horn. Their few cultural traditions revolve around mating and egg laying.

The most threatening member of the horde becomes the leader. Such "leadership" consists mainly of intimidation and lasts only as long as the other hordelings fear and respect that individual. The leader might be a barbarian, or occasionally a cleric, but often it's simply another hordeling that's meaner than the rest.

Whitespawn hordelings grudgingly accept the rule of other creatures, usually more intelligent and powerful spawn of Tiamat. However, they willingly serve white dragons, which the hordelings worship as embodiments of Tiamat.

Whitespawn hordelings speak a crude dialect of Draconic.

Typical Treasure

Whitespawn hordelings typically have no treasure other than their weapons. Even leaders don't carry more than what they need to fight. Always on the move and trading with no one, hordelings don't understand the concept of possessions, which would only weigh them down.

Whitespawn Hordelings with Class Levels

Whitespawn hordelings' favored class is barbarian, though few live long enough to acquire such training. Clerics are usually neutral evil and serve Tiamat, but most hordes lack them.

Level Adjustment: +1.

Whitespawn Hordelings in Eberron

Whitespawn hordelings live mainly in the Frostfell and on remote, northerly islands in the Lhazaar Principalities that even the pirate lords dare not approach. The hordelings lack the means to build boats, but every five years during the dead of winter they engage in migrations, fluttering and swimming across pack ice to other islands and even to Khorvaire. Scholars of the planes note that these migrations coincide with Risia's coterminous period and are surely related. The pirates, and occasionally the dwarves of the Mror Holds, have so far dealt with these small incursions, but they worry that a cold enough winter could form an ice bridge across the Bitter Sea. Such an event would offer an easy crossing to thousands of hordelings; if they were to establish a foothold in the Demon Wastes, nothing would prevent them from spreading across the continent.

Whitespawn Hordelings in Faerûn

Whitespawn hordelings can be found wherever white dragons live. Some sages speculate that the creatures are the result of inbreeding among half-white dragon kobolds, but this theory doesn't explain their close associations with white dragons. Metallic dragons say the hordelings appeared in Faerûn recently (as dragons reckon time) and were loosed on the world by Tiamat herself, but humanoid scholars scoff at the idea that the god would create such stupid minions.

WHITESPAWN HUNTER

A white-scaled humanoid slinks along the ice, sizing you up with reptilian eyes. Its face is reminiscent of a white dragon's, with a short crest and a beaklike nose. It carries a cruel-looking polearm.

WHITESPAWN HUNTER   CR 4

Always CE Medium monstrous humanoid (cold, dragonblood)
Init +5; **Senses** darkvision 60 ft., low-light vision; Listen +6, Spot +6
Languages Common, Draconic

AC 17, touch 11, flat-footed 16
    (+1 Dex, +5 armor, +1 natural)
hp 39 (6 HD)
Immune cold, paralysis, *sleep*
Fort +4, **Ref** +6, **Will** +6
Weakness vulnerability to fire

Speed 20 ft. (4 squares) in breastplate; base speed 30 ft.
Melee ranseur +8/+3 (2d4+3/×3) or
Melee handaxe +8/+3 (1d6+2/×3)
Ranged shortbow +7 (1d6/×3)
Base Atk +6; **Grp** +8
Space 5 ft; **Reach** 5 ft. (10 ft. with ranseur)
Combat Gear *potion of cure moderate wounds, potion of pass without trace, potion of protection from good, potion of resist fire*

Abilities Str 15, Dex 12, Con 14, Int 8, Wis 13, Cha 10
SQ ice step
Feats Alertness, Improved Initiative, Track
Skills Listen +6, Spot +6, Survival +8
Advancement by character class; **Favored Class** barbarian; see text
Possessions combat gear plus masterwork breastplate, ranseur, handaxe, shortbow with 20 arrows and 10 cold iron arrows

Ice Step (Ex) Whitespawn hunters ignore all movement penalties associated with snow or ice on the ground. They always succeed on Balance checks against effects caused by ice or by spells or special abilities with the cold descriptor.
Skills Whitespawn hunters have a +4 racial bonus on Survival checks.

Whitespawn hunters are brutish, crafty stalkers of the frozen realms. They revere Tiamat as the ultimate predator.

Strategies and Tactics

Whitespawn hunters track their prey for miles, staying out of sight for as long as possible before launching an attack. They try to trap their foes in terrain that limits escape, such as ice floes or chasms. Once confident of the kill, after harrying opponents with their shortbows, they close and attack with wild abandon. In melee, they take advantage of their weapon's reach.

Hunting groups prefer to keep one or more individuals out of sight to watch the engagement, entering when reinforcements are required or when victory seems certain.

Whitespawn Berserker

This white-scaled humanoid has a reptilian face with a short crest and a beaklike nose. It whirls a spiked chain, seemingly made from rusted iron, through the air before it.

WHITESPAWN BERSERKER (RAGING)   CR 6

Male whitespawn hunter barbarian 2
CE Medium monstrous humanoid (cold, dragonblood)
Init +6; **Senses** darkvision 60 ft., low-light vision; Listen +8, Spot +6
Languages Common, Draconic

AC 17, touch 10, flat-footed 17; uncanny dodge
    (+2 Dex, +6 armor, +1 natural, −2 rage)
hp 93 (8 HD)
Immune cold, paralysis, *sleep*
Fort +12, **Ref** +8, **Will** +9
Weakness vulnerability to fire

Speed 30 ft. (4 squares) in breastplate; base speed 40 ft.
Melee mwk spiked chain +16/+11 (2d4+10) or
Melee handaxe +15/+10 (1d6+7/×3)
Ranged mwk composite shortbow +11/+6 (1d6+5/×3)
Space 5 ft; **Reach** 5 ft. (10 ft. with spiked chain)
Base Atk +8; **Grp** +15
Atk Options rage 1/day (9 rounds)
Combat Gear *oil of magic weapon,* 3 *potions of bull's strength,* 3 *potions of cure light wounds, potion of resist fire*

Abilities Str 24, Dex 14, Con 22, Int 6, Wis 12, Cha 13
SQ fast movement, ice step
Feats Alertness, Improved Initiative, Track
Skills Listen +8, Ride +4, Spot +6, Survival +8
Possessions combat gear plus *+1 breastplate,* masterwork spiked chain, handaxe, masterwork composite shortbow (+5 Str bonus) with 20 arrows, 5 adamantine arrows, and 10 cold iron arrows, *cloak of resistance +1,* hemp rope (50 ft.), 10 pitons, ivory token of Tiamat worth 200 gp

Ice Step (Ex) As whitespawn hunter

When not raging, a whitespawn berserker has the following changed statistics:
AC 19, touch 12, flat-footed 19
hp 77 (8 HD)
Fort +10, **Will** +7
Melee mwk spiked chain +14/+9 (2d4+7) or
Melee handaxe +13/+8 (1d6+5/×3)
Grp +13
Abilities Str 20, Con 18

Whitespawn berserkers represent the ideal of the race. They are both crafty and merciless.

The whitespawn berserker presented here had the following ability scores before racial adjustments and Hit Dice ability score increases: Str 15, Dex 12, Con 14, Int 8, Wis 10, Cha 13.

Strategies and Tactics

Whitespawn berserkers use their superior wilderness skills to pursue prey more effectively, but once in combat, they yield to unbridled battle fury.

Sample Encounters

Whitespawn hunters prefer to travel in small groups, the better to bring down prey. However, they are fractious and competitive by nature and often fight among themselves, especially when dividing the spoils. Leaders often ride whitespawn iceskidders (see page 163).

Individual (EL 4): A whitespawn hunter encountered alone is usually a scout for the tribe.

EL 4: After a run-in with a band of orcs, a tribe of whitespawn hunters sends out individuals to track down their enemies.

Pair (EL 6): Most whitespawn hunters travel in pairs. When they encounter prey, one moves in to attack, and the other hangs back to make a surprise attack at the optimal moment.

EL 6: Two young whitespawn hunters are sent out to bring down the largest game possible so they can be accepted as adults in the tribe. They cooperate with each other to an extent, but only one can win the right of adulthood—the loser is to be killed or exiled.

Hunting Group (EL 10): A hunting group generally consists of two whitespawn hunters, a whitespawn berserker with a whitespawn iceskidder mount, and an additional iceskidder. The group uses coordinated tactics to track and ambush intruders into their territory. They attack anything they deem edible (that is, most creatures).

Ecology

Whitespawn hunters prowl the frozen realms far from civilization. They live a nomadic lifestyle, following herds of large, dangerous game such as dire elk, polar bears, and even remorhazes. They build and camp in easily transportable huts, which are hauled by slaves or whitespawn hordelings.

Whitespawn hunters are rapacious meat-eaters and can quickly deplete an area's stocks of game. When times are lean, they subsist on carrion, the flesh of slaves, and the bodies of fallen tribe members. They even devour the bones, leaving virtually nothing behind to indicate their presence other than bits of gore and tufts of fur.

Tribes of whitespawn hunters instinctively know when to move on to find richer game or to avoid the worst winter storms. Their paths often intersect with those of other tribes, resulting in open warfare. The winning tribe seizes slaves and mates from the loser.

Environment: Whitespawn hunters inhabit the most desolate wastes, preferring cold plains and frozen waterways. Occasionally a pack finds its way into a mountainous region where game is more plentiful.

Typical Physical Characteristics: Whitespawn hunters average 5 feet in height and 125 pounds in weight. They have white-scaled skin and wiry builds, and they move with surprising grace. Females are slightly smaller and slimmer, with less pronounced facial features than males.

Alignment: Whitespawn hunters are always chaotic evil. They are single-minded when both hunting and committing terrible acts of depravity, especially against their slaves.

Society

Life among whitespawn hunters is brutal and short, with most activity dedicated to the hunt. Status within a tribe depends strictly on strength and the willingness to defend one's position. Males are typically in charge, though in some tribes powerful females dominate. When a tribe grows too large to feed, the leader splits off, taking as many potential mates and sturdy combatants with him as he can. Massive bloodshed often results from such schisms.

After mating, female whitespawn hunters hide their eggs inside icebergs and other isolated locations where temperatures rarely rise above freezing, abandoning them to their fate. The eggs hatch after six months, and the young must survive on their own—often by devouring their weaker siblings. The survivors are deemed strong enough to join the tribe when it returns to the area, and they are taught additional skills to become better hunters. Coming of age is a brutal ritual: A pair of adolescents must undergo a hunt to bring down a large and dangerous creature. They hunt together, but only one can bring down the prey and earn adult status. The other is either killed by the rest of the tribe or flees into the wilderness in hopes of creating his own tribe—few such individuals survive.

Whitespawn berserker

Illus. by A. Swekel

Although rather unintelligent, whitespawn hunters value slave labor. They sometimes capture sentient beings to use as porters, entertainment, and food. Slaves rarely last more than a few months, succumbing to their masters' casual brutality and the landscape's bitter cold. Dead slaves are unceremoniously stripped and eaten by the tribe. Whitespawn hunters sometimes dominate whitespawn hordelings. The hunters despise their weak and inferior cousins and delight in bossing them around. However, they are just as apt to kill and eat hordelings as they are to command them.

Whitespawn hunters are uninterested in diplomacy; they either slaughter or enslave anyone unable to stop them, or they avoid more powerful creatures. Tribes occasionally trade with other evil beings, notably orcs, but only when desperate. During these liaisons, they are happy to divulge the location of other whitespawn hunter tribes to their trading partners, hoping to send potential attackers against their competition.

Unlike most spawn, whitespawn hunters do not especially venerate Tiamat. However, they do fear and respect her, and tribes leave offerings from every kill to appease her. The most elaborate altars to Tiamat boast the skull of a white dragon, with small items of treasure occasionally laid beneath the meat as additional offerings. Most hunters wear small icons of ivory crudely carved in their deity's image.

Likewise, whitespawn hunters do not revere white dragons; they respect the creatures' power and majesty but also see them as competition for food. When times are tough, whitespawn hunters have no compunction about killing white dragons. Indeed, they consider such action a testament to Tiamat's desire to see the strongest triumph.

WHITESPAWN HUNTER LORE

Characters with ranks in Knowledge (nature) can learn more about whitespawn hunters. When a character makes a successful skill check, the following lore is revealed, including the information from lower DCs. Those who recognize the creatures' ancestry can also use Knowledge (religion) to learn more.

Knowledge (Nature)

DC	Result
14	This creature is a whitespawn hunter, a monstrous humanoid related to white dragons. This result reveals all monstrous humanoid traits.
19	Whitespawn hunters are immune to cold, paralysis, and *sleep,* and they are vulnerable to fire.
24	These vicious carnivores favor stealth and ambush but quickly succumb to mindless chaos when combat begins.

Knowledge (Religion)

DC	Result
14	Whitespawn hunters are some of Tiamat's spawn.
19	Whitespawn hunters honor Tiamat and wear small ivory icons carved in her image.
24	Whitespawn hunters respect white dragons but are not beholden to them—some tribes hunt them, while others live under their thrall.

At other times, a white dragon might rule an entire tribe of hunters—as long as it is powerful enough to maintain command. The moment it shows any weakness, the tribe's strongest hunters (especially berserkers) challenge its rule.

Whitespawn berserkers often become the leaders of tribes. Some leave the business of ruling to others and focus on the sheer thrill of the hunt. A truly powerful berserker assumes the title "wastestalker."

Typical Treasure

Whitespawn hunters have standard treasure for NPCs of their Challenge Rating.

Whitespawn Hunters with Class Levels

Whitespawn hunters' favored class is barbarian. They are cunning and adept stalkers but revel in the chaos of battle.
Level Adjustment: +2.

SAMPLE LAIR: WHITESPAWN HUNTER ENCAMPMENT

This map shows a typical whitespawn hunter encampment within a winding ice floe.

1. Wastestalker Yurt (EL 8)

The inside of the yurt is dark and rank. A pile of smelly furs sits to one side, and the walls are adorned with the skulls of various animals—some not readily identifiable. A rack made of bone bears the weight of frozen hunks of meat.

The leader of the tribe, a 4th-level barbarian, lives in this crude yurt, along with his four noncombatant mates. No one else may enter his yurt.

2. Communal Yurt

This large, open yurt is filthy. Hunks of meat dangle from ropes in the center. Worn, disgusting pelts of yak, mastodon, and other large mammals are scattered across the ground, providing places to sit. Bits of bone litter the floor.

This large yurt is where the tribe gathers for feasts and meetings. The few supplies used by the tribe are stored here, as well as a small stock of meat.

3. Slave Pen (EL 7)

The back and sides of this pen butt up against a sheer wall of ice. The remainder is crafted from blocks of ice, with a gate made of an elaborate array of animal bones. The inside is utterly disgusting, filled with waste, old bones—and the corpse of a young male human.

The tribe currently has ten slaves: seven human commoners, two orc warriors, and an elf commoner. One slave has recently died, but the tribe has not yet consumed his corpse. At least three whitespawn hunters guard the pen at all times when it is occupied.

Ice Floe
(60 ft. high)

Ice Floe
(40 ft. high)

Ice Floe
(50 ft. high)

N

Whitespawn Hunter Lair

One square = 5 feet

4. Family Yurts (EL 6–7)
This yurt appears to be a family dwelling.

Each yurt shelters four to six individuals (half adults and half young). The high ice walls buttress the backs of the yurts and keep the wind out. An 80% chance exists that a whitespawn hunter occupies a yurt. Each yurt has one or two slaves inside at all times.

5. Meat Storage
This chamber has been rudely carved from the ice, providing a place to store meat. It contains the carcasses of two elk, several seals, and two humanoids. The bodies are in various states of dismemberment, and some have been roughly hacked apart.

This larder, carved into the walls of ice, stores the bulk of the tribe's meat. It is guarded at all times by two whitespawn hunters, who immediately kill anyone who dares to steal meat.

6. Shrine to Tiamat
This structure is cobbled together from the bones of several large animals, topped off with an enormous skull that must be a dragon's. Several heaps of meat, most of them frozen, rest among the bones, along with at least one humanoid skull.

The tribe has established a small temporary altar to Tiamat, where offerings are left after a successful hunt. This one includes the skull of a white dragon.

Whitespawn Hunters in Eberron
Whitespawn hunters live almost exclusively in the Frostfell, stalking the tundra on the hunt for game and slaves. During particularly harsh winters, when Risia is coterminous, hunters move farther south along drifting pack ice, sometimes making landfall in the Lhazaar Principalities and the Demon Wastes. During such campaigns, they typically command tribes of whitespawn hordelings to sweep ahead of them, softening up potential enemies and providing intelligence for a successful hunt.

Whitespawn Hunters in Faerûn
Whitespawn hunters live throughout the frozen north of Faerûn, but most are found in Icewind Dale and the High Ice north of Anauroch. They prey on the tribes of humanoid barbarians and on hunters and fishers caught alone on the windswept ice plains. Rumors persist of whitespawn hunter encampments in parts of the Glacier of the White Worm. The creatures avoid the Citadel of the White Worm, though, being too few and too weak to claim it.

"I walk the rimewastes, seeking prey for you, Great Mother. Meat for tribe! Glory for me, O Tiamat!"
—Morning prayer of the whitespawn hunter

WHITESPAWN ICESKIDDER

A long, lizardlike creature slides toward you across the ice, its toothy maw gaping open and short legs pumping in unison to propel its white-scaled body forward. Easily as big as a horse, it doesn't slow its rapid skid even when nearly touching your weapon.

WHITESPAWN ICESKIDDER   CR 6

Always CE Large magical beast (cold, dragonblood)
Init +0; **Senses** darkvision 60 ft., low-light vision; Listen +4, Spot +12
Languages —

AC 17, touch 9, flat-footed 17
   (−1 size, +8 natural)
hp 85 (9 HD); **DR** 10/magic
Immune cold
Fort +10, **Ref** +6, **Will** +5
Weakness vulnerability to fire

Speed 40 ft. (8 squares)
Melee bite +17 (2d6+12)
Space 10 ft.; **Reach** 5 ft.
Base Atk +9; **Grp** +21
Atk Options Improved Overrun, Power Attack, magic strike
Special Actions breath weapon

Abilities Str 27, Dex 10, Con 18, Int 2, Wis 14, Cha 7
SQ ice step, Tiamat's blessing (cold)
Feats Ability Focus (breath weapon), Improved Overrun, Power Attack, Weapon Focus (bite)
Skills Jump +12, Listen +4, Spot +12
Advancement 10–11 HD (Large); 12–18 HD (Huge)

Breath Weapon (Su) 30-ft. cone, once every 1d4 rounds, damage 6d6 cold, Reflex DC 20 half. Creatures that fail the save are frozen in place. Treat them as though struck by a tanglefoot bag (*PH* 128), taking a −2 penalty on attack rolls and a −4 penalty to Dexterity and unable to move unless they succeed on a DC 15 Reflex save. The effect ends after 2d4 rounds. The save DC against the freezing effect increases by 1 for each additional HD.

   In addition, surfaces within the area of a whitespawn iceskidder's breath weapon become covered with ice sheets (*DMG* 91).

Ice Step (Ex) Whitespawn iceskidders ignore all movement penalties associated with snow or ice on the ground. They always succeed on Balance checks against effects caused by ice or by spells or special abilities with the cold descriptor.

Tiamat's Blessing (Cold) (Su) All spawn of Tiamat within 5 feet of or riding on a whitespawn iceskidder gain immunity to cold.

Whitespawn iceskidders serve Tiamat's armies as mounts in cold environments. When left to themselves, they prowl the tundra in search of prey.

Strategies and Tactics

Whitespawn iceskidders are typically solitary, but mated pairs hunt together. An iceskidder attacks the weakest-looking creature in a group, hoping for a quick kill. It begins combat by loosing its freezing breath to damage prey and hold it in place. If a stronger-looking creature gets in the way, the iceskidder attempts to overrun that foe (+16 on the

Strength check). Once in melee, the iceskidder bites furiously until its target falls. It then slows down any remaining enemies with its breath weapon and makes its escape with the meal.

Sample Encounters

Whitespawn iceskidders are most likely to be encountered alone or in pairs. Other creatures (usually spawn of Tiamat) sometimes tame iceskidders for use as mounts or guard beasts.

   Pair (EL 8): A trail of shallowly buried treasure leads through the snow to an ice cave in the side of a glacier, where a mated pair of whitespawn iceskidders feed on their latest kill. Runoff from the glacier roars through the cave in a rushing stream, covering the sounds of intruders (Listen check DCs increase by 5).

   Whitespawn War Party (EL 6–9): Groups of whitespawn hordelings or hunters sometimes patrol on iceskidder mounts.

   EL 7: A war party of six whitespawn hordelings attacks, led by a 3rd-level hordeling barbarian and accompanied by a whitespawn iceskidder. The barbarian and another hordeling ride into battle on the iceskidder's back, though they don't really control its actions. When the iceskidder overruns a foe, the hordelings jump off to attack the prone creature.

   Family (EL 9–10): Adult iceskidders in a family group teach their young to hunt.

WHITESPAWN ICESKIDDER LORE

Characters with ranks in Knowledge (arcana) can learn more about whitespawn iceskidders. When a character makes a successful skill check, the following lore is revealed, including the information from lower DCs. Those who recognize the creatures' ancestry can also use Knowledge (religion) to learn more.

Knowledge (Arcana)

DC	Result
16	This creature is a whitespawn iceskidder, a predatory magical beast related to white dragons. This result reveals all magical beast traits.
21	Whitespawn iceskidders are immune to cold and vulnerable to fire. They breath a cone of cold that freezes prey in a skin of ice.
26	Whitespawn iceskidders live much like bears, but they "hibernate" in the warm season.
31	Although of only animal intelligence, whitespawn iceskidders are innately evil creatures. They sometimes return after a successful attack simply to terrorize prey.

Knowledge (Religion)

DC	Result
16	Whitespawn iceskidders are some of Tiamat's spawn.
21	Whitespawn iceskidders can sometimes be found in the company of worshipers of Tiamat, serving as mounts and guardians.

EL 9: Three whitespawn iceskidders are on the prowl for a meal: a mother and father with their adolescent child. The young iceskidder is eager for food and attacks the nearest creature immediately, forcing its parents to catch their child in their breath weapons as they follow typical iceskidder tactics. The parents won't abandon the child, so they fight until it regains complete mobility.

Ecology

Whitespawn iceskidders live much like bears, except that they estivate rather than hibernate, sleeping through the warm season. They spend most of their lives as solitary hunters but gather once a year to mate. Unlike bears, male iceskidders remain with their mates, hunting with the mother until the young reach adolescence. Just before sending off the young iceskidders, the parents lead them on a teaching hunt.

Despite their bestial natures, whitespawn iceskidders are still spawn of Tiamat, and this heritage comes to the fore in their dealings with other creatures. They relish terrorizing prey, and even after carrying off a victim from a group, a iceskidder often returns to attack again. Having enough food already, the iceskidder usually doesn't eat victims of the second attack—it kills for sheer pleasure.

Only chromatic dragons and spawn of Tiamat have any chance of taming the beasts. White dragons use iceskidders as "watchdogs," allowing them to live within their lairs. Whitespawn hordelings often brave iceskidder lairs to steal their eggs and raise the hatchlings as mounts. The two creatures are so often seen together that sages speculate they were born of the same white dragon parent.

Environment: Whitespawn iceskidders live primarily in cold marshes and plains, but any place with frozen water makes a fine home. They dwell in ice caves or dig dens in mounds of packed snow, where they eat, mate, lay eggs, and rear young.

Typical Physical Characteristics: An adult whitespawn iceskidder measures roughly 11 feet from the end of the nose to the tip of the tail. Its long, serpentine body weighs about 2,000 pounds.

Males and females look much alike. Only whitespawn iceskidders can tell the difference without close examination. Older individuals have broader scales and longer head ridges than younger members of the race. Few iceskidders live longer than about ten years.

Alignment: Cruel and animalistic, whitespawn iceskidders are always chaotic evil.

Whitespawn iceskidder

Typical Treasure

Whitespawn iceskidders carry no treasure, but sometimes they eat valuable items worn or carried by their prey. Typically, only gems and precious metals survive in an iceskidder's gullet, irritating its stomach so that it vomits them up. A 5% chance exists that an iceskidder encountered outside its lair has consumed some art objects, gems, or coins. An iceskidder lair contains standard treasure for the Encounter Level (coins, gems, and metal items only), buried amid waste in out-of-the-way spots within the cave.

Whitespawn Iceskidders in Eberron

Whitespawn iceskidders live in the Frostfell and sometimes drift to Khorvaire or northerly islands of the Lhazaar Principalities by clinging to icebergs that float across the Bitter Sea. Once on land, the creatures seek out cold lands and might inhabit unusual terrain, such as high mountain passes. One that arrives on the mainland might travel very far south, especially during the bitterly cold winters that come every five years when Risia is coterminous. These iceskidders often get stranded in marshes when the ice retreats.

Whitespawn Iceskidders in Faerûn

Whitespawn iceskidders live and hunt in many cold lands, but their populations are particularly large in the Icewind Dale and in northern Vaasa, Damara, and Narfell. Winter migrations push them farther south into Impiltur, the Great Dale, and Thesk in the east and the northern Sword Coast in the west.

Despite the beasts' unsuitability for domestication, the Red Wizards of Thay are very interested in iceskidders. They offer 5,000 gp for the capture of one and as much as 7,000 gp for an iceskidder egg.

TOMB SPIDER

Tomb spiders are arachnoid creatures suffused with negative energy. Their poison reverses healing spells and effects that target the poisoned creature.

Tomb spiders plant their eggs in the corpses of humanoids. A host animates as a web mummy, a zombielike mockery of life. As the eggs hatch, hundreds of tiny tomb spiders swarm inside the corpse. If released, they form a broodswarm that flows over opponents. Thus, the three basic life cycle stages of a tomb spider are the web mummy, broodswarm, and adult.

TOMB SPIDER

Chitin flakes off a mottled gray, spindly spider the size of a horse.

TOMB SPIDER   CR 6

Always NE Large magical beast
Init +5; **Senses** darkvision 60 ft., low-light vision,
    tremorsense 60 ft.; Listen +11, Spot +11
Languages —

AC 19, touch 14, flat-footed 14
    (−1 size, +5 Dex, +5 natural)
hp 76 (8 HD); **DR** 5/good
Fort +10, **Ref** +11, **Will** +7

Speed 30 ft. (6 squares), climb 20 ft.
Melee bite +12 (2d6+7 plus poison)
Ranged web +12 ranged touch (entangle)
Space 10 ft; **Reach** 5 ft.
Base Atk +8; **Grp** +17
Atk Options poison (DC 18,1d4 hp/1d4 hp)

Abilities Str 21, Dex 20, Con 19, Int 3, Wis 16, Cha 18
SQ tomb-tainted soul
Feats Alertness, Improved Natural Attack (bite), Iron Will
Skills Climb +13, Hide +5*, Jump +15, Listen +11, Move
    Silently +8*, Spot +11
    *Tomb spiders gain an additional +8 racial bonus on
    Hide and Move Silently checks when in their webs.
Advancement 9–12 HD (Large); 13–24 HD (Huge)

Poison (Ex) Creatures affected by tomb spider poison are
    healed by negative energy and harmed by positive energy
    as if they were undead. This effect lasts for 1 minute after
    a failed save.
Web (Ex) A tomb spider can throw a web up to three times
    per day. This is similar to an attack with a net but has a
    maximum range of 60 feet, with a range increment of
    10 feet, and is effective against targets of up to Medium
    size. The web anchors the target in place, allowing no
    movement.
        An entangled creature can escape with a DC 19
    Escape Artist check or burst the web with a DC 19
    Strength check. The check DCs are Strength-based.
    The web has 12 hit points, hardness 0, and takes double
    damage from fire.
        A tomb spider can create sheets of sticky webbing
    up to 20 feet square. It usually positions these sheets to
    snare flying creatures but can also try to trap prey on the
    ground. Approaching creatures must succeed on a DC 20
    Spot check to notice a web; otherwise they stumble into
    it and become trapped as though by a successful web
    attack. Each 5-foot section of webbing has 12 hit points
    and damage reduction 5/—.
        A tomb spider can move across its own sheet web at
    its climb speed and can determine the exact location of
    any creature touching the web.

Tomb-Tainted Soul (Ex) A tomb spider is healed by negative
    energy and harmed by positive energy as if it were an
    undead creature.
Skills Tomb spiders have a +4 racial bonus on Hide, Listen,
    and Spot checks, a +8 racial bonus on Climb checks, and
    a +10 racial bonus on Jump checks. A tomb spider can
    always choose to take 10 on Climb checks, even if rushed
    or threatened.

Tomb spiders have a strong connection to negative energy and are significantly more dangerous than ordinary monstrous vermin.

TOMB SPIDER BROODSWARM

A swarm of fist-sized, bright red spiders moves closer.

TOMB SPIDER BROODSWARM   CR 2

Always NE Tiny magical beast (swarm)
Init +5; **Senses** darkvision 60 ft., low-light vision,
    tremorsense 60 ft.; Listen +11, Spot +11
Languages —

AC 17, touch 17, flat-footed 12
    (+2 size, +5 Dex)
hp 22 (3 HD)
Resist half damage from piercing and slashing weapons
Immune swarm immunities
Fort +5, **Ref** +8, **Will** +6
Weakness swarm vulnerabilities

Speed 20 ft. (4 squares), climb 20 ft.
Melee swarm (1d6 plus poison)
Space 10 ft.; **Reach** 0 ft.
Base Atk +3; **Grp** —
Atk Options distraction, poison (DC 13, 1d4 hp/1d4 hp)

Abilities Str 7, Dex 20, Con 15, Int 1, Wis 16, Cha 2
SQ swarm traits, tomb-tainted soul, web walk
Feats Alertness, Iron Will
Skills Climb +13, Hide +11*, Jump +2, Listen +9, Move
    Silently +7*, Spot +9
    *Broodswarms gain an additional +8 racial bonus on
    Hide and Move Silently checks when moving in tomb
    spider webs.
Advancement —

Distraction (Ex) Fortitude DC 13, nauseated 1 round.
    The save DC is Constitution-based.
Poison (Ex) As tomb spider.
Tomb-Tainted Soul (Ex) As tomb spider.
Web Walk (Ex) A tomb spider broodswarm can move across
    tomb spider sheet webs at its climb speed and can
    determine the exact location of any creature touching
    the web.
Skills Tomb spider broodswarms have a +4 racial bonus
    on Hide, Listen, and Spot checks, a +8 racial bonus on
    Climb checks, and a +10 racial bonus on Jump checks.
    A broodswarm can always choose to take 10 on Climb
    checks, even if rushed or threatened. A broodswarm uses
    its Dexterity modifier instead of its Strength modifier for
    Climb checks.

Broodswarms are dangerous on their own, but even more so when a tomb spider parent is present. The swarm moves to overwhelm any creature trapped by the tomb spider's webs.

WEB MUMMY

A human-shaped creature completely wrapped in webs shambles toward you, its skin rippling slightly as if many small creatures squirm inside.

WEB MUMMY, HUMAN COMMONER — CR 4

Always NE Medium undead
Init +1; **Senses** darkvision 60 ft., tremorsense 60 ft.;
    Listen +1, Spot +1
Languages —

AC 20, touch 11, flat-footed 19
    (+1 Dex, +9 natural)
hp 29 (4 HD); **DR** 3/—
Immune webs; undead immunities
Fort +3, **Ref** +2, **Will** +5
Weakness vulnerability to fire

Speed 20 ft. (4 squares), climb 20 ft.
Melee slam +9 (1d6+10)
Space 5 ft; **Reach** 5 ft.
Base Atk +2; **Grp** +9
Atk Options enraged

Abilities Str 25, Dex 13, Con —, Int —, Wis 12, Cha 7
SQ adhesive, broodswarm host, undead traits
Feats Great Fortitude[B], Toughness[B]
Skills Climb +15, Listen +1, Spot +1
Advancement —

Immunity to Webs (Ex) A web mummy's movement is not affected by webs, including those created by the *web* spell.

Enraged (Ex) If a web mummy's creator tomb spider is destroyed, the mummy becomes enraged, gaining a +2 bonus on attack rolls and damage rolls for the next 10 minutes.

Adhesive (Ex) A web mummy is extremely sticky. A weapon that strikes it is stuck fast unless the wielder succeeds on a DC 19 Reflex save. Creatures using natural weapons are automatically grappled if they fail the save. Pulling a weapon or limb loose from a web mummy requires a DC 19 Strength check. The save and check DCs are Strength-based.

Broodswarm Host (Ex) Tomb spiders use web mummies as hosts for their young. When a Small or larger web mummy is destroyed, a broodswarm is released from the corpse and can act on the next round.

Skills A web mummy has a +8 racial bonus on Climb checks and can always choose to take 10 on Climb checks, even if rushed or threatened.

Web mummies are hosts for tomb spider young. They are found anywhere tomb spiders live and breed.

This example uses a 1st-level human commoner as the base creature. It had the following ability scores before template adjustments and Hit Dice ability score increases: Str 13, Dex 11, Con 12, Int 8, Wis 10, and Cha 9.

Creating a Web Mummy

"Web mummy" is an acquired template that can be added to any corporeal giant, humanoid, or monstrous humanoid (referred to hereafter as the base creature).

Size and Type: The creature's type changes to undead. The creature does not gain the augmented subtype but retains other subtypes except alignment and humanoid.

Hit Dice: Increase all current and future Hit Dice to d12s. The base creature's Hit Dice increase by 3.

Challenge Rating: Depends upon original Hit Dice, as follows:

TOMB SPIDER

Illus. by Daarken

Tomb spider, broodswarm, and web mummy

Hit Dice	Challenge Rating
1–2	4
3–4	5
5–7	6
8–9	7
10–11	8
12–14	9
15–17	10
18–20	11

Alignment: Always neutral evil.

Armor Class: A web mummy's natural armor bonus is +9 or the base creature's natural armor bonus, whichever is higher.

Speed: A web mummy's land speed decreases by 10 feet (to a minimum of 10 feet). The speeds for other movement modes are unchanged. A web mummy also gains a climb speed of 20 feet, if it did not already have one.

Attack: A web mummy retains all the attacks of the base creature and also gains a slam attack if it didn't already have one. If the base creature can use weapons, the web mummy retains this ability. A web mummy with natural weapons retains those natural weapons. A web mummy fighting without weapons uses either its slam attack or its primary natural weapon (if it has any). A web mummy armed with a weapon uses its slam or the weapon, as it desires.

Damage: A web mummy has a slam attack. If the base creature does not have this attack form, use the appropriate damage value from the table below according to the creature's size.

Size	Damage
Fine	1
Diminutive	1d2
Tiny	1d3
Small	1d4
Medium	1d6
Large	1d8
Huge	2d6
Gargantuan	3d6
Colossal	4d6

Attack Options: A web mummy loses all the attack options of the base creature and gains the attack option described below.

Enraged (Ex): If a web mummy's creator tomb spider is destroyed, the mummy becomes enraged, gaining a +2 bonus on attack rolls and damage rolls for the next 10 minutes.

Abilities: A web mummy's ability scores are modified as follows: Str +12, Dex +2, Wis +2, Cha –2. As a mindless undead creature, a web mummy has no Constitution or Intelligence scores.

Special Qualities: A web mummy loses all the special qualities of the base creature. It gains tremorsense out to 60 feet and the special qualities described below.

Damage Reduction (Ex): A web mummy's undead body is tough and encased in webbing, giving it damage reduction 3/—.

Immunity to Webs (Ex): A web mummy's movement is not affected by webs, including those created by the *web* spell.

Vulnerability to Fire (Ex): A web mummy takes half again as much (+50%) points of damage as normal from fire attacks.

Adhesive (Ex): A web mummy is extremely sticky. A weapon that strikes a web mummy is stuck fast unless the wielder succeeds on a Reflex save (DC 10 + 1/2 the web mummy's HD + the web mummy's Strength modifier). Creatures using natural weapons are automatically grappled if they fail the save. Pulling a weapon or limb loose from a web mummy requires a Strength check with a DC equal to that of the Reflex save.

Broodswarm Host (Ex): When a Small or larger web mummy is destroyed, a tomb spider broodswarm is released from the corpse and can act on the next round.

Feats: As a mindless creature, a web mummy loses all the feats of the base creature, but it gains Great Fortitude and Toughness as bonus feats.

Skills: A web mummy loses all the skills of the base creature. Its climb speed grants it a +8 racial bonus on Climb checks. A web mummy can always choose to take 10 on Climb checks, even if rushed or threatened.

Advancement: —.

Level Adjustment: —.

STRATEGIES AND TACTICS

Tomb spiders, broodswarms, and web mummies fight straightforwardly when encountered alone. When in a mixed group, a tomb spider ignores attacks against itself if its off-spring (broodswarms or web mummies) are threatened. It uses its webs against the most dangerous-looking foes, and any broodswarms move over the trapped creature.

SAMPLE ENCOUNTERS

Tomb spiders, broodswarms, and web mummies can be encountered individually, but the most potent threats involve combinations of multiple monsters.

Individual (EL 6): A tomb spider has recently moved to richer hunting grounds near some isolated farms. Thus far, only a few sheep and a dog have disappeared. Now that the spider is ready to lay eggs, it aggressively seeks a humanoid host.

Nest (EL 8): The trail from a tomb spider's recent kill leads back into its web-strewn lair. Two web mummies lurch around the chamber, while a broodswarm scurries about the webs. The tomb spider hides until the PCs attack, then jumps them from behind.

ECOLOGY

Tomb spiders are carnivorous and eat prey ranging from rabbits to horses. However, their life cycle requires them to live near humanoids, monstrous humanoids, or giants in order to reproduce.

All adult tomb spiders are capable of producing eggs. When ready to reproduce, a tomb spider finds a suitable corpse (or kills such a creature), implants its eggs, and wraps the corpse in webbing. The host corpse animates as a web mummy and protects its creator. The eggs swiftly hatch, and the baby spiders begin to feed on the decaying internal organs of the host. Under ideal conditions, the individual spiderlings then proceed to eat each other until a single fully-formed adult emerges some weeks later. However, a web mummy is often destroyed before the entire maturation process is complete, releasing a broodswarm of immature spiders. Rarely, an adult tomb spider can arise from an immature broodswarm, but without the protective environment of the web mummy, most such young quickly die.

Environment: Tomb spiders prefer to live in temperate forests at the fringes of civilization. They roam underground, looking for burial crypts or similar locations that have ready access to surface settlements. Once they find a suitable location, they begin infesting any corpses that they find. When they have depleted the ready supply of bodies, they begin hunting surface lands.

Typical Physical Characteristics: A Large tomb spider is a dead-gray, spindly creature approximately 10 feet in diameter and weighing 500 pounds. Individuals can be as large as 20 feet across and weigh up to 2,000 pounds.

Newly hatched spiderlings of a broodswarm are bright red in color, darkening to gray within the first few weeks of life.

A web mummy begins with the proportions and weight of the original host. As the broodswarm inside feeds on the host's organs, the mummy's weight decreases and that of the swarm increases.

Alignment: Tomb spiders are corrupted by negative energy and are always neutral evil.

An ancient crypt becomes a nest for tomb spiders

SOCIETY

While tomb spiders have basic intelligence, they have no true society, nor do they speak any language. Their sole concerns are survival and reproduction. For the most part, they are solitary, with their own hunting territories, but they share space if prey is plentiful.

Drow and driders honor all spiderkind and encourage tomb spiders to nest near the borders of their territories, whether between drider and drow settlements or beside the lands of other creatures. Prisoners and corpses become treats for the tomb spiders. The spiders look forward to these meals and don't attack their feeders unless very hungry or provoked.

TYPICAL TREASURE

Tomb spiders do not collect or hoard treasure, but their lairs contain standard treasure for their Encounter Level. This treasure represents the possessions of creatures killed for food or implantation.

TOMB SPIDERS IN EBERRON

Tomb spiders inhabit the wilds of Xen'drik. Small numbers of them have also migrated to Khorvaire in recent years in the holds of ships. Most dwell in forest areas near port towns, but individual creatures or small nests have been found in Sharn, Wyvernskull, and even Vralkek. These tomb spiders have adapted to urban environments, living in cellars and sewer systems.

TOMB SPIDERS IN FAERÛN

Although they prefer temperate forests, tomb spiders also find the Underdark to be an optimal environment. Drow like the creatures and frequently encourage their presence. The largest recorded tomb spider lives as a "pet" of House Barrison in Menzoberranzan. Visitors come to stare in awe at this massive creature, which measures 30 feet in diameter.

TOMB SPIDER LORE

Characters with ranks in Knowledge (arcana) and Knowledge (religion) can learn more about tomb spiders, broodswarms, or web mummies. When a character makes a successful skill check, the following lore is revealed, including the information from lower DCs.

Knowledge (Arcana)

DC	Result
16	Tomb spiders are magical beasts with a special connection to negative energy. This result reveals all magical beast traits.
21	Creatures affected by their poison are harmed by magical healing for a short time thereafter.

Knowledge (Religion)

DC	Result
14	Web mummies are undead creatures animated by a spider with a connection to negative energy. This result reveals all undead traits.
19	A tomb spider lays its eggs in a humanoid, monstrous humanoid, or giant's body, animating the corpse as a web mummy. The resulting creature is mindless but very tough. If the web mummy is destroyed, a tomb spider broodswarm bursts from the body.
24	Web mummies are vulnerable to fire.

VARAG

This humanoid stands close to 7 feet tall when fighting but moves and runs on all fours. It has a hunched posture, double-jointed hind legs, and thick, sinewy skin. The creature bears a slight resemblance to a hairy and ferocious hobgoblin, but it has a more primitive countenance and two curving horns that sweep away from its skull. It wields a cleaverlike scimitar.

VARAG	**CR 1**

Usually CE Medium humanoid (goblinoid)
Init +6; **Senses** darkvision 60 ft., scent; Listen +0, Spot +0
Languages Goblin

AC 18, touch 12, flat-footed 16
   (+2 Dex, +3 armor, +3 natural)
hp 16 (3 HD)
Fort +2, **Ref** +5, **Will** +1

Speed 60 ft. (12 squares); Run, Spring Attack
Melee mwk scimitar +6 (1d6+2/18–20)
Space 5 ft.; **Reach** 5 ft.
Base Atk +2; **Grp** +4
Combat Gear *potion of cure moderate wounds*

Abilities Str 15, Dex 15, Con 13, Int 6, Wis 10, Cha 10
Feats Improved Initiative, Run^B, Spring Attack^B, Weapon Focus (scimitar)
Skills Jump +17, Listen +0, Move Silently +13*, Spot +0, Survival +0 (+4 when tracking by scent)
   *A varag can always choose to take 10 on a Move Silently check, even if rushed or threatened.
Advancement by character class; **Favored Class** scout (*Complete Adventurer* 10); see text
Possessions combat gear plus masterwork studded leather, masterwork scimitar

Skills Varags have a +8 racial bonus on Move Silently checks and a +4 racial bonus on Survival checks when tracking by scent.

Varags, also known as blood chasers, are goblinoids that are faster, stronger, and more primitive than their kin. Less intelligent than other goblinoids, varags have predatory cunning.

VARAG LORE

Characters with ranks in Knowledge (nature) can learn more about varags. When a character makes a successful skill check, the following lore is revealed, including the information from lower DCs. Knowledge (local) can also be used, but all check DCs increase by 5.

Knowledge (Nature)

DC	Result
11	Varags are a feral goblinoid race. This result reveals all humanoid traits.
16	Varags pursue their quarry with unfettered abandon. Fast and agile, a varag can sweep past an opponent, strike a deadly blow, and scramble away before the target can react.
21	Varags are silent killers. Even when running at full speed, they are surprisingly quiet.
26	Varags are chaotic and difficult to control. They are easiest to defeat when forced to stand and fight.

They are vicious creatures, capable of taking opponents by surprise or by direct confrontation. Varags work as mercenary scouts and raiders for hobgoblin warbands. These creatures are proficient with all martial weapons.

VARAG PACK LEADER

This feral goblinoid being wears a necklace of human teeth. Its mouth and face are stained with dried blood, and it moves more like a beast that learned to carry a weapon than a true humanoid.

VARAG PACK LEADER	**CR 5**

Male varag scout* 4
   *Class described in *Complete Adventurer*
LE Medium humanoid (goblinoid)
Init +10; **Senses** darkvision 60 ft., scent; Listen +8, Spot +8
Languages Goblin

AC 22, touch 15, flat-footed 22; uncanny dodge
   (+5 Dex, +4 armor, +3 natural)
hp 45 (7 HD)
Fort +6, **Ref** +13, **Will** +5

Speed 70 ft. (14 squares); Run, Spring Attack
Melee *+1 scimitar* +10 (1d6+4/18–20)
Ranged mwk composite shortbow +11 (1d6+3/×3)
Space 5 ft.; **Reach** 5 ft.
Base Atk +5; **Grp** +8
Atk Options skirmish (+1d6, +1 AC)
Combat Gear *potion of bull's strength, potion of cure moderate wounds*

Abilities Str 17, Dex 20, Con 14, Int 10, Wis 10, Cha 8
SQ battle fortitude +1, trackless step, trapfinding
Feats Improved Initiative, Iron Will, Run^B, Spring Attack^B, Track^B, Weapon Focus (scimitar)
Skills Hide +13, Jump +21, Listen +8, Move Silently +21*, Spot +8, Survival +10 (+14 when tracking by scent)
   *A varag can always choose to take 10 on a Move Silently check, even if rushed or threatened.
Possessions combat gear plus *+1 studded leather armor, +1 scimitar,* masterwork composite shortbow (+3 Str bonus) with 20 arrows, *cloak of resistance +1*

Skirmish (Ex) +1d6 bonus on damage rolls and +1 to AC in any round in which the varag pack leader moves at least 10 feet. *Complete Adventurer* 12.
Battle Fortitude (Ex) Bonus on initiative checks and Fortitude saves while wearing light or no armor and carrying a light load. Included above. *Complete Adventurer* 12.
Skills Varags have a +8 racial bonus on Move Silently checks and a +4 racial bonus on Survival checks when tracking by scent.

Varags form hunting packs much as wolves do. Occasionally a talented leader takes levels in scout to direct the hunt more effectively.

The varag pack leader presented here had the following ability scores before racial adjustments and Hit Dice ability score increases: Str 13, Dex 15, Con 12, Int 14, Wis 10, Cha 8.

STRATEGIES AND TACTICS

Varags are capable of great stealth and seek to catch their opponents unaware whenever possible. They initiate combat by pouncing from afar, using their superior speed to great advantage.

Varags rely more on their sense of smell to track enemies than on sight or hearing. Feral and chaotic, they hate fighting in close formation or under the tight command of an officer. They are naturally attracted to fleeing opponents and eagerly run them down, even at great personal risk. Varags tend to scatter across the battlefield, picking off routing warriors and entering the fray only when they sense the prospect of fresh meat and loot.

Varags rely on Spring Attack to wear down opponents. They surround enemies and take turns attacking. Half the pack stands back to block escape, while the rest dart in and out of melee. Varags prefer to attack lightly armored, weaker creatures rather than tough, protected enemies.

Varags avoid static lines of battle. If faced with well-organized, numerous opponents, they employ hit-and-run tactics. By the time their enemies ready a counterattack, the varags are long gone.

Varag

"In the blink of an eye, they were upon us. By the time I readied my axe, Bertold, Dargr, and Xelden were down and the things were gone."
—Keltra, half-orc lieutenant
of the Iron Spire Brigade

SAMPLE ENCOUNTERS

Varags are natural runners that doggedly pursue retreating foes regardless of how dangerous the hunt becomes, determined to catch their quarry or die trying.

Individual (EL 1): A single varag is not an uncommon encounter when withdrawing from a hobgoblin battlefield.

EL 1: Durel is so determined to run down his quarry that he became separated by several miles from his hobgoblin allies.

Hunting Pack (EL 2–4): Hunting packs comprising two to four varags efficiently root out fleeing opponents. Each varag designates a target, then they all strike simultaneously.

EL 3: Belik, Garlon, and Thokas make sport of terrified enemies running for their lives, keeping tallies of their kills.

Driving Brigade (EL 5–9): A driving brigade consists of five to eight varags and a pack leader.

EL 7: Kilard, a 4th-level varag scout, takes his brigade of six varags deep into enemy territory to plow through and dishearten armies as they approach or leave hobgoblin battles.

ECOLOGY

In the wild, varags alternate between long periods of rest and brief, bloody spurts of violence. A pack might slowly cross a stretch of uninhabited wasteland until it nears a human settlement, then attack with murderous glee. Varags on the move are easy to track by the burning settlements, ravaged farms, and gnawed corpses they leave in their wake.

Varags require three times the normal intake of food that other Medium creatures do, in order to maintain their great speed and stamina. Those that do not meet this nutritional requirement are less effective hunters. A varag that eats only twice the normal amount of a Medium creature must spend most of its time sleeping to conserve energy. One whose daily intake is only that of a Medium creature has its speed reduced to 30 feet until it can consume adequate food.

Hobgoblins like to use these feral goblinoids to supplement their armies, but because of varags' high food demands, only the wealthy can support them. If not properly cared for, the weakened varags die off in battle or ally themselves with more powerful hobgoblin bands that can feed them regularly.

Varags understand Goblin but are barely able to speak. Their primitive physiology makes forming complex words difficult, while their low intellects leave them unable to learn much. Many varags lack language altogether, communicating among themselves with hand gestures, howls, and shrieks.

Varag females gestate for five to six months before giving birth to two or three children. A varag grows up quickly and is considered an adult by the age of eight. Mothers care for their children for half of this time. At one year of age, a young varag already consumes the same daily amount of food as an adult hobgoblin. Allowing male and female varags to freely interact can be dangerous. Left unchecked,

Illus. by S. Prescott

they continually mate until their birth rates severely tax local resources.

Environment: Varags inhabit warm hills but can survive in colder regions with no difficulty. They also sleep comfortably in underground burrows, though they are not naturally equipped to dig out such dens.

Typical Physical Characteristics: Varags stand approximately 7 feet tall when fighting and weigh 320 pounds on average. Varags move and run on all fours, in which posture they are 3 to 4 feet high at the shoulder. Females are smaller than males, but no less fleet of foot. Varag body language mimics the behavior of wolves.

Alignment: Varags encountered by PCs are usually chaotic evil. They are wild creatures that would easily devolve into a near-animal state were it not for the civilizing effect of the hobgoblins who employ them.

SOCIETY

Varags' behavior is distinctly canine, the result of special breeding. They are the magical product of commingling hobgoblins and dire wolves. The resulting race has bred true ever since.

Hobgoblins employ varags as mercenaries. In exchange for high-quality weapons, armor, and other treasures, the varags serve as scouts and marauders. Varags' chaotic nature makes them difficult to control, so hobgoblin warlords simply allow them to run rampant. A varag pack that accepts payment to overrun a kingdom loots farms, burns settlements to the ground, and kills all in its path.

Varags are highly valued members of any hobgoblin warband. They offer strong backup during battlefield engagements and ruthlessly pursue retreating enemies. Varags can also follow simple orders, such as the ferrying of healing potions to wounded soldiers. They naturally look for strong role models to guide them and offer encouragement.

Hobgoblins are exceedingly fond of varags. Every member of a warband knows that a varag could easily flatten him in combat without breaking a sweat, and none take for granted the dim-witted creatures' dependence. Varags receive generous praise for even the smallest accomplishments and always eat well. The creatures in turn have developed an instinctive affection for all hobgoblins, which they openly and unabashedly express. Varags protect hobgoblins at all costs. Whenever one witnesses a hobgoblin being attacked or in need of help, it immediately rushes to aid without the slightest concern for its safety.

Varags' intense devotion wanes when food becomes scarce. The more they are forced to provide sustenance for themselves, the more restless they become, seeking out other hobgoblins who can feed them. If they become desperate enough, varags might even serve goblins and orcs. To control the creatures' population growth and avoid overtaxing food resources, one central and well-protected warband keeps a stable of only female varags. Breeding occurs only in controlled meetings when more varags are desired.

TYPICAL TREASURE

Varags have standard treasure for NPCs of their Challenge Rating, about 600 gp. Their fighting style precludes the use of shields; reroll any such result.

VARAGS WITH CLASS LEVELS

Varags' favored class is scout, whose abilities complement their quickness and hunting talents. Varag clerics worship Maglubiyet. His domains are Chaos, Destruction, Evil, and Trickery. His favored weapon is the battleaxe.

Level Adjustment: +2.

FOR PLAYER CHARACTERS: THE VARAG RACIAL CLASS

If your DM allows it, you can play a varag character. While these creatures are vile and evil in most settings, they can be viable characters. This is especially true in the EBERRON campaign setting, where alignment is less restrictive, and monstrous creatures often share settlements with normal player races.

Normally, you can't begin with a 1st-level varag character because of the race's level adjustment. With your DM's permission, however, you can use the varag racial class presented here to begin play, though you don't gain the full complement of abilities granted by the race until you are more experienced. In essence, you are applying the varag's level adjustment to your character over time, increasing effective character level (ECL) gradually rather than all at once. Effective character level equals the varag's racial level on the Varag Racial Class table that follows.

THE VARAG RACIAL CLASS

Racial Level	Class Level	Special
1st	0	Racial Hit Die (1d8), varag base traits, natural armor +1, feat
2nd	0	Racial Hit Die (2d8), +2 Dex, scent 10 ft., Run
3rd	0	+2 Con, natural armor +2, scent 20 ft., Move Silently (+8)
4th	0	Racial Hit Die (3d8), +2 Dex, scent 30 ft., feat
5th	0	+2 Str, natural armor +3, Spring Attack, Move Silently (take 10)
6th	1st	Ability score increase
7th	2nd	—
8th	3rd	Feat
9th	4th	—
10th	5th	Ability score increase
11th	6th	Feat
12th	7th	—
13th	8th	—
14th	9th	Ability score increase, feat
15th	10th	—
16th	11th	—
17th	12th	Feat
18th	13th	Ability score increase
19th	14th	—
20th	15th	Feat

The varag racial class must be taken at character creation. It cannot be gained later during a character's career if it is not initially chosen.

Class Features

The following features are gained by characters who take varag racial levels that are integrated with a standard class.

Class Level: The Class Level column of the varag racial class table indicates whether a varag gains a standard class level at any given racial level. Some racial levels provide a standard class level, while others provide a varag-specific ability. Class levels grant all the benefits normally associated with a level increase, including another Hit Die and increasing base attack bonus, base saves, and ability scores, along with other class features.

Racial Hit Die: 1st- through 5th-level varags do not possess class levels. Instead, they gain racial Hit Dice and abilities.

At 1st level, the varag's first racial Hit Die grants 8 hit points and +0 base attack bonus, and base saves of Fortitude +0, Reflex +2, and Will +0. A 1st-level varag gains a number of skill points equal to (2 + Int modifier [minimum 1]) × 4. Its racial class skills are Jump, Move Silently, and Survival.

At 2nd level, a varag gains an additional 1d8 hit points and +1 base attack bonus, and base saves of Fortitude +0, Reflex +3, and Will +0. A 2nd-level varag gains a number of additional skill points equal to 2 + Int modifier (minimum 1).

At 4th level, a varag gains an additional 1d8 hit points and +0 base attack bonus, and base saves of Fortitude +1, Reflex +3, and Will +1. A 4th-level varag gains a number of additional skill points equal to 2 + Int modifier (minimum 1).

Varag Base Traits: Varags have the following base racial traits.

— +2 Strength, –4 Intelligence.

— Medium size: Varags have no special bonuses or penalties due to their size.

— Humanoid (goblinoid): A varag is a humanoid that has the goblinoid subtype.

— Varag base land speed is 40 feet.

— Darkvision out to 60 feet.

— +4 racial bonus on Move Silently checks and a +4 racial bonus on Survival checks when tracking by scent.

— Automatic Languages: Goblin. Bonus Languages: Common, Draconic, Dwarven, Infernal, Giant, Orc.

— Favored Class: Scout (*Complete Adventurer* 10).

Natural Armor (Ex): A varag's skin is tough, and it toughens further as the varag does—at 1st level, a varag has a +1 natural armor bonus. At 3rd level, a varag's natural armor bonus increases to +2. The varag's natural armor bonus increases to +3 at 5th level.

Feat: Like every other character, a varag character gains one feat at 1st level and another at every Hit Dice total divisible by 3. These feats are in addition to any bonus feats granted as class features or any other bonus feats.

Ability Score Increases: At 2nd level, a varag character's Dexterity score increases by 2. At 3rd level, Constitution increases by 2. At 4th level, Dexterity increases again by 2, and at 5th level, Strength increases by 2.

Upon attaining any Hit Die total divisible by 4, a varag character increases one ability score by 1 point, as any character does. The player chooses which ability score to improve in this case. The ability improvement is permanent.

Scent (Ex): At 2nd level, a varag gains scent, but this ability has a range of 10 feet instead of the normal 30 feet. Beginning at 3rd level, the range increases to 20 feet. At 4th level, it increases to 30 feet, becoming the normal scent ability.

Run: At 2nd level, a varag gains Run as a bonus feat.

Move Silently: At 3rd level, a varag's racial bonus on Move Silently checks improves by +4, for a total of +8. Upon reaching 5th level, a varag can always choose to take 10 on Move Silently checks, even if rushed or threatened.

Spring Attack: At 5th level, a varag gains Spring Attack as a bonus feat.

Vital Statistics

You can choose your varag character's starting age, height, and weight, based on the typical physical characteristics detailed in the ecology section of the monster entry and the random ages here. Or, you can use the tables that follow to determine these statistics randomly.

RANDOM STARTING AGES

Race	Adulthood	Barbarian, Rogue, Scout, Sorcerer	Bard, Fighter, Paladin, Ranger	Cleric, Druid, Monk, Wizard
Varag	8 years	+1d3	+1d4	+2d4

AGING EFFECTS

Race	Middle Age	Old	Venerable	Maximum Age
Varag	16 years	24 years	32 years	+2d8 years

RANDOM HEIGHT AND WEIGHT

Race	Base Height	Height Modifier	Base Weight	Weight Modifier
Varag, male	5′ 11″	+2d12	230 lb.	× (2d6) lb.
Varag, female	5′ 7″	+2d12	200 lb.	× (2d6) lb.

VARAGS IN EBERRON

Long ago, Khorvaire was the playground of hobgoblins, who bred goblins and bugbears as slaves and warriors. In the same way, varags once toiled for the hobgoblins. With the fall of the Dhakaani empire, varags now roam across the land, raiding and killing as they please. Of all the goblinoids, varags are the most likely to wander far from Darguun and other humanoid lands.

VARAGS IN FAERÛN

Varags have easily carved out a corner for themselves in Faerûn through sheer physical might. Clearly stronger than hobgoblins and goblins, varags provide a challenge even for bugbears. When it comes to thinking through a challenge, however, bugbears beat the chasers every time.

VERDANT PRINCE

A figure blending nature into a humanoid form appears on a tree limb. Curved and woody antlers grow from its head, a mane of leaves spills down its back, thornlike spikes protrude from its shoulders, and lichen covers its wrists like bracers. Its eyes flicker with green light.

VERDANT PRINCE   **CR 11**

Usually NE Medium fey
Init +12; **Senses** low-light vision; Listen +12, Spot +12
Languages Elven, Common, Druidic, Sylvan

AC 26, touch 23, flat-footed 18; Dodge, Mobility
    (+8 Dex, +5 deflection, +3 natural)
hp 136 (16 HD); **DR** 10/cold iron
Resist evasion
SR 20
Fort +14, **Ref** +23, **Will** +17
Weakness double damage from cold iron

Speed 40 ft. (8 squares)
Melee *staff of the woodlands* +13/+8 (1d6+6)
Space 5 ft.; **Reach** 5 ft.
Base Atk +8; **Grp** +11
Combat Gear expended *staff of the woodlands* (acts as +2 *quarterstaff* and allows wielder to use *pass without trace* at will), *wand of magic missile* (5th)
Spell-Like Abilities (CL 16th):
    At will—*dimension door* (only when starting point and destination are adjacent to a tree or plant creature), *disguise self* (DC 16)
    1/day—*baleful polymorph* (DC 20), *call lightning storm* (DC 20), *changestaff*, *cure critical wounds*, *fire seeds* (DC 21), *repel metal or stone*, *wall of thorns*

Abilities Str 17, Dex 26, Con 18, Int 16, Wis 15, Cha 21
SQ oath bond, unearthly grace
Feats Combat Casting, Dodge, Improved Initiative, Improved Toughness (*Complete Warrior*), Mobility, Stealthy, Track[B]
Skills Appraise +8, Balance +15, Bluff +15, Climb +8, Concentration +13, Diplomacy +14, Disguise +10 (+12 acting), Escape Artist +13, Gather Information +7, Handle Animal +6, Hide +15, Intimidate +17, Jump +14, Knowledge (arcana) +8, Knowledge (local) +8, Knowledge (nature) +10, Listen +12, Move Silently +15, Search +8, Sense Motive +11, Sleight of Hand +15, Spellcraft +10 (+12 deciphering scrolls), Spot +12, Survival +11 (+13 following tracks, +13 in aboveground natural environments), Swim +8, Tumble +19, Use Magic Device +19 (+21 for scrolls), Use Rope +8 (+10 involving bindings)
Advancement by character class; **Favored Class** druid; see text

Oath Bond (Su) A verdant prince can strike a powerful supernatural bargain with another willing creature. The bargain can be nearly anything, but must involve an exchange of services or goods. A verdant prince can make an oath bond with only one creature at a time.

    If either party does not hold up its end of the bargain, it takes a –6 penalty to all ability scores and is sickened until the bargain is fulfilled. When a bargain isn't fulfilled, the wronged party becomes immediately aware of the broken oath and gains a constant awareness of the oathbreaker's distance and direction. This awareness does not extend across the boundaries of planes, but it does relate the information that an oathbreaker is not on the same plane.

    Only death or a *wish* or *miracle* spell can end an oath bond before the bargain is fulfilled or negate the penalties that a broken oath bond imposes. When the oath bond is negated by death or magic, the other party becomes aware that the oath was ended or suppressed but not how or where.

Unearthly Grace (Su) A verdant prince adds its Charisma modifier as a bonus on saving throws, and as a deflection bonus to Armor Class. Included above.

Verdant princes lend aid to those in need and grant the desires of the greedy, but those who strike a bargain with the fey understand too late what they've given up in exchange. Tyrants among faeriekind, verdant princes employ formidable spellcasting ability and magic items.

STRATEGIES AND TACTICS

A verdant prince fights much like a sorcerer or wizard. It typically begins combat by casting *changestaff* to create a treant ally to engage in melee. The prince then retreats to a hard-to-reach spot, such as a high tree branch, from which it can cast spells at foes and use magic items. The verdant prince fears foes wielding cold iron and uses *repel metal or stone* and *wall of thorns* to keep them at bay. If engaged in melee, it uses Tumble and *dimension door* to escape.

A verdant prince remains in combat for as long as possible, casting *cure critical wounds* to heal and employing spells and items until they run out. If, despite these efforts, the fey ends up in dire straits, it flees for a few rounds using *dimension door* to gain some distance and then hides and uses *disguise self* in hopes of fooling its foes. If successful in fleeing, a verdant prince often returns to the scene of the battle the next day to track foes and gain revenge through some ambush.

SAMPLE ENCOUNTERS

The first encounter with a verdant prince seems inoffensive, if a bit sinister. Princes prefer to bargain with those they encounter and to strike a favorable oath bond. They often use *disguise self* to appear less threatening and offer aid in exchange for something they desire. Verdant princes often employ evil fey or plant creatures as allies in battle, using them as shields against melee combat.

Woodland Seraglio (EL 13): A verdant prince uses a beautiful forest glade to entrap travelers. Three satyrs gambol

VERDANT PRINCE LORE

Characters with ranks in Knowledge (nature) can learn more about verdant princes. When a character makes a successful skill check, the following lore is revealed, including the information from lower DCs.

Knowledge (Nature)

DC	Result
21	This creature is a verdant prince, a kind of fey that often aids others in exchange for a service or gift. This result reveals all fey traits.
26	Verdant princes cast some druid spells and possess powerful protections against magic. As with many fey, cold iron weapons deal more damage to them—even more than is typical for creatures of their type.
31	Verdant princes are evil and cruel, and they enjoy entrapping victims in supernatural oaths that seem beneficial but are not.

about the nearby woods playing their pipes, four evil dryads live in oak trees surrounding the glade, and two evil nymph sisters luxuriate in a pool in the glade's center. The satyrs hope to attract sentient creatures into the verdant prince's trap with their music and tales of pleasant times to be had. The other fey lie in wait, listening for the change in a satyr's music that signals an approaching victim. When the targets enter the glade, the dryads and satyrs attempt to pacify them with *suggestion* and *charm person*. If that ploy works, the verdant prince shows itself to make an oath bond with the most pliable person. If the ploy fails, the nymphs reveal themselves to blind and stun foes, then everyone attacks.

Verdant prince

ECOLOGY

Dryads or nymphs who mate with verdant princes, or who are themselves evil, sometimes give birth to verdant princes. Verdant princes mature swiftly after birth, becoming full-grown and independent after a season. Powerful and convinced of their superiority, verdant princes care little for their mothers and typically despise their fathers, even if either parent was also a verdant prince. Like many other fey, verdant princes are nearly immortal.

Verdant princes have a diet much like that of humans but require one-third of the food a human of the same size needs. Thus, verdant princes have little impact on the environment and often rely on fey servants to fetch them what they require.

Environment: Verdant princes prefer temperate forests but can live in any environment that sustains humans.

Typical Physical Characteristics: A verdant prince stands about 6 feet in height. Slender yet muscular, it looks humanoid with a number of plant features. Most verdant princes' leaves and moss remain green throughout the year. A few, however, turn color with the seasons; some princes even lose their leaves in the fall.

Alignment: Verdant princes are born mischievous; their cruel streak increases as they mature over the course of a season. By maturity, nearly all become evil, but a few might be more lawful or chaotic than others. Students of fey lore hypothesize that a verdant prince's alignment and vile nature varies according to the season of birth. Spring princes tend to be chaotic but less cruel, while winter princes cleave rigidly to their words (even when not an oath bond) but are more despicably black-hearted than most.

SOCIETY

Verdant princes are leaders of evil fey and plant creatures. Those that reside long in a verdant prince's realm often become evil over time as they repeatedly acquiesce to their lord's will and participate in its plots.

A verdant prince lives to fulfill its selfish desires. The creature lairs in a home built by its subjects, sups on the fruit of their labor, benefits from them as spies, and takes whatever it desires. Although frequently cruel and imperious to individuals, a verdant prince makes an effort to appear magnanimous and forgiving to its subjects at large.

This fey delights in tricking a creature into an oath bond that leads to anguish and despair. The verdant prince takes care to fulfill its end of the bargain while requesting something that seems innocuous but will cause strife.

TYPICAL TREASURE

A verdant prince typically possesses double standard treasure for its Challenge Rating, approximately 15,000 gp. This treasure is almost always magic items from defeated foes. Having no power to detect magic, verdant princes plunder only obvious magic such as wands, scrolls, potions, and staffs. They give other treasure to underlings or to creatures who enter into oath bonds with them.

VERDANT PRINCES WITH CLASS LEVELS

Verdant princes' favored class is druid. Rogue and scout (see *Complete Adventurer*) are associated classes for the purpose of advancement.

Level Adjustment: +4.

VERDANT PRINCES IN FAERÛN

Unknown to all but the eldest son and daughter of each generation, the Adarbrent noble family of Waterdeep has for decades sent their firstborn to the Kryptgarden forest to pledge an oath to King Witchthorn, a verdant prince. These children must perform an unspecified service for the prince by their eleventh year. In exchange, the family's businesses and homes gain secret fey guardians. The bargain has worked well for the family; King Witchthorn has never asked anything of them. Now the Adarbrents view the verdant prince as a fatherly benefactor, thinking nothing of chaining another generation to whatever dark plans the fey has in store.

VITREOUS DRINKER

This hunched, shambling figure might be able to pass for human except for the bulging, wet eyes that cover every inch of its skin, and the long, repulsively prehensile tongue that lolls from its gaping mouth. Several translucent, shadowy ravens circle the creature's head, their beaks open in silent cries.

VITREOUS DRINKER
CR 11

Always NE Medium undead
Init +8; **Senses** darkvision 120 ft.; Listen +2, Spot +19
Languages Abyssal, Common, Draconic, Infernal

AC 27, touch 17, flat-footed 23
(+4 Dex, +3 deflection, +10 natural)
hp 91 (14 HD); **DR** 10/good
Immune undead immunities
Resist +6 turn resistance; **SR** 22
Fort +7, **Ref** +13, **Will** +14

Speed 30 ft. (6 squares)
Melee tongue lash +12/+7 (2d4+1 plus eye drinking)
Space 5 ft.; **Reach** 5 ft. (10 ft. with tongue lash)
Base Atk +7; **Grp** +8
Special Actions eye drinking, horrific gaze
Spell-Like Abilities (CL 14th):
  At will—*arcane eye, detect thoughts* (DC 15), *tongues*
  3/day—*eyebite* (DC 21), *vampiric touch* (+11 touch)
  1/day—*dimension door, finger of death* (DC 20)

Abilities Str 12, Dex 19, Con —, Int 18, Wis 15, Cha 16
SQ spectral ravens, undead traits, unholy grace
Feats Ability Focus (*eyebite*), Improved Initiative, Lightning Reflexes, Weapon Finesse, Weapon Focus (tongue lash)
Skills Bluff +10, Concentration +17, Decipher Script +17, Diplomacy +17, Gather Information +15, Intimidate +15, Knowledge (arcana) +14, Knowledge (local) +11, Knowledge (nature) +8, Knowledge (religion) +8, Knowledge (the planes) +8, Listen +2, Sense Motive +12, Spot +19, Use Magic Device +19 (+21 scrolls)
Advancement 15–20 HD (Medium); 21–42 HD (Large)

Eye Drinking (Su) A vitreous drinker can use its lashing tongue to magically steal a creature's ability to see. This ability has no effect on creatures that lack sight. A creature struck by the drinker's tongue must succeed on a DC 20 Fortitude save. On a failed save, the creature's eyes become covered with thick, milky cataracts. The creature cannot see farther than 60 feet, and all melee and ranged attacks it makes within this range have a 20% miss chance. This effect can be removed only with *greater restoration* or *miracle*, or by the destruction of the drinker that stole the victim's sight. The save DC is Charisma-based.

A creature who has its sight stolen has a –4 penalty on Will saves made to resist the vitreous drinker's abilities and any of its spell-like abilities. The victim cannot avert its eyes to avoid the drinker's horrific gaze (see below).

A vitreous drinker can see through the eyes of a creature whose eyes it drinks, using the victim's full, normal sight. It does not suffer the restrictions and penalties imposed on a victim of eye drinking. The range and duration of this ability have no limit, though the drinker can view through only one victim's eyes at a time. A drinker uses its own Spot skill to view details through the victim's eyes and benefits from its darkvision.

Horrific Gaze (Su) A vitreous drinker's disgusting visage revolts even the strongest soul. A drinker has a gaze attack with a range of 60 feet that causes a creature to be nauseated for 1 round. A successful DC 20 Fortitude save negates this effect, but a creature must attempt another save each round it remains within range of the gaze. The save DC is Charisma-based.

Spectral Ravens (Su) A vitreous drinker is accompanied at all times by spectral ravens that serve the drinker unconditionally. The drinker shares a powerful symbiotic link with the spectral ravens. It is constantly aware of what they see and hear and can direct them as a free action. The ravens are incorporeal, and a vitreous drinker can control them as long as they remain on the same plane as the drinker. The ravens are not creatures, but rather objects spawned by the drinker. Each raven has 5 hit points and AC 15. Otherwise, treat them as unattended, Tiny objects. A vitreous drinker is accompanied by up to twenty-four ravens, and if any are destroyed, the creature can restore them at a rate of one per day.

The ravens have a fly speed of 100 feet and perfect maneuverability. They cannot take independent action, nor can they do anything to physically affect the world around them. They exist solely to observe.

Unholy Grace (Su) A vitreous drinker adds its Charisma modifier as a bonus on its saving throws and as a deflection bonus to its AC. Included above.

A vitreous drinker is a horrific undead servitor of Vecna. This creature steals its prey's sight, rendering the victim partially blind. Worst of all, a vitreous drinker can see through its victims' eyes. As servitors of Vecna, vitreous drinkers use their ability to pry secrets away from sages, wizards, and other wise folk. The knowledge a vitreous drinker accumulates is as fearsome a weapon as its deadly magical and physical abilities.

STRATEGIES AND TACTICS

Vitreous drinkers settle within towns, cities, or other civilized areas. They use their eye drinking ability on a wide range of animals and people within the city or region they haunt. A single vitreous drinker might ambush and drink the sight of beggars across the city. These victims are unwitting sentinels for the drinker, forming a living network of spies

VITREOUS DRINKER LORE

Characters with ranks in Knowledge (religion) can learn more about vitreous drinkers. When a character makes a successful skill check, the following lore is revealed, including the information from lower DCs.

Knowledge (Religion)

DC	Result
21	This creature is a vitreous drinker, an undead creature that steals sight from its victims. This result reveals all undead traits.
26	Vitreous drinkers can employ *eyebite, vampiric touch,* and *finger of death* as spell-like abilities.
31	Spectral ravens accompany a vitreous drinker, manifestations of the negative energy that animates it. The drinker can see whatever the ravens can see.
36	Vitreous drinkers can see through their victims' eyes.

and watchers that it can access at a moment's notice. A crafty drinker that plans ahead can track every movement that an adventuring party or other target makes in town. If a creature it has targeted wanders to a spot where it lacks spies, a vitreous drinker uses its spectral ravens to tail the target.

A vitreous drinker is a spy, infiltrator, and information broker. It shies away from direct confrontation unless doing so is in its best interest. Instead, a vitreous drinker prefers to ambush its enemies, use its eye drinking ability, and then retreat to spy upon the victim and its allies. With its excellent Spot skill, the drinker attempts to read the lips of anyone its victim can see.

In most cases, a vitreous drinker works with powerful clerics of Vecna. A single drinker might sit at the center of a wide-ranging network of spies, informants, and infiltrators. It gathers information for whatever goals it pursues. Some drinkers seek to destabilize an area, weakening its government and institutions to help usher in a wave of chaos. Others help various evil groups achieve their goals, either by passing along information to the group or harassing and slaying its foes.

A vitreous drinker is most dangerous when it has powerful allies to call on. A drinker might work with an assassins' guild, for example, helping the killers formulate plans to cut down a paladin, cleric of good, or other heroic figure.

In combat, a vitreous drinker flees unless it is cornered or it feels it can defeat its enemies. It uses *finger of death* early in the battle to strike down someone who looks vulnerable (such as an arcane spellcaster or rogue), followed by *eyebite*. Its goal is to weaken its foes, then use *vampiric touch* to sap their strength while steadying itself against any counterattacks. It saves *dimension door* as a last resort to escape harm.

SAMPLE ENCOUNTER

When a vitreous drinker goes on the offensive, it prefers to use hit-and-run tactics. It attempts to strike a victim with its eye drinking ability, flee, and then view its enemies to learn as much about their tactics as possible. It then plans an appropriate second attack.

Individual (EL 11): A vitreous drinker uses its spectral ravens to track a party's movement. Over the course of several days, it ventures out to use its eye drinking ability on beggars and other unfortunates in the area. Once the drinker can watch as much of the party's movements as possible, it makes plans to ambush and attack the weakest member. Even then, it avoids a direct fight. It uses *eye-bite* to hamper a victim, then drinks the creature's eyes.

ECOLOGY

As undead, vitreous drinkers have no true ecology. The creatures were reputedly created by Vecna for some nefarious purpose. Some legends state that Vecna actually advises each of the vitreous drinkers, directing them to some unknown end. Across countless worlds and the infinite planes, vitreous drinkers work together to fulfill Vecna's unguessable aims.

Environment: Vitreous drinkers can be found in any climate and any terrain. Urban slums with high crime rates, charnel houses, and battlefields are common places to encounter vitreous drinkers, but they can be found anywhere where death has a foothold.

Typical Physical Characteristics: Vitreous drinkers are bipedal, human-shaped beings roughly 6 feet tall and weighing 150 pounds. Their bodies are genderless, and as undead, they do not age.

Alignment: Vitreous drinkers are always neutral evil, as befits creatures so closely aligned with Vecna.

SOCIETY

Vitreous drinkers dwell alone. They rarely work together, since their abilities are best suited for a wide, dispersed effort. They do work with clerics of Vecna, but they pass the information they gather along to anyone who can help them achieve their mysterious goals. A vitreous drinker is just as likely to give information to an orc warlord as to a brave paladin if it feels that either would use the information in a manner that helps the drinker. An adventuring party could even unwittingly serve Vecna under the right circumstances. A drinker usually has humanoid allies responsible for passing information from the drinker to others in town, who then pass it higher up the chain of command to Vecna's senior mortal representatives.

TYPICAL TREASURE

Vitreous drinkers have standard treasure for their Challenge Rating, about 7,500 gp, which serves as bribes or tools. Much of a vitreous drinker's treasure is in the form of scrolls and wands, which it uses to make unexpected magical attacks against enemies.

Illus. by W. Reynolds

Vitreous drinker

WINDBLADE

In the windswept depths of Pandemonium, where icy gales scour the endless tunnels and create a constant howling, creatures known as windblades flit through the lightless labyrinths, committing murder and mayhem in the name of Erythnul, their lord and creator. Windscythes are the greater of the windblades; windrazors the lesser.

WINDBLADES IN EBERRON

Windblades make their homes in the constantly changing, chaotic plane of Kythri. Within the Churning Chaos, they practice and perfect their techniques of slaughter on those slaadi and githzerai unlucky enough to cross their path. Windscythe sages speak of the times when Kythri was coterminous, and their people brought great slaughter into the material world.

Windblades might also be encountered within manifest zones linked to Kythri. Some tribes have survived on Eberron since the plane's last coterminous phase. They form small groups in high, windy, mountainous regions, such as the peaks of Adar in southern Sarlona and the Skyraker Claws mountains along the north coast of Xen'drik.

Erythnul is unknown in Eberron; instead, windscythe clerics revere the Fury, embodying the passion the god represents.

WINDBLADES IN FAERÛN

In the FORGOTTEN REALMS setting, the windblades were created by Talos the Destroyer as a force to ride the currents of his storms and bring destruction in their wake. They make their home within Fury's Heart, traveling to Toril when called by servants of the Storm Lord. Clerics of Talos often call windblades to augment the destruction wrought by true believers. A small tribe of windblades is also rumored to be moving around the Sea of Fallen Stars, sticking to regions of high cliffs and peaks around the Inner Sea.

WINDRAZOR

A gangly creature, all gawky limbs and flaps of leathery skin, drifts through the air. At the tips of its wings are short, sharp, bony blades. Its elongated skull boasts knobby, hornlike protrusions, and its mouth is full of long, sharp teeth.

WINDRAZOR   CR 1
Always CE Small outsider (extraplanar)
Init +2; **Senses** darkvision 60 ft., keen senses; Listen +6, Spot +6
Languages Auran, Windsong

AC 13, touch 13, flat-footed 11
    (+1 size, +2 Dex)
hp 9 (2 HD)
Fort +3, **Ref** +5, **Will** +4

Speed 10 ft. (2 squares), climb 10 ft., fly 40 ft. (good); Flyby Attack
Melee 2 claws +4 each (1d4+1/19–20) and bite –1 (1d6/19–20)
Space 5 ft.; **Reach** 5 ft.
Base Atk +2; **Grp** –1
Atk Options fearsome critical, rend 2d4+2

Abilities Str 13, Dex 15, Con 11, Int 8, Wis 12, Cha 6
Feats Flyby Attack, Improved Critical (claw)[B], Improved Critical (bite)[B]
Skills Balance +4, Climb +14, Hide +6, Knowledge (the planes) +4, Listen +6, Move Silently +7, Spot +6, Survival +6 (+8 on other planes), Tumble +7
Advancement by character class; **Favored Class** ranger; see text

---

Keen Senses (Ex) A windrazor sees four times as well a human in shadowy illumination.
Rend (Ex) A windrazor that hits with both claw attacks latches onto the opponent's body and tears the flesh. This attack automatically deals an extra 2d4+2 points of damage.
Fearsome Critical (Ex) Whenever a windrazor scores a critical hit, all creatures within 10 feet must succeed on a DC 9 Will saving throw or become shaken. This is a mind-affecting fear effect. The save DC is Charisma-based.
Skills Windrazors have a +8 racial bonus on Climb checks and can choose to take 10 on Climb checks, even if rushed or threatened.

Windrazors are the scouts and hunters of the windblades. Vicious, bloodthirsty creatures, they travel in groups of up to a dozen, seeking prey for themselves or sport for their masters. Created by Erythnul, the god of slaughter, they revel in battle and blood, constantly seeking new thrills and levels of brutality.

Windrazor

Illus. by A. Swekel

Strategies and Tactics

Windrazors are pack hunters. They seek prey together, and together they bring it down.

In combat, windrazors make effective use of Flyby Attack, approaching in waves, swooping in, delivering claw attacks, and flying away again. This ensures that only foes who ready attacks ever get a chance to strike back in melee, while maximizing the number of windrazors that can attack.

The influence of their brutal patron deity leads windrazors to favor full attacks (with the potential for rending) against wounded foes. Otherwise, the creatures linger near an opponent only if it is poorly armored and otherwise easy to hit (not protected by magical effects, for example).

WINDSCYTHE

A heavily muscled creature, long of limb with flaps of leathery skin, powers through the air, its extended, bladelike tail sweeping along behind it. At the tips of its wings, short, bony blades clutch at the wind, as though grasping at the flesh of unseen prey. The flier's narrow skull is crowned with knobby, hornlike protrusions, and its mouth is full of sharp teeth. It wears a tunic of chain armor, and a quiver of javelins is slung low across its back.

Windscythe

WINDSCYTHE	**CR 4**

Always CE Large outsider (extraplanar)
Init +1; **Senses** darkvision 60 ft., keen senses;
Listen +10, Spot +10
Languages Auran, Windsong

AC 18, touch 10, flat-footed 17
(–1 size, +4 armor, +1 Dex, +4 natural)
hp 52 (8 HD)
Fort +8, **Ref** +7, **Will** +6

Speed 10 ft. (2 squares), fly 60 feet (average); Flyby Attack,
Wingover
Melee 2 claws +12 each (1d6+5/18–20/×3) and
bite +7 (1d8+2)
Ranged javelin +9 (1d6+5)
Space 10 ft.; **Reach** 10 ft.
Base Atk +8; **Grp** +17
Atk Options augmented critical, fearsome critical, rend
2d6+7

Abilities Str 21, Dex 12, Con 14, Int 9, Wis 11, Cha 8
Feats Armor Proficiency (light), Flyby Attack, Wingover
Skills Balance +1, Climb +21, Craft +4, Intimidate +9,
Knowledge (the planes) +10, Listen +10, Move
Silently +9, Spot +10, Survival +10 (+12 on other planes),
Tumble +5
Advancement by character class; **Favored Class** fighter;
see text
Possessions chain shirt, 3 javelins

Keen Senses (Ex) As windrazor.
Augmented Critical (Ex) A windscythe's claws are
extraordinarily sharp. They threaten a critical hit on a
natural attack roll of 18–20, dealing triple damage on
a successful critical hit. A windscythe's claws are not
subject to effects such as *keen edge* that would further
improve their threat range.
Fearsome Critical (Ex) As windrazor; Will save DC 13.
Rend (Ex) As windrazor; damage 2d6+7.

Windscythes are the warriors, nobles, tyrants, and priests of the windblades. Brutish, violent creatures with a voracious appetite for raw flesh, windscythes soar through their domain with the bearing of royalty. Like other windblades, they were created by Erythnul, god of slaughter, and they exult in fulfilling his brutal desires, spreading death and fear whenever they can.

"... of the depths of Pandemonium, the dangers are many, not the least of which are the razors on the winds, for they hunt and kill with great fervor, slicing with unseen blades; call on them with caution ..."
—Excerpt from *On Summoning*

Strategies and Tactics

Windscythes are cunning killers, willing to use any stratagem to accomplish their goals, from hunting alone to employing packs of windrazors.

A windscythe's favorite combat tactic is a Flyby Attack through a group, attempting to shake opponents with its fearsome critical ability. It continues this strategy until the foes have dispersed, then selects one of the isolated creatures to attack with its claws or bite. Multiple windscythes work in concert to speed up the dispersal process, then combine their attacks on isolated foes—preferably spellcasters first.

When hunting with windrazors, windscythes let their smaller cousins lead the charge, employing them as shock

Illus. by J. Nelson

troops or directing them to herd opponents into convenient groupings for the windscythes to slice through.

SAMPLE ENCOUNTERS

Windrazors usually hunt in packs, sometimes led by windscythes or demons in the service of Erythnul. They are also occasionally sent to the Material Plane to guard temples of Erythnul, where they can be found in the company of mortal priests, bugbears, trolls, and other fell creatures. The windrazor flight is the most common encounter.

Windscythes rarely hunt alone; they know that they are more dangerous in numbers and more vulnerable singly. A windscythe tries to travel with an escort of at least two windrazors. Windscythes are frequently found in the company of other creatures that serve Erythnul, and with them, windscythes find their way to the Material Plane.

Windrazor Pair (EL 2): Fuuar and Thuafin are scouts sent to the Material Plane to serve a powerful bugbear shaman dedicated to Erythnul. The creatures have little respect for their savage hosts, so they spend most of their time away from the bugbear encampment. They are likely to run afoul of the adventurers either during one of their scouting runs or when the party has been drawn into the area in response to the depredations of the bugbear tribe.

Windrazor Flight (EL 4): Surrussh, Fllist, Hwool, and Luluru are engaged in a prisoner hunt for their windscythe masters. They are most interested in a creature that moves quickly, to provide their masters more sport.

Escort (EL 4+): Windrazors sometimes accompany other servants of the god of slaughter as guards.

EL 4: Thurush and Lishae, two windrazors brought to the Material Plane by priests of Erythnul, serve as escorts for a quasit named Kamatherdin. The quasit carries important messages from one temple to another. With a higher speed and the ability to turn invisible, the quasit is quite willing to abandon its windrazor escorts to delay any attackers while it makes its escape.

Individual Windscythe (EL 4): Hurrall is a bold young male windscythe who has set off on his own to prove his bravery to the rest of his wing. Now, apart from them for days and growing increasingly worried that he could fall victim to an even more deadly predator, Hurrall has become recklessly eager to attack and kill the first thing he sees.

Raid (EL 8+): Windscythes often join with other brutal chaotic creatures, particularly those that leave them free to conduct aerial attacks.

EL 8: A group of two windscythes and two trolls is based in a shrine to Erythnul, carefully hidden beneath the sewers of a major city. The raiders, bent only on slaughter, rampage through half a dozen households before the adventurers are alerted to their presence.

Slaughter (EL 10+): Happy to accompany those devoted to the god of slaughter, windscythes are a fast strike force.

EL 10: Four windscythes and two trolls, led by a 5th-level bugbear cleric of Erythnul, fall upon an unsuspecting village, leaving devastation in their wake. The ruined village becomes a haven for disease, and neighboring communities are deeply troubled by the attack.

ECOLOGY

Windblades regard the entirety of Pandemonium as their domain and aggressively pursue intruders—everything from the Banished (humanoids, goblinoids, and giants who have been trapped in Pandemonium for ages) to the occasional slaadi or fiends that attempt to carve out some of Pandemonium's territory for themselves.

Environment: The tunnels and caverns where windblades dwell are grim, lightless places, through which the winds of Pandemonium constantly howl. Here and there, though, the winds erode enough of the surrounding stone to create cul-de-sacs, and there the windblades make their homes.

Typical Physical Characteristics: Windrazors range in height from 3 feet to 3 feet 10 inches, weighing 38 to 52 pounds. Though both genders possess the hornlike protrusions common to the race, male windrazors have four while females have only two.

Windscythes range in height from 10 to 12 feet, weighing from 550 to 800 pounds. Their tails add another 10 to 12 feet to their overall length. Both genders possess the hornlike protrusions common to the race, running the length of their skulls. The more such horns, the older the windscythe.

Alignment: Windblades are always chaotic evil, finding their calling in violent slaughter and cruel torture.

SOCIETY

Windblades believe that they were the original manifestations of Erythnul's will, and that they were the first to serve his brutal whims. This belief fuels their philosophy that Pandemonium is theirs alone, provided they can drive out all invaders. When drawn to the mortal realm by the spells of

WINDBLADE LORE

Characters with ranks in Knowledge (the planes) can learn more about windblades. When a character makes a successful skill check, the following lore is revealed, including the information from lower DCs.

Knowledge (the Planes)

DC	Result
11	Windblades are natives of the Windswept Depths of Pandemonium. This result reveals all outsider traits.
16	Windrazors are weaker windblades. Windscythes are much larger and more powerful. All windblades were created by Erythnul, god of slaughter, and usually accompany other servants of their foul patron.
21	Windrazors hunt in groups, employing flyby tactics to confuse and overwhelm their opponents. Windscythes slash with their bladelike tails during such attacks, attempting to scatter groups of foes.
26	Windscythes rarely go anywhere alone; they are nearly always accompanied by at least two windrazors each.

Erythnul's servants, they find every excuse possible to shed mortal blood and cause death and mayhem.

In windblade society, windscythes are the lords and masters. Windrazors are treated as something between servants and pets. They care for the young of the windscythes, guard the communal lairs, and patrol the tunnels and caverns of Pandemonium against intruders and possible invaders. Windrazors are always second-class citizens, afforded few rights and considered of minor importance compared to their larger cousins. They allow this system to continue, despite their superior numbers, because they fear the power and spellcasting abilities of the windscythe clerics.

Windblades have their own language, called Windsong.

TYPICAL TREASURE

Windblades have standard treasure for their Challenge Rating (about 600 gp for windrazors, and 1,200 gp for windscythes). They never carry scrolls or oils, which are difficult to use in the windy conditions of Pandemonium.

Windblades with class levels have treasure appropriate to NPCs of their Challenge Rating.

"The windrazors are fearsome, yet not the most fearsome of their kind. Their nobles are larger beasts still, with tails like scythes."

—Margin note in *On Summoning*

WINDBLADES AS CHARACTERS

Windrazor leaders tend to be rangers or rogues. Windrazor clerics are virtually unheard-of; windscythes jealously reserve for themselves the right to commune with the gods. Similarly, very few windrazors are wizards, though windrazor sorcerers are relatively common.

Windscythe leaders tend to be fighters or clerics. Some are wizards, but these are exceedingly rare; the winds of Pandemonium make the required study nearly impossible. More windscythes become sorcerers, but that class is far more common among the windrazors.

Windrazor Characters

Windrazor characters possess the following racial traits.

—+2 Strength, +4 Dexterity, –2 Intelligence, +2 Wisdom, –4 Charisma.

—Small size. +1 bonus to Armor Class, +1 bonus on attack rolls, +4 bonus on Hide checks, –4 penalty on grapple checks, lifting and carrying limits 3/4 those of Medium characters.

—A windrazor's base land speed is 10 feet. It has a base climb speed of 10 feet and a base fly speed of 40 feet, with good maneuverability.

—Darkvision out to 60 feet. A windrazor can also see four times as well as a human in shadowy illumination.

—Racial Hit Dice: A windrazor begins with two levels of outsider, which provide 2d8 Hit Dice, a base attack bonus of +2, and base saving throw bonuses of Fort +3, Ref +3, and Will +3.

—Racial Skills: A windrazor's outsider levels give it skill points equal to 5 × (8 + Int modifier, minimum 1). Its class skills are Climb, Knowledge (the planes), Listen, Move Silently, Spot, Survival, and Tumble.

—Racial Feats: A windrazor's outsider levels give it one feat. A windrazor receives Improved Critical (claw) and Improved Critical (bite) as bonus feats.

—Natural Weapons: 2 claws (1d4) and bite (1d6).

—Special Abilities (see above): Fearsome critical, keen senses, rend.

—Automatic Languages: Auran, Windsong. Bonus Languages: Abyssal, Common, Undercommon.

—Favored Class: Ranger.

—Level Adjustment: +2.

Windscythe Characters

Windscythe characters possess the following racial traits.

—+10 Strength, +2 Dexterity, +4 Constitution, –2 Intelligence, –2 Charisma.

—Large size. –1 penalty to Armor Class, –1 penalty on attack rolls, –4 penalty on Hide checks, +4 bonus on grapple checks.

—A windscythe's base land speed is 10 feet. It has a base climb speed of 10 feet and a base fly speed of 60 feet, with average maneuverability.

—Darkvision out to 60 feet. A windscythe can also see four times as well as a human in shadowy light.

—Racial Hit Dice: A windscythe begins with eight levels of outsider, which provide 8d8 Hit Dice, a base attack bonus of +8, and base saving throw bonuses of Fort +6, Ref +6, and Will +6.

—Racial Skills: A windscythe's outsider levels give it skill points equal to 11 × (8 + Int modifier, minimum 1). Its class skills are Climb, Intimidate, Knowledge (the planes), Listen, Move Silently, Spot, Survival, and Tumble.

—Racial Feats: A windscythe's outsider levels give it three feats.

—Natural Weapons: 2 claws (1d6) and bite (1d8).

—Special Abilities (see above): Augmented critical, fearsome critical, keen senses, rend.

—Automatic Languages: Windsong, Auran. Bonus Languages: Abyssal, Common, Undercommon.

—Favored Class: Fighter.

—Level Adjustment: +5.

FOR PLAYER CHARACTERS

A windrazor can be called using a *lesser planar ally* spell. It can also be summoned by *summon monster III* or a higher-level *summon monster* spell. Treat the windrazor as if it were on the 3rd-level list on the Summon Monster table (PH 287).

A windscythe can be called using a *planar ally* spell. It can also be summoned by *summon monster VI* or a higher-level *summon monster* spell. Treat the windscythe as if it were on the 6th-level list on the Summon Monster table (PH 287).

WIZENED ELDER

What at first you took for a twisted shrub unfurls to become an ancient-looking creature the size of a dwarf. Lichen-covered bark hangs in shreds from its body, and clumps of stunted leaves sprout from its limbs. Suspicious eyes glare at you from deep crevices.

WIZENED ELDER	**CR 2**

Usually CN Medium plant
Init +0; **Senses** low-light vision; Listen +3, Spot +3
Language speak with plants, Sylvan

AC 14, touch 10, flat-footed 14
   (+4 natural)
hp 30 (4 HD); **DR** 5/slashing
Immune plant immunities
Resist cold 5
Fort +7, **Ref** +1, **Will** +2
Weakness vulnerability to fire

Speed 20 ft. (4 squares); improved woodland stride
Melee 2 slams +5 each (1d8+1)
Space 5 ft.; **Reach** 5 ft.
Base Atk +3; **Grp** +4
Special Actions entangle

Abilities Str 13, Dex 10, Con 17, Int 8, Wis 12, Cha 13
SQ plant traits
Feats Alertness, Weapon Focus (slam)
Skills Hide +0*, Knowledge (nature) +4, Listen +3, Spot +3,
   Survival +3 (+5 in aboveground natural environments)
   *Wizened elders gain a +8 racial bonus on Hide checks in
   forested areas.
Advancement by character class; **Favored Class** druid;
   see text

Speak with Plants (Su) As the *speak with plants* spell; at will;
   caster level 4th.
Improved Woodland Stride (Ex) A wizened elder can move
   through any sort of undergrowth (such as natural thorns,
   briars, overgrown areas, and similar terrain) at its normal
   speed and without taking damage or suffering any other
   impairment. In addition, thorns, briars, and overgrown
   areas that have been magically manipulated do not
   impede its motion or otherwise affect it.
Entangle (Su) As the *entangle* spell; at will; DC 15; caster
   level 4th. This ability affects a 60-foot-radius area around
   the wizened elder and lasts for 1 minute. The save DC is
   Constitution-based.

A wizened elder is a stunted, ancient-looking plant creature related to treants but inhabiting forbidding lands at the very edge of the tree line. Although not evil, wizened elders are bitter, cruel creatures that blend perfectly with their harsh environment. They creep across the desolate landscape, watching for and driving off intruders.

Strategies and Tactics

Wizened elders patrol singly or in small groups (copses). They have excellent camouflage, being virtually indistinguishable from other stunted trees and shrubs, even to the point of having one side mossier than the rest, just like a real, ancient tree. They prefer to wait, standing still and observing the situation, then catch enemies off guard.

If a foe does not appear too dangerous, a wizened elder uses its *entangle* ability to ensnare it, then flails at the immobilized enemy with its limbs. Even if the foe is not held, its reduced speed means it can't easily outrun the slow plant creature.

Obviously, such tactics don't work against enemies with ranged attacks. The elder's thick bark protects it from most arrow damage, though, and slings are almost ineffective against it. When necessary, it simply retreats. If confronted by enemies wielding fire, a wizened elder immobilizes them if possible, then seeks others to overwhelm the threat.

Copses of wizened elders work together to defeat more powerful enemies. They use intelligent tactics, granting flanking bonuses and assisting one another with attacks or defense as the situation merits. They attack one enemy at a time, starting with those who use slashing weapons or anyone wielding fire. If outmatched, they retreat, leaving the enemy stuck in the impeding terrain, and hide among other shrubs once they are out of the enemy's sight.

SAMPLE ENCOUNTER

Wizened elders are not especially cooperative and rarely initiate combat. A solitary specimen is the most common encounter, but groups do gather.

Pair (EL 4): Two wizened elders keep watch over a warm spring that flows year-round despite the arctic cold. Travelers often stop here, making it an ideal spot for an ambush. The elders use *entangle* to slow their foes. They gang up on a single opponent, attempting to grapple it, drag it into the water, and drown it.

ECOLOGY

Wizened elders are found at high elevations or at the edge of tundra, where trees grow small and bonsailike at the very edge of habitability. They live a very long time but never get larger than shrubs. Immature specimens are rarely seen, since they are virtually indistinguishable from the ground cover and berry bushes of their surroundings. This puts them in danger from browsing herbivores, but they remain alert to possible threats by listening to the nearby plants. They can drive off most animals easily—it's not often that a bit of greenery slaps back! The mature plants also protect any area that harbors younglings, for not many exist.

After a century or so, a wizened elder is able to live independently and finds its own patch of licheny rock or bogland to inhabit. At this age, it is capable of reproducing. However,

WIZENED ELDER LORE

Characters with ranks in Knowledge (nature) can learn more about wizened elders. When a character makes a successful skill check, the following lore is revealed, including the information from lower DCs.

Knowledge (Nature)

DC	Result
12	This creature is a wizened elder, an arctic relative of treants. This result reveals all plant traits.
17	A wizened elder's tough hide is difficult to penetrate with piercing or bludgeoning weapons.
22	Wizened elders can cause nearby plants to animate and entangle their enemies.
27	While the animated plants entangle the elders' foes, the elders can walk through such areas without hindrance.

so few exist that finding a mate is a protracted and often unsuccessful quest. Both sexes seek potential mates by querying the local plant life. Should two elders meet and find each other compatible, they form a lifelong relationship. Reproduction is a complex process, filled with ritual. The result is a single seed, which the parents plant nearby. The offspring roots there as it grows (unless forced to move by a threat) and remains in the area for the next century or two.

A wizened elder roots itself shallowly in its chosen spot and feeds as a plant does, extracting water and what nutrients it can from the thin, sour soil. Decomposing flesh provides additional nutrients, so a wizened elder is not above slaying an incautious creature to supplement its diet. Intruders' corpses always go to feed the soil.

The elders themselves are not appetizing to plant-eaters, although in a harsh winter even such bitter browse might attract animals. The plants are quite capable of driving off ordinary beasts, but savage monsters sometimes devour them. They are especially vulnerable to brantas (*Frostburn* 113), which are adapted to such tough fare.

Wizened elder

Environment: Wizened elders are most often found in cold plains, but the chilly subalpine zones of mountains also host them. They move slowly about their region and occasionally drift into other kinds of terrain, although they do not remain there long.

Typical Physical Characteristics: A wizened elder rarely exceeds a dwarf in height, usually standing 4 to 5 feet tall and weighing around 150 pounds.

Males and females are about the same size, and both produce growths resembling pine cones every other year. The male cones have broadly flaring fins and grow at joints just below the creature's "face"; female cones are quite small and ring the elder's trunk. The two have differing patterns of leaf growth as well, with males sprouting clumps mostly along their backs while females' leaves are distributed more evenly about their bodies. Leaves are tough and waxy, and they stay green year round.

Alignment: Wizened elders are usually chaotic neutral, an attitude born of solitary watching. Those who become druids are more likely to be neutral, neutral good, or neutral evil. Particularly bitter individuals drift toward neutral evil or even chaotic evil behavior, especially in extreme old age.

SOCIETY
Wizened elders consider themselves the last, lonely defenders against the creep of "civilization" into their wastes. They consider treants to be distant and overly soft cousins who abandoned them to inhospitable lands. They are indifferent to hostile toward most other races, although they are more likely to be communicative with druids. Uldras (*Frostburn* 38) share their environment, and wizened elders consider these arctic fey to be kindred spirits (though the gentle uldras might not agree).

In general, religion isn't important in their lives. Those who are spiritually inclined usually follow druidic or shamanistic paths, though a few might offer prayers to grim winter deities. Wizened elder druids are more adventuresome than most of their kin and are the most likely to form partnerships with uldras or other druids.

Life is hard. Life is cold. These basic tenets of wizened elders' existence influence their outlook and values system. They have no patience with any (including their own kind) who cannot survive a harsh environment. Their scions quickly learn to defend themselves against predation.

Each wizened elder is a nation unto itself. Central government is unknown to these grim folk, and it isn't necessary when they are so few and widely scattered. Within a copse, authority naturally goes to the eldest. Wizened elders who become druids often assume leadership roles; they are usually the oldest as well.

TYPICAL TREASURE
Wizened elders have standard treasure for their Challenge Rating, about 600 gp, usually consisting of equipment and coins dropped by creatures they have overcome. Such items might be partly grown over by an elder's bark.

WIZENED ELDERS WITH CLASS LEVELS
Druid levels stack with a wizened elder's Hit Dice for the purpose of its entangle and speak with plants abilities. Racial Hit Dice do not stack with druid levels for spellcasting.

Wizened elder clerics usually worship Telchur (*Frostburn* 43). His domains are Air, Chaos, Cold*, Strength, and Winter*. His favored weapon is the shortspear or shortbow.

*Domain described on page 85 of *Frostburn*.

Level Adjustment: +3.

WIZENED ELDERS IN FAERÛN
Wizened elders inhabit cold, forbidding wastes, such as Narfell and Icewind Dale, or sometimes the high slopes of mountain ranges. Occasionally a Harper travels to speak to these lonely sentinels about the activities of evil beings in their lands. Some Uthgardt barbarians share the same region and pay respect to the ancient treefolk. A small offshoot of the Grandfather Tree tribe is dedicated to protecting the elders.

Illus. by W. England

WRACKSPAWN

This misshapen monstrosity seems to have been both flayed and burned, its limbs twisted into dreadful parodies. It is eyeless and shrieks with mad battle lust.

WRACKSPAWN   **CR 3**

Always CE Medium outsider (chaotic, evil, extraplanar)
Init +0; **Senses** blind, blindsight 120 ft.; Listen +10
Languages understands Abyssal

AC 14, touch 10, flat-footed 14
  (+2 armor, +2 natural)
hp 45 (4 HD); **DR** 5/—
Immune gaze attacks, illusions, visual effects
Resist fire 10
Fort +10, **Ref** +4, **Will** +4

Speed 20 ft. (4 squares)
Melee bone shortspear +8 (1d6+4 plus pain) and
  double claw +3 (2d4+2) or
Melee double claw +8 (2d4+6)
Ranged bone shortspear +4 (1d6+4 plus pain)
Space 5 ft.; **Reach** 5 ft.
Base Atk +4; **Grp** +8
Atk Options aligned strike (chaotic, evil), pain

Abilities Str 19, Dex 10, Con 22, Int 6, Wis 11, Cha 12
Feats Skill Focus (Listen), Toughness
Skills Climb +11, Hide +7, Intimidate +8, Jump +5,
  Listen +10, Move Silently +7
Advancement 5–8 HD (Medium)
Possessions piecemeal armor (counts as leather), bone
  shortspear

Pain (Su) A living creature injured by the wrackspawn's bone shortspear takes an extra 2d6 points of damage and is sickened with pain for 1 round. A DC 18 Fortitude save halves the damage and negates the sickened effect. The save DC is Constitution-based.

Wrackspawns exist because the evil of demons knows no bounds. The remnants of good souls captured and tortured in the Abyss, wrackspawns live to inflict pain upon others. Fear and pain made them what they are, and these are what they wish to bring to all forms of life.

STRATEGIES AND TACTICS

Wrackspawns charge into combat heedless of any danger to themselves. They use no strategy beyond attacking the nearest living being. Wrackspawns typically ignore undead and constructs unless attacked by them, and even then they swiftly turn toward foes who can feel pain. The only exceptions are their own kind and demons. Wrackspawns innately fear demons and fiendish creatures, and they shy away from them in combat.

Wrackspawns wield ugly shortspears created from their own broken bones. They rarely throw these treasured objects, preferring to use them in melee. Faced with no alternative, a wrackspawn might throw its spear at an opponent it's sure it can kill.

SAMPLE ENCOUNTER

Wrackspawns do not parlay or accept surrender. They exist only to make others feel pain, and they relentlessly pursue that goal. Fiends use wrackspawns as fodder, bullying the creatures into combat before them. Those employing wrackspawns typically bring four or more along with them, having emptied their Abyssal torture chambers of victims. Mortals sometimes gain control of wrackspawns through the use of summoning spells or as "gifts" from a fiend.

Pack (EL 10): A vrock named Azrath discovered an open *gate* to the Material Plane while transporting four wrackspawns to the service of a marilith. The *gate* closed behind Azrath as it went through, and now the vrock roams the countryside looking for the being who opened the portal in hopes of controlling that power. Azrath follows its pack of wrackspawns from the air as they chase and attack any creature larger than a hare. Occasionally the vrock herds the wrackspawns toward some target they cannot yet see. When confronting foes worthy of its trouble, Azrath allows the wrackspawns to attack for a few rounds while casting *mirror image* and *heroism* on itself. Then Azrath uses its stunning screech on foes from the air before landing to attack with spores and melee attacks.

ECOLOGY

Wrackspawns contribute nothing to an ecology beyond destruction. Although they do not eat, they maim and kill at will. Typically, they ignore Tiny or smaller creatures in favor of larger prey, but with nothing else to attack, they even resort to smashing insects. Wrackspawns never attack demons or each other, and they care little for creatures that can't feel pain, such as undead and constructs. If they are allowed to roam unchecked through an area, their depredations can lead to the loss of large predators and herbivores.

Environment: Wrackspawns are native to the Infinite Layers of the Abyss. As demonic footsoldiers, they are most often found in the torture chambers where they come into

---

WRACKSPAWN LORE

Characters with ranks in Knowledge (the planes) can learn more about wrackspawns. When a character makes a successful skill check, the following lore is revealed, including the information from lower DCs.

Knowledge (the Planes)

DC	Result
13	This creature is a wrackspawn, a minor demon. This result reveals all outsider traits.
18	Wrackspawns are the remains of good souls tortured beyond sanity. They exist only to cause suffering to others. Their bone shortspears can cause sickening pain to living things.
23	A wrackspawn often ignores nonliving targets and Tiny or smaller creatures. Despite lacking eyes, it can detect victims up to 120 feet away—it's impossible to hide from a wrackspawn within that range.

being or massing in armies on the Plain of Infinite Portals. Sometimes small groups serve demon lords as guardians or for use in blood sport (such as hunting condemned souls).

Typical Physical Characteristics: A wrackspawn is the twisted wreckage of a humanoid being, although it is barely recognizable as such. The skin has been burned and torn from its body, and the exposed muscles are blackened. Its joints are bent in unnatural directions, limbs sometimes truncated or split. The ravaged face no longer has eyes, and few distinguishing features remain.

Most wrackspawns stand about 5 feet tall and weigh 250 pounds.

SOCIETY

Wrackspawns come into being when demons torture captive good souls in the Abyss. The process of transformation takes longer for some than others, but most good souls endure several years of mistreatment at the hands of their captors before succumbing to their ministrations and becoming wrackspawns.

After creation, wrackspawns continue their own suffering by pulling broken bones from their bodies to craft into jagged shortspears. These awful weapons channel the wrackspawns' pain and rage, allowing them to inflict that pain upon others. A wrackspawn that loses its bone shortspear does everything it can to retrieve it. If a wrackspawn cannot regain its weapon, it cannot imbue its attacks with pain or make a new weapon. Bone shortspears separated from wrackspawns have no special qualities.

Other demons have little concern for the fate of these creatures. In most cases, they are accidental results of torture. When a good soul is transformed into a wrackspawn, it becomes a creature of pure evil, and demons find torturing it far less entertaining. Even so, wrackspawns are more useful in combat than dretches, and demons sometimes use them as expendable troops.

TYPICAL TREASURE

Wrackspawns possess nothing other than their bone weapons and piecemeal scraps of armor looted from infernal battlefields.

FOR PLAYER CHARACTERS

A wrackspawn can be summoned using *summon monster IV* or a higher-level *summon monster* spell. Treat the wrackspawn as if it were on the 4th-level list on the Summon Monster table (PH 287).

WRACKSPAWNS IN EBERRON

The nightmarish origin of wrackspawns suggests that they are products of Xoriat. If this is so, they are most likely the remnants of beings who crossed between the planar boundaries when last the Realm of Madness was coterminous with Eberron thousands of years ago. Another possibility is that the daelkyr created these twisted beings from humanoids, much like they did the dolgaunts and the dolgrims. Their burnt and flayed appearance is a physical manifestation of the mental anguish a normal creature experiences when plunged into the mind-shattering environment of Xoriat.

Whatever the truth of the wrackspawns' origin, they are unmistakably alien to the Material Plane now. Most are in the service of demonic armies that fight endlessly on the barren plains of Shavarath. Do these tortured souls find release in death? Even the eternal gray of Dolurrh would be welcome after such an existence. Or do they reconstitute on the battlefield, perhaps as even more wretched minions?

Wrackspawn

WRACKSPAWNS IN FAERÛN

Mortals who refuse to accept the gods' existence (the Faithless) receive harsh punishment from Kelemvor, the Lord of the Dead. The Faithless are transformed into a living wall around his City of Judgment, and over time their individual consciousness breaks down until nothing of their souls remains. Occasionally, a demon prince opens a *portal* to the Fugue Plane and sends through raiding fiends that rend the wall and release some of those trapped within, carrying them back to the Abyss. There the maddened souls endure cruel torment that makes the doom of the wall seem a kindness until, through pain, they are transformed into wrackspawns.

Illus. by J. Zhang

As detailed in the *Monster Manual*, the deadly yuan-ti are masters of intrigue and deception, constantly plotting and scheming for power. To the yuan-ti, open warfare is a waste of resources. A dagger in the back, a vial of poison slipped into a drink, an insurrection fomented among trusted retainers—these are the weapons of choice. Confident in their effectiveness, the yuan-ti employ these methods against their own kind and against other races.

This section presents three sample yuan-ti agents. The pureblood slayer is a spy and assassin who ventures into human society. The halfblood deceiver performs a similar role among the savage humanoids. Where the slayer targets powerful warriors, politicians, and spellcasters, the deceiver seizes control of a tribe and turns it into an unwitting weapon of the yuan-ti. The abomination cult leader is an example of a powerful yuan-ti who stands at the center of a vast network of underlings, conspiracies, and shadowy plans. It manipulates events to suit its needs, sets its enemies against each other, and uses its skill at diplomacy to win allies and to isolate enemies.

Yuan-ti racial traits are summarized on page 263 of the *Monster Manual*.

PUREBLOOD SLAYER

The humanoid figure before you is clad in form-fitting black clothing. The glint of chainmail can be seen from beneath a fold in her shirt. She appears human, but for a moment her eyes take on a snakelike appearance. Without a sound, she draws a rapier and leaps to attack.

PUREBLOOD SLAYER   CR 10
Female yuan-ti pureblood rogue 1/assassin 7
NE Medium monstrous humanoid
Init +4; Senses darkvision 60 ft.; Listen +17, Spot +17
Languages Abyssal, Common, Draconic, Elven, Yuan-Ti

AC 21, touch 14, flat-footed 21; Dodge, Mobility, improved uncanny dodge, uncanny dodge
(+4 Dex, +6 armor, +1 natural)
hp 60 (12 HD)
SR 22
Fort +4 (+7 against poison), Ref +15, Will +6

Speed 30 ft. (6 squares); Spring Attack
Melee +1 human bane rapier +14/+9 (1d6+1/18–20 plus poison) or
Melee +1 human bane rapier +16/+11 (1d6+3/18–20 plus 2d6 plus poison) against humans
Ranged mwk composite longbow +14/+9 (1d8+1/×3 plus poison)
Space 5 ft.; Reach 5 ft.
Base Atk +9; Grp +10
Atk Options Blind-Fight, death attack, poison (Large scorpion venom, DC 14, 1d4 Con/1d4 Con), sneak attack +5d6
Special Actions alternate form
Combat Gear 3 doses of Large scorpion venom, 1 dose of purple worm poison (DC 24, 1d6 Str/2d6 Str), 1 dose of shadow essence (DC 17, 1 Str drain/2d6 Str)
Assassin Spells Known (CL 7th, 10% arcane spell failure chance):
3rd (3/day)—*deep slumber* (DC 16), *false life*, *magic circle against good*
2nd (4/day)—*alter self*, *cat's grace*, *fox's cunning*, *invisibility*
1st (4/day)—*feather fall*, *jump*, *obscuring mist*, *true strike*
Spell-Like Abilities (CL 12th):
At will—*detect poison* (CL 6th)
1/day—*animal trance* (DC 12), *cause fear* (DC 11), *charm person* (DC 11), *darkness*, *entangle* (DC 11)

Abilities Str 12, Dex 18, Con 13, Int 16, Wis 11, Cha 11
SQ alternate form, poison use, trapfinding
Feats Alertness^B, Blind-Fight^B, Dodge, Mobility, Spring Attack, Weapon Finesse
Skills Balance +6, Concentration +8, Disguise +14 (+19 when impersonating a human), Hide +19, Listen +17, Move Silently +19, Spot +17, Tumble +18
Possessions +2 mithral shirt, +1 human bane rapier, masterwork composite longbow (+1 Str bonus) with 40 arrows

Death Attack (Ex) DC 20, paralysis effect lasts 1d6+7 rounds (*DMG* 180).

A pureblood slayer is a highly trained assassin charged with venturing into human lands in disguise, identifying powerful figures and potential threats to yuan-ti plans, and either slaying them or subverting them with bribes, promises of power, and other temptations.

The pureblood slayer presented here had the following ability scores before racial adjustments and Hit Dice ability score increases: Str 12, Dex 15, Con 13, Int 14, Wis 10, Cha 8.

Strategies and Tactics
A pureblood slayer always enters a fight with a clear plan and well-considered preparations. Unless she has surprise or can ambush her foes, she chooses discretion as the better part of valor. The typical slayer is well aware that she cannot stand toe-to-toe with a heavily armored paladin, a raging barbarian, or a skilled fighter. Only when she strikes with surprise can she defeat her enemies.

The slayer uses her Disguise skill to draw close to an opponent and observe him for a time. Once she has watched him long enough to use her death attack ability, she hides, casts *invisibility*, poisons her rapier, and moves in for the kill. If possible, she begins her preparation while watching her quarry. By using Spring Attack, she can slash at her opponent and move away before he can react.

The exact approach that a slayer uses depends on where she plans to make her attack. She prefers public places with large

YUAN-TI LORE
Characters with ranks in Knowledge (nature) can learn more about yuan-ti. When a character makes a successful skill check, the following lore is revealed, including the information from lower DCs.

Knowledge (Nature)
DC	Result
13	This is a yuan-ti, an evil snakelike being. This result reveals all monstrous humanoid traits.
18	Yuan-ti have deadly poisonous bites, and some can also burn enemies with acid.
23	Some yuan-ti can disguise themselves to infiltrate humanoid societies and sow discord.
28	Yuan-ti consider themselves to be favored by their evil deity and wish to advance their own status.

crowds and background noise, such as a tavern or inn. The slayer adopts the guise of a traveler or adventurer, observes her target as he eats or drinks, and then strikes at him from the anonymity of the crowd of patrons. This tactic allows her to use a variety of disguises and keep her opponents off balance.

In the wilds, the slayer relies on her alternate form ability to draw close to her victims. She hides in the grass, watches her foe, and strikes at him while still in snake form. This tactic is also useful against a victim's mount or allies. A well-placed bite can kill a horse, leaving the victim stranded in the middle of nowhere and giving the slayer plenty of time to plot her next move.

When the slayer is forced into a confrontation, such as when defending a yuan-ti lair, she relies on Spring Attack to defeat opponents. She poisons several arrows and uses ranged attacks to soften up resistance before darting in to attack. If possible, she uses *invisibility* to stand in the open and observe a foe.

HALFBLOOD DECEIVER

This creature is built like an orc warlord, but it moves with greater speed and confidence. It studies you with the probing eye of a master tactician. It licks its lips as if carefully weighing its options.

HALFBLOOD DECEIVER	**CR 6**

Male yuan-ti halfblood barbarian 2
CE Medium monstrous humanoid
Init +6; **Senses** darkvision 60 ft.; Listen +15, Spot +15
Languages Common, Draconic, Giant, Goblin, Orc, Undercommon, Yuan-ti

AC 21, touch 14, flat-footed 21; uncanny dodge (+2 Dex, +5 armor, +4 natural)
hp 77 (9 HD)
SR 18
Fort +8, **Ref** +7, **Will** +8

Speed 40 ft. (8 squares)
Melee mwk greataxe +12/+7 (1d12+3/×3) and bite +10 (1d6+1/×3 plus poison)
Ranged mwk composite longbow +12/+7 (1d8+2/×3)
Space 5 ft.; **Reach** 5 ft.
Base Atk +9; **Grp** +11
Atk Options Blind-Fight, poison (DC 16, 1d6 Con/1d6 Con), *produce acid* (3d6 acid damage)
Special Actions rage 1/day (8 rounds)
Combat Gear *potion of invisibility*
Spell-Like Abilities (CL 9th):
　At will—*detect poison* (CL 6th)
　3/day—*animal trance* (DC 18), *cause fear* (DC 17), *entangle* (DC 17)
　1/day—*deeper darkness*, *neutralize poison*, *suggestion* (DC 19)

Abilities Str 14, Dex 15, Con 16, Int 20, Wis 16, Cha 22
SQ alternate form, *chameleon power*, fast movement, trapfinding
Feats Alertness[B], Blind-Fight[B], Improved Initiative, Multiattack, Skill Focus (Disguise), Weapon Focus (bite)
Skills Bluff +18, Concentration +10, Diplomacy +14, Disguise +21, Hide +10 (+20 with *chameleon power*), Intimidate +8, Jump +6, Listen +15, Move Silently +10, Spot +15
Possessions combat gear plus +1 *mithral shirt*, masterwork greataxe, masterwork composite longbow (+2 Str bonus) with 20 arrows, *Quaal's feather token (bird)*

Produce Acid (Sp) A halfblood deceiver has the ability to psionically exude acid from its body, dealing 3d6 points of acid damage to the next creature it touches, including a creature hit by its bite attack. If the halfblood deceiver is grappling or pinning a foe when it uses this power, its grasp deals 5d6 points of acid damage. The acid becomes inert when it leaves the halfblood deceiver's body, and the halfblood deceiver is immune to its effects.

Chameleon Power (Sp) A halfblood can psionically change the color of his equipment and skin, granting it a +10 circumstance bonus on Hide checks.

A halfblood deceiver infiltrates orc, goblin, and ogre tribes while in disguise, assassinates the current chieftain or helps a puppet rise to power, and then manipulates the humanoids to serve his ends. In this manner, the yuan-ti turns potential enemies into useful allies. A sudden orc attack or similar calamity could very well be the work of a halfblood furthering some unguessable yuan-ti machination.

The halfblood deceiver presented here had the following ability scores before racial adjustments and Hit Dice ability score increases: Str 10, Dex 13, Con 14, Int 12, Wis 8, Cha 15.

Strategies and Tactics

A halfblood deceiver relies on trickery. His combat training and wild rage make him a skilled warrior, but underneath that berserker façade lurks a cunning, calculating mind. A deceiver rages only when doing so is a surprise tactic or when necessary for its survival. The deceiver wields the tribe he leads or influences like a rapier, carefully guiding it against the yuan-ti's enemies. The deceiver slips from tribe to tribe, using each of them in turn and abandoning them when they no longer serve his purposes.

A deceiver's campaigns of terror are wide in scope and difficult to detect. In the fall, he leads his orc tribe to raid and burn a kingdom's crops, cutting into the food supply. When the orcs are finally run down and slain, the deceiver escapes. Over the winter, he infiltrates a goblin tribe in the mountains. When spring comes, the deceiver leads the goblins on raids against granaries and other storage centers. These attacks might appear unrelated but combine to put immense, continual pressure on the region's food supply. Burnt crops, raided caravans, and destroyed stores all add up to famine, even during years with excellent weather.

Deceivers seize power through careful manipulation and intelligent planning. Their overwhelming personalities and potent intellects allow them to easily outmaneuver the simple goblin and orc chieftains they encounter. Usually, a deceiver helps a subchief attain power and then rules through that proxy. While a deceiver invariably draws some suspicion, he can deflect the simple-minded orcs and goblins by leading them on successful raids. Few evil humanoids question a leader who brings them gold, slaves, food, and strong drink.

When confronted in battle, a deceiver weighs the risks of exposing himself against the reward of victory. A deceiver never feels loyalty to the tribe he leads. After all, he need only adopt a new disguise and find a new tribe to begin manipulating anew. The deceiver's long-term, strategic view of situations leads him to cut and run rather than fight, unless he feels the odds are absolutely in his favor.

ABOMINATION CULT LEADER

A bizarre cross between a serpent and a humanoid stands before you. It wears a chainmail shirt and carries a flaming falchion. A horde of snaky humanoids, ogres, and other creatures surround it. With a single hissed threat, it transforms the rabble into an attentive body of soldiers that move with well-trained precision.

ABOMINATION CULT LEADER	**CR 9**

Yuan-ti abomination marshal* 4
  *Class described in *Miniatures Handbook*
CE Large monstrous humanoid
Init +4; **Senses** darkvision 60 ft., scent; Listen +21, Spot +21
Languages Common, Draconic, Giant, Gnoll, Goblin, Orc, Undercommon, Yuan-Ti

---

AC 24, touch 9, flat-footed 24
  (–1 size, +5 armor, +10 natural)
hp 127 (13 HD)
SR 22
Fort +12, **Ref** +7, **Will** +15

Speed 30 ft. (6 squares), climb 20 ft., swim 20 ft.
Melee +1 flaming falchion +17/+12/+7 (2d6+8/15–20 plus 1d6 fire) and
  bite +15 (2d6+2 plus poison)
Ranged longbow +11/+6/+1 (2d6/×3)
Space 10 ft.; **Reach** 10 ft.
Base Atk +12; **Grp** +21
Atk Options Blind-Fight, auras, constrict 1d6+7, improved grab, poison (DC 19, 1d6 Con/1d6 Con), *produce acid*
Special Actions *aversion*, grant move action 1/day
Spell-Like Abilities (CL 13th):
  At will—*animal trance* (DC 19), *detect poison* (CL 6th), *entangle* (DC 18)
  3/day—*deeper darkness*, *neutralize poison* (DC 21), *suggestion* (DC 20)
  1/day—*baleful polymorph* (DC 22; snake form only), *fear* (DC 21)

Abilities Str 21, Dex 10, Con 20, Int 22, Wis 20, Cha 24
SQ alternate form, chameleon power
Feats Alertness[B], Blind-Fight[B], Combat Casting, Improved Critical (falchion), Improved Initiative, Multiattack, Skill Focus[B] (Diplomacy), Weapon Focus (bite)
Skills Bluff +19, Climb +13, Concentration +21, Diplomacy +22, Intimidate +21, Knowledge (history) +18, Listen +21, Sense Motive +19, Spot +21, Swim +25
Possessions +1 mithral shirt, +1 flaming falchion, longbow with 20 arrows, *brooch of shielding*

Auras (Ex) Affects all allies within 60 feet who can hear an abomination cult leader, have Int 3 or higher, and understand the abomination. The abomination's aura is dismissed if it is dazed, unconscious, stunned, paralyzed, or otherwise unable to be heard or understood by its allies. *Miniatures Handbook* 13.

  The abomination can project one of the following minor auras and can switch auras as a swift action. *Master of Tactics:* +7 bonus on damage rolls when flanking. *Motivate Dexterity:* +7 bonus on Dexterity-based checks, including initiative checks.

  The abomination projects the following major aura in addition to whichever minor aura it chooses to use. *Motivate Attack:* +1 bonus on melee attack rolls.
Constrict (Ex) An abomination cult leader deals 1d6+7 points of damage with a successful grapple check.
Improved Grab (Ex) To use this ability, an abomination cult leader must hit an opponent of up to Large size with a bite attack. It can then attempt to start a grapple as a free

action without provoking attacks of opportunity. If it wins the grapple check, it establishes a hold and can constrict.
Aversion (Sp) As the *antipathy* spell; at will; caster level 16th. This is a psionic compulsion effect targeting one creature within 30 feet. The target must succeed on a DC 25 Will save or gain an aversion to snakes and yuan-ti for 10 minutes. Affected creatures must stay at least 20 feet away from any snakes or yuan-ti, alive or dead; if already within 20 feet, they move away. A subject unable to move away, or one attacked by a snake or yuan-ti, is overcome with revulsion. This revulsion reduces the creature's Dexterity score by 4 points until the effect wears off or the subject is no longer within 20 feet of a snake or yuan-ti.
Grant Move Action (Ex) As a standard action, grant an extra move action to all allies (but not self) within 30 feet. Each of the affected allies takes this extra move action immediately. *Miniatures Handbook* 13.
Produce Acid (Sp) As the halfblood deceiver.
Chameleon Power (Sp) As the halfblood deceiver.
Skills A yuan-ti abomination has a +8 racial bonus on Climb checks and can always choose to take 10 on a Climb check, even if rushed or threatened. It also has a +8 racial bonus on any Swim check to perform some special action or avoid a hazard. It can always choose to take 10 on a Swim check, even if distracted or endangered. It can use the run action while swimming, provided it swims in a straight line.

An abomination cult leader is a commander and mastermind among the yuan-ti. It leads a small cell of purebloods and halfbloods, and a variety of orcs, ogres, and other brutish creatures who serve as mercenaries, slaves, and allies. The cult leader's magnetic personality allows it to transform even the most fumbling rookie into a confident, hard-fighting warrior.

The cult leader presented here had the following ability scores before racial adjustments and Hit Dice ability score increases: Str 13, Dex 8, Con 14, Int 12, Wis 10, Cha 15.

Strategies and Tactics

An abomination cult leader is at its best when surrounded by a number of underlings. Its marshal class levels grant it enormous leadership abilities. Even puny goblins or kobolds are dangerous when commanded by a cult leader.

Usually, a cult leader acquires followers from among the survivors of tribes and clans subverted by a halfblood deceiver. As intended, the tribe causes enough trouble for civilized lands that a local ruler raises an army to defeat it. At that point, the deceiver leads the survivors to the cult leader that commands him. These survivors become virtual slaves, forced to choose between serving the yuan-ti and trying to survive in the wilds.

With orc, ogre, goblin, and gnoll servants gathered in this manner, the abomination cult leader is a daunting foe. Followers quickly learn that servitude has its rewards as the abomination leads them to victory in battle and rewards them with treasure. The yuan-ti weeds out malcontents and incompetents, then executes them.

The cult leader keeps its motivate dexterity aura active most of the time. When battle begins, it and its allies gain a significant bonus on initiative. Once battle is joined, the abomination switches to its master of tactics aura. It then grants a move action to allies to get them into flanking positions. At that point, they cut through the enemy.

While the battle rages, the abomination keeps its allies between it and its enemies. It uses its reach to lash out with its falchion. *Baleful polymorph* and *suggestion* allow it to handle foes that are too strong for its allies. When faced with large numbers of opponents, it relies on its *fear* ability.

An abomination cult leader seeks power, wealth, and strength. It deals openly with other evil creatures. Even the mightiest necromancer or evil priest cannot resist the abomination's honeyed words, well-considered plans, and thoughtful counsel. With both Intelligence and Charisma over 20, the abomination is smart enough to create intricate, effective plans and influential enough to win allies to help see them through.

Yuan-ti pureblood slayer, abomination cult leader, and halfblood deceiver

Cult leaders command both halfblood deceivers and pureblood slayers, setting them both to advance its subtle aims and plans. Even the yuan-ti under its command have little idea of the true scope of their master's goals.

ECOLOGY

Yuan-ti build elaborate cities, erecting temples to their evil pantheon and snatching slaves and sacrifices from the surrounding inhabitants.

Yuan-ti consider themselves favored and devote considerable attention to breeding ever more perfect specimens. Affection has nothing to do with the process. After mating, females lay their eggs in brood chambers and then abandon the clutch to the care of servants called broodguards. Young receive training almost from hatching and mature quickly.

Environment: Yuan-ti are most comfortable in warm forests, usually steaming jungles. Sometimes they inhabit subterranean passages, even right beneath human cities.

Typical Physical Characteristics: Purebloods closely resemble humans and have similar builds. Halfbloods have a variety of serpentine features, such as snake heads or tails. They are otherwise about the size of humans. Abominations are entirely snakelike; they can reach 12 feet in length and weigh up to 300 pounds.

Alignment: Interested only in advancing their own status within their cruel society, yuan-ti are usually chaotic evil.

SOCIETY

Yuan-ti society revolves around status, with the bigger and more powerful abominations at the top of the heap. Individual yuan-ti continually strive to increase their status, even at the expense of their fellows.

Yuan-ti worship a fiendish entity called Merrshaulk, a great, serpentine demigod. They believe themselves to be the deity's favored children and see other creatures as fit only for exploitation and slaughter. All yuan-ti are coldly intelligent, but the abominations rule through both brains and physical intimidation. The lesser yuan-ti dare not disobey their terrifying leaders.

TYPICAL TREASURE

Yuan-ti have double standard treasure for NPCs of their Challenge Rating. They gather wealth for themselves and especially seek magic items to give them an edge.

YUAN-TI AS CHARACTERS

See page 263 of the *Monster Manual* for information on yuan-ti purebloods as characters.

Illus. by D. Hudnut

187

YUAN-TI IGNAN

The creature before you resembles a giant serpent with a human-oid upper body. Long, sharp horns crown its head, and its tail splits about two-thirds of the way along its length, ending in sharp hooks. It carries a heavy mace in one hand and a small shield in the other. The colors of its scales shift from dull brown to dark red, and a slight heat haze surrounds it.

Yuan-ti Ignan	**CR 7**

Always CE Large monstrous humanoid (fire)
Init +1; **Senses** darkvision 60 ft.; Listen +8, Spot +8
Languages Common, Ignan, Yuan-Ti

AC 19, touch 10, flat-footed 18
    (−1 size, +1 Dex, +1 shield, +8 natural)
hp 93 (11 HD); **DR** 10/magic
Immune fire
SR 15
Fort +7, **Ref** +8, **Will** +9
Weakness vulnerable to cold

Speed 30 ft. (6 squares)
Melee heavy mace +16/+11/+6 (2d6+5 plus 1d6 fire) and
    gore +13 (1d8+2 plus 1d6 fire) and
    tail slap +13 (1d8+2 plus 1d6 fire)
Space 10 ft.; **Reach** 10 ft.
Base Atk +11; **Grp** +20
Atk Options Power Attack, constrict, improved grab, magic strike, tail grapple

Abilities Str 21, Dex 13, Con 18, Int 6, Wis 14, Cha 11
Feats Alertness, Multiattack, Power Attack, Weapon Focus (heavy mace)
Skills Listen +8, Move Silently +4, Spot +8, Survival +5
Advancement by character class; **Favored Class** barbarian; see text
Possessions light steel shield, heavy mace

Constrict (Ex) A yuan-ti ignan deals automatic tail slap damage (including fire damage) with a successful grapple check. It also deals this damage when it successfully uses improved grab with its tail slap attack.

Improved Grab (Ex) To use this ability, a yuan-ti ignan must hit an opponent of up to Large size with a tail slap attack. It can then attempt to start a grapple as a free action without provoking attacks of opportunity. If it wins the grapple check, it establishes a hold and can constrict.

Tail Grapple (Ex) A yuan-ti ignan's long, powerful tail allows it to coil around a foe without hampering its ability to defend itself or to fight with the weapons it wields. If the ignan grapples a foe using its improved grab ability, it does not lose its Dexterity bonus to AC. It can make a single grapple check against the foe grappled in this manner as a swift action each round. The ignan is free to perform most other actions as normal; if it wants to move, it must obey the standard rules for moving while in a grapple.

The yuan-ti ignan loses the option to spend its swift action in this manner if it uses a standard or full action to grapple the foe trapped in its tail. The reverse is also true. Once the yuan-ti ignan uses its swift action in this manner, it cannot take a standard or full action to grapple the foe already trapped in its tail.

A yuan-ti ignan can use armed or natural attacks against a creature grappled in this manner.

Ignans are the product of yuan-ti experimentation designed to create a creature resembling an abomination with elemental qualities, in this case fire. Some part of yuan-ti ignans' bloodline includes salamanders, but they are still mostly serpent.

STRATEGIES AND TACTICS

Yuan-ti ignans are fiercely aggressive creatures, more inclined to charge into melee combat than to lay traps or spring ambushes. They are simple, brutish fighters. When the yuan-ti must repel invaders, or when they prefer a blatant display of pure force, they deploy the ignans.

Working alone, a yuan-ti ignan seeks to pin down enemy spellcasters by grappling them with its tail, then uses its heavy mace to deal with other opponents in melee combat. Because yuan-ti ignans are so cruel, though, they often save the last strike in a full attack to deliver a quick mace blow to a grappled opponent.

When working in groups (usually two to four), yuan-ti ignans are actually less effective. Their bloodlust overrides their puny common sense. When one ignan successfully grapples an opponent, the others virtually ignore any remaining enemies and instead attempt to seize control of the grappled creature in a ghastly tug-of-war. (The highest grapple check wins; if the grappled opponent has the highest result, it takes advantage of the confusion to pull free.) Once the grappled creature is dead or beyond their reach, the others turn their full attention back to the remaining foes. Without the commanding presence of a smarter yuan-ti, ignans do not use battle tactics.

SAMPLE ENCOUNTERS

Yuan-ti ignans generally fight for their more intelligent yuan-ti masters. Those encountered alone are usually the

YUAN-TI IGNAN LORE

Characters with ranks in Knowledge (nature) can learn more about yuan-ti ignans. When a character makes a successful skill check, the following lore is revealed, including the information from lower DCs.

Knowledge (Nature)

DC	Result
17	This creature is a yuan-ti ignan, the result of bizarre yuan-ti breeding experiments with elementals. This result reveals all monstrous humanoid traits and the fire subtype.
22	Yuan-ti ignans are aggressive fighters, their bloodlust fueling their fiery nature. Their skin is searing hot to the touch, and they are immune to fire attacks.
27	The yuan-ti ignan's forked, barbed tail allows it to grab and crush an opponent with a single attack.
32	A yuan-ti ignan attacks by trapping its enemies within its coils. Even when the ignan has a victim grappled, it still fights and dodges its enemies without any hindrance.

survivors of a battle that destroyed a yuan-ti stronghold. With their great strength and physical toughness, ignans are better at surviving the chaos of battle or a surprise raid than their superiors.

Individual (EL 7): A lone yuan-ti ignan seeks to begin an encounter as close to its opponents as possible. This lone brute patrols the jungle around a yuan-ti stronghold. It slips from one copse of trees to another. Rather than travel a steady circuit through an area, it waits at one sentry point for a time before moving to the next spot.

Bodyguard (EL 9): A yuan-ti abomination keeps a single ignan as a personal bodyguard. In battle, the abomination waits for its ignan servant to grapple a foe. It then uses its *aversion* ability to force the grappled creature's allies to move away, making it difficult for them to help.

ECOLOGY

Like yuan-ti, ignans settle wherever they can establish a temple—anywhere from remote ruins to forgotten passageways underneath human settlements.

Despite their formidable combat prowess, ignans are not trusted by the majority of yuanti, and are considered highly expendable. Their unpredictable cruelty makes them a danger to the tribe, and when not sufficiently occupied, they commit acts of wanton destruction out of sheer boredom. Stories persist of yuan-ti fortresses overrun and now controlled by renegade ignans. Thus, the yuan-ti take care to keep beasts and slaves on hand when they must breed enough ignans to form a fighting force. These creatures form a ready supply of sport to keep the ignans occupied.

As a result of this risk of insurrection, yuan-ti leaders frequently manufacture reasons for ignan gangs to undertake lengthy missions outside the enclave. Wise yuan-ti gather their ignans on the eve of battle, rarely sooner.

Sometimes, a yuan-ti ignan that breaks away from its masters forms its own tribe. These creatures sometimes see value in forcing others to obey their will, especially if doing so nets them more captives. Weaker humanoid creatures, especially goblins and kobolds, are prime candidates for servitude.

Environment: As with all yuan-ti, yuan-ti ignans are found most often in warm forests. Their part of the yuan-ti

enclave is easily identified by the scorched appearance of the surroundings. When the rest of the tribe lairs underground (say, in the ruins of an old temple), yuan-ti ignans generally occupy the deepest parts of the enclave, where their intense body heat actually serves the tribe by keeping the tunnels warm.

Typical Physical Characteristics: A yuan-ti ignan is 10 to 14 feet long and weighs 250 to 400 pounds. Females are usually darker than males, tending toward grays and browns rather than reds.

Yuan-ti ignan

TYPICAL TREASURE

Yuan-ti ignans have standard treasure for their Challenge Rating, about 3,600 gp, but never carry flammable items. These creatures enjoy burning and destroying items too much to keep such fragile goods. They prefer gems, which are difficult to damage with flames.

Ignans with class levels have treasure appropriate to NPCs of their Challenge Rating.

YUAN-TI IGNANS WITH CLASS LEVELS

Yuan-ti worship Merrshaulk, who prompted and directed the formation of the yuan-ti bloodline. Yuan-ti ignans very rarely become clerics. They leave spellcasting to the yuan-ti purebloods.

Level Adjustment: +8.

YUAN-TI IGNANS IN EBERRON

Yuan-ti ignans have been spotted in the jungles of Xen'drik. Rumors persist of a great stone fortress overrun with these creatures, who fan out in raids on the surrounding area. Woe to any expedition caught in the jungle when the ignans seek victims to sate their boundless appetite for violence.

YUAN-TI IGNANS IN FAERÛN

The yuan-ti of the Serpent Hills created ignans as a favor to the red dragons who make their lairs there, in return for certain magical treasures. Red dragons employ yuan-ti ignans as guards for their lairs or shock troops in battle against the area's copper dragons.

Illus. by A. Stokes

YUGOLOTH

Greedy, malicious, and beholden to no standard of honor, yugoloths are fiends native to the Bleak Eternity of Gehenna. They happily offer their services to the highest bidder, serving demons and devils alike in the eternal clashes of the Lower Planes. They enjoy nothing more than causing suffering.

The glossary lists racial traits common to all yugoloths.

CORRUPTOR OF FATE

A corpulent creature with sickly yellow skin wears black studded leather armor. It is armed with a short sword and shortbow. As it attacks, a smell of brimstone emanates from its body and the faint sound of rolling dice can be heard.

CORRUPTOR OF FATE   CR 5
Always NE Medium outsider (evil, extraplanar, yugoloth)
Init +8; **Senses** darkvision 60 ft.; Listen +10, Spot +10
Languages Abyssal, Draconic, Infernal; telepathy 100 ft.

AC 18, touch 14, flat-footed 14; Dodge
   (+4 Dex, +4 armor)
hp 52 (7 HD)
Immune acid, energy drain, necromantic effects, negative
   energy effects, poison
Resist cold 10, fire 10, electricity 10; **SR** 14
Fort +8, **Ref** +9, **Will** +5

Speed 30 ft. (6 squares)
Melee mwk short sword +12/+7 (1d6+2/19–20 plus bestow
   curse)
Ranged composite shortbow +11/+6 (1d6/×3)
Space 5 ft.; **Reach** 5 ft.
Base Atk +7; **Grp** +9
Atk Options aligned strike (evil), bestow curse
Special Actions corrupting gaze

Abilities Str 15, Dex 19, Con 17, Int 10, Wis 10, Cha 10
SQ unluck, yugoloth traits
Feats Dodge, Improved Initiative, Weapon Finesse
Skills Balance +6, Disguise +10, Escape Artist +14,
   Hide +14, Jump +4, Listen +10, Move Silently +14,
   Sleight of Hand +14, Spot +10, Tumble +14, Use Rope +4
   (+6 involving bindings)
Advancement by character class; **Favored Class** rogue;
   see text
Possessions +1 studded leather armor, masterwork short
   sword, composite shortbow with 20 arrows

Bestow Curse (Su) As the *bestow curse* spell; at will; Will
   DC 16; caster level 7th.
This ability affects those touching or touched by a corruptor of fate or its weapons. A cursed subject must roll percentile dice each turn. On a roll of 01–50, it can take no action. On a roll of 51–100, it can act normally. This is a necromantic effect. Undead are unaffected by a corruptor of fate's bestow curse ability. The save DC is Constitution-based.
Corrupting Gaze (Su) A corruptor of fate can blast its enemies with a glance, at a range of up to 30 feet. Creatures that meet the corruptor's gaze must succeed on a DC 13 Fortitude save or take 1d6 points of damage and a –1 penalty on attack rolls, skill checks, and saving throws for 1 minute. The save DC is Charisma-based.
Unluck (Su) Roll twice for attacks and damage against a corruptor of fate; the attacker must use the lower result. This is a mind-affecting necromantic effect.

A corruptor of fate is a strange creature that brings bad luck. It favors stealth and cunning to inflict suffering.

Corruptor of Fate Assassin

This corpulent creature covers most of its sickly yellow skin with loose black clothing and black studded leather armor.

CORRUPTOR OF FATE ASSASSIN   CR 10
Male corruptor of fate assassin 5
NE Medium outsider (evil, extraplanar, yugoloth)
Init +11; **Senses** darkvision 60 ft.; Listen +15, Spot +15
Languages Abyssal, Draconic, Infernal; telepathy 100 ft.

AC 24, touch 18, flat-footed 24; Dodge, Mobility, improved
   uncanny dodge, uncanny dodge
   (+7 Dex, +5 armor, +1 deflection, +1 natural)
hp 111 (12 HD)
Immune acid, energy drain, necromantic effects, negative
   energy effects, poison
Resist cold 10, fire 10, electricity 10; **SR** 19
Fort +11 (+13 against poison), **Ref** +16, **Will** +6

Speed 30 ft. (6 squares)
Melee +1 short sword +18/+13 (1d6+4/19–20 plus bestow
   curse)
Ranged +1 composite shortbow +18/+13 (1d6+4/×3 plus
   poison)
Space 5 ft.; **Reach** 5 ft.
Base Atk +10; **Grp** +13
Atk Options aligned strike (evil), death attack, poison
   (shadow essence, DC 17, 1 Str drain/2d6 Str), sneak
   attack +3d6
Special Actions corrupting gaze
Combat Gear 3 doses of shadow essence, 2 *potions of cure
   serious wounds*, *potion of fly*
Assassin Spells Known (CL 5th):
   2nd (2/day)—*cat's grace*, *invisibility*, *spider climb*
   1st (4/day)—*feather fall*, *jump*, *obscuring mist*, *true strike*

Abilities Str 16, Dex 25, Con 20, Int 13, Wis 10, Cha 8
SQ poison use, unluck, yugoloth traits
Feats Dodge, Improved Initiative, Mobility, Weapon Finesse
Skills Balance +19, Disguise +9, Escape Artist +17,
   Hide +22, Jump +5, Listen +15, Move Silently +22,
   Sleight of Hand +17, Spot +15, Tumble +22, Use Rope +7
   (+9 involving bindings)
Possessions combat gear plus +2 studded leather armor, +1
   short sword, +1 composite shortbow (+3 Str bonus) with 20
   arrows, *amulet of natural armor +1*, *ring of protection +1*

Unluck (Su) As corruptor of fate.
Bestow Curse (Su) As corruptor of fate; Will DC 18; caster
   level 12th.
Death Attack (Ex) DC 16, paralysis effect lasts 1d6+5 rounds
   (*DMG* 180).
Corrupting Gaze (Su) As corruptor of fate; Fort DC 15
   negates.

In keeping with its solitary and stealthy ways, a corruptor of fate often takes levels of assassin to complement its cruel abilities.

The corruptor of fate assassin presented here had the following ability scores before racial adjustments and Hit Dice ability score increases: Str 12, Dex 15, Con 14, Int 13, Wis 10, Cha 8.

Strategies and Tactics

Corruptors of fate work alone or sometimes with a group of undead or a construct or two. They rarely team up with other corruptors of fate.

When encountered, corruptors are usually in mercenary service. Their assignments emphasize assassination, but occasionally they're used to guard a valuable asset, especially if the owner expects a threat.

Corruptors of fate take their assignments very seriously, but also have a strong instinct for self-preservation. If a corruptor is clearly outmatched, it retreats with the intent to return shortly with reinforcements.

Sample Encounters

Unlike many yugoloths, corruptors of fate don't have the innate ability to use *plane shift*. Transportation is usually arranged by a corruptor's patron or by a summoning or calling spell.

Individual (EL 5): A lone corruptor of fate might be encountered under a wide variety of circumstances.

EL 5: A corruptor of fate named Misfortune is on an assassination mission. Her target is the mayor of a small town. Why the mayor? Misfortune doesn't know. She suspects the assignment is part of a much larger and convoluted plot conceived by her patron, a mind flayer.

Guard Duty (EL 6–8): A corruptor of fate is often accompanied by undead or constructs. It prefers the company of intelligent undead such as wraiths or even shadows, but can be found with skeletons and zombies.

EL 7: Malefactor, a corruptor of fate, and two shadows guard a half-fiend's abode.

Corruptor of fate

Planar Ally (EL 5–10): A *planar ally* spell can call one corruptor of fate with up to 5 class levels. A *greater planar ally* spell can call two corruptors of fate with up to 2 class levels each.

EL 10: Malfeasance (male corruptor of fate assassin 5) has been called to the Material Plane by a powerful cleric to eliminate the threat of a pesky enemy—possibly the PCs.

Raiding Party (EL 8–12): A corruptor of fate might lead a company of other yugoloths, undead, or constructs on a mission to retrieve an item, kidnap a person, or kill a target.

EL 9: Twisted Fate, a corruptor of fate, and three canoloth yugoloths (*MM III* 200) make a strategic strike against a small village to get a holy relic from the local church. Their patron is a powerful nycaloth commander (*MM III* 202) named General Commander Render, who gives orders without explanations.

Gatekeepers (EL 12–14): Guarding an important site, such as a planar gate, is the province of a skilled corruptor of fate assassin, usually accompanied by one or more allies.

EL 12: Calamity (female corruptor of fate assassin 5) and a stone golem guard a gate that leads to Gehenna in an abandoned monastery on the Material Plane.

Mercenary Troopers (EL 12–18): As mercenary yugoloths, corruptors of fate might be hired by demons, devils, or more powerful yugoloths.

EL 14: Two yugoloth commanders dispute the deadliness of the devourer compared to the dread wraith. They each wager their patronage of a thriving corruptor of fate crèche. To settle the bet, they have formed a team of a devourer and a dread wraith to travel together on a killing spree on the Material Plane. They have added a corruptor of fate 5th-level assassin named Malice to keep track of which undead made the killing blow against a creature. Each commander believes that Malice will act to further her patron's interest. Malice has taken bribes from both and doesn't care which undead triumphs. In fact, she intends to announce a tie upon her return, no matter what the result.

EL 16: Soulbinder, an 11th-level male human wizard lich, is quite cunning. He resides in a sunken lair, like an inverted tower, under the sewers of a great metropolis. To protect him, he has an iron golem crafted by his late mentor and Malign, a corruptor of fate assassin 5, as his guards.

Ecology

Corruptors of fate are outsiders with no need to sleep, eat, or breathe. Their apparent fatness is their natural form and entirely unconnected with food intake. From birth, a corruptor has the basic body proportions of an adult.

Once a year for about a week, each adult corruptor of fate feels the urge to return to Gehenna and mate. This is the only time a corruptor of fate willingly seeks the company of another of its kind. A young corruptor reaches maturity at about ten years of age.

The mother has no maternal feelings toward a newborn corruptor. She deposits it in a crèche (a shared nursery) in Gehenna to be raised by constructs or undead slaves, which are immune to the necromantic abilities of the infant corruptors.

Environment: Corruptors of fate are native to the Bleak Eternity of Gehenna. Like other yugoloths, they're planar mercenaries that go wherever their employers send them.

Typical Physical Characteristics: A corruptor of fate stands about 5 feet tall and weighs about 200 pounds. Its body

Illus. by J. Zhang

resembles that of a very chubby humanoid. In contrast, its face looks emaciated, with thin yellow skin stretched tightly across its skull. Its eyes glow with a lurid light.

Male and female corruptors of fate look very similar. Both have bosomlike rolls of fat on their chests, so most perceive them as female (DC 20 Spot check to correctly determine a corruptor's gender).

The smell of brimstone is typical of all corruptors of fate, a by-product of their biology. It is generally noticeable only when a corruptor attacks. Skills checks to track a corruptor of fate using scent receive a +2 bonus.

A corruptor of fate is accompanied by a faint sound of rolling dice, a supernatural illusion telepathically "heard" by anyone in combat with the corruptor. It is an automatic response and cannot be stopped.

Alignment: Corruptors of fate, like all yugoloths, are always neutral evil.

Society

Life for a corruptor of fate is generally one violent assignment after another. From birth, a corruptor learns to look to its own survival, even before the demands of a mercenary role.

Growing up is difficult. Older corruptors of fate torment weaker or younger creatures. A powerful yugoloth, usually of commander level or higher, sponsors each crèche. Often the stewardship of the crèche changes hands according to political machinations and upheavals in yugoloth society, which affect the growing young as well.

The constructs or undead that raise the children are far from nurturing or maternal. They are entrusted only with providing the most basic needs, little more than keeping the young safe from external threats. Guardians occasionally intervene if their young charges are liable to kill each other during sibling conflicts.

The safest course of action for a young corruptor is to avoid notice. This environment creates an ideal training ground for potential assassins: They learn the merits of stealth and disguise, and they hone their desire to kill. They come to despise all creatures, especially other corruptors of fate, and feel most at home with undead and constructs.

Once it reaches maturity, a corruptor of fate leaves the crèche to begin its mercenary career. The crèche's current patron gives a corruptor its first assignment (usually to kill one of the patron's rivals). If the newcomer is successful, the young adult's skills are considered sufficient to enter the assassin prestige class. If unsuccessful—a result that usually means death—the patron sends a team with a more experienced corruptor to finish the job.

A yugoloth patron uses corruptors of fate for both lethal assignments and devastating "warnings" to rivals or disobedient underlings. These "warnings" usually involve near-lethal attacks that leave the target cursed. Through regular, challenging assignments, a patron endeavors to keep a corruptor busy and content.

A corruptor of fate might occasionally decide to disobey its patron's orders. Corruptors aren't apt to seize power themselves, though, being happiest in service. One that goes rogue seeks a different patron, such as a fiend or a mind flayer. Corruptors prefer evil masters but aren't picky; some even find their way into the service of an immoral ruler on the Material Plane.

Typical Treasure

Corruptors of fate without class levels have standard treasure for their Challenge Rating, about 1,600 gp. They invest in their equipment, demonstrating a keen sense of self-preservation. Most of their items are durable armor or weapons with perhaps one or two potions or other consumable items. Assassins carry two to five vials of their favorite poison.

For Player Characters

A corruptor of fate can be called using a *planar ally* spell. It can also be summoned by *summon monster VI* or a higher-level *summon monster* spell. Treat the corruptor of fate as if it were on the 6th-level list on the Summon Monster table (PH 287).

Corruptors of Fate with Class Levels

Corruptors' favored class is rogue, and many take levels of the assassin prestige class. The rare corruptor of fate that chooses to become a cleric owes allegiance to no deity but to its racial philosophy of bringing ill luck and death to others. Corruptor clerics choose from the Death, Evil, and Luck domains.

Spell Resistance: A corruptor of fate has spell resistance equal to 14 + 1 per class level.

Level Adjustment: +4.

Corruptors of Fate in Eberron

Corruptors of fate are active participants as mercenaries in the conflicts on Shavarath, the Battleground. Although they are inhabitants of Mabar, their crèches are located on Dolurrh, the Realm of the Dead. They are considered native to both planes.

Corruptors of Fate in Faerûn

Corruptors of fate inhabit the Barrens of Doom and Despair. They're often found on raids into Hammergrim because of the many *portals* that link the two planes, and they sometimes make their way through *portals* to the Material Plane.

Corruptor of fate clerics in Faerûn choose from the Fate, Hatred, and Luck domains.

CORRUPTOR OF FATE LORE

Characters with ranks in Knowledge (the planes) can learn more about corruptors of fate. When a character makes a successful skill check, the following lore is revealed, including the information from lower DCs.

Knowledge (the Planes)

DC	Result
15	Corruptors of fate are a kind of yugoloth, sharing many of their traits. This result reveals all outsider and yugoloth traits.
20	Touching or being touched by a corruptor of fate brings ill fortune.
25	A corruptor of fate has a gaze that damages those it looks at as well as bringing bad luck.
25	Attacks made against a corruptor of fate miss regularly. Even successful attacks and spells deal reduced damage, though the creature doesn't seem to have damage reduction.

VOOR

This hulking creature waddles toward you on stubby legs. Its enormous arms end in vicious claws. Its armored face has no eyes, and ropelike tentacles constantly shoot out from its arms and back.

VOOR   CR 4

Always NE Large outsider (evil, extraplanar, yugoloth)
Init +2; **Senses** blind, blindsense 120 ft.; Listen +11
Languages Abyssal, Infernal; telepathy 100 ft.

AC 17, touch 11, flat-footed 15
   (−1 size, +2 Dex, +6 natural)
hp 37 (5 HD); **DR** 5/good
Immune acid, fire, gaze attacks, illusions, poison, visual
   effects
Resist cold 10, electricity 10; **SR** 15
Fort +7, **Ref** +6, **Will** +3

Speed 30 ft. (6 squares), climb 20 ft.
Melee 4 piercing tentacles +10 each (1d6+6) and
   2 claws +8 each (1d6+3)
Space 10 ft.; **Reach** 10 ft. (20 ft. with tentacles)
Base Atk +5; **Grp** +19
Atk Options Combat Reflexes, aligned strike (evil), rend
   2d6+9

Abilities Str 22, Dex 15, Con 17, Int 5, Wis 9, Cha 7
SQ scentless, yugoloth traits
Feats Combat Reflexes, Multiattack
Skills Climb +22, Diplomacy +0, Listen +11, Move Silently
   +10, Sense Motive +7, Survival +7
Advancement 6–10 HD (Large); 11–30 HD (Huge); 31+ HD
   (Gargantuan)

Rend (Ex) A voor that hits with both claw attacks latches
   onto the opponent's body and tears the flesh. This
   attack automatically deals an extra 2d6+9 points of
   damage.
Scentless (Ex) A voor exudes no natural smell and is
   usually undetectable by scent. A voor that has been in
   combat within the past hour stinks of the blood of its
   foes and so can be detected by scent, but only at half
   the normal range.
Skills A voor has a +8 racial bonus on Climb checks, and
   can always choose to take 10 on Climb checks, even if
   rushed or threatened. It also gains a +4 racial bonus
   on Listen and grapple checks.

Voors, known among fiends as "lashers," are hulking brutes primarily used as guardians and protectors of a fixed location, or as the bodyguards and enforcers of a lesser fiend or underling.

"Indeed they are stupid, but the power of the voor comes in their loyalty, willingness to wait for interlopers, and ability to take orders. They are ideal expendable servants."
     —Xerveramas, horned devil commander of the
                "Teeth of Hell" unit

DREADFUL LASHER

An enormous, cruelly clawed fiend rips at you with flailing tentacles. Jagged teeth gnash in an eyeless, domed head.

DREADFUL LASHER   CR 9

Always NE Huge outsider (evil, extraplanar, yugoloth)
Init +5; **Senses** blind, blindsense 120 ft.; Listen +21
Languages Abyssal, Infernal; telepathy 100 ft.

AC 20, touch 9, flat-footed 19
   (−2 size, +1 Dex, +11 natural)
hp 142 (15 HD); **DR** 10/good
Immune acid, fire, gaze attacks, illusion, poison, visual
   effects
Resist cold 10, electricity 10; **SR** 20
Fort +14, **Ref** +10, **Will** +8

Speed 30 ft. (6 squares), climb 20 ft.
Melee 4 piercing tentacles +24 each (1d8+11) and
   2 claws +23 each (1d8+5)
Space 15 ft.; **Reach** 15 ft. (30 ft. with tentacles)
Base Atk +15; **Grp** +38
Atk Options Combat Reflexes, aligned strike (evil), rend
   2d8+16

Abilities Str 32, Dex 13, Con 21, Int 5, Wis 8, Cha 7
SQ scentless, yugoloth traits
Feats Combat Reflexes, Improved Initiative, Improved
   Natural Armor (2), Multiattack, Weapon Focus (claw)
Skills Climb +37, Diplomacy +0, Listen +21, Move Silently
   +19, Sense Motive +17, Survival +17

Rend (Ex) As standard voor; damage 2d8+16.
Scentless (Ex) As standard voor.

A dreadful lasher is an especially massive voor, bred and nurtured to guard the fortress of a yugoloth general. Such a monster might stand guard for millennia, growing ever fatter on the flesh of intruders.

Strategies and Tactics

Voors work best as guardians, patiently waiting for foes to approach. Their blindsense often locates creatures long before they themselves are spotted. If possible, they climb onto a wall or other high spot, allowing them to attack with their tentacles at range.

VOOR KNOWLEDGE

Characters with ranks in Knowledge (the planes) can learn more about voors. When a character makes a successful skill check, the following lore is revealed, including the information from lower DCs.

Knowledge (the Planes)

DC	Result
14	This creature is a voor, a kind of yugoloth also called a lasher. This result reveals all outsider and yugoloth traits.
19	Voors are blind and are immune to fire and poison. They attack with numerous lashing tentacles and rending claws.
24	Voors are not particularly intelligent and are commonly used as guardians for temples and other important sites.

A single voor might be content to pick off targets one by one but is just as likely to rush into the middle of a group, targeting a weak-looking foe with its claws while using its tentacles to keep others at bay. In groups, voors descend upon their prey en masse, spreading out to threaten overlapping spaces.

Because of their capacity as guardians, voors have a keen sense of determining intent and are difficult to trick with orders that are counter to their original commands. Still, they aren't quite bright enough to look beyond the letter of their instructions, so they take commands literally.

Sample Encounters

Voors are most likely encountered guarding a fiendish shrine or other important site. Occasionally, one or two might be assigned bodyguard duty for a priest or other figure of authority.

Individual (EL 4): A sole voor protects an evil temple, a cache of magic items, or a portal to another realm.

Bodyguards (EL 7): Two voors have been charged with guarding a priest of the Elder Elemental Eye (see page 7). The priest (NE human cleric 5) fights until reduced to half hit points, then attempts to surrender—at which point the voors immediately attack him for his treachery.

Ecology

Voors relish the taste of flesh and especially blood. Their impact on a region is a rampage of slaughter and cruelty.

Voors periodically spawn broods. After five years, a juvenile voor reaches its mature form and is ready for duty. It remains near the voor that spawned it, observing the best techniques for guarding a location and capturing prey.

Environment: Voors hail from the Bleak Eternity of Gehenna, specifically the smoldering layer of Khalas. Their proximity to the Nine Hells means that they are typically employed by devils, though others also summon them.

Voors prefer underground locations or those with lots of high terrain, such as walls or rock outcroppings, that allow them to climb and better ambush foes. Areas of flame and magma remind them of home, so they are also attracted to such locations.

Typical Physical Characteristics: Voors are humanoid in shape, but the resemblance ends there. A voor stands 9 feet tall and weighs about 800 pounds. Its body is heavily armored and covered in tiny maws that the voor uses to rend opponents and drink their blood. The face of a voor is an eyeless dome of chitin and bone, ending in a terrible mouth filled with sharp teeth.

The massive arms of a voor end in sharp talons. Each arm has tentacles that extend and retract in a flash. Voors do not use these tentacles to grapple, but instead spear creatures with the sharp ends. Additional tentacles extend from a voor's shoulders, which it uses to hold an opponent or occasionally to transport a charge.

Alignment: Voors are capricious and cruel, loyal only to those whom they serve. They are always neutral evil.

Society

Voors serve as guardians, bodyguards, and enforcers for more powerful fiends. They are tough and dangerous but rather dim-witted. They readily take orders from stronger fiends without question. Voors are incredibly patient; one might be content to sit and guard an area without moving for weeks on end, all the while awaiting the opportunity to wreak havoc and destruction. Voors can obey only relatively simple commands, such as "guard this area" or "let only humans that say 'Orcus' pass." Anything more complex is lost on them.

Although more subservient than most fiends, voors still delight in bullying lesser creatures, perhaps as a way to express their bloodlust. Unless given specific orders to the contrary, they attack and destroy any lesser fiend that dares to venture into an area they have been charged with protecting. They then place the carcasses about as a warning to others.

Typical Treasure

Voors have standard treasure for their Challenge Rating, about 1,200 gp for a basic version. Since the creatures are unconcerned with acquiring wealth, this treasure represents the scattered gear of those unfortunate enough to have fallen prey to a voor ambush.

For Player Characters

A typical voor can be called using a *lesser planar ally* spell. (More powerful voors might require *planar ally* or *greater planar ally*.) It can also be summoned by *summon monster IV* or a higher-level *summon monster* spell. Treat the voor as if it were on the 4th-level list on the Summon Monster table (PH 287).

Voor

ZERN

A tall, lanky humanoid watches you warily. Its body is covered in ropy muscles, and it has short tentacles where hair would be. It carries a longspear.

ZERN   CR 6

Usually NE Medium monstrous humanoid
Init +3; **Senses** darkvision 60 ft.; Listen +6, Spot +7
Languages Common, Draconic, Dwarven, Zern

AC 19, touch 13, flat-footed 16
  (+3 Dex, +6 natural)
hp 68 (8 HD); fast healing 5
Immune poison, paralysis, stunning
SR 18
Fort +6, **Ref** +9, **Will** +7; adaptive defenses

Speed 30 ft. (6 squares)
Melee warping energy +12 (4d6+2) or
Melee mwk longspear +12/+7 (1d8+4/×3)
Ranged warping energy +12 (4d6+2)
Space 5 ft.; **Reach** 5 ft.
Base Atk +8; **Grp** +11
Atk Options Point Blank Shot, Precise Shot, malleable form, warping energy
Spell-Like Abilities (CL 8th):
  At will—*reduce person* (DC 15)
  1/day—*baleful polymorph* (DC 19), *gaseous form*

Abilities Str 16, Dex 17, Con 18, Int 15, Wis 12, Cha 11
SQ shifting guise, transmutation affinity
Feats Point Blank Shot, Precise Shot, Weapon Focus (warping energy)
Skills Craft (flesh sculpting) +13, Escape Artist +10, Heal +12, Intimidate +4, Listen +6, Spot +7, Use Rope +3 (+5 involving bindings)
Advancement by character class; **Favored Class** transmuter; see text
Possessions masterwork longspear

Adaptive Defenses (Ex) A zern's ever-changing physiology allows it to shrug off effects that attack its endurance or disrupt its bodily functions. It is immune to all spells and effects that require a Fortitude save unless the effect also works on objects or is harmless. A zern can choose to allow an effect that requires a Fortitude save to affect it.

Warping Energy (Su) A zern can produce energy that rends and tears at its opponent's flesh. As a standard action, a zern can use this ability to make a melee or ranged attack that deals 1d6 points of damage per 2 HD plus the zern's Intelligence modifier. The ranged version of this attack can reach to 120 feet and has no range increment.

Malleable Form (Ex) A zern can rapidly alter its metabolism, internal structures, organs, and other bodily systems to cope with a variety of environments and situations. As a swift action, a zern can gain one of the following benefits. Each benefit has an unlimited duration. Generally, a zern remains in one form, and then slips into another one as the situation dictates. When a zern uses a swift action to gain

one of these forms, it loses the benefits of the form it previously held.

Adrenal Surge: The zern's upper-body muscles bulge and grow with enhanced power. It gains a +2 bonus on attack rolls and a +4 bonus on damage rolls, including those using its warping energy ability.

Boneless Form: The zern's body seems to melt into a puddle of goo as its bones liquefy. It gains a +8 bonus on Escape Artist checks, which increases to +16 on checks made to squeeze through a tight area.

Impervious Hide: The zern's skin shifts into plates of armor. It gains a +4 bonus to AC and DR 5/piercing.

Size Shift: The zern can shift to Large or Small size. A Large zern gains a +2 bonus to Strength, and its space and reach increase to 10 feet; one that shifts to Small takes a −2 Strength penalty. The zern gains the standard size bonuses or penalties on attacks, Hide checks, and so forth.

Speed Burst: The zern's legs lengthen and its lower body muscles bulge and grow. Its base speed increases by 30 feet.

Shifting Guise (Su) As the *alter self* spell; at will; caster level 8th. A zern can choose to shift into a different monstrous humanoid form or any humanoid form.

Transmutation Affinity (Ex) The save DCs of any transmutation spells or spell-like abilities used by a zern increase by 4.

Zerns are hideous, malevolent creatures who see other living beings as mere playthings. They warp and shift other creatures into new forms in an attempt to "improve" them. A zern can magically alter its form to disguise its true nature.

Zern

STRATEGIES AND TACTICS

Zerns use their body-altering abilities to adapt to specific combat situations. A zern usually activates its impervious hide form to protect against unexpected attacks or ambushes. Once engaged, it uses size shift to reach or corner opponents. If the zern has the upper hand, it uses adrenal surge to hasten its victory. It saves speed burst to escape if the opposition is tougher than expected.

A zern's shifting guise ability allows it to adopt a multitude of forms, especially when setting up an ambush. A zern might even pose as one of its targets. In this guise, it can observe its opponents and strike when the time is right.

A zern holds back on using its spell-like abilities until it learns how its enemies fight, preferably before they close to melee range. It prefers to use *baleful polymorph* to neutralize enemy spellcasters

Illus. by W. Reynolds

195

and *reduce person* to hamper warriors and other primary physical threats. Otherwise, it merely blasts away with its warping energy.

Zerns rely on their blade thralls, creatures forged in their hideous workshops, to do much of their fighting. A zern prefers to blast its enemies from behind a squad of blade thralls and other servant creatures such as gibbering mouthers, otyughs, and gricks. Sometimes zerns hire grimlock mercenaries.

SAMPLE ENCOUNTER

Zerns are most likely to be encountered during a slaving raid. They prefer to travel in groups, although individuals are occasionally sent out to scout an area before an assault.

Individual (EL 6): A lone zern targets a single creature to capture and enslave. It adopts a disguise and seeks out a tavern, inn, or other place where travelers gather, and it tries to poison its target's food with oil of taggit (*DMG* 297). Once the poison takes hold, the zern claims that the victim had a few drinks too many and offers to carry him up to his room. From there, it spirits the victim away.

ECOLOGY

The vast majority of zerns live in small enclaves hidden in the dark corners of the world. They prefer to dig hideouts within deep forests, in a city's sewer systems, and even within relatively peaceful corners of the underground realm. Zerns prey on all creatures, including humans, wild animals, and even drow and giants. A zern enclave must be far enough from potential victims to remain safe, but close enough to plan and execute raids easily.

All zerns begin life as male. At around age forty, they undergo a process that turns them female. Once a zern has given birth to a child (gestation takes a full year), it reverts to a sterile neutral gender, although parents are still responsible for the care and education of their young.

Environment: Zerns keep on the move, although they prefer wetter climates to drier ones. They set up temporary camps, keeping prisoners in corrals, and move on once they reach their quota.

Typical Physical Characteristics: Zerns are tall, lanky humanoids, standing around 6 feet tall and weighing 170 pounds. A zern's frame belies its incredible toughness and ability to shrug off wounds. Its skin covers ropy muscles that shift and twist in unsettling ways when it moves. Instead of hair, zerns have several delicate tentacles that also serve as olfactory organs. Like starfish, zerns can slowly regrow severed digits and limbs.

Alignment: Zerns see themselves as the only true sentient creatures in the cosmos. They experiment on other beings in the same way that a child plays with toys. Supremely self-centered, zerns are usually neutral evil.

SOCIETY

Zern society is predicated on the concept that only the zerns are truly sentient. To them, all other living things are mere playthings for experimentation. A zern sees itself as the pinnacle of biological development. Other creatures—those too primitive to control their bodies and alter their forms to suit their needs—are obviously evolutionary dead ends.

Zerns seek to discover the perfect biological form by altering creatures to produce new races. By discovering this final form, they believe they can finally achieve true transcendence and bodily perfection. Unfortunately for other creatures, zerns experiment only on the strongest, smartest, and most successful subjects. They also believe in practicing their art as often as possible, learning from the process of trial and error.

Zerns sculpt creatures into twisted, deformed beings that usually die on the operating table. Sometimes they use mystic processes to turn a subject into one of a variety of horrors, including arcanovores (see page 197), blade thralls (see page 198), chokers, ettercaps, gibbering mouthers, gricks, and otyughs. Such monsters are normally found guarding zerns' lairs or helping them capture test subjects.

Although zerns consider all other creatures to be inferior beings, they sometimes sell their bizarre creations as living weapons. A zern community in need of money to hire mercenaries or buy a fresh crop of slaves might trade a gibbering mouther, a few blade thralls, or even an arcanovore to a drow outpost, a temple of the Elder Elemental Eye, or a gang of demons.

ZERN LORE

Characters with ranks in Knowledge (nature) can learn more about zerns. When a character makes a successful skill check, the following lore is revealed, including the information from lower DCs.

Knowledge (Nature)

DC	Result
16	This creature is a zern, a form-shifting predator. This result reveals all monstrous humanoid traits.
21	Zerns are immune to poisons, stunning attacks, and other abilities that require Fortitude saves. Their malleable biology allows them to rapidly adapt to such attacks.
26	Zerns can shift their bodies to improve their defenses, strengthen their attacks, and increase their speed.
31	Zerns are masters of transmutation magic. They can assume new forms and polymorph other creatures.

TYPICAL TREASURE

Zerns have standard treasure for their Challenge Rating, about 2,000 gp. They covet items of transmutation magic, especially wands and wondrous items.

ZERNS WITH CLASS LEVELS

Zerns' favored class is transmuter, in keeping with their aptitude for transmutation magic. Levels of transmuter do not increase the DCs of zerns' spell-like abilities. Zern clerics (which are rare) worship Nerull. They see the deity as a herald who will one day wipe all imperfect life, other than zerns, from the world.

Level Adjustment: +7.

ZERN EXPERIMENTS

Zerns (see page 195) crafted other living creatures into bizarre forms. Some of these monstrous experiments survive the process and serve their creators as guards. Zerns also sell their creations to other, "inferior" beings.

ZERN ARCANOVORE

A bulbous head with pulsing blood-red veins is perched atop a mottled body with bony protrusions extending from its back. A small beak protrudes from the front of its seemingly eyeless head. Long, birdlike legs ending in wicked talons emerge from the base of its crouching body.

ZERN ARCANOVORE	**CR 7**

Always LE Small aberration
Init +7; **Senses** darkvision 60 ft.; Listen +0, Spot +0
Languages understands Common

AC 19, touch 14, flat-footed 16; Dodge, Mobility
   (+1 size, +3 Dex, +5 natural)
Miss Chance 20% (weapon repulsion)
hp 65 (10 HD)
SR 23
Fort +5, **Ref** +6, **Will** +7

Speed 30 ft. (6 squares)
Melee 2 claws +7 each (1d4–1)
Space 5 ft.; **Reach** 5 ft.
Base Atk +7; **Grp** +2
Special Actions antimagic field 3/day
Spell-Like Abilities (CL 10th):
   At will—*arcane sight, dispel magic, see invisibility*

Abilities Str 8, Dex 17, Con 14, Int 6, Wis 11, Cha 6
Feats Combat Casting, Dodge, Improved Initiative, Mobility
Skills Concentration +5, Hide +7, Listen +0, Spellcraft +4,
   Spot +0
Advancement 11–15 HD (Medium); see text

Weapon Repulsion (Su) A zern arcanovore constantly exudes a field of telekinetic energy that imposes a 20% miss chance on all attacks against it. This ability does not function while the zern arcanovore's antimagic field is active.

Antimagic Field (Su) As the *antimagic field* spell; 3/day; CL 7th. This field emanates from the creature, has a 20-foot radius and lasts until the beginning of the arcanovore's next turn.

Arcanovores, among the zerns' most successful creations, are anathema to magic of all kinds. They can dispel existing magical effects at will and exude an aura of antimagic that quashes all magic for a short time.

Strategies and Tactics

Zern arcanovores rely on the protection and direction of more powerful creatures. The zerns sell arcanovores to mind flayers, demons, devils, and other evil masters. Created and bred by the zerns to serve loyally, the arcanovores fulfill support roles in whatever plans and encounters their masters concoct. Arcanovores are far from bright, but they perform their specific role in combat ably, targeting and removing the magical protections of their foes in order to make the attacks of their allies more effective.

Once in combat, a zern arcanovore uses its *dispel magic* ability against the opponent with the largest number of existing magical auras. If a spellcaster is causing difficulties, the arcanovore moves close and activates its antimagic field.

Sample Encounters

Whether in the company of their original creators or other evil masters, zern arcanovores prefer not to enter a fight alone. They are most commonly found with mind flayers, rakshasas, evil outsiders, and evil priests.

Slaving Party (EL 10): Xal'xanorix, a mind flayer slaver, has set out to gather thralls and perhaps acquire a few items of magical power to increase its influence in its home city. Accompanied by two loyal troll thralls and a zern arcanovore, the mind flayer could be encountered by adventurers traveling overland or through the underground. One of Xal'xanorix's favorite tactics is to quietly gain control of a small human community with its mental powers. The mind flayer considers such simple folk uninteresting, but once the community is dominated, it has the villagers call for help, bringing it a steady stream of adventurers. The mind flayer ambushes the adventurers (preferably one by one), takes their magic equipment, and perhaps adds them to its collection of guards if they have significant abilities.

Demonic Gang (EL 13): A gang of demons led by Ballhanaroth, a hezrou, has gone to ground underneath a temple of Hextor. The demons were part of a host that was broken by a group of powerful heroes and a gold wyrm. Ballhanaroth leads two vrocks and one zern arcanovore, and he is willing to aid the temple in return for shelter from the pursuing

Zern arcanovore

Illus. by S. Wood

adventurers. This service might be to attack a group of less powerful adventurers that has been thwarting the temple's plans of late.

Ecology

The majority of arcanovores make their permanent homes with zerns. These creatures are sold to a variety of planar beings but serve best when used to thwart mortal spellcasters aligned against their masters. Very rarely, a demon- or devil-purchased arcanovore accompanies its master to other planes of existence.

Zern arcanovores feed off the dissipating magical energy of effects they dispel and those suppressed by their antimagic fields.

Environment: Arcanovores' existence is dictated by those who purchase them from the zerns. Most find a place within underground lairs, but a few are kept in aboveground sites, particularly temples dedicated to the Elder Elemental Eye (see page 7).

Typical Physical Characteristics: A zern arcanovore stands between 3 and 4 feet in height and typically weighs between 80 and 100 pounds. Arcanovores cannot speak, but they understand Common and follow instructions from their owners.

An arcanovore's talons resemble those of a bird of prey but possess prominent opposable claws for grasping and fine manipulation.

Alignment: Zern arcanovores are always lawful evil and loyally follow their masters, however cruel or irresolute. Like other evil creatures, they revel in cruelty and take every opportunity to cause pain and fear in those they see as weaker than themselves.

Society

Zern arcanovores are social creatures, preferring the company of their owners or creators to solitary existence.

Because of their usefulness against powerful magical effects, arcanovores are usually treated well and protected by their masters. Other minions, even some more powerful than the arcanovores, have strict orders regarding the care and preservation of these creations.

ZERN ARCANOVORE LORE

Characters with ranks in Knowledge (dungeoneering) can learn more about zern arcanovores. When a character makes a successful skill check, the following lore is revealed, including the information from lower DCs.

Knowledge (Dungeoneering)

DC	Result
17	Zern arcanovores are hideous aberrations. This result reveals all aberration traits.
22	Zern arcanovores were created by the zerns, an evil race skilled in the transmutation of living flesh. Zerns often sell their arcanovores to other races.
27	Zern arcanovores feed off magic and have powerful abilities to dispel and suppress magical effects. The energy of these dispelled effects sustains them.

Typical Treasure

Zern arcanovores rarely have any treasure, although a wealthy owner might equip one with a protective magic item.

Advanced Zern Arcanovores

For every 2 HD gained, the caster level for an arcanovore's spell-like abilities increases by 1. A zern arcanovore whose caster level reaches 11th or higher uses *greater dispel magic*, instead of *dispel magic*, as a spell-like ability.

ZERN BLADE THRALL

This creature is a bizarre cross between a humanoid and a great worm. Its lower body slithers along the ground, while its humanoid torso has two arms that end in long bone and cartilage blades.

ZERN BLADE THRALL   CR 4
Always NE Large monstrous humanoid
Init +1; **Senses** darkvision 60 ft.; Listen +3, Spot +3
Languages Zern

AC 15, touch 10, flat-footed 14
   (−1 size, +1 Dex, +5 natural)
hp 47 (5 HD); fast healing 2
Immune poison, paralysis, stunning
Fort +6, **Ref** +5, **Will** +3; adaptive defenses

Speed 40 ft. (8 squares)
Melee 2 bone blades +9 each (2d6+4)
Ranged net +6 touch (entangle, PH 119)
Space 10 ft.; **Reach** 10 ft.
Base Atk +5; **Grp** +13

Abilities Str 18, Dex 12, Con 21, Int 6, Wis 9, Cha 7
Feats Weapon Focus (bone blade), Weapon Focus (net)
Skills Jump +8, Listen +3, Spot +3
Advancement by character class; **Favored Class** fighter; see text
Possessions net

Adaptive Defenses (Ex) A zern blade thrall's resilient physiology allows it to shrug off effects that attack its endurance or disrupt its bodily functions. It is immune to all spells and effects that require a Fortitude save unless the effect also works on objects or is harmless. A blade thrall can choose to allow an effect that requires a Fortitude save to affect it.

Like arcanovores, blade thralls are products of the zerns' insidious biological experiments. They serve as warriors, sentinels, and bodyguards. Their great strength, toughness, and skill in combat makes them fearsome enemies, while their poor intelligence and weak personalities make them ideally suited as expendable troops. A blade thrall obeys its zern masters with suicidal fanaticism.

Strategies and Tactics

A zern blade thrall fights to protect its masters and obeys their every command. Typically, a blade thrall uses its bulk to shield a zern. While the zern blasts its enemies with its warping energy, the blade thrall fends off attackers and provides cover.

A blade thrall employs simple tactics without a zern to guide it. It charges toward the nearest opponent and fights until the foe is dead. It then switches to a different opponent, and so on, until it dies or its opponents are all defeated.

Zerns see blade thralls as disposable resources. A zern always puts its safety above a thrall's well-being, and the thralls are bred to willingly accept even suicidal orders from their masters. For example, a thrall might barrel through a rank of enemy fighters, accepting attacks of opportunity, to attack an enemy spellcaster or archer.

Although blade thralls are skilled combatants capable of dealing great damage, most zerns see them as little more than mobile shields. Usually, a thrall makes a few attacks at the start of a battle. If its attacks are ineffective, the zern commands it to focus on defense, especially when facing a foe that the thrall cannot possibly overcome. In this case, the thrall's sole task is to protect the zern. It fights defensively or even takes the total defense action to hold out as long as possible. A blade thrall might also use the aid another action, usually to improve the zern's AC.

Blade thralls also serve zerns by capturing living creatures. They are trained to wield nets and use them to entangle and neutralize promising test subjects. Once a creature is trapped and subdued, the blade thralls drag it back to the zerns' lair.

Sometimes the zerns sell blade thralls to other races. The thralls obey their new masters as faithfully as they would zerns.

Sample Encounter

Blade thralls travel with zerns to protect them from harm and provide physical labor.

Collecting Party (EL 8): A zern and two blade thralls travel through a dungeon level in search of fresh victims. The zern disguises itself as a dwarf cornered and trapped in a net by the two thralls, who make a show of attacking it. Once the adventurers leap to help the "dwarf," the thralls attack with their nets. The disguised zern watches the battle, gladly sacrificing the thralls to learn more about its potential subjects. If the adventurers clearly outclass the blade thralls, the zern waits for them to finish off the creatures while mentally noting their talents, abilities, and tactics. After

Zern blade thrall

the battle is over, it thanks them for their help and leaves to fetch reinforcements. If it thinks it can defeat the survivors, it shifts form and attacks.

Ecology

Zern blade thralls exist wherever zerns settle. They are servants and slaves, and their dim intellects keep them from being more independent. A blade thrall left to its own devices becomes little more than a wild animal.

Blade thralls have no gender and cannot reproduce. They can only be shaped by zerns from other living creatures. Being unaffected by diseases, poisons, and other physical ailments, blade thralls are theoretically immortal, though most die in combat after a few years of service.

Environment: Blade thralls have no preferred environment. They go wherever the zerns command them.

Typical Physical Characteristics: Blade thralls stand roughly 7 feet tall and weigh 2,100 pounds on average.

Alignment: Blade thralls are always lawful evil, loyally devoted to their masters.

Zern Blade Thralls with Class Levels

Zern blade thralls rarely advance, but especially devoted specimens might receive training as fighters. Zern blade thralls never become spellcasters—it isn't in their nature.

Level Adjustment: +4.

ZERN BLADE THRALL LORE

Characters with ranks in Knowledge (nature) can learn more about zern blade thralls. When a character makes a successful skill check, the following lore is revealed, including the information from lower DCs.

Knowledge (Nature)

DC	Result
14	This creature is a zern blade thrall, an unnatural monstrous humanoid. This result reveals all monstrous humanoid traits.
19	Blade thralls were created to be slaves by a vicious race called the zerns. The two are usually found together, with the thralls protecting their zern masters.
24	Zern blade thralls are immune to poisons, stunning attacks, and abilities that require Fortitude saves.

Illus. by E. Widermann

SAMPLE LAIR:
THE DEEPHOLLOWS

The slow drip of water gradually hollowed out this series of caverns, which are suitable for habitation by subterranean creatures.

1. Antechamber

Water seeped through a surface crack to begin forming this series of caves. The original opening to the surface has since been sealed with a stone plug, and the ground above shows no obvious entrance (Search DC 25 to locate). A tunnel connects it to other underground areas.

The floor slopes down gradually at first, then steeply. Civilized creatures inhabiting this area might carve rough steps into the slick stone.

2. Dead End

This series of steep-walled caverns is connected by extremely narrow passages, some barely wide enough to admit a Medium creature. The passages eventually end in a blind alley in which a little stale water has collected. Civilized peoples consign their common criminals (as well as those too poor to pay rent) to this "waste" area, where mere survival is a brutal, constant fight. Uncivilized beings exile the diseased, cursed, or malformed, and those shunned through superstition.

The cavern walls are rough, with many ledges and shelves that afford a bit of surface for sleeping or pitching a small shelter. Individuals with the highest status inhabit the lower caves, closer to the meager supply of water. The lower areas are also less traveled and allow a bit of privacy. Fights over this territory are frequent.

3. The Bridge

A 5-foot-wide natural bridge spans this cave. It is slick with dampness, meaning that 2 squares of movement are needed to enter each square, and running and charging are prohibited. Civilized creatures might install railings, which allows movement at normal speed as long as a character holds on. (Running and charging are still not allowed.)

A hole worn in the cavern's bottom opens into a lower space into which civilized residents dump waste (giving this area a noisome stench). Guards might be posted at the far end of the bridge.

4. The Funnel

Ancient eddies swirled about the rock here, resulting in a series of spiraling ledges that serve as footpaths. They are narrow and treacherous (DC 7 Balance check to avoid slipping) but allow passage to the wider tunnel at the bottom. Civilized creatures might construct a lift system for faster and safer transport.

5. Main Dwellings

This high-ceilinged cave is about 150 feet across at its widest point, big enough to contain a good-sized encampment or several dozen buildings. The floor slopes down gradually, with a 10-foot-wide tunnel opening from a side wall into area 6. A very large opening leads into area 7. At the lowest point of the cavern is an opening into yet lower caves (area 8). A stone slab and a mound of rubble cover the opening. If inhabited by civilized creatures, this cave might contain multistory buildings or cliff dwellings carved into the walls, as well as artificial light sources. Barbaric inhabitants simply camp on the floor.

A wide ledge midway up the far wall forms an entrance to a dead-end network of narrow tunnels. Civilized creatures might use this area for storage or military barracks.

Near the cavern's ceiling is a narrow opening into twisting hollows that connect with area 4 as well as opening to the surface, thus allowing air to flow through the complex.

6. Secondary Dwellings

A second large cave, about 60 feet across at the widest, serves as additional living space. If the inhabitants are civilized, this area is home to the wealthy and influential members of society. Smaller spaces branching off the main cave might form private estates within this privileged district.

Uncivilized inhabitants might instead use this area for noncombatant housing, child-rearing, and the like.

7. Downbelow

These smaller caves connected by sinuous tunnels form less desirable living space. Brackish water pools in the lowest cave, drinkable in a pinch but not pleasant (especially since trash and wastes tend to spill into it).

Civilized beings relegate their lowest classes to this area. Laborers, foreigners, and transient renters dwell in hovels here and travel into area 5 to work or trade. Barbaric creatures throw garbage into this area or perhaps keep beasts or slaves here.

8. The Deeps

Ancient water flows opened the floor of the large cavern into a deep gap within the rock. Its nearly vertical sides make it unsuitable for humanoid dwellings. However, flying and climbing monsters sometimes hunt here, such as monstrous vermin, carrion crawlers, cloakers, driders, hook horrors, ropers, and other typical underground threats.

A few smaller openings, as well as tunnels dug by burrowing creatures, open off the bottom of this area. A stagnant pool is home to a variety of oozes. The network of tunnels grows every year, and eventually a monster might burrow into the inhabited caves.

9. Reservoir

A lake has formed at the bottom of this enormous cave fed by an underground stream. The water is mineral rich but fresh, and it supplies the dwellings above.

Civilized creatures install winches and cables to bring up the water, or use a system of pipes and pumps. Less technologically advanced beings use a bucket at the end of a rope.

Enormous stalactites hang from the ceiling. They are strong enough to support hanging structures, such as nests or hammocks, or even industrial buildings.

The Deephollows

(side view)

One square = 20 feet

MONSTER FEATS

Presented below are a number of feats that are typically used by monsters. Some of them (such as Craft Construct) can also be useful to NPCs and player characters.

ABILITY FOCUS

A particular special ability of a creature with this feat is more potent than normal.

Prerequisite: Special ability that allows a saving throw.

Benefit: Add 2 to the DC for all saving throws against the special ability on which the creature focuses.

Special: A creature can gain this feat multiple times. Its effects do not stack. Each time the creature takes the feat, it applies to a different special ability.

AWESOME BLOW

A creature with this feat can choose to deliver blows that send its smaller opponents flying like bowling pins.

Prerequisites: Str 25, Power Attack, Improved Bull Rush, size Large or larger.

Benefit: As a standard action, the creature can choose to subtract 4 from its melee attack roll and deliver an awesome blow. If the creature hits a corporeal opponent smaller than itself with an awesome blow, its opponent must succeed on a Reflex save (DC equal to damage dealt) or be knocked flying 10 feet in a direction of the attacking creature's choice and fall prone. The attacking creature can only push the opponent in a straight line, and the opponent can't move closer to the attacking creature than the square it started in. If an obstacle prevents the completion of the opponent's move, the opponent and the obstacle each take 1d6 points of damage, and the opponent stops in the space adjacent to the obstacle.

Special: A fighter can select Awesome Blow as one of his fighter bonus feats.

CLINGING BREATH

This feat enables a creature's breath weapon to cling to creatures and continue to affect them after it has breathed.

Prerequisites: Con 13, breath weapon with recharge time expressed in rounds.

Benefit: When a creature uses its breath weapon, it can choose for it to deal additional damage in the next round to all creatures and objects affected by it. This additional damage is equal to half the damage the breath weapon dealt to that creature or object. A second save is not allowed, but any creature or object that avoided all damage from the breath weapon in the first round (such as from evasion) does not take any extra damage.

As a full-round action, a targeted creature can attempt a Reflex save (using the breath weapon's original save DC) to remove the clinging breath weapon and negate further damage. Rolling around on the ground grants a +2 bonus on this save.

This feat only works on a breath weapon that has instantaneous duration and that deals damage.

When a creature uses this feat, add 1 to the number of rounds it must wait before using its breath weapon again.

Special: This feat originally appeared in *Draconomicon*; this is a revised version. If you have *Draconomicon*, Clinging Breath is treated as a Metabreath feat.

CRAFT CONSTRUCT [ITEM CREATION]

A creature with this feat can create golems and other magic automatons that obey its orders.

Prerequisites: Craft Magic Arms and Armor, Craft Wondrous Item.

Benefit: The creature can create any construct whose prerequisites it meets. Enchanting a construct takes one day for each 1,000 gp in its market price. To enchant a construct, a spellcaster must spend 1/25 the item's price in XP and use up raw materials costing half of this price.

The creature can repair constructs that have taken damage. In one day of work, the creature can repair up to 20 points of damage by expending 50 gp per point of damage repaired.

A newly created construct has average hit points for its Hit Dice.

FLYBY ATTACK

A creature with this feat can attack on the wing.

Prerequisite: Fly speed.

Benefit: When flying, the creature can take a move action (including a dive) and another standard action at any point during the move. The creature cannot take a second move action during a round when it makes a flyby attack.

Normal: Without this feat, the creature takes a standard action either before or after its move.

GITHYANKI BATTLECASTER

A creature with this feat ignores arcane spell failure chances when wearing light armor.

Prerequisites: Githyanki, ability to cast 2nd-level arcane spells, base attack bonus +3.

Benefit: The creature ignores arcane spell failure chances for any kind of light armor it wears. If it wears medium or heavy armor or carries a shield, it has the normal arcane spell failure chance.

Special: A fighter or wizard can choose this feat as one of the bonus feats those classes grant.

GITHYANKI DRAGONRIDER [RACIAL]

A creature with this feat has a knack for getting along with red dragons.

Prerequisites: Githyanki, ride 5 ranks.

Benefit: The creature gains a +2 bonus on Diplomacy checks when dealing with red dragons and a +2 on Ride checks it attempts when riding a red dragon. While the creature is mounted on a red dragon, it and its mount gain a +1 bonus on Reflex saves and a +1 insight bonus to Armor Class.

Special: The Diplomacy bonus from this feat stacks with the githyanki racial bonus on Diplomacy checks when dealing with red dragons. A githyanki fighter can choose this feat as a bonus feat.

IMPROVED NATURAL ATTACK

The natural attacks of a creature with this feat are more dangerous than its size and type would otherwise dictate.

Prerequisite: Natural weapon, base attack bonus +4.

Benefit: The damage for one of the creature's natural attack forms increases by one step, as if the creature's size had increased by one category: 1d2, 1d3, 1d4, 1d6, 1d8, 2d6, 3d6, 4d6, 6d6, 8d6, 12d6. A weapon or attack that deals 1d10 points of damage increases as follows: 1d10, 2d8, 3d8, 4d8, 6d8, 8d8, 12d8.

IMPROVED TOUGHNESS

A creature with this feat is significantly tougher than normal.

Prerequisite: Base Fortitude save bonus +2.

Benefit: The creature gains a number of hit points equal to its current Hit Dice. Each time it gains a Hit Die (such as by gaining a level or advancing), it gains 1 additional hit point. If it loses a Hit Die (such as by losing a level), it loses 1 hit point permanently.

Special: A fighter can select Improved Toughness as one of his fighter bonus feats.

LINGERING BREATH

The breath weapon of a creature with this feat forms a lingering cloud.

Prerequisites: Con 15, breath weapon with recharge time expressed in rounds, Clinging Breath.

Benefit: When the creature uses its breath weapon, it can choose for the effect to remain for 1 round as a lingering cloud of the same shape and size as the original breath weapon.

Anyone who enters the cloud takes one-half of the breath weapon's normal effects; any saving throw the breath weapon normally allows still applies. Damaging breath weapons deal one-half their normal damage, and breath weapons with effects that have durations last for one-half the normal time. If a creature is affected by the same nondamaging breath weapon twice, the effects do not stack (use only the longer duration).

Any creature in the area of the original breath weapon takes no additional effect from the cloud, provided it is outside the cloud by the end of its next turn.

When a creature uses this feat, add 2 to the number of rounds it must wait before using its breath weapon again.

Special: This feat originally appeared in *Draconomicon*; this is a revised version. If you have *Draconomicon*, Lingering Breath is treated as a Metabreath feat.

MULTIATTACK

A creature with this feat is adept at using all its natural weapons at once.

Prerequisite: Three or more natural attacks.

Benefit: The creature's secondary attacks with natural weapons take only a –2 penalty.

Normal: Without this feat, the creature's secondary attacks with natural weapons take a –5 penalty.

POWERFUL CHARGE

A creature with this feat can charge with extra force.

Prerequisites: Medium or larger, base attack bonus +1.

Benefit: When the creature charges, if its melee attack hits, it deals an extra 1d8 points of damage (if it is of Medium size). For Large creatures, the extra damage is 2d6 points; for Huge, 3d6; for Gargantuan, 4d6; and for Colossal, 6d6.

This feat only works when the creature makes a charge. It does not work when the creature is mounted. If the creature has the ability to make multiple attacks after a charge, it can only apply this extra damage to one of those attacks.

Special: A fighter can select Powerful Charge as one of his fighter bonus feats.

QUICKEN SPELL-LIKE ABILITY

A creature with this feat can employ a spell-like ability with a moment's thought.

Prerequisite: Spell-like ability at caster level 10th or higher.

Benefit: The creature can use one of its spell-like abilities as a quickened spell-like ability three times per day (or less, if the ability is normally usable only once or twice per day).

Using a quickened spell-like ability is a swift action (see page 219) that does not provoke attacks of opportunity. The creature can perform another action—including the use of another spell-like ability– in the same round that it uses a quickened spell-like ability. The creature can use only one quickened spell-like ability per round.

The creature can only select a spell-like ability duplicating a spell with a level less than or equal to half its caster level (round down) minus 4. For a summary, see the table below. For example, a creature that uses its spell-like abilities as a 15th-level caster can only quicken spell-like abilities duplicating spells of 3rd level or lower. In addition, a spell-like ability that duplicates a spell with a casting time greater than 1 full round cannot be quickened.

Normal: Normally the use of a spell-like ability requires a standard action and provokes attacks of opportunity unless otherwise noted.

Special: This feat can be taken multiple times. Each time it is taken, the creature can apply it to a different one of its spell-like abilities.

QUICKEN SPELL-LIKE ABILITY

Spell Level	Caster Level to Quicken
0	8th
1st	10th
2nd	12th
3rd	14th
4th	16th
5th	18th
6th	20th
7th	—
8th	—
9th	—

MONSTERS RANKED BY CHALLENGE RATING

LIST OF MONSTERS BY ECL

MONSTER TABLES

GLOSSARY

This section of *Monster Manual IV* provides definitions and descriptions of monster characteristics. If you have come across a term used earlier in this book that you're not familiar with, this is the place to find out more.

Aberration Type: An aberration has a bizarre anatomy, strange abilities, an alien mindset, or any combination of the three.

Features: An aberration has the following features.

—d8 Hit Dice.

—Base attack bonus equal to 3/4 total Hit Dice (as cleric).

—Good Will saves.

—Skill points equal to (2 + Int modifier, minimum 1) per Hit Die, with quadruple skill points for the first Hit Die.

Traits: An aberration possesses the following traits (unless otherwise noted in a creature's entry).

—Darkvision out to 60 feet.

—Proficient with its natural weapons. If generally humanoid in form, proficient with all simple weapons and any weapon it is described as using.

—Proficient with whatever type of armor (light, medium, or heavy) it is described as wearing, as well as all lighter types. Aberrations not indicated as wearing armor are not proficient with armor. Aberrations are proficient with shields if they are proficient with any form of armor.

—Aberrations eat, sleep, and breathe.

Ability Score Loss (Su): Some attacks reduce the opponent's score in one or more abilities. This loss can be temporary (ability damage) or permanent (ability drain).

Ability Damage: This attack damages an opponent's ability score. The creature's descriptive text gives the ability and the amount of damage. If an attack that causes ability damage scores a critical hit, it deals twice the indicated amount of damage (if the damage is expressed as a die range, roll two dice). Ability damage returns at the rate of 1 point per day for each affected ability.

Ability Drain: This effect permanently reduces a living opponent's ability score when the creature hits with a melee attack. The creature's descriptive text gives the ability and the amount drained. If an attack that causes ability drain scores a critical hit, it drains twice the indicated amount (if the damage is expressed as a die range, roll two dice). Unless otherwise specified in the creature's description, a draining creature gains 5 temporary hit points (10 on a critical hit) whenever it drains an ability score no matter how many points it drains. Temporary hit points gained in this fashion last for up to 1 hour.

Some ability drain attacks allow a Fortitude save (DC 10 + 1/2 draining creature's racial HD + draining creature's Cha modifier; the exact DC is given in the creature's descriptive text). If no saving throw is mentioned, none is allowed.

Air Subtype: This subtype usually is used for elementals and outsiders with a connection to the Elemental Plane of Air. Air creatures always have fly speeds and usually have perfect maneuverability (see Movement Modes, page 213).

Aligned Strike: Attacks made by a creature that has this ability are treated as aligned for the purpose of overcoming damage reduction. When it applies, "aligned strike" appears in the Atk Options line of a creature's statistics block, followed in parentheses by a specific alignment (chaotic, evil, good, or lawful).

Alignment: This line in a monster entry gives the alignment that the creature is most likely to have. Every entry includes a qualifier that indicates how broadly that alignment applies to all monsters of that kind.

Always: The creature is born with the indicated alignment. The creature might have a hereditary predisposition to the alignment or come from a plane that predetermines it. It is possible for individuals to change alignment, but such individuals are either unique or rare exceptions.

Usually: The majority (more than 50%) of these creatures have the given alignment. This could be due to strong cultural influences, or it could be a legacy of the creatures' origin. For example, most elves inherited their chaotic good alignment from their creator, the deity Corellon Larethian.

Often: The creature tends toward the given alignment, either by nature or nurture, but not strongly. A plurality (40–50%) of individuals have the given alignment, but exceptions are common.

Animal Type: An animal is a living, nonhuman creature, usually a vertebrate that has no magical abilities and no innate capacity for language or culture.

Features: An animal has the following features (unless otherwise noted in a creature's entry).

—d8 Hit Dice.

—Base attack bonus equal to 3/4 total Hit Dice (as cleric).

—Good Fortitude and Reflex saves (certain animals have different good saves).

—Skill points equal to (2 + Int modifier, minimum 1) per Hit Die, with quadruple skill points for the first Hit Die.

Traits: An animal possesses the following traits (unless otherwise noted in a creature's entry).

—Intelligence score of 1 or 2 (no creature that has an Intelligence score of 3 or higher can be an animal).

—Low-light vision.

—Alignment: Always neutral.

—Treasure: None.

—Proficient with its natural weapons only. A noncombative herbivore uses its natural weapons as a secondary attack. Such attacks are made with a –5 penalty on the creature's attack rolls, and the animal receives only 1/2 its Strength modifier as a damage adjustment.

—Proficient with no armor unless trained for war.

—Animals eat, sleep, and breathe.

Aquatic Subtype: Creatures that has the aquatic subtype always have swim speeds and thus can move in water without making Swim checks. An aquatic creature can breathe underwater. It cannot also breathe air unless it has the amphibious special quality.

Archon Subtype: The plane of Celestia is home to a race of good outsiders known as the archons.

Traits: An archon possesses the following traits (unless otherwise noted in a creature's entry).

—Darkvision out to 60 feet and low-light vision.

—Aura of Menace (Su): A righteous aura surrounds archons that fight or get angry. Any hostile creature within a 20-foot radius of an archon must succeed on a Will save to resist its effects. The save DC varies with the kind of archon, is Charisma-based, and includes a +2 racial bonus. Those who fail take a –2 penalty on attacks, AC, and saves for 24 hours or until they successfully hit the archon that generated the aura. A creature that has resisted or broken the effect cannot be affected again by the same archon's aura for 24 hours.

—Immunity to electricity and petrification.

— +4 racial bonus on saves against poison.

—Magic Circle against Evil (Su): A magic circle against evil effect always surrounds an archon (caster level equals the archon's Hit Dice). (The defensive benefits from the circle are not included in an archon's statistics block.)

—Teleport (Su): Archons can use greater teleport at will, as the spell (caster level 14th), except that the creature can transport only itself and up to 50 pounds of objects.

—Tongues (Su): All archons can speak with any creature that has a language, as though using a *tongues* spell (caster level 14th). This ability is always active.

Augmented Subtype: A creature receives this subtype whenever something happens to change its original type. Some creatures (those with an inherited template) are born with this subtype; others acquire it when they take on an acquired template. The augmented subtype is always paired with the creature's original type. For example, a wizard's raven familiar is a magical beast (augmented animal). A creature with the augmented subtype usually has the traits of its current type, but the features of its original type. For example, a wizard's raven familiar has an animal's features and the traits of a magical beast.

Blindsense (Ex): Using nonvisual senses, such as acute smell or hearing, a creature that has blindsense notices things it cannot see. The creature usually does not need to make Spot or Listen checks to pinpoint the location of a creature within range of its blindsense ability, provided that it has line of effect to that creature. Any opponent the creature cannot see still has total concealment against the creature that has blindsense, and the creature still has the normal miss chance when attacking foes that have concealment. Visibility still affects the movement of a creature with blindsense. A creature that has blindsense is still denied its Dexterity bonus to Armor Class against attacks from creatures it cannot see.

Blindsight (Ex): This ability is similar to blindsense, but is far more discerning. Using nonvisual senses, such as sensitivity to vibrations, keen smell, acute hearing, or echolocation, a creature that has blindsight maneuvers and fights as well as a sighted creature. Invisibility, darkness, and most kinds of concealment are irrelevant, though the creature must have line of effect to a creature or object to discern that creature or object. The ability's range is specified in the creature's descriptive text. The creature usually does not need to make Spot or Listen checks to notice creatures within range of its blindsight ability. Unless otherwise noted, blindsight is continuous, and the creature need do nothing to use it. Some forms of blindsight, however, must be triggered as a free action. If so, this is noted in the creature's description. If a creature must trigger its blindsight ability, the creature gains the benefits of blindsight only during its turn.

Breath Weapon (Su): A breath weapon attack usually deals damage and is often based on some type of energy (such as fire). Such breath weapons allow a Reflex save for half damage (DC 10 + 1/2 breathing creature's racial HD + breathing creature's Con modifier; the exact DC is given in the creature's descriptive text). A creature is immune to its own breath weapon unless otherwise noted. Some breath weapons allow a Fortitude save or a Will save instead of a Reflex save.

Change Shape (Su): A creature that has this special quality can assume the appearance of a specific creature or type of creature (usually a humanoid), but retains most of its own physical qualities. A creature cannot change shape to a form more than one size category smaller or larger than its original form. Changing shape results in the following changes to the creature:

—The creature retains the type and subtype of its original form. It gains the size of its new form.

—The creature loses the natural weapons, movement modes, and extraordinary abilities and attacks of its original form.

—The creature gains the natural weapons, movement modes, and extraordinary abilities and attacks of its new form.

—The creature retains all other attacks and special qualities of its original form, except for breath weapons and gaze attacks.

—The creature retains the ability scores of its original form.

—The creature retains its hit points and saves.

—The creature retains any spellcasting ability it had in its original form, although it must be able to speak intelligibly to cast spells with verbal components and it must have humanlike hands to cast spells with somatic components.

—The creature is effectively camouflaged as a creature of its new form, and gains a +10 bonus on Disguise checks if it uses this ability to create a disguise.

Chaotic Subtype: A subtype usually applied only to outsiders native to the chaotic-aligned Outer Planes. Most creatures that have this subtype also have chaotic alignments; however, if their alignments change they still retain the subtype. Any effect that depends on alignment affects a creature that has this subtype as if the creature has a chaotic alignment, no matter what its alignment actually is. The creature also suffers effects according to its actual alignment. A creature that has the chaotic subtype overcomes damage reduction as if its natural weapons and any weapons it wields were chaotic-aligned (see Damage Reduction, below).

Class Skills: Any skill in which a monster has acquired at least one rank or in which the creature has a racial bonus is considered a class skill for that kind of creature. Some monsters, such as the true dragons, have their class skills explicitly listed. Other monsters' class skills can be determined from their statistics blocks.

Creatures that have a swim speed always have Swim as a class skill. Creatures that have a climb speed always have Climb as a class skill. Skills listed in an entry merely because of synergy with another skill are not class skills. For example, a whisper demon's class skills are Bluff, Concentration, Diplomacy, Knowledge (history), Knowledge (local), Knowledge (nobility), Knowledge (the planes), Listen, Sense Motive, Spellcraft, and Spot. It has other skill modifiers, such as Disguise, Intimidate, and Survival, due to synergy benefits granted by other skills. The statistics block for the inferno spider also includes a Jump modifier due to its speed, even though Jump is not a class skill for the creature.

Cold Subtype: A creature that has the cold subtype has immunity to cold. It has vulnerability to fire, which means it takes half again as much (+50%) damage as normal from fire, regardless of whether a saving throw is allowed, or if the save is a success or failure.

Constrict (Ex): A creature that has this ability can crush an opponent, dealing bludgeoning damage, after making a successful grapple check. The amount of damage is given in the creature's entry. If the creature also has the improved grab ability (see page 214), it deals constriction damage in addition to damage dealt by the weapon used to grab.

Construct Type: A construct is an animated object or artificially constructed creature.

Features: A construct has the following features.
—10-sided Hit Dice.
—Base attack bonus equal to 3/4 total Hit Dice (as cleric).
—No good saving throws.
—Skill points equal to (2 + Int modifier, minimum 1) per Hit Die, with quadruple skill points for the first Hit Die, if the construct has an Intelligence score. However, most constructs are mindless and gain no skill points or feats.

Traits: A construct possesses the following traits (unless otherwise noted in a creature's entry).
—No Constitution score.
—Low-light vision.
—Darkvision out to 60 feet.
—Immunity to all mind-affecting spells and abilities (charms, compulsions, phantasms, patterns, and morale effects).
—Immunity to poison, sleep effects, paralysis, stunning, disease, death effects, and necromancy effects.
—Cannot heal damage on their own, but often can be repaired by exposing them to a certain kind of effect (see the creature's description for details) or through the use of the Craft Construct feat (see page 203). A construct that has the fast healing special quality still benefits from that quality.
—Not subject to extra damage from critical hits, nonlethal damage, ability damage, ability drain, fatigue, exhaustion, or energy drain.

—Immunity to any effect that requires a Fortitude save (unless the effect also works on objects, or is harmless).
—Not at risk of death from massive damage (PH 145). Immediately destroyed when reduced to 0 hit points or less.
—Since it was never alive, a construct cannot be raised or resurrected.
—Because its body is a mass of unliving matter, a construct is hard to destroy. It gains bonus hit points based on size, as shown on the following table.

Construct Size	Bonus Hit Points	Construct Size	Bonus Hit Points
Fine	—	Large	30
Diminutive	—	Huge	40
Tiny	—	Gargantuan	60
Small	10	Colossal	80
Madium	20		

—Proficient with its natural weapons only, unless generally humanoid in form, in which case proficient with any weapon mentioned in its entry.
—Proficient with no armor.
—Constructs do not eat, sleep, or breathe.

Damage Reduction (Ex or Su): A creature that has this special quality ignores damage from most weapons and natural attacks. Wounds heal immediately, or the weapon bounces off harmlessly (in either case, the opponent knows the attack was ineffective). The creature takes normal damage from energy attacks (even nonmagical ones), spells, spell-like abilities, and supernatural abilities. A certain kind of weapon can sometimes damage the creature normally, as noted below.

The entry indicates the amount of damage ignored (usually 5 to 15 points) and the type of weapon that negates the ability. For example, the werewolf's entry reads "damage reduction 10/silver": Each time a foe hits a werewolf with a weapon, the damage dealt by that attack is reduced by 10 points (to a minimum of 0). However, a silvered weapon deals full damage.

Some monsters are vulnerable to piercing, bludgeoning, or slashing damage. For example, the wizened elder has damage reduction 5/slashing. When it is hit with bludgeoning or piercing weapons, the damage dealt by each attack is reduced by 5 points, but slashing weapons deal full damage.

Some monsters are vulnerable to certain materials, such as alchemical silver, adamantine, or cold-forged iron. Attacks from weapons that are not made of the correct material have their damage reduced, even if the weapon has an enhancement bonus. Examples: the dwarf ancestor's damage reduction 10/adamantine, the joystealer's damage reduction 5/cold iron, and the defacer's damage reduction 10/silver.

Some monsters are vulnerable to magic weapons. Any weapon that has at least a +1 magical enhancement bonus on attack rolls and damage rolls overcomes the damage reduction of these monsters. Such creatures' natural weapons (but not their attacks with weapons) are treated as magic weapons for the purpose of overcoming damage reduction (See Magic

Strike, page 213). For example, the balhannoth has damage reduction 15/magic and can strike as a magic weapon for the purpose of overcoming damage reduction.

Some monsters are vulnerable to chaotic-, evil-, good-, or lawful-aligned weapons. When a cleric casts *align weapon*, affected weapons might gain one or more of these properties, and certain magic weapons have these properties as well. For example, many demons such as Lolth-touched bebelith have damage reduction 10/good, while the justice archon has damage reduction 10/evil. A creature that has an alignment subtype (chaotic, evil, good, or lawful) can overcome this type of damage reduction with its natural weapons and weapons it wields as if the weapons or natural weapons had an alignment (or alignments) that match the subtype(s) of the creature. A nashrou demon, for instance, has the chaotic and evil subtypes, and thus can overcome damage reduction as if its weapons and natural weapons were chaotic-aligned and evil-aligned (see Aligned Strike, page 205).

When a damage reduction entry has a dash (–) after the slash, no weapon overcomes the damage reduction.

A few creatures are harmed by more than one kind of weapon. The kashtigur demon, for example, has damage reduction 5/cold iron or good. Either kind of weapon—cold iron or good—overcomes its damage reduction.

A few other creatures require combinations of different types of attacks to overcome their damage reduction. For example, the deathdrinker demon has damage reduction 15/good and lawful, meaning that a weapon must be good-aligned and lawful-aligned in order to overcome the demon's damage reduction.

Darkvision (Ex): A creature that has this special ability can see in the dark, out to the distance given in the creature's entry. Darkvision is black and white only, but it is otherwise like normal sight, and a creature that has darkvision can function just fine with no light at all.

Dragon Type: A dragon is a reptilelike creature, usually winged, that has magical or unusual abilities.

Features: A dragon has the following features.
—12-sided Hit Dice.
—Base attack bonus equal to total Hit Dice (as fighter).
—Good Fortitude, Reflex, and Will saves.
—Skill points equal to (6 + Int modifier) per Hit Die, with quadruple skill points for the first Hit Die.

Traits: A dragon possesses the following traits (unless otherwise noted in the description of a particular kind).
—Darkvision out to 60 feet and low-light vision.
—Immunity to magic *sleep* effects and paralysis effects.
—Proficient with its natural weapons only unless humanoid in form (or capable of assuming humanoid form), in which case proficient with all simple weapons and any weapons mentioned in its entry.
—Proficient with no armor.
—Dragons eat, sleep, and breathe.

Dragonblood Subtype: A creature that has the dragonblood subtype has a strong affinity to dragons—which means that spells, effects, powers, and abilities that affect or target dragons also affect it. The subtype qualifies a creature to use magic items normally only usable by dragons, and qualifies the creature to take feats that have the subtype as a prerequisite. The dragonblood subtype also makes creatures subject to harmful effects that affect dragons.

The dragonblood subtype does not confer the dragon type or any traits associated with that type. For instance, it does not give a creature frightful presence.

Dragons automatically qualify for any classes, prestige classes, racial substitution levels, feats, powers, or spells that require the dragonblood subtype. Creatures presented in this book that have the dragonblood subtype include all the spawn of Tiamat (see pages 128–163). Should a creature acquire the dragon type, it loses the dragonblood subtype.

Earth Subtype: This subtype usually is used for elementals and outsiders that have a connection to the Elemental Plane of Earth. Earth creatures usually have burrow speeds, and most earth creatures can burrow through solid rock.

Effective Character Level (ECL): This number represents a creature's overall power relative to that of a character from the *Player's Handbook*. A creature that has an ECL of 10 is roughly equivalent to a 10th-level character. A creature's ECL is the sum of its Hit Dice (including class levels) and level adjustment. For instance, a blackspawn raider has 8 HD and a +3 level adjustment. It is the equivalent of an 11th-level character.

Elemental Type: An elemental is a being composed of one of the four classical elements: air, earth, fire, or water.
Features: An elemental has the following features.
—8-sided Hit Dice.
—Base attack bonus equal to 3/4 total Hit Dice (as cleric).
—Good saves depend on the element: Fortitude (earth, water) or Reflex (air, fire).
—Skill points equal to (2 + Int modifier, minimum 1) per Hit Die, with quadruple skill points for the first Hit Die.
Traits: An elemental possesses the following traits (unless otherwise noted in a creature's entry).
—Darkvision out to 60 feet.
—Immunity to poison, sleep effects, paralysis, and stunning.
—Not subject to extra damage from critical hits or flanking.
—Unlike most other living creatures, an elemental does not have a dual nature—its soul and body form one unit. When an elemental is slain, no soul is set loose. Spells that restore souls to their bodies, such as *raise dead, reincarnate,* and *resurrection,* don't work on an elemental. It takes a different magical effect, such as *limited wish, wish, miracle,* or *true resurrection,* to restore it to life.
—Proficient with natural weapons only, unless generally humanoid in form, in which case proficient with all simple weapons and any weapons mentioned in its entry.
—Proficient with whatever type of armor (light, medium, or heavy) it is described as wearing, as well as all lighter types.

Elementals not indicated as wearing armor are not proficient with armor. Elementals are proficient with shields if they are proficient with any form of armor.

—Elementals do not eat, sleep, or breathe.

Energy Drain (Su): This attack saps a living opponent's vital energy and happens automatically when a melee or ranged attack hits. Each successful energy drain bestows one or more negative levels (the creature's description specifies how many). If an attack that includes an energy drain scores a critical hit, it drains twice the given amount. Unless otherwise specified in the creature's description, a draining creature gains 5 temporary hit points (10 on a critical hit) for each negative level it bestows on an opponent. These temporary hit points last for up to 1 hour.

An affected opponent takes a –1 penalty on skill checks and ability checks, attack rolls, and saving throws, and loses one effective level or Hit Die (whenever level is used in a die roll or calculation) for each negative level. A spellcaster loses one spell slot of the highest level of spells she can cast and (if applicable) one prepared spell of that level; this loss persists until the negative level is removed.

Negative levels remain until 24 hours have passed or until they are removed by a spell, such as *restoration*. If a negative level is not removed before 24 hours have passed, the affected creature must attempt a Fortitude save (DC 10 + 1/2 draining creature's racial HD + draining creature's Cha modifier; the exact DC is given in the creature's descriptive text). On a success, the negative level goes away with no harm to the creature. On a failure, the negative level goes away, but the creature's level (or HD) is also reduced by one. A separate saving throw is required for each negative level.

Environment: This entry in a monster description provides the climate and terrain (as defined in Chapter 3 of the *Dungeon Master's Guide*) where the creature is typically found. Note that these environments can also exist in portions of dungeons due to magical effects or other supernatural interference, or as features in dungeons or other environment areas.

Evil Subtype: A subtype usually applied only to outsiders native to the evil-aligned Outer Planes. Evil outsiders are also called fiends. Most creatures that have this subtype also have evil alignments; however, if their alignments change, they still retain the subtype. Any effect that depends on alignment affects a creature that has this subtype as if the creature has an evil alignment, no matter what its alignment actually is. The creature also suffers effects according to its actual alignment. A creature that has the evil subtype overcomes damage reduction as if its natural weapons and any weapons it wields were evil-aligned (see Damage Reduction, above).

Extraordinary (Ex) Abilities: Extraordinary abilities are nonmagical, don't become ineffective in an antimagic field, and are not subject to any effect that disrupts magic. Using an extraordinary ability is a free action unless otherwise noted.

Extraplanar Subtype: A subtype applied to any creature when it is on a plane other than its native plane. A creature that travels the planes can gain or lose this subtype as it goes from plane to plane. This book assumes that encounters with creatures take place on the Material Plane, and every creature whose native plane is not the Material Plane has the extraplanar subtype (but would not have when on its home plane). Every extraplanar creature in this book has a home plane mentioned in its description. These home planes are taken from the Great Wheel cosmology of the D&D game (see Chapter 5 of the *Dungeon Master's Guide*). If your campaign uses a different cosmology, you will need to assign different home planes to extraplanar creatures.

Creatures not labeled as extraplanar are natives of the Material Plane, and they gain the extraplanar subtype if they leave the Material Plane. No creature has the extraplanar subtype when it is on a transitive plane; the transitive planes in the D&D cosmology are the Astral Plane, the Ethereal Plane, and the Plane of Shadow.

Fast Healing (Ex): A creature that has the fast healing special quality regains hit points at an exceptionally fast rate, usually 1 or more hit points per round, as given in the creature's entry (for example, a bloodfire ooze has fast healing 8). Except where noted here, fast healing is just like natural healing (PH 146). Fast healing does not restore hit points lost from starvation, thirst, or suffocation, and it does not allow a creature to regrow lost body parts. Unless otherwise stated, it does not allow lost body parts to be reattached.

Favored Class: A monster that takes levels in a class (or more than one class) has a favored class, just as player characters do. In addition, a monster's racial Hit Dice also count as a favored class, in effect: If the monster becomes a multiclass character, neither its favored class nor its racial Hit Dice count when determining whether the creature takes an experience point penalty.

Fear (Su or Sp): Fear attacks can have various effects.

Fear Aura (Su) The use of this ability is a free action. The aura can freeze an opponent (such as a mummy's despair) or function like the *fear* spell (for example, the aura of a gorefang spider). Other effects are possible. A fear aura is an area effect. The descriptive text gives the size and kind of area.

Fear Cones (Sp) and *Rays (Su)* These effects usually work like the *fear* spell.

If a fear effect allows a saving throw, it is a Will save (DC 10 + 1/2 fearsome creature's racial HD + creature's Cha modifier; the exact DC is given in the creature's descriptive text). All fear attacks are mind-affecting fear effects.

Fey Type: A fey is a creature that has supernatural abilities and connections to nature or to some other force or place. Fey are usually human-shaped.

Features: A fey has the following features.

—6-sided Hit Dice.

—Base attack bonus equal to 1/2 total Hit Dice (as wizard).

—Good Reflex and Will saves.

—Skill points equal to (6 + Int modifier) per Hit Die, with quadruple skill points for the first Hit Die.

Traits: A fey possesses the following traits (unless otherwise noted in a creature's entry).

—Low-light vision.

—Proficient with all simple weapons and any weapons mentioned in its entry.

—Proficient with whatever type of armor (light, medium, or heavy) it is described as wearing, as well as all lighter types. Fey not indicated as wearing armor are not proficient with armor. Fey are proficient with shields if they are proficient with any form of armor.

—Fey eat, sleep, and breathe.

Fire Subtype: A creature that has the fire subtype has immunity to fire. It has vulnerability to cold, which means it takes half again as much (+50%) damage as normal from cold, regardless of whether a saving throw is allowed, or if the save is a success or failure.

Frightful Presence (Ex): This special quality makes a creature's very presence unsettling to foes. It takes effect automatically when the creature performs some sort of dramatic action (such as charging, attacking, or snarling). Opponents within range who witness the action might become frightened or shaken.

Actions required to trigger the ability are given in the creature's descriptive text. The range is usually 30 feet, and the duration is usually 5d6 rounds.

This ability affects only opponents that have fewer Hit Dice or levels than the creature has. An affected opponent can resist the effects by making a successful Will save (DC 10 + 1/2 frightful creature's racial HD + frightful creature's Cha modifier; the exact DC is given in the creature's descriptive text). An opponent that succeeds on the saving throw is immune to that same creature's frightful presence for 24 hours. Frightful presence is a mind-affecting fear effect.

Gaze (Su): A gaze attack takes effect when opponents look at the creature's eyes. The attack can have almost any sort of effect: petrification, death, charm, and so on. The typical range is 30 feet, but check the creature's entry for details.

The type of saving throw for a gaze attack varies, but it is usually a Will or Fortitude save (DC 10 + 1/2 gazing creature's racial HD + gazing creature's Cha modifier; the exact DC is given in the creature's descriptive text). A successful saving throw negates the effect. A monster's gaze attack is described in abbreviated form in its description.

Each opponent within range of a gaze attack must attempt a saving throw each round at the beginning of his or her turn in the initiative order. Only looking directly at a creature that has a gaze attack leaves an opponent vulnerable. Opponents can avoid the need to attempt the saving throw by not looking at the creature, in one of two ways.

Averting Eyes: The opponent avoids looking at the creature's face, instead looking at its body, watching its shadow, tracking it in a reflective surface, and so on. Each round, the opponent has a 50% chance to not need to attempt a saving throw against the gaze attack. The creature that has the gaze attack, however, gains concealment against that opponent.

Wearing a Blindfold: The opponent cannot see the creature at all (also possible to achieve by turning one's back on the creature or shutting one's eyes). The creature that has the gaze attack gains total concealment against the opponent.

A creature that has a gaze attack can actively gaze as an attack action by choosing a target within range. That opponent must attempt a saving throw but can try to avoid this as described above. Thus, it is possible for an opponent to save against a creature's gaze twice during the same round, once before the opponent's action and once during the creature's turn.

Gaze attacks can affect ethereal opponents. A creature is immune to gaze attacks of others of its kind unless otherwise noted. Allies of a creature that has a gaze attack might be affected. All the creature's allies are considered to be averting their eyes from the creature that has the gaze attack, and have a 50% chance to not need to attempt a saving throw against the gaze attack each round. The creature also can veil its eyes, thus negating its gaze ability.

Giant Type: A giant is a humanoid-shaped creature of great strength, usually of at least Large size.

Features: A giant has the following features.

—8-sided Hit Dice.

—Base attack bonus equal to 3/4 total Hit Dice (as cleric).

—Good Fortitude saves.

—Skill points equal to (2 + Int modifier, minimum 1) per Hit Die, with quadruple skill points for the first Hit Die.

Traits: A giant possesses the following traits (unless otherwise noted in a creature's entry).

—Low-light vision.

—Proficient with all simple and martial weapons, as well as any natural weapons.

—Proficient with whatever type of armor (light, medium or heavy) it is described as wearing, as well as all lighter types. Giants not described as wearing armor are not proficient with armor. Giants are proficient with shields if they are proficient with any form of armor.

—Giants eat, sleep, and breathe.

Goblinoid Subtype: Goblinoids are stealthy humanoids who live by hunting and raiding and who all speak Goblin.

Good Subtype: A subtype usually applied only to outsiders native to the good-aligned Outer Planes. Most creatures that have this subtype also have good alignments; however, if their alignments change, they still retain the subtype. Any effect that depends on alignment affects a creature that has this subtype as if the creature has a good alignment, no matter what its alignment actually is. The creature also suffers effects according to its actual alignment. A creature that has the good subtype overcomes damage reduction as if its natural weapons and any weapons it wields were good-aligned (see Damage Reduction, above).

Humanoid Type: A humanoid usually has two arms, two legs, and one head, or a humanlike torso, arms, and a head. Humanoids have few or no supernatural or extraordinary abilities, but most can speak and usually have well-developed societies. They usually are Small or Medium. Every humanoid creature also has a subtype, such as elf, goblinoid, or reptilian.

Humanoids that have 1 Hit Die exchange the features of their humanoid Hit Die for the class features of a PC or NPC class. Humanoids of this sort are presented as 1st-level warriors, which means that they have average combat ability and poor saving throws.

Humanoids that have more than 1 Hit Die (for example, gnolls and bugbears) are the only humanoids who make use of the features of the humanoid type.

Features: A humanoid has the following features (unless otherwise noted in a creature's entry).

—8-sided Hit Dice, or by character class.

—Base attack bonus equal to 3/4 total Hit Dice (as cleric).

—Good Reflex saves (usually; a humanoid's good save varies).

—Skill points equal to (2 + Int modifier, minimum 1) per Hit Die, with quadruple skill points for the first Hit Die, or by character class.

Traits: A humanoid possesses the following traits (unless otherwise noted in a creature's entry).

—Proficient with all simple weapons, or by character class.

—Proficient with whatever type of armor (light, medium, or heavy) it is described as wearing, or by character class. If a humanoid does not have a class and wears armor, it is proficient with that type of armor and all lighter types. Humanoids not indicated as wearing armor are not proficient with armor. Humanoids are proficient with shields if they are proficient with any form of armor.

—Humanoids breathe, eat, and sleep.

Immediate Action: Some monsters have special abilities that they can employ by taking an immediate action. Much like a swift action (see page 219), an immediate action consumes a very small amount of time, but represents a larger expenditure of effort and energy than a free action. Unlike a swift action, an immediate action can be performed at any time—even if it's not the creature's turn.

When a creature uses an immediate action on its turn, that is the same as using a swift action, and that action counts as the creature's swift action for that turn. A creature cannot use another immediate action or a swift action until after its next turn if it has used an immediate action when it is not currently its turn. A creature also cannot use an immediate action if it is currently flat-footed.

Immunity: A creature that has immunity to an effect is never harmed (or helped) by that effect. A creature cannot suppress an immunity in order to receive a beneficial effect.

Improved Grab (Ex): If a creature that has this ability hits with a melee weapon (usually a claw or bite attack), it deals normal damage and attempts to start a grapple as a free action

without provoking attacks of opportunity (see Grapple, PH 155). No initial touch attack is required.

Unless otherwise noted, improved grab works only against opponents at least one size category smaller than the creature. The creature has the option to conduct the grapple normally, or simply use the part of its body it used in the improved grab to hold the opponent. If it chooses to do the latter, it takes a –20 penalty on grapple checks, but is not considered grappled itself; the creature does not lose its Dexterity bonus to AC, still threatens an area, and can use its remaining attacks against other opponents.

A successful hold does not deal any extra damage unless the creature also has the constrict ability. If the creature does not constrict, each successful grapple check it makes during successive rounds automatically deals the damage indicated for the attack that established the hold. Otherwise, it deals constriction damage as well (the amount is given in the creature's descriptive text).

When a creature gets a hold after an improved grab attack, it pulls the opponent into its space. This act does not provoke attacks of opportunity. It can even move (possibly carrying away the opponent), provided it can drag the opponent's weight.

Incorporeal Subtype: Some creatures are incorporeal by nature, while others (such as those that become ghosts) can acquire the incorporeal subtype. An incorporeal creature has no physical body. It can be harmed only by other incorporeal creatures, magic weapons or creatures that strike as magic weapons, and spells, spell-like abilities, or supernatural abilities. It is immune to all nonmagical attack forms. Even when hit by spells, including touch spells, or magic weapons, it has a 50% chance to ignore any damage from a corporeal source (except for positive energy, negative energy, force effects such as *magic missile*, or attacks made with ghost touch weapons). Nondamaging spell effects affect incorporeal creatures normally unless they require corporeal targets to function (such as *implosion*) or they create a corporeal effect that incorporeal creatures would normally be unaffected by (such as a *web* or *wall of stone* spell). Although it is not a magical attack, holy water can affect incorporeal undead, but a hit with holy water has a 50% chance of not affecting an incorporeal creature.

An incorporeal creature's attacks pass through (ignore) natural armor, armor, and shields, although deflection bonuses and force effects (such as *mage armor*) work normally against it. Nonmagical attacks made by an incorporeal creature with a melee weapon have no effect on corporeal targets, and any melee attack an incorporeal creature makes with a magic weapon against a corporeal target has a 50% miss chance, except for attacks it makes with a ghost touch weapon, while are made normally (no miss chance).

Any equipment worn or carried by an incorporeal creature is also incorporeal as long as it remains in the creature's possession. An object that the creature relinquishes loses its incorporeal quality (and the creature loses the ability to manipulate the object). If an incorporeal creature uses a thrown weapon or a ranged weapon, the projectile becomes corporeal as soon as it is fired and can affect a corporeal target normally (no miss chance). Magic items possessed by an incorporeal creature work normally with respect to their effects on the creature or on another target. Similarly, spells cast by an incorporeal creature affect corporeal creatures normally.

An incorporeal creature has no natural armor bonus but has a deflection bonus equal to its Charisma bonus (always at least +1, even if the creature's Charisma score does not normally provide a bonus).

An incorporeal creature can enter or pass through solid objects, but must remain adjacent to the object's exterior, and so cannot pass entirely through an object whose space is larger than its own. It can sense the presence of creatures or objects within a square adjacent to its current location, but enemies have total concealment (50% miss chance) from an incorporeal creature that is inside an object. In order to see farther from the object it is in and attack normally, the incorporeal creature must emerge. An incorporeal creature inside an object has total cover, but when it attacks a creature outside the object it only has cover, so a creature outside with a readied action could strike at it as it attacks. An incorporeal creature cannot pass through a force effect.

Incorporeal creatures pass through and operate in water as easily as they do in air. Incorporeal creatures cannot fall or take falling damage. Incorporeal creatures cannot make trip or grapple attempts, nor can they be tripped or grappled. In fact, they cannot take any physical action that would move or manipulate an opponent or its equipment, nor are they subject to such actions. Incorporeal creatures have no weight and do not set off traps that are triggered by weight.

An incorporeal creature moves silently and cannot be heard with Listen checks if it doesn't wish to be. It has no Strength score, so its Dexterity modifier applies to both its melee attacks and its ranged attacks. Nonvisual senses, such as scent and blindsight, are either ineffective or only partly effective with regard to incorporeal creatures. Incorporeal creatures have an innate sense of direction and can move at full speed even when they cannot see.

Lawful Subtype: The lawful subtype usually applies only to outsiders native to the lawful-aligned Outer Planes. Most creatures that have this subtype also have lawful alignments; however, if their alignments change, they still retain the subtype. Any effect that depends on alignment affects a creature that has this subtype as if the creature has a lawful alignment, no matter what its alignment actually is. The creature also suffers effects according to its actual alignment. A creature that has the lawful subtype overcomes damage reduction as if its natural weapons and any weapons it wields were lawful-aligned (see Damage Reduction, above).

Level Adjustment: Certain monsters can used as the basis for interesting, viable player characters. These creatures have a level adjustment entry, which is a number that is added to the creature's total Hit Dice to arrive at its effective character level. A creature that has multiple special abilities is more powerful as a player character than its Hit Dice alone would indicate. For example, a drow elf has spell resistance, bonuses to its ability scores, and spell-like abilities. Its level adjustment of +2 indicates that a 1st-level drow wizard is the equivalent of a 3rd-level character.

Some creatures' level adjustment entries include the word "(cohort)." Although these creatures might be problematic as PCs, they make good companions for a character who has taken the Leadership feat. Some other creatures aren't intended for use as PCs or cohorts but can become companions through the use of the Improved Familiar feat. In these cases, the level adjustment entry is a dash followed by the words "(Improved Familiar)."

Level adjustment is not the same thing as an adjustment to a creature's Challenge Rating because of some special qualities it possesses. Challenge Rating reflects how difficult an opponent is to fight in a limited number of encounters. Level adjustment shows how powerful a creature is as a player character or cohort in campaign play. For instance, a drow receives a +1 adjustment to its Challenge Rating to account for its special abilities, indicating that it's tougher in a fight than its Hit Dice would suggest, but its level adjustment is +2 to balance its abilities over long-term play.

Living: Any creature that has a Constitution score is a living creature. Constructs and undead are not living creatures.

Living Construct Subtype: A living construct is a new subtype of construct, a created being given sentience and free will through powerful and complex creation enchantments. Living constructs combine aspects of both constructs and living creatures, as detailed below.

Features: A living construct derives its Hit Dice, base attack bonus progression, saving throws, and skill points from the class it selects.

Traits: A living construct possesses the following traits (unless otherwise noted in a creature's entry).

—Unlike other constructs, a living construct has a Constitution score. A living construct does not gain bonus hit points by size but gains (or loses) bonus hit points through a Constitution bonus (or penalty) as with other living creatures.

—Unlike other constructs, a living construct does not have low-light vision or darkvision.

—Unlike other constructs, a living construct is not immune to mind-influencing effects.

—Immunity to poison, sleep effects, paralysis, disease, nausea, fatigue, exhaustion, and energy drain.

—A living construct cannot heal damage naturally.

—Unlike other constructs, living constructs are subject to extra damage from critical hits, effects requiring a Fortitude save, death from massive damage, nonlethal damage, stunning, ability damage, ability drain, and death effects or necromancy effects.

—Unlike other constructs, a living construct can use the run action.

—Living constructs can be affected by spells that target living creatures as well as by those that target constructs. Damage dealt to a living construct can be healed by a *cure light wounds* spell or a *repair light damage* spell, for example, and a living construct is vulnerable to a *harm* spell. However, spells from the healing subschool provide only half effect to a living construct.

—A living construct responds slightly differently from other living creatures when reduced to 0 hit points. A living construct that has 0 hit points is disabled, just like a living creature. He can only take a single move action or standard action in each round, but strenuous activity does not risk further injury. When his hit points are less than 0 and greater than –10, a living construct is inert. He is unconscious and helpless, and he cannot perform any actions. However, an inert living construct does not lose additional hit points unless more damage is dealt to him, as with a living creature that is stable.

—Can be raised or resurrected.

—Does not need to eat, sleep, or breathe, but can still benefit from the effects of consumable spells and magic items such as *heroes' feast* and potions.

—Does not need to sleep, but must rest for 8 hours before preparing spells.

Low-Light Vision (Ex): A creature that has low-light vision can see twice as far as a human in starlight, moonlight, torchlight, and similar conditions of shadowy illumination. It retains the ability to distinguish color and detail under these conditions.

Magic Strike: Natural weapon attacks made by a creature that has this ability are treated as magic for the purpose of overcoming damage reduction. When it applies, "magic strike" appears in the Atk Options line of a creature's statistics block.

Magical Beast Type: Magical beasts are similar to animals but can have Intelligence scores higher than 2. Magical beasts usually have supernatural or extraordinary abilities, but sometimes are merely bizarre in appearance or habits.

Features: A magical beast has the following features.

—10-sided Hit Dice.

—Base attack bonus equal to total Hit Dice (as fighter).

—Good Fortitude and Reflex saves.

—Skill points equal to (2 + Int modifier, minimum 1) per Hit Die, with quadruple skill points for the first Hit Die.

Traits: A magical beast possesses the following traits (unless otherwise noted in a creature's entry).

—Darkvision out to 60 feet and low-light vision.

—Proficient with its natural weapons only.

—Proficient with no armor.

—Magical beasts eat, sleep, and breathe.

Manufactured Weapons: Some monsters employ manufactured weapons when they attack. Creatures that use swords, bows, spears, and the like follow the same rules as characters, including those for additional attacks from a high base attack bonus and two-weapon fighting penalties. This category also includes "found items," such as rocks and logs, that a creature wields in combat—in essence, any weapon that is not intrinsic to the creature.

Some creatures combine attacks with natural and manufactured weapons when they make a full attack. When they do so, the manufactured weapon attack is considered the primary attack unless the creature's description indicates otherwise (using the manufactured weapon consumes most of the creature's attention), and any natural weapons the creature also uses are considered secondary natural attacks. These secondary attacks do not interfere with the primary attack as attacking with an off-hand weapon does, but they take the usual –5 penalty (or –2 with the Multiattack feat) for such attacks, even if the natural weapon used is normally the creature's primary natural weapon.

Monstrous Humanoid Type: Monstrous humanoids are similar to humanoids, but they have monstrous or animalistic features. They often have magical abilities as well.

Features: A monstrous humanoid has the following features.

—8-sided Hit Dice.

—Base attack bonus equal to total Hit Dice (as fighter).

—Good Reflex and Will saves.

—Skill points equal to (2 + Int modifier, minimum 1) per Hit Die, with quadruple skill points for the first Hit Die.

Traits: A monstrous humanoid possesses the following traits (unless otherwise noted in a creature's entry).

—Darkvision out to 60 feet.

—Proficient with all simple weapons and any weapons mentioned in its entry.

—Proficient with whatever type of armor (light, medium, or heavy) it is described as wearing, as well as all lighter types. Monstrous humanoids not indicated as wearing armor are not proficient with armor. Monstrous humanoids are proficient with shields if they are proficient with any form of armor.

—Monstrous humanoids eat, sleep, and breathe.

Movement Modes: Creatures can have modes of movement other than walking and running. These are natural, not magical, unless specifically noted in a monster description.

Burrow: A creature that has a burrow speed can tunnel through dirt, but not through rock unless the descriptive text says otherwise. Creatures cannot charge or run while burrowing. Most burrowing creatures do not leave behind tunnels other creatures can use (either because the material they tunnel through fills in behind them or because they do not actually dislocate any material when burrowing); see the individual creature descriptions for details.

Climb: A creature that has a climb speed has a +8 racial bonus on Climb checks. The creature must succeed on a Climb check to climb any wall or slope that has a DC higher than 0, but it always can choose to take 10 (see Checks without Rolls, PH 65), even if rushed or threatened while climbing. The creature climbs at the given speed while climbing. If it chooses an accelerated climb (see the Climb skill, PH 69), it moves at double the given climb speed (or its base land speed, whichever is lower) and attempts a single Climb check at a –5 penalty. Creatures cannot run while climbing. A creature retains its Dexterity bonus to Armor Class (if any) while climbing, and opponents get no special bonus on their attacks against a climbing creature.

Fly: A creature that has a fly speed can move through the air at the indicated speed if carrying no more than a light load;

see Carrying Capacity, PH 161. (Note that medium armor does not necessarily constitute a medium load.) All fly speeds include a parenthetical note indicating maneuverability, as follows:

—Perfect: The creature can perform almost any aerial maneuver it wishes. It moves through the air as well as a human moves over smooth ground.

—Good: The creature is very agile in the air (like a housefly or a hummingbird), but cannot change direction as readily as those that have perfect maneuverability.

—Average: The creature can fly as adroitly as a small bird.

—Poor: The creature flies as well as a very large bird.

—Clumsy: The creature can barely maneuver at all.

A creature that flies can make dive attacks. A dive attack works just like a charge, but the diving creature must move a minimum of 30 feet and descend at least 10 feet. It can make only claw or talon attacks, but these deal double damage. A creature can use the run action while flying, provided it flies in a straight line.

For more information, see Tactical Aerial Movement, DMG 20.

Swim: A creature that has a swim speed can move through water at that speed without making Swim checks. It has a +8 racial bonus on any Swim check to perform some special action or avoid a hazard. The creature can always can choose to take 10 on a Swim check, even if distracted or endangered. The creature can use the run action while swimming, provided it swims in a straight line.

Native Subtype: A subtype applied only to outsiders. These creatures have mortal ancestors or a strong connection to the Material Plane and can be raised, reincarnated, or resurrected just as other living creatures can be. Creatures that have this subtype are native to the Material Plane (hence the subtype's name).

Unlike true outsiders, native outsiders need to eat and sleep.

Natural Weapons: Natural weapons are weapons that are physically a part of a creature. A creature making a melee attack with a natural weapon is considered armed and does not provoke attacks of opportunity. Likewise, it threatens any space it can reach.

Creatures do not receive additional attacks from a high base attack bonus when using natural weapons. The number of attacks a creature can make with its natural weapons depends on the type of the attack—generally, a creature can make one bite attack, one attack per claw or tentacle, one gore attack, one sting attack, or one slam attack (although Large creatures that have arms or armlike limbs can make a slam attack with each arm). Refer to the individual monster descriptions.

Unless otherwise noted, a natural weapon threatens a critical hit on a natural attack roll of 20.

When a creature has more than one natural weapon, one of them (or sometimes a pair or set of them) is the primary weapon. All the creature's remaining natural weapons are secondary.

The primary weapon is given in the creature's Attack entry, and the primary weapon or weapons is given first in the creature's Full Attack entry. A creature's primary natural weapon is its most effective natural attack, usually by virtue of the creature's physiology, training, or innate talent with the weapon. An attack with a primary natural weapon uses the creature's full attack bonus. Attacks with secondary natural weapons are less effective and are made with a –5 penalty on the attack roll, no matter how many there are. (Creatures that have the Multiattack feat take only a –2 penalty on secondary attacks.)

Natural weapons have types just as other weapons do. The most common are summarized below.

Bite: The creature attacks with its mouth, dealing piercing, slashing, and bludgeoning damage.

Claw or Talon: The creature rips with a sharp appendage, dealing piercing and slashing damage.

Gore: The creature spears the opponent with an antler, horn, or similar appendage, dealing piercing damage.

Slap or Slam: The creature batters opponents with an appendage, dealing bludgeoning damage.

Sting: The creature stabs with a stinger, dealing piercing damage. Sting attacks usually deal damage from poison in addition to hit point damage.

Tentacle: The creature flails at opponents with a powerful tentacle, dealing bludgeoning (and sometimes slashing) damage.

Nonabilities: Some creatures lack certain ability scores. These creatures do not have an ability score of 0—they lack the ability altogether. The modifier for a nonability is +0. Other effects of nonabilities are detailed below.

Strength: Any creature that can physically manipulate other objects has at least 1 point of Strength.

A creature that has no Strength score can't exert force, usually because it has no physical body (a whisper demon, for example). The creature automatically fails Strength checks. If the creature can attack, it applies its Dexterity modifier to its base attack bonus instead of a Strength modifier.

Dexterity: Any creature that can move has at least 1 point of Dexterity.

A creature that has no Dexterity score can't move. If it can perform actions (such as casting spells), it applies its Intelligence modifier to initiative checks instead of a Dexterity modifier. The creature automatically fails Reflex saves and Dexterity checks.

Constitution: Any living creature has at least 1 point of Constitution.

A creature that has no Constitution has no body (a stone specter, for example) or no metabolism (a clockwork stallion). It is immune to any effect that requires a Fortitude save unless the effect works on objects or is harmless. For example, a zombie is unaffected by any kind of poison but is susceptible to a *disintegrate* spell. The creature is also immune to ability damage, ability drain, and energy drain, and automatically fails Constitution checks. A creature that has no Constitution cannot tire and thus can run indefinitely without tiring (unless the creature's description says it cannot run).

Intelligence: Any creature that can think, learn, or remember has at least 1 point of Intelligence.

A creature that has no Intelligence score (such as a bloodsilk spider) is mindless, an automaton operating on simple instincts or programmed instructions. It has immunity to mind-affecting spells and abilities (charms, compulsions, phantasms, patterns, and morale effects) and automatically fails Intelligence checks.

Mindless creatures do not gain feats or skills, although they might have bonus feats or racial skill bonuses.

Wisdom: Any creature that can perceive its environment in any fashion has at least 1 point of Wisdom.

Anything that has no Wisdom score is an object, not a creature. Anything without a Wisdom score also has no Charisma score.

Charisma: Any creature capable of telling the difference between itself and things that are not itself has at least 1 point of Charisma.

Anything that has no Charisma score is an object, not a creature. Anything without a Charisma score also has no Wisdom score.

Ooze Type: An ooze is an amorphous or mutable creature, usually mindless.

Features: An ooze has the following features.

—10-sided Hit Dice.

—Base attack bonus equal to 3/4 total Hit Dice (as cleric).

—No good saving throws.

—Skill points equal to (2 + Int modifier, minimum 1) per Hit Die, with quadruple skill points for the first Hit Die, if the ooze has an Intelligence score. However, most oozes are mindless and gain no skill points or feats.

Traits: An ooze possesses the following traits (unless otherwise noted in a creature's entry).

—Mindless: No Intelligence score, and immunity to all mind-affecting spells and abilities (charms, compulsions, phantasms, patterns, and morale effects).

—Blind (but have the blindsight special quality), with immunity to gaze attacks, visual effects, illusions, and other attack forms that rely on sight.

—Immunity to poison, sleep effects, paralysis, polymorph, and stunning.

—Some oozes have the ability to deal acid damage to objects. In such a case, the amount of damage is equal to 10 + 1/2 ooze's HD + ooze's Con modifier per full round of contact.

—Not subject to extra damage from critical hits or flanking.

—Proficient with its natural weapons only.

—Proficient with no armor.

—Oozes eat and breathe, but do not sleep.

Outsider Type: An outsider is at least partially composed of the essence (but not necessarily the material) of some plane other than the Material Plane. Some creatures start out as some other type and become outsiders when they attain a higher (or lower) state of spiritual existence.

Features: An outsider has the following features.

—8-sided Hit Dice.

—Base attack bonus equal to total Hit Dice (as fighter).

—Good Fortitude, Reflex, and Will saves.

—Skill points equal to (8 + Int modifier) per Hit Die, with quadruple skill points for the first Hit Die.

Traits: An outsider possesses the following traits (unless otherwise noted in a creature's entry).

—Darkvision out to 60 feet.

—Unlike most other living creatures, an outsider does not have a dual nature—its soul and body form one unit. When an outsider is slain, no soul is set loose. Spells that restore souls to their bodies, such as *raise dead, reincarnate,* and *resurrection,* don't work on an outsider. It takes a different magical effect, such as *limited wish, wish, miracle,* or *true resurrection* to restore it to life. An outsider that has the native subtype (see page 214) can be raised, reincarnated, or resurrected just as other living creatures can be.

—Proficient with all simple and martial weapons and any weapons mentioned in its entry.

—Proficient with whatever type of armor (light, medium, or heavy) it is described as wearing, as well as all lighter types. Outsiders not indicated as wearing armor are not proficient with armor. Outsiders are proficient with shields if they are proficient with any form of armor.

—Outsiders breathe, but do not need to eat or sleep (although they can do so if they wish). Native outsiders breathe, eat, and sleep.

Paralysis (Ex or Su): A paralysis attack renders the victim immobile. Paralyzed creatures cannot move, speak, or take any physical actions. The creature is rooted to the spot, frozen and helpless. Paralysis works on the body, and a character can usually resist it with a successful Fortitude saving throw (the DC is given in the creature's description). Unlike *hold person* and similar effects, a paralysis effect does not allow a new save each round. A winged creature flying in the air at the time that it is paralyzed cannot flap its wings and falls. A swimmer can't swim and might drown.

Plant Type: This type comprises vegetable creatures. Note that regular plants, such as one finds growing in gardens and fields, lack Wisdom and Charisma scores (see Nonabilities, above) and are not creatures, but objects, even though they are alive.

Features: A plant creature has the following features.

—8-sided Hit Dice.

—Base attack bonus equal to 3/4 total Hit Dice (as cleric).

—Good Fortitude saves.

—Skill points equal to (2 + Int modifier, minimum 1) per Hit Die, with quadruple skill points for the first Hit Die, if the plant creature has an Intelligence score. However, some plant creatures are mindless and gain no skill points or feats.

Traits: A plant creature possesses the following traits (unless otherwise noted in a creature's entry).

—Low-light vision.

—Immunity to all mind-affecting spells or abilities (charms, compulsions, phantasms, patterns, and morale effects).

—Immunity to poison, sleep effects, paralysis, polymorph, and stunning.

—Not subject to extra damage from critical hits.

—Proficient with its natural weapons only.

—Proficient with no armor.

—Plants breathe and eat, but do not sleep.

Poison (Ex): Poison attacks deal initial damage, such as ability damage (see page 205) or some other effect, to the opponent on a failed Fortitude save. Unless otherwise noted, another saving throw is required 1 minute later (regardless of the first save's result) to avoid secondary damage. A creature's descriptive text provides the details.

A creature that has a poison attack is immune to its own poison and the poison of others of its kind.

The Fortitude save DC against a poison attack is equal to 10 + 1/2 poisoning creature's racial HD + poisoning creature's Con modifier (the exact DC is given in the creature's descriptive text). A successful save avoids (negates) the damage.

Pounce (Ex): When a creature that has this ability makes a charge, it can follow with a full attack—including rake attacks if the creature also has the rake ability.

Psionics (Sp): These are spell-like abilities that a creature generates with the power of its mind. The saving throw (if any) against a psionic ability is 10 + the level of the spell the ability resembles or duplicates + the creature's Cha modifier.

Racial Hit Dice: The Hit Dice a monster has by virtue of what type of creature it is. Hit Dice gained from taking class levels are not racial Hit Dice. For example, the corruptor of fate assassin described in this book is a 12 HD creature because of its five levels of assassin, but it has 7 racial Hit Dice (the same number as a typical corruptor of fate without any class levels).

Rake (Ex): A creature that has this ability gains extra natural attacks when it grapples its foe. Normally, a monster can attack with only one of its natural weapons while grappling, but a monster that has the rake ability usually gains two additional claw attacks that it can use only against a grappled foe. Rake attacks are not subject to the usual –4 penalty for attacking with a natural weapon in a grapple.

A monster that has the rake ability must begin its turn grappling to use its rake—it can't begin a grapple and rake in the same turn.

Ray (Su or Sp): This form of attack works like a ranged attack (see Aiming a Spell, *PH* 175). Hitting with a ray attack requires a successful ranged touch attack roll, ignoring armor, natural armor, and shield and using the creature's ranged attack bonus. Ray attacks have no range increment. The creature's descriptive text specifies the maximum range, effects, and any applicable saving throw.

Regeneration (Ex): A creature that has this ability is difficult to kill. Damage dealt to the creature is treated as nonlethal damage. The creature automatically heals nonlethal damage at a fixed rate per round, as given in the entry (for example, a dread blossom swarm has regeneration 5). Certain attack forms, typically fire and acid, deal lethal damage to the creature, which doesn't go away. The creature's descriptive text describes the details.

A regenerating creature that has been rendered unconscious through nonlethal damage can be killed with a coup de grace (*PH* 153). The attack cannot be of a type that automatically converts to nonlethal damage.

Attack forms that don't deal hit point damage (for example, most poisons) ignore regeneration. Regeneration also does not restore hit points lost from starvation, thirst, or suffocation.

Regenerating creatures can regrow lost portions of their bodies and can reattach severed limbs or body parts; details are in the creature's descriptive text. Severed parts that are not reattached wither and die normally.

A creature must have a Constitution score to have the regeneration ability.

Rend (Ex): If a creature that has this ability hits with the specified natural attack, it latches onto the opponent's body and tears the flesh. A rend attack deals damage equal to the creature's natural attack + 1-1/2 times its Str modifier. The creature's descriptive text gives the exact amount.

Reptilian Subtype: These creatures are scaly and usually cold-blooded. The reptilian subtype is only used to describe a set of humanoid races, not all animals and monsters that are truly reptiles.

Resistance to Energy (Ex): A creature that has this special quality ignores some damage of the indicated type each time it takes damage of that kind (commonly acid, cold, fire, or electricity). The entry indicates the amount and type of damage ignored. For example, a wrackspawn has resistance to fire 5, so it ignores the first 5 points of fire damage dealt to it anytime it takes fire damage.

Scent (Ex) This special quality allows a creature to detect approaching enemies, sniff out hidden foes, and track by sense of smell. Creatures that have the scent ability can identify familiar odors just as humans do familiar sights.

The creature can detect opponents within 30 feet by sense of smell. If the opponent is upwind, the range increases to 60 feet; if downwind, it drops to 15 feet. Strong scents, such as smoke or rotting garbage, can be detected at twice the ranges noted above. Overpowering scents, such as skunk musk or troglodyte stench, can be detected at triple normal range.

When a creature detects a scent, the exact location of the source is not revealed—only its presence somewhere within range. The creature can take a move action to note the direction of the scent. Whenever the creature comes within 5 feet of the source, the creature pinpoints the source's location.

A creature that has the Track feat and the scent ability can follow tracks by smell, making a sucessful Wisdom (or Survival) check to find or follow a track. The typical DC for a fresh trail is 10 (no matter what kind of surface holds the scent). This DC increases or decreases depending on how strong the quarry's odor is, the number of creatures, and the

CREATURE SIZES

Size Category	AC/Attack Modifier	Grapple Modifier	Hide Modifier	Dimension*	Weight**	Space (in squares)	Reach (Tall) (in squares)	Reach (Long) (in squares)
Fine	+8	−16	+16	6 in. or less	1/8 lb. or less	1/2 ft. (1/100)	0 ft. (0)	—
Diminutive	+4	−12	+12	6 in.–1 ft.	1/8 lb. – 1 lb.	1 ft. (1/25)	0 ft. (0)	—
Tiny	+2	−8	+8	1 ft.–2 ft.	1 – 8 lb.	2-1/2 ft. (1/4)	0 ft. (0)	—
Small	+1	−4	+4	2 ft.–4 ft.	8 – 60 lb.	5 ft. (1)	5 ft. (1)	—
Medium	+0	+0	+0	4 ft.–8 ft.	60 – 500 lb.	5 ft. (1)	5 ft. (1)	5 ft. (1)
Large	−1	+4	−4	8 ft.–16 ft.	500 – 4,000 lb.	10 ft. (2 × 2)	10 ft. (2)	5 ft. (1)
Huge	−2	+8	−8	16 ft.–32 ft.	2 – 16 tons	15 ft. (3 × 3)	15 ft. (3)	10 ft. (2)
Gargantuan	−4	+12	−12	32 ft.–64 ft.	16 – 125 tons	20 ft. (4 × 4)	20 ft. (4)	15 ft. (3)
Colossal	−8	+16	−16	64 ft. or more	125 tons or more	30 ft.+ (6 × 6+)	30 ft.+ (6+)	20 ft.+ (4+)

* Biped's height, quadruped's body length (nose to base of tail).
** Assumes that the creature is roughly as dense as a regular animal. A creature made of stone will weigh considerably more. A gaseous creature will weigh much less.

age of the trail. For each hour that the trail is cold, the DC increases by 2. The ability otherwise follows the rules for the Track feat. Creatures tracking by scent ignore the effects of surface conditions and poor visibility.

Shapechanger Subtype: A shapechanger has the supernatural ability to assume one or more alternate forms. Many magical effects allow some kind of shape shifting, and not every creature that can change shapes has the shapechanger subtype.

Traits: A shapechanger possesses the following traits (unless otherwise noted in a creature's entry).

—Proficient with its natural weapons, with simple weapons, and with any weapons mentioned in the creature's description.

—Proficient with any armor mentioned in the creature's description, as well as all lighter forms. If no form of armor is mentioned, the shapechanger is not proficient with armor. A shapechanger is proficient with shields if it is proficient with any type of armor.

Size: The nine size categories are (in ascending order) Fine, Diminutive, Tiny, Small, Medium, Large, Huge, Gargantuan, and Colossal. A creature's size provides a modifier to its Armor Class and attack bonus, a modifier on grapple checks it attempts, and a modifier on Hide checks. The Creature Sizes table above provides a summary of the attributes that apply to each size category.

Sonic Attacks (Su): Unless otherwise noted, a sonic attack follows the rules for spreads (see Aiming a Spell, PH 175). The range of the spread is measured from the creature using the sonic attack. Once a sonic attack has taken effect, deafening the subject or stopping its ears does not end the effect. Stopping one's ears ahead of time allows opponents to avoid having to attempt saving throws against mind-affecting sonic attacks, but not other kinds of sonic attacks (such as those that deal damage). Stopping one's ears is a full-round action and requires wax or other soundproof material to stuff into the ears.

Spell-Like (Sp) Abilities: Spell-like abilities are magical and work just like spells (though they are not spells and so have no verbal, somatic, material, focus, or XP components). They go away in an antimagic field and are subject to spell

resistance if the spell the ability resembles or duplicates would be subject to spell resistance.

A spell-like ability usually has a limit on how often it can be used. A spell-like ability that can be used at will has no use limit. Using a spell-like ability is a standard action unless otherwise noted, and doing so while threatened provokes attacks of opportunity. It is possible to make a successful Concentration check to use a spell-like ability defensively and avoid provoking attacks of opportunity, just as when casting a spell. A spell-like ability can be disrupted just as a spell can be. Spell-like abilities cannot be used to counterspell, nor can they be counterspelled.

For creatures that have spell-like abilities, a designated caster level defines how difficult it is to dispel their spell-like effects and to define any level-dependent variables (such as range and duration) the abilities might have. The creature's caster level never affects which spell-like abilities the creature has; sometimes the given caster level is lower than the level a spellcasting character would need to cast the spell of the same name. If no caster level is specified, the caster level is equal to the creature's racial Hit Dice.

The saving throw (if any) against a spell-like ability is 10 + the level of the spell the ability resembles or duplicates + the creature's Cha modifier.

Some spell-like abilities duplicate spells that might work differently or be of a different level when cast by characters of different classes. A monster's spell-like abilities are presumed to be the sorcerer/wizard versions. If the spell in question is not a sorcerer/wizard spell, then default to cleric, druid, bard, paladin, and ranger, in that order.

Spell Resistance (Ex): A creature that has spell resistance can avoid the effects of spells and spell-like abilities that directly affect it. To determine if a spell or spell-like ability works against a creature that has spell resistance, the caster must attempt a caster level check (1d20 + caster level). If the check result equals or exceeds the creature's spell resistance, the spell works normally, although the creature is still allowed a saving throw.

Spells: Sometimes a creature can cast arcane or divine spells just as a member of a spellcasting class can (and can activate magic items accordingly). Such creatures are subject to the same spellcasting rules that characters are, except as follows.

A spellcasting creature that lacks hands or arms can provide any somatic component a spell might require by moving its body. Such a creature also does need material components for its spells. The creature can cast the spell by either touching the required component (but not if the component is in another creature's possession) or having the required component on its person. Sometimes spellcasting creatures utilize the Eschew Materials feat to avoid fussing with noncostly components.

A spellcasting creature is not actually a member of a class unless its entry says so, and it does not gain any class abilities. For example, a creature that casts arcane spells as a sorcerer cannot acquire a familiar. A creature that has access to cleric spells must prepare them in the normal manner and receives domain spells if noted, but it does not receive domain granted powers unless it has at least one level in the cleric class.

Summon (Sp): A creature that has the *summon* ability can summon specific other creatures of its kind much as though casting a *summon monster* spell, but it usually has only a limited chance of success (as specified in the creature's entry). Roll d%: On a failure, no creature answers the summons. Summoned creatures automatically return whence they came after 1 hour. A creature that has just been summoned cannot use its own summon ability for 1 hour.

Most creatures that have the ability to summon do not use it lightly, since it leaves them beholden to the summoned creature. In general, they use it only when necessary to save their own lives.

An appropriate spell level is given for each summoning ability for purposes of Concentration checks and attempts to dispel the summoned creature. As stated on page 37 of the *Dungeon Master's Guide*, no experience points are awarded for summoned monsters.

Supernatural (Su) Abilities: Supernatural abilities are magical and go away in an antimagic field but are not subject to spell resistance. Supernatural abilities cannot be dispelled. Using a supernatural ability is a standard action unless otherwise noted. Supernatural abilities might have a use limit or be usable at will, just like spell-like abilities. However, supernatural abilities do not provoke attacks of opportunity and never require Concentration checks. Unless otherwise noted, a supernatural ability has an effective caster level equal to the creature's Hit Dice.

The saving throw (if any) against a supernatural ability is 10 + 1/2 the creature's HD + the creature's ability modifier (usually Charisma).

Swallow Whole (Ex): If a creature that has this ability begins its turn with an opponent held in its mouth (see Improved Grab, page 211), it can attempt a new grapple check (as though attempting to pin the opponent). If it succeeds, it swallows its prey, and the opponent takes bite damage. Unless otherwise noted, the opponent can be up to one size category smaller than the swallowing creature.

Being swallowed has various consequences, depending on the creature doing the swallowing. A swallowed creature is considered to be grappled, while the creature that did the swallowing is not. A swallowed creature can try to cut its way free with any light slashing or piercing weapon (the amount of cutting damage required to get free is noted in the creature description), or it can just try to escape the grapple. The Armor Class of the interior of a creature that swallows whole is normally 10 + 1/2 its natural armor bonus, with no modifiers for size or Dexterity. If the swallowed creature escapes the grapple, success puts it back in the attacker's mouth, where it might be bitten or swallowed again.

Swarm Subtype: A swarm is a collection of Fine, Diminutive, or Tiny creatures that acts as a single creature. A swarm has the characteristics of its type, except as noted here. A swarm has a single pool of Hit Dice and hit points, a single initiative modifier, a single speed, and a single Armor Class. A swarm attempts saving throws as a single creature.

A single swarm occupies a square (if it is made up of nonflying creatures) or a cube (of flying creatures) 10 feet on a side, but its reach is 0 feet, like its component creatures. In order to attack, it moves into an opponent's space, which provokes attacks of opportunity. It can occupy the same space as a creature of any size, since it crawls all over its prey. A swarm can move through squares occupied by enemies and vice versa without impediment, although the swarm provokes attacks of opportunity if it does so. A swarm can move through cracks or holes large enough for its component creatures.

A swarm of Tiny creatures consists of 300 nonflying creatures or 1,000 flying creatures. A swarm of Diminutive creatures consists of 1,500 nonflying creatures or 5,000 flying creatures. A swarm of Fine creatures consists of 10,000 creatures, whether they are flying or not. Swarms of nonflying creatures include many more creatures than could normally fit in a 10-foot square based on their normal space, because creatures in a swarm are packed tightly together and generally crawl over each other and their prey when moving or attacking. Larger swarms are represented by multiples of single swarms. (A swarm of 15,000 centipedes is ten centipede swarms, each swarm occupying a 10-foot square.) The area occupied by a large swarm is completely shapeable, though the swarm usually remains in contiguous squares.

Traits: A swarm has no clear front or back and no discernible anatomy, so it is not subject to extra damage from critical hits or flanking. A swarm made up of Tiny creatures takes half damage from slashing and piercing weapons. A swarm composed of Fine or Diminutive creatures is immune to all weapon damage.

Reducing a swarm to 0 hit points or lower causes it to break up, though damage taken until that point does not degrade its ability to attack or resist attack. Swarms are never staggered or reduced to a dying state by damage. Also, they cannot be tripped, grappled, or bull rushed, and they cannot grapple an opponent.

A swarm is immune to any spell or effect that targets a specific number of creatures (including single-target spells such as disintegrate), with the exception of mind-affecting spells and abilities (charms, compulsions, phantasms, patterns, and morale effects) if the swarm has an Intelligence score and a hive mind. A swarm takes half again as much damage (+50%) from spells or effects that affect an area, such as splash weapons and many evocation spells.

Swarms made up of Diminutive or Fine creatures are susceptible to high winds such as that created by a *gust of wind* spell. For purposes of determining the effects of wind on a swarm, treat the swarm as a creature of the same size as its constituent creatures (see Winds, *DMG* 95). For example, a clockwork mender swarm (Diminutive creatures) can be blown away by a severe wind. Wind effects deal 1d6 points of nonlethal damage to a swarm per spell level (or Hit Dice of the originating creature, in the case of effects such as an air elemental's whirlwind). A swarm rendered unconscious by means of nonlethal damage becomes disorganized and dispersed, and does not re-form until its hit points exceed its nonlethal damage.

Swarm Attack: Creatures that have the swarm subtype don't make standard melee attacks. Instead, they deal automatic damage to any creature whose space they occupy at the end of their move, with no attack roll needed. Swarm attacks are not subject to a miss chance for concealment or cover. A swarm's statistics block has "swarm" in the Attack and Full Attack entries, with no attack bonus given. The amount of damage a swarm deals is based on its Hit Dice, as shown below.

Swarm HD	Swarm Base Damage
1–5	1d6
6–10	2d6
11–15	3d6
16–20	4d6
21 or more	5d6

A swarm's attacks are nonmagical, unless the swarm's description states otherwise. Damage reduction sufficient to reduce a swarm attack's damage to 0, being incorporeal, and other special abilities usually give a creature immunity (or at least resistance) to damage from a swarm. Some swarms also have acid, poison, blood drain, or other kinds of attacks in addition to normal damage.

Swarms do not threaten creatures in their square, and do not make attacks of opportunity with their swarm attack. However, they distract foes whose squares they occupy, as described below.

Distraction (Ex) Any living creature vulnerable to a swarm's damage that begins its turn with a swarm in its square is nauseated for 1 round; a Fortitude save (DC 10 + 1/2 swarm's HD + swarm's Con modifier; the exact DC is given in a swarm's description) negates the effect. Spellcasting or concentrating on spells within the area of a swarm requires a Concentration check (DC 20 + spell level). Using skills that involve patience and concentration requires a DC 20 Concentration check.

Swift Action: Some monsters have special abilities that they can employ by taking a swift action. A swift action consumes a very small amount of time, but represents a larger expenditure of effort and energy than a free action. A creature can perform one swift action per turn without affecting its ability to perform other actions. In that regard, a swift action is like a free action. However, it can perform only a single swift action per turn, regardless of what other actions it takes.

Tanar'ri Subtype: Many demons belong to the race of evil outsiders known as the tanar'ri.

Traits: A tanar'ri possesses the following traits (unless otherwise noted in a creature's entry).

—Immunity to electricity and poison.

—Resistance to acid 10, cold 10, and fire 10.

—Summon (Sp) Tanar'ri share the ability to summon others of their kind (the success chance and kind of tanar'ri summoned are noted in each monster description).

—Telepathy.

Telepathic Link (Ex): Creatures that have this ability share a communal consciousness, enabling them to communicate telepathically with other creatures of their kind. A group of such creatures within a certain distance of each other (specified in the creature's entry) are in constant contact. If one is aware of a particular danger, they all are. If one in the group is not flat-footed, none of them are. No creature in the group is considered flanked unless all are.

Telepathy (Su): A creature that has this ability can communicate telepathically with any other creature within a certain range (specified in the creature's entry, usually 100 feet) that has a language. It is possible to address multiple creatures at once telepathically, although maintaining a telepathic conversation with more than one creature at a time is just as difficult as simultaneously speaking and listening to multiple people at the same time.

Trample (Ex): As a full-round action, a creature that has this ability can move up to twice its speed and literally run over any opponents at least one size category smaller than itself. The creature merely has to move over the opponents in its path; any creature whose space is completely covered by the trampling creature's space is subject to the trample attack.

If a target's space is larger than 5 feet, it is only considered trampled if the trampling creature moves over all the squares it occupies. If the trampling creature moves over only some of a target's space, the target can make an attack of opportunity against the trampling creature at a –4 penalty. A trampling creature that accidentally ends its movement in an illegal space returns to the last legal position it occupied, or the closest legal position, if there's a legal position that's closer.

A trample attack deals bludgeoning damage (the creature's slam damage + 1-1/2 times its Str modifier). The creature's descriptive text gives the exact amount.

Trampled opponents can attempt attacks of opportunity, but these take a –4 penalty. If they do not make attacks of opportunity, trampled opponents can attempt Reflex saves to take half damage. The save DC against a creature's trample attack is 10 + 1/2 creature's HD + creature's Str modifier (the exact DC is given in the creature's descriptive text). A trampling creature can only deal trampling damage to each target once per round, no matter how many times its movement takes it over a target creature.

Tremorsense (Ex): A creature that has tremorsense is sensitive to vibrations in the ground and can automatically pinpoint the location of anything that is in contact with the ground. Aquatic creatures that have tremorsense can also sense the location of creatures moving through water. The ability's range is specified in the creature's descriptive text.

Turn Resistance (Ex): A creature that has this special quality (usually an undead) is less easily affected by clerics or paladins (see Turn or Rebuke Undead, PH 159). When resolving a turn, rebuke, command, or bolster attempt, add the indicated number to the creature's Hit Dice total. For example, a vitreous drinker has 14 Hit Dice and +6 turn resistance. Attempts to turn, rebuke, command, or bolster treat a vitreous drinker as though it had 20 Hit Dice, though it is a 14 HD creature for any other purpose.

Typical Treasure: This entry in a monster description describes how much wealth a creature owns. (See DMG 52–56 for details about treasure, particularly Tables 3–5 through 3–8.) In most cases, a creature keeps valuables in its home or lair and has no treasure with it when it travels. Intelligent creatures that own useful, portable treasure (such as magic items) tend to carry and use these, leaving bulky items at home.

Undead Type: Undead are once-living creatures animated by spiritual or supernatural forces.

Features: An undead creature has the following features.

—12-sided Hit Dice.

—Base attack bonus equal to 1/2 total Hit Dice (as wizard).

—Good Will saves.

—Skill points equal to (4 + Int modifier, minimum 1) per Hit Die, with quadruple skill points for the first Hit Die, if the undead creature has an Intelligence score. However, many undead are mindless and gain no skill points or feats.

Traits: An undead creature possesses the following traits (unless otherwise noted in a creature's entry).

—No Constitution score.

—Darkvision out to 60 feet.

—Immunity to all mind-affecting spells and abilities (charms, compulsions, phantasms, patterns, and morale effects).

—Immunity to poison, sleep effects, paralysis, stunning, disease, and death effects.

—Not subject to extra damage from critical hits, nonlethal damage, ability drain, or energy drain. Immune to damage to its physical ability scores (Strength, Dexterity, and Constitution), as well as to fatigue and exhaustion effects.

—Cannot heal damage on its own if it has no Intelligence score, although it can be healed. Negative energy (such as an *inflict* spell) can heal undead creatures. The fast healing special quality works regardless of the creature's Intelligence score.

—Immunity to any effect that requires a Fortitude save (unless the effect also works on objects or is harmless).

—Uses its Charisma modifier for Concentration checks.

—Not at risk of death from massive damage, but when reduced to 0 hit points or less, it is immediately destroyed.

—Not affected by *raise dead* and *reincarnate* spells or abilities. *Resurrection* and *true resurrection* can affect undead

creatures. These spells turn undead creatures back into the living creatures they were before becoming undead.

—Proficient with its natural weapons, all simple weapons, and any weapons mentioned in its entry.

—Proficient with whatever type of armor (light, medium, or heavy) it is described as wearing, as well as all lighter types. Undead not indicated as wearing armor are not proficient with armor. Undead are proficient with shields if they are proficient with any form of armor.

—Undead do not breathe, eat, or sleep.

Vermin Type: This type includes insects, arachnids, other arthropods, worms, and similar invertebrates.

Features: Vermin have the following features.

—8-sided Hit Dice.

—Base attack bonus equal to 3/4 total Hit Dice (as cleric).

—Good Fortitude saves.

—Skill points equal to (2 + Int modifier, minimum 1) per Hit Die, with quadruple skill points for the first Hit Die, if the vermin has an Intelligence score. However, most vermin are mindless and gain no skill points or feats.

Traits: Vermin possess the following traits (unless otherwise noted in a creature's entry).

—Mindless: No Intelligence score, and immunity to all mind-affecting spells and abilities (charms, compulsions, phantasms, patterns, and morale effects).

—Darkvision out to 60 feet.

—Proficient with their natural weapons only.

—Proficient with no armor.

—Vermin breathe, eat, and sleep.

Vulnerability to Energy: Some creatures have vulnerability to a certain kind of energy effect (typically either cold or fire). Such a creature takes half again as much (+50%) damage as normal from the effect, regardless of whether a saving throw is allowed, or if the save is a success or failure.

Water Subtype: This subtype usually is used for elementals and outsiders that have a connection to the Elemental Plane of Water. Creatures that have the water subtype always have swim speeds and can move in water without making Swim checks. A water creature can breathe underwater and usually can breathe air as well.

Yugoloth Subtype: Possibly the greediest, most selfish beings in the Outer Planes, yugoloths reign supreme among the evil outsiders of Gehenna.

Traits: A yugoloth possesses the following traits (unless otherwise noted in a creature's entry).

—Immunity to acid and poison.

—Resistance to cold 10, electricity 10, and fire 10.

—Telepathy.

MONSTERS BY TYPE (AND SUBTYPE)

Aberration: balhannoth, howler wasp, lodestone marauder, mageripper swarm, zern arcanovore.
(Air): cyclonic ravager.
Animal: sailsnake.
(Aquatic): corrupture.
(Archon): justice archons.
(Augmented Humanoid): half-fiend gnoll warlock, orc plague speaker.
(Chaotic): demons, Lolth-touched bebilith, wrackspawn.
(Cold): whitespawn hordeling, whitespawn hunter, whitespawn iceskidder.
Construct: clockroach, clockwork mender, clockwork steed, fang golem.
(Dragonblood): spawn of Tiamat (all).
(Earth): black rock triskelion, craa'ghoran giant, greathorn minotaur.
Elemental: black rock triskelion, cyclonic ravager, holocaust disciple, waterveiled assassin, inferno spider.
(Elf): drow (all), Lolth-touched drow ranger.
(Evil): corruptor of fate, demons, demonhive, Lolth-touched bebilith, orc plague speaker, wrackspawn, voors.
(Extraplanar): black rock triskelion, clockwork mender, concordant killer, corruptor of fate, cyclonic ravager, demons, demonhive, githyanki, holocaust disciple, inferno spider, justice archons, Lolth-touched bebilith, skiurid, voors, waterveiled assassin, windrazor, windscythe, wrackspawn.
Fey: joystealer, lunar ravager, verdant prince.
(Fire): bloodfire ooze, holocaust disciple, inferno spider, redspawn arcaniss, redspawn firebelcher, yuan-ti ignan.
Giant: craa'ghoran giant, ogres.

(Goblinoid): varag.
(Good): justice archons.
Humanoid: drow (all), fiendish cleric of Yeenoghu, githyanki, gnoll slave-taker, lizardfolk, Lolth-touched drow ranger, orcs, varag.
(Incorporeal): joystealer, whisper demon.
(Lawful): clockwork mender, justice archons.
Magical Beast: blackspawn stalker, bloodsilk spider, bluespawn ambusher, bluespawn burrower, bluespawn stormlizard, greenspawn leaper, greenspawn razorfiend, quanlos, redspawn firebelcher, skiurid, tomb spider, tomb spider broodswarm, whitespawn iceskidder.
Monstrous Humanoid: blackspawn raider, blackspawn exterminator, bluespawn godslayer, greathorn minotaur, greenspawn sneak, greenspawn sneak raid leader, nagatha, redspawn arcaniss, whitespawn hordeling, whitespawn hunter, yuan-ti (all), yuan-ti ignan, zern, zern blade thrall.
(Native): dwarf ancestor, half-fiend gnoll warlock, orc plague speaker.
Ooze: bloodfire ooze, corrupture.
Outsider: concordant killer, corruptor of fate, demons, demonhive, dwarf ancestor, half-fiend gnoll warlock, justice archons, Lolth-touched bebilith, orc plague speaker, voors, windrazor, windscythe, wrackspawn.
Plant: briarvex, oaken defender, wizened elder.
(Reptilian): lizardfolk.
(Swarm): mageripper swarm, tomb spider broodswarm.
(Tanar'ri): kastighur demon.
Undead: bloodhulk, defacer, necrosis carnex, plague walker, vitreous drinker, web mummy.
Vermin: Lolth-touched monstrous spider.
(Water): waterveiled assassin.
(Yugoloth): corruptor of fate, voors.

ABOUT THE DESIGNERS

GWENDOLYN F.M. KESTREL works for Wizards of the Coast as a game designer. Her previous design credits include *Fantastic Locations: Fane of the Drow*, *Races of the Dragon*, and *Monster Manual III*. Gwendolyn lives in Washington State with her husband, game developer Andy Collins. They host a gaming convention, appropriately titled "GwenCon," each fall.

JENNIFER CLARKE WILKES works for Wizards of the Coast as a roleplaying and miniatures editor. Her previous design credits include *Savage Species*, *Sandstorm*, *Stormwrack*, and *Races of the Dragon*.

MATTHEW SERNETT worked for Paizo Publishing as the editor-in-chief of *Dragon* Magazine before joining Wizards of the Coast as a game designer. His previous design credits include *Monster Manual III*, *Fiend Folio*, and *Tome of Magic*.

ERIC CAGLE has done several design jobs for Wizards of the Coast, including *d20 Apocalypse*, *Races of Destiny*, and *Monster Manual III*. He has also written for *Dragon* Magazine, the Game Mechanics, and Green Ronin.

ANDREW FINCH has played D&D for 25 years and worked at Wizards of the Coast for the last 10 years. In addition to putting in his 2 cents on the creation of D&D 3rd Edition, Andrew did a two-year stint as RPG Development Manager before becoming the Director of New Business for R&D. *Monster Manual III* is the D&D book he is the most proud of having worked on.

CHRISTOPHER LINDSAY's credits include *Complete Psionic*, in addition to his many contributions to the D&D website and the RPGA. Christopher spends his hours outside gaming studying various martial arts and spending time with his wife, a horde of kids, and a cat that is gracious enough to share the same living space.

KOLJA RAVEN LIQUETTE is perhaps best known for creating The Waking Lands website, but has also written material for *Races of the Dragon*, *Weapons of Legacy*, and various articles and enhancements for the Wizards of the Coast website.

OWEN K.C. STEPHENS, a freelance writer living in Oklahoma, has written numerous articles for the Wizards of the Coast

website, including d20 MODERN adventures and advice columns. His roleplaying game design credits include *d20 Apocalypse*, *d20 Cyberscape*, and *d20 Critical Locations*.

TRAVIS STOUT works as a freelance game designer. In addition to writing several articles for *Dragon* Magazine, Travis also contributed to *Player's Guide to Faerûn*.

JD WIKER is currently freelancing while also working as president of The Game Mechanics, a d20 design studio. Some of JD's recent titles include *d20 Future*, the *Star Wars Hero's Guide*, and the *Galactic Campaign Guide*.

SKIP WILLIAMS freelances from his home in Wisconsin, where he tends a garden and a growing orchard when not creating new fantasy heroes and villains. His numerous design credits include *Monster Manual*, *Races of the Wild*, and *Draconomicon*.

EXPAND YOUR  EXPERIENCE

D&D Introductory Products

D&D® is easy to learn, but can be hard to teach. With the DUNGEONS & DRAGONS® Basic Game, you can quickly bring your friends up to speed and get them ready for more adventure.

❖ *DUNGEONS & DRAGONS Basic Game* ☐ 0-7869-3409-3 $24.99 _____

❖ *DUNGEONS & DRAGONS Miniatures Starter Set* ☐ 0-7869-3500-6 $19.99 _____

D&D Accessories

Keep your game moving with essential tools that put information at your fingertips. And add excitement to every session with ready-made adventures, maps, and more.

❖ *Deluxe Character Sheets* ☐ 0-7869-3421-2 $14.95 _____

❖ *Deluxe Dungeon Master's Screen* ☐ 0-7869-3422-0 $14.95 _____

❖ *DUNGEONS & DRAGONS Dice* ☐ 0-7869-3513-8 $9.95 _____

❖ *Map Folio 3D* ☐ 0-7869-3437-9 $9.95 _____

❖ *D&D Miniatures Underdark Booster Pack* ☐ 0-7869-3522-7 $12.99 _____

D&D Supplements

Add options for developing characters, creating adventures, and building campaigns with books filled with new races, feats, equipment, spells, monsters, magic items, and more.

❖ *Lords of Madness: The Book of Aberrations* ☐ 0-7869-3657-6 $34.95 _____

❖ *Complete Adventurer* ☐ 0-7869-2880-8 $29.95 _____

❖ *Libris Mortis: The Book of Undead* ☐ 0-7869-3433-6 $29.95 _____

❖ *Spell Compendium* ☐ 0-7869-3702-5 $39.95 _____

D&D Campaign Settings

Explore detailed worlds filled with inspiration, excitement, and adventure. Even if your game is set in a different setting, you'll find maps, monsters, villains, spells, races, and other options that you can use to add depth and detail to your campaign and characters.

❖ *EBERRON® Campaign Setting* ☐ 0-7869-3274-0 $39.95 _____

❖ *FORGOTTEN REALMS® Campaign Setting* ☐ 0-7869-1836-5 $39.95 _____

Total: _____

Use this sheet to help friends and family find the products you want and when ordering from your favorite hobby shop or bookstore.

Name: _____ Telephone: _____

Address: _____

City: _____ State: _____ Zip: _____

GET YOUR HANDS ON A FIGHT

Encounter a menagerie of monsters ready to invade your **D&D**® game.
Fiend Folio, *Monster Manual II*, and *Monster Manual III* come packed with
hundreds of creatures ready to challenge heroes of any level.

Look for them at your favorite hobby shop or bookstore.

 wizards.com/dnd

FIND THE EDGE
YOU NEED TO SUCCEED

DUNGEONS & DRAGONS

COMPLETE DIVINE
A Player's Guide to Divine magic for All Classes

David Noonan

DUNGEONS & DRAGONS

COMPLETE ADVENTURER
A Player's Guide to Extraordinary Abilities for All Classes

Jesse Decker

DUNGEONS & DRAGONS Supplement

COMPLETE WARRIOR
A Player's Guide to Combat for All Classes

Andy Collins, David Noonan, Ed Stark

Whether you swing steel or sling spells, you want to make sure your character
has what it takes to walk out of every encounter with treasure and a tale to tell.
Inside *Complete Divine*, *Complete Adventurer*, and *Complete Warrior*,
you'll find the stuff of which legends are made.

Look for them at your favorite hobby shop or bookstore.

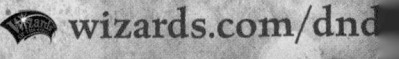